Jean Toomer and the Terrors of American History

Jean Toomer and the Terrors of American History

Charles Scruggs
and Lee VanDemarr

PENN

University of Pennsylvania Press

Philadelphia

10 9 8 7 6 5 4 3 2 1

Published by
University of Pennsylvania Press
Philadelphia, Pennsylvania 19104-4011

Library of Congress Cataloging-in-Publication Data
Scruggs, Charles.
Jean Toomer and the terrors of American history / Charles Scruggs and Lee VanDemarr.
    p.   cm.
  Includes bibliographical references (p.   ) and index.
  ISBN 0-8122-3451-0 (alk. paper)
    1. Toomer, Jean, 1894–1967. Cane.   2. Literature and history—United States—History—
20th century.   3. Toomer, Jean, 1894–1967—Criticism and interpretation—History.
4. Afro-Americans in literature.   I. VanDemarr, Lee.   II. Title.
PS3539.0478C337   1998
813′.52—dc21   98-17686
                                                                                 CIP

For Our Parents

Contents

Introduction: The Witness of History

Jean Toomer and the Terrors of American History is about a literary life and its complicated relationships to the social, political, and economic worlds in which the writer lived and worked. In particular it is about the African-American writer Jean Toomer and his major book, the hybrid short story cycle *Cane*, first published in 1923. For more than three decades a kind of subterranean text, not forgotten but unavailable, *Cane* had been a critical success rather than a popular one in 1923, and though its publisher reprinted it in 1927 (no doubt to capitalize on the rise of the Harlem Renaissance), it would not be reprinted again until 1969, two years after Toomer's death. In 1969, in the midst of a revival of interest in black writing, Robert Bone's review of the first paperback edition appeared in the *New York Times Book Review* with the headline "The Black Classic That Discovered 'Soul' Is Rediscovered after 45 Years," and *Cane*'s revival was securely launched. The New York literary world's approval was something Toomer the author would have appreciated.[1]

Cane became a canonic text rather late, but it was never quite a lost text; despite the *Times*'s headline, *Cane* was "rediscovered" only in the sense that the mass-market edition made it available, as Bone remarked, "to the general reader." The importance of reprinting for a book's long-term survival should not be underestimated, but in this case the critical effort to remember *Cane*, which can be traced in Therman B. O'Daniel's excellent bibliography of Toomer, was equally important. Though excluded from "mainstream" anthologies of American literature, selections from *Cane*, a few poems and stories, were more or less continuously in print between 1927 and 1969—this despite the fact that Toomer himself sometimes declined to appear in "Negro" anthologies. Some critics of African-American writing also made sure Toomer's work was not forgotten: Alain Locke, Sterling Brown, J. Saunders Redding, Hugh M. Gloster, and particularly Bone and Arna Bontemps.[2]

Since 1970 *Cane* has become an important text, and Jean Toomer has become the subject of biographies and book-length literary studies. After

1923 Toomer continued writing almost until the year of his death, accumulating a huge archive of unpublished work, most of it now collected at Yale University's Beinecke Rare Book and Manuscript Library. Understandably, much of the recent interest in Toomer has focused on this unpublished writing, particularly parts of his multiple autobiographies and the record of his "spiritualist" work after 1923; there has also been a tendency to read backward and interpret *Cane* in light of selected bits of this material. However, in part because of this concentration on the later writing, the now considerable body of scholarship about Toomer leaves important areas of his life and work untouched, especially the historical contexts within which Toomer began to write: the social and political milieus of the post–World War I period. Neglected in most previous commentaries, these matters are central to understanding *Cane* and cast light as well on Toomer's other works.

Two words in our title, "terrors" and "history," describe what we have found to be lacking from studies of Toomer and what we have tried to begin recovering. A significant project for recent critics of American literature has been the rediscovery of books and authors excluded from the New Critical canon, and a part of this work has also been to investigate the dimensions of literature which the New Critics were little interested in studying. Not coincidentally, the literary circles of Jean Toomer worked on a similar project; as Waldo Frank observed in *Our America*, criticizing the canon established by the "Genteel Tradition" and the "New Humanists": "Whatever consciousness we have had so far has been the result of vast and deliberate exclusions." Cary Nelson's critique of literary history as it has been written since the 1950s summarizes one kind of exclusion:

> The New Critics were at pains to point out that "literary history" generally omitted and obscured what was specifically *literary* about poetry and fiction, the textual qualities that distinguish literary language from other discourses. It may now, however, be more crucial to argue that literary history is typically (and improperly) detached from history as it may be more broadly construed—not only the familiar history of nations but also the still less familiar history of everyday life.[3]

The background to *Cane* and the story of how Toomer came to write the book involve both "everyday" and national histories that had been "detached" from the text even as the complete text itself virtually disappeared for thirty years. *Con-texts* have been there to be uncovered, but for various reasons they have remained hidden.

There is one obvious reason for the loss of historical—especially political—contexts for *Cane*. Toomer's life after 1923 turned away from the social circumstances and urgencies that led him to begin writing, and this move toward religious and personal concerns undoubtedly encouraged critics and biographers to regard him as a mystic and spiritualist rather than as a political writer. After 1923 Toomer formed a series of attachments to spiritualists like George Gurdjieff and religious groups like the Quakers which continued virtually until the end of his life. It seems clear that Toomer's commitment to a "spiritual quest" was serious and deeply felt, but our study is not concerned with that part of his career, except to point out that the political Toomer who wrote *Cane* resurfaced in later years. We have tried to outline the historical context from which *Cane* emerged, examining ignored or neglected evidence about the specific background within which Toomer wrote his book, and to show how that background helps explain the political meanings of *Cane*.[4]

The politics of Jean Toomer the writer and of *Cane* have been obscured by intentional disregard (even by Toomer himself) and by scholarly neglect. Although we did not begin our work with the idea of revising Toomer's biography, in the process of writing we came up against serious errors and omissions in the scholarship dealing with Toomer's life through 1923; correcting this record has made us, in effect, involuntary biographers. The most complete biography of Toomer is Cynthia Earl Kerman and Richard Eldridge's *The Lives of Jean Toomer: A Hunger for Wholeness*—the subtitle of which indicates its concern with the "spiritual" Toomer. In fact, Kerman and Eldridge devote only two short chapters to *Cane*, whereas almost three-quarters of their book is given over to the religious quests of Toomer's later life. More important in our view, *Lives* contains factual errors and questionable interpretations and overlooks crucial biographical materials, particularly in its discussion of the writing of *Cane* and the social, political, and intellectual milieus that influenced it. We address specific errors in the notes to our main text, but the major problem is what has been omitted from the discussion of Toomer's life.[5]

These omissions include a lack of attention to Toomer's earliest published writings, which are specifically political and which illuminate the crucial literary relationship between Toomer and his mentor, Waldo Frank. In *Lives* as, indeed, in all the published biographical writings on Toomer, there is no mention of the three articles he published between 1919 and 1920 in the *New York Call*, a prominent socialist newspaper. Although Toomer avoided any mention of the *Call* essays in his autobiographies, references to these articles appear three times in Toomer's unpublished writings, twice in the correspondence between Waldo Frank and Toomer and again in the biographical sketch that Toomer wrote for Horace Liveright on the eve of *Cane*'s publication.[6]

Most of the writing about Toomer has understated, or even ignored, the essential contribution Waldo Frank made to *Cane*, and this problem becomes more troublesome when combined with critical misunderstandings about the meaning of Frank's own books, particularly his key work, *Our America*. Kerman and Eldridge, for instance, largely reduce Frank's significance for Toomer to the "spiritual" and the "religious," viewing *Our America* as a work focused on the idea of the nation's "organic mystical

Whole." This phrase, however, offers little help in coming to terms with a book whose real foundation is political and social, as Toomer's defense of Frank in his final *Call* article, "Americans and Mary Austin," shows he well understood. Austin had attacked Frank as a Jew, condemning *Our America* because it presumptuously challenged the cultural hierarchy that Austin, as an Anglo-American, was determined to uphold, and Toomer defended Frank on precisely those issues of "race," culture, and politics that were at the heart of *Our America*.[7]

In 1919, when *Our America* was published, Frank and others of his generation faced a repressive government. Bolshevik paranoia and war hysteria defined the national temper; anti-Semitism was at its zenith; civil liberties remained under "wartime" suspension; members of the liberal and radical Left were being harassed, jailed, or deported; major race riots (attacks by whites on black communities) erupted throughout the year. Randolph Bourne, Frank's friend and fellow contributor to the brilliant little magazine *The Seven Arts* (1916–17), wrote a brutal but unfinished satire on the tenor of the times called "The State." Published posthumously in the same year as *Our America*, it conceived of America's future as a totalitarian nightmare. Some of Bourne's politics found their way into *Our America* as part of an extended socialist critique of American history, but Frank's book placed hope for resistance more in the cultural arena than in the political one. This choice was not a retreat in his view: he believed the artist rather than the revolutionary could radically remake American society, just as marginalized groups (Jews, Hispanics, Native Americans, African-Americans, immigrants from southern Italy and eastern Europe) might redefine an America as "ours" and not "theirs." Frank thought "culture" was a political force that might change society rather than simply reflect it, and his use of *religion* was tied to the social: art is "religious" (from *religare*: "to bind") because it serves in the creation of the Beloved Community.[8]

Although by the end of 1923 Toomer was on his way to embracing Gurdjieffism, this future choice is largely irrelevant to *Cane*'s meaning. The "spiritual" always appears in *Cane* within a political context, that is, within a context concerned with issues involving the American polis. Toomer's politics in the period from 1918 to 1923—roughly the time during which he was learning the craft of writing and then completing *Cane*—were centered on socialism and on the "New Negro"; his first published essays drew ideas from both movements, which were contemporary currents in postwar New York City and which coincided in radical African-American magazines like Cyril Briggs's *Crusader* and the *Messenger* of A. Philip Randolph and Chandler Owen.[9]

Toomer criticism has largely dismissed socialism as a significant influence on his thought at the time he was writing *Cane*. Critics paraphrase Toomer's remarks in the 1931–32 version of his autobiography, that ten days of working in the shipyards of New Jersey in 1919 "finished socialism for me." But the shipyard experience did not finish socialism for Toomer. He continued to move in the world of the New York Left after 1919, and in 1936 he wrote another version of his autobiography which completely revised his understanding of those days in the shipyard. Where the 1931–32 autobiography is satirical, even cynical—the shipyard workers "had only two main interests: playing craps and sleeping with women"—in the 1936 autobiography this satiric perspective shifts to the Gothic: Toomer admits his own fear of working-class life, that he did not want "to be confined in the death-house with doomed men." [10]

The lot of these workers represented a brutal actuality that underlay society; working as a common laborer had shown Toomer "that the underlying conditions of human existence were ruthless and terrible beyond anything written in books or glimpsed in those forms of society wherein men, their behavior and manners, are veneered by the amenities of civilization. This is what the shipyard experience had done to me—and done for me." He was also convinced that socialism was a necessary solution to the soul-deadening, exhausting work of the shipyards: "I realized as never before the *need* of socialism, the *need* of a radical change of the conditions of human society." Like George Orwell—and indeed this part of the 1936 autobiography reads like *Down and Out in Paris and London*—Toomer would escape back to "normal" middle-class life, but the world of the shipyards would be present in *Cane*, in its keen social analysis of class and caste and in its Gothic portrayal of the terrors of American history. [11]

Also missing from the biographical record are essential facts about Toomer's engagement with African-American politics and civil rights. The second *Call* essay Toomer wrote, "Reflections on the Race Riots," published in August 1919, raises important questions: Where was Toomer during the Washington, D.C., race riots of July 1919, and what was his reaction to them? Some of the worst fighting of July 21–22 took place in the streets virtually fronting the apartment Toomer occupied with his elderly grandparents, yet there is no mention of this in Darwin T. Turner's *The Wayward and the Seeking* or in Toomer's other autobiographical writings. Toomer's contemporary reaction, a militant leftist one, is evident from his *Call* essay, but his later decision to "forget" that public history points up how difficult it is to determine exactly what can be trusted in the autobiographies. [12]

One of the problems in Toomer criticism has been the use of Turner's autobiographical collage in *The Wayward and the Seeking* as an accurate record of Toomer's life. Turner's book has been valuable as a source for long-unavailable portions of Toomer's published and unpublished work, and Turner himself was clear in his introduction about the selective nature of the autobiographical fragments he joined together to produce a narrative of Toomer's life through 1923. But inevitably the largest portion of the autobiographical writings were excluded from this anthology, and some of those excluded pages are of crucial significance for understanding

Toomer's political life. It is absurd that the half-dozen lines about working in the shipyards from the 1931–32 "Outline of an Autobiography" should be quoted repeatedly even as Toomer's many pages of reflection on the same experience written in 1936 remain unmentioned.[13]

To a considerable degree the difficulty in establishing the basic facts of Toomer's life has been due to his own evasiveness. The problem with Toomer's discussions of *Cane* and its composition presented in *The Wayward and the Seeking* is a matter not primarily of which documents were selected, but of Toomer's own deliberate misrepresentation of those circumstances. After comparing Toomer's extensive 1922–23 correspondence with Waldo Frank, Gorham Munson, and others against the record of the same period in "On Being an American," one becomes very cautious of Toomer's selective memory, especially in any matter involving his racial identity. Similarly, the exclusion of the *Call* articles from Toomer's autobiography was his own choice, a choice that successfully "buried" them for a surprisingly long time. Such was also the case with the events of his life during the summer of 1919, though it is now possible—with the *Call* article and various hints in Toomer's unpublished autobiographies—to piece together a probable narrative for those months.[14]

Beyond mistaking specific facts of Toomer's life, scholarship about *Cane* has never adequately treated the intellectual and historical settings of that work, though there are important exceptions in the criticism of Vera M. Kutzinski, George B. Hutchinson, Michael North, and Barbara Foley, who have made valuable contributions to the recovery of *Cane*'s background. That background, the political circumstances behind *Cane*, was varied, and included Toomer's activist engagement in polemics ("Reflections on the Race Riots" and "Americans and Mary Austin"), the traumatic circumstances of his stay in Sparta, his attempt to understand the mulatto-elite milieu of his hometown, Washington, D.C., and its ideology of racial uplift, and his ongoing effort to define himself as an "American." Although he wrote about these experiences before he renewed his acquaintance with Waldo Frank in 1922, it was Frank's influence that led him to think of developing this diverse material into a book. The euphoria Toomer felt over being associated with Waldo Frank and the group of intellectuals known during the Great War as "Young America" cannot be overestimated. The members of that group were to move in different directions after the war, but the ideas emanating from their vortex would give Toomer an intellectual context for *Cane*.[15]

The brief mention of "Young America" in *The Lives of Jean Toomer* is the best available discussion of Toomer's relationship to this group, but it is sketchy and incomplete. Nor is it useful to characterize these people as part of the "Lost Generation." Whatever that phrase meant when Gertrude Stein dropped it to Ernest Hemingway in Paris, it has a very limited relevance to Toomer's circle of New York intellectuals. Lewis Mumford, a member of "Young America," put the difference directly:

In contrast to the disillusioned expatriates of the "lost generation" who were travelling in the opposite direction, we [Mumford and Van Wyck Brooks] felt—as did Randolph Bourne, Waldo Frank, and Paul Rosenfeld—that this [task of reclaiming our American literary heritage] was an essential preparation for America's cultural "Coming of Age." For Brooks this remained a lifelong mission; and between 1921 and 1931, partly under his influence, I made it my concern too.[16]

Mumford would say elsewhere that "what united me in comradeship" to this group was the idea of "re-discovery." Although he probably took that word from the title of Waldo Frank's *The Re-discovery of America* (1929), the sequel to *Our America*, he may have been thinking of Van Wyck Brooks's seminal article in the *Dial* (1918), "On Creating a Usable Past," in which Brooks saw American history, and especially American literary history, an "inexhaustable storehouse" of multiple pasts. Mumford, Frank, Hart Crane, and eventually Kenneth Burke came to see that America's usable pasts might be reclaimed in order to express a utopian future. The renewal of American life was also Toomer's concern, but Toomer's racial perspective on American society, past and present, complicated this theme in *Cane*. As much as he wanted to embrace the optimism of Frank and others, he came face to face in *Cane* not with a usable past but with the terrors of American history.[17]

As Kerman and Eldridge's plural *Lives* suggests, and as most readers looking at *Cane* and the post-*Cane* work are likely to feel, Jean Toomer's life changed dramatically after 1923. Since we have read Toomer primarily because of *Cane*, we will look at only a few of his later writings, and those in light of the vexed question of what became of the author whom Waldo Frank at one time regarded as the most promising writer in America. Our sense of *Cane*'s importance has led us to try to uncover the background for the book and to clarify its political meanings; we find little point in the current anachronistic tendency that attempts to link *Cane* with Toomer's New Age thinking after he came under the influence of George Gurdjieff and to read the book via Gurdjieffism or some other "spiritual" system. Fixing on the illusory search for "spiritual wholeness" in the text reduces, intentionally or not, its social and political dimensions, and ignores the historical background of the times and Toomer's intricate and evolving connection to them. To insist that *Cane* be a "spiritual autobiography" is to disregard his text's most important enactment: the transformation of the isolated spectator into the witness of history.

Chapter 1
Sparta

NOT very long ago
  A lady come to town
HER business here, she said
  WAS to a mission found

SHE meant to teach drawing
  TO the colored kids
BUT before she got started
  WE put her on skids.

There is another verse but we can't think of anything to rhyme with
"She left in a hurry."
— *Sparta Ishmaelite*, Dec. 23, 1921

Sparta, Georgia, is located almost at the center of Hancock County, a little over one hundred miles southeast of Atlanta, seventy-five miles southwest of Augusta. Hancock County is in the upper half of what was historically the "Black Belt" of the state, the cotton-growing heartland where the plantation system of antebellum Georgia was established, to be succeeded in Reconstruction and the following years by the system of tenant farming and sharecropping, piece-work labor, and peonage which would last well into the twentieth century. The term "Black Belt" was a reference to the predominantly African-American population of the area; according to the census of 1920, Hancock County's population of 18,257 was 74.4 percent black.[1]

The 1906 *Cyclopedia of Georgia* briefly characterizes Hancock County in volume 2:

The northern part of the county is hilly and has a red, aluminous soil. In the south the land is level and covered with pine forests. The best soil is along Shoulderbone creek and its tributaries. The staple productions are cotton, the cereals, sweet and Irish potatoes, sorghum, sugar-cane, field and ground peas. Vegetables and various varieties of fruit are raised, the melons, grapes and berries being excellent quality and many are shipped. The timber is of the various hardwood species, mostly oak, sweet-gum, maple and hickory. There is also some pine.

Sparta is the county seat, and near the town was located the Mt. Zion Academy, "so long presided over by Dr. Beman and later by William J. Northen, afterward governor of the state. Many of Georgia's most noted sons received their early training in this school."[2]

Sparta acquired another school in 1910, when Linton S. Ingraham opened the Sparta Agricultural and Industrial School, intended to provide an elementary education and vocational training to the county's African-American children. The school appears in Thomas Jesse Jones's 1917 study, *Negro Education*: "A small elementary school owned by the county. It was founded in 1910 by the principal. In 1914 the building and 5 acres of land were transferred to the county board of education. The original trustees were all local white men of influence." The study lists a "reported enrollment" of 124 pupils and suggests that there should be a more careful accounting of the school's budget; it recommends that "aid for the institution be given under the direction of the State supervisor of colored schools." Ingraham's school was provided with minimal state support, and in a tradition extending back to the days of Reconstruction, its principal sought funds from wealthy Northerners. In 1921 he made a trip north and stopped at Washington, D.C., in search of a "substitute principal" to serve in his absence. He found one, and in September 1921 Jean Toomer traveled south to Sparta as Ingraham's replacement.[3]

Two years later, in 1923, Toomer would publish *Cane*, which became for the 1920s one of the major texts of a new African-American literature and, after its rediscovery in the 1960s, was equally important to another generation of African-American writers. Toomer would continue writing for another thirty years, but would never produce anything as remotely successful or influential as *Cane*. One of his long-term projects would be an autobiography, which he would attempt in several versions over a period of at least fifteen years (1929 to the 1940s).[4]

In one of these autobiographies he emphasizes the connection between the writing of *Cane* and the time he spent in Sparta: "I left Georgia in late November of that year [1921], after having been there three months. On the train coming north I began to write the things that later on appeared in that book [*Cane*]." Toomer's letters from this time are also clear about the Sparta connection. To the editors of the magazine *The Liberator* he said that "a visit to Georgia last fall was the starting point of almost everything of worth that I have done." Yet despite the importance of the experiences in Sparta for Toomer and his writing, he was curiously reticent about providing any details of his months there. The Georgia visit is characterized in both letters and autobiographies by the lyric images, pastoral landscapes, and spontaneous folksongs that are scattered throughout *Cane*, suggesting that the book celebrated the vitality, tenacity, and spiritual cohesiveness of the black peasant world of Sparta and that the poet who sang of this world found the "seed" of himself in his songs.[5]

However, *Cane*'s long concluding story, "Kabnis," suggests an experience other than the lyric, and there are three letters that Toomer wrote to his mentor and friend Waldo Frank that at least hint at the nature of this experience. On April 26, 1922, early in their correspondence, Toomer wrote to Frank: "Kabnis sprang up almost in a day, it now seems to me. It is the direct result of a trip I made down into Georgia this past fall. That trip (my actual experience down there will interest you. I barely avoided a serious time.) by the way, is more or less responsible for most of my stuff that you like." A few months later, as Toomer and Frank discussed plans for a trip to the South together (Frank was working on his novel about the South, *Holiday*, and Toomer thought he might find material to continue *Cane*), Toomer wrote to him about possible destinations: "There's always Georgia to fall back on. I'd have suggested it in the first place were it not for the fact that certain conditions there (in Sparta . . .) make it not the best place in the world at this time." His remark has the tone of a carefully considered understatement.[6]

There is also the somewhat more ambiguous text of what was probably the draft of a letter to Frank in September 1923. Toomer says of writing *Cane* that "it was born in an agony of internal tightness, conflict, and chaos." He never clearly identifies the source of these feelings, except perhaps in a remark further on in the text about Sherwood Anderson. Anderson was an important influence for Toomer, and the two corresponded while Toomer was working on *Cane*. Toomer, however, objected to Anderson's focus on the African-American world in Toomer's writing; as he put it, Anderson "limits me to Negro." In the draft letter Toomer closes with the remark that "when they, in all good faith have advised me, as Sherwood Anderson did, to keep close to the conditions which produced Cane, I have denied them. Never again in life do I want a repetition of those conditions."[7]

The world Toomer had entered in Sparta in some way represented "those conditions," and it is possible by examining contemporary sources to recover at least part of that world. Something of Toomer's experience there was central to the writing of *Cane*, and perhaps to the rest of his life as well. The weekly country newspaper, the *Sparta Ishmaelite*, published six items in 1921 about Linton S. Ingraham and the Sparta Agricultural and Industrial School. The first appeared on February 4, reprinted from the *Boston Globe* and headlined "Boston Globe Boosts Ingraham's School." The story is unusual in that the *Ishmaelite*, in this year at any rate, rarely or never published pieces from the Northern press. The paper's content was a mix of local news provided by various correspondents (usually uncredited) and "filler" items from the various syndicating groups that supplied Southern country newspapers. Perhaps Ingraham himself provided a copy of the article, which generously praises the school and its founder. Perhaps the *Ishmael-ite* couldn't resist the attention of a large metropolitan daily, though on at least one crucial point the *Globe* story violated the tenets of white supremacy which the Sparta paper routinely maintained. It suggested that the condition of African-American people in the South was "due to the lack of education facilities."[8]

Ingraham's cultivation of Northern benefactors bore fruit in a visit to his school described by an *Ishmaelite* correspondent on March 25 under the heading "A Visit to Industrial College." The visitor was "Miss Annie Brown, Supt. of the Lend a Hand Mission movement of Boston, Mass," and she spoke to the assembled students and staff, the county school superintendent, his wife, and the reporter. The reporter notes that "music, sight-singing[,] physical culture, agriculture, arts and crafts, drawing etc. [are] being taught in connection with the well regulated grade school." The reporter also carefully remarks that "we were all served with a delicious luncheon[;] at noon hour covers were laid for four, two of the senior girls rendered most excellent service." By mentioning that the lunch was served for just four—the reporter, the woman from Boston, and the local white school supervisor and his wife—the reporter assures the reader there was no mixed-race dining of the kind for which the South had never forgiven Theodore Roosevelt.[9]

Ingraham next appears in the *Ishmaelite* of April 29 in a letter written by him but given the heading "Colored Citizens Write a Card." He is representing a group called "The Hancock Improvement League" (his name is misprinted as "Ingram"), and his letter begins with a familiar American reference that a "crime wave seems to be abroad in the land." Ingraham goes on to mention his approval of the work of the local court system, "showing to the county that crime will be punished irrespective of person." The letter would seem pointlessly commonplace out of context, but two phrases make clear that its coded subject is lynching or other extralegal action by local whites. The first is Ingraham's praise of "the peaceable relations between the two races" in Hancock County, and the second is his assurance to "law abiding white citizens that we stand for law and order." The meaning here depends on what is not said, the implied opposites of "peaceable relations" and "law abiding white citizens." Nine black people had been lynched in Georgia in 1920; twenty-one had been lynched in 1919. In 1921 eight more blacks were lynched, and nine black bodies were found in unmarked graves on John S. Williams's plantation in Jasper County. In 1922 thirteen more black people would be lynched. During this period, however, there were no lynchings in Hancock County.[10]

The remaining three Ingraham items in the *Ishmaelite* for 1921 deal with his fund-raising activities for his school, and two of them must approximately bracket Jean Toomer's time in Sparta. On July 22 Ingraham's letter headlined "Communication" appeared. It is primarily an appeal for money, one that chides the locals since "the school gets its support largely from northern people." It also affirms the school's Booker T. Washington model, which was to instill "right ideas into the life of the young Negro so that he will have a higher regard for honest labor." Shortly after this letter's publication, Ingraham must have visited Washington, D.C., been introduced to Jean Toomer, and thereupon hired him as a substitute principal for the Sparta school, since Toomer left for Georgia in September. On November 4 the *Ishmaelite* carried a small item titled "Ingraham Returns from Trip through North." He had been to Boston and other cities "working in the interest of his school." Within three weeks of his return, Jean Toomer departed Sparta, and so would have missed Ingraham's single appearance on the front page of the *Ishmaelite* on December 23, under the headline "Tourists Appreciate the Southern Hospitality."

This last story records the odd culmination of Ingraham's work in the North, as his school hosted a visit by "fifty wealthy New Englanders . . . enroute to Southern Florida." The Northerners were driving south, led by a Mr. McGee who planned "a stop-over for the party at Prof. L. S. Ingraham's Negro Industrial School. The tourists were delighted to find so good a school for negroes in the South. Tradition has unfortunately and falsely accused the South of mistreatment of the negro." During the stopover, a Mr. W. W. Driskell spoke to the visitors in "defense of the South in explaining our true feeling toward the Negro," and the group took up a "free-will offering" that raised $44.50 for the school. The story concludes with a menu of the dinner Ingraham's wife prepared and a list of all fifty party members and the cars they were driving—a Haynes, a Hupmobile, a National, a Franklin, an Essex, a Marmon.

The *Ishmaelite* and its readership, or at least its reporters and editor, were fascinated with the display of Northern wealth passing through Sparta in December 1921. The concern with cars already was reflected in the paper's advertising columns; every issue in October and November 1921 carried a large ad for Buick: "Presenting the New Buick Four." Ads for motor oil, garages, and repair services were also common. But cars were still expensive items in the rural South, and the *Ishmaelite* ads were for an agent in Atlanta. The main headline for the December 23 paper announces that "Sparta Must Have Business Men's Club—Now!" The story begins, "Our people really do not seem to realize the serious predicament our county is in, caused by the ravages of the boll weevil and the panic prices being given for all farm produce." It goes on to claim that a business club will "put Sparta on the map and get new business concerns to come in here." Hancock County, like most of the rural South, was falling into a postwar depression as prices for agricultural products declined.[11]

In Georgia the state's prosperity was still tied to cotton markets, more than fifty years after the Civil War and the end of slavery. The working of large plantation farms by wage laborers or sharecroppers continued to leave the land owning planter at the top of an economic pyramid. Since cotton cultivation required intensive labor at every stage, from planting to picking, the planter's profits depended not only on the market price being set in New York or London but also on the price of local labor. To ensure profits the planters required access to a large pool of cheap labor, which meant that landowners needed in some form or other to replicate the control over African-American farm workers which they had maintained during the period of slavery. The system they created was what W. J. Cash in 1941 called "the pattern of essential peonage which had generally persisted ever since the Civil War." Two extreme forms of control under this system were the convict lease system and labor contract peonage; beyond these quasi legal means there were a range of coercive methods and, ultimately, the Southern ritual of lynching.[12]

Among the white planters there was also an intermittent fear, particularly strong at the end of World War I, after the Great Migration of blacks to the North had already begun, that the pool of cheap labor would dry up, and many Southern states, including Georgia, passed laws to halt outmigration. On the front page of the *Ishmaelite* for April 16, 1920, appears a story titled "Stanley Talks About Labob [*sic*]," a letter from the Georgia Commissioner of Commerce and Labor "published for the information of the people generally." Stanley reminds his readers that recruiting laborers to work outside of Georgia without acquiring a set of licenses and paying extravagant fees (amounting to more than two thousand dollars per county) is illegal, and urges the arrest of anyone suspected of such activities. He warns that "there is every indication that a great many laborers are being carried out of Georgia into other states in violation of the Georgia law. It is the usual method for a white man to employ a negro helpers [*sic*] in securing this labor." To thwart them the commissioner suggests that any movement of labor should be "carefully watched," and he offers his bureau's assistance to local sheriffs and farmers. This was the economic system supporting the world in which Jean Toomer found himself in Sparta in the fall of 1921, and in *Cane* it would be the threat of violence, lynching, and surveillance that would define Southern society.[13]

The *Ishmaelite*'s pages for the early 1920s frequently illustrate the contradiction implicit in the South's desire both to modernize its economy and to retain its feudal social system. On June 4, 1920, appears a story headlined "Congressman Vinson Writes People Card," an open letter from the congressional representative for Hancock County on the matter of federal funding for local schools. He opposes such funding because it might lead to some diminution of "the blessings of home rule and local self-government." Of course, since 1908 Georgia had essentially disfranchised African-American voters, who made up nearly 75 percent of the county's population. The same set of statutes, particularly the poll tax, served to keep some poor whites from voting. "Home rule," then, among Congressman Vinson's constituency, represented probably less than 20 percent of Hancock's population. Members of this ruling elite were, as the *Ishmaelite*'s pages show, concerned with the county's economic plight, but they were also wary of the danger to their own authority implicit in educating the general population. Before Ingraham had managed to open his school in 1910, an earlier effort to establish a school for black children in Sparta had been blocked. In 1903 a Miss Carrie Bemus proposed "a Normal and Industrial School for the Negro youth of the state." Despite gathering some local support for her idea, she was thwarted when the *Ishmaelite*'s editor, Sidney Lewis, denounced it, saying "the outlook is that we are going to have trouble too much without the addition of its complications." His remark was an allusion to the charge of attempted rape made against a local black youth by two white women shortly after the school proposal was presented.[14]

The *Ishmaelite*, of course, like any newspaper, provided not only the "news" but a continuous cultural context for the town's sacred myths. A weekly newspaper, it was founded in 1879, replacing the *Sparta Times and Planter* just as Reconstruction ended; like Sparta itself, it took on its unusual name as an act of myth-making in response to history. Alluding to the fierce warfare between the Native Americans and the early emigrating Anglo-Scottish settlers, the name "Sparta" looked back to a classical past to project a heroic present and future. The name of the town reminded its citizens that they possessed the "Spartan" virtues necessary to conquer both the indigenous people and the wilderness. Calling the newspaper the "Ishmaelite" followed in this same tradition of symbolic inscription: the biblical reference implied that the inhabitants of this town rebelled against the order of a Reconstruction that had placed political power in the hands of the black majority.[15]

Sparta's resistance to education for African-Americans was part of a long tradition in the South. In the slave states before the Civil War, it was illegal to teach slaves to read and write. After the war, a concerted effort by the victorious Abolition groups of the North sent instructors to the defeated South to teach the freedmen, and the region fixed on the figure of the "Northern schoolmarm" as the primary symbol of the attack on Southern social mores. In *The Mind of the South*, W. J. Cash singles out the "schoolmarm" figure as having "no little part in developing Southern bitterness as a whole," and although his characterization fosters an absurd stereotype and his remarks about her role in the "mind" of the South are at best misleading, he properly recognizes the symbolic threat she represented. After the Civil War Southern society developed a way of life intended to maintain antebellum social relations as far as possible, and without the legal fact of slavery and its supporting arguments of biblical or "civilized" tradition, it relied increasingly on scientific racism to justify the oppression or virtual reenslavement of the emancipated African-Americans. The theory of white supremacy required black inferiority, a "natural incapacity," a "racial inheritance." The empirical evidence of these "natural" conditions, of course, could be guaranteed only by denying former slaves an education that might allow them to show themselves as equal. Schoolmarms, then, threatened the new order the white South was establishing, an order based on a new version of white supremacy.[16]

Yet the South wanted "progress," as manifested in economic development and material wealth. As C. Vann Woodward observed, "The paradoxical combination of white supremacy and progressivism was not new to the region, but it never ceased to be a cause of puzzlement and confusion above the Potomac—and not a little, below." In 1921 that conflict was expressed in a series of exchanges between outgoing Georgia governor Hugh Dorsey and other state officials, as well as by the rapidly expanding Ku Klux Klan. Dorsey criticized the endemic violence directed against black citizens, while his opponents both denied that violence occurred and defended it as necessary to protect white supremacy. These exchanges even reached the New York media, and it's likely the stories were read by Jean Toomer before he traveled south. The conflict also frequently appeared in the pages of the *Ishmaelite*, never more openly perhaps than in the issue of December 23, 1921, which joined an admiration and envy of Northern wealth with apologetics for Southern racial attitudes, a call for new business organization and industrial development with a savage little verse attacking the Northern schoolteacher and her plan to educate the black children of the South.[17]

Jean Toomer's position when he arrived in Sparta to become the temporary principal for Ingraham's school was not unlike that of the despised schoolmarm. In his history of Hancock County, Forrest Shivers summarizes the ambiguous position the school held from the moment of its founding:

The establishment of Sparta A & I represented quite an achievement. It had been only seven years since Mell Duggan's attempt to establish a school for blacks on the Tuskegee model had foundered and those who sought to establish advanced colored schools no doubt met with a great deal of suspicion. Ingraham proceeded with due circumspection and the first board of trustees of his school were all prominent white citizens. By 1914 white suspicions were sufficiently allayed that A & I was taken into the county school system. Ingraham never forgot the necessity of maintaining good relations with the white community while struggling to maintain and improve his school. A measure of his success were the favorable comments that appeared from time to time in the local press.[18]

Of course, as the briefest examination of the 1921 *Ishmaelite* quickly uncovers, "favorable comments" have to be understood in the context of Southern apartheid. White supremacy ultimately depended on a politically maintained denial of black opportunity, but it would be increasingly hard for the South to introduce modern technologies and exclude modernist ideologies. When Toomer spoke after the publication of *Cane* of writing a "swan-song," and of the book as "a song of an end," he wasn't only being a pastoral elegist; he understood that "with Negroes also the trend was towards the small town and then towards the city—and industry and commerce and machines." Education is a reciprocal process, and the evidence of *Cane* is that Toomer learned more in Georgia than he taught. In his book's long concluding story, "education" is a figure not only for the contradictions of the New South but for the painful initiation of Kabnis into the world of "due circumspection," "white suspicions," and things much worse.[19]

Sparta and Sempter

Toomer said in his autobiographical writings that he began work on *Cane* during his train ride home from Georgia, but, in fact, he had already begun writing while he was still in Georgia; he submitted at least one long story, "Georgia Night," to the *Liberator* in New York before he left Sparta. It's not surprising, then, that the town and the landscape of central Georgia are so closely observed in "Kabnis" and the stories of the book's first section. Toomer took the name "Sempter" for his fictional town, but he adopted other local names literally. He also sketched through the stories of *Cane* a kind of fictional map that has a close resemblance to the Sparta of 1921, as it can be partially reconstructed or even, in some cases, still discovered in the present-day town. However, what becomes clear from such comparisons is that while Toomer modeled his imaginary Sempter on the actual Sparta, he was primarily interested in creating a symbolic geography of Sempter, not a literal transcription of Sparta. As a modernist, Toomer assembled a mosaic of topographical images by which he revealed the silent spaces and buried secrets within the map of his small town, secrets arising from a hidden history of racial oppression.[20]

The official map of Sparta, Georgia, blurs the distinction between town and country. A major road, Dixie Street, is included within Sparta's city limits, though it deviates from the pattern of Sparta's basic grid, curving off to the northwest, breaking away from Sparta's formal arrangement of streets that cross each other at right angles. Dixie Street is really a country road and, as well, the center of Sparta's black district on the western edge of town. Intersecting Dixie Street is an unnamed dirt road, not marked on the map, which runs south to the site of the Sparta Agricultural and Industrial School, in 1995 a group of empty buildings boarded up and fenced off. Today this unnamed dirt road serves as a shortcut to Dixie Street, representing an invisible boundary line of the black neighborhood known to its inhabitants as "Sander's Quarters."[21] The school itself was located on the top of a small hill about a mile from town, just a few yards from the present-day Highway 22. From this spot one can see the tower of the courthouse in town, as Kabnis does at the beginning of "Kabnis." Directly across this dirt road to the west is the "Big House" of the school's former principal and founder, Linton Ingraham, the model for Hanby in "Kabnis." The unnamed dirt road would have been the path along which Kabnis fled in panic from the rock thrown through Halsey's window in the final story of *Cane*.[22]

In *Cane*, Dixie Street becomes the "Dixie Pike," and at dusk, a transformation occurs along this meandering road that crosses the railroad tracks, hinted at by Toomer's figure in "Carma": "Dusk takes the polish from the rails."[23] At "dusk"—the moment of transition from light to dark—the visible polish of the daylight world disappears, soon to be replaced by a night world redefined by black sounds and songs; the rails, which occupy a prominent place on Sparta's official map because they indicate the town's connection to the modern world, also serve to bring black laborers home. Toomer often fixes upon the spot where Dixie Pike meets the railroad track. He refers to it in both "Carma" and "Fern"; most important, it is the place where Becky's house is "islandized." The narrator of "Carma" watches Carma drive her wagon on the Dixie Pike as it "crosses the railroad track"; at the end of "Fern" the narrator, watching from his train window, says, "I saw her [Fern] as I crossed her road" (16, 33). Carma's disappearance "at some indefinite point along the road" foreshadows her tale, whose meaning eludes him, just as he continues to remain puzzled by Fern's anguished song in the forest. In both cases, the narrator bears witness to something he doesn't quite understand, and, as in "Becky," there doesn't seem to be any "true word" that will do justice to the witnessed experience (13). The islandized space at the crossroad of dirt track and railroad track represents that indefinite boundary between inside and outside.

If Toomer was precise in his memory of Dixie Street, he also remembered and used real places and place names from the town of Sparta itself. Esther walks from home "toward her father's grocery store," turning "in Broad from Maple Street [probably "Miles Street"]." This small detail suggests the significant class difference between Esther and those who live outside town, even Kabnis's ambitious employer, Hanby (36). Her father, Jim Crane, may be modeled after Richard Johnson, a man light enough to pass for white who owned a block of businesses in Sparta and ran them through white front men. In "Kabnis," Halsey's wagon shop occupies a building a few yards off "Broad Street" (to the south). In this instance, Toomer was probably thinking of the Old Rock Shop. Built in 1819, it was first a stagecoach stop, then a wheelwright shop, and finally, in 1927, a gas station. It stood on the southeast corner of Broad and Boland streets. In terms of its actual history, the Old Rock Shop ironically predicts Halsey's fate as a wheelwright, for automobiles, as the *Ishmaelite* ads promise, are in the process of replacing wagons and buggies. In "Kabnis," Halsey's business has fallen off: "Not much work these days," he tells Lewis; when work does come, he eagerly watches "for the wagon to turn from Broad Street into his road" (191, 196).[24]

Several blocks south of Broad Street, off Spring Street, was an area known as Montour Village. The place was not a "village" but, as Elizabeth Wiley Smith says, a "municipality within another municipality." The forty acres that defined Montour Village had been incorporated in 1857, and a textile factory was built at its center; Toomer confirms these urban origins by calling Montour "Factory Town," the site of Tom Burwell's lynching in "Blood-Burning Moon." Slavery had already negated the pastoral myth to which the South tardily laid claim, and as one historian has observed, plantations were "factories in the fields," the dilapidated factory in Toomer's story being an extension of a system that was a kind of agribusiness.[25]

In the center of a square at the western end of Sparta's commercial district stands the building that dominates the landscape: the Hancock County courthouse. The courthouse fronts "Broad Street" and is a door west of the Edwards House Hotel where Toomer's father once stayed. Since Sparta was (and is still) the county seat of Hancock County, the courthouse—built in the Palladian style and completed in 1883 at the height of the town's economic prosperity—suggests, as does its name, that this village saw itself as a city. The courthouse is both a symbol of law and order and one of sentiment, for as a *monument* it memorializes a heroic past. In her 1930s history of Hancock County, Elizabeth Wiley Smith quotes the English historian Thomas Macaulay in a caption accompanying a photograph of the courthouse: "A people who take no pride in the noble achievements of a remote ancestry, will never achieve anything worthy to be remembered with pride by a remote posterity." As Victor Walter observes of "ancient times through the Middle Ages," there were "two ways . . . to glorify a city: one by erecting splendid buildings, and the other by composing eulogies." Smith does both by coupling Macaulay's words with Sparta's monument.[26]

Smith also implies that the courthouse is the middle link in a historical narrative: its continuing presence connects past and future. To commemorate that sense of temporal continuity, a clock was placed in the courthouse tower with a face for each of the four compass points. But narratives are also political, and another expression of that temporal continuity appeared as an announcement in the *Sparta Ishmaelite* of February 18, 1921: "On Monday night, February 21st, at 8 o'clock in the court house a speaker from the Imperial Palace of the Knights of the KU KLUX KLAN will deliver an address on the Klan of 'Yesterday today and forever.'" Esther hears the "town clock striking twelve" as she leaves for her misadventure with Barlo, and Kabnis imagines himself lynched under the courthouse tower as the town's white citizens "juggle justice and a nigger" (45, 163). But Toomer also twice mentions a black woman who "saw the mother of Christ and drew her in charcoal on the courthouse wall," once in "Fern" (31) and again in "Esther":

"an inspired Negress, of wide reputation for being sanctified, drew a portrait of a black madonna on the court-house wall" (40).

The symbolic placement of the courthouse in the center of a square points to an important characteristic of cartography in the history of the New World. William Boelhower observes that "the function of the first maps was not at all to report a place, but to impose an *idea* of place on the new continent." The effect of this was not only to inscribe an ideology on a place but to erase what was already there: "The global strategy of the map is a strategy of deterritorialization, an aesthetic of corporeal disappearance." Simon Ryan calls this the "cartographic double movement," one of "erasure and projection, creating a blank, and filling that blank with a legend (both in the sense of a myth and a cartographical inscription)." The map, then, strives for accuracy, but also serves to define place as "sites for mythical projections." These myths represent authority, the economic authority of a railroad line, the political authority of a sheriff's jurisdiction. Of course, whoever lives in a place may project their own mythic understanding onto their map of the land. Pierre Nora notes that "memory attaches itself to sites, whereas history attaches itself to events." Thus, the drawing in charcoal on the courthouse wall restores the site to local memory and, in reclaiming that memory, rewrites Southern history; in repeating the figure of the "sanctified Negress," who was inspired by Barlo's origin story of the enchained African giant, Toomer restores a religious dimension to the secular map. Throughout *Cane* the reader is confronted with maps depicting contradictory realities, and often the conflict is between an official reality and a communal or private one.[27]

The Hancock County courthouse in Sparta is a site of "mythic projections" as a monument to civilization and to a heroic past. Of course, in a conflict of maps not all pasts will be memorialized, and peoples who possess the wrong kinds of monuments can be defined as "savages," as Thomas Jefferson observes in *Notes on the State of Virginia*: "I know of no such thing existing as an Indian monument: for I would not honour with that name arrow points, stone hatchets, stone pipes, and half-shapen images." In this view the whole question of "honour" itself hinges on this matter of monuments: those who have them are civilized because they have a conception of honor. Yet the folk artist in *Cane* who refigures Christ's mother as a black woman ("in charcoal") on the courthouse wall has not only remapped the history of Christianity but also called into question the monument's relationship to honor and abstract justice, a rule of masculine law.[28]

The courthouse has not been the instrument of justice but rather the site of a history of oppression and terror, its system serving to distort justice for the sake of power. A monument to the Confederate war dead in front of the Hancock County courthouse is inscribed: "Georgia's was the word, and theirs the will to die." The biblical echo ("the word") gives historical sanction to the defense of the Lost Cause, a cause that is forever inscribed on the monument itself. The inscription implies that although the cause was lost, the white "will" remains, or as Kirk Savage puts it in his essay on the Civil War monument, "The South . . . renounced its proslavery ideology without tearing down the fundamental structure of white supremacy." The Civil War monument testifies to the permanence of that structure: "That the common soldier is also always white and Anglo-Saxon in physiognomy suggests that memorials offer up not a neutral individual body but a collective body conceived within certain boundaries and allegiances." The inscription on the monument that stands in front of the Hancock County courthouse suggests, too, that justice is hardly neutral. It says that justice is defined (from *definire*: "to set bounds to") by whiteness, a definition sanctified by history, the event of the Civil War.[29]

"Did He Have Negro Blood?"

Although Toomer went to Sparta in 1921 as a stranger, he had his own connections to the South and even, indirectly, to Hancock County. His maternal grandfather, P. B. S. Pinchback, who raised him after his mother's death in 1908, was the son of a white planter and a mulatto slave woman who had been manumitted shortly before the child's birth. The family's legal status was uncertain enough that when the planter died in Mississippi in 1848, the mother moved with her children to Cincinnati, to avoid the possibility that they might be reenslaved. Pinchback became a prominent Republican in Louisiana's Reconstruction politics, was elected lieutenant governor of the state in 1871, and served briefly as acting governor. He was also elected U.S. senator in 1873, but his election was contested as Republican support for Reconstruction faded, and he never entered the Senate. In 1893 he moved to Washington, D.C., his money and political connections giving him quick entry into that city's "mulatto elite," the mixed-race middle-class society closely tied to the Republican party and the federal administrative offices of the city. At a Christmas party at the new Pinchback home in 1893, his daughter Nina met Nathan Toomer, a gentleman of apparent means from Georgia; shortly thereafter they were engaged, and Nathan gave Nina twelve thousand dollars in cash to purchase a house. Three months later they were married, and on December 26, 1894, Jean Toomer was born.[30]

Jean Toomer's father, Nathan, had been married twice previously, the last time to Amanda America Dickson, briefly famous as "the richest colored woman alive." Amanda Dickson, born in 1849, was the daughter of David Dickson, Hancock County's most prominent, and richest, planter, and his slave mistress, Julia Lewis. Amanda had inherited her father's estate, worth around four hundred thousand dollars, at his death in 1885, despite Georgia laws that specifically prohibited such inheritance. The Dickson will also provided that on Amanda's death the estate would pass to her children and not to her husband. When she died in 1893 Nathan was immediately embroiled with her sons in legal disputes over the disposition of the estate, wrangles that continued until 1901 and left Nathan in possession of some of the Dickson property. He died in 1906, without a will, and whatever estate he had evidently passed to his daughters by his first marriage.[31]

It is not clear how much Jean Toomer knew about his father. Nathan essentially abandoned his wife and son after a year of marriage, and Jean had only one memory of seeing him. Nina was granted a divorce in 1899. In an autobiographical fragment Toomer recorded that when he was in Sparta in 1921 he learned, during a conversation in the local black barbershop, that his father had "stayed at the white hotel," and that "some white men were trying to get his money away from him." These separate remarks by the two black barbers probably indicate Nathan Toomer's ambiguous racial identity, though even to have "stayed at the white hotel" was no small accomplishment for someone identified as black in rural Georgia of 1900. Nathan had been born into slavery in North Carolina in 1839. He was sold twice and taken to Houston County, Georgia, about fifty miles southwest of Hancock, with his mother, to become a servant to Henry Toomer. By 1870, only five years after Emancipation, he somehow managed to become a wealthy farmer, with real estate worth twenty thousand dollars, personal property worth ten thousand dollars, and two live-in "domestic servants." His connection to Hancock County began with his involvement with the Dickson estates, and he evidently lived in Sparta or visited the town frequently in the last years of his life.[32]

If Toomer heard stories about his father in Hancock County he may have known that Nathan had been born in slavery, though Toomer does not say so directly in his autobiographical writings. In "On Being an American" he says of Nathan: "His father, a plantation owner, had left him some money, and Toomer lived as a gentleman of leisure with a taste for luxury and elegance. He was of English-Dutch-Spanish stock. I gather that he lived in the south as a white man. Did he have Negro blood? It is possible." In the draft fragments of "Incredible Journey," he is more direct, noting that "my father's father was a southern planter of considerable wealth and culture, his mother a woman of mixed blood." Nathan Toomer in fact was a working, prosperous farmer for most of his life, classed as a black or mulatto in various census and legal documents. As Kent Anderson Leslie and Willard Gatewood, Jr., report, "Tax digest records from 1875 to 1892 depict Toomer as a freedman slowly accumulating capital, mostly in stock, and eventually purchasing land." Thus, "in 1879 he hired five colored laborers and produced $3500 worth of farm products." The question remains of how Nathan Toomer acquired his initial stake of money or land. If Jean Toomer had an accurate source for the story that Nathan's father was a planter who "left him some money," that would fit a pattern of white-black kinship relations which has been suggested as an important cause for the growth of the mulatto middle-class in the nineteenth-century South, especially in Hancock County, Georgia.[33]

The mulatto child of a white planter and a slave woman might be given special treatment by his father, and even after Emancipation economic aid of one kind or another might be continued to that individual or perhaps to an extended family. Joel Williamson in *New People* discusses not only how commonplace miscegenation was in the antebellum South, but how it sometimes led to such ties: "A final important consequence of the mixing in late slavery of upper-class white men in the South with mulatto women was that the offspring were often well cared for in terms of property, occupations and education. It was not so much the quantity of the new mulatto issue that was important as it was their quality. When freedom came, they were prepared to leap to the fore in leadership, and did so." This general pattern describes the career of P. B. S. Pinchback, and it may also have fit Nathan Toomer.[34]

No doubt the most famous example of such support was Amanda Dickson's inheritance of her father's large estate, some part of which passed to Nathan Toomer. Jean Toomer, then, probably knew of planter inheritances to each of his mulatto parents (though very little of that wealth would be passed down to him), and it's possible one reason he went to Georgia was to inquire about his father's estate. In any case, after Toomer arrived in Sparta in the fall of 1921, he would almost certainly have heard stories of mixed-racial families, besides the Dicksons, in Hancock County. Indeed, his account of Halsey's white ancestors in "Kabnis" indicates that he knew something about Sparta's secret racial history. In her book *Ambiguous Lives*, Adele Logan Alexander refers to a nineteenth-century account of Judge Nathan Sayre's house in Sparta as having "more doors, intricate passageways & cul de sacs . . . [than] the Castle of Otranto." This hidden part of his Pomegranate Hall housed his common-law wife, Susan Hunt, a woman of color, and their two children. A prominent citizen, an eligible bachelor, and a member of Georgia's supreme court, Sayre arranged his house so that there was both public space where he could entertain and private space where he lived with his black family. The historian Mark Schultz was able to trace ten such families in postbellum Hancock, most of them located in rural areas; further, as Schultz notes, "eight of the ten postbellum mixed relationships . . . were initiated between 1860 and 1900. Only two of the unions . . . existed after 1921." The mixed relationship was disappearing because the conditions that favored it—rural isolation of white planters and, perhaps, a "tradition" of such relationships—were changing.[35]

Antimiscegenation laws were rarely enforced against white males, but as the pressure of Jim Crow attitudes increased from the 1890s on, it became harder to maintain an open mixed-race liaison. Such relationships didn't disappear entirely, of course, but they became even more private and secretive. Schultz notes that "Hancock County holds a reputation among surrounding counties for having an unusually strong tradition of recognized interracial kinship." However, he believes such kinship was probably equally common in other Black Belt counties, and that the fame, and scandal, of the David Dickson example accounts for Hancock's reputation. Pointing out that most white aid to black relatives was a matter of discreet transfers of land, money, or goods, Schultz says, "Dickson's celebrity, and the breathtaking completeness of his gift, turned a somewhat acceptable, privately quiet exchange into an 'embarrassing' public affair."[36]

Open Secrets: The Roots of a Modernist

Secrecy and miscegenation are the major themes in the first section of *Cane*. They underlie the mystery of "Karintha," and they appear directly in "Becky"; they emerge as hints and glimpses through the rest of the section's stories and poems until they erupt in the apocalyptic conclusion of "Blood-Burning Moon." The questions of origins and of racial identity which concerned Toomer sprang directly from miscegenation—the mulatto class into which he was born was created by miscegenation. And the secrecy that had long surrounded mixed-race sexual relations in the United States had a particular history associated with the hierarchy of race status which was central to Southern society.

Race, as biologists and anthropologists have made clear in this century, is a social category, not a biological one. Physical characteristics associated with a "race" may be statistically more common in groups that have been largely endogamous for a long period of time, but this statistical grouping does not constitute a biologically significant division. As Barbara Fields has aptly stated, "There is only one human species, and the most dramatic differences of appearance can be wiped out in one act of miscegenation." Nor are there such things as "pure races"; no human group has not been mixed, to some extent, at some time or other. For most groups, including Africans and Europeans, this mixing has been continuous, if not large-scale, for all of recorded history, and no doubt long before. In the early colonies of Virginia, English indentured servants and African imported laborers were producing children whose appearance mixed their parents' traits, and who were called mulattoes. This mixing would continue throughout American history, occasionally on a large scale.[37]

As the South imported the vast majority of African slaves brought to the United States and, after the end of the slave trade, encouraged the increase of the native slave population, it became home to the majority of the nation's black and mulatto people. The idea of slavery and of racial definition developed together and came to be linked; as the Southern economy was increasingly based on plantation crops worked by black slave labor, the definition became fixed in custom and law. Beginning with an economic system, the South, of course, developed a cultural mythology to justify and support the basis of its profits.

After slavery was institutionalized, the growing mulatto population was largely a result of sexual contacts between slave owners and their female slaves. Masters held essentially the "right to rape," whether or not the slave agreed to her concubinage; as Deborah Gray White says, "The choice put before many slave women was between miscegenation and the worst experiences that slavery had to offer. Not surprisingly, many chose the former, though they were hardly naive." That is, slave women knew there was a tradeoff involved in their actions; while they might hope to gain something from their choice (if it was a choice), or at least to avoid further trouble, that was not always possible. The sexual exploitation of slave women produced not only mulatto children but the cultural myth of the lascivious African-American woman, what White refers to as the "Jezebel myth." This myth rationalized, by a circular reasoning, the very sexual exploitation that gave rise to it, and would remain a stigma attached to black women long after slavery was defunct.[38]

In both the North and the South, commentary on the sexual practices of slavery made miscegenation an "open secret" well before the Civil War. Northern abolitionists attacked the obvious hypocrisy of "Christian gentlemen" who sexually used their slaves. To defend itself the South devised a number of replies, from the outright denial that miscegenation took place to the argument by the chancellor of the University of South Carolina that of course it took place, but black women couldn't be harmed by the practice, and it was preferable to the prostitution of white women in the North. Contradiction and sophistry inevitably plagued Southern attempts to reply to their attackers, and so finally silence was held to be the best answer.[39]

After Reconstruction the new ideologues of white supremacy would develop the "Jezebel myth" to propose the notion that African-American women, sensual by nature, had seduced their white masters, and, in fact, continued (especially mulattas) to be dangerous seducers. But beyond the public discussion and mythologizing carried on in books, articles, sermons, and so forth, the local dynamics of race and sex in the South remained secretive. White describes what was at stake:

Of course, the slaves on a given plantation could have advised their mistress of the paternity of a mulatto child, for they usually knew with which slave women the master was sleeping. Out of fear they dared not, and these secrets of slavery remained, as Linda Brent reported, "concealed like those of the Inquisition."[40]

Despite the fact that some white men acknowledged their mulatto offspring and attempted to provide for them outside the system of slavery, in general mulattoes and free blacks were disconcertingly subversive of the South's developing racial ideology. Still, before 1850 there were many local variations in social attitudes toward mulattoes, and, as Joel Williamson points out, parts of the South (coastal South Carolina and south Louisiana in particular) more or less adopted the Latin American code by which mulattoes were seen as a group intermediate between blacks and whites. Whatever were the "moral" attitudes toward race mixing, South Carolina, for instance, never passed a law forbidding racial intermarriage before the Civil War. During the 1850s, however, the division between North and South widened: Northern Abolitionist attacks on slavery intensified, and the South responded in part by trying to clarify its racial order. The social position of mulattoes and free blacks everywhere eroded in the face of this new Southern fear, and the separate status of mulattoes began to disappear; as the South advocated more absolute versions of racial definition, mulattoes and blacks were pushed together under the new designations.[41]

The Civil War and the Reconstruction that lasted in parts of the South until 1880 ended legal slavery in the United States, but those huge, disruptive events did not mark a halt in the nation's willingness to contest racial identities and racial definition. In the South the passion to define and control became more all-consuming, more bitter, more ferocious. Southerners of the elite classes recognized that the economic basis of their way of life had been destroyed, but whites of all classes felt their social worlds threatened. Those worlds had in common some ideology that presumed "natural" white superiority, a presumption now without a universal legal framework to support it, or, where Union troops were present, without the automatic resort of extralegal violence. When the North abandoned Reconstruction in the 1870s, the South was left to effectively recreate both the extralegal and legal means to enforce a social order constructed around white supremacy. This new order still maintained as its elite the planter class whose wealth depended on the labor of black peasants, formerly slaves, now primarily tenant farmers or wage laborers. But while the South after 1880 reconstituted important parts of the antebellum order, it had to do so on terms different from those existing before the Civil War. Barbara Fields captures the contradictory sense of change and continuity: "There is . . . a profound difference in social meaning between a planter who experiences black people as ungrateful, untrustworthy, and half-witted slaves and a planter who experiences black people as undisciplined, irregular, and refractory employees."[42]

Among the changes that African-Americans demanded as they began to take stock of the consequences of Emancipation and the defeat of the South was that black women should no longer be subject to the sexual control of their former owners or of white men in general. After Emancipation, and particularly during Reconstruction, African-American women were able to offer physical resistance to sexual exploitation, and could turn as well to the Freedman's Bureau or the newly accessible state legal systems for protection. With the end of Reconstruction, effective resistance no doubt became more difficult, even though the South, publicly at least, proclaimed that its sexual code was part of the growing "Jim Crow" system for separating the races. John G. Mencke has shown that up to the 1890s whites were relatively disinclined to view amalgamation as a threat, but with the spread of "radical racism" in the South, a rash of books and pamphlets appeared describing miscegenation as "a crime" against God and man that "will spread like a bubonic plague."[43]

In a sense a kind of pornography was created by the new literature, with the terms "pollution," "unclean," "the mire of mongrelism," and "the abomination of miscegenation" revealing both fear and fascination. The act of sexual congress between the races was like incest, the ultimate taboo, and thus provoked description even though the act was said to be indescribable and indefensible. In 1891, the Reverend William H. Campbell warned that miscegenation would result in "all the evils we now contemplate with horror and alarm." Dr. Josiah Nott (*Types of Mankind*, 1854) believed in polygenesis, which not only accounted for mulattoes as "unnatural" hybrids, but also placed them in biblical lore as descendants of Cain, who married a black woman after he left Eden. One of Nott's articles was entitled "The Mulatto a Hybrid—Probable Extermination of the Two Races if the Whites and Blacks Are Allowed to Intermarry" (1843). Indeed, a common notion throughout the nineteenth century held that mulattoes were infertile unless they mated with "pure" whites or blacks. Therefore what was imagined to be at stake was not only racial purity or social hegemony, but species survival.[44]

With or without these dire predictions, the opinion of many travelers and writers who passed through the South in the early 1900s was that miscegenation had by no means ended with slavery. Albert Hart, in *The Southern South* (1910), spends several pages retelling "the testimony of Southern Whites now living down there," which revealed that sexual relations between white men and black women were still commonplace. Hart, a history professor from Harvard, held strongly racist views about African-Americans, yet he pointed out that "there are two million deplorable reasons in the South for believing that there is no divinely implanted race instinct against miscegenation; that while a Southern author is writing that 'the idea of the race is far more sacred than that of the family. It is, in fact, *the most sacred thing on earth*,' his neighbors, and possibly his acquaintances, by their acts are disproving the argument."[45] The "two million deplorable reasons" were, of course, the South's estimated mulatto population. Hart's characterization is a reminder of the contempt for mulattoes frequently expressed during the period. Since the Civil War the South, and indeed the nation, had been moving toward the "one-drop rule" of racial definition, by which any trace of black "blood" categorized a person as "Negro." However, the absolute separation between black and white which the legal systems of Southern states attempted to create was made impossible by the uncertain nature of distribution for "racial" characteristics: a "white" person might appear swarthy; a "black" person might appear pale. South-ern courts often fell back on questionable means of definition, including whether a person was "known" as black or white in their local community, a reliance that made a mockery of the science of the new "rational" racism. But Hart saw what moved the extraordinary fear of miscegenation and mu-lattoes when he observed, "The point is, however, not only that miscegena-tion in the South is evil, but that it is the most glaring contradiction of the supposed infallible principles of race separation and social inequality." [46]

If various white commentators were convinced that miscegenation con-tinued to be common in the South after the end of Reconstruction, there was an even stronger opinion, both more extensive and more angry, among African-Americans. For black people, miscegenation was understood as the rape, concubinage, or prostitution of black women by Southern white men. "Secret" though this activity might have nominally been, there is a great deal of evidence for the continuity of white men's sexual exploita-tion of black women in the South well into the twentieth century. Rape or coercive sexual demands were part of the system of maintaining white su-premacy, and resistance by either black women or black men was usually met with extreme violence. The sets of mythic stereotypes whites attached to both genders of both races—bestial black man, chivalrous white man, pure white woman, libidinous black woman—were intended to conceal the actual relations of the sexes: the white South's fury against the black man–white woman relationship helped to conceal its own brutal treatment of black women during slavery and afterward.[47]

African-Americans who were able to speak out—virtually all of them from the educated class living in the North—were not silent on the sub-ject. In his address of 1883, "The Black Woman of the South: Her Neglects and Her Needs," Alexander Crummell said in reference to slavery that "the evil of gross and monstrous abominations, the evil of great organic institu-tions crop out long after the departure of the institutions themselves." His meaning was made explicit as he went on to note that, in the rural South, "in large districts the white man has not forgotten the olden times of slavery, and, with, indeed, the deepest sentimental abhorrence of 'amalga-mation,' still thinks that the black girl is to be perpetually the victim of his lust!" Crummell's point, and anger, was replayed by black women like Anna Cooper in *A Voice from the South* and even by one of the few black people to speak at the Chicago Exposition in 1893, Fannie Barrier Williams.[48]

Joel Williamson has argued that after the Civil War miscegenation in the South declined dramatically, claiming that Emancipation "resulted in a large measure of physical separation between the races. Throughout the South, as plantations fragmented into farms and slave gangs dissolved into Negro families, opportunities for miscegenation decreased. Moreover, Negro servants tended to desert the big houses." However, the evidence he assembles is convincing only in terms of public attitudes toward mulattoes and the public taboo against miscegenation; it seems much less conclusive about private acts of miscegenation. Evidence from sources such as the records of the Freedman's Bureau and personal memoirs, as well as the investigations of Albert Hart and Ray Stannard Baker, offer substantial anecdotal proof of white sexual attacks on black women and of the continuing practice of concubinage. Of course, African-Americans were rarely able to maintain economic independence in the rural South—most black people were still tied to the plantation system, though as laborers rather than slaves. If African-American women left the planter's home on emancipation, they were often forced to return as domestic workers in the years following, and they might frequently find themselves in danger of being economically or physically coerced by white men.[49]

The white myths of black sexuality—the black man as rapist of white women and the black woman as inevitably licentious—were even absorbed into the legal systems of the Southern states, enshrining white supremacy within the region's court procedures. Peter W. Bardaglio points out that "social customs founded on race differences" were admissable considerations in Southern rape trials. "If the accused was black and the victim white, according to this judicial rule, the jury had a reasonable basis for inferring that he intended to rape her. No other evidence was necessary to establish intent." Since African-American women were, by white definition, immoral, and a reputation for chastity was important in rape trials, it followed that black women could not be raped by white men. Thus, "out of about 345 appeals by males convicted for rape or attempted rape that appear in the published records of state courts in the South between 1865 and 1899, only 2 identifiable cases involving a white man and black female could be found; in both instances, the appeals by the men were successful." Such prejudice did not operate only in the judicial branches of Southern governments. Before 1918, the age of consent for women in Georgia was ten. When various women's groups lobbied the Georgia legislature to have that age raised, they were told that the all-white, all-male legislators did not wish to give a legally protected status to African-American girls.[50]

Jean Toomer, growing up as P. B. S. Pinchback's grandson, was certainly aware of the history and functioning of white supremacy, and he clearly understood that miscegenation was the critical fact calling into question the racial myths that underlay the whole of Southern life. Secrecy was the means of covering over this contradiction, but a mulatto child exposed that secret and brought the private fact into public life, where it might become literally a matter of life and death. In his recollection of the Sparta barbershop where he asked about his father, Toomer describes how his conversation with the three black barbers ended:

I was rather startled out of my thoughts by the voice of the younger barber. Up till now he had said nothing. Suddenly, apropos of nothing so it seemed, he came out with—the leading white man in this town is said to have some colored blood. His enemies call him nigger behind his back. Then dead silence. I could see and almost feel their lips shut tight. All three suddenly felt that too much had been said. Forbidden words had been forced out. It was too late to recall them, but silence might cover them. Silence had to cover them, had to knock them down from the walls so that the walls could not echo them around the town.[51]

The attribution of "mixed blood," the hint of miscegenation, was not the stuff of casual conversation in Sparta, Georgia, in 1921. Racial identity was a deadly serious matter.

Toomer would write his book around that secrecy and deadliness. *Cane* is a modernist text in that its narration is fragmented and indirect; it hides what it is finally talking about and yet makes the hidden its actual topic. Toomer draws threads of meaning between stories and poems, threads composed of a single repeated word or phrase or image or idea. The meaning of the text derives not only from a complete story or sequence of stories, but from those accumulated repetitions that, beneath surface narrations, join scene to scene or character to character. The techniques of modernism served Toomer because the culture of secret miscegenation in the South could be powerfully represented by indirection. To put it in another way, Toomer made W. E. B. Du Bois's veil of double vision into a modernist mode of storytelling.

A Mulatto Aristocracy

When Toomer left Georgia in late November 1921, he returned to Washington, D.C., where his grandfather P. B. S. Pinchback was in his final illness. Pinchback died in December, and Toomer returned to the South, this time accompanying his grandfather's body on its burial journey to Louisiana. Pinchback was interred in the family vault in New Orleans, and Toomer went to Washington D.C. and continued to work on the sketches that would become *Cane*. The trip from New Orleans to Washington, D.C., in some way represented the axis of Pinchback's later life, the connection between his initial political career in Reconstruction Louisiana and the center of political power in Washington, where he had tried to maintain some influence on Black Republican politics. Pinchback's move north in 1891 was also a retreat, of course; an intelligent insider in Southern politics and a close observer of Southern life, he saw that Reconstruction had been abandoned and that the white South would be able to deal with its black people as it pleased. He left as the system of Jim Crow was being instituted and black people were being disfranchised. In Washington, Pinchback was a member of the city's mulatto upper class, a social world with origins in the antebellum era but which achieved its clearest definition and greatest prominence by the turn of the century. In his study of the postbellum African-American elite, Willard B. Gatewood, Jr., says that "from the end of Reconstruction until at least World War I Washington was the center of the black aristocracy in the United States."[52]

In one of his autobiographical sketches, "On Being an American," Jean Toomer offered his own recollection of the society he was born into and to which he belonged for part of his youth:

In the Washington of those days—and those days have gone now—there was a flowering of a natural but transient aristocracy, thrown up by the, for them, creative conditions of the post-war period. These people, whose racial strains were mixed and for the most part unknown, happened to find themselves in the colored group. They had a personal refinement, a certain inward culture and beauty, a warmth of feeling such as I have seldom encountered elsewhere or again. A few held or had held political posts of prominence. Some were in government positions. Others were in the professions. One was a municipal court judge. Several were in the real estate business. All were comfortably fixed financially, and they had a social life that satisfied them. They were not pushing to get anywhere or be anything other than what they were. Without bitterness, but with a sweetness and warmth that I will never forget, they were conscious that they were and had something in themselves. The children of these families became my friends.

Toomer's remarks mix history and nostalgia: he speaks of the particular circumstances that produced his class—they are "transient," rising by the "for them, creative conditions of the post-war [postbellum] period." He also essentializes them—they formed a "natural" aristocracy. He recognizes the economic basis of their position, that they held professional or white-collar jobs and "were comfortably fixed financially," yet also implies that they were somehow above or beyond the mundane world, possessing an "inward culture and beauty," "conscious that they were and had something in themselves." Toomer may suggest that the cultural confidence of this class is linked to their financial comfort, but he remembers, too, of his childhood friends in this group, that "their quality of person was considerably higher" than children he had known from other backgrounds, and he concludes that "they were my kind."[53]

The world described here is the mulatto aristocracy in Washington around 1910; after his mother's death Toomer returned there to live with his grandparents and to graduate from M Street High School (later Paul Laurence Dunbar High School), the excellent school for children of the African-American elite. Understanding that his society began in large part with Reconstruction politics, Toomer saw it as having largely vanished by 1934, though he gives no reason for that disappearance. The middle section of *Cane*, all but one of its stories set in Washington, narrates that decline in sketches of the social milieu of the city's black elite and the isolation and uncertain status of its members. And *Cane* suggests reasons for the decline which the autobiography ignores.

Two important reasons for the changing fortunes of the mulatto aristocracy were the gradual breakdown of the system of patronage for black Republicans and, somewhat later, the mass migration of African-Americans from the South into Northern cities. When Woodrow Wilson became president in 1913—just the second Democrat elected since the Civil War—he not only cut back on appointments for black politicians but also allowed the systematic segregation of parts of the civil service in Washington. His actions (or in some views, his inactions) allowed subordinates and Southern politicians to pursue their own racial agendas, and the segregationist movement was encouraged in the city at large. Increasingly after 1913 the Jim Crow rules that prominent mulattoes had escaped by moving north followed them to the nation's capital. The growing migration of poor black people from the South to the North also frequently sharpened the black elite's sense of class difference; as Kevin Gaines says, "What was good for black elites became increasingly worrisome if the masses followed suit."[54]

The mulatto aristocracy assumed public leadership in African-American life after Emancipation, yet they were always at best ambivalent about their connections to the black masses. As Gatewood observes,

in the late nineteenth century the light-skinned colored aristocrats exhibited a self-conscious elitism: on some occasions it led to condescension and even arrogance toward other blacks, especially the poor, uneducated masses at the bottom of the class structure, who were sometimes referred to as "vicious" and "degraded"; on others this same elitism produced a sense of awesome responsibility that translated itself into a commitment to improve the lot of the race in general.[55]

While white America tried to lump all black people together, the mulatto elite continued to believe in their distinctness, even as they were forced either to try to "pass" as white or to observe the ever-stricter lines of racial demarcation.

Jean Toomer's claim of his adolescent society, that "these new friends of mine were not conscious of being either colored or white," may well have a degree of truth to it. "Ideas about color," as Barbara Fields has said, "derive their importance, indeed their very definition, from their context." The context of that largely secure, still confident mulatto world might have minimized questions or discussions of race. But to say, as Toomer does further, that "they had never run up against the color line," is less a suggestion of serene self-confidence than of social isolation. There is some question, however, as to whether or not Toomer is telling the whole story. Not only was his grandfather still deeply involved in political wars and racial maneuvers at least through the 1912 election—he received a short-lived political appointment for his speech-making to black audiences in support of Taft in 1912—but the M Street High School that Toomer attended was the scene of discussion and argument against Wilson administration policies toward African-Americans in 1913.[56]

The more gradual and long-term alterations in African-American life were part of the sea change of economic and social life in the United

States that had been accelerating at least since the Civil War. The Great Migration of black people to the North produced a more virulent Northern racism and at the same time created new opportunities for a different kind of black middle class. Gatewood says that "by the 1920s a new economic elite had emerged in urban black communities and posed a serious threat to the place traditionally occupied by the old upper class in the black social structures." This new elite, "unlike the old upper class, whose occupations brought it into frequent contact with upper-class whites, was tied almost exclusively to the black ghetto and less concerned about assimilation into the larger society." The changes were not only economic or social, of course, but cultural as well. The American genteel tradition of higher culture was one the old black elite embraced as a proof of its own worth; the new black masses of the cities were carrying the seed of a popular and mass culture which media technology would make ubiquitous in the next twenty years. The avant-garde culture of modernism would replace the one while attempting to absorb, celebrate, and critique the other.[57]

Toomer's opening line in his quoted recollection, "and those days have gone now," echoes a remark made in 1914 by the widow of a prominent member of Washington's black elite. She said to a British journalist, "but alas those days are gone," in reference to her world of social order and hierarchy. This elegaic sentiment would take various forms of expression in the middle section of *Cane*, which is partly about a time of transition and its consequences for Toomer's class, a class defined by its Southern origins and its Northern decline. Indeed, when Toomer began composing the *Cane* material, he wrote a play about Washington's vanishing mulatto elite called *Natalie Mann*. The play's setting is divided between Washington's fastidious social circles and a mixed, open New York world. Mrs. Hart, one of the Washington hostesses, observes of the black masses' spirituals that "we havent been working these many years to get away from those low conditions simply to have them served up on a silver or any other kind of platter by the name of art." But in New York the play's hero, Nathan Merilh, has his triumph when, accompanied by guitar and mandolin, he reads his prose poem "Karintha" to a group of young intellectuals. New York doesn't appear in *Cane*, yet it was to be the most important city for the creation of Toomer's book. It would give him intellectual stimulation, social ideas, and the larger frame within which to understand Georgia and Washington, D.C. It was to provide the circle of friends and critics Nathan Merilh names, after Van Wyck Brooks and Waldo Frank, "Young America": "Jews and Germans and Irish and Russian and Latin, God Almighty's Anglo-Saxon, and Niggers! Wheeee!"[58]

Chapter 2
The New Metropolitan

The radical forces in New York City have recently embarked on a great
new field of revolutionary endeavor, the education through agitation
of the southern Negro into the mysteries and desirability of revolutionary Bolshevism.

— *New York World*, 1919

Washington, D.C., and New York

In his "Outline of an Autobiography" Jean Toomer described the period
from 1915 through 1920 as his "years of wandering." Figuratively, he meant
those were years spent attempting to discover his calling; literally, they were
years in which Toomer was often on the move—from Washington, D.C., to
Wisconsin, to Chicago, to New York City—along paths he retraced several
times. After graduating from M Street High School, Toomer enrolled in an
agricultural course at the University of Wisconsin for the summer of 1914,
but remained to complete only the fall semester. During the next three
years he attended, or at least enrolled, in five other colleges: two in Chicago, one in Amherst, and two in New York City. His grandfather, P. B. S.
Pinchback, was largely supporting these often interrupted studies, and he
and Toomer argued frequently over money and Toomer's apparent indi-
gence.[1]

In Toomer's wanderings the two cities he kept returning to were Washington and New York. Washington remained a refuge, the familiar home
that offered room, board, and, eventually, time to write. If Pinchback was
antagonistic to his grandson, he was also aging and sick; Toomer increasingly took over the care of his grandparents when he stayed with them.
But New York came to represent something almost opposite to Washington in Toomer's world. As the contrasted passages from *Natalie Mann* indicate, New York was the place where Toomer found his milieu as a writer.
Even more specifically, New York would come to mean a circle of other
writers, "Young America," the group of artists who would connect Toomer

with contemporary American literature. *Cane* is set in rural Georgia and in urban Washington and Chicago, but the metropolis behind the book is New York City.

When Nina Pinchback remarried in 1906, she and her son moved from Washington to Brooklyn with her new husband, where they lived for about a year. On his own in late 1915, after deciding not to attend school in Amherst, Toomer stayed for a time in New York City before returning to Washington. In the summer and fall of 1917, he took courses at both New York University and City College, and, after side trips to Chicago, Milwaukee, and Washington, again moved to New York in 1918, where he worked for the grocery firm Acker, Merrall and Condit, which would employ him off and on for the next three years. After yet another sojourn in Washington, Toomer moved back to New York in early 1919—his fourth separate residence in the city in as many years. Toomer regarded these years as a period of intellectual awakening, as a gradual accession to the circles of writers, artists, activists, editors, and journalists among whom he discovered his calling. The center for these circles was New York City, and Toomer was like many other young aspiring writers in finding the city irresistible.

Toomer recalled an English teacher in Wisconsin in 1914 "who [had] urged me to read magazines such as the *Nation*, the *New Republic* and the *Manchester Guardian*." If he was not ready then to understand what those publications—two of them important journals in New York's intellectual and literary life—represented, he remembered them in retrospect. Toomer had already made his first attempts at writing—"pretty poor stuff" he called it, but the impulse to write continued; he was reading widely and had encountered ideas that challenged the largely conventional religious and social ideologies with which he had been raised. As he later recognized, "This was the first time I'd ever seriously thought about society at all. All of my thinking had been individualistic, highly so. As for my political and social views—they merely existed in me as my grandfather, school, and reading had deposited them." Toomer's introduction to radical social thought took place in Chicago, where he attended the American College of Physical Training, a school that took students from a wide variety of backgrounds. He said of the college's atmosphere: "Here was democracy. None of us had much money; all, somehow, managed to have enough. Snobbery did not exist. There were no prejudices, no ill will or meanness. . . . It was, if you will, a one-class society. . . . Grouped as one body we lived as a simple community, pursuing our interest, aided by a common work, unhindered by artificial competitions and acquisitive rivalries."[2]

In the fall of 1916 the school and the friends he made there led Toomer into the social mix of Chicago's radical working-class culture; he not only read and absorbed socialist ideas, he also attended lectures and discussions and debated with the people around him. At a talk by Arthur Lewis on the scientific critique of religion, Toomer was impressed by the concentration of the audience: "It was not well-dressed. . . . This audience was intent and serious and eager to learn to the point of self-forgetfulness. Most of the people were sort of crude and uncouth, but they were simple and unassuming and they too had a vitality, a hunger to take in, which complemented Lewis' passion to give out." Toomer's sartorial observations—he was always concerned with a "gentlemanly appearance"—didn't obscure for him the impressive demeanor of the audience. It was, as he later recognized, "a radical Chicago audience, Chicago radicals with a history of radicalism in ideas and in actions stemming behind them into the history of the vital movements of this huge city." It is probable this experience of radical Chicago directed Toomer toward the similar milieu he would discover in New York, one that would become the intellectual and social focus of his life for the next seven years.[3]

The Rise of the City, the Crux of Modernity

The changes in American life brought about by the great economic expansion following the Civil War were the transformations of modernity. By the turn of the century that expansion had industrialized and urbanized much of the northeast quarter of the nation; expansion had pushed the railroads to the Pacific coast and was slowly creating a New South, economically if not yet socially. In 1893 Frederick Jackson Turner, pointing to data from the census of 1890, announced that the American frontier was closed. A nation which, by its own mythos, was primarily one of rural communities and small towns, of independent farmers and artisans, had become in fact a nation of industry and cities whose physical expansion would fill in the shrinking spaces between those cities. The self-sufficiency and independence Thomas Jefferson had idealized for its citizens—and which he made a basis for sustaining democracy—were harder and harder to imagine in a society that was every year more interdependent and more hierarchical.

The corporation became the dominant economic organization in the United States, and hierarchies of efficiency and control came to be the hallmarks of corporate operation. The rise of corporations did not make the path toward modernization smooth or orderly, however; their concentration of power upset the economic, social, and cultural orders. Devastating and long-term depressions had marked the 1870s, 1880s, and 1890s. These dislocations of modernity and incorporation fostered movements for labor unions, the rise of rural populism, and the broad reformist impulse of Progressivism. The populists organized a political party that rose and fell in the 1890s; meanwhile the political expression of labor was concentrated in the Socialist party, which remained prominent until the 1920s. The radical world Toomer discovered in Chicago was the world of labor and socialist politics.[4]

Progressivism arose in part as a political reaction to the populists and socialists. Most directly it was a response to the problems of the new American city, a city remade by industrial and commercial growth, by technology and by immigration. While Progressivism began as a reformist effort, with many of the same sources in Protestant religious thought that had motivated the Abolitionists, it became a much more ambitious and broadly based movement. The Protestant moral intention remained important to many Progressives, even as it was largely displaced as a justification for their actions by the belief in the possibility of a rational social order. This scientific spirit also attracted Progressives to radical and critical views of American society, although they generally maintained their middle-class outlook. In implementing their reformist programs, they most often became mediators in the struggles between capital and labor which modernity had made central to the political life of the United States.

Progressive reform was closely tied to urban problems associated with the vast new immigrant population of the cities. The history of immigration to the United States, indeed, was always one of conflict and cultural tension, even if the nation remained in theory an "open" society. Almost from the moment of its founding, American "nativists" had become uneasy with the mixture of the national citizenry; the seemingly endless frontier and the relatively small size of the non-English population had allayed their fears into the early nineteenth century. The first "mass" immigration of the Irish in the 1830s and 1840s, however, produced an angry anti-Irish response; a splinter political party, the "Know-Nothings," was formed with the intention of keeping the new Americans out of politics and mainstream culture. After the Civil War, a new development again changed the nature of the urban population: whereas the earlier large-scale immigrations to the United States had gathered in people mainly from northern Europe—Britain, Germany, Scandanavia, and Ireland—the majority of immigrants after the 1870s came from southern and eastern Europe—Italy, Poland, and Russia. In New York City, the Italian population grew from 3,000 in 1870 to 145,433 in 1900; from 1880 to 1900, nearly 500,000 Jews immigrated to the city, primarily from Russia and Poland.[5]

If the differences in national origins did not at first seem especially important, they would eventually become central to a debate about American identity that would continue far into the twentieth century—indeed, in a sense, this debate has never ended. After 1890, the issues were framed by the question of whether or not the new immigrants could ever become proper "Americans." The nativist position was that they could not: their culture and appearance, their "racial" makeup, was too alien ever to be "naturalized." Since many of these immigrants were already citizens, their de facto exclusion marked a major division within the legal American polis. As Alan Trachtenberg has put it, this division was (and is) based on the requirement that "immigrants must assent to the foundational historical memory which renders *American* a cultural term that the ideology of 'America,' the nation's theoretical basis, distinctly denies." The culture wars that erupted alongside the economic and political conflicts in the first decades of the twentieth century were partly about trying to break down that "foundation" by evoking the "theory" of America to open its canonical memory.[6]

If the Progressives' initial hope was to reform American life by rationalizing it, in the process fulfilling a moral obligation of ameliorating the worst excesses in industrial and urban conditions, that general program led to ends that were not discussed so openly. The urge to regularize ultimately meant social control had to be exerted over the portion of the polis they could reach, in the name of the state and the state institutions the Progressives fostered. This control produced some regulation of corporate activity but a great deal more restriction of immigrant and working-class life and, finally, of the radical politics rooted in these groups. Nor were Progressives able, at least before 1910, to see more value than danger in that life; the usefulness of variety was overwhelmed by the threat of difference. Probably as much reform effort was devoted to "Americanizing" the masses as to improving their living conditions; the assumption, of course, was that those two projects were closely related. Concentrating on the poor and the new immigrants to the cities, the Progressives thus were able to carry out reform, but they also created the means to exclude and suppress cultural and political difference.[7]

By 1910 the Progressives not only had formulated theoretical justifications for social intervention (the philosophy of John Dewey, the historical interpretations of Charles Beard) and joined in social action (the stories by muckraking journalists and the settlement houses organized by Jane Addams), they also had combined theory and practice by producing influential journals and books and by becoming advisors to the politicians who enacted policy. Theodore Roosevelt left the Republican party in 1912 to run on the new Progressive ticket, adopting as one of his major slogans the promise to promote a "New Nationalism," a phrase and idea taken from Herbert Croly's *The Promise of American Life*, published in 1909. The phrase promised a compromise solution to the seeming disorder and divisiveness in American society, a solution to overcome divisions of class, ethnicity, or region. Woodrow Wilson, who defeated Roosevelt and the Republican incumbent Taft in 1912, would also focus in his inaugural speech on the agenda of national problems which the Progressives had been addressing for more than ten years, the social crisis created by the effects of modernity.

In Wilson's administration Progressive reform would flower, and, with the entry of the United States into World War I, so too would the bureaucratic security state. Many Progressives who began by promoting reform would find themselves drawn into supporting the political suppression of domestic opponents of the war. The resultant splintering and effective demise of the Progressives as a coherent movement by the end of the war left some young intellectuals at odds with both their older peers and the government that had been their hope for social reform. In New York City these people would become important figures in the literary and political culture of the 1920s, and among them Jean Toomer would find his artistic home as he began the writing of *Cane*.

Progressive Reform and the Politics of Race

The populist, laborite, and Progressive responses to the changes being produced by modernity were those of specific interest groups within American society; the political argument could always be made that the general good was involved in any agenda of reform, but the heart of that agenda spoke to a particular constituency. Although its defenders argued for the promise of universal progress, modernity created social and economic hierarchies that fragmented society and culture along familiar fault lines, since the differences on which these hierarchies were based already existed within American society—the differences between owners and workers, skilled and unskilled workers, landowners and tenant farmers, old and new immigrants, as well as the differences of gender and racial definition. By the middle of the 1890s, the group that had been made effectively anomalous by the postbellum reordering were African-Americans.

The sympathy, always mixed, with which the North regarded black people under slavery gradually faded after Emancipation, and the stresses of foreign immigration and the uncertainty of "American" identity promoted a more overt and virulent American racism. As Nina Silber says,

One of the most noteworthy features of the [postbellum] reunion process was the transformation in white northerners' racial outlook. Never known for racial enlightenment, northern opinion, nonetheless, underwent a noticeable change from the 1860s, a period characterized by a certain optimism regarding the position of African Americans, to the 1890s, when northerners seemed uninterested, pessimistic, and derisive regarding the status of southern blacks. Increasingly, northern whites bowed to the racial pressures of reunion, to a process that depoliticized the legacy of sectionalism, overlooked the history of American slavery, and came to view southern blacks as a strange and foreign population.[8]

The political and social isolation of African-Americans in the United States during and after the 1890s can be seen in terms of how they fared with the various groups trying to organize in response to the crises of the day. Populism, which became a major force in the South, initially tried to include blacks in an alliance of farmers and workers. But, as C. Vann Woodward observes, "The exciting vision of 1892, picturing black and white farmer and laborer marching together toward a new era, had by 1898 become dimmed by old prejudices and suspicions. It had been a precarious and handicapped experiment from the start." The Georgia politician and editor Tom Watson represented the transformation of Southern populism;

an advocate for black civil rights and black-white cooperation in the 1890s, he had become by 1905 a zealous racist and an advocate of black disfranchisement.[9]

Labor unions and the Socialist party had similar relations with African-Americans. While the first major national labor organization, the Knights of Labor, had accepted black members in the 1880s (60,000 black workers had joined by 1886), its successor, the American Federation of Labor, adopted a substantially racist program, allowing member unions to write articles into their constitutions specifically excluding black workers. The Socialist party was equally closed, refusing to admit that black workers were under any special handicaps in the United States and catering to a Southern membership that worked to keep blacks out. The party's ongoing attempt to affiliate with the conservative American Federation of Labor also made its leadership evasive or reactionary regarding racial questions. At least one prominent Northern socialist leader, Victor Berger of Milwaukee, was openly antagonistic to blacks; he wrote in 1902 that "there can be no doubt that negroes and mulattoes constitute a lower race" and worked at socialist conventions to block consideration of antilynching motions.[10]

There were exceptions to this policy. The IWW (International Workers of the World) consistently denounced racism, called for black-white solidarity, and recruited black members; and in New York City several socialist leaders began trying after 1903 to work more directly for black civil rights. These New York socialists would be important activists in the founding of the NAACP in 1909; Oswald Garrison Villard wrote at the time that, "the most ardent workers who are really accomplishing something, Miss Ovington, Miss Blascoer, Walling, Mrs. Maclean, etc., are all Socialists." After 1910 elements of the Socialist party, notably its leader, Eugene V. Debs, and its New York City branch, moved toward recognizing the special problems of black workers and the advocacy of their civil rights.[11]

The Progressives had a more complicated relationship to African-Americans, one that varied according to regions and individuals. In the South, Progressive leaders almost universally accepted the Jim Crow organization of society. As William Link describes, "Southern social reformers often expressed a strange combination of ideas: a fervent belief in white supremacy along with a belief in the necessity of black progress." This meant that Southern Progressives were hesitant to address directly such questions as lynching; they preferred to raise the specter of class war, suggesting that lynching was dangerous because it paved the way to social anarchy. When Progressive reform movements such as prohibition and suffragism for women appeared in the South, they were often presented as a means for reinforcing white supremacy.[12]

In the North many Progressives, particularly the "muckraking" journalists who helped initiate so much social reform, had little interest in black problems or the racial question. A major exception to this neglect was Ray

Stannard Baker's *Following the Color Line: An Account of Negro Citizenship in the American Democracy*, which was published as a series of magazine articles in 1904–5 and then as a book in 1908. The book in some ways was remarkably liberal in its view of black Americans, but it also demonstrated the limits of the Progressive racial agenda. Baker presented numerous examples to show that African-Americans were capable of economic, political, or intellectual achievement if given equal opportunities. He was also unsparing in his depiction of Southern Jim Crow and the economic exploitation of black labor, though he was less attentive to Northern racism. He offered counter-arguments to the attack on black women's morals; he pointed out how few lynching victims were accused of sexual crimes; and he even discussed the practical absurdity of legal attempts to define "race." Baker, however, in his attempt to present a "balanced" view of racial antagonisms, also gave credence to the white South's version of Reconstruction and favored restriction of the franchise until African-Americans were "worthy" of the vote. He wouldn't say that lynching helped maintain Southern economic relations, though he recognized that white violence was intended to "keep the Negro in his place."[13]

In general Baker supported Booker T. Washington against W.E.B. Du Bois, depending on the advance of modernity to improve the position of blacks in the United States, but even his moderate criticism of the racial status quo sounds radical in the context of the early 1900s. Most often, when whites spoke out about race they tended to repeat the definitions and strictures inherited from the world of Southern slavery. Herbert Croly's *The Promise of American Life*, regarded as a primary text of Progressive thought, argued for the rational "reconstruction" of American society. Yet in his section discussing the crisis of the Civil War he wrote:

They [Southern slave owners] were right in believing that the negroes were a race possessed of moral and intellectual qualities inferior to those of the white men; and, however much they overworked their conviction of negro inferiority, they could clearly see that the Abolitionists were applying a narrow and perverted political theory to a complicated and delicate set of economic and social conditions.[14]

Croly's nationalist bent saw the justification of the Civil War in the Union's preservation and slavery as an unfortunate contradiction within American democracy. Most important, he accepted the Southern myths of the largely benevolent nature of slavery, of the "baleful spirit" of Reconstruction, and of the criminality of lynch victims. Lynching was not a matter of the maintenance of white supremacy, but an organizational problem that would be corrected by developing adequate state and local police forces.[15]

Croly's attitudes were in no way atypical of Northern Progressives. The most directly engaged of the Progressives were the settlement house workers of the major cities, who ran social service centers to aid the new urban immigrants arriving from Europe. When black migrants from the South began appearing in Northern cities in large numbers, however, "the majority of settlement houses either excluded blacks, conducted segregated activities, closed down completely, or followed their former white neighbors out of black neighborhoods." Even those in the settlement movement who paid attention to black needs continued to see African-American migrants as essentially different from white immigrants, and that difference was framed according to the stereotypes created in Jim Crow mythology. It is a measure of African-Americans' exclusion from the American polis that they were rarely included in the Progressive discussion of how that polis might be democratized. It was into this hostile and disbelieving public arena that a few black intellectuals entered with their own articles and books.[16]

The Background: Jim Crow, Du Bois, and Washington

The retreat from the radical Reconstruction of the South after the Civil War took less than ten years in most areas. By 1880 the Reconstruction state governments had been replaced by white-dominated legislatures and governors, "Redemptionists," who largely represented the surviving planter class; black representatives or their white sympathizers were removed from office, frequently by violence or threats of violence and by blatant electoral fraud. The freedmen, mostly poor farmers living in the rural South, had limited resources to meet this new oppression. Black leadership, composed primarily of the mulatto elite and Northern blacks, vacillated over how to respond to the growing restrictions on their civil rights and economic opportunities. August Meier reports a convention of African-American newspaper editors meeting in 1875 whose pronouncements "stressed racial self-confidence and self-reliance. . . . A reference to the denial of African-American civil rights in a committee report caused considerable debate. A few delegates 'could see no use of keeping up the same old whine.' Others supported the statement on civil rights, one delegate asserting that the only way for Negroes to obtain their rights was to keep on asking for them." The convention concluded by recommending "not agitation and political activity, but education and the co-operative acquisition of landed wealth in the South or elsewhere."[17]

The line being drawn here between political engagement and economic striving would divide "civil rights" from "self-help" in all future discussions of how African-Americans might be joined to the American polis; it would also divide the class of the black leadership, and in the first two decades of the twentieth century that division was personified by the conflict between Booker T. Washington and W.E.B. Du Bois, between Tuskegee's model of "self-help" and the NAACP's pursuit of civil rights. The division between these concerns was never in any sense absolute, of course; no African-American leader could ignore the economic problems blacks lived with, and Du Bois was one of the most thorough and unrelenting investigators of those problems. In public life Booker T. Washington made a political practice out of his disavowal of political interest, while he secretly worked for (and financed) an extensive political agenda, part of it directed against black rivals and part against the erosion of black civil rights.

For thirty years, however, until perhaps 1910, self-help was the dominant African-American strategy for accommodating blacks to their tenuous and uncertain position within the economic and civil society of the United States. More than 90 percent of black people lived in the South, and the Southern states from the 1880s steadily promulgated the Jim Crow system intended to produce the legal exclusion of these blacks from participation in public life. Violence against black persons and property, disfranchisement of black voters, and attempts to block or limit black economic success went hand in hand with the Jim Crow laws. In this environment the idea of self-help, which was understood to mean social solidarity as well as personal ambition, appeared to many as the only option. When Booker T. Washington made his speech to the Atlanta Exposition in 1895, the program of economic progress and political quietism he advocated was not new, but rather a summary of the retrenchments and adjustments African-Americans had been making since the 1870s. It was also, of course, in accord with the dominant economic ideology of the era, the gospel of wealth, which roughly associated virtue with success and success with material prosperity. It convinced some black people at least that, as Booker T. Washington said, "no race that has anything to contribute to the markets of the world is long in any degree ostracized."[18]

Washington's program pleased many Southern businessmen and some politicians. It also pleased Northern Republicans, who were trying to retain the black vote—which had been theirs since the Civil War—while also catering to white racism in the North and making an appeal for white votes in the South. Booker T. Washington became the center of the patronage system by which Republican politicians and Northern philanthropists disbursed federal appointments and charitable gifts to black individuals and institutions, particularly those who were part of the movement for black vocational training. This system became so well established that in Sparta, Georgia, Linton S. Ingraham's school, built on the Tuskegee model, could still successfully solicit Northern aid in the 1920s, several years after Washington's death and the opening of the era of the urban New Negro.

The break between Washington and Du Bois should not have been unexpected. They were of different generations and of very different backgrounds. Washington was born and raised in slavery in the South and educated at the Hampton Institute in Virginia, a school that promoted exactly the moral/agricultural/artisanal program that he would make famous at Tuskegee. Du Bois was born into a free black family in a mostly white Northern community and educated at elite schools: Fisk, Harvard, and the University of Berlin. The division between them, then, was partly that between Northern mulatto elite and Southern peasant freedman (though Washington was also mulatto). Both men tried to develop a system of leadership for the black masses whose way of life and culture they were critical of, each one imagining that his own class should provide the ideal leaders; such programs were, of course, very much the order of the day, and the "uplift ideology" of the black elite was similar to other social engagements of the Progressive era. In fact, Washington and Du Bois were scarcely at odds during the 1890s, and Du Bois was invited more than once to teach at Tuskegee. Only after 1900 did Du Bois gradually develop a critique of Washington, first because of his heavy-handed domination of black political life, and then because Du Bois felt Washington's accommodationist policies were actually undermining the conditions of black economic and civic life.[19]

From his attack on Washington in *The Souls of Black Folk* (1903) through 1905's Niagara Movement and the founding of the NAACP in 1909, Du Bois was crucially involved in the opposition to what he called the "Tuskegee Machine." When he became editor of the NAACP's magazine, *The Crisis*, in 1910, he gained a forum that he would make into the most important outlet for the public expression of African-American opinion for the next fifteen years. Expanded literacy and a new print media with a national market had allowed the Progressive muckrakers and publicists to influence public policy debates; the African-American leadership joined in this discussion wherever possible and argued their positions in their own newspapers and periodicals as well. One of Washington's political strategies was to control as much of the black press as he could, either through paying direct (or more often, secret) subsidies, or through pressures and hints to black or white sponsors of the publications. Washington controlled the most important black newspaper in New York, the *New York Age*, and after 1908 he had significant influence over the District of Columbia's *Washington Bee*. In 1904 Pauline Hopkins was removed as editor of the important *Colored American Magazine*, "soon after the magazine came under the control of persons sympathetic to Booker T. Washington," because her editorial politics weren't accommodationist.[20]

The Washington–Du Bois struggle was carried on simultaneously, but often separately, within both the black and white communities. Among whites Washington had the support of most establishment politicians (virtually all Republicans) and major philanthropists like Andrew Carnegie and George Eastland. Du Bois's white support would eventually come from a small group of radical Progressives, mainly centered in New York City, as well as more conservative inheritors of the Abolitionist tradition such as the wealthy businessman John Milholland. Among blacks Du Bois was followed mainly by the older, established middle class of the Northern cities, his famous "Talented Tenth"; Washington, in contrast, appealed to a new emerging black middle class associated particularly with African-American urban communities in the South and North. Washington's broad base of support was built up in no small part by patronage; the Tuskegee Machine had, as Louis Harlan says, "many recruits even from the Talented Tenth, [and] made rewards and punishments a central feature of its recruitment and retention of its followers."[21]

One of Washington's prominent followers in the Talented Tenth was Jean Toomer's grandfather, P.B.S. Pinchback. After fighting for black political and civil rights in Louisiana during Reconstruction, Pinchback had reached an understanding with the redemptionist state government which allowed him to continue as an influence in Louisiana politics, though of steadily diminishing authority, into the 1880s. In 1890 he was a founder of the American Citizens' Equal Rights Association, which attempted to stem the flood of antiblack legislation; it was this association that brought the suit on behalf of Homer Plessy which resulted in the Supreme Court's 1896 Plessy–Ferguson decision and the legal establishment of a Jim Crow code, hidden behind the facade of "separate but equal." But well before the case was tried, Pinchback had given up on the South and moved on to New York and later Washington. He remained a defender of black civil rights and retained a close connection to the Republican patronage system. Campaigning for McKinley in 1896, Pinchback made a speech at the Cooper Union in New York City that rejected the accommodationist position, asserting that "a voteless class has no rights that anybody is bound to respect."[22]

By 1901, however, Pinchback's authority was in decline, and his correspondence with Booker T. Washington beginning in that year traces his shift into the Tuskegee camp. The editors of Washington's *Collected Papers* characterize him as a political aide-de-camp: "A close friend of Whitefield McKinlay in Washington, Pinchback was an adviser to BTW on national capital affairs and made frequent visits to the White House and to congressional committees in BTW's behalf, particularly in patronage matters."[23] At least some of the patronage Pinchback hoped to promote was to benefit himself. One estimate in 1895 assessed his wealth at approximately $95,000, a sizable fortune for the time. Yet by January 1902 John H. Lewis, a friend of Pinchback's, would write to Booker T. Washington that he had learned "ex-gov P.B.S. Pinchback was sadly in need of something to do, and also that he had gone thro' nearly all he possessed, and was quietly asking his friends to interest themselves in his behalf, and I had a little quiet talk with some of his friends, and they promised their level best to see if they could not get something from the government for him." Lewis went on to ask for help in finding Pinchback government work; Washington ultimately supported Toomer's grandfather for various appointed positions. The "Governor," as Washington's circle referred to him, continued to monitor black politics in the capital and elsewhere on Washington's behalf, to meet him when he visited the District of Columbia, and to serve as an advisor and political speaker for Washington's Republican party allies.

Although his usefulness and importance to the Tuskegee group declined along with Republican patronage, Pinchback remained loyal to Washington and, after the latter's death in 1915, even tried to join in the maneuvering to choose his successor at Tuskegee.[24]

Though Jean Toomer knew something of his grandfather's political career, he appears never to have directly discussed Pinchback's continuous involvement with black politics or, in particular, his connection to Booker T. Washington. In *The Wayward and the Seeking*, Toomer says he doesn't know the facts of Pinchback's racial background and suspects that his grandfather's claim to being a black leader in Reconstruction Louisiana was a matter of political expediency. Yet Toomer also saw Pinchback as "the dominant overshadowing figure of us all," and up until 1920 he was in an important sense the figure Toomer measured himself against, as well as the one he struggled against. At least two references mention the distance he put between himself and his grandfather's politics. In Ellenville, New York, in 1919 Toomer says he wrote "long letters which usually dealt with world-matters as I saw them." His grandfather replied and "often disagreed with me, but I could detect in the wording his surprise and even his admiration that I had such ideas." Later that year Toomer announced a more comprehensive disillusionment to Pinchback: "If you didn't have pull, or if you didn't get a fortunate break, you just stayed down there where the majority of the workmen of the world were, and always would be. . . . Once I told grandfather these ideas, and they shocked him."[25]

It is hard to imagine that some of the arguments between Toomer and Pinchback didn't concern race and the position of African-Americans in the United States. Toomer's autobiographies are so selective, or evasive, regarding racial matters, however, that they have to be read with some caution, and preferably in tandem with sources roughly contemporary to the writing of *Cane*. The most important of these sources are Toomer's own published writings, which began in 1919, and which appeared exclusively in radical publications that might well have "shocked" the elder Pinchback.

The American Metropolis

The New York City that attracted Jean Toomer was the new metropolis of the United States, a position it had assumed before the turn of the century and which had been consolidated in the following years. Herbert Croly suggested this designation in an essay of 1903, "New York as the American Metropolis," which recognized that New York took on this role as a result of the changed and changing nature of the national economy and society. The agrarian world was gone, and in its place would be New York, a city that must be more than a concentration of population and industry: it must offer a national example to the hinterlands (and by implication must "nationalize" them), and it must provide a meeting point where the many strands of the nation's culture could be joined to produce some orderly and recognizable pattern. The cultural authority of the city, then, would make it inevitable that "men will be attracted [to it] in proportion as their enterprises, intellectual and practical, are far-reaching and important." The suggestion that *only* New York could foster an important national culture would help ignite the contention between the national and the local, the center and the provinces, that was behind the populist movement.[26]

The pell-mell economic development that drove New York is captured in Page Smith's statistical litany:

In 1874 almost 61 percent of all American exports were shipped from the wharves of New York City. By 1884 nearly 70 percent of all imports were unloaded on its docks. The city was also unquestioned as the financial capital of the country. In a twenty-year period its banking resources increased by almost 250 percent, as opposed to 26 percent for the nation. Of the country's 185 largest industries, 69 controlling 2,416 plants around the country had their headquarters in New York. The odoriferous leather district was located near Brooklyn Bridge. Newspaper Row was near the Fulton Fish Market, the largest in the world. The garment industry was rapidly expanding north and west from the Lower East Side. Between 1870 and 1915 the population of Manhattan doubled, while that of Queens, the Bronx, and Brooklyn increased nine, four and sixteen times respectively.[27]

After 1900 New York's development did not slow down, but it became somewhat more "metropolitan," as "the sectors in which New York City manufacturers increasingly specialized, particularly apparel and publishing, were linked to the city's position as a center of communication and control in the nation's economy. Clothing manufacturers had to be attuned to the latest in fashions, and publishers to the latest in ideas. In no other American city was this information more readily available than in New York." Publishing and ideas, literary culture, intellectual culture, books and magazines were to be associated with New York as assuredly as the parallel developments of popular and mass cultures—Broadway, Tin Pan Alley, and Madison Square Garden. Important Progressive journals and journalists were in New York, as well as the major publishing houses and the large-circulation magazines, a presence that "provided the financial basis for the emergence of the American writer as a professional." [28]

New York was the home, as well, of a political radicalism that partly originated in the city's huge European immigrant population, and which in turn helped to organize that population. These politics also inspired a political and literary intellectual milieu that included many migrants from the American provinces and the more critical and adventuresome of the Progressives. Their political voice, the Socialist party of New York, was activist and agitational but not revolutionary, and a good deal of its energy went into union organizing among the immigrant masses made up prominently of Jews, but also Italians, Poles, Hungarians, and the other nationalities of the later nineteenth-century migration. The unions, the Socialist party, and the radical intellectuals created a semiautonomous cultural world that spread over much of lower Manhattan and flourished between the turn of the century and the 1940s. After the Red Scare of 1919–20 and the accompanying postwar suppression of the Left, the Socialist party declined and the surviving unions went their own ways, but a remnant group of radical intellectuals carried on, bolstered by occasional recruits, to reemerge with new strength in the 1930s. Literary radicalism, in particular, came to be defined by "its close identification with New York City and its involvement in the rise of New York as a cultural center."[29]

The geographical focus of New York's literary radicals was Greenwich Village, a neighborhood of predominantly Italian working-class residents near the southwestern end of Manhattan. The area had escaped the skyscraper development that was altering the financial district to the south and Midtown to the north; it was bounded by the more affluent Chelsea, the more industrial Soho, and the Lower East Side, where Jewish immigrants and garment industries clustered. Village rents were cheap, and so by 1905 there was already a history of writers in residence, notably the young Stephen Crane. The most famous Village literary culture, however, existed during the decade of World War I, the years of Max Eastman, Floyd Dell, and John Reed and of Mabel Dodge's salon just three blocks north of Washington Square, the primary public space of the Village.[30]

The connection of the writers and artists to their working-class neighbors was not without complications. If their meeting point was a politics of reform or revolution (and that difference could be a crucial one), their political expression was notably distinct: working people would organize unions, agitate, and strike; writers would write and publish. If both groups worked generally toward the same end—as was the case at least for journals such as *The Masses* or *Rogue*—their experiences of the work remained separate. Most of the Village radicals came from middle-class backgrounds, and they attacked not only a system of economic exploitation but what they viewed as a repressive Puritan social order. The idea of a personal liberation (often reduced in the popular press of the time to the question of "free love") was not of first importance and might well be antagonistic to working-class Italians, Irish, or Jews still living within traditional cultures. This class/cultural difference gave Progressive reform its paternalistic cast; it was implicit in Du Bois's concept of the Talented Tenth and "uplift," and it bedeviled the radical intellectuals. The solution Antonio Gramsci would arrive at, the "organic intellectual," remained impossible while individual liberation was a primary goal. When Jean Toomer recalled his observation of the working-class audience in Chicago, his distance as onlooker admitted the difference of class which literary radicals more frequently tried to ignore. That distance would become central to the narrative of *Cane*, where the representation of race, class, and gender difference shifts unpredictably between characters and narrators. And Toomer's stories would powerfully represent these differences as a mystery not only of alienation, but of empathy.[31]

There were some institutions within the socialist and working-class life of lower Manhattan which provided links to the city's intelligentsia. Both the Cooper Union and the Rand School offered courses, lectures, and speeches intended for worker education, and a portion of the socialist press accepted a steady stream of contributions by Village writers and activists. The Cooper Union for the Advancement of Science and Art was located on Seventh Street in the East Village. It had opened in 1859 as a "workingman's institute" and continued in that capacity. The Rand School was founded in 1906 and eventually settled at East Fifteenth Street on the northern edge of the Village, functioning as a "worker's university" with "courses in public speaking, English Grammar, composition, Socialist theory and history, American history, and stenography." The historians Charles Beard and David Muzzey and the sociologist Franklin Giddings taught at the Rand. Besides its basic curriculum the school offered specialized courses taught by union organizers, writers, or other city radicals. Originally funded by a bequest from Mrs. Carrie D. Rand, the school later was managed by the American Socialist Society and supported by New York's labor unions.[32]

New York's huge publishing industry had an important leftist contingent, initially in newspapers and magazines and after 1918 in book publishing as well. Between 1913 and 1918 there were sixteen socialist periodicals published in New York City, including three daily papers, the Russian *Novy Mir*, Abraham Cahan's *Jewish Daily Forward*, published in Yiddish, and the *New York Call*, the English-language paper of the New York Socialist party. The *Forward* had a circulation of nearly 200,000, while the *Call* never exceeded 25,000, but both were important voices in the city's radical milieus. The major expression of the Village radicals was *The Masses*, begun in 1911 by Max Eastman as a leftist journal of culture, with offices at 91 Greenwich Avenue, and published monthly until its suppression by the government in 1917. It was revived as the more directly political *Liberator* in 1918, and in 1923 would become the cultural magazine of the Communist party.[33]

The "little magazines" became a good deal more significant after 1910. They frequently appeared and disappeared within the space of a year or two, depending on financial exigencies or, after the entry of the United States into World War I, on government censorship; yet they published work that would endure, and they contributed immensely to the energy and sense of common purpose among New York writers, especially young writers. One of the best of these magazines was the *Seven Arts*, started by James Oppenheim and Waldo Frank in 1916 from an office near Alfred Stieglitz's gallery "291" on Fifth Avenue—another rallying point for Village artists. There was also the *Messenger* of A. Philip Randolph and Chandler Owen, begun in November 1917 as the first radical socialist African-

American publication. And New York City, of course, was the home of Du Bois's *Crisis*, the major black magazine in the country during the decade of war, and one that often favorably addressed socialist positions.[34]

The book-publishing business of New York also had a left wing, more or less moderate at Alfred Knopf and B. W. Huebsch, more or less radical with the Boni brothers, Thomas Seltzer, and Horace Liveright. Huebsch, who began publishing in 1902, was the first Jewish publisher in the city, the sponsor of *The Freeman*, which Van Wyck Brooks edited in the early 1920s, and a founder of the American Civil Liberties Union. Albert and Charles Boni started the Washington Square Book Shop on MacDougal Street in the Village in 1912, "a gathering place for both new and established writers," and began publishing social criticism and avant-garde literature. They backed Alfred Kreymborg's *The Glebe* for ten issues, including the one that introduced Ezra Pound's imagist anthology, and founded a series of classic reprints that eventually became the famous Modern Library editions of Random House.

The Washington Square Book Shop was as much a radical institution as was the Rand School, but with a different following:

As leaders in Greenwich Village bohemian life, the Bonis were interested in all the arts. The Theatre Guild was founded in the shop's backroom, and the Washington Square Players [the seed of the Provincetown Players] presented the Guild's initial production there. Naturally, there were political activities too, made easier when a door was cut between the bookshop and its neighbor, the Liberal Club, which occupied the brownstone next door, providing access to the Bonis' stock for such radical figures of the day as Emma Goldman, John Reed, Margaret Sanger, Theodore Dreiser, Big Bill Heywood and Dr. A. A. Brill, who had come to introduce Freud to America.[35]

The Boni brothers passed their bookstore on to one of the Provincetown Players, but Albert then met Horace Liveright, and in the spring of 1917 the two launched Boni & Liveright, a publishing firm that specialized in Modern Library classic reprints. They were so successful that they began publishing newer works, among the first of them Trotsky's *The Bolsheviki and World Peace* and a reissue of Dreiser's *Sister Carrie*. Boni, Liveright, and the firm's third principal member, Thomas Seltzer, agreed on radical politics, but not about whether their house should emphasize American or European authors; in 1918 they parted ways, and Horace Liveright became sole head of Boni & Liveright (by virtue of a coin-toss, according to a famous story). In the early 1920s the Boni brothers and Thomas Seltzer would both head separate publishing houses, which merged in 1926. Their lists included Marcel Proust, D. H. Lawrence, Ford Madox Ford, Upton Sinclair, and Thornton Wilder. Meanwhile, Liveright "at last turned to the native-born radicals—political and literary—of Greenwich Village."[36]

Liveright would become the most important publisher of new American literature in the 1920s, though not only with writers from the Village.

Along with the Bonis and Seltzer, Huebsch, and Alfred Knopf, Liveright was a liberalizing, innovative publisher who adapted the book business to the cultural conditions of the developing media age. These men were also the first Jewish publishers to break into what had been in effect an Anglo-American monopoly:

> Young Jews interested in publishing careers either were refused jobs outright when they applied at old-line houses or were told that for *them* there would be no opportunity for advancement. As a result, they established their own houses which lacked any allegiance to the entrenched Anglo-American literary heritage, that foundation of respectable conservatism which had proved so profitable for their older rivals.[37]

Liveright published Theodore Dreiser, Sherwood Anderson, Ernest Hemingway's first book, William Faulkner's first two novels, Robinson Jeffers, Hart Crane, and Eugene O'Neill. He also gave the first American book publication to T. S. Eliot's *The Waste Land* and Ezra Pound's *Collected Poems* (both poets, of course, would go on to publish other, notoriously anti-Semitic works). Liveright also became Waldo Frank's publisher, bringing out *Our America* in 1919 and then publishing seven more of his books in the next ten years. Liveright incurred an eventual net loss of nearly $10,000 on Frank's books, but he continued to publish them, and Frank brought him other young authors, including Lewis Mumford, Hart Crane, and Gorham Munson. Frank also brought Liveright Jean Toomer's *Cane*, which he would publish in 1923.[38]

A Writer in the City

What was remarkable about New York's cultural authority in the first three decades of this century was its concentration and its extension: how much of American culture emerged from the tiny area between Battery Park and Washington Heights and how widely influential this culture became in the world beyond Manhattan. The new American literature was not primarily about New York or created only by New Yorkers or produced only in New York City, but it passed through the city, inevitably as it came to seem, to be read by the country at large. Horace Liveright, in his offices on West Forty-eighth Street, would publish not only Greenwich Village figures like John Reed (from Portland, Oregon) or Floyd Dell (from Chicago), but also William Faulkner from Mississippi and Robinson Jeffers from the wilds of northern California. The metropolitan effect of New York also drew to the city the talented, curious, and restless from the rest of the country, a phenomenon Waldo Frank regarded in *Our America* as the hope of American culture: "This throw-back upon the city from the West, the South, the North brings to New York its restless inquiry, its insatiate search. A true leaven." The leaven of immigrants from the hinterlands and immigrants from Europe was to enliven and renew an American civilization that had been reduced to the material and the mechanical.[39]

Jean Toomer's first serious connection to New York was formed in the summer of 1917 when, he says, inspired by a reading of Lester Ward's *Dynamic Sociology*, he enrolled for sociology and history courses taught at New York University around Washington Square. He interrupted his studies in the fall for one of his sprees of wandering, to Washington, then Chicago, and finally Milwaukee, where he was rescued by a train ticket home sent reluctantly by Pinchback. In the spring of 1918 he moved back to New York, this time taking a job with the firm of Acker, Merrall and Condit and renting a room on Thirteenth Street, just off Sixth Avenue, at the northern end of Greenwich Village. In Toomer's boardinghouse lived a girl named Eleanor Minne, "and she, or one of her friends, introduced me to the Rand School—and this was the beginning of my contact with radical, and, later, with literary New York." As he had in Chicago two years earlier, Toomer willingly embraced this radical milieu. "I attended lectures at the Rand School. I went to Cooper Union. I went everywhere and did everything possible in line with my entrance to and expansion in my chosen world."[40]

Eleanor Minne may have been the woman who worked at the office of the *Dial*, and it may have been on a visit to Minne that Toomer met Lewis Mumford. Mumford, Toomer notes, "among the other things he came to mean to me—was the first flesh-and-blood writer to enter my life." The most important part of this "chosen world" was Toomer's exhilarating realization that New York City grounded him: "I began to feel myself 'connected.' I felt I was beginning to connect. What a marvel that I actually knew people in 'The Dial.' What a miracle that I could actually talk with women and men, if only a few, who knew Shaw and Ibsen and the scientists and the philosophers as well as I, if not better. Truly I had done the right thing in coming to New York this time." Toomer could have met Mumford at the *Dial* office no earlier than March 1919, the month Mumford began working as an associate editor for the magazine; the date of their meeting is of interest because Toomer's whereabouts from the spring to the fall of that crucial year are something of a mystery.[41]

In his autobiography published in *The Wayward and the Seeking* Toomer says he spent the summer of 1918 working for Acker, Merrall in Ossining, about twenty miles north of New York City. That fall, in the city again, he took on a strenuous regime of work and study "for six months," suffered some kind of physical breakdown, and retreated to Ellenville, New York, in the foothills of the Catskills to recover. If his dates and time periods are approximately correct, this would be the spring of 1919. At Ellenville, he says, "I was suddenly seized by a passion for writing." He wrote and sent copies of what he wrote "to friends and acquaintances, in Washington, New York, Chicago, . . . my long letters which usually dealt with world-matters as I saw them." These were the letters Toomer also sent to his grandfather. After recovering his health, Toomer says he returned to Washington, where, "in the early summer," a friend from Chicago, Walt Palmer, proposed they spend the summer tramping about. They hitched to New York City, then made their way to the far west of the state to Walt's home in Salamanca, and they spent the summer there: "I, reading Shelley." In the "early fall" they returned to New York, and Toomer continued on to his home in Washington: "This was the fall of 1919. I was twenty-five years old."[42]

There is a second version of Toomer's summer of 1919 which appears in a later untitled autobiographical notebook written in 1936. This version repeats some of the events narrated in *The Wayward and the Seeking*, though it provides more detail of the trip to western New York state and adds, crucially, that Toomer was gone from Washington for only "a month." In this version there is no indication of when he left the capital, although Toomer says that "once at Walt's home we lived happily. Bill Tenes, another American College friend, came on. The three of us had a swell out door time until fall came. Walt had a job awaiting him. Bill had a job. My job, it seemed, was to return to Washington and face the music. Which I did." If Toomer stayed in Salamanca for a month, "until fall came," he might have left Washington in mid- or late August.[43]

"Facing the music" is a reference to his grandfather's anger at Toomer's "careening off on a bat like this at just this time when I was going well and he with me." Evidently what had been "going well" was Toomer's writing, which his grandfather had begun to appreciate. Toomer had returned to Pinchback's Washington apartment in "early spring" of 1919, and "during the months immediately following he not only did not oppose me but he became my companion as never before, entering into talks and discussions with me, reading my papers, praising as well as criticizing them." Pinchback was probably Toomer's first serious reader, critic, and editor. The most interesting thing about this account, however, is that it neglects to mention that during the summer of 1919 Toomer published his first pieces of writing, two sketches about politics and race that appeared in a prominent socialist newspaper in New York City.

Choosing the Appropriate Forum

On June 15, 1919, the *New York Call* printed a short sketch titled "Ghouls," by Jean Toomer in its Sunday supplement, the *Call Magazine*. Less than two months later Toomer's "Reflections on the Race Riots" appeared on the *Call*'s editorial page for August 2. Apparently the only public mention Toomer ever made of these early publications was in a short biographical sketch he composed for Boni & Liveright as they were preparing to bring out *Cane*. There he said: "His first published writing was a prose sketch called the Profiteers. This appeared in the New York Call. It was followed by two articles[,] The Americans and Mary Austin, and Reflections on the Race Riots, printed in the same paper. But the satisfaction derived from this writing was superficial and slight." Toomer misremembered the publication title of his first piece, "Ghouls," or perhaps that title was provided by a *Call* editor. He also reversed the order of the pieces on Mary Austin and on the race riots; the Mary Austin article was not published until 1920.[44]

The references to writing about "world-matters" in Ellenville, and to his grandfather's interest in his work in Washington, are probably veiled allusions to Toomer's first two *Call* articles. Certainly he could have written "Ghouls," which has the subject of war profiteering, anytime after the armistice, and he may have sent it to the *Call* or dropped it by the paper's offices on a trip to the city. War profiteering was a taboo subject before November 1918, but it became a frequent topic in the *Call* after the war's end; Toomer's brief, melodramatic sketch would have been welcome material during 1919. The *Call* was, of course, opposed to the entry of the United States into World War I and critical of government actions after its entry; the paper was banned from the mails by the postmaster general from 1917 until more than a year after the armistice.

Toomer's war sketch begins with a looter robbing corpses: "Hither and thither among the dead and dying of the battle-field moved the crouched shadow of the ghoul. His practiced hands went about their business with a precision almost machine-like." The parallel between the looter's "machine-like" hands and an assembly-line workforce in a factory emphasizes the economic nature of the war; the second part of the sketch is set in the boardroom of the "war profiteers," as "slaves entered obsequiously and deposited upon the broad table" the spoils collected from the battlefield. Here, as elsewhere in the piece, Toomer's prose strains for melodramatic effect; the "coins" on the table are "stained with tears of children, coins wrung from the breasts of mothers." At last one group of "slaves" — "a peculiar look in their eyes" — places a bundle on the table, and when the "profiteers" open it they find not gold but a ghoulish surprise: "They recoiled, afraid, for they had touched there the hearts of men."

What begins as a satire, then, ends with the Gothic motif where something hidden and unexpected is discovered. There is a possible echo here of Poe's "The Tell-Tale Heart," but what is more important for Toomer's future writing is his treatment of eyes and "seeing." In the beginning the looter has "trained eyes" for his work, but when he looks into a corpse's "two eyes, luminous in their death stare," he is unnerved. In the boardroom, war profiteers' "eyes glowed with the light of conquest," but they miss the dangerous "light" in the eyes of the slaves who bring the final bundle. So too, in *Cane*, what is seen will be all important; "eyes" that see, "eyes" that bear witness, "eyes" that are blind create or destroy a moral world.

The publication of "Ghouls" is possible, if curiously unmentioned, within the autobiographical frame of *The Wayward and the Seeking*; however, the writing of Toomer's second *Call* piece, "Reflections on the Race Riots," presents a significant problem. Of his visit to Salamanca Toomer says, "all summer we stayed there." Yet in late July 1919 large-scale race riots erupted in his hometown of Washington, D. C. From Saturday night, July 18, through Tuesday, July 22, mobs of whites, many of them soldiers or discharged soldiers from local military camps, attacked blacks and black residential areas in the city in what became virtually a "race war." The fighting, which would result in six deaths, at least seventy-five seriously injured, and numerous arrests, was centered around Seventh Street and the black district of northwestern Washington, where the apartment of Toomer's grandparents was located. If Toomer was indeed in Salamanca, it is difficult to imagine he wasn't shocked by this news when it came to him and concerned to learn what had happened to his grandparents and other family and friends in Washington. He might have been able to contact Washington by telegraph from western New York; it seems more likely he would have tried to return home, or at least to New York City, where he could have readier access to news reports.[45]

However, the time frame of Toomer's later autobiography, while vague, offers a more plausible outline of what happened that summer. If Toomer had departed Washington in mid-August or later, he would have been in the city during the riots, which would also explain how he was able by August 2, barely more than a week after the fighting had ended, to publish his rather specific article on those riots in the *Call*. This scenario would explain, too, some of the conflict between Toomer and his grandfather. If Toomer wrote his article, showed it to Pinchback, and then got it published in New York, the old defender of African-American civil rights would probably have been impressed, as well as expectant that Toomer would follow up the *Call* piece with more political writing. Instead, his grandson abandoned the city—and what may have become a mutual writing project—and, in effect, retreated to the country with white friends.[46]

Whatever the circumstances of its composition, Toomer's article is unique among his surviving work. Its introductory paragraph takes as militant a stand on American race relations as he was ever to assume:

The central fact emerging from the recent series of race riots is not so much that the Negro has developed an essentially new psychology, characterized by a fighting attitude. The Negro has always been conspicuous for his aggressiveness when arrayed against a foreign enemy. What is significant is that the Negro, for the first time in American history, has directed his "fight" against the iniquities of the white man in the United States.

Notwithstanding Toomer's "first time in American history" error, this account is incisive and accurate; his observation that the indifference of the "civil authorities" to threats against black life helped to inspire African-American resistance indicates that he has seen the riots, has had firsthand reports of them, or has read accounts detailed enough to trace the course of the four days' fighting. Without using the phrase, Toomer plays on the idea of the "New Negro," which had become a kind of rallying cry for African-American writers and intellectuals in the North after 1910; Ernest Allen, Jr., defines this movement as "a broad array of radical political, economic and cultural tendencies emerging from a black avant-garde located primarily in New York City."[47] While the first two days of the Washington riots showed a pattern of white mob attacks on black people, the second two were marked by determined, violent black resistance and even reprisal. Toomer was not the only one to note this fact—it was generally remarked upon, either with triumph or with dismay, in public commentary after the event—but in Toomer's argument this resistance becomes opportunity, and he insists that reformation from within the system seems unlikely. The only real cure must be radical.[48]

As Toomer sees it, solutions offered for racial injustice are not meant to end that injustice. One group "would have the fist of the white man educate the brain of the black." Fire, guns, lynchings—this is their answer to black recalcitrance. A second group urges restraint, but of course the restraint is to be all on one side: the Negro must believe that their "constitutional rights" are their protection. But, Toomer responds, if they haven't been effective before, what makes anyone think these "rights" will be effective now? Indeed, "it should be apparent that under this very constitution the country has come to this crisis." Moreover, "race riots are prevalent in Chicago, where Negroes enjoy political privilege," and yet this "privilege"—the fact that black voters control some elected positions in the city—did not protect them: "The solution, then, must lie deeper than mere suffrage."

Throughout the article, Toomer confronts those who deplore "the new spirit and attitude" of the Negro, and, echoing Frederick Douglass in his famous 1876 Fourth of July speech, he notes that "not a few who condemn the Negro's 'fight' would be themselves the first to fight under the like circumstances." These people want the Negro docile, but, adds Toomer, a Negro unwilling "to submit to injustices" is also a "Negro . . . difficult to exploit." Having made the economic connection, Toomer proceeds to his conclusion: "Those, then, who would aid in the present crisis would do well to focus on those fundamental and determining causes which have irresistibly drawn the Negro into his present position. To do this brings one adjacent to the thought and action of the labor movement."

Toomer then proceeds with an analysis of "fundamental causes" in terms of economics: "the causes of race prejudice may be primarily found in the economic structure that compels one worker to compete with another." These causes anticipate the solution, for socialism offers "a rational explanation of the causes of racial hatred," and a rational solution promotes "the substitution of a socialized community for a competitive one." Unless this happens, "America will remain a grotesque storm-center, torn by passion and hatred, until our democratic pretensions are replaced by a socialized reality." Toomer's argument is not only radical, it also closely resembles the arguments of such African-American radicals as A. Philip Randolph. In March 1919, for instance, Randolph had written, "When the motive for promoting race prejudice is removed, viz., profits, by the social ownership, control and operation of the machinery and sources of production . . . the effects of prejudice, race riots, lynching, etc., will also be removed." [49]

This reasoning had historical substance: the race riots in St. Louis in 1917 and Chicago in 1919, at least, were most directly the result of labor competition between local white workers and black workers migrating from the deep South. Employers encouraged and aided that migration, both to find replacement workers for employees lost to military service or the wartime halt of immigration and to have available strikebreakers in the event of labor disputes. Certainly one of the major subjects of *Cane* would be the "grotesque storm-center" of American racial attitudes, though their nature would not be reduced to such an absolute economic formula as in the final paragraph of "Reflections on the Race Riots." But while Toomer would adopt a much more complex attitude toward the question of racism and its causes in his later writing, he would never abandon his sense of how economic matters motivate human action and underlay the habits of everyday life. [50]

One thing that is striking about Toomer's second *Call* piece is the fluency of his argument; writing evidently on short notice, he is able to present a coherent and convincing argument, most of it devoted to the justification of violent black resistance to white attacks. While the history of racial confrontations in the United States shows that black resistance, where it was possible, was the rule rather than the exception, this was not a fact that was part of *public* myth or the subject of public discussion. Toomer, in other words, is wrong about his history—African-Americans had resisted white violence in the past—but right in his sense that acknowledging black resistance in a public forum *was* uncommon.

Revealing the New Negro

Toomer's omission in his autobiographies of any reference to the "Red Summer" of 1919 is unaccountable. As Philip Foner summarizes, "From May through September 1919, major race riots broke out in Charleston, Longview (Texas), Knoxville, Omaha, Washington, D.C., Chicago, and Phillips County, Arkansas. In addition, these same months produced no fewer than thirteen lesser conflicts between blacks and whites, excluding lynchings." Toomer's response to this violence in "Reflections" was not restrained; if he did read Shelley that summer, it was "The Mask of Anarchy" or "England, 1819." In fact, Toomer's position was uncommon enough that it seems likely he was influenced not primarily by white radicals, who generally gave little attention to the question of African-American civil rights or the physical oppression of black people, but by the radical New Negroes of Harlem, who championed black resistance. That kind of influence, or association, however, was something that Toomer would later be at pains to erase from his background. His silence about the *Call* articles probably had to do with the subject matter of race rather than with their socialist positions. Even in the autobiography of 1936, where he discusses his leftist politics freely, Toomer would still say, musing over the possibility of a journalistic career, that he "never even reached the stage of submitting a manuscript to the press." This erasure would seem to be deliberate.[51]

Despite this later obfuscation, it is probable that, during his time in New York, Toomer had been reading A. Philip Randolph and Chandler Owen's *Messenger*, Cyril V. Briggs's *Crusader*, Hubert Harrison's *Voice*, or W. A. Domingo's *Emancipator*, all radical New Negro publications. The single most famous African-American response to the Red Summer of 1919 was a poem by Claude McKay, "If We Must Die," published, along with six other McKay poems, by Max Eastman in the July issue of the *Liberator* and quickly picked up and reprinted by both the *Messenger* and the *Crusader*. When Toomer began writing the pieces that would become *Cane*, the first publication he would submit them to was the *Liberator*, whose literary editor by then was McKay. Toomer also was certain to have known of Randolph and Owen; in the spring of 1919 they were both part-time teachers at the Rand, offering a course on "The Economics and Sociology of the Negro Problem." Less than two weeks after the *Call* published Toomer's first article, the paper carried an editorial praising the work of the two black radicals and their "sound interpretation of the economic history of this country."[52]

The evidence for Toomer's relation to the Harlem radicals remains circumstantial, a coincidence of time, place, and associations, except for the clues offered by "Reflections on the Race Riots" and perhaps "Banking Coal," a Toomer poem published in the *Crisis* in June 1922. "Banking Coal" was the second piece Jessie Fauset had taken for the magazine (along with "Song of the Son," published in April), and in one sense it was the less original piece, its style and method much indebted to Robert Frost. As a good Frost imitation, its subject matter was ambiguous enough that the *Crisis* felt they could publish it, though without the full-page flourish given to "Song of the Son." "Banking Coal" could be read as a carpe diem piece, or as a critique of the black middle class on the order of *Cane*'s "Rhobert"; it might also be a poem about the repression of radicalism in the United States during the postwar years and, in particular, the decline of the New Negro radicals. The poem begins with praise of "whoever it was" that started "the fire," though since then:

Somehow the fire was furnaced,
And then the time was ripe for some to say,
"Right banking of the furnace saves the coal."
I've seen them set to work, each in his way,
Though all with shovels and with ashes,
Never resting till the fire seemed most dead.

Small flames flicker beneath the ashes, but "roaring fires" aren't made through such caution. Whether the poem's final "one grand flare" refers to the Russian Revolution or to African-American resistance during the Washington riots, Toomer concludes that the memory of that conflagration "is worth a life."[53]

Chapter 3
Cultural Politics, 1920

What kind of fire of pure passion are you going to keep burning under the pot in order that the mixture that comes out may be purged of its dross and may be the fine gold of untainted Americanism?
—Woodrow Wilson, Public Address, May 20, 1916

To preach a pure and undiluted Americanism with the spectacle of suicidal Europe before us is to invite disaster and destruction.
—Randolph Bourne, "The Jew and Trans-National America," 1916

Bourne braced against the war, hence against all that is vicious in this nation.
—Jean Toomer, "Paul Rosenfeld in *Port of New York*," 1924

Jean Toomer's conflict with his grandfather in the fall of 1919 was serious enough to prompt his return to New York. At the end of December he rented a room "on 9th Street near 5th Avenue," again in the Village. He took a job in the shipyards of New Jersey, an experience that was illuminating for a "parlor socialist," as he described himself. His remarks about the job in *The Wayward and the Seeking* are brief: "I was called a fitter. I got $22.00 a week. After ten days of it, I quit. And that, by the way, finished socialism for me. The men who worked in those yards—and they were real realistic workmen—had two main interests: playing craps and sleeping with women. Not God himself could have done anything with those men. Socialism . . ? Well, it was for people like [G. B.] Shaw and Sidney Webb."[1]

Toomer's biographers have relied on that single passage—selected from the "Outline of an Autobiography," written in 1931 or 1932—to conclude that work in the shipyards ended Toomer's attachment to radical politics. In 1920, however, there had been no apparent change in his political attitudes; he continued to visit the Rand School, he wrote again for the *Call*, and he submitted his stories and poems to radical journals in New York and further afield even three years later. The radical side of Toomer's politics would also continue to appear in his post-*Cane* writings, notably his essay on race for the *Problems of Civilization* anthology, and in the discussion of his shipyard job in his autobiography of 1935–36. In "Race Problems and Modern Society," published in 1929, Toomer was not optimistic about the prospects for significant social change since, "irrespective of the example and influence of the Soviet Union from without, and of radical and liberal labor and political forces from within, the World War notwithstanding, and despite the protests and revolts of foreign peoples, the business, political, legal, and military organizations and expansion of Western nations have advanced." He went on to critique a civilization that was materially obsessed and yet where "the fact that most of us are just one step ahead of the sheriff is a thing that one mentions less and less." Finally, speaking about the advantages gained for the economic status quo as a result of racial antagonisms, Toomer concluded that "Americans of all colors and of most descriptions are crawling about their social prison, which is still called Democracy."[2]

One of the most extensive revisions in Toomer's autobiographical writings concerned those ten days he spent in the shipyards in December of 1919. The brief, dismissive paragraph of the early "Outline of an Autobiography" became in his 1936 version a painstaking analysis of what that experience meant for him, taking up thirty-one pages of a small spiral-bound notebook and seventeen pages of a large one. He now wrote:

That I was disillusioned with these workers did not mean that I was disillusioned with socialism. On the contrary. Just because I saw at first hand the wretched character of the worker and his life, just because I myself had shared his peril and his plight, I realized as never before the *need* of socialism, the *need* of a radical change of the conditions of human society. Whereas before, socialism had been for me a reasoned and a felt *value*, now it became more deeply rooted in me as *the* most urgent need of life for the majority of living people.

In this later account of the shipyards, Toomer concentrated on how men were alienated from their work by the "savagery" of their working conditions, while both workers and employers—like "slaves and masters"—were caught in the same vicious economic system: "despite the class-difference . . . a general pattern and similar traits [were] stamped on owners and workers alike." Owners and workers alike were indifferent to the ships they built, which "didn't mean anything to anyone." Toomer's empathy, however, was with the workers, "spoiled for working" by the system of production, and so degraded by drudgery that their "faculties of speech and feeling and understanding had been paralyzed if not destroyed."[3]

As he represented the South in *Cane* by Gothic imagery, Toomer recalled the shipyards with a similar kind of terror. He had tried at first to aestheticize his experience there, to focus on the beauty of the ships themselves: "At such times I was happy, even in the midst of inferno, happy as the artist is happy who sees the beauty of forms and visions to the exclusion of actual human conditions." But he could not forget the conditions of the work—"brutal, ruthless, unadorned"—nor could he forget the men he worked with: "They haunted me, these men, they and their plight. With open eyes I'd see their ravaged faces. If I closed my eyes, they'd haunt me, not their faces only, not their eyes only, but their spirits crucified in life, up against it and nailed there." Even months later, while he worked at a white-collar job for Acker, Merrall, that memory continued to haunt him: "sometimes while at work in the store, sometimes in my room or walking the streets at night, my habitual views and feelings of myself and of life would be suddenly pushed aside, as dreams are pushed back when one awakes, and I'd see and realize the terrible core of life's reality. In fear and terror I'd shrink back, struggling to forget, trying to hide this vision from sight." In 1920, he said, "Some deep center of me came awake . . . an essence-eye that saw the skeleton beneath the flesh."[4]

Toomer's narrative was both an attempt to understand why he found it impossible to cross the class lines that separated him from the other shipyard workers and an apology for his separateness. He felt that "these men and these conditions were not mine. This was the fact—and it too made me feel wretched, and made me wonder if I were committing a betrayal, and made me ask myself in all possible sincerity if my 'deep knowing' were not merely a rationalization of, on the one hand, my dislikes and inadequacies in the proletarian world, and, on the other hand, my preferences and ego-urges for the middle class." Toomer was determined not to be "a bourgiose [*sic*] leader of the proletariat," but to find a way to embrace his own "conditions." If he wouldn't be proletarian in New York, Toomer would become part of the leftist literary and political group descended from the magazine *Seven Arts*, an association he maintained into the late 1930s.[5]

In early 1920 Toomer went back to work for Acker, Merrall and continued to frequent the socialist world of the Village. Sometime that spring Pinchback decided to sell the Washington house he held in Toomer's name in order to get back the money he had loaned his grandson against it; there was a surplus of six hundred dollars after the sale, and Pinchback sent this to Toomer, who promptly quit his job at Acker, Merrall and used the small legacy to live on while he continued writing and taking music lessons. That spring he also attended a lecture at the Rand School "on Romain Rolland and Jean Christophe, by Helena DeKay." Introducing himself to DeKay, Toomer was eventually invited to a party at Lola Ridge's, "my first literary party," as he calls it. An author of a book on the Jewish East Side, Ridge was a member of the radical left and the future editor of the avant-garde magazine *Broom*. It was at her party that Toomer saw Waldo Frank, though he did not speak to him there. Then, he relates, "a week or so later I chanced to be walking through Central Park. A man passed me. In a flash I seemed to recognize him. . . . Now I knew it was the person I had marked at Lola

Ridge's. We introduced ourselves. He was Waldo Frank. I vaguely remembered having heard of him through my friend Ehrlich. Ehrlich had said Frank had written a remarkable book called *Our America*. I had not read it. This was all I knew of Waldo Frank."[6] Toomer says the two discussed his interest in studying music and in writing, and Toomer was evidently impressed enough by this conversation that he went on to read Frank's *Our America*. This meeting with Frank was to be the most important literary contact of Toomer's life.

By summer the money from the house was gone, and Toomer returned to his grandfather's apartment in Washington once again. This time, he says, he was determined on a "long apprenticeship": "I was going to Washington and remain there until my literary work lifted me out." He was still three years away from the publication of *Cane*, though by 1922 his work would begin appearing in prominent little magazines. Toomer would also place one more article in the *Call*, and that article would join him to the literary circles of Waldo Frank and involve him in the cultural wars of the 1920s, wars ignited by questions of American identity, ethnicity and "race."[7]

Suppression and the "Acceptable" Patriot

In April 1917 the United States had entered World War I, despite Woodrow Wilson's reelection the preceding year under the slogan "He kept us out of war." The war had by no means been a universally popular cause; there were strong objections to America's entry from Progressive senators and congressmen and from two-time Democratic/Populist presidential candidate William Jennings Bryan, among others. However, the opposition was comprised of individual voices rather than an organized force, and the more general reaction of the nation seemed to be a fatalistic apathy. The major exception occurred the day after the declaration of war, at a meeting of Socialist party leaders in St. Louis that produced a manifesto denouncing "the war just declared by the Government of the United States" and promising to "uphold the ideal of international working-class solidarity." With unfortunate prescience they described the social effect of wars:

They breed a sinister spirit of passion, unreason, race hatred, and false patriotism. They obscure the struggles of the workers for life, liberty, and social justice. They tend to sever the vital bonds of solidarity between them and their brothers in other countries, to destroy their organizations, and to curtail their civil and political rights and liberties.[8]

The manifesto was prophetic. Shortly after the declaration of war, Wilson's administration initiated an elaborate campaign to eliminate domestic opposition to his policies, and, as the socialists had predicted, political support for this suppression was generated in particular by playing on the nation's racial and economic fears. Political radicals, immigrant and "hyphenated" Americans, farm and labor groups, any organization that could be identified as potentially critical or resistant was subject to surveillance, censorship, arrest, and attack. Since a crucial part of this policy intentionally stirred up antagonisms based on existing differences and distrusts within the American population, its consequences could not be limited to the brief period of the war.[9]

The policies promulgated by the government, the media, and private corporations and agencies helped create a national war hysteria. For the government's part Wilson oversaw the establishment of an extensive security apparatus intended for propaganda production as well as for stifling dissent. Various Progressives and a few socialist figures participated in that apparatus, either as appointed administrators or as apologists for the "right" of government to suspend civil liberties. Even John Dewey would weigh in with articles for the *New Republic* that defended the necessity of censorship. Private organizations like the National Security League, ostensibly "patriotic societies," joined patriotism to their conservative economic agendas, and "their major contributions came from corporations and businessmen who saw in the patriotic crusade an opportunity to benefit the position of organized capital."[10]

The official and unofficial apparatus of suppression became so effective and so politically useful that, even after the armistice of November 1918, neither the government nor the private enforcers of patriotism wished to give it up. In December 1919, President Wilson requested that Congress pass a peacetime sedition bill; he then refused to sign a bill that would have ended emergency measures giving police powers to his cabinet officers. According to historian Harry N. Scheiber, "Until the day before he left office Wilson refused to surrender wartime powers." The defense of economic conservatism was also extended as a campaign against anyone who could be defined as "un-American," a category determined by ethnic and racial criteria as well as political ones; in effect, the wartime attacks on opponents of the war became peacetime attacks on union organizers and "non–Anglo-Saxons." The large number of immigrants in the working classes made it easier to identify labor organizing with "foreign" influence, so the postwar campaigns against the Left and labor were energized by the extended campaign against ethnic Americans that had been carried out as wartime propaganda.[11]

These various "patriotic" appeals were joined in the phrase "100 percent Americanism," used both by the Ku Klux Klan and by middle-of-the-road politicians in 1919. The acceptable patriot held an uncritical view of American history and economic arrangements, a view in which distortion or misdirection was brought in by "aliens," either nonwhite or non–Anglo-Saxon, depending on how closely the circle was being drawn. Of course, beyond this general formula was a vast culture of race theory and myth, propagated in universities and congressional committees and mainstream periodicals as well as in saloons and revival meetings and movie theaters. In February 1921 Vice President–elect Calvin Coolidge published an article in *Good Housekeeping* entitled "Whose Country Is This?" Among his observations on American identity, Coolidge noted that "biological laws tell us that certain divergent people will not mix or blend. The Nordics propagate themselves successfully. With other races, the outcome shows deterioration on both sides. Quality of mind and body suggests that observance of ethnic law is as great a necessity to a nation as immigration law."[12]

Coolidge joined the danger of miscegenation to the need for immigration restriction, and miscegenation in this context was not the mating of black and white but the mixing of "Nordic" and "non-Nordic," or "100 percent Americans" and "others." The hyphenated Americans—Irish-Americans, German-Americans, Russian-Americans, particularly Jewish-Americans—were suspect patriots and, as government committees investigating the "new" immigration had been claiming since at least 1911, were also regarded as racially inferior. The long history and basic assumptions of white supremacy in the United States could easily be adapted to the latest "scientific" definition of "white" based on Madison Grant's race theories in *The Passing of a Great Race* (1916); to the new racial-purity-as-Americanism ideal were attached political ideas that defended the economic and social status quo.[13]

In 1919, then, the United States fell, or was pushed, into a state of extreme reaction. Race riots, labor struggles, and government repression were continuous. In Michigan Henry Ford made the *Dearborn Independent* over into an anti-Semitic newspaper and began publishing a series on "The International Jew" that was based on the bogus *Protocols of the Learned Elders of Zion.* By 1922 the revived Ku Klux Klan was headed toward its membership peak of two million, attacking Catholics as well as African-Americans and Jews. In 1921 Congress had passed the first stage of the Immigration Act, a law whose chief purpose was understood to be "to keep out the Jews." The Immigration Act of 1924 would be even more specifically written along racial lines, and it would effectively end large-scale legal migration into the United States.[14]

Frederic Howe, the prominent Progressive writer and Woodrow Wilson's Commissioner of Immigration for New York, wrote a memoir about the period of the war and the "Red Scare." In a chapter titled "Liberals and the War," Howe reflected on the fate of friends and followers, especially those he had known as director of the People's Institute of the Cooper Union in New York City:

Few people know of the state of terror that prevailed during these years, few would believe the extent to which private hates and prejudices were permitted to usurp government powers. It was quite apparent that the alleged offenses for which people were being persecuted were not the real offenses. The prosecution was directed against liberals, radicals, persons who had been identified with municipal-ownership fights, with labor movements, with forums, with liberal papers which were under the ban. Many of them were young people, many were college men and women. . . . I hated the new state that had arisen, hated its brutalities, its ignorance, its unpatriotic patriotism, that made profit from our sacrifices and used its power to suppress criticism of its acts. I hated the suggestion of disloyalty of myself, and my friends; suggestions that were directed against liberals, never against profiteers. I wanted to protest against the destruction of *my* government, *my* democracy, *my* America.[15]

Howe's "my America" overlapped with, if it was not identical to, Waldo Frank's *Our America*; Frank's *Seven Arts* was one of the "liberal papers" effectively banned, as was the *New York Call*, the single publication that had printed the work of Jean Toomer. The pressure of censorship and surveillance, of threatened or actual violence would continue through the early 1920s, acting to suppress the American Left and the labor movement. But, despite that violence and repression, the question of whose America it was would continue to be argued.[16]

Toomer and Mary Austin

Jean Toomer's final *Call* article, "Americans and Mary Austin," appeared on October 10, 1920, in reply to a piece Austin had published in the *Nation* two months earlier, "New York: Dictator of American Criticism." At the center of Austin's attack on "New York," and at the core of Toomer's defense of it, was *Our America*, the book Waldo Frank had brought out with Boni & Liveright in 1919. It's probable that literary envy was one motive behind Austin's article. By casting New York as "dictator," Austin evoked the power of the city's literary community to publish, review, publicize, or ignore the written word, thereby contributing significantly to a work's commercial success or failure. *Our America* may have stirred her ire partly because it was the object of a major publicity campaign by Boni & Liveright, while Liveright had recently issued a new edition of Austin's 1910 novel, *Outland*, without such special attention. In addition, Austin's novel of the New York immigrant and radical world, *No. 26 Jayne Street*, was poorly received in 1920. Whatever the literary jealousies involved, the public debate about Frank's book became part of the larger struggle over the question of American identity: the cultural politics invested in conceptions of "race" or ethnicity, of language, class, and region, of city and country, of center and periphery.[17]

Mary Austin, born and raised in the Midwest, had lived in New York City since 1912, writing novels, reviews, and plays and becoming part of the new artistic ferment of the city. She was associated with the suffragette movement, the salon of Mable Dodge, and with such prominent editors and writers as Carl Van Doren, Lincoln Steffens, and Van Wyck Brooks. Her move to New York, in fact, like Sherwood Anderson's move from Chicago and Hart Crane's from Cleveland, reflected the rise of the city's literary culture, and she was well known within that culture. Although she lived in New York and wrote about the life of the city, her most important attachment was to the far western United States, particularly California and the Southwest, where she had lived for twenty years before traveling abroad and settling on the East Coast.[18]

Austin's Western pedigree provided her rationale for attacking New York's "dictatorship" of American criticism: "It is totally void of any reference to such writers as Fewkes, Hodges, Lumholtz, Lummis, Cather, Matthews, Cushing, and Alice Fletcher." Her plea for the provinces as against the center looked back to the populist revolt of the 1890s (still alive in 1920 in the Midwest's Non-Partisan League) and to rural America's distrust of the eastern metropolis. Austin set her Western writers against such New York names as "Stieglitz, Stein, Ornstein, Rosenfeld, Oppenheim, Mencken, Littell, Hackett, and Brooks"—and, of course, Waldo Frank, from whose book *Our America* she compiled her list. Of the ten names she censured, six were Jewish, and the others were suspect to the Anglo-American tradition: the Irish-American Francis Hackett supported the Irish Free State and, as literary editor of the *New Republic*, he was tainted by his association with Jews, as was Philip Littell; the Anglo-American Brooks was linked to the Jewish writers of the *Seven Arts*. Mencken, of course, was German-American, an identification that in 1920 would still banish him to the margins. Austin was by no means the first writer to enter into the period's rabid literary ethnic-baiting, a practice given intellectual cachet by the "New Humanists," but she quickly learned the rules of the game.[19]

Of course, the custodians of the American literary canon in the 1890s or 1900 would have been appalled by the idea that a suffragette (Mary Austin), a Jew (Waldo Frank), and a black (Jean Toomer) would presume to address a subject of "national" importance. Even in 1920, though the intellectual door had been opened somewhat, there was no automatic assumption that anyone might speak about such matters, and Mary Austin may have been looking for approval or support from the traditional cultural power brokers. Austin's damning list, in fact, closely resembles the one contested by Ludwig Lewisohn and Stuart Sherman in their long-running debate over what should constitute the future of American literature.[20] In his autobiography, *Upstream* (1922), Lewisohn, a German-Jewish intellectual who suffered during World War I for both his "race" and his "nationality," pointed to the major issue in this battle of the books. An American since age ten, he was, nevertheless, "to be Americanized." Having mastered the "Anglo-American Tradition" in literature, "I am even now to be assimilated." But, he continued, "Suppose I intend rather to assimilate America, to mitigate Puritan barbarism by the influence of my spirit and the example of my life? Then a writer named, let us say, Stuart Sherman, declares that I pervert the national genius. But suppose I am the national genius—Dreiser and Mencken and Francis Hackett and I—rather than Stuart Sherman?"[21]

Thus, despite her credentials as an "outsider"—Westerner, feminist, participant in radical salons—Austin's object of attack in her *Nation* article was leftist Manhattan or, specifically, the Jewish heart of Manhattan, "authors [who] have never lived west of Broadway or north of Fifty-ninth." Austin claimed that "a small New York group," most of whose members are "under forty," dictated literary taste to the rest of the country, and she defined the city as "only a half-way house of immigration, a little less than a half-way house for European thinking." New York was a nest of outsiders ("the foreign born or foreignly derived," in Austin's all-purpose phrase) and home to the Jew, the source of a "schism" that prevented an authentic national culture from being established: "One wonders what part is played in this schism between literature and the process of nationalism by the preponderance of Jews among our critical writers." Generously conceding that "there is nothing un-American in being a Jew," she yet demurred about Jewish writers:

It is only when the Jew attempts the role of interpreter of our American expression that the validity of the racial bias comes into question. Can the Jew, with his profound complex of election, his need of sensuous satisfaction qualifying his every expression of personal life, and his short pendulum-swing between mystical orthodoxy and a sterile ethical culture—can he become the commentator, the arbiter, of American art and American thinking?[22]

Waldo Frank's *Our America* became the exemplar of all these Jewish defects, its attention focused on New York and Chicago, with the rest of the country "magnificently predicated from a car window." Austin identified a poet Frank praised, Louis Untermeyer, as "the well-found, smartly schooled, urban American," applying just the faintest, coded hint of anti-Semitism; she then remarked on the inappropriateness of comparing Untermeyer with the English poet Alfred Noyes, for "if writing and the criticism of writing is to become an aid to that development of the American consciousness to which the New York critic is devoted, some relating of the work to its generating sources is indispensable." That is, Jews must be identified as Jews, not as Americans. Gertrude Atherton would give this idea its critically logical and mad extension in an essay for the *Bookman*, "The Alpine School of Fiction," two years later.[23]

Toomer's reply to Austin was the work of someone familiar with the terrain of American racism: he read her acutely. His opening remarks outlined what would remain his consistent view of race in America, that "the race to be known as the American . . . will be a composite one, including within itself, in complementing harmony, all races." This ideal "composite" was the "First American" of the Whitmanesque poem Toomer may have been working on at the time of this essay; it would become "the man of blue or purple" in his long poem *The Blue Meridian*, finally published in 1936, and its ultimate reference was always to Toomer himself and his "five or six" bloodlines. Toomer's critique of Austin revealed that, though she spoke of the need for a "national consciousness" and of "the vast America of our affections," she really aimed to enforce exclusion and produce divisiveness. "Desiring the inevitable amalgamation and consequent cultural unity, Miss Austin's article has given new cause for old race consciousness."

Toomer saw through Austin's "Americanist" stance to her "drawing room" prejudices: "many energies, directed at our evolution, have been degraded, producing no salutary or compensating effects." He defended New York's cultural ascension as having occurred through merit; the problem with the provinces was that they remained provincial. He understood that Austin's defense of the essential unity of Native American culture was not necessarily at odds with the nativist probity of a Madison Grant. When Toomer said, "New York and the New Yorkers are dictators of American criticism for the same reason that Moscow and the Bolsheviki are dictators of the present course of Russia, namely, that they are doing the job better than any others are now capable of doing it," he had perhaps unwittingly noted the metropolis's ideal situation for contending with the process of modernization and its bewildering diversity. And when he turned to criticize Austin's attack on Jews, he evoked the fears of localism and the hopes for the metropolis which American minorities and outsiders experienced in 1920.[24]

Toomer rejected Austin's claim that Jews were producing a "schism" in American civilization, and he praised the value of the writers Waldo Frank celebrated in *Our America*. Linking her anti-Semitism to the feeling "of the average Southern white in his attitude toward the Negro," Toomer effectively exposed her rhetorical ploys: " 'There is nothing un-American in being a Jew,' says Miss Austin. Certainly not. But why state the obvious? Once made, such statements are never without their contrary implications." And he reminded the reader, again, that Austin's sanctimonious claim for America's "dearest tradition" of tolerance "does not now obtain," either in New York or in her favored California.

The most unusual point in Toomer's essay was his inclusion of African-Americans and Japanese-Americans within the discussion of American identity and culture. In the "identity" debates of the war and postwar eras, race was always present, in shouts or whispers, but black or Asian people were infrequently mentioned, partly because they were people associated with distant regions, the rural South and the far West, rather than with the metropolitan East, where the debate had developed along the path of Madison Grant's race theories and the movement to restrict immigration. But, more precisely, African-Americans or Japanese-Americans were unmentioned because they were beyond consideration; in a "whiteman's country" they were the anomaly, the exception, the problem, a separate category, and the argument as framed by Grant and his followers centered on which "whites" were "really white." Were Jews? Were Slavs? Were "Alpines" or "Mediterraneans"? Toomer employed the usual terms of "assimilation," "fusion," and "amalgamation" to describe the creation of a new American "race," but he was unequivocally frank about the inevitable mixing of "blood-lines." And against the nativist tide of exclusion, Toomer argued to imagine everyone as American within a "community of cultured differences."[25]

Toomer joined the cultural to the political, as Randolph Bourne and Waldo Frank had in their writings. Austin, ostensibly advocating "cultural unity," in fact promoted an "old race consciousness." Though Toomer gave her the benefit of the doubt, it's questionable whether Austin actually wanted anything like a "community of cultured differences." Toomer's elegant phrase expressed an ideal that was situated on one side of the cultural wars being fought in 1920, and Austin's writings placed her increasingly on the other side. If Jews caused a cultural "schism," it was because they didn't recognize or abide by established standards; their understanding of America was somehow "alien." In 1920 Mary Austin was slated to teach a course at the Rand School titled "American Literature as an Expression of American Life," and a brief description, almost certainly her own, was published in the *Call*: "Mrs. Austin is not herself a Socialist, but she has become convinced that much of the social unrest of the half-Americanized is due to their not being able to find any suitable medium of expression." The foreign mediums they employ "do not get to the American public, or, if they do, it is with an alien flavor offensive to the American taste." In this view "social unrest" was not the result of working or living conditions but of "alien" difference, and Austin's course offered not the acceptance of difference, but its elimination.[26]

Most of the intellectual debate over "Americanism" and American identity assumed that the result of assimilation would be the dissolution of at least the major cultural differences between American citizens. There was, however, extreme disagreement as to what that resulting culture might be like or how it could be achieved. The metaphor of the "melting pot," made famous in Israel Zangwill's play, *The Melting-Pot*, of 1908, was frequently evoked to portray the process of immigrant assimilation, and no doubt one reason for the metaphor's popularity and resonance was its essential ambiguity. As Toomer used it, for instance, the melting pot was to produce a new human type altogether, "a continent of Walt Whitmans . . . universal in their sympathies and godlike of soul." Toomer assumed a progressive social and "racial" evolution, one that was "inevitable" and which moved toward a "cosmopolitan" ideal based on universal standards of cultural amalgamation rather than the parochial affiliations of any specific group. For Mary Austin, however, the point of assimilation was to remake the "alien" as an American modeled after the "good stock" of the Plains or the far West. As

Philip Gleason has observed, after 1920 "the melting pot came to be looked upon as almost exclusively a purger of 'foreign dross' and 'impurities'; the melting pot 'theory' tended to lose all association with the idea that immigrants could make valuable contributions to a yet unfinished American culture."[27]

Toomer assumed that the cosmopolitan ideal of the American future would include both a mixing of races and the creation of a new American culture, represented in his essay by the universal Walt Whitman and the younger writers of Frank's *Our America*. In 1920 this idea was, as Toomer himself admits, "some distance" from acceptance. A more common argument at the time was the racialist claim that the new immigrants lacked any "inherited" capacity to understand or adapt to American — that is, "Anglo-Saxon" — culture. John Higham identifies as part of the postwar nativist eruption "a whole school of literary traditionalists in the early twenties [who] looked on American literature as a battleground where old-stock writers were defending the nation's spiritual heritage against onslaught from the spokesmen of alien races." The defense of an academic canon of literature easily became a defense of Anglo-Saxon ideals, and then of the "purity" of the "race." That is not to say that every writer who defended one of these ideals went on to link it to the others, but the continuity and progression of the argument were generally understood.[28]

Thus when Toomer defended Frank and then modeled his own writing after the young modernists of Frank's group, he was making not only aesthetic choices but political ones, and was joining himself to the "outsiders." These allegiances were formed to a degree during the preceding years, when Toomer had experienced the radical worlds of Chicago and New York; similarly, the ideal of racial amalgamation was an assumption, however much debated, rooted in Toomer's background among the mulatto elite of Washington, D.C. Waldo Frank had his own intellectual debts, of course, and thus Toomer's discussion of cultural politics in his *Call* essay, formulated in Frank's terms, had its origins in the writings of Frank's own mentors among the *Seven Arts* group.[29]

Brooks and Bourne: Cultural Theory and the *Seven Arts*

In 1916 three young Jewish intellectuals, James Oppenheim, Waldo Frank, and Paul Rosenfeld, discussed the possibility of starting their own magazine of culture and politics. When Oppenheim was able to find financial backing for their project, the *Seven Arts* was born, with Oppenheim as chief editor, Frank as his assistant, and Rosenfeld as music critic. In his 1930 memoir about the magazine, Oppenheim reflected on the two central ideals it was to represent: First was the belief that "America could be regenerated by art." This was a constant theme, beginning with the introductory circular that announced: "The *Seven Arts* is not a magazine for artists, but an expression of artists for the community." The second ideal sprang from the expectation of where this new cultural vitality would be found. In Thomas Bender's words, the *Seven Arts* "was the first example of an ethnic collaboration, Christian and Jew, that sought to speak for an American national culture embracing 'different national strains.' "[30]

The primary theorists for this new culture were two "Anglo-Saxons," initially Van Wyck Brooks, then, a few months later, Randolph Bourne. Brooks's addition, Oppenheim ironically noted, helped by "relieving us of the onus of being non–Anglo-Saxon," but his presence was more important for other reasons. Bourne was "the greatest thing that happened to the *Seven Arts*, though in the end it was the main cause of our shutting down." Bourne's essays attacking the U.S. role in World War I would eventually lead to the magazine's loss of financial support. Brooks never agreed with the other editors' opposition to the war and was a lukewarm supporter of America's involvement; he concentrated on cultural questions while Bourne, Oppenheim, and others increasingly turned to immediate political matters. Nevertheless, Brooks and Bourne together provided a critical approach to American history and culture that became an intellectual starting point for Frank, Rosenfeld, and those attracted to their circle, including Jean Toomer.[31]

Van Wyck Brooks was the senior writer of the group; his *Wine of the Puritans* had appeared from an English publisher in 1908, and in 1915 he published *America's Coming-of-Age*, a book Frank and Oppenheim saw as the "prologemena [*sic*] to our Future Seven Arts magazine." They offered him a fulltime position as an associate editor soon after opening their offices. With some notable exceptions, Brooks's early criticism of American life has been neglected or reduced to a few clichéd phrases: "highbrow/lowbrow," "usable past," "cultural nationalism." These catchwords have overshadowed the remarkable suggestiveness of his metaphors and the incisiveness of his comic wit, as well as the vital ideas behind those familiar phrases. The phrase "a usable past" has become so commonplace that many have forgotten that Brooks coined it in the context of a particular argument, the express aim of which was to challenge "the accepted canon of American literature." The essay in which it appears shows why Brooks was important to young writers like Frank and Toomer, and illustrates how durable has been the subject matter of American cultural wars.[32]

Brooks's argument attacked the authority of professors in the academy who tried to regulate America's literary history by reducing it to a single tradition, their aim being "apparently no sort of desire to fertilize the present, but rather to shame the present with the example of the past." Brooks had in mind the New Humanists—Irving Babbitt, Paul Elmer More, Stuart Sherman—as well as members of the older Genteel Tradition, all opponents of the "Young America" in whom Brooks placed his hope. As Brooks said, "The spiritual past has no objective reality; it yields only what we are able to look for in it." What modern writers needed to find, if they were to "grow and ripen," were alternative pasts that might replace the mono-myth that had produced a cultural sterility.[33]

There was a problem, however, in Brooks's desire both to escape a sterile gentility and to inspire an "organic" culture that could somehow represent the American nation in common. Brooks explained his usable pasts by the example of relationships between "national" cultures:

Every people selects from the experience of every other people whatever contributes most vitally to its own development. The history of France that survives in the mind of Italy is totally different from the history of France that survives in the mind of England, and *from this point of view there are as many histories of America as there are nations to possess them.* (Emphasis added)

By implication, a people *within* a nation of multiple cultural heritages will have its own view of America's past and may have its own "literary" tradition, even if that tradition is an oral rather than a written one. As Brooks himself would note, rejecting the Arnoldian notion of a single cultural definition of "the best," "When Matthew Arnold once objected to Sainte-Beuve that he did not consider Lamartine an important writer, Sainte-Beuve replied, 'Perhaps not, but he is important *for us.*' "[34]

It was Brooks's italicized phrase "*for us*" that in a sense inspired Waldo Frank's *Our America*, for it implied that a writer had the right to find his or her own ancestors, to define literature on his or her own terms. And that definition, Brooks elaborated, could be "racial," for "the European writer, whatever his personal education may be, has his racial past, in the first place, and then he has had his racial past *made available* for him. The American writer, on the other hand, not only has the most meager of birthrights but is cheated out of that." "On Creating a Usable Past" was concerned with a "national" literature to be created by the "American" writer. Despite his concession in *Letters and Leadership* to the "hyphenates," of whom Randolph Bourne helped make him aware, Brooks's intention, here and elsewhere, was to make America more like Europe—more like the organic societies he thought existed in England and France. It is doubtful that he imagined his words could have special meaning for an African-American writer, that "racial" and "birthright" would reverberate on a different frequency for someone like Jean Toomer. Nor did he resolve the implied tensions of several "national" cultures coexisting within one social body, the problem that would occupy Randolph Bourne.[35]

Brooks's goal was the creation of an organic culture in the industrial wasteland bequeathed to Americans by Puritans and pioneers. As early as *The Wine of the Puritans* (1908), he outlined his "Utopia" within the ruins he perceived in the American scene: "The vague ideal of every soul that has a thought in every age is for that communion of citizens in some body, some city or state, some Utopia. . . . Those artificial communities—Brook

Farms and East Auroras—are so pathetically suggestive of the situation we are all in! 'We get together' (what an American phrase that is!) because we *aren't* together."[36] The problem, as Brooks saw it, was how to make "Utopia" a possibility without making it "artificial"; one answer seemed to lay in making available to the American writer those multiple pasts that lay outside the Puritan-pioneer hegemony.

One of the metaphors Brooks used to describe that act of discovery appeared in *The World of H. G. Wells* (1915): "a bridge thrown out across the void," filaments, like those cast by Whitman's spider, that would connect self and other. Brooks's whole conception of a "usable past" was based on the notion of a bridge connecting past, present, and future. Those writers who had lived in an organic society—Friedrich Nietzsche and William Morris, for instance—"kept alive the tradition of a great society and great ways of living. . . . They made it impossible for men to forget the degradation of society and the poverty of their lives and built a bridge between the greatness of the few in the past and the greatness of the many, perhaps, in the future."[37]

This "bridge" became the Brooklyn Bridge in Frank's *The Unwelcome Man* (1917) and a central metaphor in *Our America* (1919); the same Brooklyn Bridge emerged in Paul Rosenfeld's analysis of John Marin's painting in *Port of New York* (1924), and in Lewis Mumford's study of symbolic architecture in *Sticks and Stones* (1924). Brooks's use of the bridge metaphor was taken over by Hart Crane, and may have influenced Kenneth Burke's concern with the linguistic forms of "pontification" in his later books about language and culture. For *Cane*, the "bridge" would express Toomer's concern to find a link between North and South, country and city, black and white.[38]

There was an optimism implicit in Brooks's early view of American culture, despite his harsh criticisms of it; the metaphor of the bridge suggested the possibilities of connection, of joining, of crossing over, and the younger writers of the *Seven Arts* embraced those possibilities. That optimism did not survive the war and its aftermath. In *The Wine of the Puritans* in 1908, Brooks observed that "American history is so unloveable"; nine years later, as the United States was about to enter the war, he said that American intellectuals could feel only "the chill of the grave as we look back over the spiritual history of our own race." That "chill"—or as he would say in another context, that unmeltable "splinter of ice"—began to preoccupy him more and more between 1917 and 1923. By 1922 even an admirer like Paul Rosenfeld felt that Brooks was no longer in touch with the younger generation.[39]

Brooks turned away from a criticism that offered ways out of a historical dilemma to one that observed the nature of American failure, even the "failure" of a Mark Twain, Jack London, or Henry James. Focusing almost entirely on those forces that destroyed the American artist, Brooks could find no exit from this cul-de-sac of history. In 1923 he suffered a nervous breakdown that disabled him for almost eight years; he finally emerged to focus on "the more smiling aspects of life . . . as the more American," a choice for which he had earlier faulted W. D. Howells. In the early 1930s, Brooks began the *Makers and Finders* series to which he would devote the rest of his life, and where the "usable past" that he celebrated as multiple in 1918 would be reduced to the controllable, single past of the New England tradition.[40]

With the exception of Lewis Mumford, the other writers around the *Seven Arts* group were withdrawing from Brooks's influence by 1920, or perhaps even earlier. In *Our America* (1919), a sympathetic Waldo Frank complained of those critics who could not escape a "disabling past," and in *America and the Young Intellectual* (1921), an equally sympathetic Harold Stearns would note that Brooks "shrinks a little from the practical world, as if it were in a kind of malign collective conspiracy to destroy one's interest in the true things of the spirit." In his poem *The Blue Meridian* (begun in 1921–22 and influenced by *Our America*), Toomer singled Brooks out as "someone" who had yielded prematurely to a pessimistic assessment of American life:

> Someone said:
>> Blood cannot mix with stuff upon our boards
>> As water with flour to make bread,
>> Nor have we yeast, nor have we fire.
>> Not iron, not chemicals or money
>> Are animate to suffer and rejoice,
>> Not what we have become, this angel-dough,
>> But slowly die, never attaining birth.

Brooks had said that America failed to provide its artists with "yeast" to make the "angel-dough" rise, an organic culture that would have nourished them. Although *The Blue Meridian* evokes the early Brooks throughout, Toomer's "someone said" dismisses the Brooks of the postwar years as blind to an emerging "new people," the very cultural "yeast" Brooks despaired of finding.[41]

Yet in *Cane* a poem like "Harvest Song" has themes of isolation and the despair of the disconnected individual that echo this later Brooks. The poem's voiceless singer ("My throat is dry") cannot hear the songs of his fellow workers in the fields: "My ears are caked with dust of oatfields at harvest-time." Its Brooksian imagery of sterility in the midst of plenty contrasts strikingly with the "singing tree" that the "seed" becomes in "Song of the Son," and *Cane* itself seems to alternate between the same two poles of possibility and impossibility which tormented Brooks. Toomer was to create two Brooksian protagonists after *Cane*, the homeless Costyve Duditch (a Brooksian Henry James in miniature) and the surreal Drackman, a corporate executive whose "friends" are clones of himself and whose skyscraper takes his human shape, thus illustrating the thoroughness with which the

American environment hardens "angel-dough" into stone. And, of course, Kabnis is a kind of Brooksian intellectual, "suspended a few feet above the soil whose touch would resurrect him." [42]

What *America's Coming-of-Age* and *Letters and Leadership* seemed to promise was a heroic endeavor that might, in helping to create a new national culture, integrate a fragmented personality and a fragmented people. What Brooks missed, at least on a conscious level, was the limitation of his word "invent": "If we need another past so badly, is it not conceivable that we might discover one, that we might even invent one." "Inventing" a past could offer new understandings of the present that might be liberating, but it could not overcome the literal present as an act of will. Banned journals and intimidated writers would not be restored only by invention. In *Cane*, similarly, any "usable past" is hedged around by the nightmare of history that Toomer's characters cannot "invent" away. [43]

What Van Wyck Brooks was unwilling to admit about the American polis at the end of the war his friend Randolph Bourne had already unflinchingly addressed. Both men began their careers within the zeitgeist of the Progressive era, and their early writings shared the optimism of the period, the belief, in Walter Lippmann's words, that "drift" could be mastered. World War I and its aftermath would blight the hopes of many intellectuals who thought they might help build a rational social order. Though he was not to live into 1919—he died of influenza in December 1918—Randolph Bourne attempted to come to terms with the meaning of the war and its social and political consequences well before it ended; if his preliminary conclusions were misunderstood, or went largely unheeded, they still represented a situation which Brooks and the *Seven Arts* group could not quite ignore.

Indeed, Woodrow Wilson's war was to show that the "State," as Bourne defined it, was by no means a benevolent or neutral institution, and Bourne came to see World War I as the event that had ushered in an American totalitarianism. His essays on Dewey and the pragmatist intellectuals who supported America's entry into the war were not pacifist position papers; they were acute analyses of how completely democracy had disappeared in America, how thoroughly Progressive hopes for *enlightened* self-interest and government based on intelligence were bankrupt. This was not a view the Progressive left was happy to hear or necessarily willing to accept. Bourne's shift in the last two years of his life from cultural critic to acute political analyst was a significant event in the history of the American intellectual class; but it was symptomatic of the *Seven Arts* group that while Bourne emerged for them in the 1920s as a martyred hero, they more or less deliberately averted their eyes from what he was writing near the end of his life.

Van Wyck Brooks would remain concerned with Bourne and his ideas, from his editing of the first collection of Bourne's essays in 1920 to his long essay on Bourne in 1962, the year of Brooks's own death. Each time Brooks wrote of Bourne—and he wrote about him on four different occasions—

the essays expanded and Brooks's admiration increased. Yet these essays also kept returning to what he saw as Bourne's mistaken direction in 1917: "the obsessions of the war," the antiwar articles in the *Seven Arts*, the essay on "The State." As he said on two different occasions about Bourne's *Seven Arts* articles, "It was his writing largely that killed *The Seven Arts*, for the donor could not accept this anti-war position, nor could I, for it seemed to me that to oppose the war was scarcely less futile than opposing an earthquake."[44]

Brooks had begun to revise Bourne's intellectual legacy in his selection for the posthumous collection of essays, *The History of a Literary Radical* (1920), which emphasized cultural criticism and omitted the unfinished but vital essay "The State." James Oppenheim, upset by what he saw as a distortion of Bourne's legacy, quickly assembled the late political writings and had them published in 1919 as *Untimely Papers*. Brooks never seemed to understand that Bourne's essays on the war were intended to make the "intellectuals" see that by joining the military procession they were abandoning essential principles. As Bourne said to Brooks in a letter of 1918, "We find a liberal war undertaken which could not fail to do far more damage to American democracy at home than it could ever do to the enemy abroad." With the capitulation of the intellectuals there would be much less resistance to a political absolutism that would make censorship, as well as many other oppressions, the social norm.[45]

Brooks would not openly admit that the processes of history might render art meaningless, because he wanted to believe that artists could renew society despite external conditions. Here was the major source of his crisis: the war appeared to demonstrate that art and "culture" were simply more debris on his "Sargasso Sea" of American life. What Brooks failed to say about the *Seven Arts* was that his own articles were sometimes as pessimistic as Bourne's—the "splinter of ice" in the "American mind" that he hoped American artists would melt was more resistant than he had imagined; art would not change the hardened forms within the culture, and his attention to a debilitating environment in his articles and books after 1919 must be seen as his own alienation from the effects of the war.[46]

A Usable Future or the Future as Nightmare?

Although Brooks and Bourne both spoke of the need for the artist and intellectual to discover a "usable past," Bourne more often emphasized a "usable" future:

Looking into the future he [the man of culture] will have to do what Van Wyck Brooks calls "invent a usable past." Finding little in the American tradition that is not tainted with sweetness and light and burdened with the terrible patronage of bourgeois society, the new classicist will yet rescue Thoreau and Whitman and Mark

Twain and try to tap through them a certain eternal human tradition of boundless vitality and moral freedom and so build out the future.[47]

The debt here to Brooks is clear: Bourne, too, thought that cultural criticism might weld old to new, past to future, vitality to discipline in such a way as to create a new America. Like Brooks, Bourne began thinking of American culture on the model of the ostensibly coherent European nation-states. Traveling in Europe after graduating from Columbia, Bourne wrote four articles in 1914–15 which expressed that ideal. For Bourne the rich cohesiveness of French society stood in marked contrast to the spiritual sterility of the United States, which borrowed the artifacts and ideas of other nations to create an artificial "Culture" that had little to do with the lived experience of most Americans. Bourne's ideas in these early essays had their roots in the Progressive era and reflected the hope that a managerial elite could reshape American lives by reorganizing society, particularly the life of American cities.[48]

In contrast to Brooks, however, Bourne used his background in sociology to broaden his conception of the aesthetic experience. Anticipating Mumford, Bourne would write essays on architecture, city planning, politics, and literary criticism. This catholicity of interests meant he was more engaged than Brooks in the process of modernity, in the culture beyond Emerson's Concord, in the hurly-burly metropolis into which the new immigrants from southern and eastern Europe were flooding every day. He was fascinated by the changes wrought within America by the immigrants' unassimilated presence, and the metaphor of the Sargasso Sea that an uneasy Brooks had used to represent America—"a prodigious welter of unconscious life"—Bourne saw as the hope of America's future.[49]

The model of European nationalism, of an "organic" culture, had lost some of its luster with the outbreak of World War I. By 1916, as Wilsonian "democracy" stepped up its campaign to enlist American support for England in the war, Bourne also began to see "Anglo-Saxondom" in a more serious light, and he wrote three essays that expressed his different hopes for the future: "Trans-National America," "The Jew and Trans-National America," and the unpublished "A Sociological Poet." "Trans-National America" was Bourne's first direct engagement with the arguments over American identity that had become even more prominent since 1914. World War I showed that immigrant Americans still held attachments to their native countries, and this became an excuse for attacks on "hyphenated" Americans even before the U.S. declaration of war. In February 1915, in this atmosphere of growing recrimination, Horace Kallen published in the *Nation* a two-part essay on "American nationality" titled "Democracy Versus the Melting-Pot."[50]

Kallen's essay sketched the history of "nationality" in the United States and rejected the feasibility of the "melting pot" for either producing an "organic culture" or creating a new "American race." Instead he advocated what he would later call "cultural pluralism," nationality as a cultural federation in which different ethnic groups existed in mutual toleration. In the first two of its three parts, Bourne's "Trans-National America" was largely a recapitulation of Kallen's essay, but Bourne, writing in the *Atlantic* in July 1916, was importantly concerned with the growing pressure on the United States to enter the world war; in the current treatment of the "unpopular and dreaded German-American," he already had intimations of the official suppression that was to come. Bourne's difference with Kallen in this essay was one of emphasis more than doctrine; like Kallen, he advocated the preservation of ethnic cultures and asserted that the "American" culture of the genteel tradition was actually just the preserved canon of an Anglo-American ruling class: "We are all foreign-born or the descendants of foreign-born." However, where Kallen closed his essay with his vision of a culturally pluralistic "Federal republic," Bourne in his essay's third part attempted to outline what new "cosmopolitan" or "trans-national" culture might arise from such a republic.[51]

Bourne defended difference and saw it as necessary for "social advance," yet as a modernist he also saw that "difference" itself was a temporary condition. "We are not dealing with static factors, but with fluid and dynamic generations." The ethnic friends who changed and broadened the "Anglo-Saxon's" outlook were in turn changed by his outlook. "Cosmopolitanism," then, attempted to construct a cultural ship that might stay afloat, preserving both the local and the international, in the huge seas of modern history. Bourne didn't emphasize Kallen's discrete *natios* because he didn't really imagine such "static" ideals would survive.[52]

Bourne saw America as the site of modernity at work. Though an American traveling abroad must adjust to foreign cultures,

after wandering about through many races and civilizations he may return to America to find them all here living vividly and crudely, seeking the same adjustment that he made. He sees the new people here with a new vision. They are no longer masses of aliens, waiting to be "assimilated," waiting to be melted down into the indistinguishable dough of Anglo-Saxonism. They are rather threads of living and potent cultures, blindly striving to weave themselves into a novel international nation, the first the world has seen.[53]

One definition of modernity might be that it is a condition of permanent immigration, of the mass circulation of people, goods, and ideas on such a scale that boundary lines of any kind are continually erased—not over a period of generations, but within a decade or a year. Bourne was trying to imagine a cultural matrix that might survive melting down or erasure, something adaptable to a world in process. What was needed, therefore, was a future "plastic" in its possibilities, a new world defined in terms of "the paradox that our American cultural tradition lies in the future."[54]

Bourne's insight foreshadows Brooks's view that the "usable past" may be multiple and outside the mainstream American perspective; his essay argued that diversity should be the country's greatest asset, not its liability, as the nativists argued. The appeal in this for someone like Jean Toomer was that it made *difference* the locus of an integrating force. Because the governing impulse of ethnic stocks was centripetal, it was possible for Americans to escape the narrow orbit of a monolithic nation-state and yet, given the broadening influences of modernity, substitute for it a "cosmopolitan ideal" that could serve as a kind of "spiritual welding." Here was a vision of community that was open yet centered, held together by a common ideal. As Kallen had said, common understanding suggested that heterogeneity might be more binding than homogeneity, that a country which respected difference would receive more loyalty than one which demanded uniformity. It was, of course, a utopian conception of society, but as Bourne came to believe, watching his generation of intellectuals drift toward war, pragmatism was not always the best way to deal with reality. His favorite quotation from the Bible reflected the Emersonian need for dealing with experience on a level other than that of brutish empiricism: "For lack of a vision the people perish." [55]

In "The Jew and Trans-National America," a revised version of his essay printed in the *Menorah Journal* in December 1916, Bourne was clearer about the difference between "cultural pluralism" and "cosmopolitanism." He insisted that it was not enough for ethnic groups to remain attached to the cultural customs and mores of their place of origin. The Anglo-Americans had remained "true" to English ways, and they had ended with a culture that was "petrified." There was a real danger that other groups, like the Irish or the Germans, would make a similar mistake: "[Trans-nationalism] is a spirit and not any particular form. A genuine trans-nationalism would be modern, reflecting not only the peculiar gifts and temperament of the people, but reflecting it in its contemporary form." In the face of a modernity that changes constantly, all cultures must become modern if they are to endure. The past tradition could be preserved, but only if it was a flexible tradition, one continually adapting itself to experience. Only in that way would it become "usable." [56]

Bourne, like many others, came to see the great metropolis as the home of modernity, both in the United States and in Europe. Rather than recording urban destructiveness, he tried, at least part of the time, to celebrate urban energy; in the cosmopolitan spirit he hoped to join the city's common life to a larger international culture. In an unpublished essay on the French writer Jules Romains ("A Sociological Poet"), Bourne found in the author's *unanimisme*, "the group-life of the city," a counter to modern angst and the isolation of solipsism. The word "dynamic" was part of the reason Romains appealed to Bourne; Romains spoke of the urban "group" as a body that "flows together" then "disperses," only to come together again like an amoeba in a new form. The rhythms of the city create this new expression of the "Beloved Community": "The mystery and glamor of railroad yards at night, the surge of the tugs and barges on the river, the heave and strain of great steel buildings in the course of erection, the bells and dissonances of the cars and engines, the variegated flow of the boulevards." These forces, not Nature, reflect the great primal energies of the universe: "What is the universe, cries the poet, but one vast city?" For Bourne, Romains was able to reimagine this metropolis as a cultural mix made coherent by the common patterns of daily life and the community they generated.[57]

Bourne also had reservations about modernity, and these revolved around the same cultural questions that discouraged Van Wyck Brooks and alienated T. S. Eliot (and still antagonize curriculum committees in contemporary universities). The "new spirit of the time" had "two aspects—one, what Nietzsche calls the 'herd instinct,' the blind compressing forces of conventionality; the other, the liberating forces of democratic camaraderie, the common life." Romains's *unanimisme* created a culture from the common life, but in "Trans-National America" there was another kind of American openness, an emptiness into which rushed the continually proliferating mass culture whose "home" was also the modern city. To the extent that the center disappeared from ethnic life in the sprawling urban areas, what might replace it was a culture of the "herd instinct," featureless architecture, and cultural "half-breeds" who lived in a kind of disconnected netherworld, where "letting slip from them whatever native culture they had, they have substituted for it only the most rudimentary American—the American culture of the cheap newspaper, the 'movies,' the popular song, the ubiquitous automobile."[58]

The tension in Bourne between the modern city as the locus for a new kind of community and as the place where the institutions of mass culture substituted a false, meretricious community was a political as much as a cultural tension. The society that promoted the "melting pot" as a social ideal taught a "sentimentalizing and moralizing history" in which the Anglo-Saxon myth equaled patriotism and "the inflections of other voices have been drowned." To eliminate these other voices was to disable critical thinking and disallow "future social goals in which all can participate." In his "Trans-National" essays, Bourne's fear of this possible end was still mostly implicit; the energy of his writing was directed toward an exhortation, as he concludes that "to make real this striving amid dangers and apathies is work for a younger *intelligentsia* of America."[59]

War and "The State"

The "dangers and apathies" Bourne spoke of were clearly a reference to the world war and the social reaction it was generating. As a Progressive activist before the war, he recognized the paradox in himself of having a "scorn for institutions, combined with a belief in their reform," but it was only with America's declared entry that he realized the paradox could not be sustained. "The difficulty with the liberal," he wrote Van Wyck Brooks in 1918, "is that so far he has felt that he could ride two horses at once; he could be a patriot and still frown on greed and violence and predatory militarism; he could desire social reconstruction and yet be most reverent toward the traditional institutions." Not only had those "traditional institutions" failed to ensure the survival of civil liberties during the war, they had in fact been used to abolish them. Congress passed the Espionage Act (1917) and the Sedition Act (1918), and Wilson's government created the Committee on Public Information (1917) and the Bureau of Investigation (1918), an unofficial secret police.[60]

When Wilson appealed to Congress for a declaration of war, he asked, "Why is it that all nations turn to us with the instinctive feeling that if anything touches humanity it touches us? Because it knows that ever since we were born as a Nation we have undertaken to be the champions of humanity and the rights of men." Given what followed, it was not surprising that Bourne wrote "The State." What surprises, perhaps, is that no one besides him wrote anything comparable. After the armistice, intellectuals who had supported Wilson began, at first slowly, grudgingly, to revise their positions; by the time of the Treaty of Versailles there had been a wholesale defection from the president's camp that included even the *New Republic*. But the criticisms of the mainstream political writers were mild in light of the threats to their own civil liberties that had taken place and continued to take place.[61]

Bourne's unfinished masterpiece, "The State," was much more a radical critique of the American system than any objection to a particular politician or set of policies. In his view from what seemed the nadir of fortune for the young intelligentsia, governance by and for the people had never been more than a convenient fiction to be dragged out on Independence Day and for ceremonial elections. The continuation of the Anglo-American ascendancy into the present had made possible the "mystical" conception of the "state" as it emerged with the U.S. entrance into the war. With the flag as the visible sign of its invisible presence, the "state" would require unwavering loyalty and a consensus of sentiment. For Bourne, the "state" became a demonic version of the "Beloved Community," where hysteria replaced *caritas*, uniformity replaced diversity, hierarchy replaced democracy. In essence, the "state" demanded that racial or ethnic memory be erased, that history dissolve into nostalgia, and that intelligence succumb to the eternal moment of emotional patriotism.[62]

Before he died in December 1918, Bourne came to feel that he had lived to see another "mystical" America, not the "integrated" future promised by "Trans-Nationalism," not the "bridge" thrown between present and future, but a nightmare vision out of Hobbes. If there was some initial recognition for his vision—Oppenheim and others worked, at least, to get it into print—there quickly grew up a reluctance to face the political or cultural consequences of Bourne's conclusions. It was too bleak a prospect, and in 1920 probably seemed too dangerous as well. Yet, in a sense, that prospect informs Jean Toomer's *Cane*. Bourne's famous remark in his final essay—"War is the health of the state"—would not have surprised Toomer, as it would not have surprised Du Bois; the state had been making war on African-Americans for centuries, and it had been using traditional institutions to support and justify that war.[63]

At the same time he was writing his "Trans-National" essays, Bourne had also dealt briefly with American race relations in a piece for the *New Republic*, "The Will-to-Lynch," published in October 1916. Although too inclined to accept the South's historical justifications for lynching, Bourne was clear that the practice had come to represent "an act of faith by which certain classes in the community express their hatred of an 'inferior race,' their contempt for law, their sense of the predominance of the Anglo-Saxon, the gallantry of the predatory male." He saw an economic basis for lynching in the South where poor whites were "in open competition with the Negro, and economic rivalry fans into flame the traditional social hatred." But he also saw the shocking, Gothic nature of the crime:

The quiet towns in which we live we cannot conceive in our most feverish moments to be the scene of such orgies. Yet in just such towns, and in just such public squares and through just such streets, in this very year and this very United States in which we live, savage mobs, springing from the earth, have done men and women to death with the utmost torture human cruelty could devise. One gets the sense of a country afflicted by a loathsome plague, mysterious in its infection and transmission.[64]

Both the economic roots and the mob "springing from the earth" would appear in Toomer's lynching story, "Blood-Burning Moon."

Although it is unlikely that Toomer wrote *Cane* with Bourne's late work in mind, *Cane*'s view of America, filtered through the veil of black life, North and South, made it the only work from the "Young America" of the 1920s to comprehend the terror depicted in Bourne's unfinished essay. Waldo Frank, Paul Rosenfeld, Lewis Mumford, and Van Wyck Brooks all wrote significantly about Bourne after his death, and each suggested that somehow he had escaped definition or had been misrepresented; none of them quite addressed the political or cultural questions raised by "The State," though Frank at least attempted to approach them. No doubt these issues seemed a dead end at a time when they needed to find hopeful possibilities. They turned to the Bourne of cultural and literary criticism instead of the political writer, and that turn directed much of their work in the next decade. If they retained a cause in common, it was one that embraced the Bourne of the "Trans-National" essays, which had asked with youthful confidence, "Our question is, What shall we do with our America?"[65]

Chapter 4
Whose America?

I dreamed years ago, that the time of Association, the time of battalioning the Spirit had come to America. When I wrote *Our America* I thought I was heralding a fact, not prophesying.
— Waldo Frank to Jean Toomer, 1922

This book [*Our America*] is not a mere compilation of critical opinions and cultural attitudes; deeper than even its psychoanalytic content are to be found "the artistic milieu that nurtured Frank, and a complete statement of this temperament."
— Jean Toomer, "The Critic of Waldo Frank," 1924

Jean Toomer was thirty years old when *Cane* was published. The evidence of that book, his development from the *Call* articles of 1919–20 to the completed volume of fiction, poetry, and adapted drama of 1923, indicated that he could emerge as an important American writer. But *Cane* would be the high point of Toomer's writing career; only a few other stories, essays, and poems appeared in print during his life, and he published only one other book, a small collection of aphorisms entitled *Essentials*, which was privately printed in 1931.[1]

It is impossible to know exactly why Toomer never wrote anything to equal *Cane*; it is possible, however, to look at the particular circumstances under which *Cane* was written, and to suggest why those circumstances were so important to the book. Toomer's work on *Cane* coincided with two unique situations—his identification with black America and his association with Waldo Frank and the writers descended from the *Seven Arts* group in New York. Toomer's identity as an African-American writer was perhaps strongest in 1919–22, judging not only from *Cane* but from his *Call* essays, his association with the Washington, D.C., circle of Alain Locke, his decision to travel to Sparta, Georgia, and his correspondence with both black and white friends. But this identity would hardly survive beyond 1925. Similarly, his close association with Waldo Frank, Gorham Munson, and other young intellectuals and writers who were promoting a modernist literature would never again be quite as close as it had been during and immediately following the composition of *Cane*. Those writers represented Toomer's connection to an avant-garde literature, a cultural "lifeline" to the cosmopolitan world beyond his relative isolation in Washington, D.C., but they also associated him with a book about the African-American world which he would soon be at pains to deny. Even as Toomer finally moved to New York and saw the publication of *Cane*, his most important friendship, his relationship with Waldo Frank, cooled and ended in a serious estrangement.[2]

The writers of the *Seven Arts* and the small magazines that followed it maintained their literary connections through the 1920s, but their initial common impulse was largely exhausted by 1923. While the dynamics of the group's dispersion are complex, the consequences for Toomer as a writer seem clear: he lost the critical connection that had been so vital to finishing *Cane*, as well as the social impetus that had encouraged his continued writing. At about the same time Toomer became interested in, and then preoccupied with, the ideas of George Gurdjieff, the Russian mystic and forerunner of New Age thinking. Toomer had been attracted to the vaguely "spiritual" elements in the writings of Frank, Hart Crane, and even Sherwood Anderson, and he noted that Mumford, having recognized "in me a certain mystic strain," introduced him to the *Bhagavad-Gita*. Much later, in his unpublished autobiography, Toomer was to justify his transformation by saying, "I would far rather form a man than form a book," but he also admitted that, as he moved toward Gurdjieffism, he moved away from his black identity, as he found that his reputation as a black writer "hindered" his new work. This change came about after his break with Waldo Frank, as Toomer's equivocal feelings about the critical success of *Cane* began to surface.[3]

Frank and "Young America" made up the loosely joined literary group practicing the new cultural criticism that emerged in the work of Van Wyck Brooks and Randolph Bourne after 1914. The members of this group wrote and edited books and magazines, they knew publishers and patrons, they reviewed and encouraged each other's work, and in the case of *Cane* they offered Toomer not only formal models and personal support for his writing but also detailed and ongoing critical suggestions. For a young writer trying to complete his first book, this was an immensely valuable aid. Further, these two crucial factors—Toomer's identification as an African-American and his connection to the group of Waldo Frank—were interrelated; Toomer encouraged Frank and others to regard him as a black writer in his initial contacts with them.[4]

In addition to Waldo Frank and Gorham Munson, these writers included Paul Rosenfeld, Lewis Mumford, Anderson, and Crane, as well as a number of other figures—Alfred Stieglitz, Lola Ridge, Kenneth Burke, Matthew Josephson—who were significant to Toomer but less directly aligned with

Frank. Most of these people Toomer would not meet until after he moved to New York in 1923, but he corresponded with some of them (Frank, Munson, Ridge, and Anderson), and he read the work of the others in literary journals. They formed the intellectual background—or at least part of the background—from which *Cane* emerged. They were important not only in terms of what they taught Toomer, but in terms of what they forced him to redefine, to revise, and to reject. *Cane* emerged from both inside and outside the vortex of "Young America," in a space somewhere between the myths of "Our America" and the history of Toomer's black America.[5]

Beyond High Culture: *Our America*

Waldo Frank first wrote to Jean Toomer on October 21, 1920, thanking Toomer for his defense of *Our America* in the *Call* essay of October 10; Frank said that he admired "your answer to Mary Austin. Your paper was a remarkably clear and keen piece of work." Toomer's article had shown that he was familiar with the general arguments over "race" and American identity and culture, and he knew that Frank's analysis had its intellectual antecedents as part of an ongoing critique of American culture, although it is not clear how familiar Toomer was with those antecedents. He would read Van Wyck Brooks's *Letters and Leadership* while he was writing *Cane*, and Frank evidently loaned him his copies of the *Seven Arts* to read, though probably some time after *Cane* was completed. It seems most likely that *Our America* was the main source for Toomer's understanding of the intellectual opening Brooks and Bourne had begun, and while Frank's book was in general a synthesis of Brooks's and Bourne's ideas, it also extended those ideas in new directions. Further, it had a kind of eclectic, patchwork form that would be the distinguishing feature of *Cane*; it was part travel book, part seat-of-the-pants history, part prophetic text, and it belonged to a literary tradition of books, like Tocqueville's *Democracy in America*, that explained America to the Old World.[6]

As "Americans and Mary Austin" made clear, Toomer found in Frank's book a program for work yet to be done and a guide to contemporary cultural politics. *Our America* attempted to "fuse" the political and the literary, drawing on the *Seven Arts* program and the examples of Brooks and Bourne. For Frank, Brooks was the scholar uncovering "a usable past" within American culture, but he had "essentially a non-political mind" (197). It was Bourne whose example showed the possibility of "the joining, through his work, of the political and the cultural currents of advance" (199). The enemy in Frank's book was the "Machine," the mechanical, materialistic and stultifying conditions of American life, the end result of the Puritan-pioneer character that had dominated American history; that history measured a "spiritual" loss, but its causes were economic and political. Bourne "pointed the path of fusion" because "his political discussions were actually lit by a spiritual viewpoint. They took into account the content of the human soul, the individual soul, the values of *being*" (200).

Our America was not a spiritualist or "mystical" tract, although "spirit" and "mystic," along with "religious" and "consciousness," appear frequently in its text. As Frank used them, these terms always had a social reference. He repeated with approval Thomas Carlyle's criticism of Emerson, "that he had not applied such spiritual vehemence to the reality of life" (70). Emerson became for Frank the false spiritualist for whom "the gesture of human aspiration was a transcending leap away from all that was mortal-human." He measured him against the ideal of Walt Whitman, from whom Frank quotes, "I will make the poems of materials, for I think they are to be the most spiritual poems" (71). The difference Frank saw between Whitman and Emerson was between "the mystic whose Mystery is consciousness of All, and the mystic whose Mystery is escape." What Frank valued as "spiritual" was the "*mystical sense of life* . . . as an end in itself" (52). Thus his "spirit" was a means of redeeming the actual, of ascending a Hegelian "hierarchy of consciousness" to Whitman's all-embracing view of the interrelation of things (202–3). And Frank's idealist speculations were always rooted in the actual: "spiritual growth without the facing of the world is an impossible conception" (32).[7]

Frank defined the "spirit" as what attached people to their world: "The spiritual power is man's capacity to feel life as a whole. It is that part of us which dwells within and yet may merge us with the world" (20). In a social sense, then, to be "spiritual" was not to be alienated, to avoid that sense of disaffection which Frank saw as the legacy of the Puritan-pioneer and the common condition of his society; thus, "we are in revolt as well against that organized anarchy to-day expressed in Industrialism which would deny to America any life—hence any unity at all—beyond the ties of traffic and the arteries of trade" (9). In Frank's view contemporary social conditions—in effect, modernity—produced an alienation that could be escaped only by analyzing and working to change those conditions, a program he sometimes formulated as a religious one: "For the more surely a man finds himself, and finds the world he lives in, the more surely he finds God" (186–87).[8]

The elements in Frank's critique of American society were mostly practical matters of economics and politics and cultural definitions. He attacked not only the alienation created by modern industrial society but the class structure and cultural apparatus that both sustained and benefitted from that society. Borrowing from Charles Beard's economic history of the Constitution, Frank asserted that the colonies' "revolution against England in 1775 was one of the first clear-cut struggles between bourgeois capitalism and the old feudality" (14). The Founding Fathers "wanted to make money for themselves: that was what they meant by Liberty. They were eager to rule America in accord with their own lights: that was what they meant by Freedom" (15). Nor had things changed very much in Frank's view. The American establishment still supported "the whole set of myths required by a Democracy in which five per cent. of the people owned sixty-five per cent. of the world they lived in: and controlled all of the political, cultural and economic channels" (156). Those myths provided the basis of both American class relations and American culture. The American Dream served to soothe class antagonisms, since "Labor in this country is cheated of its own resurgence by the common myth that any workman may reach the employer's class" (179).

High culture, created particularly in New England and maintained by an institutional network of Anglophiles, provided "an apt means to the suppression of a nascent, non-Anglo-Saxon culture of our own" (163). Frank's critique of Puritan culture named the enemy—"W. C. Brownell, Barrett Wendell, William Lyon Phelps," and "the *Atlantic Monthly*, the *Boston Transcript*, the *New York Evening Post*"—and it mounted an attack on the canon of American literature (crediting Van Wyck Brooks): "Whatever consciousness we have had so far has been the result of vast and deliberate exclusions. A consciousness that would fit the citizen for pioneering, prepare him to exploit, or to remain the victim of exploitation" (196–97). This "deliberate" exclusion was possible, Frank said, because the "Printed Word" was largely produced by the same industrial conglomerates that ran the rest of American life, including the universities. During the world war and the Russian Revolution, "professors in leading universities found themselves suddenly in the streets because of a liberal attitude toward social change" (210). *Our America*, a book Frank hoped would announce the dawn of radical change in the United States, was much less optimistic in its analysis of American conditions than it was in its prophesying.[9]

The Rise of the Lower Orders

In 1919 and 1920 there was plentiful evidence that the government and the ruling classes were actively suppressing any movements for social change in the United States. The most hopeful signs in *Our America*, therefore, were the corners of resistance and the critical social trends to which Frank devoted most of his book. Toomer would claim one of those corners as his own. In the chapter "The Land of Buried Cultures," Frank outlined the way in which modernity had broken down and replaced traditional societies with examples drawn from the Mexican-American and Native-American cultures of the Southwest. He distinguished between the pioneer, whose urge it was to dominate and move on, and the "Mexican," who "has really dwelt with his soil, cultivated his spirit in it, not alone his maize" (96). The Mexican produced the superior culture, but "the growing dominion of the 'gringo' is stamping out the impulse from which this native culture sprang, . . . [and] the Mexican is already lost in the spell of the tin-can and the lithograph" (96–97).

In explicit detail and with attention to its coherence and "spiritual" unity, Frank described the Native American life that was being obliterated by "the iron march of the Caucasian" (115). The irony of the "buried cultures," though, was that the Puritan and the pioneer had been buried also, lost in the "ban of the Industrial world." In turning to "the land of the buried cultures," Frank saw that the "stream" of modernity, symbolized by the westward movement across the American continent, had "overwhelmed the life that stood in its way" (97), thus describing the same process Karl Marx summarized in his famous phrase "all that is solid melts into air." Facing the dissolution of traditional cultures, Frank tried to mark what was being lost and to find a means to imagine what might be born from the "industrial chaos." He understood, though, like Bourne in "The Jew and Trans-National America," that modernity would not permit holding actions or turning back. In his final chapter Frank attacked William Jennings Bryan's populism for its nostalgia: "Bryan was a voice without a mind. Speaking in 1896, as if Karl Marx had never lived" (223). Frank's remark on the Mexican way of life, "what has been buried must die surely," was the single allusive gleam of hope he could foresee, at least for those who remembered the "seed" that must die to be "reborn." Frank suggested that others might recover and record some of these "buried cultures":

Some day some one who is fitted for the task will take the subject of this Chapter and make a book of it. He will study the cultures of the German, the Latin, the Celt, the Slav, the Anglo-Saxon and the African on the American continent: plot their reactions one upon the other, and their disappearance as integral worlds in the vast puddling of our pioneering life. I have no space and no knowledge for so huge a picture. I must be content with the suggestion of a single curve. (97)

Frank's "suggestion" would reappear as the curves introducing the three sections of *Cane*, an acknowledgment of Toomer's part in the project of *Our America*.

Though Frank traced pioneer expansion to the Pacific and chose his "buried cultures" from the far Southwest, his major concern was with the eastern heartland and its great metropolitan areas. Turning to those cities in the last half of his book, he sketched out a future that would revise the frontier thesis of Frederick Jackson Turner. Turner had praised the first generations of American settlers, pioneers of Anglo-Saxon stock who had settled New England and those of Nordic stock who had pushed the frontier west, but he criticized in racialist terms the new immigrants from southern and eastern Europe who settled in the cities of the Atlantic seaboard. For him they represented the "Old World," a corrupting influence that threatened the American character established by the contest of the

Western frontier. In Frank's history, however, the frontier did not energize the pioneer impulse but rather exhausted it. Los Angeles was characterless and trivial because the long passage to the West Coast had stripped the pioneer of any cultural definition. Los Angeles, Frank claimed, "is not a city, [but only] a country town that has outgrown its rural voice and found no other" (103); if Los Angeles had any spiritual center, it lay with the "buried" culture of the Hispanics. Only as Frank's book returned east did it find the hopeful signs of renaissance, beginning with Chicago, the "City of the Big Shoulders." [10]

Frank's measures of hopefulness were the cultural stirrings, the new works of writing that promised to understand and illuminate American life. In Chicago Frank found Edgar Lee Masters's *The Spoon River Anthology* a depiction of the voices of a "Puritan" town full of rancor and bitterness: "The whole burden of Masters' song [*Spoon River Anthology*] is the burial of love and life beneath the crass deposits of the American world" (128). His poem represented the Brooks-Frank thesis in microcosm, for it debunked the conception of America's Puritan-pioneer history as a heroic adventure. In Frank's view, Chicago was on its way to escaping that history. Although it sometimes imitated New York—its citizens celebrated size and industrial might—the city's materialism had not yet cut off its roots in the New World. Despite Chicagoans' passion for empire, their feet were still "planted on the prairie," in their city the grass still pushed up through the sidewalk, and Carl Sandburg was the city's poet, his "tender shoots of verse . . . pushing up through the filth like grass upon the prairie" (135).[11] However, it was Sherwood Anderson—his life and his books—who became for Frank the symbolic figure of the city's future promise. Anderson was the businessman who discovered an artist buried within himself, thus becoming a parable of Chicago, the sleeping giant that must awaken to its spiritual destiny: "He wrote his first story, as five hundred years ago his forebears might have gone to Church and to confession. But there were no Cathedrals in Anderson's Middle-West" (138). Anderson the advertising canvasser, Chicago the city with Big Plans—they were alike, except Anderson had "learned to venerate the truth that gushed like a hidden spring from his pent life." Anderson's "revolt" would be repeated in Chicago, then spread across America:

For what . . . Anderson [did] in person, America must fulfill in her social and spiritual life. She has come to the climax of material wealth. She must discover that she is empty, that she is hungry and unclean. She must learn to the last bitter lesson, the sterility and falsehood of her Puritan, possessive world. She must go forth, and she must go within, to create her own salvation. (141)

Unlike *The Spoon River Anthology*, Anderson's stories in *Winesburg, Ohio* were not simply tales of hidden frustration and loneliness but were "drawn, for the most part, with a curve and a line that reveal infinite distance" (142). The "curve" Frank pointed to in the best of Anderson's stories symbolized the nonlinear nature of his book's structure; form and content matched, as Frank said: "One may puzzle over the disparate value of these simple tales and the vision they unfold. *But one cannot sever.* In other words, Anderson's stories have true aesthetic form. They are material impregnate" (143; emphasis added). This observation was not "mystical" but practical, a recognition of the modernist technique Anderson used in his books. Sherwood Anderson's short-story cycles of *Winesburg* and *The Triumph of the Egg* would be, along with Waldo Frank's writing, the major influences on *Cane.*

Frank's greatest hopes were reserved for the city of New York, the choice that so displeased Mary Austin. At first glance, New York seemed as lifeless as Los Angeles. The city absorbed human energy so that its citizens were dehumanized: "Their feet shuffle, their voices are shrill, their eyes do not shine" (171). Yet Frank insisted that in recent years there had been "two leavens" working on New York, an influx of energy from two sources outside the city. One source was the American provinces, home to young men and women unhappy with the past and present their ancestors had made. Desperately moving about but not finding what they were looking for in the hinterlands, they reversed direction and came to New York, the center of the nation, despite its shortcomings: "This throw-back upon the city from the West, the South, the North brings to New York its restless inquiry, its insatiate search. . . . Quite like their fathers, they go forth to hunt— though in an opposite direction." What they "seek," argued Frank, "is a world nearer their hearts" (176–77). Their energy was reinforced by the influx from Europe of the immigrant millions, the second "leaven" or "seed" of Bourne's "Trans-National America," who joined the sons and daughters of Old America to infuse the city of stone with a new spirit: "New York lies between invading Europe and America. A frontier city. . . . The rebels from the West met Europe in New York and made it theirs" (180, 177–78).

Frank saw that New York's cosmopolitan mixture attracted the most energetic and able of the young; he also saw a new and redemptive American art emerging from "Young America" in Chicago and New York. After meeting Frank in New York and reading *Our America,* Jean Toomer followed his own route of reverse "westering," returning South as a schoolteacher and finding sources for his art in a peasant people he believed would soon be absorbed by modernity. Toomer also would argue in *Cane's* middle (and urban) section that these "buried" people not only survived in Washington and Chicago but also infused these cities with new energy, will, and spirit. New York in *Our America* would become Washington, D.C., in *Cane,* a city whose life and culture would be transformed by black immigrants from the South, by an unrecognized part of "Young America."

The American "Giant"

One reason *Our America* had a profound impact on Toomer was that its celebration of an invisible polis and the redemptive potential for the "buried
cultures" helped him to imagine his own place in the American racial conflicts of 1920. As a Jew, Frank, too, spoke as an outsider, but his reading
of history and cultural relationships offered the prospect not only of social
revisions but of the benefits of living on the "outside," a possibility Toomer
had already recognized in his essay on Mary Austin. Frank gave the Jew a
unique position in *Our America*, juxtaposing a chapter called "The Chosen
People" with chapters on the pioneer and New England, and also crediting
the Jewish intellectual as an important force behind New York's cultural
revival. That attention to Jewish life irritated people like Mary Austin, who
was not happy with the prominence given Jewish intellectuals nor with
Frank's analysis of the Jew in the New World as the locus for extending his
attack on a debased Puritan ethos.

The Jewish-American milieu that Bourne had touched on became central to Frank's cultural vision, which saw in the experience of Jewish immigrants a paradigm of Brooks's American history, where the spiritual was
suppressed and the material dominant. The contrast Frank developed between the mystical Jew and the materialistic Jew would be echoed in *Cane*'s
conflict between the black artist and the black bourgeoisie. Frank drew
parallels between the contemporary Jewish influx into New York and the
earlier Puritan invasion, arguing that while these newly arrived immigrants
shared with the Puritans a dream of earthly power and a penchant for "material aggression" (79), this excessive aggression was unnatural to the Jew
in a way that it was not unnatural to the Puritans. The Old World culture
the Puritans had inherited was already secularized; what the Jews brought
from the Old World to the New was a paradoxical combination of a "will-
to-power" and a religious mysticism. The problem was that the New World
had not allowed the spiritual element to develop:

They came to America—mostly after 1880—with their sharpened wits and will-to-
power, and America welcomed them and put these qualities to work. They came
to America also with their love of God, but for such a seed America was less fertile. . . . The psychological history of the Jew in the United States is the process of
his rather frenzied conformation to the land of new opportunity: the sharpening of
his means to power, the perfecting of his taste for comfort, the suppression of the
mystical in his heart. (83–85)

This "seed" was buried, but not destroyed: "The mystical Jew survived. But
he slept" (84).[12]

Frank's early chapter, "The Chosen People," foreshadowed his description of the contemporary generation of New York Jewish intellectuals,

whose expression of the mystical Jew promised to awaken a new art in America. In his chapter on New York, Frank was careful to emphasize examples of what Bourne called the Jew's "dual citizenship": the musician Leo Ornstein, whose song "Walt Whitman would have loved" (188); Paul Rosenfeld, whose musical criticism distills "French and Russian music [into] an experience that is American" (190); James Oppenheim, whose city poems "convey . . . the uplifted passions of the marketplace" (192). At the center of this group he placed "the Jewish mystic" Alfred Stieglitz and his photographic gallery, "291," which had been the meeting point for a community dedicated to art, a community that expanded the conception of the "chosen" to the American scene and beyond: "To him, art is simply the directest conduit to human consciousness—to self and to the world: the most urgent incentive left to man" (186).

Stieglitz, in one sense, was *Our America*'s most important figure, for in Frank's view, amid the "set" world of New York, he had willed into being a new cultural city, and his example was to inspire the continuing project of "Young America." With his camera Stieglitz spiritualized American technology, perceiving a hidden city in his vital photographs of New York; and his "place," "291," had been a refuge for a community of artists who wished to remake America. The crucial metaphor for Frank was that of art as religion: "291" was "a little altar at which life was worshipped above a dead city. . . . You were in a church consecrate to them who had lost old gods, and whose need was sore for new ones" (184). Like the cathedral in the Middle Ages, "291" bound people together as a spiritual body, and it defined the city *as* a spiritual body. In eulogizing Stieglitz, Frank described a possible city in the age of the Dynamo; it was a utopian projection not only for "set" New York, but for "Young America."

At the heart of that city was Frank's version of Bourne's "Trans-National America." In his penultimate chapter, "The Multitudes in Whitman," Frank, like Bourne, focused on the new urban immigrants, but he was more hopeful than Bourne about the effects of the city's culture on their lives. He noted with approval that German and Yiddish theaters gave a new gusto to high culture: "It is here, not on Broadway, that the European masters, classic and modern, receive competent attention" (213). He also observed that these ethnic theaters not only preserved their own cultural traditions but allowed these traditions to "merge" with the new mass culture to create something vital and different:

In cities like New York, still unassimilated cultural groups—Jewish, Italian, German—have their playhouses where dramas, actors, audiences meet on a common mental and emotional level. Here, the naiver forms of dramatic art still strive: melodrama that is sincere, musical shows that are fresh, curious *melanges*, like those of the Yiddish stage, where Synagogic chants merge with the latest ragtime of Broadway. These performances often surprise by their value. (213)

Mixing "Synagogic chants" and "ragtime," Frank anticipates Al Jolson's *The Jazz Singer* by almost ten years. Toomer would develop similar ideas about African-American music and dance in his urban stories "Theater" and "Box Seat," where the tension between mass and folk culture helps create an art of modernity.[13]

In *Our America*, Frank's ethnic theater became a metaphor for social coherence, a world whose center provided the space for artist and audience to meet and become one: "A theater without an audience is as unthinkable as a painting without paint. A man may write a good novel, sing a fair song in the dark. . . . He cannot produce a theater without an audience. For the multitude is the pigment of the dramatic picture" (219). That "multitude" concerned Toomer in a similar way in *Cane*'s middle section, as the streets and alleys of Washington, D.C., became "theaters" where the essential dramas of the black masses were enacted. In those stories and poems Toomer looked for the city's center, juxtaposing Washington's monuments and its "whitewashed wood" with the vitality of the Howard and Lincoln theaters and the folk life that supplied them with song.

Jean Toomer saw that Frank's ideas about cultural renewal springing from marginalized groups in America might be true of black life, that the African-American could, through music and dance or literary art, bring about a renaissance in the urban North. The rooted black peasant culture of America's South might create a New World to be born in America's cities, as the "seed" dying in Georgia or Mississippi would bloom in Washington, D.C., or Chicago or New York. Patterns of images, metaphors, and repeated themes provide structure to *Our America*, as they do to *Cane*, and in *Cane* Toomer would borrow one of Frank's figures for the potential contained in "trans-national" American life, the image of the mute giant.

The potential of the American "giant" was manifest both in Frank's "buried cultures" and in the work of individual artists who might redeem the American promise:

Mark Twain was a giant. Or a giant he would have grown to be, had he been nurtured at his nation's breast. But the centrifugal force was overwhelming. . . . Nietzsche, Flaubert, Whitman, Tolstoi, Dostoievski—such were the last giants to float. Then the world went under. . . . With them [the Chicago writers], new gods come out of the corn: and shoulder their way across the iron streets. (44, 92, 147)

The giant manqué, the fallen giants, the emerging giants—Frank returns to this image throughout *Our America*, and always to invoke the theme of Bourne's "Trans-National America":

America is a turmoiled giant who cannot speak. The giant's eyes wander about the clouds: his feet are sunk in the quicksands of racial and material passion. One hand grasps the mountains, and the other falls bruised and limp upon the lowlands of the world. His need is great, and what moves across his eyes is universal. But his tongue is tied. (4)

What will allow the giant to speak, to wake from sleep, will be the voices of the "trans-nationals," creating a new cultural frontier of limitless space, limitless possibility.

The giant would reappear in *Cane*, and then in Alain Locke's Foreword to *The New Negro*. Toomer adapted Frank's giant for the story "Esther," where the prophet and confidence man Barlo has a vision of an African giant carried off to the New World:

I saw a vision. I saw a man arise, an he was big an black and powerful . . . but his head was caught up in the clouds. An while he was agazin at th heavens, heart filled up with th Lord, some little white-ant biddies came an tied his feet to chains. They led him t th coast, they led him to the sea, they led him across th ocean and they didnt set him free. The old coast didnt miss him, an the new coast wasnt free, he left the old-coast brothers, t give birth t you and me.[14]

Barlo's vision is of a giant enchained and so becomes the story of African enslavement in the New World; but his black giant has the same symbolic dimension as the mute giants of *Our America*, and he is chained by "little white-ant biddies" who represent the same kind of material forces that Frank felt had constrained American culture. As his adaptation shows, Toomer saw the importance of *Our America*'s ideas about cultural renewal, but he would choose areas for his own work which Frank had passed over— the "buried" life of African-Americans and the region of the American South, a culture and a locale barely mentioned in Frank's book.

A Call to Arms

Late in his life, Frank said that writing *Our America* was a reaction to the fall of the *Seven Arts*: "I agreed with Brooks that 'the time had come to write books.' My *Our America* was the first result of that withdrawal from the magazine field." Thematically, of course, *Our America* was not a "withdrawal," for it continued the program of cultural renewal promoted by the *Seven Arts*. With a different emphasis, it held to the magazine's belief that "we are living in the first days of a renascent period," that in such a time the "arts . . . become not only the expression of the national life but a means to its enhancement." *Our America* followed Bourne's courageous critique of American nativism, capitalism, and the corporate "state," though at the same time it was clearly a postwar book that attempted to replace the Progressive (and pragmatic) ideals shattered by the war with another political agenda. Political and social change would be subsumed within a cultural revolution; the energy of the religious impulse, the "spiritual," would be directed into an art that would change society. Despite Frank's millennial predictions, even this new, limited agenda was so uncertain in postwar America that by 1922 he began to feel his book had been an erroneous prophecy.[15]

The idea that artists could remake American culture virtually by an act of will was one of the great appeals of *Our America,* for Toomer and for others (including Hart Crane and Gorham Munson). The book began with Frank's vision, "I saw that America was a conception to be created" (4), and ended with the declaration that "in a dying world, creation is revolution" (232). By "creation" Frank meant art, especially the literary art in which words might become "the Bridge which all true artists seek, between themselves—expressers of a world—and the world that they express" (195). *Our America* thus became a prophetic text: by expressing his vision of a future America ("ours") opposed to that of the present ("theirs"), Frank would help to bring the future into being. His words were the "seeds" that would blossom in the art of others or serve as the connective tissue (a "bridge") between self and other, a reminder that in his dream of a new America he was not alone. As Gorham Munson said many years later, "At the onset of the Twenties, Frank probably did more than any other writer of the avant-garde to reveal the opportunity for a new turning point of our culture. . . . A second printing of *Our America* was called for before 1919 ended, and a third printing was ordered a few months later."[16]

Our America's appeal to young artists was a call to arms, a universalizing and connective act; it offered a vision of a literary-political community wherein admission was based on a set of fairly abstract beliefs rather than on distinctions of ethnicity, race, or class. Toomer was struck not only by its heady combination of historical analysis and prophecy, but by his recognition that Frank's concerns closely paralleled his own situation. Both men occupied anomalous positions as members of an elite class that was at the same time part of an excluded group. Frank was the son of a well-to-do German-Jewish family, his father a successful Wall Street lawyer and his mother descended from "the Alabama branch of a Jewish clan of international business men." When Frank identified with the Yiddish theater, he was crossing class lines, for the immigrants who made up the audience for this theater were the Jewish masses only recently arrived in the city from eastern Europe and Russia. Toomer was descended from the mulatto elite of the nineteenth century—a background so "respectable" that people of his class looked askance on the nouveau middle-class of black doctors, lawyers, and undertakers emerging from the late nineteenth century to service the new black communities in the Northern and Southern cities. Toomer crossed class lines in identifying with the black masses in "Seventh Street," "Theater," and "Box Seat."[17]

Neither wealthy Jews nor well-off mulatto aristocrats were likely to find themselves accepted in the mainstream of 1920s America. In 1919, when *Our America* was published, Frank knew that he was writing about Jews in the context of a virulent anti-Semitism that had emerged on the American scene at all social levels well before the turn of the century. From Madison Grant's *The Passing of a Great Race* (1916) to a revived Ku Klux Klan, from polite exclusion from "eating clubs" in Ivy League schools to Congress's immigration law of 1921, from scurrilous articles in the *Saturday Evening Post* in 1920–21 to the restrictive quota system initiated by President Abbott Lowell of Harvard in 1922, attacks on Jews as cultural and racial "un-Americans" became almost as commonplace as Negro-baiting. In 1911, the year Frank graduated from Yale, one of the university's "senior societies voted unanimously that 'Jews should be denied recognition at Yale.'" Two years later, the lynching of New Yorker Leo Frank in Georgia illustrated that "race" phobia at the ground level might make no distinction between black and Jew.[18]

According to John Higham, so thoroughly had anti-Semitism permeated the American mind by 1900 that earlier class distinctions among the Jewish population had disappeared:

Because immigration became a general problem toward the end of the nineteenth century and because the east European Jews looked as bizarre and unkempt as any of the other immigrants, they aroused distaste among native Americans from the moment they landed. At first public comment (abetted by assimilation-minded German Jews) often distinguished between the new and older population to the latter's clear advantage. But after 1900 the differentiation almost vanished from popular consciousness.[19]

In *Our America*, Frank recognized that the gap between his father's German-Jewish world and the Jewish masses from eastern Europe had closed, and in the chapter entitled "The Chosen People," he focused on the distinction between the mystical Jew and the materialistic Jew. Frank thus revised the distinction that his father's generation made between the assimilated and the unassimilated, between the German-Jewish middle class and the new Jewish working class. In Frank's America the distinction between old and new Jew was false: both groups were socialized to want the same thing, and both were products of American materialism—the only difference being that one had grasped what the other continued to pursue. In this context, however, it was the "mystic Jew," with a spiritual impulse still intact, who offered an escape from America's closed system.

Our America, then, answered the prejudice of anti-Semitism in a new way, arguing not for assimilation or separatism, but for a version of Bourne's cosmopolitanism. The Jews would change and be changed by America, offering their particular religious sensibility to counter a materialism that was destructive of culture and human values. It's not difficult to see how this outlook might have a direct appeal for Toomer, a light-skinned mulatto in a world that categorized all blacks as a "Negro problem." Cosmopolitanism, however, was a distinctly minority aspiration in 1920; the fear and anger generated by the war, the continuing government persecution of "un-Americans," the related attacks by organized capital on labor and the political Left, all these contaminated the cultural and political life of the country. Furthermore, Toomer's place in this unsettled and unsettling social context was ambiguous in ways different from Frank's—identified as a black man, Toomer faced a different world. For all their literary agreement and mutual support, this difference was finally to be the most critical defining point of their relationship.

Representations of Race

If *Our America* offered Toomer a historical and political framework within which to set his own examination of "Negro and mixed blood America," it did not finally answer the questions and problems that examination raised. The friendship and collaboration between Frank and Toomer was played out over a contested field of American ideas about race and racial identity, and the misunderstandings between the two men grew as each tried to find some accommodation in a society where "race" and color were primary social categories.

In Toomer's initial correspondence with Frank, he presented himself as both an insider and an outsider with regard to African-American life. His letter of March 24, 1922, probably the first contact with Frank since 1920, stated:

in your Our America I missed your not including the Negro. I have often wondered about it. My own life has been about equally divided between the two racial groups. My grandfather, owing to his emphasis upon a fraction of Negro blood in his veins, attained prominence in Reconstruction politics. And the family, for the most part, ever since, has lived between the two worlds, now dipping into the Negro, now into the white. Some few are definitely white; others definitely colored. I alone have stood for a synthesis in the matters of the mind and spirit analogous, perhaps, to the actual fact of at least six blood minglings.[20]

After establishing his racial authenticity (albeit with a carefully worded caveat), Toomer went on to note his expertise in the "history, traditions, and culture" of black life, which had been so often misrepresented that he had to "spend a disproportionate time in Negro study. Recently, facts and possibilities discovered have led to an interest mainly artistic and interpretive." In the final paragraph of his letter, Toomer asked if Frank would like to read some of his poems and sketches, the latter of which he described as "attempts at an artistic record of Negro and mixed-blood America." Whether or not he remembered Frank's call for a study of "the African on the American continent" (97), Toomer seemed to be offering to fill out Frank's "suggestion of a single curve" in *Our America*.[21]

Toomer's ambiguity about his racial identity didn't contradict his own growing conviction that "race" was an artificial distinction, but Frank's conception of racial identity was much more conventional than Toomer's. When Frank thought in terms of Randolph Bourne's "dual citizenship," he imagined a cosmopolitan position where "whiteness" was a given, because that assumption infected the racialist structures of the culture at large. After 1910 various American polemicists about race—Tom Watson, Henry Ford, Mary Austin, and many others—were concerned to exclude Jews from the category of "whiteness," often by linking them racially and culturally to African-Americans or "Orientals." Some Jewish artists developed their own ways of resisting that exclusion, further complicating the terms of the public debate. In the American obsession with color, the old Irish distinction of those "beyond the Pale" was a horrible and bloody pun.[22]

The cultures in *Our America*, including Jewish culture, were attached to races, but whereas cultures might alter and influence each other, racial identities remained fixed to individuals. Frank accepted a racial essentialism that was the "common sense" of his time. Yet Toomer told Frank that some of his family lived as blacks and others as whites, the implication being that race was a matter of choice. The usual term for such choices, of course, was "passing": a light-complexioned African-American might "pass" as white (or a Jew might "pass" as gentile). Toomer didn't address the question of passing to Frank, probably because he expected Frank to recognize his rejection of stark racial divisions. Toomer, of course, did write about "passing": directly in "Withered Skin of Berries," less directly in "Bona and Paul." However, when Toomer presented himself as black, or as attached to African-American culture and society, as he had to Frank, the careful reservation he set out escaped his white correspondent. To one degree or another this confusion dogged Toomer's correspondence with Sherwood Anderson, with John McClure, and with his publisher, Horace Liveright. It also led to misunderstandings with acquaintances who regarded themselves as unambiguously African-American.

Yet on some level Frank recognized Toomer's qualification of his racial identity, even if he never fully accepted or understood it. In the letters between the two men written from March 1922 through the fall of 1923, the question of racial identity—and the deeper puzzle of what "race" itself might be—appears frequently, sometimes submerged, sometimes more explicit. Four related matters brought up the racial question most directly: the planning of Frank and Toomer's trip to Spartanburg, South Carolina, in the early fall of 1922; the exchanges between the two about *Holiday*, Frank's novel of black and white relations in the South; their discussion of Sherwood Anderson and his attitude toward Toomer; and, finally, the introductory remarks Frank was to write for *Cane*.

The trip to Spartanburg was intended to give background for Frank's novel and also to give Toomer an impetus to complete *Cane*. In discussing the trip Toomer wrote a letter that described, perhaps unintentionally, his own racial dilemma as well as he ever would:

One phase of the trip which I have thus far said nothing about, I think best to mention now. At whatever town we stay, I'll have to be known as Negro. First, because only by experiencing white pressure can the venture bear its fullest fruit for me. Second, because the color of my skin (it is nearly black from the sun) at the present time makes such a course a physical necessity.[23]

Toomer says he will have to be "known as Negro" in the South, implying the socially determined nature of the designation, but the reasons he gives for this designation support the idea of race as both arbitrary and inescapably determined—Toomer "chooses" to be Negro in order to witness white racism, but his skin color at the end of summer also makes the "choice" unavoidable. For the rest of his life Toomer maintained a view of "race" as primarily learned rather than inherited, a socially constructed form of identity, yet he confronted a society that fiercely maintained traditional racial divisions, particularly according to color, even in the face of scientific refutation and social transformations. In that world to be "known as Negro" was to suffer consignment to the bottom of the racial caste system.[24]

Frank formulated a dramatic reply to Toomer's rather matter-of-fact letter:

If you go as Negro, can't I also? What is a Negro? Doubtless, if the Southerner could see in my heart my feeling for "the negro," my love of his great qualities, my profound sympathy for his trials and respect for the great way he bears them, that Southerner would say "why you're worse than a nigger!" . . . So if you go as a Negro, so go I.[25]

Frank is not only speaking of a political solidarity with Toomer in this passage; he also recognizes in some way the idea of race as a "choice," or at least as dependent to a degree on social circumstances, and he suggests that he can "pass" as a black man. But embedded in Frank's words, too, is the suggestion of race as masquerade, an association that raises the question of minstrelsy, and of the Jewish player in blackface, which Michael Rogin has persuasively argued underlies so much of American mass culture. In the original sound film of *The Jazz Singer* (1927), Al Jolson rises to fame and fortune as a Jewish boy who puts on blackface to become a minstrel performer. Rogin asks the question, "But why should the member of one pariah group hide his identity under the mask of another?" His answer is that by performing in blackface "the jazz singer acquires exchange value at the expense of blacks." This "exchange value" includes both the admired "jazz" qualities of black performers, which the jazz singer puts on with his blackface, and his proof of "whiteness," which the act of "blacking up" validates in a form of backstage ritual. Thus, performing in blackface allows the Jewish player to cross to the "white" side of the great American racial divide and yet to appropriate (perhaps as parody in this case) the performance of the black artist.[26]

Since the purpose of the Spartanburg trip was to gather "background" for Frank's novel on race (the idea for the trip was his), Frank in a sense was putting on blackface in order to "perform," or attempt to create, black characters for his fiction. That he was aware of the moral and creative complications in such an act is made clear by his correspondence with Toomer; Frank repeatedly seeks assurance that his novel will be authentic but not "presumptuous." After Toomer had written to ask about the absence of the Negro in *Our America*, Frank planned a revision to include "the chapter on the Negro which I am preparing, together with one on the Jew." Part of the source for this revision was to be his trip with Toomer into the South, a trip that would also allow Frank to complete "a short novel that sprang into being one night in the pinewoods of an Alabama village, full of the songs and calls of the black folk." This became *Holiday*.[27]

Toomer's reply was both supportive and modestly assertive of his own authority: "It is a fine thing you are going to put the Negro in Our America. It will be an organic inclusion. What little I know is freely open to you." As Frank had already read much of the material that would become the first part of *Cane*, as well as the early version of "Kabnis," he might have recognized an irony in Toomer's understatement, and his own reply was apologetic: "I am probably presumptuous to write about the Negro, and particularly since I know you who are creating a new phase of American literature (O there's no doubt of that my friend). Of course, what my book will be is something far apart from your own." [28]

Toomer appreciated Frank's ongoing support for the writing of *Cane*, and he was quick to reassure him of the integrity of *Holiday*: "There is no poaching in the domain of pure art. I think that we (postulating my own maturity) could take the identical subject and create works similar only in such broad things as impulse and purpose." However, while he acknowledged Frank's seniority as a writer and recognized the broad possibilities of literary creation, the phrase "pure art" probably represented a qualification of his "no poaching" observation. As he would show in other letters and in *Cane*, Toomer understood the dependence of American popular and mass culture on African-American models; he appreciated, in other words, that Paul Whiteman's "jazz" was mostly poached from black players. After the two friends returned from South Carolina and Frank set to work on *Holiday*, an extensive and anxious exchange ensued that blended with a related discussion of Sherwood Anderson and the foreword Frank proposed to write for *Cane*. Beneath it all ran a barely concealed tension over race—what it was and how it should be represented.[29]

Criticism and Collaboration

In the fall of 1922, after reading the pieces the younger writer had submitted to the *Double Dealer*, Sherwood Anderson wrote to Toomer, praising and encouraging him to continue with "a note I have long been wanting to hear come from one of your race." Toomer responded to Anderson in terms that seemed to acknowledge his African-American identity, but he soon wrote to Frank with a very different tone: "Sherwood Anderson and I have exchanged a few letters. I dont think we will go very far. He limits me to Negro. As an approach, as a constant element (part of a larger whole) of interest, Negro is good. But to try to tie me to one of my parts is surely to loose me." Toomer probably meant these remarks both to comment on Anderson and to further clarify his ideas about racial identity for Frank. By this time Horace Liveright had agreed to publish *Cane*, and Frank had offered to write a foreword for the book, matters Toomer brings up later in the letter. Thus Anderson's attitude may have pointed up precisely how Toomer did *not* want to be understood in racial terms.[30]

It seems clear that Frank understood Toomer's intention, for when he responded to the comments on Anderson he tried to embrace Toomer's "cosmopolitan" position: "But I want to say now: that the day you write as a negro, or as an American, or as anything but a human part of *life* your work will lose a dimension. How typical that is of most recognition: that effort immediately to limit you, to put you in a cubbyhole and stick a label underneath." Yet as Frank went on to outline his approach to the foreword for *Cane*, a serious difference emerged between his conception of "race" and the more fluid, socially ambiguous terms Toomer had used: "I intend, possibly above all else, in my introduction to *Cane* to point out that the important thing which has at length released you to the creating of literature is that you do not write as a Negro . . . that you take your race or your races naturally, as a white man takes his." If taking one's race as a "white man" does is "natural," the state to which everyone aspires, then Toomer's achievement becomes the equivalent of putting on whiteface; and the negative result, that he does "not write as a Negro," nevertheless identifies Toomer as a Negro.[31]

Frank went on to suggest that a combination of race and class awareness will fatally inhibit the artist:

The few talented writers among the negroes have been ruined because they could not forget . . . that they were negroes. For analogous reasons, when the Jews were first liberated from ghettos, they produced second rate books and music and pictures: they were too conscious of the limiting details of their race and consciousness of race became the norm of their creations, instead of consciousness of Life itself.

Randolph Bourne's ideal of "dual citizenship" demanded that individuals perform a balancing act between the mores of their ethnic group of origin and the national or international culture of modernism. Frank assured Toomer that he had passed from the parochial to the cosmopolitan: "Precisely because you have been able to go South as a human being, among negroes as one of them *because you are a human being first* your work is released into real creation." The hidden paradox of dual citizenship was resolved here in favor of the universal over the particular.

Frank claimed that he, too, had transcended the ordinary order of American racism, that his racial masquerade with Toomer in Spartanburg allowed him to pass beyond "surfaces": "And the miracle that came to me at last last Fall with you, after several years of loving and understanding the South, was that I also was able to get to the deep reality in which color and race disappeared as entities: and took their place as mere surfaces." How was Toomer to understand Frank's claim of having escaped a racial essentialism, joined with his remarks about the "naturalness" of the white race and his characterization of Toomer as a Negro who did not write like a Negro? In his reply Toomer appeared to accept Frank's claim of a "miracle":

Even before last fall I am certain that you saw race and color as surfaces. Perhaps your mind still retained a few inhibiting wraiths. But the fact is, that you were *ready* for the miracle to happen. For myself, I could sense no dissonance or qualification whatsoever. I dont look for these things. I dont have to. If they're there, I simply *know* it. Nothing could have been more natural and real than our experience in Spartanburg.[32]

However, the two men were still writing from different frames of reference. "Race and color as surfaces" may still amount to a racial definition, and to be "natural and real" in Spartanburg would seem to deny the "naturalness" of the white race. These subtle differences in meaning would become crucial only when each man tried to evaluate the other's work in a public forum. In the same letter, Toomer elaborated on his opinion of Sherwood Anderson and "race":

Sherwood Anderson has doubtless had a very deep and beautiful emotion by way of the Negro. Here and there he has succeeded in expressing this. But he is not satisfied. He wants more. He is hungry for it. I come along. I express it. It is natural for him to see me in terms of this expression. I see myself that way. But also I see myself expressing *myself*, expressing *Life*. I expect artists to recognize the circle of expression.

Toomer reiterates that he doesn't want to be "limited to Negro," but there may be another suggestion here as well—the implication that Toomer's writing about African-American life expresses things beyond the reach of a racial outsider. Given Frank's uneasiness about *Holiday*, this idea could not have provided much encouragement, especially since Toomer then continued with a long passage on the position of blacks under the new conditions of modernity and the transformation of their culture from the rural South to the urban North, matters which Frank touched on only indirectly in his own work. Toomer ends his letter with praise for the project of *Holiday* which seems unfeigned, yet, significantly, he treats the text as a record of Frank's "spiritual experience" rather than as a book about race and the South.

These misunderstandings and misjudgments between the two men, always twined about the question of "race," finally collided in Frank's foreword to *Cane* and Toomer's review of *Holiday*. Frank stressed Toomer's identity as a Negro even as he proclaimed the author as "the artist who is not interested in races, whose domain is Life." When Toomer saw the piece he praised it—"I was sure of *you*. I knew you could do the thing. You *have*"—but he also hinted at misgivings that were to become much more manifest in the future: "The facts for a curious public to toss about, are there." In later years Toomer was to blame the publication of *Cane* for fostering the misperceptions surrounding his racial identity among a "curious public," and the original irritation he felt at Frank's "cataloguing" of the book and its author may have prompted his criticism of *Holiday*.[33]

Toomer's review of *Holiday* appeared in the *Dial* of October 1923. Incorporating remarks Frank had made to him in their earlier correspondence about the novel, Toomer praised the book as sustaining "Waldo Frank's high achievement as a literary artist." But, Toomer also opened and closed the review by claiming that the novel expressed "the artistic personality of Waldo Frank" rather than the life of the South, and that the main African-American character, John Cloud, was more Frank than authentic "southern Negro." Stressing the work's "subjective design," Toomer said that "whatever local or racial truth or untruth the work may contain, must be considered as a purely secondary factor." Upon reading the review, Frank wrote to Toomer in disappointment:

You [*sic*] opening paragraph *suggests* that in your opinion there is no meeting ground between my reality in Holiday and the reality which exists fundamentally in the South. I know you do not say this, and you do not believe it. But in your omission of the opposite, there is a suggestion of this. And I regret it, because practically all the critics are jumping on me for not knowing the South, and you are the one man who knows I do, who was in a position to state so with some authority.[34]

Toomer's review was an ironic reversal of Frank's foreword: where Frank began by stressing the "regionalism" of *Cane* ("this book *is* the South"), Toomer began with an assertion that *Holiday* was not "sectional," but rather portrayed "the artistic personality of Waldo Frank." When he went on to point out that his reservations toward the novel had to do specifically with "local or racial truth or untruth" and with the character of the black man John Cloud, Toomer was indirectly saying that the black characters were not "black," because, as he said earlier to Frank, *Holiday* was primarily an element in Frank's "spiritual experience." In fact, Toomer did not believe that Frank understood the dynamics of the Southern racial conflict, a point most definitively made in his story "Blood-Burning Moon."

"Blood-Burning Moon" echoes *Holiday* in two important ways: a lynching ends each work, and triangular relationships structure both narratives (Tom Burwell, Bob Stone, and Louisa versus Bob Hade, Virginia Hade, and John Cloud in the latter). But in Toomer's work white Virginia is replaced by black Louisa in the former. Whereas both women react to the lynching of their lovers by a retreat into madness in the face of a horrible reality, Virginia evades her personal responsibility for John Cloud's death, while Louisa's insanity is the product of the terror of history whose elaborate "web" envelops all of Toomer's characters. Toomer complicates "Blood-Burning Moon" in a manner that critiques Frank's dualistic essentialism —Niggertown/whitetown, repressed whites/emotionally liberated blacks— and suggests that there are other economic and political dimensions to the history of race.[35]

Finally, Toomer and Frank each felt the other had missed a crucial point in public commentary on their books, and these differences arose from their different conceptions of race, racial identity, and the historic circumstances behind these conceptions. Toomer's position had its contradictory elements: he said he was not really an African-American yet spoke as the final arbiter on matters of African-American life and culture ("I don't look for these things. I don't have to. If they're there, I simply *know* it"). But Frank's position was equally problematic in its attempt to hold a conception of race as both a "surface" and an essence. In his posthumously published memoirs, Frank spoke of Toomer's "need to forget that he was Negro," a remark which even at that late date misses the point of Toomer's racial position. The idea of "race" Toomer tried to live by, utopian though it may have been, escaped those essentialist categories that have continued to fix color and identity in American culture.[36]

Toomer tried to live his life as if the ideal of the mulatto aristocracy he was born into were a fact: as if "amalgamation" of black people and white people had taken place, or at least was imminent. If he were the "First American," everyone after him could follow his example; given the status of African-Americans in the United States, his choice made perfect sense. But Toomer found a crucial difference between his experience and that of Waldo Frank, who could pass as a black man in South Carolina for two weeks and then return easily to his white identity; the fact that Toomer was "known as Negro" had a more permanent status. Toomer had his own lynching story (or stories) in *Cane*, and they offered a different history of Southern racial violence. *These* differences, which Toomer understood only too well, meant that *Cane* would be a book about the other side of the utopian image prefigured in *Our America*.

Revising a Life

By his own account, Jean Toomer stopped writing and turned to Gurd-jieffism sometime in the winter of 1923–24. It was at this time that he had begun to reach a decision regarding the matter of his racial identity. If American society insisted on classifying him as African-American, then with equal insistence he would deny that classification. He continued to be engaged with racial questions and would write about racial matters for most of his life (little of this material would be published), but he always maintained a spectator's distance that emphasized a rational, objective analysis of the American race mania. While Toomer continued to associate with many of the white writers he had met through Waldo Frank and as a result of the publication of *Cane*, he began withdrawing from the world of the black writers and the intellectuals he had cultivated when he first sought support for and publication of his work.[37]

This withdrawal did not come about all at once; Toomer's initial attempt to lead groups in Gurdjieffian training took place in Harlem, and he was listed in the 1927 *Who's Who in Colored America*. When Du Bois wrote him in Paris in 1925 requesting material for the *Crisis*, Toomer replied politely, "I too feel that I should like to touch Crisis readers, and have them keep in touch with me," though he had no new work to send. While he objected to parts of *Cane* appearing as fragments, he allowed pieces from the book to be printed in anthologies of black writing at least three times in the decade, the last in V. F. Calverton's *Anthology of American Negro Literature*, which appeared from the Modern Library in 1929.[38]

In 1924, however, Toomer had declined to appear at Charles S. Johnson's famous *Opportunity* magazine dinner to honor the newly arrived Negro literati, and in introducing the selection of his poems in Countee Cullen's 1927 anthology, *Caroling Dusk*, Toomer would pointedly identify himself with "a literary and artistic group in New York composed of such men as Waldo Frank, Alfred Stieglitz, Paul Rosenfeld, Gorham B. Munson, and others." George Hutchinson notes that Toomer did remain in contact with some African-American friends after 1923: "Toomer was not, then, avoiding contact with black artists at this time, although he did not count himself one of them." Toomer was attempting gradually to divide his private life from his public identity. By 1930 he refused to appear in an anthology of African-American writing because "I see our art and literature as primarily American art and literature. I do not see it as Negro, Anglo-Saxon, and so on."[39]

However, to be the "First American" rather than an African-American, Toomer not only had to restrict his public associations, he also had to revise or, more strongly, to "erase" some of his personal history from 1919 to 1923, from the time he wrote his articles for the *New York Call* until the publication of *Cane*. As we noted in Chapter 2, Toomer's autobiography as excerpted in *The Wayward and the Seeking*—the version of his life he wrote between 1929 and 1934—omitted or rearranged significant facts. If one compares this account of the writing of *Cane* (which Darwin Turner took from "On Being an American") to the surviving correspondence between

Toomer and Frank and the various editors and critics they were in touch with, one sees evidence of further revisions to the story.[40]

In those pages of autobiography Toomer obscured the ambivalence he projected about his own racial awareness in 1920–22, a period when his identity as an African-American was strongly affirmed in letters to Mae Wright, strongly implied in letters to Claude McKay, Sherwood Anderson, and John McClure, and at least ambiguously recognized in the letters to Waldo Frank. Additionally, in revising the record of *Cane*'s composition, Toomer greatly reduced Frank's role as literary mentor (and antagonist), practical editor, and, in effect, literary agent. In these matters Frank's influence was equal in importance to the intellectual connection *Our America* had provided Toomer, but they were matters also enmeshed in the misunderstandings about race between the two men.

In *The Wayward and the Seeking*, Toomer says he began writing the *Cane* material on his train trip back from Sparta in 1921. After his grandfather's death and the funeral in New Orleans, he returned to the work: "Some of the pieces were impure and formless. But some, I knew, were really written. These authentic ones I began sending out. The *Double Dealer* of New Orleans was the first to accept. Then the *Liberator* and, later, *Broom*. In these literary magazines I made my mark. Beyond them was Waldo Frank and the possibility of a book."[41] The first piece from *Cane* to be published, however, was the "Song of the Son," which Jessie Fauset accepted for the *Crisis*, where it appeared in a full-page layout in April 1922. Toomer apparently never mentioned this publication to Frank, nor is there any mention of it in the autobiographies. This omission is significant, because questions of publication were a frequent topic in Toomer and Frank's letters. Despite what Toomer says, the publication in the *Crisis* was the only appearance in print of *Cane* material before he sent his manuscripts to Frank and received his initial criticisms; further, it was Frank who suggested trying *Broom* and who spoke to Lola Ridge on Toomer's behalf. Thus early in the correspondence, in April 1922, Toomer wrote to Frank that he had sent "Becky" to the *Dial* and "Carma" to the *Liberator*, and that "I shall send something to Broom. I do not know it; I do know the calibre of Lola Ridge."[42]

Toomer's exchanges with John McClure of the *Double Dealer* also began after Frank had criticized the first *Cane* pieces. McClure's letter to Toomer in early July 1922 refers to "the work which you showed us three weeks ago," which would place Toomer's initial submission to the magazine sometime in June. In his earlier letter to McClure, Toomer indeed mentions that he had given Frank his manuscripts to read "two months ago." Those manuscripts included the play "Natalie Mann," with its "lovely poem that M [Merilh] recites in NY," as Frank described the piece that would be detached from the play and eventually published in *Broom* as "Karintha." McClure's July letter judges Toomer's submissions: " 'Fern' and 'Karintha' were excellent, more excellent than the other manuscripts, we felt, though all were good."

It seems clear, then, that Toomer, probably acting on Frank's criticism, had already salvaged "Karintha" from his play and was submitting it as a separate prose poem to the *Double Dealer*.[43]

Toomer's autobiography is most misleading on the point of the writing of *Cane* in the section where he describes his decision to finish the book:

> But I had not enough for a book. I had at most a hundred typed pages. These were about Georgia. It seemed that I had said all I had to say about it. So what, then? I'd fill out. The middle section of *Cane* was thus manufactured. I sent the manuscript to Frank. He took it to Horace Liveright. Liveright accepted it, but wanted a foreword written by Frank. Frank himself had a book to write, based on Negro life. It was arranged that he come to Washington and then both of us would go South.[44]

Several pieces about Washington, D.C., and the world of the mulatto aristocracy—"Seventh Street" and "Avey" at least—had been sent to Frank in March 1922, but the key stories "Theater" and "Box Seat" would not be written until the fall of 1922, *after* Toomer and Frank visited Spartanburg, South Carolina, together. In addition, the concluding story of *Cane*'s first section, "Blood-Burning Moon," was written after their return and after Toomer knew about, and no doubt had discussed, Frank's lynching story, *Holiday*. "Bona and Paul," the final story of part 2, was revised at this time as well. Finally, Frank began discussing the possibility of *Cane*'s publication with Liveright in November or December 1922, and the book was accepted sometime after Christmas of that year.[45]

It is possible that Toomer misremembered some of the events of 1922 when he was working on his autobiography eight or ten years later. However, he could have consulted his correspondence, and it is difficult to believe that he could have forgotten so entirely the order of such important dates as the trip to Spartanburg and Liveright's acceptance of *Cane*. Certainly he could not have believed, as the autobiography suggests, that he had "made his mark" in the little magazines and that *Cane* was largely complete before he contacted Waldo Frank. His version of events in "On Being an American" is intended not only to obscure the part Frank (and others) played in putting *Cane* together, but to dismiss the care and extended concern given to the *form* of Toomer's book. When he says "the middle section of *Cane* was thus manufactured," he speaks as if it were only for the commercial requirements of publication that he bothered to write about black life in Washington, D.C., or about the subject of "passing." But of course it is the connection between the rural South and the urban North, between "passing" and miscegenation, that makes *Cane* the powerful, complex representation of African-American life that it is; and this representation depends also on the modernist forms that Toomer took—and improved upon—from Waldo Frank and Sherwood Anderson.

In "On Being an American," Toomer attempts to dramatize his differences with Frank over the matter of racial identity. He says that when Frank visited him in Washington before they traveled south, "I took this opportunity to convey to him my position in America. I read to him 'The First American.' I explained my actuality and my ideas to the point where I felt sure he understood them." Toomer's intention was to make sure that Frank's foreword to *Cane*, "this introduction of myself to the literary world," would be "accurate and right." Toomer may have read the poem to Frank when they were in Washington preparing for their trip, but it was a text with which Frank was already familiar; "The First American" had been included in the original group of manuscripts Toomer mailed to him in March, and Frank had evaluated this work by noting that "some of the things are mere statement, not fleshed not living . . . like The First American." Toomer's memoir tries to depict their discussion about "race" as direct and unambiguous, but his correspondence with Frank shows their exchange to be much more subtle and circuitous.[46]

In explaining his attitude about race, Toomer's assessment of "Waldo Frank's lack of understanding of, or failure to accept, my actuality" seems accurate. But in attempting to present his version of how that "actuality" was misunderstood or ignored, Toomer buried the history behind the writing of *Cane* and thereby distorted the book's meaning. In his desire to distance himself from the unalterable rule of the American racial order, Toomer needed to create a "manufactured" *Cane*, written from the objective perspective of an observer, a spectator rather than a witness. That ambiguity was already embedded in the book, in the person of the narrator who can't decide the nature of his relationship to Fern or Avey, whose understanding and *participation* transform him from spectator to witness. At the end of a long letter confirming his request that Frank write *Cane*'s foreword, Toomer suddenly says, "Kabnis is *Me*." Significantly, this identification was not one he was willing to make after 1923.[47]

Chapter 5
Writing *Cane*

Brother mine . . . you certainly are the engineer and locomotive in this
landing of CANE. And by god but you have a steady pull and a sharp
clear eye going up grade.

—Jean Toomer to Waldo Frank, 1922

You have helped me too, Jean. Who can measure the balance one way
or the other?

—Waldo Frank to Jean Toomer, 1922

Jean Toomer wrote *Cane* over a period of two years, from its beginnings
in Georgia in the fall of 1921 until it was published by Boni & Liveright in
the fall of 1923. The task of making a book out of Toomer's various poems,
sketches, and stories was largely accomplished between March and December 1922. By the evidence of their correspondence, Waldo Frank worked
closely with Toomer throughout that time, continuing on into 1923 as
final revisions to the manuscript were made. Frank selected and critiqued
pieces, influenced the ideas and forms for individual stories, suggested at
least the theoretical conception for the book's structure, and edited the
text line by line.

Toomer, of course, had written important parts of what would become
Cane before he showed his work to Frank, and by the time he was writing
the Washington section late in 1922 he was moving in his own direction
both thematically and formally. But the 1922 correspondence between the
two men shows in some detail the central role Frank played in *Cane*'s creation—and not only as critic and editor. As confidant, mentor, and established author, Frank told Toomer where to send his early tales and poems
and offered encouragement when the small magazines first rejected his
work: "Damn Dial for not having sense to accept your stuff," he wrote
Toomer after Gilbert Seldes turned down "Fern" and "Karintha." It was
Frank who had spoken to Seldes in the first place, as he did to Van Wyck

Brooks at the *Freeman*, to Lola Ridge at *Broom*, to Gorham Munson at *Secession*, and to Oscar Williams at *Rhythmus*. His letter to Toomer added the highest praise he could manage: "If the Seven Arts were going, I would run ten pages of you instanter."[1]

To associate Toomer with the group of the *Seven Arts*, of course, was to admit him to the project of revitalizing American culture, the work of Brooks, Randolph Bourne, Sherwood Anderson, and even Walt Whitman. On October 29, 1922, Toomer received *Secession*'s letter of rejection for "Theater," and he immediately informed Frank. Knowing something of Toomer's precarious situation at home and his uncertainty about his writing, Frank sent him a reassuring reminder of their sacred calling: "There is no doubt about you, brother. You have an extraordinary gift. The flame of you is pure and strong, and you are not fragile either. You have the protection of a prophetic vision concerning yourself. You're in a good state deep down. . . . Never forget: we are the intimately sanctified priests of the new Vision, and of the eternal God." The "we" in this exalted conception of the artist was the "we" of *Our America*, the artists who would redeem the betrayed promise of the country's origins. That encouragement was precisely what the despondent author needed, as Toomer's response clearly shows: "Your love and confidence are elements of my striving. There is no rest in them. They are elements of my creation. And the real critic will be he who sees these in my work over and above what ever you may have to give me in the way of form."[2] Toomer here mentions, as an aside, Frank's most important contribution to *Cane*: a notion of "form." When Toomer sent Frank his hodgepodge of manuscripts, Frank's critique repeatedly stressed the need for "form." Toomer would be stirred by his mentor's ideas about American culture (especially, as we have seen, in *Our America*) and by specific characters and situations in Frank's novels and short stories—all of which he would read during the period he was writing *Cane*. But, most important, Frank's ideas about literary form were embodied in his novels and the short-story cycle *City Block* (1922), and were expressed as well in his critical prose. The direction those examples gave Toomer was vital: what he would ultimately draw from them were lessons in modernist form that he would use to shape the materials of *Cane*.

There were other literary influences on Toomer before 1922: contemporary writers like Anderson, W.E.B. Du Bois, Robert Frost, Carl Sandburg, and Hart Crane, and European authors like Goethe, Victor Hugo, and Romain Rolland, as well as nineteenth-century American writers like Whitman and Herman Melville. A number of other critics—Lola Ridge, John McClure, Gorham Munson, Kenneth Burke—gave Toomer suggestions for improving the work he sent to the small literary magazines. However, it is clear that Waldo Frank's critical ideas and fiction were the major influences on Toomer's book, even though *Cane* would become something very different from anything Frank had written. In fact, by the end of their literary relationship, the student began to teach the teacher, for the novel Frank wrote immediately after *Holiday* (1923), *Chalk Face* (1924), was Frank's own attempt to match the Gothic horror story that Toomer told in *Cane*.

"The Reality of Experience"

Toomer returned to Washington, D.C., in 1921 with a passionate desire to be a writer; the "flesh and blood" intellectuals he had met in New York, Mumford and Frank especially, had encouraged his ambition and given him a sense of at least a tenuous connection to their world. In addition, he had succeeded in publishing work in the *Call*, with one piece printed on the same page as a piece by H. L. Mencken. Frank, too, had dropped out of the New York scene for a year, spending the first six months of 1921 in Alabama, where he researched *Rahab* and got the idea for *Holiday*; he lived for the next six months in France, where he completed *Rahab* and worked on *City Block*. Yet before he left for Alabama, Frank sent off a short note to Toomer to praise his incisive "answer to Mary Austin in the [New York] Call." Frank's gratefulness and praise must have encouraged Toomer to think of himself as a writer: "Your paper was a remarkably clear and keen piece of work. You are doubtless, by your findings a musician, but you have a mind that does not show to disadvantage in writing either." [3]

Later, although their correspondence had lapsed for more than a year, Toomer wrote to Frank on March 24, 1922: "If you have thought of me, I guess it has been to wonder in terms of mere survival. Music has gone under." But, Toomer says,

I have thrown my energies into writing. I have written any number of poems, several sketches in play form, and one long piece which I call a Play in Three Acts. The poems are largely impersonal, and have no relation to any definite segment of life. The sketches are attempts at an artistic record of Negro and mixed-blood America. [4]

Toomer added that his writing reflected "an impulse to self-expression that is maturing, growing," despite the fact that Washington, D.C., hardly provided the atmosphere for creativity or a "creative friendship": "Almost the first and surely the last real talk was the one I had with you in Central Park. Such spiritual asceticism develops a strength whose reverse face is marked with sterility. I am reaching out. I have to. I wonder if you wouldnt like to read a few of my things?" Frank answered this letter in less than two weeks, assuring Toomer that he had not forgotten him:

You are the sort of life one doesn't forget . . . nor do you grow dim. The contrary! Let me see what you wish to send me. . . . We must still persevere alone . . . all of us, scattered, suffering, fighting the pain and menace of under-nutrition of which you speak. Perhaps in the very scatter of ourselves, a seed is being planted more widely than it could be otherwise . . . and perhaps not. I believe, sometimes I think it is a credo quia absurdum. But I go on believing. Your letter helped enormously. I wish I could think I could be of help to you. You are one of those men one must see but once to know the timbre and the truth of.[5]

The scattering Frank speaks of was the dissolution of the group connected with the *Seven Arts*, the disaffection of Van Wyck Brooks, and the death of Randolph Bourne; yet Frank, true to the optimism of *Our America*, still hoped to create a new group, one centered around younger writers such as Munson, Anderson, Crane, and possibly Kenneth Burke. He soon saw Toomer as an addition to this circle, and an especially useful one given his unique perspective on American life.[6]

A grateful Toomer sent his manuscripts to Frank the next day: "I have never had such a deep and wonderful experience from a letter. When I had read it, before I was through reading it, an emotion and thrill surged upward, filling out the curves of my spirit, and filling my eyes with tears." Frank must have been pleasantly surprised by the work's high quality, because he in turn replied almost immediately: "The hurried glimpse I have been able to give your batch of writing makes me feel the need of going through it carefully. The vital and original nature of it seems evident." Here he suggested sending "some of the shorter things" to *Broom* and the *Dial* "as the very lovely Washington Vignettes, the Negro portraits," and added that he had already spoken to Lola Ridge at *Broom* "about your stuff."[7]

Toomer reacted to Frank's friendly letters immediately, even before receiving the favorable response to his manuscripts, and he wrote to Frank again, offering complimentary comments on his recently published essay "A Note on the Novel." This important letter shows, by virtue of its focus on several of the essay's themes, Toomer's sympathetic appreciation of its critical modernism, beginning with his admiration for Frank's attack on the critics who would limit art's scope: "I have the desire to receive the most varied forms of life, not merely as so many convenient packages of pleasure and pain (narcotics or tooth-aches), but as elements of spiritual fertility." Frank's conception of the high significance of art, already given prominence in *Our America*, probably answered Toomer's own need to be engaged with important subjects, whether political or "spiritual" or, as in Frank, with the two combined.[8]

Toomer's letter sounds rather cryptic, since he quoted only words or phrases or partial sentences from Frank's essay and layered between them his own brief responses; but when the context for the quotes and responses is provided, the letter shows Toomer absorbing a theoretical background for modernist art:

Your treatment of "Receptivity to Material" and "Program" has helped me quite a bit. I have always felt that "every artist that has lived in the world is a realist insofar as he [*sic*] himself is real and as his material, determined by himself and the world, must be real also." A dream is real; a dray is real. Program-making . . . assimilates . . . etc. Surely. Programs form "schools." The very implications of the term sustains your position. "For the intellect possesses what was created before." That is a fine and timely distinction.

"The aesthetic value of any novel is the end-product of its related elements of life." Good. I dance. I express myself. I create. Perhaps those who see me will feel beauty. Perhaps in looking back I too may be conscious of beauty. But if I were to strike some pose for the sake of beauty, and not for the sake of self-expression, all would be lost.

In his essay, Frank attacked those who judged the novel in terms of its adherence to "accuracy" in life, for that judgment, Frank insisted, was based on a preconceived notion of what constitutes reality. Critics take their view of aesthetic reality from artists and codify that "reality" into a program, whereas true artists are always striking out to find new versions of the "real." This is the contrast Toomer found so useful, that between the artist who was receptive to life (shows "receptivity to *fresh* material"—Toomer leaves out the original's "fresh") and one who simply tried to find a program and then judged other artists by the program's tenets. As Frank said, "Zola . . . framed the Naturalistic novel which [he] never wrote. . . . Only the disciples of Zola, whose names we forget, wrote Naturalistic novels according to the program."[9]

According to Frank, the terms "realist" and "romanticist" were misleading, for they suggested a false dichotomy between the real and the unreal. Actually, "the fresh material of the romanticist became the reality of the realist," that is, the historical period called "romantic" provided, in essence, a new view of reality, and those who fought for that new view saw themselves as "realists." This discussion leads to the statement Toomer quoted above, but that statement's full meaning depends on the sentences that follow it:

Every artist that has lived in the world is a realist insofar as himself is real and as his material, determined by himself and the world, must be real also. But no artist conceivable to man can be a realist in the sense of our critical implication—the sense of an absolute reality which true scientists would not arrogate to mathematics and certainly not to man. "It is the highest glory of man," said Remy de Gourmont, "that there is no science of man." *Our standard of reality is an accumulating, gyrating and disappearing flux of subjective contributions.* If there is a science of man, its name is aesthetics, and its axiom: that each new contribution shall be gauged by the inner law of its own genesis. (Emphasis added)[10]

Frank's conceptualization of "our standard of reality" formed part of his idea of *unanimisme*, his adaptation of Jules Romain for American modernism, but it also describes his understanding of how his short-story cycle, *City Block,* worked.

Toomer's real "dream" and real "dray" were a step toward Frank's conception of an inclusive ("accumulating") but unstable ("disappearing") reality. Frank argued that the "absolute reality" critics applied to a work of art was beyond anyone's understanding, but he would attempt to show in *City Block* that short stories in a sequence might accumulate a multidimensional reality that transcended the temporal, finite world they described. In other words, what approached a science of "absolute reality" was a modernist aesthetic form, one that by its relativity and multiplicity could reveal a truer, more complete reality than what lay on the surface—the kind of "realism" written by Sinclair Lewis. This was the connection between the epigraph from Spinoza that introduced *City Block* ("By reality and perfection I understand the same thing") and Frank's lines prefacing the contents page, which insisted "that *CITY BLOCK* is a single organism and that its parts should be read in order." Around this time Toomer, perhaps thinking of *Cane* or *City Block*, wrote in a journal: "Perfection is real. But not all reality is perfect. For perfection implies harmony, and it may be defined as a harmonious *aggregate* of realities" (emphasis added).[11]

"Programs" of literature form "schools," a reduction Toomer joined to the quotation "for the intellect possesses what was created *before*." In Frank's words:

The value of imaginative literature, even pragmatically as *nourishment to life*, lies in the fact that it creates what the intellect—theory, program, apriori standards of good, bad, right and wrong—does not yet possess. For the intellect possesses what was created *before*. Hence contemporary art can never fall within the scope of pre-existing programs.[12]

Frank's ethos sounds like a variation on Pound's "make it new," but, of course, it was an older argument, at least as old as Coleridge's theory of the creative imagination that is capable of assembling parts into new wholes which extend the boundaries of knowledge. The intellect, working by itself, could only apprehend that knowledge, but could not extend it. Toomer liked a definition of art that went beyond the photographic realism of such contemporary novels as T. S. Stribling's *Birthright* (1922), not least because that "realism" might reduce him to "Negro." "Programs" in art were similar to the social strictures and divisions of American life, and Toomer was looking for a way to escape those restrictions.[13]

In Frank's view, all great art was the expression of an inner vision. The critic's job was to facilitate "the process of assimilating the novelist's contribution to the sum of social experience," but he should not presume to judge the uniqueness of the artist's vision. Of course, the novelist could not escape the zeitgeist and the minutia of his social existence: "Let the novelist think that he is primarily concerned with socialism, housing problems, psycho-analysis and the like. If he is an artist, his thinking will be but a detail of his work; but if he is not an artist his work will be but a negligible detail of this thinking." Still, Frank continued, art does not directly create an abstraction called "Beauty"; what is seen as beautiful is rather a by-product of the formal combination of the "elements of life":

The aesthetic value of any novel is the end-product of its related elements of life. The novelist who deals with, and relates into organic form, elements of life, with whatever intellectual conviction, may create Beauty if he has that virtue in him. But the novelist who tries to deal directly with Beauty, get at it directly, short-cutting the elements of life, is doomed. The artist in the act of creation can afford to be anything rather than an aesthete.[14]

Toomer noted that the "related elements of life" had to be included in the work of art. Otherwise, "Beauty" was simply an empty shell, or as Toomer put it, a "pose." Frank's distinction here resembled the one he made in *Our America*, between the mysticism of Emerson and that of Whitman, between a conception in flight from actuality and one rooted in the "material."

Within its limits Frank's essay was an excellent introduction to modernist literary ideas, and as such it was very useful to Toomer. The theoretical problems it raised, which Kenneth Burke would later point out, were perhaps also useful to the younger writer, for *Cane* was to qualify Frank's idealism with the realities of African-American life. Although Frank rejected aestheticism, his conception of the "reality of experience" neglected the reality of the world outside the artist's subjectivity, and Frank admitted to Toomer that "the spirit of this world [in *Holiday*] is nearer to me than its body." The one thing Toomer could not escape would be the world's body, and in *Cane* the color of bodies and the identification of races are inescapable themes.[15]

Frank's "Note on the Novel" is also problematic regarding subjectivity: Frank's view of art seemed to exclude the possibility of criticizing it. How could one criticize what Frank insisted only the artist could understand? This point was especially troubling for a theory of art that proclaimed the artist a restorer and creator of American culture. Frank desperately wanted an audience, for only an audience could finally ensure that American culture would be renewed, yet he would tolerate no criticism of his own creative work, even from Paul Rosenfeld and Lewis Mumford, fellow writers who were close to him. These contradictions came together in Frank's reaction to Toomer's review of *Holiday*. Frank wanted to be regarded as "knowing the South" even though, according to his own critical parameters, that knowledge—his "thinking" about the South—should be secondary in critiques of his novel; thus when Toomer emphasized the "subjective" and imaginative success of the book, Frank understood him to be implying that the story was not "realistic."[16]

Perfecting the Free Form of Narrative

Although Waldo Frank's own creative work suffered because he refused to accept criticism, he was an excellent critic, as Sherwood Anderson and Hart Crane both knew. He was, indeed, the best kind of critic: appreciative, sympathetic, and honest, with an acute eye for what worked and what didn't. Writing to Toomer on April 25, 1922, about the material Toomer had sent him, Frank included a two-page, single-spaced, typed critique. It was an extraordinary response: detailed yet general in a helpfully theoretical way, critical yet encouraging in a way that was all the more valuable in that it came from an established author like Frank. Indeed, when one looks at the range of work Toomer sent to Frank, it seems clear he had little sense of the quality of his own work until Frank praised the odd assortment of plays ("Kabnis" and "Natalie Mann"), sketches, and poems. Toomer accepted almost every judgment in that critique and acted on almost every suggestion made. Eventually, he would also accept Frank's ideas about the formal organization of his book, ideas Toomer had first responded to in "A Note on the Novel."[17]

Frank began with what he felt was the weakest of Toomer's works, "Natalie Mann": "the central drama of Natalie, Merilh, Mertis, Law, etc. is smothered by the form of the other stuff . . . the teaparties, the talk of the incidental . . . the trouble is not with the density and amount of this milieu but with the deadness of the texture." There was simply too much "discussive talk," a judgment that anyone who reads "Natalie Mann" today is also likely to make. Yet, Frank said, "What is clear is: that you have a vision . . . the start of a true Form, but that Form is not there yet," though, he noted, "in individual scenes, there is a very beautiful glow of life." He singled out the excellence of "Karintha," the prose poem that would open *Cane* but which seems out of place in the problem drama Toomer had constructed, via Shaw and Ibsen, as "Natalie Mann."[18]

Although Frank thought "Kabnis" needed work ("the texture is superb, but there is a sacrifice in the bone-structure"), it was "very near to its state of fusing." And it was brilliant:

Kabnis has in it the embryon of an expression which America has not even the faintest inkling of, and which America demands if it is to become a real part of the human adventure. Color, spiritual penetration, counterpoint of human wills, the intuition that they are harmonics of a Unit, the power to convey line and volume in words, intellectual cleansing-capacity . . . all here, but not yet fused into the final art.

Frank had two immediate suggestions, both of which Toomer would follow: first, Toomer should create a "freer form of narrative in which your dialog, which has no kinship with the theatric, might [thrive] more successfully," and, second, he should cut the speech of Father John: "I felt that the speech of the Ancient at the end was a sudden drop into particulars failing to take along and light with itself the general atmosphere you had built about his relationship with Kabnis."

Clearly, Frank wanted Toomer to avoid the conversational idiom of "Natalie Mann." He understood that realistic dialogue was not Toomer's forte, but that symbolic or poetic dialogue could be. Cutting the Ancient's speech to the enigmatic line, "the sin th whit folks 'mitted when they made the Bible lie" would illuminate Father John's relationship with Kabnis by creating an ambiguously symbolic figure, a voice from the past that challenged, questioned, and underlined the decisions and compromises made by the present generation. The "freer form of narrative" would allow what had been stage directions in the dramatic version of "Kabnis" to function in a similarly symbolic manner; thus, at the end of "Kabnis," Toomer, as the camera eye, can both freeze-frame Carrie K and the Ancient in a tableau and retreat through the window of the cellar to witness the sun rising from the pine trees. The "freer form" allowed him to escape the discursive for the poetic and symbolic, joining this hybrid poetic drama to the patterns of imagery, symbol, and myth that Toomer developed in his other material. Both suggestions pushed the work toward a modernist form of narration.

The "freer form of narrative" was one of a series of suggestions Frank peppered throughout his critique regarding the matter of "form." Concluding his remarks on "Natalie Mann," he noted, "Your whole aim is so new, that the work of formulation must needs be absolutely independent: and to create Form out of chaos, as must all true American artists, takes time time time." The chaos was not only American, of course, it was modern, and Frank told Toomer he must discover his own form because there were no adequate models for what he was trying to write. Frank had just finished *City Block*, his own short-story cycle that attempted to discover a unity of American life within separate lives linked by the unifying device of an apartment building. *City Block* is at least partly Sherwood Anderson's *Winesburg, Ohio* subjected to the compression and fusion of an urban environment; that fusion, based on Frank's understanding of Jules Romains's *unanimisme*, must produce a new social spirit, "the harmonics of a Unit," a communal relationship that would manifest itself beyond the individual's awareness. *City Block* demonstrated the spirit of *unanimisme* through the technique of *Winesburg*, where later stories in the book completed or complicated the meaning of earlier ones, linking them by patterns of imagery, doubled characters, recurring themes, and a broken or intermittent narrative.

It was perhaps with the form of *City Block* in mind that Frank said of the "Kabnis" manuscript, "the thing lies in the retrospective mind in its parts, in its details and . . . in the reading the mind does not catch on to a uniformly moving Life that conveys it whole to the end, but rather steps from piece to piece as if adventuring through the pieces of a still unorganized mosaic." Frank might have thought of *City Block* as an "organized" mosaic, a group of fragments (stories) which, read in the correct order (as Frank demanded in the note prefacing the book), would make up a meaningful whole. Frank saw the whole of his short-story cycle as depicting the invisible unity and spirit of the characters within the city block rather than the isolation and separateness of the characters in *Winesburg*; the development of *City Block* was the revelation of an invisible unity, not the growth of an individual experience like that experienced by Anderson's George Willard. For Frank the evolution toward "Spirit," toward the recognition of unity, must always take place in and "through" the unstable finite; it was the expression of "the form of God in matter." Once they perceived this, artists could order their discoveries into works of art: "To see is to order. The principle of order is to unify a heterogeneity of things. The method of order is to give these things a focus; and the result of order is *form*."[19]

Again, when Frank came to consider Toomer's "poems," he focused beyond the individual lyrics:

> although you are a poet, I don't think you'll find your final satisfaction in the mere direct lyric. Something in the way of a free woven narrative that includes the song of Nathan Merilh and gives the texture of the world he springs from will include you all. Some of the poems are quite perfect. Seventh Street, Becky, Avey, (Daniel less so), Carma are lovely transcripts of a world old in America but new in American expression.

Frank's description here might be considered a cogent synopsis of *Cane*. The "free woven narrative," repeating the "freer form of narrative" Frank recommended earlier in the letter, is the lyric short-story cycle that will begin with Merilh's "song" ("Karintha") and include Merilh's world (Washington, white and black, the masses, the bourgeoisie, and the mulatto elite) and the world of "Kabnis" that produced the "song"—which is, ultimately, the world Merilh (Toomer) came from. Thus Frank told Toomer not to restrict himself to the lyric, but implied that he might include the lyric (as Frank himself had done in *Rahab* and in *City Block*) within a narrative *not* defined by conventional genres. A work need not be a "novel" or even a collection of short stories or book of poems linked by a single locale (like Robert Frost's *North of Boston* or Edgar Lee Masters's *Spoon River Anthology*), but might make use of elements from all three genres to create a new form uniquely suited to the complicated world–"mixed-blood" America and the Negro's unknown peasant past—whose stories Toomer wished to tell. In Frank's words, these materials were "transcripts of a world old in America but new in American expression," and they required a new form of "expression" to describe them.

In Search of a Form for *Cane*

Frank's remarks in his April 25, 1922, critique referred indirectly to the form of *City Block*, but Toomer had not yet read that short-story cycle, and for some time he missed the point of Frank's narrative theory. Thus, writing from Harpers Ferry on July 19, Toomer first brought up his idea for a book:

> I've had the impulse to collect my sketches and poems under the title perhaps of CANE. Such pieces as Karintha, Carma, Avey, and Kabnis (revised) coming under

the sub head of Cane Stalks and Chorouses [*sic*]. Poems under the sub head of Leaves and Syrup Songs. And my vignettes, of which I have any number, under Leaf Traceries in Washington.[20]

What Toomer had in mind was a "collection," a miscellany organized roughly according to genre, as stories, poems, and "vignettes" or prose poems. He did not yet have even the idea of dividing the book between South and North, or rural and urban, since "Avey" was to be included with "Karintha" and "Carma," and there was no sign of the complicated order he would finally work out, no suggestion of the patterns of imagery, the pairing and doubling of stories, the matching poems as commentary on the stories, or any of the devices by which *Cane* was transformed from a collection into a collage. Four days after his letter to Frank, Toomer wrote to John McClure of the *Double Dealer*, again describing the proposed book:

I think I shall call it CANE. Having as sub-heads Cane Stalks and Chorouses (Karintha, Fern, etc. and two longer pieces), Leaves (poems), and Leaf Traciers, in Washington, under which I shall group such things as "For M.W., and other sharp, brief vignettes of which I have any number.[21]

Toomer mentions slightly different contents, but the form of the book was still essentially to be a selection of his best work, as identified by Frank and his other editorial readers.

Between the end of July, when Toomer first described his idea for a miscellaneous *Cane*, and the completion of the carefully structured book that Frank took to Liveright in December, Toomer read *City Block* and carried on extensive literary discussions with Frank during their time together in Washington and on the trip to Spartanburg. Immediately after outlining his first conception of *Cane*, he said to Frank, "Well, I'll get a chance to talk to you, and that is what I deeply want." Frank was publishing and selling *City Block* privately—Liveright feared prosecution by New York censors for its "obscene" content if he published it—and he asked Toomer if he would sell the book in Washington among his friends. Toomer agreed, and their letters discussing arrangements for selling the books continued into July and August. Even as he promoted the book, however, Toomer had yet to read it; in a postscript to the August 21 letter concluding plans for their trip to Spartanburg, Toomer repeats his question from an earlier letter, "Will you have a copy of City Block when you come?" Clearly, he was anxious to see what Frank had done with his short-story cycle.[22]

Toomer had already read at least one of the stories from *City Block*, "Murder," which had appeared in *Broom*, and he remarked on it twice in his July letters to Frank. He praised first its "form and design, . . . depth and directness." A week later he expanded on this theme: "I belive [*sic*] it is that Abstract Design that makes your work so significant for me. Murder, for example. . . . My own form-impulse, strong as it is, seems as yet mostly concerned with what is concrete and strictly literary. But I believe that higher perceptions will come, if for no other reason than that I somehow sense them in you." In *City Block* the "higher perceptions" are intended to be an expression of *unanimisme*, the spirit of social coherence within the potentially alienating urban setting of the stories. As Frank was to explain years later, the conventional "novel-form" creates the illusion "that human lives are separate," but in truth "human individuality is deeply embedded in a texture of family, heredity, town—in the whole intricate context of its time." Moreover, "at any moment," this fluid "*reality* within and around us has many dimensions, many forms and . . . many 'times,'" and thus is capable of linking past and present, self and other. The formal pattern of *City Block*'s stories, characters, themes, and imagery tried to express that fluid "*reality*," and must have been crucially important for Toomer, especially if, as seems likely from the circumstances of their weeks together, he read the book and was immediately able to discuss it with Frank. His conception of a form for *Cane* probably originated at this time.[23]

One of the writing projects Toomer had in mind during the summer of 1922 was an essay on Frank's work which he had been planning even before the trip to Spartanburg. Frank approved the idea and advised him, "Be sure and read Burke on my two novels before you tackle your own essay. It will help you." Kenneth Burke reviewed *Rahab* and *City Block* in the October 1922 *Dial*, and he had run a perceptive paragraph about Frank in a review of Evelyn Scott in the September *Dial*. On October 4, after their return from the South, Toomer wrote to Frank, commenting at length on the October review. Burke had argued that Frank too readily leaped into metaphysical conceptualizing without grounding his fiction in physical reality, that his creations were "completely erroneous as a gauge of our environment." Toomer angrily sprang to Frank's defense: "Your purpose is not to gauge an isolated physical environment, but to create spiritual realities, and the milieu seen in terms of these." Burke was critical of Frank's "distortion" of reality; he claimed that "for the last fifty years the world has been pressionistic (read, volitional) first im and then ex," and that Frank's "expressionism" was "false," not "statistically true," nor was it "a whole and proper valuation of life." Burke's most damning remark was that Frank was not "*superbly* false," that he was not a beautiful or eloquent writer, but the point Toomer chose to argue for a page of his letter to Frank was the matter of "distortion."[24]

The argument inevitably turned on questions modernism had made prominent, and Frank and Toomer felt, as true modernists, that all literature was relative in its point of view: as Toomer said with some impatience, "doesn't every writer 'stack the cards'? How esle [*sic*] can he possibly write? What in hell's the matter with these fellows?" Toomer now understood Frank's antirealist position from his "Note on the Novel" essay well enough to appreciate its application as a formal method, thus Burke's criticism "sees no relation, no spiritual tangency and implication." The point of "distortion" was to show something more accurately ("create spiritual realities") than realism could. Frank wasn't concerned with an "isolated physical environment" but with "relation" and "implication," that is, with the "spirit," the social connectedness of his settings.

But Toomer did seem to accept one part of Burke's criticism of Frank in observing that "Burke's questioning of the structural significance of CB [_City Block_] is his best taken point. Just this, with the serious critics, will dog you." Burke had questioned the effectiveness of the form, the "abstract design," around which Frank had written his book: "What, for instance, is the structural significance of the City Block cycle? What is the _inevitable_ centre about which it revolves? It should force itself upon us from the complexion of the work. Structure is not so priestly a thing that only the elect can glimpse it. Structure is the first principle of a work, not the last." One way of interpreting Toomer's reaction to these remarks is to say that he understood Frank's design—the order of the stories and their interconnectedness—as intentional, but he agreed with Burke that its intention was too obscure. Another possibility is that Toomer knew precisely what Frank's intention was from the design of _City Block_, but that his own intention would be different when he came to assemble _Cane_'s parts. When Toomer put together _Cane_ he would be at once more subtle and less ambiguous than Frank about his book's "inevitable centre." [25]

Into the South

July 1922 was perhaps the most intense period of Toomer and Frank's collaboration, with letters passing between them almost every third day. In the middle of the month, Frank suggested they take their trip to the South; Toomer agreed, looking forward no doubt to the opportunity to meet Frank again and discuss their writing at length. Frank wanted more material to fill out the story he had been thinking about since his 1921 trip to Alabama; he had finished _City Block_ and was anxious to apply _unanimisme_ to a Southern, rural environment (the novel Toomer speaks of would become _Holiday_). Toomer began to send Frank suggestions as to whether they should go first to Harpers Ferry, West Virginia, or to Virginia, but he revealed a reluctance to return to the Deep South. His letter of July 19 from Harpers Ferry outlined the difference he felt between the upper and lower South: "Life here has not the vividity and distinction of that of middle Georgia. Racial attitudes, on both sides, are ever so much more tolerant, even friendly. Oppression and ugly emotions seem nowhere in evidence. And there are no folk-songs. A more stringent grip, I guess, is necessary to force them through." Of Harpers Ferry he concluded, "While [it is] not the best place for our trip, it would be an easy matter to go farther and fare worse. It has this distinct advantage: transition and intercourse between the races is neither difficult nor hazardous." [26]

Frank, however, wanted the Deep South, not, he wrote to Toomer, "the sort of border place you describe in W Va." Toomer in return suggested Kentucky as a destination, but Frank again demurred and set down his ideas specifically:

Here is my need, Jean, as regards town. My novel is to be called HOLIDAY. And it is simply the story of a lynching. The picture of the drab hideous unpainted town of the whites, the niggertown next-door, possibly in a marshy pinewood: and the gradual tumescence that ends in the Passion of the burning. A short swift novel, all living in my head except the actual words. Now what I want, just incidentally, is to be once again in such a town . . . where there are such white persons, and such black ones. Is Kentucky the place? Is it sufficiently *south*? What about one of the Carolinas? [27]

Toomer finally agreed to set up a visit to South Carolina, which he described to Frank as "more of the crude South, less of the semi-crude North." Toomer's unwillingness to return to the "crude South" was something Frank either missed or chose to ignore, and when one compares Frank's reaction to their Spartanburg trip to Toomer's, the great difference between the two men's understanding of race and the South becomes apparent. Frank told Toomer that Spartanburg gave him a "liberation": "the possibility of writing about a negro without seeing and saying negro all the time. Anymore than when I write about a white man, I say white skin, white skin, all the time." Toomer never confessed his real feelings about the trip to Frank, but he wrote openly about them to a correspondent named "Moses." On October 9, 1922, he apologized to Moses for not answering his letter—it had been forwarded to Spartanburg: "I had gone down there with Waldo Frank. I simply could not answer it at the time. The city, with all its beauty and hideousness had come inside me; I wasn't Jean but a sort of sensitized embodiment of the place." Frank's question to Toomer, "What is a Negro?" could not be so glibly answered, as "Blood-Burning Moon" showed. Facing "white pressure" for Toomer meant facing the possibility of being caught in a place and in a sociological condition from which there was no escape; facing "white pressure" for Frank meant an experience that would result in a novel.[28]

Between Toomer and Frank in July and August there was much planning; they talked of the small literary magazines, of Frank's *City Block*, and, above all, of the joint venture of creating a new American literature. In speaking of *Holiday*, Toomer assured Frank that "I cannot think of myself as being separated from you in the dual task of creating an American literature, and of developing a public, however large or small, capable of responding to our creations. Those who read and know me, should read and know you."

Toomer assured Frank that his desire to promote *City Block* and to sell it in Washington was connected to his own work: "it will pioneer and set a high standard for those who read it—they will the better absorb my own." The values he praised in Frank were those he desired for his own work: "intensity of vision, depth of perception, originality of execution"—everything that the realists Sinclair Lewis and T. S. Stribling lacked.[29]

The correspondence of July and August suggests that Toomer saw *Cane* as largely complete in terms of the "collection" he planned. It was to be a book about the South, one that would outdo *Birthright*. Perhaps Toomer could imagine his book with that single focus because he saw Washington as in some sense *part* of the South. He had, after all, asked Frank to consider Washington as a possible destination for their Southern trip, and he was even more explicit in a letter he wrote at this time to Claude McKay: "I love this southland of my ancestors. In New York I have been nostalgic for the streets and faces of Washington. In Paris or Moscow I think I would be the same."[30]

However, Toomer would return from Spartanburg to write "Theater" and "Box Seat"—stories that saw Washington as a representative modern city, where previously he had treated it primarily in symbolic terms, as in "Withered Skin of Berries" and "Avey." Indeed, he made a point of saying to Frank that he had exploited the symbolic aspect of the city in "Withered Skin of Berries." In "Box Seat" and "Theater" he would further explore the theme introduced in "Seventh Street," that of mass culture and the masses in the new urban context; from this subject grew the contrast and clash between the different classes of African-Americans in the city. It is possible that Frank's reaction to Washington and his observations of the city gave Toomer a different perspective; at the conclusion of his long letter to Frank about the fate of African-American culture, he wrote, "both Theatre and Box-Seat, of course, spring from a complex civilization, and are directed to it." Thus the middle section of *Cane* emerged with a far more complicated view of Washington than Toomer had originally conceived—he juxtaposed old (colored aristocrats) with new (masses, new bourgeois), the city of symbolic architecture and monuments with jazz palaces and cabarets of modern life.[31]

Toomer also returned from Spartanburg to write the most horrific story in *Cane*, "Blood-Burning Moon." In part, the story was written in response to Frank's descriptions of *Holiday* in letters and conversations (Toomer did not actually see the novel's first section until late January 1923); in part, it reflected Toomer's deep-seated fears about his racial position within America and his uncertainty about his partnership with Frank, by which he had committed himself to creating a new American literature and a new American culture.[32]

Revising *Cane*: Finding an Organic Form

Cane began to take on its new dimensions in October, when Toomer worked for two weeks as assistant manager at the Howard Theater in Washington. He told Frank that the job led directly to "Theater" and then "Box Seat," though there were probably a number of other inspirations, including those that moved his new perception of Washington as "modern." The confrontation between the intellectual John and the passionate Dorris is an answer to *Birthright*, and probably to elements in Frank's *Holiday* as well. In July, before their trip, Frank had written Toomer that his "short, swift novel" was going to be a "work something far apart from your own . . . a dynamic Form, a rather abstract Design of this juxtaposition of repression and passion. My book will be of its source . . . probably the most subjective Design I have ever created, precisely because of the extreme objectivity of its subject."[33]

"Repression and passion" would be a theme of "Theater," but Toomer's particular social setting gave his story meanings not easily contained within an "abstract design." In one letter he wrote to Frank he said that he used race merely for an effect in his writing:

The only time I think "Negro" is when I want a peculiar emotion which is associated with this name. As a usual thing, I actually do not see differences of color and contour. I see differences of life and experience, and often enough these lead me to physical coverings. But not always, and, from the stand point of conventional criticism, not often enough. I'm very likely to be satisfied with a character whose body one knows nothing of.[34]

Toomer here appears to have fully embraced Frank's aesthetic. In his fiction, Frank tended to distill experience into an essential meaning, so that social contexts dissolved into confrontations of souls, whether it be "niggertown" versus "whitetown" or John Cloud versus Virginia Hade. And yet in *Cane* Toomer paid close attention to color differences, and the book's most important stories develop around the social meaning given to "physical coverings."

In a letter discussing the confrontation between Dorris and John in "Theater," Toomer argued to Gorham Munson that his story had followed an "abstract design." When *Secession* rejected "Theater," Munson explained to Toomer that the pattern of the story was ruined by too many "pulsation[s]," which violated "the principle of the crescendo." Toomer responded with his own detailed analysis of the story, explaining first what took place in the narrative, then trying to analyze the action in terms of Munson's "crescendo": "John's curve starts with intellection, swings down to passion in Dorris, and sweeps upward into dream." The formalism, even proto–New Criticism, in this exchange perhaps offered Toomer a way to think about his writing, but it had little to do with the meaning of "Theater." As one of the cofounders of _Secession,_ Munson saw himself charting a new direction in American letters—away from the old Puritan-pioneer fixation, away from naturalism and realism (Dreiser and Anderson were laboring in "exhausted forms"), and toward questions of aesthetics, with a special emphasis on literary form. He promoted a new "cerebral quality" in literature and criticism that diverged sharply from the emotional effusiveness of Rosenfeld or the cultural criticism of Brooks. He disliked "good taste" but favored "strangeness," "abstraction," "simplicity," and especially literature that was not hostile to the machine.[35]

Munson's conception of form put rather strict limits on how he might read a story, as his overly reductive comparison of Toomer's "Theater" and Frank's story "Hope" shows. Munson did not understand the meaning of Toomer's word "dictie" and, more important, did not recognize that Toomer's character John was mulatto—thus he missed the indicators of both class and color. When Toomer pointed these issues out to him, Munson grudgingly admitted that "Theater" was "more subtle than I thought it was," but Toomer's letter also failed to discuss other factors of color and class so crucial to understanding the story. Toomer generalized his theme as the gap between art and life, or between stage folk ("not respectable") and audience, but he did not explain how the gap between John and Dorris also reflected the gap between Washington's mulatto elite and the newly arrived Southern masses, nor did he bother to explain that the artist/audience split was ambiguous. Although this ambiguity escaped Munson, it would make a good deal of sense to the later Harlem Renaissance. Who was the real artist—the educated, intellectual John or the blues performer Dorris? Munson recognized the situational resemblance between Frank's "Hope" and Toomer's story, but he was unable to appreciate how Toomer had fleshed out, and so essentially changed, Frank's abstract pattern.[36]

In the ongoing discussion among Toomer, Frank, and Munson over matters of literary form, Toomer's most explicit remarks appeared in a letter he wrote to Munson in March 1923. Responding to Munson's just-published book, _Waldo Frank: A Study,_ Toomer wrote:

from this study, perhaps more than from any single source, I see the importance of form. The tree as a symbol comes to mind. A tree in summer. Trunk, branches: structure. Leaves: the fillers out, one might also say the padding. The sap is carried in the trunk etc. From it the leaves get their sustenance, and _from their arrangement comes their meaning,_ or at least, leaves upon the ground do not make a tree. Etc. This symbol is wanting, of course, because a tree is stationary, because it has no progressions, no dynamic movements. A machine has these, but a machine is all form, it has no leaves. Its very abstraction is now the death of it. Perhaps it is the purpose of our age to fecundate it. But its flower, unlike growing things, will bud from within the human spirit.[37]

Toomer's extended metaphor is awkward, but his sense is generally clear: a work's meaning derives from the combination of form and subject, or of structure and substance. "Leaves upon the ground do not make a tree," and the separate poems and stories of *Cane* did not comprise a finished work until they were arranged in a meaningful pattern.

Toomer also understood that form was not an end in itself. In late December, he read Munson's article in the November *S4N*, "The Mechanics for a Literary 'Secession.'" He wrote to Munson that he "liked your piece: the concentration on America. The acceptance of the machine, the attitude (the only healthy, the only *art* attitude) which uses modern forms, and not the hurt caused by them, as the basis of literature." In his enthusiasm, he began to sound like a futurist: "I had been in every power-house in the city years, years before I dragged myself into the Corcoran Gallery of Art. . . . There is not a statue in Washington . . . that has the lines and balance of certain Pierce Arrow cars." After this praise, however, Toomer pointed out that "there is something lacking in your program," and that was "Power, friend. Power!" Toomer was insisting that form must have a *significant* subject: "the dualism of form and substance is largely specious. That great design cannot rise from puny matter." Or, as he put it in a postscript to the same letter, "I want great art. This means that I want great design. As a means to this end, I want great substance, great power." There is a suggestion here of the implied critique Toomer already had made of Frank's *City Block*, that a concentration on form for its own sake might obscure meaning. As he said in his "Open Letter" to Munson, "Whatever its design, what significance is there to a machine rusting in a junkman's yard? what to a poem or a sketch or a novel that lacks stuff, power, deep organic functioning? that can do no work?"[38]

While Toomer probably continued to go over all the pieces of *Cane* after his return from Spartanburg in September, his correspondence suggests that he concentrated on the second and third parts of the book, the city stories and "Kabnis." "Blood-Burning Moon," "Theater," "Box Seat" and "Esther" were stories Frank had not seen in Toomer's first manuscript because they had yet to be written. "Kabnis," besides being the longest piece in *Cane*, presented special problems because it had to be converted from a play to a story. Once Toomer had settled on the idea of a lyric short-story cycle and began working out the intricate order of *Cane*, "Kabnis" not only had to be integrated with the other pieces, it had also to function as a conclusion, or, in Toomer's circular form, at least to seem continuous with parts 1 and 2.[39]

It was probably October before Toomer was able to determine how to revise "Kabnis," and he immediately sent Frank word that the work was underway:

I'm in Kabnis! Yea. Four sections parctically [*sic*] done and I'm storing power for that last one. Two more days should see me finished. Curious, isnt it? for almost a year now I've been held away. Couldnt touch it. Even the thought of going over it tired me. And here I've plunged in, gripped it, and within a week shall round it off. I'm adding things here and there. Bringing things into relief and fusing them. But I am not re-creating. The bulk of the old Kabnis will still be there. And the dialogue basis of the old form.[40]

What Toomer seems to have done is to convert "Kabnis" from a play in scenes to a story in sections, creating a "freer narrative"; he also added material that would connect his conclusion to the earlier poems and stories in part 1 of *Cane*. The "bulk of the old Kabnis" included the play's dialogue and songs that were retained in the new story, and the stage settings and directions were translated into the story's descriptive passages. What Toomer was "adding" in "bringing things into relief and fusing them" was probably a group of images and thematic references that specifically linked this closing story to what had come before. As Toomer described the work to Frank, "I want Kabnis to remain as an immediate record of my first contact with southern life. Such, it is. And for this reason I see it as an organic part of CANE." In other words, in rewriting "Kabnis" as prose narrative Toomer didn't "re-create" it as a new tale; instead, he rewrote it as a deliberate extension of the earlier parts of *Cane*, the material "organic" to his initial experiences in Sparta.

Frank's critique of "Kabnis" in March had been phrased in very general terms, but Toomer had another critic who read the play and made more specific remarks. Frank had recommended sending the *Cane* materials to *Broom*, where Lola Ridge, whom Toomer had already met in New York, was an editor. Ridge criticized the character of Lewis in the dramatic version of "Kabnis" as "not convincing . . . he seems to have been yanked into your story from some other source entirely without your own experience and therefore he is not authentic—he has not been felt by you." Her criticism is perceptive: even in the revised "Kabnis," Lewis seems to belong more to "Natalie Mann." As Toomer began to see when he responded to Ridge's letter, Lewis works in "Kabnis" only as a foil to Kabnis, "an imperfect incarnation of possibilities . . . a projection of Kabnis' possibilities." Toomer admitted that "Kabnis has the emotion which I could not possibly give to Lewis without bringing Lewis into the foreground more than I care to in this instance." As Toomer recognized, Lewis threatened to become an intrusive deus ex machina who would resolve problems posed in "Kabnis" that were, in fact, not resolvable.[41]

The heroes and narrators Toomer created in *Cane*, particularly in "Kabnis," were much different from the superhuman Nathan Merilh in "Natalie Mann" or the flawless David Teyy of "Withered Skin of Berries," both of whom overwhelm whatever dramatic form exists in their respective texts. While Lola Ridge made Toomer think about how Lewis's dynamic character unbalanced the structure of "Kabnis," it was Frank and Sherwood Anderson whose work offered Toomer examples of the potential power of flawed characters. Toomer read Anderson's *Winesburg, Ohio* and *The Triumph of the Egg* just before his time in Sparta. He read all of Frank's fiction while he was writing *Cane*, and the impetus to revise "Kabnis" coincided with his reading Frank's first novel, *The Unwelcome Man*. Toomer thought the novel was "formative" apprentice work, but he appreciated the main character: "Quincy's struggle, his strength and weakness, his inabiltiy [*sic*] to give himself, are real."[42]

The Unwelcome Man reflected a darker side of *Our America*; it shared many of its themes and recurrent metaphors ("seed," "giant," "bridge") but ended in loss and defeat. In the foreword to the novel's second edition (1923), Frank described his subject as "a tale of the seed that rotted and did not rise." What Frank did not say was that it was the tale of his adolescence and young manhood, and was thus autobiographical in a way similar to "Kabnis." Toomer would refer to the novel's "dead levels," arguing that *Our America* was its "antidote," yet the novel's hero, Quincy Burt, might have been important to Toomer's writing of *Cane* because of his status as an outsider alienated from the world by his uncertain social identity.[43]

The Unwelcome Man is divided between the ordered, theoretical world of college and the common world of New York City. The college episode is perhaps the most autobiographical section of the novel, though in writing about the outsider Frank makes Quincy's intellectuality, sensitivity, and shyness the reasons for his alienation from the Ivy League institution. Nothing is said of anti-Semitism, which is replaced by the school's vacuous philistinism. The novel's major conflict is between the ideal and the quotidian. Talking to his friend Garsted, Quincy can't accept that he is connected to the harshness of the world represented by the city of New York: "A sense of harmony with filthy hovels and cruel skycrapers!" But Garsted retorts, "Absolutely. Something in them is in you,—is truth." Although Garsted forces Quincy to admit that his visit to the city is "a visit to myself in extension," Quincy's parting words foreshadow the young man's ultimate defeat: "If I belong to the world, there's that within me objects to it. It cries out, objecting. It felt the beauty, that day. And, as you say, that meant that it recognized a fellowship, a harmony. But it hurt, Garsted,—it hurt like being crushed!" Here is Kabnis's retreat from Georgia's contraries: its stunning beauty, its apalling brutality and ugliness. And in Garsted's analysis of Quincy is a situation very close to the exchanges between Kabnis and Lewis near the end of *Cane*.[44]

The Unwelcome Man presented a picture of the "stranger" different from that of *Our America*. In *Our America* Frank was unhesitant about celebrating innovative Jewish artists like Stieglitz and Rosenfeld, but in *The Unwelcome Man* he was much more cautious about matters of "race" or ethnicity. Though Frank would explain that he made his protagonist an Anglo-Saxon because being an "outsider" in America crossed class or race lines, he also

knew, as Toomer most certainly knew, that there was a great difference between bohemian rebellion and American racial antagonisms. Behind his
affirmation of a renewed America created by an act of will was an America
violently resistant to any "cosmopolitan" ideal. In making Quincy a weak,
Gentile hero, Frank avoided admitting that what destroyed him lay beyond
character, and within society.

In the same letter in which he commented on _The Unwelcome Man,_ Toomer
asked Frank about the negotiations with Liveright for _Cane's_ publication
and updated him on the progress of the book:

> Since last writing you, I've written a new piece, and have rewitten [_sic_] Theatre. Only
> one sketch more, and Cane will be ready. The design for this is clear in my mind.
> Another week like the two just past will see it finished. If pushed, there's no reason
> why Cane cant be sent to you by the first of next week. All I have to do is to double
> type certain of the things. And then, when Box Seat (thats the title of the piece I
> have still to write) is ready, I can send it on, for you to insert where I indicate.[45]

The "new piece" was "Blood-Burning Moon," and Toomer also mentions
that he has "sent Kabnis to Lola Ridge," indicating that the major revision
of that long piece was complete. _Broom_ would publish selections from "Kabnis," with further revisions, in August and September 1923. Shortly after
this, on December 12, Toomer sent Frank the rough draft of _Cane,_ announcing "Cane is on its way to you! For two weeks I have worked steadily
at it. The book is done." [46]

Frank had approached his own publisher, Horace Liveright, to recommend publication of Toomer's manuscript sometime after their return from
Spartanburg in the fall of 1922. Toomer appears to have had no contact
with Liveright until after _Cane_ was accepted, though he said to Frank, "I
admire Boni and Liveright as publishers. I consider them the best." After
receiving the rough draft in December, Frank read it and passed it on to
Horace Liveright. Sometime around New Year's Liveright agreed to publish the book, and Frank sent a telegram announcing the news to Toomer.
He followed with a letter saying he was to meet with Liveright on January 8,
"at which time I will talk matters over with him. I shall bring back the ms
to Darien [Frank's Connecticut home] and go over it carefully. . . . He will
then of course send you a contract." Frank's later criticisms of the middle
section of _Cane_ probably date from this rereading of the rough draft.[47]

At Darien Frank gave the manuscript a close reading. He praised most of
it, but remarked of several poems, " 'Something is Melting Down in Washington,' 'Tell me,' 'Glaciers of Dusk,' and 'Prayer' I consider _failures_—and I
heartily recommend that you do not publish them in so beautiful a book."
Toomer's reply, undated but probably written in mid-January, illustrates
just how closely involved Frank was in the final version of _Cane._ Toomer
opens with, "Here's how your points strike me," and continues:

Yes, cut out Something is Melting etc., Tell Me, Sonnet, and Glaciers of Dusk. I rejected poems as good as these. I retained these fellows on grounds that have no real artistic validity. So cut em out. I'm not so sure about Prayer. I know it is an imperfect realization. As you say, some day I'll write it. But its *idea* is essential to the spiritual phase of CANE. And it is the companion piece, the only companion piece to Harvest Song. I am almost willing to sacrifice the artistic to the spiritual curve in this instance. Think over it, will you brother, and give me your final thought. I'm enclosing two new poems. If you like them, if you think they fit, I'll include them.[48]

As he had followed Frank's selection from the initial group of manuscripts in April, Toomer now gave Frank final choice among the poems to be included in *Cane*'s middle section, and, judging from the rejected titles that we know, Frank made good choices. "Prayer," which did appear in *Cane*, is perhaps the weakest piece in the book, but Toomer's remark that "Prayer" is "the only companion piece to Harvest Song" also points to a structural order in which the poems were linked to other poems as well as to stories.[49] Frank's poem selections evidently disrupted Toomer's original order for the second part of the book, as Toomer says:

These rejections and inclusions call for a rearrangement of the Washington cycle. Here's my offhand grouping:
Seventh Street.
Rhobert.
Calling Jesus?
Avey.
Bee-hive.
Storm Ending.
Theatre.
Her lips are copper wire.
3 in 1.
Box Seat.
Prayer.
Harvest Song.
Bona and Paul.[50]

"Calling Jesus," which Toomer tentatively listed after "Rhobert" here, would eventually replace "3 in 1"; otherwise, this order is what would appear in the published *Cane*. Frank had approved the revision of "Kabnis," and Toomer noted, "I am mighty glad that Kabnis stands with you. You know what it is. It took a year to grow within me. For it to have been wrong—foundations and everything else would shake." Toomer depended on Frank's judgment both for selecting what to include in *Cane* and for the line editing of the manuscript: "Your marginal notes through out the mss are splendid. I do use 'curious' loosely. I was half aware of the fact, but never strictly checked myself up. Your sensitivity to muddy, ragged lines and passages is unerring. Thanks brother, thanks!"[51]

Frank's criticism of the first draft of *Cane* included some reservations about the latest stories added to the manuscript, and Toomer agreed to continue working on them:

Box Seat should have come off good. It is a first writing but I had the thing completely in hand before I began to write. It was written however at the very end of my rush to get CANE off (and so was B-B Moon). I was tired and sort of dry. This may account for the lack you feel in it. And of course, all of my stuff gains in the second trial. When my mind clears up, I'll see what I can do. Likewise Bona and Paul. When should I get the mss back to you?[52]

Toomer's revision of "Box Seat" must have altered it in a substantial way, however, because when Frank saw it he complained that the story was breaking out into "formlessness" and that the proposed revision belonged to "another phase." Toomer, in turn, explained that in his first version of the story he wanted his hero, Dan Moore, "to be sensitive, but weak." In the new version Dan "expanded," became stronger, and "this new energy is ragged, dynamic, perhaps vicious." But the new Dan posed a problem, since his characterization needed to be consonant with the first version's ending: "Can this new energy, this greater strength slough off up the alley?" Frank preferred the old ending, and Toomer let it stand, but he also left in the line Frank disliked: "JESUS WAS ONCE A LEPER." The conflict between Frank's preference for a weak character (Toomer was reading *The Unwelcome Man* as he wrote "Box Seat") and Toomer's urge to make him more heroic finally produced one of the most complicated and interesting figures in *Cane.*[53]

The discussions about the stories in the middle section of *Cane* continued nearly into the spring of 1923, well after the book had been accepted for publication. On February 27 Toomer sent the revised manuscript of *Cane* to Horace Liveright, and by the summer of 1923 Toomer and Frank were discussing errors and corrections in the page proofs for the book. In a letter of August 1923 Frank wrote, "Rushing through Cane hurriedly as I have, I am struck quite afresh by its colossal power. Box-Seat strikes me right, now." But growing tensions had been apparent in the letters between the two men during that spring. Within a year after *Cane*'s September publication Toomer had become a student of Gurdjieff at Fontainebleau, outside Paris. From France he wrote to Frank, "I am inarticulate. Never before have I been so intense and conscious; and I cannot recall the time when I have been so dead." It seems, then, that the high point of the literary friendship between the two men had been reached in the letter Frank sent in early January of 1923 confirming Liveright's acceptance of *Cane.* Frank had concluded, "I say quite openly to you that I know no one now in America in whom I have higher hopes, and no one to whom I feel quite so close."[54]

The Son of Two Fathers

Toomer's ability to absorb, reconstitute, and refigure his sources was re-markable, and this skill was a mark of his modernism. Although Waldo Frank was the primary influence on the writing of *Cane*, the book is very different from any of Frank's fictional work. Indeed, one can see in the style of *Cane* a balance between the styles of Frank and Sherwood Anderson. Toomer chose Frank as his model in part because his fiction had those mystical "elements" that Toomer thought all art should have (or, as Toomer put it, it had the elements "that I need"). In contrast, Toomer told Gorham Munson, Anderson's artistic vision after *Winesburg* was mired in the commonplace, "all prose, not a thought that one can bite into, and even that curiously golden emotion that came out in his Winesburg sketches seems thinning." Toomer would even complain to Frank, the man most responsible for creating an audience for Anderson, that Anderson was "like a carriage dog nosing the dust and flowers of a mid-western roadside," always moving in a straight line, his perception of reality circumscribed by the road.[55]

Anderson's fiction does smell of the "dust and flowers," while Frank's approach to "roadside" reality is almost always filtered through an abstract realm of ideas. Yet despite Toomer's apparent preference for Frank, *Cane* represents a kind of fusion of Anderson and Frank, a balance of opposites that gives the book its special blend of the visceral and the cerebral. *Cane* also illustrates Toomer's relationship to Anderson and Frank as one that combines his respect for the older writers with his real desire to best them at their own game. In *Cane* Toomer took a phrase, a character, and a situation from Anderson and complicated it with themes of caste and class; he used Frank's metaphysics to develop the tensions between wholeness and division, and the conflicts within the race as well as outside it.[56]

The Sherwood Anderson that Toomer admired was the Anderson of *Our America*. In the letters he exchanged with Anderson after completing *Cane* were echoes of Frank's assessment of *Winesburg*:

There is a golden strength about your art that can come from nothing less than a creative elevation of experience, however bitter or abortive the experience may have been. Your images are clean, glowing, healthy, vibrant: sunlight on forks of trees, on mellow piles of pine boards. Your acute sense of the separateness of life could easily have led to a lean pessimism in a less abundant soul. Your Yea! to life is one of the clear fine tones in our medley of harsh discordant sounds.[57]

The echoes from *Our America*—the religious impulse, the affirmation of life—are obvious but are here given a Toomerian twist in the son/sun of "The Song of the Son," the poet in search of images to describe the South as "down home": "sunlight on forks of trees, on mellow piles of pine boards." This was not the Toomer who wrote of the Gothic house in "Becky" as

the South in ruins, nor the Toomer who identified with Kabnis, the disconnected writer whose "words"—"split-gut, tortured, twisted"—feed the
nightmare ("th form") "thats burned int my soul." Still, the South in "Kabnis" revealed another Anderson influence, the night world of *Winesburg*
that reappeared among the lonely, anguished souls in Halsey's cellar.[58]

Perhaps Toomer's reservations about Anderson were a rejection of a
commonplace side of himself which he did not want to believe existed. He
accepted Gorham Munson's judgment of Anderson's art because it was a
kind of reassurance that Toomer was *not* like Anderson, and as a writer he
depended on Frank's appreciation of his "spiritual" qualities. Yet, despite
his superb editing, his necessary encouragements, and other assistance, it
is not clear that Frank ever really understood *Cane*. His foreword described
Cane as "the aesthetic equivalent to the land," as if modernity and urbanization were not equally important issues. Even more misleading, he spoke of
Toomer's view of the South as a kind of idyll: "For Toomer, the Southland is
not a problem to be solved; it is a field of loveliness to be sung: the Georgia
Negro is not a downtrodden soul to be uplifted; he is material for gorgeous
painting." And, finally, he mentioned the "looseness" of *Cane*'s "form" as
though he had shut his eyes to its intricate, collage structure, an error that
is especially surprising in light of his knowledge of Toomer's admiration
for *City Block*. In a letter, Toomer insisted that sending Frank those manuscripts was "a natural step in their *expression*," and he seemed to expect that
the "Introduction" Frank was to write for *Cane* would be a tangible embodiment of the book's spirit and the "spiritual bond" between the two men.
Ultimately, Frank seemed more interested in answering Mary Austin's attack on him as a New York critic who knew nothing about the hinterlands
than in confronting *Cane*'s Gothicism, its modernism, and its brilliant and
complex treatment of black life, particularly the theme of miscegenation.[59]

Toomer's understanding of the position of African-Americans in the
United States also led him away from Frank's vision of American culture
and politics, even though Toomer wanted to abide by the optimism of *Our
America*. Frank saw Anderson as the American folk's historian, and in the
case of *Winesburg* as a witness to the folk's "passing" from the American
scene. "For that which is in each one of them [the American Folk] to love,
frail and tenuous and passing is incarnate in you. You are in a miraculous
way the soul of this people," Frank wrote to Anderson in 1919. However,
"Seventh Street" in *Cane* illustrated an optimism different from Frank's,
one that was based on a conception of a "folk" who retained their ability
to resist the hegemony of a "mechanical civilization." The energy there—
its "crude new life"—was "pure Negro" in conflict with both the Puritan-
pioneer tradition ("the whitewashed wood of Washington") and American
modernity. Instead of America "absorbing" the Negro, Toomer depicted
the Negro absorbing America, taking the "Ballooned" Cadillac and integrating it into *their* culture. What makes the middle section of *Cane* so fas-

cinating is just this tension between a mass culture that absorbs black life and a black folk that in turn absorbs mass culture but recreates it in terms of a new black life.[60]

That new black life retained its integrity because of American racism. Segregation also, ironically, revitalized the black peasant world, as the Dixie Pike came alive at night, "grown from a goat path in Africa," *because* the system of segregation ensured an unbroken connection between past and present, ensuring the creation of a unique black culture separate from the American mainstream. Thus, in one sense time has stood still—racism is the constant in American culture. *Cane* continually recalls how racism in the South and the North keeps bringing the past to the surface of the present, how in fact little has changed between then and now, despite the "new life" of Seventh Street that Anderson could not understand. Finally, the meanings of "Karintha" and "Fern" had little to do with the melding of black life into some American "common soul." Fern's "spirit" preserved an inviolate connection with the history and community outside of the white man's laws or religion, and Karintha's dead child was a reminder that the terrors of history are hardly ended. The smoke from the sawdust pile that rises above the grave and "spreads itself out over the valley" is a metaphor for how thoroughly the past continues to permeate the present. Prohibition and the war created the "bastard" of Seventh Street, a figurative expression of the miscegenation that created Karintha's child. The street as "bastard" was a triumph of black life's ability to absorb the impact of the white world; the corpse under the sawdust pile reflected the devastating effect of white upon black. Thus when Anderson told Toomer to keep close to the conditions that produced *Cane*, even though his life as a Negro writer would be "hellish," he saw something that had entirely eluded Frank. He saw that the demonic was as important to *Cane* as the sun/son.

Chapter 6
The Gothic Detective Story

> The race-sex-sin spiral had begun. The more trails the white man made to back-yard cabins, the higher he raised his white wife on her pedestal when he returned to the big house. . . . Guilt, shame, fear, lust spiralled each other.
>
> —Lillian Smith, *Killers of the Dream*, 1949

> I went to the rock to hide my face;
> the rock cried out, "No hiding place,
> No hiding place down here."
>
> —African-American spiritual

As a work of modernism *Cane* surpassed Toomer's models—the works of Sherwood Anderson and Waldo Frank—in the sophistication of its narrative. Additionally, however, the book was related to the popular genres of the detective and the Gothic, and Toomer used those generic backdrops to direct and characterize his own revelation of "our America." Plotted with modernist indirection, Toomer's book is a mystery, and his various narrators act as detectives, with each story, sketch, or poem contributing a clue toward the mystery's solution or, in Waldo Frank's terms, a piece of the yet incomplete "mosaic." The solution will not solve a particular murder, but will illuminate a *kind* of American murder, native to a culture in which the contradictions of the nation's origins manifest themselves in relations of race, gender, and class. What is more, *Cane*, like the stories of Edgar Allan Poe, will be a mystery invested with Gothic horror.

Terry Eagleton has pointed out that there are interconnections among "Gothic horror tale, detective mystery, autobiography, [and] political history." What these genres have in common is their concern with the past: "In Gothic, history weighs like a nightmare on the present; in consumerist capitalism, the present eradicates the past. Detective stories, by contrast, put time in reverse: they start with the culmination of a history—a corpse—and then reconstruct what led up to it. So too does autobiography, which strives to reclaim the past from the vantage-point of the present."[1] Like Eagleton's mystery story, *Cane* begins with a corpse and from that beginning looks back in time for a solution; what it gradually reveals is not *who* the murderer was, but *why* the murder took place.

The past is eradicated not only by consumer societies: in the South, racist myth and the Lost Cause created a redemptionist history that served to deny and disguise the nature of race relations in the region. Because they are moving in a society defined by a history that has been erased, and which cannot be safely mentioned, Toomer's narrators in the first part of *Cane* and in "Kabnis" can never quite say what they see nor, at times, make sense of what they see: there is always a disjunction between the characters' actions and the secret social terms by which they act. Their indirection results both from fear and from misunderstanding, the dilemma of the singer in "Harvest Song" who both "hungers" and "fears knowledge of my hunger." Toomer's narrators want to look and want not to look, for what they see always draws them deeply into the matters of "race" and American identity. Where the writing is at its most brilliant is where that tension between looking and not looking creates a tortured, imagistic text.

In *Cane*'s opening sketch, Karintha kills her newborn baby and buries the corpse in the sawdust heap of a sawmill. This story, told with indirection and by the accumulation of details, forces the reader to interpret these "clues" in order to understand what happened. The corpse will be visible only as "smoke" from the "pyramidal sawdust pile" rising in the air, its trace the "odd wraiths" that the smoke makes "about the trees."[2] The Enlightenment banished ghosts, just as the Founding Fathers promised to restore liberty to the new American commonwealth, but the presence of slavery in enlightenment America denied liberty and reintroduced ghosts through the back door of domestic space; the trace of the corpse, the smoke from the "pyramidal sawdust pile [that] spreads itself out over the valley," rises from the history of violence at the heart of the American polis. In the book's first section, that history is made explicit in its concluding story, "Blood-Burning Moon," but even then *Cane* remains an "analytical" detective story wherein the solution opens up yet another mystery.[3]

The narrator of "Karintha" speaks in the secret manner by which racial matters are expressed in Sempter. He says enough for the careful reader to understand what happens to the child but omits a crucial fact, which the reader (as an outsider to the community and its immediate concerns) is unlikely even to notice. The missing fact—"Who gave it to her?" Who is the child's father?—is brought up in the following story, "Becky," but the continuously unraveling mystery, the act of uncovering the solution to a crime, does not move only from point A to point B along a straight line. As Eve Sedgwick notes, the theme of "live burial," a convention common to the Gothic, points to the narrative structure of "within"-ness: "a story within a story within a story within a story." So the thread or clue of

Karintha's buried child is repeated by "dead birds . . . found / In wells a hundred feet below the ground" in "November Cotton Flower"; by Becky's "live burial" under her fallen chimney in "Becky"; by the lynchers' intention to have Tom Burwell's burned body fall to the "bottom" of the well in "Blood-Burning Moon"; in Rhobert's sinking into the mud of the river bottom in "Rhobert." Similarly, the final clues about Karintha's child will appear only in "Kabnis," the long story that ends *Cane*, where the images of "live burial" also come to full realization in the portraits of the walking dead in Halsey's cellar.[4]

Like Gothic narratives, *Cane* progresses through circular repetition that both reveals and conceals. The ubiquitous dead child is one source of *Cane*'s Gothicism, as are the lynched man or woman ("Portrait in Georgia," "Blood-Burning Moon," "Kabnis"), decaying flesh ("Face"), maimed or murdered animals ("Reapers," "Kabnis," "November Cotton Flower")— and these figures also bear witness to something hidden. Gothicism in *Cane* depends for its effects on the hidden past erupting into the present, upsetting the social order, and raising questions about good and evil that conventional morality cannot answer. In the post-Reconstruction South, that morality revolved around the issue of black-white relationships and especially the "moral" issue of lynching. The most obvious extension of the white authority of the slave era, lynching demolished claims for a "New South" or "white civilization." Lynching is central to *Cane*, as violent fact and as whispered fear, reflecting both the society of the New South— where, after 1880, in the words of one contemporary observer, it became "a popular sport"—and the precise historical situation in Georgia that stood "first in the list of states in the matter of lynching." Gothicism often deals with the fantastic made commonplace, the ghastly as part of the normal, the realization that no nightmare is ever as terrifying as the reality of waking "from a dream and find[ing] it true."[5]

Southern lynching was a variety of Gothic murder, replete with mutilation and macabre rituals, and it came to infect every aspect of the society that specialized in it. A popular Southern writer at the turn of the century, Thomas Nelson Page, wrote on the subject as the South's spokesman to the North. One of his typical essays, "The Lynching of Negroes—Its Cause and Its Prevention," claimed to discuss the subject dispassionately so that "the matter shall be clearly and thoroughly understood." He deplored lynching "as a serious menace to our civilization," and in his concern for its "real injury"—not to its victims but to the "perpetrators"—he observed that it destroyed the legal and moral foundations of community and culture. Thus, although he ended by tacitly defending the necessity of lynching, he embodied the voice of "reason" crying out to the wilderness of misunderstanding in both North and South.[6]

Page's explanation of lynching repeated by rote the South's standard justification: lynching had become common practice in the South because black men, freed from the constraints of slavery, raped white women. "Talk of social equality" during Reconstruction and an "absence of a strong restraining public opinion among the negroes" themselves had released brutal passions in "the inferior race" (44). In Page's argument the empirical evidence of this crime was assumed or proclaimed as evident: "in the last twenty years . . . hundreds of [white] women and a number of children have been ravished and slain" (42). In the Southern justice system, the intention to rape was proof enough, especially when it involved the proximity of a black man and a white woman. The solution, too, was obvious: return blacks to a plantation condition where they were once content and convince them that their best interests demand that they remain there.

Up to a point Page presented his case as a reasoned argument, yet the Gothic implications of what he said seemed to accumulate, to demand an outlet. They burst forth at last in a long passage about the suffering of white women at the hands of black rapists. Page evoked "the unnamable brutality with which the causing crime was, in nearly every case, attended . . . [horrors] so unspeakable that they have never been put in print . . . unnamable horrors which have outraged the minds of those who live in regions where they have occurred, and where they might occur again, and, upsetting reason, have swept from their bearings cool men and changed them into madmen, drunk with the lust of revenge" (38). There have been many careful studies of lynching, beginning with the work of Page's contemporary Ida B. Wells, and none has ever discovered charges of black men's sexual assault on white women as the major cause of lynching in the South. W. Fitzhugh Brundage's detailed study of lynching in Georgia shows that of the 236 lynchings in the state between 1900 and 1919 only 45 were even *alleged* to be retribution for sexual offenses. In fact, the evidence is clear that the intimidation of black people to ensure their subordination in the racial hierarchy was always the primary purpose of lynching. That subordination was primarily economic, but also social; African-Americans were oppressed according to both class and caste.[7]

The "unnamable" and the "unspeakable" infected Page's prose at the point where his denunciation of lynching changed inevitably into its justification. The Gothic slipped into his speech not from the imaginary reign of a "black terror," but as the secret heritage of slavery, of lynching as the enforcement of a new slavery, and of a white supremacy that included the sexual exploitation of black women. Page ended his plea for rationality by dwelling on the irrational in human nature: if reason did not prevail, if these "suggestions . . . cannot be carried out, it is because the ravishings by negroes and the murders by mobs have their roots so deep in racial instincts that nothing can eradicate them, and in such case the ultimate issue will be a resort to the final test of might, which in the last analysis underlies everything" (48).

From the perspective of another century Page's essay reads like "A Modest Proposal" without irony. Its last sentence, indebted to the social Darwinism popular at the time, illuminates the Gothic nightmare: there is no place of grace because power/desire "underlies everything." The system of Southern agriculture needed cheap, intimidated labor, even as the Southern caste system depended on the ritual subordination of African-Americans. Lynching served both interconnected systems, as did attacks on black women, and only changing Page's victims from white women to black women would reveal what was hidden, truly "unnamable," in his essay.[8]

Miscegenation is the thing in *Cane* not *named* but always there, like the corpse beneath the sawdust pile. It is the "hidden truth" the detective-author uncovers which surfaces like an angry moon: "Up from the dusk the full moon came." In the context of the traditional South, as W.E.B. Du Bois saw in *Darkwater* (1920), it also meant the "damnation of women," especially black women. In slavery, the child followed the condition of the mother, because "paternity is always ambiguous, whereas maternity is not. Slaveholders eventually recognized the advantage of a different and unambiguous rule of descent, one that would guarantee to owners all offspring of slave women, however fathered." "However fathered" explains why for Toomer the theme of miscegenation was an intricate web, involving not only white men and black women, white women and black men, but black men and black women. The question repeatedly asked about the women in these stories is "Who gave them their child?"[9]

Cane depicts a world in which black men and women cannot escape their racial history. Black women had endured coerced sexual relations with white men under slavery and after Emancipation; because black men could not prevent this rape, a gap was created between the two sexes that misunderstanding, mistrust, and violence might fill. Each story in *Cane*'s first section is about the pressure, communal, sexual, or familial, that men put on women. Courtship, a romantic relation between the sexes, always returns here to the matter of masculine control—in fact, the constant theme in the first section is of women trying to control their lives while men try to deny them that control. In *Darkwater*, W.E.B. Du Bois remembered "four women of my boyhood" who "were not beings, they were relations and these relations were enfilmed with mystery and secrecy." What Du Bois described was how women were denied existence outside of their social "relations" with men, while even those "relations" were "enfilmed with mystery." The women in *Cane*'s first section must attempt to negotiate an identity within the context of "relations" with both black and white men.[10]

Those relations might involve miscegenation, and because of the culture's racial codes that act necessarily generated "mystery." Social barriers are also thresholds, and once crossed they open up spaces that are unknown, making the familiar suddenly strange, producing the "uncanny." A miscegenated child was evidence that a boundary had been crossed; as Mary V. Dearborn observes, "The connection between the uncanny and miscegenation is clear: the mulatto . . . is a kind of uncanny text about the coherence and limits of the self." He or she was a visible expression of the broken taboo, the figure bearing witness to the innerconnection of past and present and "the site of the hybridity of histories." When there was no ocular proof of blackness, no "mark" that could be seen, the figure yet functioned as hidden history.[11]

Karintha's baby is such a figure. The image of "Karintha carrying beauty, perfect as dusk" is an ephemeral expression in the material world. On the threshold of puberty—"at twelve"—she "was a wild flash that told the other folks just what it was to live." That *perfection* can only be captured in a kinetic moment, "her sudden darting past you was a bit of vivid color, like a black bird that flashes in light" (1–2). Why do the black men of her community wish to hasten Karintha into maturity—"to ripen a growing thing too soon"? The desire of the men who count "time" is an attempt both to control her developing sexuality and to fix "in time" the emanation of the divine—to reduce Karintha's kinetic beauty to something static. "Karintha's running was a whir. It had the sound of the red dust that sometimes makes a spiral in the road" (3). Karintha creates a *figura* of eternity ("a spiral"), like Waldo Frank's "form of God in matter," the divine breaking through the finite clay. The story ends with an image of "her skin . . . like dusk on the eastern horizon" and Karintha's child entombed beneath a "pyramidal sawdust pile" that will take the cycle of a year to burn. The images connect Karintha with the east and with the myth of origins that lies beyond in Africa.[12]

The "spiral" associated with Karintha is a sign of circularity, of a rising that falls back to the same point, of the incarnation of matter within unseen forms, and of the movement of history. The young black men who have been counting time to mate with Karintha find they are too late. They have returned from the road or from the big cities to woo her, "but Karintha is a woman, and she has had a child. A child fell out of her womb onto a bed of pine needles in the forest" (4). It is the unspoken thing, the missing fact, that is crucial to the story's "mystery": Who gave Karintha that child? It is the question that is asked in the first lines of the following story, "Becky," and so inevitably reflects back on "Karintha"; but the secrecy surrounding Karintha's child means the question is asked only implicitly. The clue that answers the question is given earlier, in the "but" of "But Karintha is a woman," for it separates the black men who pursue her from the man who seduced or raped her.

Karintha's child "fell out of her womb onto a bed of pine-needles in the forest. Pine needles are smooth and sweet. They are elastic to the feet of rabbits." The ambiguity of this incomplete description is deepened in the imagist poem "Nullo," where falling "pine-needles" are lit by the "western horizon gold" that opposes Karintha's "eastern" beauty. The poem's central image is of the empty "dry moulds of cow-hoofs," a state of absence or nothingness ("nullo") in which the horror of the child's death goes unrecognized. Images of the spiral and of the pine smoke, of the falling child and killing, appear prominently in "Kabnis" in lines that extend "Karintha" and "Nullo" and weave together the simultaneous presence of beauty and terror. This is the effect Toomer referred to as "fusing" in the letter he wrote to Waldo Frank about his revision of "Kabnis," and these are lines in which Toomer's poetic prose slides into modernist poetry, fragments of a lullaby juxtaposed with fragments of folklore.

Kabnis has awakened from an uneasy half-sleep and jumps from his bed to capture a hen that has invaded his flimsy cabin:

With his fingers about her neck, he thrusts open the outside door and steps out into the serene loveliness of Georgian autumn moonlight. Some distance off, down in the valley, a band of pine-smoke, silvered gauze, drifts steadily. The half-moon is a white child that sleeps upon the tree-tops of the forest. White winds croon its sleep-song:
rock a-by baby . . .
Black mother sways, holding a white child on her bosom.
when the bough bends . . .
Her breath hums through pine-cones.
cradle will fall . . .
Teat moon-children at your breasts,
down will come baby . . .
Black mother.
Kabnis whirls the chicken by its neck, and throws the head away. Picks up the hopping body, warm, sticky, and hides it in a clump of bushes. (160–61)

The phrase "the half-moon is a white child" follows directly on the drifting "pine-smoke" of Karintha's burning sawdust pile, and leads to the "black mother [who] sways, holding a white child on her bosom." Lines from "Rock-a-By Baby" alternate with images from the pine forest, and the broken nursery rhyme is bracketed by Kabnis's killing the chicken and hiding its body under a bush, repeating the fate of Karintha's child. Toomer combines white and black in the image of the "half-moon," suggesting that the child at the breast of the black mother is a "half-breed"; as a mulatto child is like a changeling left by fairies, its identity is a mystery because it is neither black nor white. The ominous fall of the cradle recalls Karintha's child as it falls to Earth: the white winds' "sleep-song" is a death song, and as "her breath hums through pine-cones" the black mother drops the white child.[13]

The clues pointing to infanticide and miscegenation appear as images and phrases in "Karintha," but their meaning is not clarified until the last long story in *Cane*. Even there these clues remain indirect intimations rather than statements, unmistakable only in light of all that occurs between beginning and end. As Toomer said to Gorham Munson, "Mystery cannot help but accompany a deep, clear-cut image." The image of the child is like the ghostly presence of miscegenation, not "pictorial" yet "clear-cut" in the way it haunts the landscape throughout *Cane*. The mystery that accompanies it "spreads" like the curling smoke from the sawdust pile, permeating everything, even the water; the murder, though undiscovered, will have its effect. As Du Bois suggests in *Darkwater*, if one destroys the power of Isis, the goddess of the moon, someday the life force will enact its revenge.[14]

The delayed link between "Karintha" and "Kabnis" illustrates Toomer's modernist narration technique. Frederick Karl has described a similar method in Joseph Conrad's and Ford Madox Ford's "progression d'effet," a method "by which they meant objects and people became clarified progressively as the narrative proceeded; what was ambiguous and murky, even disguised, gained substance in successive stages." One of the supplementary effects of a "murky" narrative is to give particular significance to what is "missing" in the story, as "the void or absence of something gives meaning, *there* by virtue of its negation." Thus Karintha's child becomes a powerful presence because it is *not* mentioned, its vanishing always associated with "bands" of pine smoke.[15]

The narrator of "Karintha" apparently knows what has taken place, the circumstances behind the story, yet chooses to tell it in an oblique and incomplete way. That narration reproduces the aura of secrecy, the concealment—as well as the countering gossip that tries to reveal—which will characterize all the stories in *Cane*'s first section. Before Layman tells the story of Mame Lamkins in "Kabnis" he says, "White folks know that niggers talk, an they dont mind jes so long as nothing come of it" (178). Yet Layman is still reluctant to talk because he can't be sure how "white folks" might judge the talk: to reveal a secret history is to open the possibility that something may "come of it." The line between amused white tolerance and lynching is dangerously vague, and Layman knows that vagueness is deliberate.

Toomer's narrative is constructed with political purpose. As Allon White observes of modernist writing, "Obscurity, then, is the linguistic defense of vulnerable offenders against public codes." Toomer's story is not accidentally obscure; in fact, one of its subjects is the circumstances that necessitate obscurity, the constraints African-Americans in the South faced in their day-to-day negotiation of the dangerous territory between private histories and the white myths of public life. This reflects, again, on the barbershop talk in Sparta which Toomer recorded, where it was said that enemies of the "leading white man" in town called him "nigger behind his back." This remark brought the talk to a sudden end:

Then dead silence. I could see and almost feel their lips shut tight. All three suddenly felt that too much had been said. Forbidden words had been forced out. It was too late to recall them, but silence might cover them. Silence had to cover them, had to knock them down from the walls so that the walls could not echo them around the town.

"Lips shut tight," "forbidden words," and "silence" are parts of the narrative method Toomer devised for the first section of *Cane*. Through the openings of that narrative some forbidden words appear, as "night winds" ("vagrant poets") whisper secret, coded messages through the "cracks" of Kabnis's walls (157).[16]

The white South defined miscegenation practically as the rape of white women by black men. Within the black community, of course, the understanding was very different—by 1920 an estimated 70 percent of African-Americans were of mixed race, and that huge total had nothing to do with black men's rape of white women.[17] Karintha's secrecy about her child indicates some communal violation beyond mere illegitimacy, and that disruption is hinted at in the poem that follows her story. "Reapers" describes a mechanical mower drawn by "black horses" that cuts up a squealing "field rat." More antipastoral than the work of Robert Burns, the poem depicts the suppressed anger of the black field hands, whose motivation is both economic and sexual. Killing the rat, they foreshadow Bane's slashing his friend in "Carma" and the death of Bob Stone in "Blood-Burning Moon." In the post-Reconstruction South, sexual exploitation of black women was an act of political terror, a way of intimidating both black women and black men. And although Karintha's child is a private scandal, the world of whispered facts and gossip, like secret miscegenation, powerfully affects the action in *Cane*.[18]

One of Toomer's usual structural devices is to balance pairs of stories or poems, allowing each piece to play against the other. The matching poem to "Reapers," the sonnet "November Cotton Flower," looks forward to something "never seen before," and in the following story, "Becky," a "poor Catholic poor-white" woman gives birth to a mulatto child and ignites a public scandal. The townspeople ask of Becky's child, "Who gave it to her?" They try to contain the event within the meaning of madness, although the child calls up other original mysteries, including the immaculate conception. The "words" of the townspeople change Becky into a mechanical doll: "Mouth setting in a twist that held her eyes, harsh, vacant, staring" (8). She is exiled to a cabin that mirrors her dispossession, on "ground islandized between the road and the railroad track." Like Karintha's child, Becky's sign becomes a "wraith of smoke," and no one, in fact, discovers who fathered her child, or even if Becky is under the fallen chimney at the story's end.

The townspeople build the house for Becky, then they clothe and feed her, but they do so "unknown . . . to each other" (10). Their ambivalence is reflected by the "eye-shaped piece of sandy ground" (9) where they place her. They "cast her out"—the phrase is repeated three times—by putting her outside their line of sight, yet they place her on a "sandy" island nearby. Throughout the sketch Toomer uses the image of the eye to suggest the "uncanny," thereby evoking Freud's 1919 essay, "The Uncanny," a kind of modernist reflection on the nature of the Gothic. Becky's house is something "pushed up where a blue-sheen God with listless eyes could look at it." She exists in liminal space and on unstable terrain, neither this nor that. When Becky has a second miscegenated son, the townspeople imagine her dead, their wish couched in terms of a pious circumlocution that evades any personal responsibility: "Nothing was said, for the part of man that says things to the likes of that had told itself that if there was a Becky, that Becky now was dead" (10).[19]

Becky in fact had disappeared after her house was built, her only remaining sign the smoke from her chimney, which shakes when trains pass: "A creepy feeling came over all who saw that thin wraith of smoke and felt the trembling of the ground" (11). The town speaks of her as dead because she had transgressed the most absolute, and therefore the most compelling, communal taboo; fascinated by that taboo, the community continually watches the cabin, which it also pretends does not exist. Edgar Allan Poe, says Joan Dayan, understood "the power in the word *my*." That is, possession taps into the demonic: the possessor is also the possessed, as the townspeople are in "Becky" when they anxiously wait to hear the "true word" of her fate.[20]

In *Cane*, Toomer reshapes Gothic conventions to fit the American scene, particularly the South. In European Gothicism, the paranoia of a triumphant middle class took the form of fiction about decadent aristocrats, labyrinthian castles, and endangered maidens, all distorted mirrors of its own insecurity and illegitimacy. Captains of industry claimed to "free" human beings from a feudalistic order, but the ruthless rule of supply and demand meant not only that feudalism was recreated in a new form (wage-slaves replacing serfs), but that now one could fall as quickly as other people rose. American Gothicism differs from its European antecedents in that in fiction like Charles Brockden Brown's *Edgar Huntly*, Poe's "The Gold Bug," and William Faulkner's *Absalom, Absalom!* homegrown horrors from an American past—the legacy of slavery, the theft of Indian land—created new secrets and lies, and these often appear in new spatial configurations. In "Becky," the Gothic ruin is Becky's cabin—not a castle (*The Castle of Otranto*) or a monastery (*The Monk*), but domestic space or, more precisely, the symbol of domestic space: the hearth.

Yet the domestic space valorized by the South also existed within a complex of spatial configurations inherited from the Georgics and *hortus conclusus*, European literary conventions also connected to the favorite fables of the nation: the sturdy yeoman farmer, the small town as the backbone of civilization, the myth of origins. All these American social fictions conceal reality by mythologizing history, a process true also of the Old South, as W. J. Cash noted: "For more than half its cotton was sold in the European market, and the price of it was fixed, not in New Orleans or Charleston or Savannah and not even in New York or Boston but in Liverpool." If the South's economy gave the lie to its fiction of a self-sufficient, homogeneous space, the violence of the nation's founding also called into question the myth of harmony. The settlement of Georgia was a war of conquest, and the development of the state's economy was soon dependent on slave labor.[21]

In "Becky" what Homi K. Bhabha has called "the unhomely moment" destroys domestic myth, as "the world" enters the home and the house presumed to be a refuge from external danger literally falls down. The collapse of Becky's house produces the kind of revelation Freud discussed in "The Uncanny," and Toomer may have borrowed Freud's notion of *heimlich* (homelike, familiar) in the story. The connection between "homelike" and "familiar" is tied to eyesight: something seen often enough to be familiar. Yet Freud notes that *heimlich* also implies "the notion of something hidden," as closets and basements might contain things that are not seen, hence *unheimlich* (unfamiliar). When Barlo and the narrator come upon Becky's cabin, something strange happens to the two men's perception of the scene. The elements of an ordinary day suddenly seem strange and confusing—the stillness, the thin smoke from the chimney, "even the pines were stale, sticky, like the smell of food that makes you sick" (11). The narrator feels goosebumps: "Eyes left their sockets for the cabin. Ears burned and throbbed. Uncanny eclipse! Fear closed my mind" (12). Before their eyes the cabin collapses, and although both Barlo and the narrator believe Becky must have been buried under the rubble of her home, neither one sees her. Like Karintha's dead child, she is "something hidden," and because neither the child's body nor Becky's corpse is ever *seen*, they both point to what is hidden, to a secret history.[22]

The narration of "Becky" begins in the third person, and, as in "Karintha," the narrator knows as much as town rumor and gossip relate. In the fourth of the story's five short sections, however, the narrator suddenly asks of Becky's sons, "We, who had cast out their mother because of them, could we take them in?" (11). This shift into the first person plural becomes the mode of the story's final section, and that change moves the narration from the spectatorship of the third person to the terrified participation of the first-person narrator, as he and Barlo "were pulled out of their seats. Dragged to the door that had swung open" (12). Somehow compelled to witness Becky's death, the two men still don't know what they have seen, though they will become the town's only source of information. "Barlo, mumbling something, threw his bible on the pile. (No one has ever touched it.)" When Barlo and the narrator reach the town and tell their story, the townspeople want "the true word" of Becky's end as a narrative that will satisfy the communal need for completion and a restored social order.[23]

But Toomer ends the story as he began it, repeating a refrain that intimates that Becky's tale will not fit into the narratives the townspeople wish to hear:

Becky was the white woman who had two
Negro sons. She's dead; they've gone away.
The pines whisper to Jesus. The Bible flaps
its leaves with an aimless rustle on her mound. (13)

The Bible that Barlo threw on the rubble as he and the narrator fled remains silent, but it will be alluded to in Father John's single remark in
"Kabnis." The townspeople want a simple story, but the banishment of
Becky represents a situation for which there is no simple "true word." The
story begins as a mystery: "Becky had one Negro son. Who gave it to her?"
Becky herself "wouldn't tell," and the story ends with *no* witness to tell. The
story is as secret and deceptive as Karintha's, with an ending that is not an
end. The two sketches reveal the shifting boundary line between the known
and the unknown characteristic of Gothic and detective fiction.[24]

Secret Talk in "Carma" and "Fern"

"Carma" continues with the first-person narration that emerged in "Becky."
The question posed at the end of "Becky" as to what history, or whose history, may be told becomes the main subject of "Carma." Secret talk, the
meeting of rumor and public information where the "unspeakable" in fact
may be spoken, is a theme throughout *Cane*'s first part, but in the three
stories with a first-person narrator, that narrator's uncertainty further complicates the telling of the "true word." In "Carma" the narrator calls the
story within a story "the crudest melodrama," the tale as it might have
been told by the *Ishmaelite*: "Her husband's in the gang. And its her fault
he got there. Working with a contractor, he was away most of the time. She
had others" (18). The depictions of adultery, deception, and violence that
follow this opening create a story to confirm for white people that African-
Americans are essentially "other," but Carma's story is also melodramatic
because of her gender; she is a femme fatale, a bad woman, a hot-blooded
"mulatta."[25]

The "unspeakable" in "Carma" is never expressed directly, but there are
clues to its presence, clues that are already familiar. In the opening lines
framing the "crudest melodrama," "Smoke curls up. Marvelous web spun by
the spider sawdust pile" (17). There is a double allusion: to the storytelling
tradition of the African Anansi stories and to the web of mystery surrounding Karintha's child. The web spun by the sawdust pile is also "composite"
in a diabolic sense: black and white histories in the South are intertwined
like a web with a corpse at the center. That intricate web speaks of marvels,
playing on the root meaning of the word: *mirabilis*, the extraordinary *seen*
or, in the Apostle Paul's words, "the evidence of things not seen."

Melodramas are forms that demand emphatic closure. At the story's end,
Bane is back on the chain gang: "And it's her fault he got there." The nar-

rator ends this tale with a surprising question: "Should she not take others, this Carma, strong as a man, whose tale as I have told it is the crudest melodrama?" (20). But the question itself keeps the tale within the melodramatic format by reducing Carma's actions to sex and lies. The narrator's idea of "strong" is masculine ("strong as any man"), and his tale gives her a conventionally feminine role, that of the deceiver. Yet the woman singing the "sad, strong song" in the poetic second paragraph suggests another definition of "strong." What is missing from this crude tale is the political dimension, carried by the refrain of a song that opens and closes "Carma" and which prefaces the section called "the crudest melodrama." This is the true music of the story, the speaking leaves whispering of things done in secret in corn and cane fields, the mixture of rumor, gossip, and fact that dogs Karintha and mystifies Becky's story.

The intangible but visible smoke suggests that when Carma "had others" some of these others were white. Since her husband, Bane, can't kill the white man who made love to his wife, he slashes the black man who helped find her. The rumors that he hears in town about Carma are the stories that white men tell about black women, and they can lead, as in this story, to a self-fulfilling prophecy. The implications are potentially tragic for the black community: how can the call-response pattern that takes place in the church be effective outside of it if blacks believe the stories that whites make up about them? Bane's "cutting" repeats other scenes where reactions by black men to acts of miscegenation have resulted in cutting and bleeding. The "Carma" the title refers to is, in Martin Buber's words, "the *karma* of an earlier life of which we are unconscious" and which "has shut us in a prison we cannot break in this life."[26]

The rumors that Carma "had others" also explain the extremity of her reaction, her pretended suicide. Carma herself, with her "yellow flower face," is a product of miscegenation, and the "flower" of miscegenation appears in "Kabnis" as a metaphor for rape: "White faces, pain-pollen, settle downward through a cane-sweet mist and touch the ovaries of yellow flowers" (214–15). The suggestion is that if Carma had other lovers, and some of them were white, she has not been a willing partner. Neither the story's narrator nor Bane know for certain that Carma has taken others—they rely on the "boasts and rumors" around town which, like the stories of Karintha's early promiscuity (playing " 'home' with a small boy who was not afraid to do her bidding"), are only male "rumors" (3, 18). Fleeing to a cane field where "time and space have no meaning," Carma attempts to flee history, and the shot fired "like a dying hornet through the cane" is the frustrated action of a woman made voiceless. Only the corn and the cane, "rusty with talk," know the true word of the true story, but that story involves history: the cane's "talk" witnesses the past and present.[27]

Although Carma cannot answer accusations based on others' ideas about her reputation, the story shows that she possesses her own kind of strength.

There is a special irony in putting the paragraph that precedes the "crudest melodrama" in parentheses, as if nothing within this inconsequential black peasant world at dusk would be news in the pages of the *Ishmaelite*. But here at dusk occurs an invisible refiguring of the map along the Dixie Pike, and within this paragraph is also the suggestion that Carma cannot be confined by the parameters of a newspaper story or men's words. Carma retains her ambiguity: is she "Foxie, the bitch," in heat and howling at the moon, or is she the black woman outside her shack singing a "sad strong song"? Whoever she is, Carma's song is so strong that it permeates the landscape like a "fragrance," and that story eludes the narrator: "Using reins to slap the mule, she disappears in a cloudy rumble at some indefinite point along the road" (16).

The narrator in "Carma" has been a witness to her story even though he doesn't quite realize what it means. As Carma crosses the railroad tracks in the opening paragraph, she turns to look at the narrator: there is a point of connection, a mutual "gaze" the narrator reads as sexual but which also links storyteller and protagonist, as if that "gaze"—the recognition that is both sexual and transsexual—implies that the narrator bears a responsibility to tell her tale: if he does not do so, only the *Ishmaelite* will. That narration is not a straightforward matter, however; if the narrator is aware of the prison of melodrama, seeing in terms of convention rather than understanding, he still cannot entirely escape its forms. His words are still related to the words of the men who define Carma, though he tries to convey a further meaning through fragments, images that respect the mystery that lies behind them. His equivocal position is further undermined in the story of "Fern," and the narratives of both Carma and Fern question the confidence and the assumed authority of the intervening poem, "Song of the Son."

Carma resorts to a faked suicide to escape her husband's anger, and she succeeds in her own way. Fern, however, isolates herself with a mysterious passivity, and the black town transforms her into something sacred without ever specifying exactly what she represents. The absurd belief that her virginity is miraculously restored ("She became a virgin") expresses the needs of the black community and protects Fern from both black and white men: "What white men thought of Fern I can arrive at only by analogy. They let her alone" (26). The analogy, of course, is ironic; they leave her alone because they think she's mad; the further implication is that white men ordinarily do *not* leave black women alone. The narrator thinks "men are apt to idolize or fear that which they cannot understand, especially if it be a woman." Although he attempts to explain Fern, assuming he is above the "superstition" that surrounds her, the narrator, too, feels lost in her presence; by imagining various scenarios for her—serving as a white man's mistress, walking the streets of Harlem, and so forth—he attempts to place her and so control her mystery.[28]

As an outsider, an urban Northerner in the small town, the narrator also takes Fern out into the cane fields. In his frustration, he ends up like all the other men, feeling that he would do "some fine unnamed thing" for her. He has come to the South hoping to discover something: "When one is on the soil of one's ancestors, most anything can come to one" (31). But vision does not come to him, because he has compromised it—his interest in Fern is more sexual than he admits: "From force of habit, I suppose, I held Fern in my arms." Lying in his arms, Fern is the one who has the vision:

She spring up. Rushed some distance from me. Fell to her knees, and began swaying, swaying. Her body was tortured with something it could not let out. Like boiling sap it flooded arms and fingers till she shook them as if they burned her. It found her throat, and spattered inarticulately in plaintive, convulsive sounds, mingled with calls to Christ Jesus. And then she sang, brokenly. A Jewish cantor singing with a broken voice. A child's voice, uncertain, or an old man's. (32)

This last voice is that of Father John, from "Kabnis," who also speaks "inarticulately in plaintive, convulsive sounds." At this moment Fern's voice is not her own but the voice of "race memories" (22), a phrase from the poem "Georgia Dusk," which precedes "Fern." Fern, like the lynched victim of "Portrait in Georgia," seems to physically experience the pain of being burned, but as she struggles to release the voices of the past, her utterance is the song the narrator longs to sing. It is a song of anguish, of the many thousands gone in the diaspora, which she sings as she is hidden by the dusk, the narrator hearing "only her song."

In the opening lines of "Fern," Toomer brings her within the orbit of Waldo Frank's *Our America*: "If you have heard a Jewish cantor sing, if he has touched you and made your own sorrow seem trivial when compared with his, you will know my feeling when I follow the curves of her profile, like mobile rivers, to their common delta" (24). Fern's face is a racial map of memory, the "mobile rivers" of her features leading to the longed-for home of her "strange eyes," the "common delta" into which seemed to flow "the whole countryside." Fern's mysticism is "prophetic," because she speaks for her community as a historical witness and as a link to communal origins. Her role is one that Frank saw as the most important contribution that Jews could make to America's future, but in "Carma" Toomer had already suggested that "God has left the Moses-people for the nigger" (16).

The final irony of the story's ending is that the narrator passes on the burden of pursuing Fern's mystery to someone else ("And friend, you?"). When the narrator mentions her name for the first time in the story's last sentence, it is "Fernie May Rosen"—the Jewish-sounding name reveals a miscegenated past, although the past she articulates in her vision is not Jewish but African-American. Her face may remind the narrator of a Jewish cantor (her nose is "aquiline, Semitic"), but the sorrows in Fern's face speak to a different history. That last line also speaks to Frank's definition of "races" and subtly comments on *Our America*, in which there is no chapter for the African experience in the New World.[29]

The narrator's final view of Fern is from a train as he leaves to return North; he sees her in her familiar place, standing against the wall, her "head tilted a little forward where the nail was." He has not had the vision he seeks because he remains outside the terrors of history, a spectator not yet become a witness. To paraphrase a line from "Georgia Dusk," to express black life the true "genius of the South" will have "blood-hot eyes" and "cane-lipped scented mouth." He will not be a timid voyeur. The allusion to "Kubla Klan" ("His flashing eyes, his floating hair /. . . . / For he on honey-dew hath fed") is unmistakable: to build that "pleasure dome" the poet must be prepared to immerse himself in the destructive element. Visions come only to those willing to confront the blue ghosts of the past and present.

At the beginning of "Fern," Toomer's Northern narrator finds himself attracted to Fern's mystery. He believes he can understand her, although the local people apparently cannot. He does not grasp her role as the town's storyteller, one who records/reenacts the mystery of origins. That mystery bears witness both to the birth of the African in the New World and to all its attendant horrors, for, as Walter Benjamin notes, the storyteller "has borrowed his authority from death." The narrator wishes to link her to *his* memory—his final desperate appeal to the reader as "you" is an attempt to create a community to mitigate the homelessness he feels, and this is nowhere better revealed than in his final voyeuristic view of Fern from a train window. The real basis of his attraction to her, as Esther's is to Barlo, lies in her authenticity, which derives from the context of this place; part of the pathos of the narrator's various scenarios that place her elsewhere is that it reflects his own uprootedness, not hers. Although he says, "I felt that things unseen to men were tangibly immediate. . . . When one is on the soil of one's ancestors, most anything can come to one" (31), these "unseen" things do not come to him, at least not yet.[30]

The African-American folk culture Toomer adapts and creates for the first section of *Cane*, the sorrow songs and blues lines between and within the stories, is a politicized culture. The subtle menace of "Reapers" and the direct challenge of "Cotton Song" both speak against the white South and its economic, social, and political systems. The songlike verses in "Carma" are not lyrics to nature, but refer to the secret history of miscegenation and its disruption of black family and society, as do the key images and lines from "Karintha" that are repeated in "Georgia Dusk," "Nullo," and eventually "Kabnis." Even an apparently simple lyric like "Evening Song," with its "Lakes and moon and fires" (35), anticipates "Blood-Burning Moon." Toomer also recognizes how black folk culture embraces Christianity, for slaves the religion of submission, and adapts it for resistance, as in the lines from "Cotton Song": "Shackles fall upon the Judgement Day / But lets not wait for it" (15). Toomer extends this adaptation by incorporating African traditions, the "juju-man" and the "Guardian of Souls," and visionary stories of racial history and origin that begin to provide a continuous background between *Cane*'s individual pieces. But miscegenation is a taboo mystery *and* a source of origins, a reason for murder *and* for creation. The mosaic assembled in *Cane*'s first part portrays the setting in which these contradictions exist simultaneously.

Returning to a third-person narration, Toomer makes the final two stories of *Cane*'s first section specifically historical and political. The connecting link between "Fern" and "Esther" lies in the visions of origin that center each story. In "Esther," King Barlo has a vision on the public sidewalk, "on a spot called the Spittoon," where white men sit and spit tobacco juice. That vision, like Fern's, is an origin story: a black giant in chains who "left the old coast brothers, t give birth t you an me" (39). A witness to the event at age nine, Esther, the "chalk-white" daughter of the richest black man in town, is transformed by what she sees and hears: Barlo "became the starting point of the only living patterns that her mind was to know" (40).

The Changing Face of Modernity: "Esther" and "Blood-Burning Moon"

At sixteen Esther has two dreams, each one about having a child. There are no labor pains and, as with Karintha and Becky, no visible fathers in the dreams. They are her children, for only she claims them, and yet they are orphans, as she is herself. In the first dream firemen rescue a colorless "dimpled infant" from a burning building and Esther "claims [the child] for her own": "How had she come by it? She must think of it immaculately. It is a sin to think of it immaculately" (40–41). In Esther's second dream, the baby is black, "ugly as sin," and emerges from a fire fed by streetcorner loafers squirting "tobacco juice." This infant—"black, singed, woolly, tobacco-juice baby"—suddenly appears among black and white women, pulling "their skirts above their heads," displaying "ludicrous underclothes," and only Esther "is left to take the baby in her arms" (41).[31]

Esther's obsession with Barlo crosses lines of both color and class. Daughter of a mulatto storeowner, Esther belongs neither with the whites of the town nor quite with the blacks, though community "law" classifies her as African-American. The colorless dream child is what her father would want, a sign of near-whiteness, "immaculate," and in this sense *he* is its father. "How had she come by it?" (40) is a variation on the question asked about Becky—"Who gave it to her?"—but it is a question Esther does not wish to answer, because answering it would mean naming her father as *the* father. Thinking about it "immaculately" avoids the questions of sex, kinship, and incest which are intimately tied to her family's social class. The "tobacco-juice baby" is also "ugly as sin," ugly because it's black, and sin-ful because it is Barlo's. Since it is Barlo's child, Esther loves it "frantically," attracted not only to Barlo's sexual vitality but to the vitality of his class, the black peasantry. Yet having Barlo's child would be a serious transgres-sion within the circles of her social world, and the black child in the dream seems repulsive even as she loves it, because it carries a legacy of black history that Esther's family wants no part of. Dirt, violence ("singed"), stig-mata ("woolly")—these features of the child symbolize the psychic fears of the mulatto elite. This is another version of a recurrent theme in *Cane*: the possibility of the past returning unexpectedly.

Esther's social confusion emerges in her job as clerk in her father's gro-cery store, where she is "learning to make distinctions between the business and the social worlds" (42). Unlike Carma, who drives a wagon, or Louisa, who works in a kitchen, Esther is involved in the exchange of money. She works for her father " 'to keep the money in the family,' as he said," and he provides her with a very flexible measure for racial identity: "Be just as black as any man who has a silver dollar" (42). Her father is explaining just when and where to draw the color line within the race: "Good business comes from remembering that the white folks don't divide the niggers, Esther." "White folks" give his class a business edge, for white racism unites the "niggers"; because Esther's family is considered black, "niggers" trade at their store. However, her father wants the identification of blackness only within the store, and although "whiteness" is denied to him by the one-drop rule, the father uses the word "niggers" to let Esther know that social distinctions should be maintained outside the store. Yet if Esther's family cannot *be* white because the community knows her family is "black" by reputation, and if blackness is of value only in business transactions, what kind of identity is left for her?[32]

Esther's family turns away from its black past by emulating the white middle class and adopting from the white world the ethos of capitalism, which is always grounded in the present moment: "Be just as black as any man who has a silver dollar." In Marxist terms, the economic arrangements of capitalism insist that the human history that lies behind money must dis-appear: currency is always both current and colorless, that is, the human exchange on which it is based remains hidden. The story of "Esther" is a Marxist version of Freud's "family romance." The father makes his money from "niggers" but wishes to distinguish his social class within the race from such people. "Keeping the money within the family" is a pretense of self-sufficiency, but it also suggests that family values mean an interconnec-tion between money and incest. These values also mean social and political isolation—a fear of the common life—the theme that will be central to *Cane*'s second part. Moreover, "keeping the money in the family" also ex-poses the father's business as a kind of minstrel show. The image of Esther's deracination is a "chalk-white face," the opposite of burnt cork, as if she pays for the sins of her father by becoming a grotesque parody of what he aspires to be.

Esther dreams of her miscegenated "tobacco-juice" child in an atmosphere of carnival, and her memory of the time she witnessed Barlo's humiliation and triumph takes the form in her dream of a street life full of promiscuous events and people. The "tobacco-juice" child is the loathed/loved object, the vital Barlo who can free her from her father's world and the feared Barlo who represents a threat to that world. Esther's class, however, is not only passive in its actions. Toomer describes its equivocation in a curious image: "Her mind is a pink meshbag filled with babytoes" (45). The "babytoes" in the meshbag have an eerie relation to the parts of bodies sought after by lynchers. There is nothing innocent, finally, about this image in her mind, as there is nothing innocent about the father's desire to "keep the money in the family." Black capitalism, as the father practices it, is a murderous business. It pretends to be colorless, impartial ("just as black"), but its consequences fragment African-American life as effectively as does the diaspora.

While the world of *Cane* is one of repetitions and recurrences, it is never outside of history. Before the Great War, Barlo was a jack-of-all-trades—cotton-picker, preacher, gambler, all within a working-class milieu; when he returns to Sempter after the war, he is "as rich as anyone," even Esther's father. Barlo's success represents not only the forces of modernity that will transform the small towns, but a new black middle class that will replace Esther's father as the town's leading black citizen and will eventually replace, and intermarry with, the mulatto elite of the Northern cities. Toomer, however, mocks the Booker T. Washington model of black success by making Barlo a combination of visionary and confidence man, and by implying that his material success is due to shrewd speculation in the wartime cotton boom rather than to diligent labor. Thus when Esther sees Barlo a second time, her obssession is renewed, but her animation is due less to his vision of the African giant than to the aura of his "large new car [which] passes her window" (44).

In the story's final scene Esther goes to claim Barlo, but cannot embrace her long fixed desire. Her loss of nerve is the failure of her social class; Esther is afraid to do what she most wants to do, and when "like a somnambulist" she walks down the steps of the whorehouse where she has found him, she has no world to return to: "There is no air, no street, and the town has completely disappeared" (48). At the story's end Esther has witnessed the prophet for a third time, and in one sense the two have changed places: Barlo began as a visionary and ends as a good-time man, and Esther *sees* this change. "His faculties are jogged"—Barlo's drunken response to what he thinks is Esther's lust is a perverted distortion of the "religious trance" of the story's beginning. So she is not entirely wrong when she perceives Barlo as "hideous." For all her flaws, Esther is right about Barlo at the beginning and at the end. A member of the working class before the war, he has now become one of the predators from Toomer's *New York Call* article "Ghouls," or one of the "blood suckers of the War" in "Seventh Street."

If the storyteller has lost his aura, the story itself remains inviolate. At the beginning of "Esther" the spittle on Barlo's face does not discredit his fable—rather, that politic humiliation helps give the story its power. The past embodied in Barlo's vision is seen as the only hope for an authentic future. It is a utopian moment, the death of one world and the anticipated birth of another: "the old coast didn't miss him, an the new coast wasn't free." That visionary moment also has an impact on the white world: "old Limp Underwood, who hated niggers, woke up next morning to find that he held a black man in his arms" (40). This sexual pun is slapstick comedy out of vaudeville, but its implication is serious: miscegenation is a part of the origin story. Once the "little white-ant biddies" put the African giant in chains and took him "across the ocean," whites and blacks in the New World were inextricably bound to one another, united in every way. The hope for the future, if there is one, lies in a miscegenated culture.

In "Esther," there is another witness to Barlo's origin story, "an inspired Negress, of wide reputation for being sanctified," mentioned also in "Fern," who after hearing Barlo "drew a portrait of a black madonna on the court-house wall" (40). Barlo is a kind of Nat Turner, using a Christian device to hide a political message, its militancy cloaked by the spot of humiliation ("the Spittoon") that protects him. Tobacco juice streaming down his face, Barlo hides his male anger by the imitation of a humbled Christ who has a vision of a visionary African, also humbled by slavery. Although Esther's attraction to Barlo reflects her sexual frustration and her desire to flee her social class, it is also connected to the black experience of homelessness in the New World, an experience to which Barlo's vision had spoken. Indeed, when she comes to Nat Bowle's whorehouse to find Barlo, "her voice sounds like a frightened child's that calls homeward from some point miles away" (47).

Barlo's vision is passed on to the black female artist who brazenly translates the male hero into a mother figure, a miscegenated (Christian/pagan) Isis. In a sense, Barlo becomes a combination of Damballah and the God of the New Testament, impregnating both the "inspired negress" and Esther, but it is the folk artist who is truly fecund, giving birth to her double, a black madonna who in turn becomes midwife and mother. Like Barlo's visionary African, the black madonna signifies; it is a militant image in disguise. She symbolizes the suffering and endurance of betrayed black mothers hidden in the recesses of the South's Gothic past, and in linking Fern and Esther she joins the experience of women across color and class lines.

The theme of Barlo's vision at the "Spittoon" is of a lost home and a conversion to a new condition, that of slavery. "Conversion," the poem that follows "Esther," repeats Barlo's origin story from a "sardonic" perspective; Christianity becomes a means of suppressing black people and a source of Esther's repressions. The poem links the conversion to slavery with the conversion to Christianity and Barlo's drunkenness before Esther with the slaver's rum. The result of the slave's conversion to the gods of Western civilization appears in the poem "Portrait in Georgia" where the lynched body of the young woman/man is *converted* to white ash. The great power of "Portrait in Georgia" resides in the relations between Petrarchan enumeration of parts ("Hair . . . / Eyes . . . / Lips . . . / Breath . . . / body) and their transformation in death. The "clear-cut" images of the poem not only create a "mystery" of identity within the poem but point to the larger mystery of miscegenation within the text itself. "Portrait in Georgia" becomes a microcosm of the collage structure of *Cane*, the narrative technique which, by taking away the connectives, compels the reader to look for "the evidence of things not seen." As something unseen, miscegenation was a sin condemned in public but practiced in private.[33]

Everything that was unseen and implicit in the previous stories and poems emerges violently in "Blood-Burning Moon": miscegenation, black rage, lynching—the heritage of the slave South and the yet-undefined ambitions of the new South. The figure uniting these themes is the bloodred moon, the sign both of impermanence and change and of repeated cycles:

> Up from the skeleton stone walls, up from the rotting floor boards and the solid hand-hewn beams of oak of the pre-war cotton factory, dusk came. Up from the dusk the full moon came. Glowing like a fired pine-knot, it illuminated the great door and soft showered the Negro shanties aligned along the single street of factory town. The full moon in the great door was an omen. Negro women improvised songs against its spell. (51)

The bloody moon is a residue of Southern history; it is also Isis, the goddess of renewal and fertility, and "the red-eyed" Erzuli, the seductress, and her agent in the story, Louisa. The moon is an omen of death, as its metaphor, "a fired pine-knot" (itself a circle), alludes to the lynching of "Portrait in Georgia." The ruined prewar cotton factory out of which the moon rises, rotting from beneath yet still solid in its superstructure of "hand-hewn" beams, is the past that should have vanished but somehow endures.[34]

As both innocent and femme fatale, Louisa stands at the secret center of Southern life, hidden because, as a black woman, she cannot be publicly acknowledged. She is loved by a black man and a white man, her innocence an ironic counterpart to the South's pretense that miscegenation is about black men who rape white women. Thinking of her two lovers, Louisa cannot keep them separate—"they jumbled when her eyes gazed vacantly at the rising moon" (52). Both the white Bob Stone and the black Tom Burwell want Louisa, but their conflict is much more complicated than a sexual rivalry. For each she stands as a kind of trophy by which they try to measure their social position, their honor, even their economic prospects. That she wants them both is something neither is willing to consider.

The history that moves the story has black and white versions. Tom Burwell's comment to Louisa about Bob's gifts—that "silk stockings an purple dresses" mean nothing because "white folks aint up t them tricks so much nowadays" (57)—reveals a fatal naiveté about the background of black-white relationships. Tom's dream of becoming a yeoman farmer "if ole Stone'll trust me," his belief that trust can exist between white landowner and black laborer, presupposes that the Southern economic exploitation of the past is dead. He compares himself to Barlo, whom he "come near to beatin" in a day's cotton-picking, but he lacks the shrewdness by which Barlo chose the Spittoon to announce his subversive vision of African-American history. Barlo will understand that the money is to be made speculating in cotton, not raising it or picking it.

Tom Burwell is a peasant New Negro: rebellious, ambitious, self-reliant. But the future he imagines is out of Booker T. Washington: he wants to become a small landowner and farmer. Even that future of modest success would be in conflict with Bob Stone's anxiety over the status of his planter class: "Some position for him to be in. Him, Bob Stone, of the old Stone family, in a scrap with a nigger over a nigger girl" (60). Bob Stone's love for Louisa threatens both his class position and his racial ideology. The fact that he must try to keep the relationship secret seems to him proof of his social decline; as he twice reflects, "His family had lost ground." Since his conception of his class requires a sexual domination of black women, he imagines a reversal of that decline in a fantasy of raping Louisa in his kitchen, even though they are already secret lovers.

Bob Stone's history leads him into further uncertainties because white supremacy has no explanation for his loving a black woman. As he steps outside on his way to meet Louisa in the canebrake, "his cheeks turned purple" (59). To counter "this outer change," this miscegenated self, "his mind became consciously a white man's." To admit the effect of Louisa would be to cross the line of his racial identity, and to hopelessly confuse his relations to his family and peers. Intentionally making Louisa "different"— she is not just a "gal" but a "nigger gal"—he engages in circular reasoning: he loves her because she's a "nigger," but because she's a "nigger" he can't love her. Miscegenation as a crime, as something hidden, leaves him with a conundrum: "Was there something about niggers that you couldnt know?" (60). He cannot imagine how the history of racism has created the unknowable because he is too thoroughly emeshed in that history. His only solution to the mystery is to cut through it by insisting upon his "whiteness."

"Blood-Burning Moon" develops like an inevitable tragedy, and behind the three protagonists black choruses comment on the action. The men around the fire laugh at David Georgia's ribald stories about "sweet nigger gals," but an incautious remark by one of them about Louisa and Bob Stone almost leads to disaster. They forget the history of sexual and economic exploitation behind the "silk stockings" that Bob Stone gave Louisa, and their talk leads Burwell and Stone toward their confrontation. All the clues, hints, and warnings of the previous stories and poems are gathered into the triangle of black woman, black man, and white man. The black women of the story "improvized" songs to try and deflect the moon's "spell," but because the moon represents history, it only *seems* to act as a supernatural force. The songs articulate sorrow but are helpless to prevent it; the music is the community's voice, adapting to each new crisis, but its power for resistance is limited, as the women realize: "Their songs were cotton wads to stop their ears" (53).

The women know what the moon means because they have inherited a repository of stories from their mothers and their mothers' mothers. They are witnesses to witnesses who have seen this thing happen before, in similar kitchens and in similar canebrakes, and their songs are the "rusty talk" of the cane in "Carma." The black women in the story contain the real font of African-American communal wisdom; they preserve the secret history, and their songs recall the terror behind Bob's courtship of Louisa. They don't want to hear the chaos the moon provokes: "all over the countryside dogs barked and roosters crowed as if heralding a weird dawn or some ungodly awakening" (53). The barking dogs and the crowing roosters refer to an old blues refrain, just as the phrase "showered upon Negro shanties" echoes Charlie Patton's blues line, "An the blues comes down, baby, like showers of rain." At the story's end, the whites have disappeared into their lynching party and the blacks into their homes, and Tom's "eyes were set and stony." Louisa remains the sole surviving witness to the disaster; she is the blues singer as witness.[35]

The bloodred moon that creates an illusion of a "weird dawn" and an "ungodly awakening" is an ironic comment on the New South—it foreshadows the bloody acts that consume Bob Stone and Tom Burwell: "Roosters crowed, heralding the bloodshot eyes of southern awakening. Singers in the town were silenced" (63). The terror that rains down on the black village muffles the storytellers; it also creates a border world, like Nathaniel Hawthorne's Gothic "moon shining through an attic window," turning the familiar to the unfamiliar, the uncanny "weird dawn." The dawn will not rise on either man's history—the white man's redemptionist nostalgia and the false hope of the black man are balanced in a terrible equipoise, and a new future cannot be born from the "fact'ry door" of the song's refrain:

Red nigger moon. Sinner!
Blood-burning moon. Sinner!
Come out that fact'ry door.

The bloodred moon that once rose over slave laborers in the "pre-war cotton factory" continues to shed its influence over the course of events in black lives. The "red nigger moon" belongs to Tom and Louisa, but the "blood-burning moon" belongs to the lynchers led by Bob Stone; dying, he had called out Tom Burwell's name in Sempter's Broad Street. The song compresses the entangled griefs of the South into the image of the red moon and the mysterious "Sinner," still unnamed in the house of Southern history. The "Sinner" links the past and the future, the animated corpse of history that refigures the "weird" combinations of character and circumstance in the present. The "Sinner" inside "that fact'ry door" remains hidden at the story's end, as so many elements of the world of Sempter remain secret. Two years after he read *Cane* and reviewed it for the *Crisis*, W. E. B. Du Bois wrote:

Georgia is beautiful. Yet on its beauty rests something disturbing and strange. . . . There lies a certain brooding on the land—there is something furtive, uncanny, at times almost a horror. Some folk it so grips that they never see the beauty—the hills to them are haunts of grim and terrible men; the world goes armed with loaded pistols on the hip; concealed but ready—always ready. There is a certain secrecy about this world. Nobody seems wholly frank—neither white nor black; neither child, woman or man.[36]

Toomer discovered that a modernist form could powerfully express the ambiguity and mystery of Georgia, and Du Bois's remarks are an unintentionally accurate assessment of what Toomer achieved.

"Blood-Burning Moon" is structurally important as the story concluding *Cane*'s first section in that it treats miscegenation openly and explicitly. In stories like "Becky," "Carma," and "Fern" (and poems like "Reapers" and "Portrait in Georgia"), miscegenation is both there and not there—deflected because Becky is white (and therefore an anomaly), or hidden in the silent rage of the black reapers, or revealed through an ironic "analogy" in "Fern," or seen obliquely in the imagery and metaphor of "Georgia Dusk." In all these instances, Toomer's modernist method is directly related to his theme of a hidden history that waits to overwhelm the present, as it finally does in "Blood-Burning Moon." Indeed, the book's first section is made up of a series of dyads—"Karintha"/"Becky," "Carma"/"Fern," "Esther"/"Blood-Burning Moon"—that circle around a single point, the "blood-burning moon" of the past that confuses and terrorizes the present.

"Gothic fiction," argues Maggie Kilgour, focuses upon "mystery, a loss of boundaries, and confusion of differences." These words also apply to miscegenation, the "crime" that springs from the primal crime of slavery. All the mysteries in *Cane*'s first section are linked to the secret of miscegenation, from the hint that Karintha's dead child under the smoldering sawdust pile is mulatto, to the love affair between Louisa and Bob Stone. This theme will be central to "Bona and Paul" and will be threaded through "Kabnis." Miscegenation, of course, created the mulatto aristocracy of Washington, D.C., which is the subject of most of *Cane*'s second part.[37]

Chapter 7
Cane in the City

Washington lay in the cup surrounded by hills. . . . But my heart swelled at this last view of the place which had been mine to love.
— Jean Toomer, *Reflections of an Earth Being*, 1929–30

The superficial inducement, the exotic, the picturesque has an effect only on the foreigner. To portray a city, a native must have other, deeper motives — motives of one who travels into the past instead of into the distance. A native's book about his city will always be related to memoirs; the writer has not spent his childhood there in vain.
— Walter Benjamin, "The Return of the Flaneurs," 1929

Jean Toomer liked cities — their textures, their special geographies, their capacity to stimulate the emotions and the intellect. He called New York "one of the few liveable places on earth," and at one point in his life he wanted to be known as "Toomer the Chicagoan." But the city he knew best was Washington, D.C., where he was born in 1894 and where he lived for seventeen of the first twenty-seven years of his life. The memory quoted above from *Reflections of an Earth Being* dates from 1907, the year he moved to Brooklyn with his mother, Nina Pinchback, and his stepfather. His description touches on characteristics of the city he admired in other contexts, a harmony of urban and rural, North and South, earth and sky. Washington, too, was not only the city in which he spent his young manhood — it was the city in which he spent his *black* manhood. When, after the publication of *Cane*, Toomer denied his African-American identity, arguing that he was "simply an American," cities became the places where his American self could find a home. In 1931–32 he would see Chicago as the home of the "First American," the purple man who emerges new from the melting pot. As a place where Toomer's mixed blood was an asset rather than a liability, Chicago became a symbolic setting for *The Blue Meridian*. Toomer's sense of Washington as a symbolic city was always complicated by what Walter Benjamin calls "the deeper motives . . . of one who travels into the past," by his unique racial past and his ambivalence toward the distinctive black urban world he lived in, one he later remembered as a creation of the social class of the mulatto aristocracy.[1]

Toomer was acutely aware that he had emerged from a class that was in decline; even before his birth, the position of the mulatto aristocracy within the city of Washington had begun to erode. Washington was in many ways a Southern city, and in the post-Reconstruction decades it began to revert to familiar racial patterns. Not only did the position of African-Americans within Washington decline after 1880, but distinct class structures within the race began to harden as well, and those two social phenomena—segregation from without and a growing social stratification within—were connected. As the African-American community within Washington was increasingly isolated in the 1890s, members of the mulatto aristocracy began to react to white pressure for segregation by distancing themselves from the black peasant masses who moved, along with foreign immigrants and rural whites, to urban centers in the North and South. The aristocracy's motive was fear of contagion; maintaining their status was seen as dependent on "appearing" white, whether that meant actually "passing" as white or living in as nearly a white, middle-class manner as possible.[2]

As de facto segregation became the empirical fact of life in Washington in the first decade of the twentieth century, so the mulatto aristocracy continued to withdraw to a citadel of culture and gentility. When Woodrow Wilson was elected President in 1912 and the de facto condition in the nation's capital moved toward a legal system of apartheid, the city's black population for a brief moment closed ranks; Toomer's own high school—M Street High School—helped lead the way in the collective social protest. The ultimate failure of this effort meant that, after the Great War, when American society returned to business as usual (what Harding would call "normalcy"), "upper-class [black] families, tired of making common cause with needy blacks, washed their hands of every group but their own."[3]

This withdrawal by the mulatto aristocracy accounts for part of the ambivalence Toomer expressed about his connection to their world. As a group, its members claimed that theirs was the most cultured black city in America, having at its center the distinguished Howard University, which was to be celebrated by Kelly Miller in *The New Negro* (1925) as the premier institution of African-American higher education. Of course, such a claim to exclusive culture on the part of a single class within the race exacerbated divisions within the black community of Washington. Although other black urban communities—Philadelphia, Brooklyn, Chicago, even Harlem—had their social divisions, Washington seemed to Toomer (as it did to Langston Hughes and Sterling Brown) to carry these divisions to an extreme.[4]

A book published four years after *Cane* offers a sense of the social values of Toomer's mulatto aristocracy in Washington, describing how tightly closed its world was and how rigidly its class lines were drawn. In 1927

William H. Jones, an African-American sociologist from Howard University, published *Recreation and Amusement Among Negroes in Washington, D.C.*, dedicated "TO ALL MOVEMENTS DESIGNED TO IMPROVE THE SOCIAL LIFE OF THE NEGRO CITY-DWELLER." Although he was clearly influenced by Robert Park's description of "moral regions" within an urban environment, Jones lacked Park's wide-ranging sympathies and tolerance. His book balanced between sociological study and cautionary tale, and attempted not so much to "improve" social life as to warn the black middle class against the dangerous world of an urban proletariat that was increasingly visible in Washington.[5]

One of Jones's major concerns, in fact, was the "encroachment" of lower-class entertainments "upon the life of the more advanced groups of Negroes in Washington," a process, he said, that "appears to be due to the fact that class stratification as a social process lacks many of those elements which might result in a more rigid exclusion of both questionable individuals and anti-social cultural patterns." Throughout the book Jones was concerned as much with separating the classes within black Washington as he was with criticizing the city's policies of racial segregation. In his "recommendations" at the book's conclusion, Jones suggested that "cultured Negroes seek to maintain higher standards in connection with their leisure-time activities by practicing more of the milder forms of social exclusion." While this exclusiveness should be based on "moral and cultural attainments rather than distinctions of color," Jones chose not to mention the strong correlation between social class and lightness of complexion within Washington's mulatto aristocracy. The extraordinary fear of contamination from the lower classes that Jones shows was the characteristic of the mulatto aristocracy on which Toomer would focus his Washington stories.[6]

The Urban Landscape

The city-centered material that found its way into *Cane* was written both early and late in the composition of the book. During the early period Toomer used Washington as a setting for two other works, a short story ("Withered Skin of Berries") and a play (*Natalie Mann*), which were not included in *Cane*. In both works Toomer focuses on the urban landscape of Washington—the symbolic structures within the nation's capital, those articulated spaces of the black community that define class divisions within the race, and an invisible geography that hints at both personal and cultural renewal.

"Withered Skin of Berries" deals with a black woman "passing" for white in the city. Vera works, lives, and hides in official Washington, but she moves through landscapes of alternate, coextensive cities, an African-American Washington whose vitality she's drawn to and a hidden city composed of the symbolic settings of the past and present—of "multi-colored leaves," in Toomer's phrase. Vera works for the government and dates a white man (Carl), but she is attracted to David Teyy, a black man who symbolizes, rather overwhelmingly, the energy of a new African-American consciousness. Teyy lives at the wrong (black) end of "Sixteenth Street"; in Toomer's geography "life . . . flowed up the blue veins of the city. Up Sixteenth Street. David was a red blood center flowing down. She [Vera] sucked his blood." [7]

Vera's anemic condition represents the personified city and a light-skinned African-American aristocracy that has depleted its own "blood-lines," an image Toomer returns to continually. The flow of blood as a figure for social and cultural vigor will appear most significantly in Toomer's sketch of "Seventh Street" in *Cane*, where it becomes the measure for all the sketches and stories that follow in the book's middle section. The character of David Teyy stands not only for a bloodline, however; he also expresses the story's historical consciousness. The narrative's key moment comes when he confronts Vera's political blindness: "What is that, Vera?" he asks, looking directly at the Masonic Temple. When she tells him, he wants to know what that temple "means to you . . . who live under the shadow of it." The Masonic Temple houses a secret society that excludes blacks from membership, and, like the city's other public monuments, it symbolizes an exclusive history, the history of institutional American racism. Vera's blindness is implicit in her choice of "passing"; riding in Carl's car, she has already seen evidence of that exclusion in the city's newest monument: "Negroes were working on the basin of an artificial lake that was to spread its smooth glass surface before the Lincoln Memorial. The shadow of their emancipator stirred them neither to bitterness nor awe." In 1922 the dedication ceremonies of the Lincoln Memorial had segregated seating for blacks and whites. [8]

Natalie Mann, the eponymous heroine of Toomer's play, has more political awareness. Nathan Merilh—another of Toomer's larger than life heroes—is both her lover and mentor, but it is he, finally, who must be taught by her. The play again uses Washington's social geography to define the essential conflict, fixing on a division between home and cabaret that would become important in the Washington stories of *Cane*. In *Natalie Mann* the black aristocrats of Washington claim the home as their special province; it symbolizes respectability, conformity—all the virtues of the "social animal." They are outraged at the apostasy of one of their members, Natalie, who attaches herself to Nathan, an artist who frequents Washington's black nightlife. His disgrace comes when he not only dances with Etty Beal, a cabaret performer, but brawls with her bootlegger lover. [9]

Hounded out of Washington, Natalie and Nathan flee to New York, a less hidebound environment. The play ends with an operatic flourish: Natalie and Nathan return to Washington for a friend's funeral, and in front of Washington's finest black citizens Nathan repeats his erotic dance with Etty

Beal, collapsing on the dance floor in a moment of ecstatic triumph. "What are you weeping over, you silly women?" Natalie gloats as she addresses the matrons who have been mesmerized by Nathan's performance and "who see him only as a man." As this last line of the play indicates, transcendence—both personal and geographical—is the play's major theme, but this theme is intimately connected to the divisions within black life and to Nathan Merilh as a black artist.[10]

The problem Toomer's play addressed did not involve the houses of the black elite—the problem lay in the ideology attached to the houses and the myopic values of their inhabitants. Defining their values according to the white world, the African-American aristocrats of Washington attacked as "other" any aspect of black city life that did not replicate white standards. The mulatto aristocracy still thought of Washington as "the Athens of colored America" and saw itself as the race's cultural vanguard, but Toomer's images of pinched lives, of a class desperately clinging to an imitative respectability, made their houses into prisons. One theme expressed in *Natalie Mann* was that the house would be "made creative" only when the idea of culture was redefined—then, possibly, even the cabaret in the city might become a "home."[11]

William Jones's *Recreation and Amusement Among Negroes in Washington, D.C.* sketches the class lines that defined approved cultural activities. Jones sets out the recreational activities he considers wholesome—tennis, golf, even baseball—but he is more interested in warning readers away from the places within the black urban scene that are unwholesome or déclassé: dance halls, theaters, and especially cabarets on or near Seventh Street. Jones doesn't condemn dancing per se—he recognizes it is a form of courtship—but his assessment of the "moral region" of dance halls delivers a class-biased sermon masquerading as sociological treatise:

Aside from the cheap and stifling places, the trouble is not with the dance hall but with the dancing. Many of the modern dances are sexual pantomimes. They are similar to many of the ancient and primitive methods of publicly arousing human passions in preparation for lascivious orgies. A careful investigation disclosed the fact that the originators of these extreme forms of behavior have clearly in view a sexual end. A large amount of illicit sex behavior is unquestionably the natural sequence of certain modern forms of dancing. There is probably no other form of conventional and socially established behavior which has such a strong tendency toward demoralization as that of the dance hall.[12]

Jones's severest censure is reserved for the cabaret, where "dance hall behavior is intensified." Frequented by the black urban masses, cabarets carry everything to "excess":

dancing, jungle laughter, and semi-alcoholic beverages are characteristic features of their life. Here, jazz music is carried to extremes. In general, there is more abandon achieved by the dancers than in the formal dance hall, and more of a tendency toward nakedness on the part of the female entertainers.[13]

Jones continues with an assessment of the cabarets along Seventh Street and streets nearby, all in the heart of the black underworld, where, to quote Jones on Cafe Cat's Meow, "The lights are dim with almost a red aspect. There are suggestive pictures on the walls. The entertainment is of a low type."[14]

Jones singles out Seventh Street as the geographical center of "low" or "pathological" behavior: prostitution, gambling, bootlegging, even theatergoing. According to his rating system, the Howard Theater, "located . . . near Seventh Street," is given a ranking of "C" because it features blues singers like Mamie Smith and "high brown dancing girls," and is responsible for "some of the principal song fads that have characterized Negro life in Washington during the last three years." On the other hand, the Lincoln Theater rates an "A" not only for its superior facilities but for its superior styles of entertainment and its location—safely distant from Seventh Street. Toomer apotheosized Seventh Street in the opening sketch of *Cane*'s middle section, and made symbolic use of the distance separating the two theaters in "Theater" and "Box Seat."[15]

Cane begins with portraits, poems, and stories set in the rural South, and Toomer defines the singer in "The Song of the Son" as the black descendant who has come back to celebrate a vanishing way of life. He is the poet-detective "returned . . . in time" to discover a peasant world before it disappears, before it fades into the common day of modernity; he is a "singing tree" whose "leaves"—the "songs" that make up *Cane*—will counter time's mutability with the permanence of art. The words "in time" convey a double meaning: the singer has returned to the South in the nick of time, but although he aspires to the universality of art, he is trapped as a mortal man in history, "in time." Indeed, the "plum" in "Song of the Son" plucked by the poet has an inescapable connection to the apple plucked from the Tree of Knowledge in the Garden of Eden. Once it is eaten, the "son," like Adam and Eve, has entered history and can only know good and evil, in Milton's words, "as two twins cleaving together." Taken by itself, "Song of the Son" only hints at this theme, but in the context of the book, the "son" soon learns that terror and beauty in the South are intertwined; the "singing tree" and the lynching tree are the same tree. Moreover, the "son's" personal history, identified by the narrators of the other stories and poems, marks him as the urban outsider, a member of Washington's light-skinned black aristocracy, and complicates his seeing the African-American peasant life of the South as a whole.[16]

Thus the stories, sketches, and poems that make up *Cane*'s first section severely qualify the optimistic purpose expressed in "Song of the Son." In these works the world Toomer's narrators would like to articulate in song continually eludes them; like the smoke from the sawdust pile in "Karintha," its incarnations reveal and conceal at the same time. The speaker in "Carma" admits that he has reduced Carma's tale to "the crudest melodrama"; the narrator of "Fern" pronounces her complete name in a final attempt to conjure up her essence; he can barely express Louisa's "mystery" by identifying her with her "song" to the moon. Only Esther, a figure who partly anticipates the world of Washington, seems understandable, and even she fades into nothingness as the "air," "street," and "town" "completely disappeared" at story's end.

The disappearance of a recognizable landscape is an important feature of *Cane*'s first section. The main hint of a familiar geography is the repeated mention of the Dixie Pike, and even that tangible thoroughfare at night mysteriously becomes "a goat path in Africa" (18). In the first section Toomer expresses the topography of the South through a consistent pattern of imagery and metaphor. Space is redefined in terms of a few elements: blood, cane, pine smoke, dusk, and night become the constituents of a world ruled by the moon. As Nathaniel Hawthorne saw, this lunar landscape is the medium of the romance, yet the "son" wants to become the "sun." He wants more than Dionysian mystery; like Apollo, the "sun" king and the God of poetry, he also wants rational knowledge, and the further clues to that knowledge of black life lie beyond Sempter, in Washington, D.C. Ironically, Dionysian energy exists in the city in the form of Seventh Street and needs a poet to describe it who has "blood-hot eyes" ("Georgia Dust").

Washington's Seventh Street is a counterpart to the Dixie Pike of Sempter (as Seventh Street continues north in the capital it actually becomes Georgia Avenue), and Toomer plays off its location in the city: "A crude-boned, soft-skinned wedge of nigger life breathing its loafer air, jazz songs and love, thrusting unconscious rhythms, black reddish blood into the white and whitewashed wood of Washington" (71). The map of Washington, D.C., shows Seventh Street running north and south midway between the White House and the Capitol; it literally *wedges* itself between the city's two most significant national buildings. The first sentence of the vignette calls attention to an intimate and illicit link between the street and the government: "Seventh Street is a bastard of Prohibition and the War." The Great War and the "Great Experiment" produced the street, an illegitimate child who nevertheless thrives and delights in its bastardy:

> Bootleggers in silken shirts
> Ballooned, zooming Cadillacs,
> Whizzing, whizzing down the street-car tracks.

The industrialism that attracted black peasants to the North during World War I has been made over by those same peasants—and the pregnant Cadillac ("Ballooned") suggests that the street continues to give birth to new permutations, all potentially disruptive of the city's social status quo.

The Great War helped to initiate the Great Migration of black people to the Northern cities, where, confined by segregation and economics into new ghettos, their cultural energies resisted the world of legality symbolized by Prohibition. Seventh Street is a "bastard" because it was created by apparently unrelated acts, and those who were responsible for both Prohibition and the Great War (making the world safe for the sober, white middle classes) could hardly have imagined Seventh Street. Yet, as Toomer sees, these disparate events—The Great War, the "Great Experiment," the Great Migration—are related. The laws that prohibit the selling of liquor are part of a Mosaic code that also tells people when they should go to war, who they should marry, or what schools to attend. The phrase "whitewashed wood of Washington" echoes Christ's indictment of the Pharisees and other hypocrites who "shut the kingdom of heaven against men"; in blindly following the letter of the law, they are like "whitewashed tombs, which outwardly appear beautiful, but within are full of dead men's bones and all uncleanness." [17]

In this opening sketch, Toomer juxtaposes institutions and "blood," the one embodied in buildings ("Stale soggy wood of Washington"), the other in the street, the human energy that can breathe life into a dead world. Toomer—like Waldo Frank and Hart Crane—associated this energy with the divine fire of the poets who, with their visions, could burn away the old and allow the new to rise from its ashes. Appropriately, then, the protagonists of the three most important stories in *Cane*'s second section have names of prophets with apocalyptic visions: John, Daniel, and Paul each rebels against a system of law that belongs to the earthly city.[18]

"Rhobert," the sketch following "Seventh Street," elaborates the theme of the death impulse embodied in the world of law. Rhobert's house, which he "wears [on his head] like a diver's helmet," pushes him down into the "mud" by the weight of convention, like Waldo Frank's symbolic dome in *City Block*. The sign of his membership in the middle class, Rhobert's house controls his life: he can only live and act within the context of a legal enclosure, an imposed definition. Part of what traps Rhobert within this enclosed space is his fear of the world outside his door: "Life is a murky, wiggling, microscopic water that compresses him. Compresses his helmet and would crush it the minute he pulled his head out" (73).

Everything in the portrait is grotesquely comic. Rhobert thinks that "God built the house," that his fate is ordained; but Rhobert's conception of God, like his conception of his own life, is a parodic social fiction: "God is a Red Cross man with a dredge and a respiration-pump who's waiting for you at the opposite periphery." This image leads to a verse from "Deep River," the African-American spiritual that Toomer evokes in the closing lines of the sketch: "Lets build a monument [to Rhobert] and set it in the ooze where he goes down. A monument of hewn oak, carved in niggerheads. Lets open our throats, brother, and sing 'Deep River,' where he goes down" (75). The monument, a satiric extension of the house, draws attention to official Washington, the city of monuments, which both supports and subordinates the mulatto aristocracy. The sting comes in the slang word Toomer puns, "nigger-heads"—discarded cigar butts. The monument is composed of useless remnants, the class of "nigger-heads" who refuse to challenge the word of law and Tocqueville's "legal fictions."[19]

Toomer treats the urban peasant world en masse in "Seventh Street," but he locates it *outside*, in the street, as energy that cannot be bottled up or contained. Toomer dissects the black middle class through an individual portrait, his satire of the American ideal of self-reliant individualism reduced to the affectation of things genteel, like Rhobert's French name. Locked inside his house, Rhobert will not allow anything to enter, and he refuses contact with the very thing—the masses—that might reanimate that suffocating space.

The sketches "Seventh Street" and "Rhobert" characterize the two poles of African-American life in Washington; the first story of this section turns back to the subject of their common ground. In the manner of Sherwood Anderson, Toomer in "Avey" underscores the narrator's obtuseness in the story's opening line: "For a long while she was nothing more to me than one of those skirted beings whom boys at a certain age disdain to play with" (76). While this opening implies Avey will become more than a "skirted being" to him, the narrative seems, ironically, to concentrate on her subsequent social decline. First desirable as a sexual object or reduced to the object of Ned's "smutty wisdom," she later appears to the narrator as "no better than a cow," and eventually he even acknowledges Ned's crueler judgment: "She was no better than a whore" (84). It is her lack of ambition that bothers the narrator most; his plans to improve himself by going to college, even his desire to be an artist, reflect the values of a social class Avey seems to disregard.

Avey's descent into prostitution or concubinage begins like an example of literary naturalism, but Toomer's anecdotal narrative and his images point in another direction. The image of a boxed tree in the street and the first of a series of images of military drill that will appear in the city stories represent an alternative view of the middle-class regimen. The narrator leads his high school drill team, and "on the days for drill, I'd let my voice down a tone and call for a complicated maneuver when I saw her coming" (79). Toomer's narrator, who is also identified with the boxed tree, employs the "complicated maneuver" as an act of mystification by which the black middle class deceives itself and others about the extent of its own power and influence. Avey, of course, is subject to the same process of social homogenization; if she graduates from the "normal school," members of the mulatto elite "could give her a job if they wanted to" (82). Her "abnormality" is her independence, set against the class ideal of the military formation, and so "Avey" develops with an imagistic logic from the themes expressed in the vignettes of "Seventh Street" and "Rhobert," those of energy and improvisation against a static order.[20]

"Avey" is told as a series of encounters between the narrator and the young woman, beginning in his adolescence and concluding with his young adulthood. Those meetings and the stories he hears about her — most important, that she has lost her teaching job, the key to middle-class status — serve to obscure his own uncertainty and uncertain prospects. He keeps reminding himself of his difference from her. In the story's final scene he longs to find Avey out of some nostalgia for a time before "the business of hunting for a job or something or other had bruised my vanity so that I could recognize it" (84).

Avey and my real relation to her, I thought I came to know. I wanted to see her. I had been told that she was in New York. As I had no money, I hiked and bummed my way there. I got work in a ship-yard and walked the streets at night, hoping to meet her. Failing in this, I saved enough to pay my fare back home. One evening in early June, just at the time when dusk is most lovely on the eastern horizon, I saw Avey, indolent as ever, leaning on the arm of a man, strolling under the recently lit arc-lights of U Street. (84)

Dusk, "lovely on the eastern horizon," links Avey to Karintha, but the crucial point of the passage is the narrator's conviction that he at last knows Avey and his "real relation to her." Avey dismisses the man she is with, and the narrator takes her to the grounds of Soldiers' Home, a federal veterans' hospital. Vacillating between the pleasure of his own monologue — "I talked, beautifully I thought, about an art that would be born" — and seduction, Toomer's narrator suddenly realizes that Avey has fallen asleep. "My passion died," he says, and what replaces it are the beginnings of compassion.

If the story ended here it would be an acceptable imitation of Sherwood Anderson, but as he watches the sleeping Avey, Toomer's narrator sees "the dawn steal over Washington," and the city is transformed in his mind from the Washington of the black bourgeoisie, who have played an ignoble part in shaping Avey's life, to the symbolic polis of the republic. The story ends with a new revelation of the real relation between the black man and woman:

The Capitol dome looked like a gray ghost ship drifting in from sea. Avey's face was pale, and her eyes were heavy. She did not have the gray crimson-splashed beauty of the dawn. I hated to wake her. Orphan-woman. . . . (88)

The Capitol dome, crowned with its statue of Freedom, symbolizes the rational principles that govern the republic and its symbolic city. Architecturally, the dome reflects the Enlightenment's revolt against the Gothic cathedral, with its spire's emphasizing mystery rather than understanding. Just as Christopher Wren, after London's Great Fire, rebuilt the old Gothic cathedral of St. Paul's on the principle of the dome, thereby illustrating the harmonious laws of nature recently discovered by Sir Isaac Newton, so did the several architects of the Capitol construct their dome on similar metaphysical foundations. The republic was to be a nation founded on law, not a king's caprice, and thus the circular dome represents a perfect and comprehensible universe: from within the dome, one can perceive the symmetry of the entire structure.[21]

The "pale" Avey and the "ghost ship" of the Capitol dome suddenly open the narrator's eyes to his own history: the Capitol dome drifts like a "ghost ship" (and like the "wraiths" of pine smoke in Georgia) because it is the ghost of a slave ship. The word "ghost" touches the mystery of origins: where did the ship come from and why? In black folklore the mark upon Cain, blanching in horror at the murder of Abel, is his white skin, and in Washington the taint of slavery, in all its forms, turns the city and its victims a ghastly white, as it does the "pale" Avey. The pun of Toomer's title (Cane/Cain) plays on the paradox of the city founder; he creates an artifice that ideally mirrors cosmic order, but he and his actual creation reflect injustice and disorder.[22]

The narrators' judgments of women in *Cane*'s opening section reflect in some way the communal prejudices of a small town, but the young man in "Avey" has judged Avey by the equally parochial standards of Washington's mulatto elite. What he finally realizes is that he doesn't know Avey and that he cannot judge her by the categories the city has created for her. Tony Tanner observes of the biblical story of the woman taken in adultery that the Pharisees' judgment of the adulteress is the voice of the city, a world that "by defining itself as a city . . . immediately creates nonsocial space outside it." According to this division, the nonsocial space outside the city walls is a world of anarchy and barbarism, whereas the social space circumscribed by the city is made visible by its laws. Yet Christ's voice—his refusal to "participate in [a] purely secular attitude to the woman and to discuss her as a category"—implies that the city's judgment is not absolute, that there is an order higher than the court of the city's laws. Of course, the illuminating epiphany at the conclusion of "Avey" does not transport Toomer's narrator and Avey into "an illumined city." Rather, the narrator sees himself linked with Avey as the city's bastard children, orphans condemned to guess at their origins from the glimpsed "ghost ship." He changes, by accident and perhaps unwillingly, from spectator to witness.[23]

The extremity of Rhobert's house-bound isolation and the fact that the narrator of "Avey" always meets Avey on the street fit the spatial opposition Toomer uses to define Washington. In *Cane*'s middle section, street and house are often antithetical points of reference, and the stories that follow "Avey"—"Theater," "Box Seat," and "Bona and Paul"—explore the tensions between "street" culture and "house" culture. The poems set between these stories, as well as the vignette "Calling Jesus," express the same binaries associated with this theme: active and passive, outside and inside, movement and fixity—the oppositions that arise between Seventh Street and the dead "stuffing" of Rhobert's house.

Toomer's urban opposites are not his unique discovery, any more than they are a product specifically of African-American class divisions. Lewis Mumford thought that the diminishment of public space—and hence the slow decline of the city as "theater"—could be laid at the door of all the middle classes. As the city changed from medieval to modern, the "desire for privacy" replaced the desire to interact with one's fellow citizens in a public arena. The open space of "the medieval dwelling house," the clutter of whose main room often appeared only as a continuation of street activities, was reconceived as enclosed space, removed from the space of the city's streets, so that it gradually came to mean "withdrawal . . . from the common life and the common interests of one's associates." In "Rhobert" Mumford's observations are confirmed: Toomer's satire shows the house as an inseparable extension of the black middle class and a symbol of its agoraphobia—its fear of the "social disharmony and conflict" expressed by the drama that takes place in the city's streets.[24]

While Toomer's observations about house and street in the city were not unique to African-American life, they were accurate depictions of his own city. In his book *Alley Life in Washington,* James Borchert describes how thoroughly alley life defined the world of the black urban peasant in the nation's capital, especially from the turn of the century to the 1920s. More than 90 percent of alley inhabitants were black in 1897, and alleys comprised the area where most migrating peasants from the South lived when they first entered the city. The locus of alley dwellings reflected patterns of segregation: alley houses did not face streets; they faced each other in an interior world that resembled a rural village. Yet this situation, according to Borchert, was not as dire as it would look to the middle-class sociologist William Jones in *Recreation and Amusement Among Negroes in Washington, D.C.,* or to the group of social analysts of the slum and ghetto (ranging from Jacob Riis to Daniel Moynihan) who have insisted on identifying the urban peasant milieu with the pathological.[25]

Borchert argues that doors fronting on each other encouraged the citizens of these "hidden communities" to create tightly knit social units. Contrary to the critical interpretations of the black urban poor by middle-class sociologists, these units were vital, protective, and nourishing, consisting of individuals who formed a variety of social arrangements: nuclear families, extended families, single-parent families whose heads preferred being single and whose children were protected by, and benefited from, invisible but well-defined codes of behavior:

Home may be private, but the front door opens out of the living room onto the street [alley], and when you go down one step or use it as a seat on a warm evening you become part of the life of the neighborhood. . . . But it is not only the frequency of using the street and the street outside the house as a place, and not simply as a path, which points up the high degree of permeability of the boundary between the dwelling unit and the immediate environing area. It is also the use of all channels between dwelling unit and environment as a bridge between inside and outside: open windows, closed windows, hallways, even walls and floors serve this purpose.[26]

Alley life obviously wasn't an ideal world, but, despite economic privation, it did possess social coherence, and it represented values of human interaction and public exchange which the middle classes were anxious to abandon. Toomer understood that the consequences of that abandonment would include cultural stagnation, political estrangement, and personal isolation.

The two poems that follow "Avey"—"Beehive" and "Storm Ending"—depict the same kind of oppositions Mumford and Borchert saw within urban life. An antipastoral, "Beehive" begins with the active image of the "black hive" and ends with the frozen image of the speaker's "wish that I might fly out past the moon / And curl forever in some far-off farmyard flower" (89). Anticipating the story "Theater," the "hive" of the city offers an extravagant fantasy of escape for the "drone" observer, who describes himself "lying on my back, / Lipping honey" that is "dripping from the swarm of bees." The exploitation of urban folk art, the "silver honey"—whether money or music or some less definable energy—requires commercial packaging of folk themes. For all its sentimentalization of the country, the pastoral, after all, is an urban art form.[27]

"Storm Ending" contains the contrasting energy Toomer associates with cabaret life. Here the imagined flower "far off" becomes the present but invisible phenomenon of "thunder blossoms." Unlike the ambiguous "silver honey," the storm of the flowers is "bleeding rain" like "golden honey." "Earth," which was a "waxen cell"—that is, static, immobile—is now "sweet" and "flying," defined by change and movement. "Silver," "moon," and "honey" in the first poem are replaced by "gold," "sun," and "blood" in the second, and the two poems taken together parallel the different classes and styles of "Seventh Street" and "Rhobert."

"Beehive" and "Storm Ending" serve as a conclusion to the preceding section and as an introduction to "Theater," the short story that follows them in sequence. "Theater" begins:

Life of nigger alleys, of pool rooms and restaurants and near-beer saloons soaks into the walls of Howard Theater and sets them throbbing jazz songs. Black skinned, they dance and shout above the tick and trill of white-walled buildings. At night, they open doors to people who come to stamp their feet and shout. At night, road-shows volley songs into the mass-heart of black people. Songs soak the walls and seep out to the nigger life of alleys and near-beer saloons, of the Poodle Dog and Black Bear cabarets. (91)[28]

The exchange of "life"—of music, dance, language—between street culture and the "road shows" at the Howard Theater is a two-way flow. Black energy from the *outside* seeps into the Howard Theater, saturating it; at the same time, mass culture—"the road shows" that visit the Howard—works its influence from *inside* to outside, its songs becoming the songs of the pool halls, streets, and cabarets. Above this exchange, the white city works at a different pitch ("trill") and operates on a different time (the "tick" of a clock). The director of the Howard Theater promotes another kind of influence, shaping "songs" and those who dance to their rhythms into "movements, appropriate to Broadway" (93). Thus commercial culture takes what it needs from street culture, homogenizes it, smooths its rough edges, and packages it as a kind of military drill: "Its three counts to the right, then three counts to the left and then you shimmy" (95–96).[29]

Toomer describes the dilution of energy involved in this transformation of street culture to commercial culture. Sitting in the audience of his brother's theater, John is moved by the chorus girls who appear on the stage "in the mass," not yet arranged in a chorus line: "as if his own body were the mass-heart of a black audience listening to them singing, he wants to stamp his feet and shout" (92). Despite his attraction, he can't join in their emotional abandonment: "His mind, contained above desires of the body, singles the girls out, and tries to trace origins and plot destinies." He prefers, finally, order to disorder: "Soon the director will *herd* you, my full-lipped, distant beauties, and *tame* you, and *blunt* your sharp thrusts" (92–93; emphasis added). John's position "above the desire of the body" thinly veils a fear of both the "crude" energy and the "individualized" self, what Dorris thrusts toward him when she breaks free of the chorus line and dances. His answer to the nakedness of Eros is to imagine transforming it into "writing," because to write about it is to escape the danger of its presence.

The transformation of the act into literature makes John and his role as both artist and audience contradictory in ways that extend Toomer's concerns about class and culture in the city. Toomer told Gorham Munson that in both "Theater" and "Box Seat" he was trying to achieve a new kind of open form, with each story based on a "central dynamic figure propelled by inherent energy." John, said Toomer, is bound by the laws of respectability until "Dorris' dancing . . . pulls his passion from him to it." Yet John, in abstracting the experience,

rebounds from the actuality of Dorris, from the reality of his own passion, into dream. . . . In this, he gives her an impossible beauty, and achieves an impossible contact. He is startled from his fancy by the bumper chord which is the actual end of Dorris' dancing. It is evident that he will never do more than dream of her. . . . The implication of the story is that of a dual separation: one, false and altogether arbitrary, the other, inherent in the nature of the two beings.[30]

The story's conclusion is ambiguous: does John's dream represent the first stage of art or is it escapist fantasy? According to Toomer's idea of a symbolic structure, the dream could be either the apex of the "curve" upward or the nadir of the "curve" downward, illustrating in microcosm the "spherical form" of *Cane* itself. Is art primarily passion (Dorris) that will be diluted in the mind of the audience (John)? Or is art the alembic (John) transforming passion into a "higher" truth? More crucially, is the story's "central dynamic figure" really John? Or is it Dorris? These implied questions are not meant to be answered. They arise from a social context that is new (the African-American city), and the flux ("solution" is Toomer's term) of modernity is recasting conceptions of origin, community, and identity.

The "arbitrary" division between John and Dorris is one of class and, by implication, color; she is a "lemon-yellow" showgirl, while John is, in his own words, "dictie, educated, stuck up"—a mulatto aristocrat (94). The "inherent" division is between their active and passive characters, categories Toomer continually returns to in *Cane*. Dorris is articulate in a way John is afraid to recognize: "The girls, catching joy from Dorris, whip up within the footlights' glow. They forget set steps; they find their own. The director forgets to bawl them out. Dorris dances" (97). To "forget set steps" and "find their own" is the essential definition of jazz, the ability to improvise beyond the routine or established form. In abstracting Dorris from her dance, John's dream reduces her to a passive, virtually anonymous spectator: "John reaches for a manuscript of his, and reads. Dorris, who has no eyes, has eyes to understand him" (99). "Her eyes"—her personality—are effaced; she is subsumed in his.[31]

The story's larger social meaning emerges here, joining gender and class. The entire rehearsal scene has been a contest between improvisation and "set steps," between the anarchic feminine energy of the dancers and the male director's attempts to control them. In John, Toomer depicts the artist who is unable to reconcile this contradiction, to bring the "illumined city" into being. There is also a lingering question as to whether what seems "inherent," in the nature of things, might be "arbitrary," socially created. Is the difference between Dorris and John the "mystery" of personality or the background of class?

"Beehive" presented a narrator who anticipates the passive nature of John's character in "Theater," the voice of the drone observer unable to enter into the life of the hive. In "Storm Ending," on the other hand, the speaker is pulled into the world of action, as the girls at the rehearsal pull "passing show-men" into their dance; he becomes a participant, not merely an observer. This poem represents Toomer's ideal, the reciprocal relationship between outside (storm) and inside (self), a situation mirrored in the cultural exchanges of the opening lines of "Theater." This ideal appears only in momentary glimpses of the characters of *Cane*, and modernism was the ideal technique for presenting this transience: collages depict the city's shifting theatrical dynamism without pretending to sum up its truth in a closed form. But in his characters Toomer also recognizes the limits of artifice; for them the separations of class and art which provide social advantage and understanding may also involve a confusion of identity.

Inside and Outside

It is clear that the structure of *Cane*'s middle section has been worked out very carefully. The opening pieces—"Seventh Street" and "Rhobert"—characterize two aspects of black life in Washington by metaphor: "Seventh Street is a bastard" and "Rhobert wears a house." The image of the house is one of separation, enclosure, while the street is open, embracing everything that comes its way. "Avey" introduces a character from one of the houses, a black middle-class narrator, and his crucial encounters with Avey in the streets. Those meetings confirm the divisions of Washington's African-American community, yet the story's ending suddenly uncovers a historical terror from which the whole community suffers together. The two poems that follow not only comment on "Avey" but introduce the themes of "Theater," which in turn is followed by a poem ("Her Lips Are Copper Wire") and a sketch ("Calling Jesus") that offer commentary on "Theater" and a preview of "Box Seat."

Using city imagery reminiscent of T. S. Eliot's early poems, Toomer in "Her Lips Are Copper Wire" again touches on themes of social connection and interchange. Toomer claimed in his autobiography that he was a "a natural poet of man's artifices. Copper sheets were as marvelous to me as the petals of flowers; the smell of electricity was as thrilling as the smell of earth after a spring shower." Unlike Eliot, Toomer does not satirize the mechanical image. The two cities in *Cane*'s middle section, the city of law (the insulated wires) and the city of vision, contradict one another—before vision is achieved, some kind of empathetic connection beyond the law must be made between human beings. When the lover in the poem asks to have the "tape" removed from his lips, he asks for the spark that a kiss will create, that will turn his lips to an "incandescent" glow.[32]

Each of the paired sketches and poems of *Cane*'s middle section presents contrasted elements; "Her Lips Are Copper Wire" is intentionally contrasted with "Calling Jesus." The lovers' ecstatic meeting in "Copper Wire" is set against the "scared" isolation of Nora in the sketch. The woman of "Calling Jesus" (nameless in *Cane*, but originally called Nora) is also a female counterpart to Rhobert, though here the satire is softened by compassion for her plight as a black peasant lost in the urban landscape of the city. The sketch hovers between sympathy and irony, balanced in the figure of the "little thrust-tailed dog" that is Nora's "soul." The dog remains in the "vestibule" when she retreats to her house for refuge from the alienation of the streets; at night, she summons it to her dreams, which mix nostalgia for rural life ("dream-fluted cane") with her Christian heaven, "where builders find no need for vestibules, for swinging on iron hinges, storm doors" (103).[33]

The dog—"her soul"—is ambivalent about her escapist dreams: "at night, when she comes home, the little dog is left in the vestibule, nosing the crack beneath the big storm door, filled with chills unto morning" (103). A "vestibule" is somewhere between outside and inside, and given a choice the dog would rather go outside into the street. Nora's fear of city life has displaced the church traditions in which her breath could "bear the life of coming song," and that fear also keeps her from potential sources of renewal in this new urban landscape:

I've seen it [the dog] tagging on behind her, up streets where chestnut trees flowered, where dusty asphalt had been freshly sprinkled with clean water. Up alleys where niggers sat on low door-steps before tumbled shanties and sang and loved. (103)

The first sentence points to nature's presence in the city, the second to the black communal life "up alleys" that shares the vitality of nature. It is these worlds of nature and community that the "dog" wishes to join when he noses "the crack beneath the big storm door." But Nora, like John in "Theater," is lost in the fantasy of dream, ignoring the alley world that could saturate her with the same vitality that enlivens the walls of the Howard Theater, where walls act as a medium "between inside and outside" to connect the theater to the "life of nigger alleys." In "Rhobert" and "Calling Jesus," the divisions between inside and outside are maintained.

The distinction between inside and outside introduces "Box Seat." The story opens with an elaborate figure posing the relationship of house and street as a courtship:

Houses are shy girls whose eyes shine reticently upon the dusk body of the street. Upon the gleaming limbs and asphalt torso of a dreaming nigger. Shake your curled wool-blossoms, nigger. Open your liver lips to the lean, white spring. Stir the root-life of a withered people. Call them from their houses, and teach them to dream.
Dark swaying forms of Negroes are street songs that woo virginal houses. (104)

Echoing the *The Waste Land*, Toomer associates the dying "root-life" of the black middle class with their sealed houses. By contrast, the story's protagonist, Dan Moore, is identified with the world *outside* the houses, with nature and the streets: "Dan Moore walks southward on Thirteenth Street. The low limbs of budding chestnut trees recede above his head. Chestnut buds and blossoms are wool he walks on." The literal and figurative chestnut blossoms describe the vividness of the streets: Dan seems to walk on cloth, cotton or wool, recalling the vitality of black peasant life.

Dan, however, is frustrated by the houses' enclosed space, in which the domestic, the feminine, and the pragmatic dominate. Mrs. Pribby, the landlady and guardian of Muriel, is also guardian of the Lares and Penates of the black middle class, her ethos circumscribed by the society pages of the newspaper that she continuously shakes. In her house, panes of glass separate and divide, and chairs assume a military function, locking people into place as in the M Street High School drill:

The house contracts about him. It is a sharp-edged, massed, metallic house. Bolted. About Mrs. Pribby. Bolted to the endless rows of metal houses. Mrs. Pribby's house. The rows of houses belong to other Mrs. Pribbys. No wonder he couldn't sing to them. (107)

When Dan visits the Lincoln Theater, the metaphor of the padlock reappears: "The seats [in the Lincoln Theater] are bolted houses." As the audience sits down, each seat is "a bolt that shoots into a slot, and is locked there." The Lincoln's audience is bolted down because they are not supposed to interact with the stage; they are purely spectators. According to sociologist William Jones, the Howard Theater and the Lincoln Theater attracted different audiences because their kinds of entertainment differed. The Howard Theater specialized in jazz and "popular" entertainment, while the Lincoln Theater's ambience and entertainment were suitable for genteel tastes. In "Box Seat," though the setting of the theater is "proper," the audience at the Lincoln is not uniform — its heterogeneous composition reflects all of Washington's black community. Highbrow and lowbrow mix, a point Dan makes by his satirical (and miscegenated) reference to Bernice, Muriel's friend, as "a cross between a washerwoman and a blue-blood lady, a washer-blue, a washer-lady" (116). Moreover, the different acts performed in the Lincoln Theater serve the audience's diverse tastes; the boxing match between two dwarves that is central to the story belongs to vaudeville, the urban art form of the masses.[34]

The sentence that follows the metaphor of the seat as a locked cell evokes the spirit of vaudeville: "Suppose the Lord should ask, where was Moses when the light went out?" (117). The joke is an old one, with both theatrical and literary sources, and it establishes the mixed culture of the theater. When Dan enters, he singles out people who cannot be locked into their seats, who do not fit the middle-class mold, in particular a "portly Negress" who joins country and city; she sends her "strong roots" beneath the floor of the theater: "They spread under the asphalt streets. Dreaming, the streets roll over on their bellies, and suck their glossy health from them. Her strong roots sink down and spread under the river and disappear in blood-lines that waver south" (119). She might heal the "root-life of a withered people" so that the "glossy health" of the streets could enter the Lincoln Theater just as it entered the Howard Theater. Vaudeville itself is a collage of disparate events — high and low, naive and sophisticated — that mirror the woman whose roots cross boundaries; indeed, Boni & Liveright referred to *Cane* on the book jacket of the first edition as a "black vaudeville," its form also a collage of ragtag odds and ends.[35]

The answer to the Moses joke is "in the dark," a metaphysical place that Toomer's heroes may inhabit or from which they may pass in and out. In "Theater," John is half in the dark as he sits waiting for rehearsal to begin: "Light streaks down upon him from a window high above. One half his face is orange in it. One half his face is in shadow" (91). When Toomer explained "Box Seat" to Waldo Frank, he said he wanted Dan Moore "to be sensitive, but weak. The minute I started to rewrite, Dan expanded." The two versions of the story are predicated on two versions of Dan, a pattern of doubling that also obtains between John and Dan and in "Kabnis" between Kabnis and Lewis. When Dan is "sensitive and weak," he is merely an observer, like John in "Theater." This is the Dan of whom Muriel complains: "Starts things he doesn't finish" (117). His revised character makes him a more active agent in the story, not merely an observer, yet this new Dan is also problematic. His acts of will have uncertain results; his assertiveness gives him greater strength, but it also seems uncontrollable or "vicious," as Toomer says.[36]

Finally, Dan is both heroic and ineffectual. He is clumsy, expending energy that spills over into chaos and inconclusion, so that he is unable to act on what he knows. The dwarves' staged boxing match—the centerpiece of the evening's entertainment—turns into a genuine brawl, and from this excitement comes the winning dwarf's song, after which he offers the bloodstained rose to Muriel. Dan sees that she takes the rose only because of the audience's expectations—their desire to see the spectacle appropriately completed—and he tries to make her realize that the dwarf, made in God's image, is therefore capable of being Christ ("the Son of God"). "JESUS," he shouts, "WAS ONCE A LEPER!" (129). The image of the "leper" raises the specter of what polite black society prefers to ignore: the heritage of slavery, and the grotesquely white, deathly pale skin of the leper which the mulatto aristocracy parodies.[37]

Muriel's reluctance to accept the rose is like the black middle class's attempt to isolate themselves from history and the present reality. Dan "shouts" the dwarf "into a possible Jesus" because he wants to break down the barrier between inside and outside (actor/audience) so that Muriel can see the connection between the potential Christ and the visible leper/dwarf. By shouting Christ into visibility, Dan urges Muriel not to be a voyeur like the other black middle-class spectators. Dan engages in an act of reading—reading the "words" in the dwarf's eyes—that makes him a participant in the dwarf's agony, and he wants Muriel to share that experience for her own salvation.[38] Toomer's reservations regarding his protagonist, partly expressed in the letter to Frank, hinge on the mixture of Dan's motives and his incomplete understanding of Muriel. Dan had intended to "sing" to the feminine houses ("shy girls") and to woo Muriel into his uncircumscribed world. Toomer even puns on Mrs. Pribby's enclosed space, when "the house contracts about him," as the social conventions of Washington act on black society with the force of a legal contract. "No wonder," Dan despairs, that "he couldn't sing to them" (107). However, despite Dan's later insight—seeing possible salvation in an image of defeat—his *sight* is incomplete because it precludes Muriel's own vision.[38]

Dan imagines himself a "dynamo" and "a god's face that will flash white light from ebony" (126). The energy of the dynamo should result in vision, and Dan seems always on the verge of having one. He hears the "new-world Christ" coming up through the walls of Mrs. Pribby's house and sees the woman at the Lincoln Theater who sinks her roots so deep beneath the building's foundations that they travel back to the South. He also remembers seeing an old man on a street who was "born a slave" and who makes him reflect on "slavery not so long ago," a figure who anticipates Father John in "Kabnis." Dan also evokes his biblical namesake: "Sometimes I think, Dan Moore, that your eyes could burn clean . . . burn clean . . . BURN CLEAN!" (123). Struggling to read the handwriting on the walls of the Lincoln Theater, he wants more than what the mass culture of watered-down jazz offers its captive audience. Yet when the dwarf flashes the mirror in his direction—"in the face of each one he sings to"—Dan is blinded by the light.

When Muriel looks at the dwarf, she, "tight in her revulsion, sees black" (128). Like Dan, she sees the dwarf symbolically, but the sight terrifies her; she can only "daintily" reach for the offered rose. Dan wants the dwarf to mediate between him and Muriel, as if each of them, looking at the dwarf, could see things that went unseen in Mrs. Pribby's house. Yet when in his anger Dan "shouts" rather than "sings," attacking Muriel and, by implication, black society, he expends his energy rather than consolidating his vision: "He is as cool as a green stem that has just shed its flower" (129). Dan's frustration with his own ambiguous situation and sense of failure, which is both racial and economic—"No, I aint a baboon. I aint Jack the Ripper. I'm a poor man out of work" (105)—blinds him to Muriel's personal fear and the real limitations of her own social position. In "Avey" the narrator has the extraordinary epiphany that allows him suddenly to understand; in "Box Seat" Dan's violent insight disappears even as he voices it, and no understanding remains.

Finally, Dan scuffles with a man in the audience and follows him outside for a fight that replays the boxing match onstage. But the dwarves' ritual performance, made authentic by their genuine anger, cannot be replicated; misunderstanding the relation between stage and street, Dan tries to imitate their real anger as if it might extend his shouted insight, the epiphany that cannot be realized as vision or translated into meaning for Muriel's life. When Dan walks away, leaving Muriel and the angry man behind, "eyes of houses, soft girl-eyes, glow reticently upon the hubbub and blink out" (130). An isolated figure at story's end, Dan walks down an alley behind the theater and disappears, followed by "smells of garbage and wet

trash" and the image of black trashmen who will pass in the morning, singing and ringing their gongs.[39]

The Divided Personality

"Box Seat" is the final piece of *Cane* to be set in Washington, although the
book's second part includes two more poems and a final story. The poem
that follows Dan's vanishing into the night is the much-debated "Prayer."
Waldo Frank did not like "Prayer," but Toomer argued strongly to include
it as part of the book's "spiritual curve." Its language is arch and abstract
compared to the imagistic mode of the other poems in *Cane*, and its style
points in the direction Toomer's writing would take after *Cane*. A kind of
free-verse sonnet, "Prayer" analyzes Dan's rage and John's distant dreami-
ness not only as active and passive responses, but as types of the divided
personality.

The poem is stated as a plea to the "Spirits" to heal the mind/body dualism; neither the rational nor the sensual fulfills the needs of the soul, which
is the third party in the poem's triad. The large soul of the "Spirits" is reflected in the finite as "a little finger," the human soul that should mediate
between mind and body. The "flesh-eye" is the pivotal image in the octave,
for its "lid" is a gateway to a spiritual realm, the link between infinite/finite
and to a reconciliation between mind and body. When the eye is open, the
"little finger" is strong, when the eye is closed, it is weak; but, as the sestet
makes clear, the speaker is unable to control the "finger" that might open
his spiritual eye. He is unable even to distinguish between body and soul or
to decide how they are related, for the "flesh-eye" only opens in rare moments which the speaker associates with the "voice," the incarnated word.
"My voice could not carry to you did you dwell in the stars," he affirms,
yet he seems unable to find a way to join himself to them. Similarly, the
inability of John and Dan to connect their visions to their lives leaves the
central ambiguity of earthly existence intact. They see imperfectly, or speak
and are not heard. The ending of "Prayer" offers only the indirect evidence
of the "voice" to signal that some resolution is possible; in a sense, the ending of "Bona and Paul" illustrates the inadequacy of language to express a
perfect vision.

While "Prayer" tries to depict an individual sense of confusion and self-
doubt, a disorganized personality, its companion piece, "Harvest Song,"
describes social alienation. The setting moves from city to country, and the
poem is linked to "Reapers" and "Song of the Son" from *Cane*'s first part; it
also anticipates the themes of "Bona and Paul" and "Kabnis." The speaker
in "Harvest Song" has cut his field of oats but now is "too chilled, and too
fatigued to bind them" (132). Like the speaker in "Prayer," he is blind but
tries to see, he is deaf but tries to hear; he wants to reach "other harvesters." In "Song of the Son" the speaker seems sure of his task, "to catch thy

plaintive soul," to record in some way a culture he believes will be "soon gone." His relationship to that "song-lit race of slaves" is presented unproblematically, perhaps because he believes he is there by choice—"I have returned to thee." The speaker of "Harvest Song," by contrast, is *part* of the rural world, where he both "hungers" to see and hear the other harvesters and is afraid "to call" to them. As he says, "I fear knowledge of my hunger."

What the speaker fears to know are the full terms of his relationship to the world of the black peasant in the South, and by extension the position of all African-Americans in the United States. The title's promise of fulfillment is ironic, for the singer's "throat is dry," and he suffers from both deprivation and disconnection; the harvesting is done, but he can't "bind" what he has harvested. The poem concludes:

> O my brothers, I beat my palms, still soft, against the
> stubble of my harvesting. (You beat your soft
> palms, too.) My pain is sweet. Sweeter than
> the oats or wheat or corn. It will not bring me
> knowledge of my hunger. (133)

Addressing the other harvesters as "brothers" (as Paul will address the black doorman in "Bona and Paul"), the speaker imagines a final, almost subliminal call and response between them, a gesture that hints at the missing drum of the slave experience. The pain of his dry isolation is suddenly made sweet by possible contact, perhaps empathy, yet that possibility will not resolve the conflict between his hunger to join and his fear of what that connection, that identity, will mean.[40]

Toomer's choice to put this antipastoral poem in his city section—even referring to it as a pivotal moment in *Cane*'s "spiritual entity"—seems at first odd: why should it preface the final city story, "Bona and Paul"? In "Seventh Street," the poetic sketch that prefaces the Washington stories, the emphasis falls on the energy of an African-American peasantry reinvigorating a dead city. As a preface to "Bona and Paul," "Harvest Song" suggests the difficulty and the danger posed by a connection that is needed and even desired. The narrator of the poem frames a paradox in which he both wishes to join the "other harvesters" and fears that he won't be able to escape them.

Outside the Garden, an Awakening

The first part of *Cane* ends with "Blood-Burning Moon," a story that in a sense explains the stories and poems that precede it; what underlies the South's system of racial terror, miscegenation and lynching, is made explicit. In a different way, "Bona and Paul" draws together the themes and ideas Toomer has woven through his book's second part, though its conclusion requires that the setting move away from Washington, D.C., to

Chicago. In fact, it is crucial that the city of "Bona and Paul" be Chicago and not Washington, for Chicago is supposedly free of the strict social codes that still control the historical Southern city. Rising from the ashes of the famous fire of 1872, Chicago seemed to promise the realization of an American ideal. In Carl Sandburg's poem "Prairie," it foreshadows a utopian future: "I sing of new cities and new men," and in Frank's *Our America* it is one of the hopeful centers of the new culture. Modern, energetic, and open to change, Chicago represents freedom from the past, a point emphasized in "Bona and Paul" as Paul reflects upon his relationship with Bona, a white girl from the South: "in Chicago you'll have the courage to neither love or hate. A priori" (148). Here "a priori" means an escape from a posteriori boundaries and definitions, from the arbitrary colors of black and white. The story is filled with colors—lavender, gray, pink, red-brown, purple—which seem to suggest how impossible that duality would be.[41]

Chicago as a symbolic city promises a terrain where social maps, if they exist, can be erased and redrawn. The story undercuts that promise on its first page, as Bona watches Paul at military drill in the school gymnasium. Although "the dance of his blue-trousered limbs thrills her," what attracts her to Paul is his difference: "he is an autumn leaf. He is a nigger. Bona! But dont all the dorm girls say so? And dont you when you are sane say so? That's why I love—Oh nonsense" (134–35). Bona's ambivalence is like Bob Stone's, an attraction to something forbidden joined to a revulsion against crossing a social line. When the young recruits stop drilling and the basketball game begins—"girls against boys"—Bona's passion surfaces: she "burns crimson . . . lunges into his body . . . squeezes him," and Paul in turn is made dizzy by the contact (136).

"Bona and Paul" transfers Toomer's repeated pattern of conflict between man and woman into a setting that should be freer than rural Georgia or conservative, segregated Washington, D.C. The basketball game is a kind of utopian moment, for within the game there is gender equality and contact between the races. Bona's images of Paul come from a pastoralized nature—he is "a candle that dances in a grove," a "harvest moon," an "autumn leaf"—and are balanced by Paul's own imaginary vision of his origins, where "a Negress chants a lullaby beneath the mate-eyes of a southern planter" (137–38). The city that includes nature also includes history, however; Bona's imagination moves from "autumn leaf" to "nigger," and Paul's benevolent planter recalls Bob Stone and the man who impregnated Karintha. Chicago is no sanctuary from America's racial obsession, and the question becomes whether it is possible to discover any countering impulse there, any "cosmopolitan" solution beyond Georgia or Washington, D.C.

Paul is accepted as a student at the school of physical education, but his racial identity still defines him in the eyes of others. In their eyes he is "passing," crossing a racial boundary that is not as rigidly drawn as in Georgia, but which is still unmistakable. Bona, Art, and Helen all want to place him as black, to force him to confess to his tincture of black blood. Paul's friend Art thinks, "If he'd only come out, one way or the other, and tell a feller" (146). Bona asks him, "Paul, tell me something about yourself" (143). The need to "answer questions," to explain, points to the enormous pressure of society's racism; Paul resists, but without reflecting on his resistance. In Paul's doubled consciousness his private musings celebrate his mixed blood and even mythologize it as the potential source of his art, while in his public life he evades the social consequences of an African-American identity.[42]

Toomer uses a mirror image to represent Paul's equivocal status and his divided mind:

> Paul is in his room of two windows
> Outside the South-Side L track cuts them in two.
> Bona is one window. One window, Paul. (137)

Toomer puns on "South-Side"/South, the two windows divided by spatial/moral regions that travel back in time, and Paul's reverie traces his roots back to the South, to the primal act of miscegenation ("A Negress . . . beneath the mate-eyes of a southern planter"). He sees the mating of the two races as taking place under the "sun," sending forth sunlit melodies, and by implication he is one of the melodies, the "son" of the sun: "Paul follows the sun into himself in Chicago" (138). His self-deception is then marked by a biblical allusion:

> He is at Bona's window
> With his own glow he looks through a dark pane. (138)

In First Corinthians 13:12, the Apostle Paul's dark "glass" stands for an immature spiritual understanding: "For now we see through a glass darkly; but then face to face: now I know in part; but then I shall know even as I am known." Paul's glow, his inheritance from the Southern "sun," isn't adequate for understanding Bona, or for fully understanding himself.[43]

When Paul takes Bona out in public to a nightclub called the Crimson Gardens, he confronts his identity "face to face." The club's patrons "leaned towards each other over ash-smeared tablecloths and highballs and whispered: What is he, a Spaniard, an Indian, an Italian, a Mexican, a Hindu, or a Japanese?" (145). The list names the "borderline" nationalities in American culture, but it omits the African-American. The club's doorman/bouncer is a large black man, perhaps instructed to exclude people with complexions slightly less ambiguous than Paul's. The pressure of the staring faces is a revelation to Paul:

Suddenly he knew that he was apart from the people around him. Apart from the pain which they had unconsciously caused. Suddenly he knew that people saw, not attractiveness in his dark skin, but difference. Their stares, giving him to himself, filled something long empty within him, and were like green blades sprouting in his consciousness. (145)

"Face to face," the stares of the crowd give Paul "to himself," his new knowledge of his difference "sprouting" into identity.[44]

In First Corinthians the Apostle Paul attempted to sort out early doctrinal disputes for the church at Corinth; a major problem was the question of whose authority was to be accepted or, more generally, the nature of the true revelation. The false "wisdom" the Apostle questions is to be replaced with the true knowledge of God: "Let no one deceive himself. If any one among you thinks that he is wise in this age, let him become a fool that he may become wise" (1 Cor. 3:18). In the Crimson Gardens Paul becomes a kind of holy fool, seeing visions and almost speaking in tongues after the revelation of his difference. Dancing with Bona, he at first continues their argument—Bona insisting that he is "cold" and Paul insisting that "mental concepts" rule her; then, as "passionate blood leaps back into their eyes," they abruptly move to the door to leave the nightclub and consummate their passion. As they leave, however, the black doorman catches Paul's eye with a "knowing" glance. Turning back to speak to him, Paul delivers an elaborately poetic peroration, explaining what his relation to Bona is to be. The story ends: "Paul and the black man shook hands. When he reached the spot where they had been standing, Bona was gone" (153).

If Paul has become a fool to become wise, his new wisdom is still inadequate for understanding the world. His assertion that "something beautiful is going to happen," "that white faces are petals of roses. That dark faces are petals of dusk. That I am going out and gather petals" (152–53), struggles to create a unifying myth that might answer his realization of difference. That ideal epiphany, like Dan's cry that Jesus was once a leper, will not resolve Bona's fear nor change the doorman's knowledge of how the world works. It remains uncertain what exactly the doorman "knows," but Paul reads his "knowing look" as racial recognition, and he hastens to inform the doorman that he does not want to "know" Bona only in the flesh. The merging of petals must be a union of opposites—not just black with white, but the actual with the ideal, involving body and soul, passion and spirit. It's a task that is beyond Paul, and, in the context of the story, it seems to be beyond anyone.

When Toomer sent the manuscript of *Cane* to Waldo Frank and sketched in his letter the form he had tried to give his book, "Bona and Paul" was described as the point of "awakening." In the Crimson Gardens Paul awakens to his "difference," to the realization that he is regarded by the others in the crowd as "racially" different. In a sense, Paul has been sleepwalking through the hostile American city, "passing" without admitting even to himself that he is "passing." His moment of truth comes when the black doorman catches his eye as he leaves with Bona. Outside, Paul looks back at the nightclub:

A strange thing happens. He sees the Gardens purple, as if he were a way off. And a spot is in the purple. The spot comes furiously towards him. Face of the black man. It leers. It smiles sweetly like a child's. Paul leaves Bona and darts back so quickly that he doesnt give the door-man a chance to open. He swings in. Stops. Before the huge bulk of the Negro.
  "Youre wrong."
  "Yassur."
  "Brother, youre wrong.
  "I came back to tell you, to shake your hand, and tell you that you are wrong."
(152)

As an "awakening," what Paul tells the doorman about his relation to Bona is much less important than the vision he has of the man's face rushing at him, first leering, then smiling like a child's: here are the contradictory plantation stereotypes of African-Americans, the "lascivious beast" or the "simple child." When Paul confronts the man with "Youre wrong," the doorman's reply—"Yassur"—is a concentrated history of racial and class hierarchies in America. Paul quickly softens his manner, "Brother, youre wrong," but his transcendent explanation is equally a condescension. In effect, the black doorman is cut out and silenced much as John silences Dorris in "Theater." In imitating the white world, Paul imitates its racism as well in his reflexive vision of the doorman and in the way he puts him in his "place." In this exchange, class is as important as race: the black doorman who is allowed only one line, "Yassur," remains *outside* the door, whereas Paul is allowed to enter.

  The irony is doubled, then, when Paul turns back to Bona and finds her gone. Paul can't have both the black and the white worlds—when he joins one, he loses the other. The ideal of amalgamation, of the new "purple" American as Toomer will imagine him in *The Blue Meridian*, is still, as Paul sees it, "way off." As an "awakening," the story of "Bona and Paul" is also a prologue to "Kabnis." South and North, city and country, black and white, body and spirit—all the divisions and conflicts in "Bona and Paul" are amplified in *Cane*'s last and longest piece. The conclusion there, whether seen as resolution or nonresolution, is also prefigured in "Bona and Paul."

Chapter 8
The Black Man in the Cellar

But some of you will ask: "Why bring up these sad memories of the past? Why distress us with these dead and departed cruelties?" Alas, my friends, these are not dead things.
—Alexander Crummell, "The Black Woman of the South," 1883

On the prefatory pages facing parts 1 and 2 of *Cane*, Toomer had Boni & Liveright print two semicircular glyphs suggesting a crescent moon and a dome, respectively. On the page facing part 3, "Kabnis," appear two curved lines that hint at the form of a circle but never meet—just as "Kabnis" ends the book not by synthesis or closure but by posing a further enigma. "Kabnis" extends the mystery story of the book's first part by parodying a traditional scene from a detective story, "where the characters are gathered together in a drawing-room of the country house to hear a will revealed or the source of the crime disclosed." In the classic detective tale, as W. H. Auden observes, the crime is the entrance of history into a timeless world, and the detective, in solving the crime, returns the world to its state of innocence. On the night of Halsey's party, when the major characters are gathered in the cellar of his shop, the "source of the crime" is only indirectly disclosed; in a sense, however, Toomer's narrator does reveal the contents of a will, a heritage that will be passed on to another generation.[1]

When Toomer sent the first rough draft of his book to Waldo Frank, he defined the form of *Cane* as a circle. Frank had been, as Toomer said, "the prime mover" in helping with the completion of *Cane*, and he was going to personally deliver the manuscript to his own publisher, Horace Liveright. Given these circumstances, it's not surprising that Toomer would be grateful and eager to affirm that he was part of Frank's project for the regeneration of American culture; Toomer's dedication of the book's third section to Frank appears on the same page as the two curves. *Cane*, in fact, repeats the general structures of Frank's *Our America*, *Rahab*, and *City Block*, narratives where the end lies in the beginning. The last story of *City Block* is named "Beginning," in which the storyteller emerges as the voice of an already dead narrator, and *Rahab*'s final chapter is called "Earth," a renewal of the false pastoral ("River Garden") that began Fanny's journey in the earthly city.[2]

The circle was for Frank a figure of wholeness and coherence representing the possibility for cycles of renewal and growth. The circle implies a pattern of continuity, one that seems to offer connection and reference within a random, chaotic moment of history. Thus, in Frank's favored Hegelian terms, the "spiral" of history in *Cane* is a series of ascending circles, all on the same axis, that subsume previous experience in such a way that nothing is ever lost, only reseen and reconfigured: "Karintha's running was a whir. It had the sound of the red dust that sometimes makes a spiral in the road." Although Karintha herself is mortal ("red dust"), her beauty is passed on to Carrie K. in "Kabnis," where "[Carrie's] red girl's-cap, catching the sun, flashes vividly" echoes a previous description of Karintha: "her sudden darting past you was a bit of vivid color, like a black bird that flashes in light." The poet's gaze links the two women, and the sun captures their beauty in a spot of time, becoming the sun/son of "The Song of the Son," the redemptive force behind the vision. So, too, when Carrie K. kneels before Father John within a "soft circle" of morning light, youth embraces age, the present encompasses the past, and the regenerative process begins anew.[3]

While acknowledging his debt in *Cane* to Frank's formal example, Toomer, in his letter to Waldo Frank of December 12, 1922, offered three different readings of how the form was embodied in the book:

From three angles, CANE's design is a circle. Aesthetically, from simple forms to complex ones, and back to simple forms. Regionally, from the South up into the North, and back into the South again. Or, from the North down into the South and then a return North. From the point of view of the spiritual entity behind the work, the curve really starts with Bona and Paul (awakening), plunges into Kabnis, emerges in Karintha etc. swings upward into Theatre and Box Seat, and ends (pauses) in Harvest Song. . . . Between each of the three sections, a curve. These, to vaguely indicate the design.

Cane alternates between story and lyric, sometimes within the same narrative, and Toomer regarded the stories of the middle section as his most complex and experimental works. The return to "simple forms" in the aesthetic reading concludes with the tableau of Father John embracing Carrie K. and the author sending his text out into the world. In describing how his narrative "regionally" circled between North and South, Toomer, of course, was referring not only to compass directions; he also evoked the contrast of different histories, cultures, and societies. The movement between North and South also moved between a literal and a symbolic geography, for a region's reality is fluid, not fixed; as Toomer knew, modern cultures were changing rapidly.

In his correspondence with Waldo Frank, Toomer's use of the phrase "spiritual entity" also had a particular meaning. As we have shown, the "spiritual" for Frank involved a sense of belonging, of self-knowledge, of personal and cultural integration, and it was this social meaning that informed the "mystical" aspect of *Our America*: "For the more surely a man finds himself, and finds the world he lives in, the more surely he finds God." In a letter probably written a few weeks after he sent his manuscript to Frank, Toomer wrote of his friend's novel: "Holiday? Brother, you are weaving yourself into the truth of the South in a most remarkable way. You need it to complete your own spiritual experience." "Spiritual experience" refers to Frank's understanding of America and his place in it that he will come to by writing *Holiday*. Similarly, the "spiritual entity" of *Cane* defined for Toomer an understanding of his own life history and that history's relation to "his" America.[4]

The Enlightenment impulse to resolve the conflicts that produce human misery was the distant problem behind Toomer's specific examination of "race" in America. However, whether it has its roots in Hegel or elsewhere, the central assumption of a cyclical history is that it needs to "ascend" in order to offer hope; to begin anew a history of exploitation and murder is the Gothic terror of repetition. In a letter to Georgia O'Keeffe in January 1924, Toomer spoke of "Bona and Paul," as if indeed "Paul resolves these contrasts ['black' and 'white'] to a unity," which marks the necessary ascension. The vision of fusion (white and black, tangible and intangible) in Paul's speech to the doorman points to the beginning of the author's spiritual journey in which, like Dante, he descends into Hell ("Kabnis") in order to ascend as the author of *Cane* (his "birth-song"). In "Karintha" the folk spirit of the race becomes the basis of an ascent "upwards" through the visions of John and Dan (in "Theater" and "Box Seat"); it finds an apotheosis in "Harvest Song," whose singer articulates a dilemma ("I hunger . . . I fear knowledge of my hunger") that is resolved in "Bona and Paul."[5]

Toomer's remarks to O'Keeffe, however, expressed a notably reductive reading of *Cane*, one that moves away from the complex situations of the individual stories and poems and toward a generalized resolution through transcendence. Toomer's conversion to Gurdjieffism, which dates from the latter part of 1923, probably played an important part in his revised conception of *Cane*—though even in the letter to O'Keeffe, Toomer recognized that his reading of "Bona and Paul" did not quite explain the story's complexity: "Someday perhaps, with a greater purity and a more perfect art, I'll do the thing." In fact, Toomer *had* done "the thing," if by that phrase he meant a brilliantly powerful depiction of how American racial categories separate and deny "unity." The "awakening" in "Bona and Paul," which he mentions to Frank, is an awakening to his racial difference. Paul cannot escape the nets of race, caught as he is between the doorman and Bona, and so the "curve" of *Cane's* "spiritual entity" begins by defining a social condition. This condition also explains "Harvest Song"—with its twin themes of "hunger" and fear ("I fear knowledge of my hunger")—which is as much at the nadir of the circle as is "Kabnis." In fact, Paul, Kabnis, John, Dan, and the singer of "Harvest Song" all occupy the same place on the circle, a point of Gothic repetition and sameness where the protagonist awakens from the dream to find it a nightmare. Indeed, "Kabnis" becomes an explication of the nightmare, a detailed examination of what Paul's "awakening" means.[6]

"Kabnis" and the Face of History

The Gothic modality that informs *Cane* assumes that there is no precise time in American history when slavery "happened": the corpse has always been under the sawdust pile. In "Blood-Burning Moon," the factory was in the garden before the Industrial Revolution began to change the South, thus the prewar cotton factory is history that is prehistory, a Gothic ruin without a date. Auden's analysis of detective fiction assumes that an act of discovery may restore the pastoral world—for Auden, the corpse is an open contradiction, like "a mess on a drawing room carpet," but it can be removed. For Toomer history is much more intractable; the corpse's trace remains as a silent menace, Kabnis's "intangible oppression" (162), which touches everything, including the detective who tries to solve the mystery.[7]

The pre–Civil War cotton factory is a monument to the economic arrangements that support slavery *and* it is a Gothic symbol, since Gothicism disguises power relationships as something else: haunted castles, evil demons, and so on. Inspired by Hegel, Orlando Patterson argues that slavery had as much to do with the issue of control and submission (social death, natal alienation, shame, and honor) as it did with the issue of goods and services, but Marx also understood that class struggle could take the form of social "nightmare": "The tradition of all the dead generations weighs like a nightmare on the brain of the living." In *Cane*, economics and naked power create a historical nightmare in which black *labor* is subject to capital and black women are subject to sexual oppression.[8]

An image that appears frequently in *Cane* is the human face, most often the face of an African-American woman, strangely insubstantial in its configuration. The two curves that preface "Kabnis" offer a graphic form of these indefinite faces, the Gothic mark of the identities given black women by the South's system of class and caste. The poem "Face," from *Cane's* first part, is not a precisely rendered portrait but a dreamlike series of images, or as Kabnis says, "some twisted awful thing . . . crept in from a dream":

Hair—
silver-gray,

like streams of stars,
Brows—
recurved canoes
quivered by ripples blown by pain,
Her eyes—
mist of tears
condensing on the flesh below
And her channeled muscles
Are cluster grapes of sorrow
purple in the evening sun
nearly ripe for worms. (14)

The form of the face is not static, as a photographic image might be, but seems constantly to shift. It is a face prematurely ripened, defined (condensed) by an accumulation of indescribable moments whose imprint distorts the features; it becomes the face of African-American history that pursues Kabnis.[9]

The poem itself is a Gothic revision of the Petrarchan conventions whereby the poet describes a woman's beauty by beginning with the hair and working downward to brows, eyes, and "the flesh below." This face expresses not only what she has experienced but what she has seen: "Her eyes— / mist of tears." The description alludes to both Becky and Karintha, "purple in the evening sun / nearly ripe for worms." The word "ripe" is connected with mortality ("to ripen a growing thing too soon"), but looks forward to "Song of the Son," in which ripeness is equated with fullness. The woman of "Face" also becomes the face of the lynched woman/man in "Portrait in Georgia," as in that poem "Hair . . . / Eyes . . . / Lips" slide into a "lyncher's rope . . . fagots . . . red blisters." The face not quite revealed recurs throughout the various stories in the first section: "Fern" begins: "Face flowed into her eyes." "Esther" begins: "Esther's hair falls in soft curls about her high-cheek-boned chalk-white face." In the opening paragraph of "Carma," the sun blinds the narrator by "shooting primitive rockets" into Carma's "yellow flower face." The crucial foreshadowing of the ambiguous curved lines before "Kabnis" appears at the conclusion of "Bona and Paul," where "white faces are petals of roses . . . dark faces are petals of dusk."

Thematically, "Kabnis" begins where "Bona and Paul" ends. In "Harvest Song," the singer-poet yearned for contact with his black brothers, yet feared the "knowledge of my hunger," a phrase that alludes to the Tree of Knowledge in the Garden of Eden. Satisfying the hunger to eat of the fruit of that tree would result in knowing an original sin he could never throw off. Once he is known as a "nigger," the aura of his mystery evaporates, and Bona disappears. Once a "nigger," he must remain outside the Gardens with the doorman, and he can no longer imagine himself in terms of his particular view of American exceptionalism. Chicago is a false frontier, a modern city where the garden myth is reimagined in terms of mass culture, and where a New World Adam and Eve act out the original curse of eating from the Tree of Knowledge. Kabnis, then, is a Paul who has tried to reenter the garden by returning to his ancestors' origins. Yet back in the South he is haunted by "faces" that know him, by a world that is both unreal and too real.

The opening monologue in "Kabnis" poses this situation in terms of identity, will, and fear represented by "faces":

Kabnis: Near me. Now. Whoever you are, my warm glowing sweetheart, do not think the *face* that rests beside you is the real Kabnis. Ralph Kabnis is a dream. And dreams are *faces* with large eyes and weak chins and broad brows that get smashed by the fists of square *faces*. The body of the world is bull-necked. A dream is a soft *face* that fits uncertainly upon it. . . . God, if I could develop that in words. Give what I know a bull-neck and a heaving body, all would go well with me, wouldn't it, sweetheart? If I could feel that I came to the South to *face* it. If I, the dream (not what is weak and afraid in me) could become the *face* of the South. (158; Emphasis added)

If Kabnis had the courage to *face* the real South, he could put a *face* on the dream—that is, make the dream take a tangible form. Yet, like John in "Theater" and Dan in "Box Seat," Kabnis finds it difficult to act on what he knows, and "things are so so immediate in Georgia" that they leave him without time to think or formulate a response (164). Toomer uses the word "immediate" in its philosophical sense—"things" that take shape before cognition has a chance to deal with them—and the *immediacy* in "Kabnis" and elsewhere is a historical terror that can erupt at any moment.[10]

In "Kabnis," the square faces of the white South sit upon its "bull-neck," multiple as hydra heads but monolithic in their force. The metaphor follows a pattern in *Cane* of active/passive: the bull-neck versus the soft face, the dancing Dorris versus the watching John. Toomer holds out the possibility that the two principles may merge when the "spectatorial artist" becomes a full witness to black life, and Kabnis makes a start in this direction when he actively returns to the South in search of origins and a usable past. In one sense, Kabnis/Toomer is the son who searches for a genealogy, for a father who can authenticate the son's existence. He anticipates Ralph Ellison's view that the artist's job is "not actually one of creating the uncreated conscience of his race, but of creating the *uncreated features of his face*." Identity precedes morality, yet the creation of identity also creates moral understanding. Throughout the story, the face of Kabnis is not given to him by a "southern planter" (like Halsey's white ancestor); as much as he would like to identify with *that* face, he is made to acknowledge (as Paul felt compelled to acknowledge the doorman) the suffering face of the black woman who has endured the planter's embraces.[11]

This clash of contradictory identities, the heritage of a past of terror, expresses itself in the land and people of Georgia, whose features Kabnis can never see "whole." In the story's first scene, Kabnis asks God not to "torture" him "with beauty." Lewis would resolve Kabnis's problem by harmonizing the contradictions: beauty/ugliness leads to the synthesis of art, a solution like that in "Song of the Son," in which death is a precursor to life (the poet as "singing tree"), or like Dan's well-meaning advice to Muriel in "Box Seat." But Kabnis's anguish has metaphysical roots in a painful history: "Whats beauty anyway but ugliness if it hurts you? God, he doesn't exist, but nevertheless He is ugly. Hence, what comes from Him is ugly" (162). Here there is no comfortable synthesis of opposites, no safe pattern to be imposed on the South; the "radiant beauty" of the Georgia night hides the invisible corpse under the sawdust pile or illuminates the charred body on the cross and at the crossroads. Toomer anticipates Kenneth Burke's paradox concerning "*being* or *essence*." God's being cannot be empirically proven, but because He is a linguistic "character," He affects human behavior, as Father John notes at the end of "Kabnis." Indeed, "th sin th white folks 'mitted when they made th Bible lie" is a truism so terrible that it can obliterate all other truths. God may not exist, but His essence as defined by the white South creates a universe so ugly that beauty can seem unreal or irrelevant.[12]

The day following his troubled sleep, Kabnis seeks reassurance from his local black friends, Halsey and Layman, that "things" are not as bad in the South as they have been made out to be: "theres lots of northern exaggeration about the South. It's not half the terror they picture it" (171). But he doesn't get this reassurance because he has not yet learned half the truth about the South, and his initiation becomes an education in horror as he hears Layman's story about Mame Lamkins and Stella's story about her father. His fears then are not just of the physical danger to himself — they concern what is happening to him as he becomes a witness to what has been done to others. When "Kabnis wants to hear the story of Mame Lamkins. He does not want to hear it" (178), this is another context for "I hunger / I fear knowledge of my hunger" in "Harvest Song." Kabnis is the detective driven to discover what he does not want to discover, driven to know even as he fears the consequences of that knowledge. And the consequences are dire: the lowest point in his spiral downward occurs in the cellar when he says: "The form that burned int my soul is some twisted awful thing that crept in from a dream, a godam nightmare, an wont stay still unless I feed it. And it lives on words" (224). The demon (mare) of the night is an insatiable parasite, converting all things to itself, especially language. The "word" that Frank thought would be the midwife to the real America becomes for Kabnis a vehicle by which the Southern nightmare is relived.

The shift of language from a mode of ordering to the expression of disorder is associated with faces and mouths, as the words "twist" or "twisted" recur in "Kabnis":

Black roots twist in a parched red soil beneath a blazing sky. (25).

Except for the twisted line of her [Stella's] mouth when she smiles or laughs, there is about her no suggestion of the life she's been through. (213)

The form that burned int my [Kabnis's] soul is some twisted awful thing. . . . An it lives on words. . . . Misshapen, split-gut, tortured, twisted words. (224)

On close inspection, her mouth is seen to be wistfully twisted. The expression of her face seems to shift before one's gaze—now ugly, repulsive; now sad, and somehow beautiful in its pain. (168)

The figure of the "twisted" represents pain and distortion, the intricate, invisible threads that make up the history of African-Americans, the complicated interrelationships between white and black. The last face described in the quotation above refers to a portrait of Halsey's black great-grandmother, one of four portraits above a mantel in a home that has served "at least seven generations of middle-class shop-owners." This picture is smaller, and stands to the left of the portrait of the English patriarch that dominates the room. That man, who has transmitted his "nature and features" to Halsey, and who was the progenitor of two families, one white, the other black (the remaining two group portraits above the mantel), appears real and consequential. The mystery of the room derives from the woman's portrait. The great-grandmother's face "shifts" in and out of focus and looks back (or forward) to the characters of Carma and Fern and Avey, women who are imperfectly seen, or who evade the danger of being "known."

In the story's opening scene, Kabnis's nerves have been peeled. Unable to sleep, he tries reading a book, but the night poets sing a more compelling song. The story's setting is a cabin reminiscent of the slave cabins of the past. The cabin illustrates Kate Ferguson Ellis's observation that Gothic novels "can be distinguished by the presence of houses in which people are locked in and locked out." Kabnis feels trapped within the cabin, yet excluded from the life outside: "Christ, how cut off from everything he is" (163). But in another sense there is no distinction between outside and inside, between home and the world:

*White*washed hearth and chimney, *black* with sooty saw-teeth. Ceiling, patterned by the fringed globe of the lamp. The walls, unpainted, are seasoned a rosin *yellow*. And cracks between the boards are *black*. These cracks are the lips the night winds use for whispering. *Night* winds in Georgia are vagrant poets, whispering. Kabnis, against his will, lets his book slip down and listens to them. The warm *whiteness* of his bed, the lamp-light, do not protect him from the weird chill of their song:
    White-man's land.
    Niggers, sing.

Burn, bear *black* children
Til poor rivers bring
Rest, and sweet glory
In Camp Ground. (157; Emphasis added)[13]

This mixture of light and shadow would be appropriate to film noir, but here it represents the secret of miscegenation, where boundaries of black and white are blended (the yellow walls, Kabnis's "lemon face"). The "cracks between the boards" through which "vagrant poets" sing the song of inexplicable suffering serve like rustling canebreaks to release the secret. The song itself suggests a slave message, filtering in from the outside, and Kabnis is forced to hear this message whether he wants to or not.

Norman Holland remarks that the Gothic castle is a "nighttime house —it admits all we can imagine into it of the dark, frightening, and unknown. . . . At the same time, [it] contains some family secret." Toomer's cabin unites these two Gothic motifs but places them within the context of African-American history. The cracks in the walls permit "powdery red dust" to settle upon Kabnis: "Dust of slavefields, dried, scattered" (159). The image recalls one from "Blood-Burning Moon," in which the moon "soft showered the Negro shanties," and foreshadows Stella's story about her father, itself foreshadowed by the image where "white faces, pain-pollen, settle downward through a cane-sweet mist and touch the ovaries of yellow flowers" (214–15).[14]

Ironically, the terror in the first scene of "Kabnis" is wholly imaginary. A squawking chicken frightens Kabnis, and he complains that he cannot smoke or drink on school grounds, self-indulgent and petty concerns. "You know, Ralph, old man,"—he says to himself, amused by the thought—"it wouldnt surprise me at all to see a ghost" (165). After his "ghost" turns out to be a stray cow, the tone has moved to farce or *Northanger Abbey* parody. As in the best writing of terror, Toomer mixes his tones, creating uncertainty, a narrative that seems unplaceable; the supernatural is absurd, yet "there must be many dead things moving in silence" (164–65). History is a "dead thing" that returns or which, to paraphrase Faulkner, may never even have left.

As the scene continues, Kabnis imagines himself "yanked" under the "court-house tower" and "sees white minds . . . juggle justice and a nigger" (163)—abruptly, the ground of the story has shifted. A stranger in Sempter, Kabnis is undergoing a process of socialization; he is being taught to live, in Michel Foucault's words, "under the shadow of the gallows." The subtlety of the South's education lies in how it creates personal fear and a climate of terror through the stories it circulates. The farcical terror of Kabnis and the chicken is first comic, then macabre, as he wrings its neck, then frightening, as the echoes of the scene and its intermittent lullaby travel back to Karintha's missing child. Halsey tells Kabnis that the rock and message he thinks are meant for him are "theatrics" out of *Uncle Tom's Cabin*, and "white folks aint in fer all them theatrics these days" (183). But the story he hears about Mame Lamkins makes the actual state of affairs in the South more direct and terrible than anything fiction can offer. The irony of Kabnis's literary imagination is that it is falsely inflated and yet inadequate to the real nightmare.[15]

The real nightmare includes both what happens to Mame Lamkins and the story of her murder as a form of "faceless," internalized surveillance. The white South intends Mame Lamkins's death to be a spectacle of terror, and its gruesomeness is even more unsettling as a story passed on within the black community. A woman beaten and murdered in the street, her infant ripped from her womb and "stuck . . . t a tree," is only the visible part of the mechanism to control and discipline—it is the invisible story that functions as the real agent of social control. As a tale whispered by the cane or told by Layman, the murder expresses the Burkean "sublime" of something so terrible that the mind cannot encompass it. Even the spoken tale somehow partakes of the unspeakable, set against a background of groans and cries.[16]

In the opening scene, Kabnis's killing of the chicken suggests the effect of this "intangible oppression" not only by the motif of transferred aggression, as in "Reapers," but also in relation to Freud's repetition-complex as the basis of the uncanny, a sense that the individual lacks agency because he or she is condemned to repeat the same reflex over and over. Kabnis has been made a grotesque, no longer in control of his own actions: "He totters as a man would who for the first time uses artificial limbs. As a completely artificial man would" (163). Later, rushing out of Halsey's house when the rock and the note come crashing through the window, he becomes a machine out of control, running on fear: "A splotchy figure drives forward along the cane- and corn-stalk hemmed-in road," imitating the terrified chicken in Kabnis's room "driving blindly at the windowpane" (160, 180). This terror reduces him to "a scarecrow replica of Kabnis"; as Kabnis tries to find his way home, Toomer describes him not as "he" but as "it," as though he has become the terrified chicken whose neck he has wrung, an act of killing that itself imitates the act of lynching. In this world social control operates as a repetition of terror, often in terms of a compulsion to mimic the crime most feared.

Foucault's notion of an omniscient, "faceless" surveillance has common points with Toomer's conception of the Gothic in *Cane*. The moon and the dome function as the all-seeing eye in "Blood-Burning Moon" and "Avey," but the menace of absolute power turns up elsewhere as things present, though unseen. The only extended description of a literal lynching occurs in "Blood-Burning Moon," but references to it through image and metaphor are everywhere in *Cane*; although white people are (with one notable exception) absent in "Kabnis," their presence, like an all-seeing eye, is felt on every page. Halsey can say facetiously that "this county's a good un," because there "aint been a stringin up I can remember" (172), but he knows, as does Layman, that effective terror lies not only in the visible lynching but in the invisible anxiety of the potential for violence. When the only white man in the story comes into Halsey's shop to have his hatchet fixed, Kabnis feels that "the whole white South weighs down upon him" (201). When Kabnis says in the cellar that "the form thats burned int my soul is some twisted awful thing crept in from a dream," he is describing an internalized terror, one produced by the world of white surveillance and control that surrounds him.[17]

The Gothic forms of power in "Kabnis" break the narration of communal history; the exchange between Kabnis, Layman, and Halsey explains the form of *Cane*'s first part, where important details are lost or omitted by narrators because their inclusion would be too dangerous. "Kabnis" then extends the investigation of the consequences of "losing" history and asks, does the "terror of power or the power of terrorism" destroy the witness's capacity to witness? That question concerns not only Kabnis and his role as artist, but the other artist-detective figures in the story: Layman, Lewis, and Halsey. At the end of "Kabnis," when Father John and Carrie K. are encircled within a "soft circle" of light and the narrator emerges like the sun to shake the "shadows" from his eyes, the poet of "Karintha" attempts to restore history. A communal history must be an exchange of experience, because, in Walter Benjamin's words, "to perceive the aura of an object we look at means to invest it with the ability to look at us in return." All of the thwarted and misunderstood gazes in *Cane* hide the "true word" of the world of the South, as narrators struggle to express the "face"—the face of the landscape, the faces of black women, the face of the man/woman on the cross.[18]

Benjamin observes that storytelling involves a reciprocal relationship between artist and audience. Similarly, according to Shoshana Felman and Dori Laub, the witness links public and private, as narrative verifies or corrects history:

the narrator-as-eyewitness is the testimonial bridge which, mediating between narrative and history, guarantees their correspondence and adherence to each other. . . . To testify—before a court of law or before the court of history and of the future; to testify, likewise, before an audience of readers or spectators—is more than simply to report a fact or an event or to relate what has been lived, recorded, and remembered. Memory is conjured here essentially in order to address another, to impress upon the listener, to appeal to a community.[19]

The storyteller as witness tries to ensure that the truth gets told and that it is incorporated within the fund of experience belonging to the community. The "vagrant poets" whispering through the cabin walls at the beginning of "Kabnis" stand for the fugitive, incomplete nature of knowledge in *Cane*'s Southern world, and for the urgent need for that knowledge to be communicated. Layman does not want to tell his story and Kabnis does not want to hear it, yet Layman talks and Kabnis listens.

Benjamin's ideal storyteller assumes that all stories form an inter-connected, continuous "web" in which individual fate is connected to communal history and destiny. But Benjamin himself observes how "the dissemination of information" in the modern world has "diminished the communicability of experience," and a commonplace in critiques of moder-nity is that diminished history is not random; particular strands and tradi-tions are singled out to be trivialized, diluted, or abolished. One effect of this is to channel memory, the storyteller's muse, into the public mode of communication known as the "news," a form that assumes the communal memory to be short-lived. The history of Sparta, therefore, will appear in the pages of the *Ishmaelite* rather than in the storytelling tradition of the city's African-American community.[20]

In "Kabnis" the web of communal memory is threatened by the intricate "web spun by the spider sawdust pile" (17). The corpse at the center of that web disrupts the connection between storyteller and audience. This is why the silent Layman and the mute Father John are linked: they are witnesses to events that they can only describe in fragments. The black commu-nity doesn't suffer from the kind of "historical amnesia" that plagues the white world, not least because the present is a continuation of past hor-rors, and the memories of past experience are so traumatic and immediate that they are unforgettable. The hesitant dialogue between Layman and Kabnis is symptomatic also of the difficulty of finding words for this kind of experience. As Felman and Laub say of the Holocaust, its "very cata-strophic . . . nature" renders the witness silent; instead of seeing a "clear *picture* of events, [he] has to literally *wake up* to a reality that is undreamt of, wake up, that is, into the unthinking realization that what he is witnessing is not simply a dream." [21]

The corpse under the sawdust pile in "Karintha" leads inexorably to Halsey's cellar, a place similar, in Kabnis's thoughts, to "where they used t throw th worked-out, no-count slaves" (233). Being down there with Father John, he relives history, and, against his will, he becomes a witness to the continuity of racial oppression. That it is the frightened Kabnis who gets the old man to speak means paradoxically that the real detective cannot be detached and cannot treat the problem to be solved as only a rational puzzle; he will have to be someone like Christ who lives with the lepers and who is himself crippled. This is the important distinction between Kabnis and Lewis.

Lewis possesses the moral rectitude Auden demands of his detective, as well as the powers of ratiocination that make him an Enlightenment man like Sherlock Holmes. He names and anoints Father John, sees the fate of Carrie K. before that fate is realized, categorizes the contradictions that beset Kabnis, and impresses Halsey with his explanation of the church "shouters": "a stream whats damned has got t cut loose somewheres" (177). However, the witness must not only be there, he/she also must not turn away. Lewis chooses not to look. At the party in the cellar, he sees the effects on the others of a Gothic system of terror that defies logic and his neat Hegelian syntheses, and he flees: "Kabnis, Carrie, Stella, Halsey, Cora, the old man, the cellar, and the work-shop, the southern town descends upon him. Their pain is too intense. He cannot stand it" (226).

Kabnis wants both to look and not to look: "Here, look at that old man there," he tells Lewis. "See him? . . . Do I look like him?" Lewis turns the tables: "You look at him, Kabnis. . . . The old man as symbol, flesh, and spirit of the past. What would he say if he could see you?" (217). And, of course, the blind Father John does *see* Kabnis, as the past judges the present. His enigmatic utterance—"O th sin th white folks 'mitted when they made th Bible lie"—exposes the illusion that the New Negro can escape a horrific past (237). On the one hand, the lie is that blackness is the mark of Cain that justifies "white folks" in their treatment of African-Americans as beasts; on the other hand, the mark of blackness is the sin Kabnis internalizes because it contaminates his "blue-blood" ancestry: "Th whole world is a conspiracy t sin . . . against me" (236).

This obsession with self is why Kabnis returns to the same question he put to Lewis: "Does he look like me?" he asks Carrie K. "Have you ever heard him say th things youve heard me say?" (236). Caught between two worlds, Kabnis cannot resolve the question of his own identity because his sociological condition also reflects a historical dilemma. The "sin" of making "the Bible lie" is an erasure not only of a usable past but of a hopeful future, for if the lie causes the open city of the New Testament to disappear, then the future becomes a nightmare of endless repetition, the chosen of the South acting out a hegemonic universe based on the law of white supremacy. To escape that prospect, Kabnis tries to separate himself from Father John, even though he realizes he cannot be a poet until he faces him. His attraction to Father John is based on his recognition that the "sin" of slavery is still his as well ("that ornery thing that's livin on my insides"), yet his fear and hatred of his black heritage cause him to identify with those who oppress him ("Aint surprising the white folks hate y so").[22]

Father John is Kabnis's hound of heaven and his tar baby: the past pursues him because he pursues it; he is stuck to it because he won't let go: "You sit there like a black hound spiked to an ivory pedestal. . . . What are y throwing it in my throat for? Whats it going to get y? A good smashin in th mouth, thats what. My fist'll sink int y black mush face clear t y guts— if you got any" (231). The threat comes from a Brer Rabbit who substitutes anger for the understanding he fears. Disturbed by the silence of that face, Kabnis seeks the Word that will release him from the twisted words that consume him. If he can just find out why Father John is where he is, he believes he can discover why "I'm what sin is."

His questions are put to a face that yields no answers, and one reason for this is that Kabnis is speaking to himself; he mocks Father John as permanently crucified on "a white pedestal," yet this figure is a better description of Kabnis himself. Kabnis's "whiteness" (as Lewis sees) immobilizes him, rendering him mute as an artist. He cannot be a running black hound because, although he identifies with the bloodhounds chasing the rabbits, he is one of the rabbits. Until he recognizes that he belongs with the anguished, "shouting" churchwomen, he can never become the trickster rabbit of black folklore. Halsey underscores his failure to identify with black life on the lower frequencies when he compares black country moonshine to Kabnis's writing: "th boys what made this stuff have got th art down like I heard you say youd like to be with words" (184).

Lewis calls Halsey "an artist in your way," and Halsey's own metaphor linking liquor and writing suggests that he is another portrait of the artist in *Cane*. Halsey represents a Southern version of the frustrated mulatto elite who are the subjects of "Esther" and the stories in the second part of *Cane*. Potentially another detective-witness in the story, he yearns for a fulfillment that he cannot articulate, and the art he creates is a diversion from the social and cultural limitations of his world. In the daylight world of his shop, he boasts: "There ain't no books what's got th feel t them of them there tools. Nassur. And I'm atellin y" (200–201). Yet when a white man walks into his shop with a "broken hatchet-handle and the severed head" that needs to be reattached, it becomes a grisly reminder of what is permitted Halsey in this small Southern town. "They like y if y work fer them," he says to Lewis and Layman, after he deftly fits together the broken parts. It is a confession of sorts, meant for Lewis, and tacitly admitting that his love of tools is also a kind of conditional surrender. Halsey expresses a passion for knowledge that he disguises with sarcasm: "Some goody-goody teachers from th North had come down t teach th niggers" (221). Halsey "couldnt stand em messing an pawin over m business like I was a child." Like the young Richard Wright in *Black Boy*, he hungered for a knowledge not available in America's institutions, not even among those possessing good intentions. His remark that the *Literary Digest* had "nothing I could sink m teeth int" separates him from Kabnis: "As f you," a drunken Kabnis tells Halsey, "youre all right f choppin things from blocks of wood [but] I've been shapin words after a design" (223).

Both Halsey and Kabnis belong to the mulatto elite, but one is a working artisan, the other a member of the middle class. Halsey is looking for form in matter, his approach practical and pragmatic; Kabnis wants matter to fit the form, an idealistic approach that measures the class distinction between the two men. Despite that distance between the pragmatic Halsey and the idealistic Kabnis, both are outcasts ("bastards") and frustrated word smiths. As a "smith," Halsey is one of Cain's children; questioning his fate in terms of its justice connects him to Byron's Cain and to Stephen

Dedalus. His position in the black community is substantial—he can stand up to Hanby—but his economic place is becoming precarious; the "busted" wagon that Mr. Marmon wants him to fix perhaps alludes to the famous vaudeville and blues song, "You've Been a Good Ole Wagon," which in the 1920s takes on a technological meaning as well as a sexual one. The wagons Halsey repairs are on the verge of being replaced by motorcars.[23]

Lewis is trying to gather the kind of facts that Kabnis wants to avoid discovering, but it is Kabnis who finally hears the stories of lynching and mutilation that control black life in the South, and he hears them from the story's central witness. Layman is a man "by turns teacher and preacher, who has traveled in almost every nook and corner of the state and hence knows more than would be good for anyone other than a silent man" (169). Unlike Lewis and Kabnis, who come from outside the community, Layman is both outside and inside, the storyteller, as Walter Benjamin notes, who "goes on a trip" and brings back new stories to be absorbed by the village. Layman is worried about the attention Lewis gives to his stories: "Noted what I said th other day, an that werent fer notin down" (177). Stories as "information" can go into an NAACP report on lynchings for the year 1921, but that will not touch the quality of black lives in Sempter, except perhaps to make them more vulnerable. Lewis can return to New York, but Layman and Halsey must continue to live under the rule of lynch law.

This is the point of the object lesson Halsey and Layman give Kabnis, who suggests that conditions around Sempter must be "better now" since a public "stir" has been made "about those peonage cases." Layman and Halsey respond to this bit of wishful thinking by speaking in proverbs:

LAYMAN: Ever hear tell of a single shot killin moren one rabbit, Professor? . . .
HALSEY: Now I know you werent born yesterday, sprung up so rapid like you aint heard of the brick thrown in th hornets' nest. (172)

Both men are convinced that the weak interventions of meddling outsiders bring danger to the local African-American community—the meaning also of the message for Lewis hurled through Halsey's window. The stir of public attention seems likely to further infuriate the whites and compound the killing.[24]

Toomer wrote an essay, probably in 1921 or 1922, that offers a collateral view of the nature of history and terror in the South. In an unpublished piece on Eugene O'Neill's *The Emperor Jones*, he discussed how O'Neill "particularize[s] the general emotion of fear in the Negro." O'Neill intensifies the main character's fear so that

it overpowers Jones, it successfully unlocks chambers of the Emperor's unconscious. Now the contents of the unconscious not only vary with individuals, they are differentiated because of race, by social conditions due to race. And in fact Brutus Jones lives through sections of an unconscious which is peculiar to the Negro. Slave ships, whipping posts, and so on. And because these things are actually real and present for him, his fear is at once expressed, intensified, and colored by them. *In a word, his fear becomes a Negro's fear, recognizably different from a similar emotion, modified by other racial experience.* (Emphasis added) [25]

Whether because of a "racial unconscious" or because of actual "social conditions," terror is a product of history and memory, a cultural as well as an individual reaction. Layman, like all the storytellers in *Cane*, is constrained by "slave ships, whipping posts, and so on." As a silenced storyteller, he is a preacher given the name "Layman."

Layman breaks his silence toward Kabnis with a series of three stories, interwoven with hesitations and cautions, each story becoming more grotesque and terrifying: lynchers "cut . . . t pieces" a person they had killed the previous day; lynchers kill two men "like you kill a cow" but allow Sam Raymon to choose his own death; and lynchers murder Mame Lamkins and her unborn child. At the end of Sam Raymon's story, the "shouting" from the church next door grows louder, and it upsets the fastidious Kabnis—he would like it stopped. Layman ironically agrees, noting that it is always the loudest drunk, the woman most gone in sin, who shouts the loudest: "Seems as if they cant control themselves out in th world; they cant control themselves in church. Now dont that sound logical, Professor?" (176). The final "Professor" is a rebuke: logic and control may not be saving virtues "out in th world" of the rural South. The "shouting" is a story in code, an unreadable text to an outsider like Kabnis. The story of Mame Lamkins is Kabnis's initiation into the meaning of that text. The shouting from the church and the story Layman tells are part of the same tale that has recurred throughout *Cane*: the wind blowing through trees or cabin walls or cornfields—Layman's "voice is uniformly low and soothing. A canebreak, murmuring the tale to its neighbor-road would be more passionate" (178). The shouted refrain that cuts through the walls of the room as Layman concludes his story of Mame Lamkins—murdered in the street, lying in her blood "like any cow," her living child stuck with a knife to a tree—is a response to the "call" of Layman's tale. "And then they all went away" is how Layman ends his story; the murderers disappear like a flood or a hurricane, inhuman forces that have nothing to do with logic or justice. "And then they all went away" is the way a traditional tale ends ("And they lived happily ever after"); the tale will not be forgotten, but there is also a silence at its center.

Mame Lamkins's story is the most problematic of the three for the storyteller. In the first story, the body is already a corpse, and in the second, Layman can diffuse the horror by placing Sam Raymon's death in a comic context; but in the third, he must describe the indescribable. Before he begins, he seems to sense this: "Whitefolks know that niggers talk, an they dont mind jes so long as nothing comes of it, so here goes." What does a witness like Layman do for the black community if "nothing comes of it," if the story itself does not change conditions in the earthly city? In the modern world, perhaps only Lewis's "information" can accomplish such change. What is problematic about Mame Lamkins's story is that it raises questions about the act of witnessing.

No Exit

It is probable that one influence on Toomer's conception of "Kabnis" was Hart Crane's 1921 poem, "Black Tambourine," and its theme of live burial. The major questions posed by Crane's poem are related to *Cane*'s conclusion: Is there a resurrection for the living dead? Can African-Americans escape their socially defined prisons? At the conclusion of "Kabnis," three male characters—Kabnis, Halsey, and Father John—are trapped in the cellar, as are the women at the "good-time" party, Cora and Stella. The last lines of Crane's poem suggest that the "mid-kingdom" of the cellar world is a permanent condition:

> The black man, forlorn in the cellar,
> Wanders in some mid-kingdom, dark, that lies,
> Between his tambourine, stuck on a wall,
> And, in Africa, a carcass quick with flies.[26]

Yet the key word in the last line of the poem is "quick," which has the archaic meaning "endowed with life." The black man's body is in the cellar, but his mind is not, for he shares the latent energy of Ralph Ellison's Invisible Man, who "couldn't be still even in hibernation." His interests place a *mark* on the door, a signature; the door may be closed, but

> Gnats *toss* in the shadow of a bottle,
> And a roach *spans* a crevice in the floor. (Emphasis added)

The metaphors (gnats, roach) are deliberately commonplace, but they form a pattern of living resistance that includes the "flies" and the "tambourine." The tambourine that defines the black man in terms of a stereotype from the minstrel show is also, like Aesop's fables, a subversive instrument.[27]

Aesop "found/Heaven" in those things tossed away by civilization as too trivial for consideration, and Africa's presence within the storyteller offers the potential for life's *quickening* into song. Crane's black man, then, is a symbol not just of an invisible history, but also of a poet who articulates its meaning:

> Aesop, driven to pondering, found
> Heaven with the tortoise and the hare;

Fox brush and sow ear top his grave
And mingling incantations on the air.

Aesop, dwarf and slave, appears in Toomer's "Box Seat," "driven to pon-
dering," attempting to tell his story by means of his song and the bloody
rose. Similarly, the black man in the cellar might tell his story with his
tambourine, a kind of African drum, a link to the past that potentially
quickens memory. Thus Crane's final stanza leads hopefully to the poem's
last phrase: "a carcass quick with flies." If the corpse of the past is the locus
for new life—a favorite theme of Waldo Frank, who influenced Crane as he
did Toomer—then the figure of the black man in the cellar is not as lost as
he seems.[28]

The cellar as either womb or grave suggests different interpretations of
Cane's ending, and these meanings are connected to Toomer's ongoing
argument with Waldo Frank about the question of American identity.
Frank's proclamation in his July 1922 letter to Toomer about the trip to
Spartanburg—"if you go as a Negro, so go I"—finds its complement in
Crane's analysis of the African-American dilemma. Crane could identify
with the black man in the cellar as artist, but ultimately the black man's
condition was not his own. A repeated situation in *Cane* involves narrators
who are drawn almost unknowingly into the American racial dilemma. In
"Black Tambourine," Crane's narrator comments from outside the cellar,
but Toomer's Kabnis is cast *into* the cellar with Father John.

Randolph Bourne's cosmopolitan ideal, which lay somewhere behind
Frank's revivified America and Toomer's "purple" man, offers an optimistic
reading of *Cane*'s ending. When Father John, Carrie K., and the narrator
form a triad, with Kabnis's absence (or death) as a seed that brings forth
new life, they reflect Toomer's idealized version of *Cane*, the circle of fulfilled vision and form that he promised Waldo Frank. The narrator, as
Bourne's ideal "trans-national" citizen, both participates in the communal
ceremony and remarks on it from a larger point of view, that of the American artist. Here Kabnis's verbal intellectuality dissolves into the eloquent
silence of a painting, yet the narrator is still providing the perspective of a
witness.

The final scene begins when Carrie K. shames Kabnis into humility the
morning after the party, chastising him for calling Father John "a black
fakir." "Brother Ralph, is that your best Amen?" she asks. In response, he
"sinks to his knees before her, ashamed, exhausted" (238). Kabnis goes upstairs, and Carrie K. kneels before the old man, as Kabnis had done before
her. She murmurs, "Jesus, come," the lines that conclude the Book of Revelation and the Bible, and the Beloved Community now replaces the lost
Garden. The lines that follow Carrie K.'s brief invocation (her "call"), probably the original stage directions, constitute the visionary response: "Light
streaks through the iron-barred cellar window. Within its soft circle, the

figures of Carrie and Father John." When Carrie K. kneels before Father John, the special aura that encircles them suggests a resolution of the conflicts that have beset the characters introduced earlier in *Cane*.[29]

The religious moment is continued in the last words of *Cane*, those of a narrator who has arisen from the ashes of the "dead coals" that Kabnis carried upstairs:

Outside, the sun arises from its cradle in the tree-tops of the forest. Shadows of pines are dreams the sun shakes from its eyes. The sun arises. Gold-glowing child, it steps into the sky and sends a birth-song slanting down gray dust streets and sleepy windows of the southern town. (239)

All the images that have been associated with miscegenation and death—cradle, treetops, pines, child, birth—are now transformed into a "birth-song" of hope. The twice-cited allusion to Ecclesiastes ("the sun arises") is the eternal return of the circle to origins, confirmed again in the aura emanating from the two figures within the "soft circle" of light and by the circle of the sun's "cradle." That sun is the poet as son, the religious significance of his sacred calling as artist linked to the aura cast around Carrie K. and Father John. It is the moment of *unanimisme* that Toomer has sought throughout *Cane*.[30]

The problem with such an optimistic reading of *Cane*'s conclusion, however, is that everything leading up to the "gold-glowing child" of the final sentence contradicts such optimism. Although the story ends with the birth-song of *Cane* itself, Toomer's book is hardly comforting when it comes to childbirth or babies, either literal or figurative. In *Cane* there are frequent images of pregnancy or children, cradles or fragments of lullaby, and there are four pregnancies: Karintha's, Becky's, Esther's, and Mame Lamkins's. Karintha kills her baby, and Becky's two boys are cursed with a "cross," the mark of miscegenation. Esther can love only a "tobacco-juice baby—ugly as sin" in her dream; Mame Lamkins has her baby ripped from her womb. If the child always symbolizes a future, what kind of future does this promise? Although the ending of *Cane* sees the cellar as a womb, birth as a symbol of the future is heavily qualified by the defamation and death of so many black children. Toomer's cellar is more Gothic than anything imagined by Crane, because it involves experiences unknown to Crane.

Section 5 of "Kabnis" begins with night as "a pregnant Negress," the possibility of birth and change, but the same image recalls Karintha's child. And as the poems "Reapers" and "Cotton Song" indicate, black labor produces black labor—black birth is the source of the South's economic fecundity, cynically underscored by the cotton-pickers themselves in the puns ("Hump . . . roll away") of their song (15). Sexual oppression affects both genders, and *Cane* gradually unveils the actual function of white supremacy—the anger of the "Reapers" is given explicit reason in the despair of

Stella's father; Karintha's dilemma is made clear by a white man's claim on Stella's mother. Dust, pollen, and moonlight shower the Southern landscape with malevolence. "A white man took m mother an it broke th old man's heart" (219) is Stella's story, in which the mother remains voiceless, like so many of the other women in Cane. Father John looks like Stella's father, and Stella's own despair and subsequent descent into the "sin" of prostitution hints at a hidden history about Avey to which the narrator remains blind until his final revelation on the hillside of Soldiers' Home.

Motherhood, the unborn child, and lynching culminate in Layman's story about Mame Lamkins, which throws into relief "Face" and "Portrait in Georgia" in part 1 and Avey and Muriel in part 2. Muriel's puritanism is the obverse face of Avey as prostitute: these are the only two public images of black women allowed. The hidden history that lies behind the condition of black women in Cane is revealed in "Kabnis" through Stella, Mame Lamkins, and Halsey's great-grandmother. Even an innocuous remark about Jim, a character who doesn't appear in the story, ties together scraps of information from other stories: "the nigger hates th sight of a black woman worse than death" (216). "Death" is one of the words that Father John utters, the curse to be visited on the "white folks" but first endured by blacks when the Bible is made to lie. Jim's gaze is a kind of death, reflecting the lie of the outer culture that beauty is white; but the gaze is returned by Fern and later by Carrie K., who shames Kabnis into humility. Despite the kinds of social powerlessness shared by all black women in Cane, they remain powerful figures—for better (Fern and Carrie K.) or for worse (Louisa and Carma).

Kabnis uses the figure of Mame Lamkins's child to represent the nightmare that feeds on him, a grotesque image of the seed that flowers into death: "I wish t God some lynchin white man ud stick his knife through it an pin it to a tree" (224–25). Thus the old man to Kabnis is the "Father of Hell," for Hell in the romance tradition is a "closed cycle of recurrence." Although Kabnis desperately wishes he could break the cycle once and for all by having the nightmare pinned to the tree, he fears, with considerable justification, that the act of child murder will be repeated again and again without end. In Cane the counterpart to the harmonious circle that encloses Father John and Carrie K. is the spiral. In "Kabnis," "a great spiral of buzzards reaches far into the heavens" above the black church, a shadow of death hovering over the congregation inside (169). The mystical, vertical line of the skyscraper, which will affirm American possibility in The Blue Meridian of 1936, is a sinister line of ascent in "Kabnis." The spiral of the buzzards reaching to "the heavens" concludes the images of rising smoke, dust, and ashes in this landscape which lead downward to the corpse under the sawdust pile, as if between heaven and earth there is no haven in this "white-man's land." [31]

The passion with which the shouters in the church release their emotions is a testimony to this terror of "the shadow," a passion ironically repeated (because Kabnis finds their "shouting" indecorous) by Kabnis's own shouting in the cellar when he, too, testifies to the "sin . . . done against th soul." This terror is a secret truth quite unlike Waldo Frank's hidden America, something more menacing than the Puritan-pioneer complex, something that is embedded within the American polis and the history of slavery. As Randolph Bourne had noted, the state is an organization for war, veiling its intentions behind a web of idealism and patriotism. In the South, the state was intimately linked with white supremacy, producing the state of terror that encloses the men sitting around the table in Halsey's parlor.

In "Kabnis" the power of the state appears first in the image of the Sempter courthouse that Kabnis imagines in his cabin: "He sees himself yanked beneath that tower. He sees white minds, with indolent assumption, juggle justice and a nigger" (163). This view of the Southern jury system— African-Americans, of course, would be excluded from the system except as prisoners—follows on Kabnis's characterization of God's Southern world as "lynchers and businessmen, and that cockroach Hanby, especially" (162). These are the people who populate the pages of the *Ishmaelite*, a newspaper that was essentially an instrument of the white supremacist state. Hanby, principal of the school where Kabnis teaches, invokes the state in evicting Kabnis from his cabin by threatening to call "Mr. Clayborn (the sheriff)." Hanby is part of the system, as Booker T. Washington's accommodation resorts to the institutions of white supremacy which it, in turn, helps support.[32]

The state was not primarily intended for punitive action against caste violations. Its function was to ensure that private enforcers of caste (the Klan, lynch mobs) went unpunished and that the rules of the economic regime were maintained: "The awesome and largely unchecked power of the state enforced crop-lien laws, ran the convict-lease system, and enacted penalties against outside labor recruiters." These powers were directed in large part against black labor, but some poor whites were punished as well; in Randolph Bourne's observation on power's final disposition, "the State thus becomes an instrument by which the power of the whole herd is wielded for the benefit of a class."[33]

Waldo Frank applied Bourne's herd theory to the American culture at large: "Whitman and his sons cry for their multitudes to be born anew: and the American powers take every step to preserve them in a state of ignorance, flatulence, complacency which shall approximate the Herd." Bourne's depiction of the oppressive potential of a nominal democracy acting as a "State" was not entirely equivalent to Frank's cultural concerns, and Toomer understood the difference between the two social critics. Frank's hopeful prophesy drew on sources that must have seemed very distant from the *Ishmaelite* or the sheriff in Sparta, Georgia: John Reed and the Russian Revolution, Floyd Dell and Max Eastman in Greenwich Village, the tradition of the "mystical Jew" or, in Frank's terms, "In the American chaos the Jew went under. We shall see how, in the American birth, he rises up." Counterposed against the new religion of Stieglitz and "291" is Kabnis standing in the doorway of his cabin and thinking, "New York? Impossible. It was a fiction. He had dreamed it" (163). Although Toomer, too, wanted to create a "conception of America" through an act of will, he was working with different materials, and thus he became in *Cane* a different kind of witness to American life than Frank was in *Our America.* His problems and his situations resisted the solution of the mere will to "creation."[34]

The gaps between the curves that preface "Kabnis" seem to reflect that uncertainty, a contradiction between what Toomer wanted to affirm and what he knew about American life. The absence of Kabnis at the conclusion is another gap as well, a mystery that makes the circle incomplete. The mystery involves a detective story that remains unsolved and a witness who cannot record or make sense of the original crime, curves that do not meet and a face whose features remain a blank. The sphere in which the author encloses Father John and Carrie K. suggests that Toomer wanted a totality of vision at the end of *Cane,* but, as the gaps between the curves indicate, he also knew that the completeness of the enclosed circle shuts out as much as it includes. The gaps point to the detective's limited perception of the mystery he is trying to solve, and Toomer can complete the circle only by making the detective disappear. Kabnis trudges upstairs a defeated man, carrying a bucket of "dead coals" and condemned to try to straighten a twisted axle. The poet's light has gone out, his center of gravity is lost. The two words that Father John gives him are "sin" and "death," the legacy of slavery whose circle of eternal recurrence must be broken. This is something that Kabnis cannot do, and that Toomer can do only by forming a new circle that excludes Kabnis.[35]

The witness who has seen the unspeakable and has returned from Hell to utter it is the Toomer who writes his own version of the Gothic novel. The shadows that haunt his pages are only fog to be burned off by the sun/son's clear "eye," but that eye is set in juxtaposition to the all-seeing eye at the top of the authoritarian pyramid of power that continues to rule the New South. Toomer's hopeful ending suggests that the circle of the poet's eye replaces the cycle of terror created and sustained by slavery, yet the text itself keeps insisting that Kabnis and others are forced to endure "the original violent act of transforming free man into slave." The contradiction cannot be resolved by an act of will or, in Frank's words, "a conception to be created." As the singer of "Harvest Song" expresses it, Toomer's "pain . . . will not bring me knowledge of my hunger." Toomer was already abandoning his African-American identity as he completed *Cane,* and the exit of Kabnis is part of that abandonment. Toomer understood that the artist could never make an American identity whole again, could never return the world to the state of innocence before the Fall. Kabnis's departure marks Toomer's denial of the chaos attendant upon a black identity, but his fate probably also represents the fate of the mulatto elite. At the conclusion of *Cane,* the future of African-Americans lies with the black masses, who, as Toomer knew, had already begun their great migration to the Northern cities. From their number would arise a new kind of detective, different from either Lewis or Kabnis.[36]

Epilogue: "An Incredibly Entangled Situation"

> Stephen's problem, like ours, was not actually one of creating the un-
> created conscience of his race, but of creating the *uncreated features of
> his face.*
>
> —Ralph Ellison, *Invisible Man*

> History, Stephen said, is a nightmare from which I am trying to awake.
> —James Joyce, *Ulysses*

In his autobiographical sketch "Incredible Journey," Jean Toomer recalled visiting Sparta's black barbershop for a haircut. Seeing two young
girls walking and laughing together on the street outside the window, one
black and the other apparently white, he asked his barber, "Isn't that unusual? Are white and black that friendly here?" The barber replied that
the white girl wasn't "white"—she was "colored." In his handwritten journal Toomer posed a single question to himself concerning the girl with the
"Caucasian features": "If a white girl is colored, who is white?"[1]

In the same passage Toomer went on to speculate about this girl's origins, adopting a tone close to that of the detective novel:

It was quite apparent that the rigid barrier that is supposed to exist between the
races at all points, and that does exist at some points, had been breached more than
once to produce her. What an incredibly entangled situation the racial situation is
in the United States. There are facts and events, plenty of them, that will never be
told; or, if told, that would not fit into any familiar category. No book could possibly contain them.

Of course, *Cane* did "contain" those facts and events, expressed in an
oblique way, through a modernist form analogous to the secret nature of
the "entangled situation" in the United States. This mode of revelation was

part of *Cane*'s brilliance; yet the question Toomer asks about the young "colored" girl anticipates the issue of his own life after *Cane*, a question he would never escape: "If a white girl is colored, who is white?"

The question itself should—as Toomer always insisted—explode the biological underpinnings of race. Beginning with "Americans and Mary Austin," Toomer's writings called attention to the falsity of the "familiar category"; he regarded the idea of race as a socially constructed barrier to the creation of the New America and the New American, but he also recognized that social fiction had serious consequences for everyday reality, such as the reality he encountered in the race riots of 1919. Toomer's view of race began with the views of his class, the mulatto elite that upheld its hope for a gradual amalgamation by distinguishing itself in mores and culture from the black masses. For Toomer this class distinction had been passed through the socialist idealism of Randolph Bourne and Waldo Frank, "Young America" and *Our America*, to emerge in "Americans and Mary Austin" as a vision of democratic amalgamation, a vision that appears occasionally, half-seen, in *Cane*. Yet despite this ideal, Toomer attempted in the years after *Cane*'s publication to pass into that very category of "whiteness" which his earlier writing had so purposefully subverted.

Kevin K. Gaines, writing of Toomer's era in *Uplifting the Race*, observed that

> because of its preferential status, whiteness meant that its subscribers would never in their right minds want to live their lives as African Americans. Small wonder that those African Americans able to "pass" for white would claim for themselves the opportunities and freedoms denied to the race, sparking anxiety in many whites, and in some African Americans as well. The bottom line was that black elites, like all black people, were demonized and terrorized by white supremacists of all social strata, and were especially vulnerable to attack when claiming full equality.[2]

Yet "passing" also meant embracing the "racial fictions" which, as Gaines shows, are woven through the uplift ideology the black elites used to set themselves apart from the black masses. Toomer's depiction of the social hurt suffered by the black middle classes as a result of this ideology—by Avey and Esther and Dan—is one of *Cane*'s major themes, culminating in Kabnis's harrowing night. For Toomer the line between race and class remained dangerously undefined; his belief in egalitarian democracy was hedged around by a fear of being "demonized and terrorized." In life and art the dilemmas of race and class continued to dog him, and even his later works, such as the short story "York Beach" or the long poem *The Blue Meridian*, struggle with the same face Kabnis confronted in the depths of Halsey's cellar.[3]

In a journal entry for 1924, Toomer described a dream where he inhabits a castle, which I own and master. Some unusual rites are to be held within. I am called to the altar by the inability of the doorkeeper to prevent a large crowd of Negroes from entering. Taking a position by the door, I indicate that I will undertake the keeper's duty. I call to the people, commanding that they withdraw. All do, immediately, with the exception of one. I ask that one to look at me. I tell him I am Jean Toomer. He smiles disparagingly, and stubbornly shakes his head, refusing to leave.[4]

Someone offers to help Toomer, but he feels "that the issue is between myself and this man." Toomer then exercises "some magic," which involves a mysterious "flesh element, a lovely element of sex," and causes the Negro to writhe in great suffering before the altar: "I say some word to relieve his agony, without releasing him." And then, without any transition, Toomer adds: "I fly. As I go up, Negroes from the roofs of buildings jeer at me. At an ultimate height, a gargoyle-negro face on a pole, grins (totem pole)." Here the journal entry abruptly ends.

Toomer's dream records an explicit parable of his ambiguous position in relation to African-Americans and his own identity. In this passage Toomer assumes the role of the doorman, determined to keep the Negroes out of *his* dwelling. The house—perhaps his new identity as fashioned by Gurdjieff—is a fortress infiltrated by his former identity as a Negro—the black man who refuses to leave would seem to be his double. The journal entry reflects both Toomer's sense of power and his fears; he flies above the black masses, but even at the zenith of his flight a grinning "gargoyle-negro face on a pole" awaits him, an image that gives a face to the mysterious "gargoyle shadows" of *The Blue Meridian*. Further, the "face on a pole" harks back to the lynching motif in *Cane*, and to the image of the leering black doorman's face rushing at Paul at the conclusion of "Bona and Paul." Toomer's parable describes not only his ambiguous racial identity but the class/color designations within African-American culture that were so important to the narrators and characters of *Cane*.[5]

While Toomer was both a member of the black aristocracy and a thoroughgoing democrat, he could not be both at the same time. *Cane*, by denying the values of the black bourgeoisie (especially their patriarchal bias), is a text proclaiming an egalitarian conception of African-American life, but Toomer's own belief in this ideal seemed to be selective. Toomer's ambivalence toward his class position crops up in the changes he made to his autobiographical writings between 1930 and 1936: the earlier texts dismiss "workers" almost with contempt and nostalgically praise the mulatto aristocrats among whom he grew up; the later texts are at pains not only to embrace the necessary reforms of socialism, but to critique the limitations of Toomer's own class attitudes.[6]

The polarities of this conflict can be seen in the two major religious affiliations that absorbed much of Toomer's life after *Cane*, Gurdjieffism and Quakerism—one movement based on a "great leader" hierarchy, the other on a doctrine of "spiritual equality." In one of his last books, *The Re-*

Discovery of Man (1958), Waldo Frank made a late attack on Gurdjieff. Pointing out Gurdjieff's debt to Buddhist philosophy, Frank noted that, while Buddhism assumed that "all existence is evil" and advocated an escape from the world, "in Gurdjieff's version, there is none of this effort to displace the ego center. The 'I' that observes the body and the world remains unchallengedly ego. If it grows strong enough, it will arrogate to itself the group and cosmic energies, becoming—as Paul Tillich has defined the term—demonic."[7] In this view the end of the Gurdjieffian ego becomes worldly power. Frank saw Gurdjieff's movement as another attempt to assert social control on the cultural flux of the 1920s: "In those postwar days, Mussolini was enthralling the world with his manifestation of demonic power. I sensed the relation between the Duce in his theater of crude power politics and Gurdjieff in his more rarefied field." Frank did not suggest that Gurdjieff was a political threat, but that his system was authoritarian and that its seemingly esoteric metaphysics had political implications.[8]

Gurdjieffism, practically, was a kind of upper-middle-class therapy. When Toomer first tried to teach the system, he held classes in Harlem, but he quickly discovered there were not enough African-Americans with funds to spare for a search for "cosmic consciousness" (to use Langston Hughes's phrase). This economic bind led Toomer away from Harlem and away from the democratic view of black life that underlies *Cane*. Moving to the "Gold Coast" of Chicago's Walton Place, Toomer had a good deal more success, recruiting five hundred fee-paying members between 1926 and 1931 according to Robert Twombly. He also enthralled feminist intellectual and Greenwich Village patron of the arts Mabel Dodge Luhan and in 1926 obtained from her a loan or contribution of $14,000 for Gurdjieffian work. But, according to Toomer, it was also in Chicago that he discovered that anthologies of Negro writing which included his work had preceded him and led to "impressions" that he was African-American. "Finding that these pictures and impressions tended to hinder my work, I began destroying them. When the occasion arose, which it did now and again, I destroyed the notions in my close acquaintances, and conveyed the facts about myself and my life which would enable them to see me in this respect as I was." The terms of American racism proscribed any image of "blackness": destroying such "pictures," Toomer attempted to blend into the haute bourgeoisie of his new environment.[9]

Toomer's story "York Beach," published in *The New American Caravan* in 1929, offers an extreme view of how uplift ideology and the Gurdjieffian system might complement each other. "York Beach" echoes the end of "Bona and Paul," as Nathan Antrum utters an impassioned speech describing utopian possibility and Alma, the woman he is courting, flees. It is a rather different utopia that Nathan imagines, however, evoked in a bizarre tour-de-force monologue that combines a Menckenian denunciation of American folly and hypocrisy with a plea for the "pure potentiality" of a race of superior men and women. And the character of Nathan, who could be yet another incarnation of Toomer, has a specific political agenda: "I can be a democrat. But I am convinced that the world cannot. No sizeable group of people for any length of time. Not so-called civilized people. And I hate democratic pretense. Bah, if men must be ruled by fear and power, give me the clean cruelty of monarchy, the candid exercise of absolute power." Nathan imagines an American political future as an empire with an emperor: "Perhaps someday when the democratic dogma is less strong in people, and when there comes a man with the genius and the power and the courage to break tradition, overrule his rivals, and declare himself. Ah, but I would hail such a man!"[10] Did Toomer imagine Gurdjieff, or a Gurdjieffian adept, as "such a man"? Of course, Nathan Antrum isn't Toomer, although he does bear Toomer's first name (before he changed it to Jean) and a last name that is an anagram of "Truman"—"True-man." Nathan's contempt for the "great lower middle class" approaches T. S. Eliot's hatred and fear of the poorer socioeconomic groups, and his desire for order and a strong leader or elite leadership resembles the political/spiritual designs of the Nobel Prize–winning poet. In a curious passage relating to the idea of a "strong leader," Toomer wrote about his most concerted effort to put Gurdjieffism into practice during the two months he spent in a cottage at Portage, Wisconsin, from July to September 1931. There, "six to ten men and women from Chicago and Portage lived communally." Toomer wrote in "Portage Potential,"

the form of the cottage life was a thing created and moulded and controlled by me. . . . No thing of any consequence was done in relation to the group as a whole unless I did it, or unless the person had previously spoken to me about it and gained my approval. I held the reins in my hands, and I held them strictly. Everyone understood this. That was why they were in the cottage. Everyone tried to govern themselves accordingly.[11]

Racial Politics and *The Blue Meridian*

Toomer's Chicago "revisions" and his Portage demagoguery were a long way from the epiphany of his narrator and Avey at Soldiers' Home in *Cane*, but they were not very different from the paternalistic cast of most middle-class attitudes toward the working classes and immigrants, black or white; at least Toomer's orders were directed to fellow Gurdjieffians. Toomer did not remain comfortable with the authoritarian stance he had assumed, however; besides the evidence recorded in his later autobiographies and his move to the Quakers, he also tried once more to come to terms with the material of the *Cane* period, and in 1936 he published *The Blue Meridian*, a long poem distantly descended from the poem "The First American," which he had sent to Waldo Frank in 1922. *The Blue Meridian* shows the whole range of the influence of "Young America" on Toomer, from

Walt Whitman to Van Wyck Brooks, Randolph Bourne, Waldo Frank, and, finally, Hart Crane. What best explains the poem, however, is its relation to *Cane*, to the general outlook and method of the earlier work and to its individual parts.[12]

In Toomer's interpretation of "Bona and Paul" which he presented to Georgia O'Keeffe in 1924 (see Chapter 8), he not only denied that "black" and "white" referred to black and white persons but also insisted that Paul, in his speech to the doorman, "resolves these contrasts to a unity." The question the reader has to ask of this solution is, if things are resolved, why is Bona gone? The resolution seems to take place inside Paul's mind and to be without consequence in the street outside the Crimson Gardens. Kenneth Burke speaks of a rhetoric of "courtship": "By the 'principle of courtship' in rhetoric we mean the use of suasive devices for the transcending of social estrangement. There is a 'mystery' of courtship when 'different kinds of beings' communicate with each other." Paul may think he is describing a mystical experience, but the speech's rhetorical motive is to persuade Bona to forget about "social difference," and the rhetoric of "courtship" is challenged by the presence of race and class, creating what Burke calls a "dramatist" dialectic between idea and action. When Toomer tried to take literally Frank's claim that "America was a conception to be created," the resolution he created dismissed race and class and ignored the experience depicted in *Cane*. In *The Blue Meridian* Toomer employed a transcendent rhetoric of courtship to persuade the finite but resistant polis.[13]

Toomer's poem is about history and place, yet its resolution depends on timelessness and placelessness. It centers on the Great Depression, which is represented as an airplane crash (219) or shipwreck (224), and is filled with the language of finance and industry (Wall Street, checks, offices, mills, stocks, currency, and so forth). The poem speaks of American regions and places ("Michigan Avenue and Walton Place," "The Palmolive Building, / Or the Empire State") which, as the poem progresses, are dissolved into a "spiritualized" new America. *The Blue Meridian* tries to provide a map to that "new America" and to identify the "new American" who appears in the visions of Brooks, Bourne, and Frank. But the poem's maps are abstracts, covered, like the works of medieval cartographers, with "flaming earth and torrent-rains" and inhabited by people whose histories are manifestations of "Nature" and "Spirit" (217). Lewis Mumford affirmed in his epigraph to *Story of Utopias* that "a Map of the World that does not include Utopia is not worth even glancing at." Mumford went on to use various utopian schemes of the past to critique the present, taking a quasi-Marxist perspective to suggest possible "seeds" of development for the chaotic, modern condition. Toomer's utopia, for all its apparent diversity, reduces the complexity of American culture to a solipsistic text.[14]

Placing himself in the center of Chicago, a city at the center of America, Toomer sees his personal transcendence as representing the Whitmanesque potential within every American. "Rooted" as he is within the American heartland, he believes he is giving birth to a new vision of the City on a Hill:

> The prairie's sweep is flat infinity
> The city's rise is perpendicular to farthest star,
> I stand where the two directions intersect,
> At Michigan Avenue and Walton Place,
> Level with my countrymen,
> Right-angled to the universe.
> It is a New America,
> To be spiritualized by each new American. (218)

But Toomer's map essentially replicates the mono-myth of the nation's conquerors. Located a block from Lake Michigan on posh Lake Shore Drive, Walton Place hardly put Toomer "level" with his countrymen, especially if he were to have looked southward down Michigan Avenue to see his black "countrymen" living in segregated poverty (as Richard Wright did four years later in *Native Son*). Missing from Toomer's map are the economic histories of both Walton Place and Michigan Avenue, especially as they are related and dependent on one another, so his map confirms the significance that the early explorers gave to roads, "not at all to report a place, but to impose an *idea* of place." Roads "represented order and guaranteed as well as directed all levels of circulation," and in *The Blue Meridian*, Toomer merely transformed the existing system of circulation into a metaphysical abstraction of the kind Nathaniel Hawthorne ridiculed in the "Celestial Railroad." Toomer's road, "a near highway just beyond where all roads end" (223), was a highway to heaven, but one lacking Hawthorne's insight of irony.[15]

In *The Blue Meridian*, race, like history and geography, dissolves into the spiritualized rebirth of America. At the poem's beginning and at its conclusion, Toomer invokes the three "old peoples": Europeans, Africans, and Native Americans. Initially, the Europeans achieve and "perish," the Africans begin their Great Migration, and the Native Americans sink "into the sacred earth" (217). In the concluding section the Europeans are revived, having "died and came alive again" (230), and the Native Americans are resurrected as "an example," but the Africans simply disappear, absorbed at last, it would seem, by that process of amalgamation which the mulatto elite always believed would eventually take place. In the stanza describing the fate of the "great African races" in America, Toomer writes:

> Earth is earth, ground is ground,
> All shining if loved.
> Love does not brand as slave or peon
> Any man, but feels his hands,
> His touch upon his work,

And welcomes death that liberates
The poet, American among Americans,
Man at large among men. (231)

This death is both a "racial" death and a death of racial identity, Toomer's own, which frees him to be just an American. Toomer's version of the cosmopolitan ideal has already affirmed that "Islanders" "must outgrow clan and class, color/Nationalism, creed" (225), "so I, once an islander, proclaim." As in "Bona and Paul," Toomer's poem holds white and black in tandem as components of thesis and antithesis which form the synthesis of the "the man of blue or purple." Yet whereas in "Bona and Paul" the utopian synthesis is subjected to a dramatist critique, the colors in *The Blue Meridian* exist in abstract space; they are adjectives attached not to human beings but to "light." Thus Toomer can invoke the "Radiant Incorporeal" to "blend our bodies to one flesh" (218). Toomer returns in his conclusion to the meeting of infinity and the perpendicular: "I stand where the two directions intersect, / In any town or county in the land / Level with my fellow men" (233). And yet Toomer must have known that in Hancock and in many other counties he would not have stood level with other men.

Toomer's poem opens by calling on the "waking forces" of a new America, forces that "must spiral on . . . / must crash the barrier to the next higher form" (214). Inevitably this spiral of direction turns outward, "and then beyond / To aid the operations of the cosmos" (234), as American history, including the history of race and class, become so many pointers leading to the stars. Kenneth Burke observes that "people tend to think that when they speak of 'the Universe,' they are actually speaking of the Universe . . . [yet] 'concepts become poorer in contents or intension in proportion as their extension increases, so that content *zero* must correspond to the extension *infinity*.'" Further, "a transcendent realm of 'pure being' is indistinguishable from 'nothing.'" Thus, as the "spiral" zooms into the infinity in *The Blue Meridian*, it cancels the "spiral" of smoke in *Cane* which pointed downward to Karintha's dead child; and as the "yeast" of Toomer's self rises above the body, it recalls Van Wyck Brooks's complaint that the dead weight of American materialism turns the "yeast" of its intellectuals into airy nothings.[16]

"Just Americans"

Toomer's desire to be just an American involved the merger of two influences: the class ideal rooted in his origins among the mulatto elite and the democratic socialism of "Young America." The real conflict came in the contradictions: the black aristocracy's need for class differentiation and the general failure of "Young America" to recognize how American racism supported class subordination for both white and black people.

Race, class, and gender were never separate categories in the history of the United States but always interlocked in changing patterns of mutual influence. One of the reasons *Cane* is a great book is the intelligent subtlety with which it traces those patterns. When Toomer came to write *The Blue Meridian*, he subordinated that understanding to a transcendental belief, or hope, in a new beginning that would somehow be an escape from designations of race or class. The escape was not tenable, but there was a certain courage in Toomer's proclamation, since he still remembered, with some bitterness, his public clash with the old America.

The social experiment at Portage had one immediate personal effect on Toomer: it was there that he fell in love with Margery Latimer, whom he had known in Chicago, and they married in October 1931, within a month of leaving the communal cottage. The newlyweds settled in Carmel, California, in March 1932, and Toomer completed "Portage Potential" at this time. Perhaps wishing to publicize his work, Toomer gave an interview about the commune at Portage to a local reporter. The piece was passed to a San Francisco newspaper, where a fact-checker discovered that Toomer had been anthologized in a book of African-American writing. "And from this," Toomer said, "[arose] the idea that I was a Negro." When reporters called to interview Toomer, "I told them definitely I was not a Negro." But the story was started; it went out nationally on the Hearst wire services and appeared in the *Milwaukee Sentinel* with the headline, "Margery Latimer, Novelist, Is Married to Negro Poet." Although Toomer imagined an America in which racial difference vanished, replaced by the "purple" man, race could not vanish from his life, he felt, because his public identity as the author of *Cane* would continue to make him known as a "Negro" writer. The contradiction between that ideal and that fact probably led Toomer into the revisions of his life story, notably in "On Being an American," which he would write in 1934.[17]

Once the Hearst papers broke the story of the Toomer-Latimer marriage as a scandal, all the white newspapers that covered the story treated it in true tabloid style, as a cautionary tale focusing on Toomer as the libidinous black male and Latimer as the naive white girl. The coverage of the *San Francisco Examiner* was especially vicious, emphasizing the "love-nest" of the Gurdjieffian "Portage Experiment." On March 17, 1932, the *Examiner* headlined its article on the marriage "Negro Poet and White Bride on Honeymoon at Cottage in Carmel" with the subtitle "Romance Started in Psychological Experiment." Toomer was quoted as saying that Portage proved "that it is entirely possible to eradicate the false veneer of civilization, with its unnatural inhibitions, its selfishness, petty meanness and unnatural behavior." Two days later the *Examiner* described the "communal" living conditions at Portage and the "Exercises Based on Tibetan Dances Which Won White Woman." Six days later, another article appeared in the

Examiner quoting Toomer on "American" versus "European" love, among other topics.[18]

Time magazine was slightly more subtle. In the "National Affairs" section for March 28, 1932, *Time* ran two stories under the subhead "RACES." The first one, with a picture of "Jean & Margery Toomer," was titled "Just Americans." It began:

No Negro can legally marry a white woman in any Southern State. But Wisconsin does not mind, nor California. Last week at Carmel, Calif., "Provincetown of the Pacific Coast," there was an intellectual charivari. A parade of Carmel artists and authors marched to the cottage of Jean Toomer, 36, Negro philosopher (*Cane*), psychologist and lecturer, and Novelist Margery Bodine Latimer (*This Is My Body*), 33. It had just been revealed that they were married four months ago at Portage, Wis. Bridegroom Toomer, who has a small mustache and few Negroid characteristics, told the story of their romance.[19]

The remainder of the article was an ironic account of the Portage "experiment" containing two long quotations from Toomer, one on the "false veneer of civilization" and the other on amalgamation:

"Americans probably do not realize it," Bridegroom Toomer told his callers last week, "but there are no racial barriers anymore, because there are so many Americans with strains of Negro, Indian and Oriental blood. As I see America, it is like a great stomach into which are thrown the elements which make up the life blood. From this source is coming a distinct race of people. They will achieve tremendous works of art, literature and music. They will not be white, black or yellow—just Americans." [20]

Toomer's statement was a restatement of the views he had published in the *Call* twelve years earlier: in "Americans and Mary Austin" he had joined the concept of "inevitable" amalgamation with Waldo Frank's vision of cultural renaissance.

Relying on heavy irony rather than outrage, *Time*'s racism nevertheless presented Toomer's marriage as a threat to the mores of middle-class white America and the system of white supremacy and segregation which united North and South in the twentieth century. Toomer's background was reduced to that of his grandfather, "Pinckney Benton Stewart Pinchback, a mulatto carpetbagger," and the media assault on the couple was termed an "intellectual charivari." The "charivari" was a ritual of public mocking and shaming practiced at one time in many traditional cultures, but by the 1930s it was mostly associated with "tar and feathering" rituals in the South. As Bertram Wyatt-Brown says, the South "ensured the permanence of popular white rule by means of charivari and lynch law," practices carried out against those whom the community recognized as "aliens, deviants, and social underlings." [21]

Following the Toomer story in *Time*'s RACES section was a second piece, titled "Tulapai," which also began in an openly racist manner:

In grim, guttural Apache, Golney ("Mac") Seymour, undersized Redskin buck, told a Federal court in Globe, Ariz. last week how he happened to attack and kill white Henrietta Schmerler, Columbia University student, last summer.

Its point of view established, the story proceeded with a long quotation from Seymour's confession and a short account of the trial that was heavy with ironic condescension for "the prisoner's stolid, blanketed kinsmen." The final line, set as a separate paragraph, read: "Found guilty, Apache Seymour was condemned to life imprisonment." The stories of the Toomers and of Golney Seymour thus were not separate stories; as *Time* had carefully joined them, they combined warning and threat, cause and effect, and made the very "civilized" case for white supremacy and racial segregation.

"Just Americans" and "Tulapai" became in particular a warning against miscegenation. The Columbia graduate student, like Margery Latimer, had flirted with forbidden fruit, for in studying the "primitive," she had conceived a fatal attraction for her subject matter. The lurid description of the killing placed more blame on her than on the Apache youth: his actions were entirely predictable, but she should have known better—just as, by implication, Margery Latimer should have known better than to become involved with a Negro in a "free-love" commune. Toomer's assertion in his remarks on racial amalgamation, that "many Americans" have strains of "Negro, Indian and Oriental blood," was rebuked by the attention to Native American "difference" in the story of Golney Seymour. The narrative developed with seeming inevitability from an "intellectual charivari" to murder and punishment, all consequences of dangerous racial transgression.

After the fiasco of Carmel, Toomer and his wife returned to Chicago; in the following year he suffered a greater tragedy when Margery died giving birth to their daughter. Toomer turned to work on his autobiographies at this point; he clearly was revising his past, but he was also rethinking his present positions. By the end of 1934 he was ready to break with Gurdjieff, "who was touring the United States, in the process alienating many followers with his crude behavior, drunkenness, sexual indiscretions, and his questionable financial dealings." Toomer's decision was at least partly based on Gurdjieff's claim that Toomer had never remitted to him the entire $14,000 received from Mabel Dodge Luhan. In 1934 Luhan again wrote to Toomer to ask what had become of the money, insisting that it had been a "loan" rather than a "contribution," but Toomer was unable to satisfy either donor or recipient. This episode of the search for wholeness ended amid financial controversy and general recriminations.[22]

In September 1934 Toomer married Marjorie Content, a wealthy friend of Georgia O'Keeffe who probably encouraged his break with Gurdjieff.

The next year Toomer began another version of his autobiography, "Book X" and its associated notebooks, in which he returned to a radical analysis of the politics of his time but not to an open discussion of racial matters. In 1932 *Time* magazine had joined a story of Wisconsin and California to one from the deserts of northern Arizona, combining them under the title "RACES" and creating a small antimorality tale; it was the perfect example of modernist technique that almost suggested that the anonymous Luce writers had been studying *Cane*. On that page and the other pages of newspaper coverage, the question of Toomer's racial identity had reverted to *Cane* and to his grandfather Pinchback: obviously, Toomer didn't want any further "repetition of those conditions." In 1953, in his last mention of Toomer, Alain Locke would observe that the major "shortcoming" of *Cane* was "that its author chose not to continue."[23]

Cane and the New Negro

Cane's republication in 1969 meant that the book had two critical histories—one associated with the Harlem Renaissance of the 1920s and a second one in the 1970s and after, as the text became familiar to new generations of readers and writers. The initial reception had shown very clearly the demarcations of race and class with which Toomer had struggled: while white critics marveled or fretted over the book's modernistic style, African-American readers weighed how much they could acknowledge of the bone beneath the racial skin of American life that *Cane* had exposed. Countee Cullen wrote to Toomer in the month *Cane* appeared in the bookstores (September 1923) and praised him for creating "a classical portrayal of things as they are." But a day later Cullen wrote to Alain Locke: "Jean Toomer's book is out, and I like parts of it immensely. He is a genuine poet, but I do wish he would look, if only for a few seconds, beyond the muck and mire of things."[24]

Cullen's reservations were in part class based; the secrecy that was *Cane*'s subject was meant to hide the "muck and mire," real or imagined, in black life, and Cullen's class was invested in protecting that secrecy. He appreciated Toomer's powerful portrayal of American racism and regretted the reality that it confirmed; and he feared too much reality would further undermine African-Americans' status. While it seemed possible in the fluid world of the 1920s that serious social change might take place, such change had not happened significantly for black people by 1923, and Cullen held to the necessity of African-Americans being very careful in the images they presented to the white world. There was nothing unique in his observation, although he would put it with unusual directness in remarks published five years later: "American life is so constituted, the wealth of power is so unequally distributed, that whether they relish the situation or not, Negroes should be concerned with making good impressions." Cullen developed this idea through the metaphor of black culture as a house whose Gothic secrets should be concealed:

Every house worthy of the name has an attic or a bin or an out-of-the way closet where one may hide the inevitable family skeleton. But who inviting a prominent guest to tea, or dinner, and hoping to make even the slightest of good impressions, feels called upon to guide the guest sedulously through every nook and corner of the house, not omitting attic, bin, and the dusty retreat of the skeleton? [25]

"Making good impressions" was a way of announcing that some black people could meet white "standards," presenting an image of African-Americans that would minimize their difference from the white middle class. If the culture of the Talented Tenth was like white culture, then it could be proclaimed that a kind of cultural amalgamation had already taken place—much as Waldo Frank had proclaimed that "revolution" was a fact in *Our America*. The black equivalent to Frank's book would be Alain Locke's 1925 anthology of African-American literature and commentary, *The New Negro*. Locke saw fresh opportunities for overcoming America's rigid institutional racism, opportunities created by the social changes of modernity, migration and urbanization: "The American mind must reckon with a fundamentally changed Negro." Locke, however, was more careful than Frank to court authority in his political outline; Locke's foreword defined the New Negro's politics as "radical on race matters, conservative on others . . . a social protestant, rather than a genuine radical." This "New Negro" was a revision of the radical black intellectual associated with New York and the postwar period, a term now appropriated for Locke's own class and cultural program. Locke also coopted the fading threat of Bolshevism, warning, "Harlem's quixotic radicalisms call for their ounce of democracy to-day lest to-morrow they be beyond cure." [26]

Like Frank, Locke offered new art as proof of the cultural change he heralded, but instead of revolution this new art was to produce a "revaluation of the Negro" which would lead to improved race relations: "He [the Negro] now becomes a conscious contributor and lays aside the status of a beneficiary and ward for that of a collaborator and participant in American civilization" (15). This new art also fit Locke's preoccupation with the essential difference between the "multitude" and the "thinking few" among black Americans—a crucial class differentiation. The masses constituted the "peasant matrix" that had enlivened the South with "the gift of [a] folk-temperament," but who were now to be replaced by "a second crop of the Negro's gifts," the material of Locke's anthology.[27]

In *The New Negro* Toomer served as an important model of that transformation: he was the prime example of the folk spirit reconstituted as conscious, modern art—in William Stanley Braithwaite's words, "the bright morning star of a new day of the race in literature." Locke wanted the new elite of New Negro artists to escape from "the arid fields of controversy and debate to the productive fields of creative expression" (15), and *Cane* might be read "creatively" because, though perceptive readers recognized its "classic portrayal" of the conditions of American racism, Toomer's modernistic form made his work seem open, not to say obscure, to other readers. Toomer helped solve the interpretive problem, because by 1925 he, too, was speaking of his book as the record of a region's disappearing folk life.[28]

In *The New Negro*, Locke quoted some of Toomer's words about Georgia to imply that this folk spirit was the single most important aspect of the South as it appeared in *Cane*:

Georgia opened me. And it may well be said that I received my initial impulse to an individual art from my experience there. For no other section of the country has so stirred me. There one finds soil, soil in the sense that Russians know it,—the soil every art and literature that is to live must be imbedded in. (51)

There is no hint that Karintha's child lies under that soil, no social anger, because Toomer was "being racial . . . purely for the sake of art." Out of context, "Song of the Son" and "Georgia Dusk"—both poems anthologized in *The New Negro*, along with "Fern" and "Carma"—made it possible for Locke and other black critics to celebrate a unified folk spirit and an ennobling past as recaptured by the modern artist.[29]

In his foreword to *The New Negro*, Locke wrote that black artists could now afford to represent the "Negro . . . even in his faults and shortcomings" (11), but most of the pieces in his anthology were carefully chosen to highlight the positive and the promising, the achievements of the "thinking few" among African-Americans. Although Countee Cullen's poem "The Black Christ" would be in many ways as starkly political as *Cane*, after the publication of *Nigger Heaven, Home to Harlem* and the single issue of *Fire!* Cullen in 1928 devoted part of his column in *Opportunity* to the need for keeping skeletons in closets. So, while there seemed to be a public disagreement between Locke and Cullen about how black life should be represented in the 1920s, each man, in a different way, supported a careful gentility in African-American art. Locke said he wanted an art that depicted "things as they are," but in fact promoted a refined art produced by the "cultured few." And Cullen would argue publicly that "Negroes should be concerned with making good impressions." In this critical climate Jean Toomer's writing could be praised and ignored.[30]

Praising Toomer in 1925, Locke had ignored *Cane*'s origins among the radical intellectuals of New York, Waldo Frank and the black journalists of Harlem. In 1950, reviewing a set of essays on black writing, Locke returned to his praise of Toomer's work, this time on the basis of its "objective universality" and its fit with "the 'new criticism' ": "I am personally surprised that no one referred to the phenomenal early appearance of such 'universal particularity' in Jean Toomer's *Cane* in 1923. Here was something admirably removed from what Mr. Chandler calls very aptly 'promotional literature,' but it is Negro through and through as well as deeply and movingly human."[31] While Locke had practiced his own careful race (and class) promotion in assembling *The New Negro*, he now saw more room for controversial topics, and in the same short piece in 1950 called for black writing to break the "tabus" of "Negro life":

Why, then, this protective silence about the ambivalence of the Negro upper classes, about the dilemmas of intra-group prejudice and rivalry, about the dramatic inner paradoxes of mixed heritage, both biological and cultural, or the tragic breach between the Negro elite and the Negro masses, or the conflict between integration and vested-interest separatism in the present-day life of the Negro? These, among others, are the great themes, but they moulder in closed closets like family skeletons.

So Locke had understood some of *Cane*'s political subject matter, even if he thought it impolitic to discuss it in 1925; in 1950, these were potentially "great themes," and he turned the meaning of Cullen's metaphor of closets and skeletons inside out—these things should not be hidden, but revealed.

The remarks quoted in *The New Negro* were not Toomer's only words on the "soil." In his poetry notebook of 1923, he wrote:

A distinction should be made between the wish to return to nature, and the desire to touch the soil. . . . Those who wish to return to nature wish to rid themselves of man in what we are pleased to term his modern associations. . . . To return is to escape. (Impossible. That people are still driven up this blind alley attests this need.) To touch is to be revivified by contact with the race's source. The moralistic temperament inclines toward nature. The artist springs from the soil, and from cities.[32]

Toomer restates the point Frank had made in *Our America* when he criticized William Jennings Bryan for not taking modernity into account—for talking as if "Karl Marx had never existed." As Toomer made clear in the middle section of *Cane*, those who return to nature embrace the pastoral in order to escape modernity and the "modern associations" that include the city ("the arts are produced through overcrowding"). "Seventh Street" just as surely as "Cotton Song" reflected the social and economic conditions that produced art. *Cane* never posits the mystical bond between blood and soil suggested by Locke, nor does it indulge in the illusion of "escape" to a timeless Nature. Its modern associations would not be lost on the generation of black writers who followed Toomer in the 1940s and 1950s, nor were they missed by those who began publishing after *Cane* reappeared in the late 1960s.[33]

If Toomer was the artist as "Apostle of Beauty," or one of the "cultured few" celebrating the race's folk spirit in Locke's program, the black writers who read *Cane* in the post-Renaissance period saw other things: they saw the democratic implications of how the book depicted common life, and they saw the noirish world within its text. In the 1930s, Richard Wright rewrote "Blood-Burning Moon" as "Long Black Song" in *Uncle Tom's Children* (1938), and James Baldwin later recast "Bona and Paul" as "Come Out the Wilderness" in *Going To Meet the Man* (1965); each short story took a black woman as its central figure. In Ralph Ellison's *Invisible Man* (1952), Hanby of "Kabnis" is the model for the sinister Dr. Bledsoe, a college president who masks his considerable power behind a persona of humility. Ironically, James Baldwin, Richard Wright, and Ralph Ellison would all claim white modernists as their literary ancestors, perhaps not only to distance themselves from the Renaissance but to give their own work critical stature as well. Toomer was simply too obscure to be cited as an influence in the immediate post-Renaissance period, but that would change with the reprinting of *Cane* in 1969.[34]

The effect of *Cane*'s revival was immediate. David Bradley described a black literature class in 1970: "I was hoping merely to stumble on one author in whose work I could immediately and instinctively recognize a paradigm for my own." Most of what he encountered made no impression on him, but when he read *Cane* he was moved by its power and beauty and its revelation of "the earthy realities of a Black past." His own novel, *The Chaneysville Incident* (1981), which he said took "ten years of preparation," was published eleven years later; like *Cane*, it was a Gothic detective story whose subject was the terrors of American history. This aspect of *Cane*, long ignored or buried by the Harlem Renaissance, came to have special appeal for other writers of Bradley's generation, as the older, homogenized versions of American history began to undergo more realistic criticism after the 1960s.[35]

Black women writers especially admired Toomer's complex treatment of gender and sex. Both Alice Walker and Gayl Jones wrote appreciative essays on Toomer's work; Jones focused in particular on Toomer's "erotic imagination," his use of "incremental repetition" as a modernist technique, and his democratic use of such black oral traditions as blues music. Citing Toomer as a major influence on her work, she wrote a fine essay about the "mystery" of Karintha, and she referred to her brilliant first novel, *Corrigadora* (1975), as a "blues novel" that "corrects" history by rewriting it from a female perspective. Toni Morrison linked history and the narration of detection in *Song of Solomon* (1977) and *Beloved* (1987), while her novel *Jazz* (1992)—also a Gothic detective story that shifts back and forth between country and city, past and present—alludes to *Cane* throughout. Her image of Joe's "apple" recalls Toomer's "plum" in "Song of the Son," and "plum" and "apple" both represent the inescapable knowledge of corpses (Karintha's child, Dorcas) that forces the detective to uncover history as the progress of a crime, and in the process to discover a new history of the republic.[36]

There are also frequent echoes of *Cane* in the recent emergence of the black detective story as a popular genre. The secret fact of miscegenation is the theme of three of Walter Mosley's novels—*The Devil in a Blue Dress* (1990), *White Butterfly* (1992), and *Black Betty* (1994). Reconstructing the history of the intricate interrelations between caste and class in Barbara Neely's *Blanche Among the Talented Tenth* (1994) becomes the key to unraveling the mystery of the "mess on a drawing room carpet." Likewise, black director Carl Franklin in the film *One False Move* (1992) uses the "thriller" as a vehicle to explore the hidden crime of miscegenation in a small Southern town. One effective twist in the script is an echo from "Kabnis": the cops from Los Angeles, white and black, are smug urban intellectuals who stare at the primal crime without seeing it—until it's too late.

Cane revealed the impossibly unstable conception of "whiteness" in American culture, a revelation that is acknowledged more at the end of the twentieth century than it was at the beginning. At least at the end of the century, when a school official refers to a mixed-race child as a "mistake," the remark draws national attention and is contested rather than accepted as an obvious truth. In *Our America*, Waldo Frank insisted that the horrors of America's origins could be redeemed through an act of will, but after editing, proofreading, and reflecting upon *Cane*, he wrote his own mystery tale, *Chalk Face* (1924), in which a detective from an "old" American family—a "leader" and "creator"—discovers that the corpse's pallor is also that of the killer's, a man whose face appears "chalk-white" when he kills. Frank's detective—an unwilling one, like Kabnis—also discovers, to his horror, that the face is his own, an emblem not of his "darker" side but of his desire to embrace a pure "whiteness." Thus perhaps the true companion pieces to derive from the Toomer-Frank collaboration were not *Cane* and *Holiday* but *Cane* and *Chalk Face*—Gothic fictions which, taken together, represented a profound critique of both "Young America" and the Harlem Renaissance.[37]

Jean Toomer died in Pennsylvania in March 1967, two years before *Cane* was to be reissued in its entirety for the first time since the 1920s. Two months earlier, Waldo Frank had died in White Plains, New York. Frank had remained an activist and radical to the last, serving as temporary chairman of the Fair Play for Cuba Committee and publishing his last book in 1961 on the Cuban revolution. Toomer's spiritual seeking continued through his final decades, although nothing important seems to have been recorded about his late social or political views. It is impossible, of course, to do more than speculate about how Toomer would have reacted to *Cane*'s evolving status as a central text of African-American literature, but he might well have been pleased. His argument had always been that the contradiction between the world of *Cane* and the world he chose to live in was not his private contradiction, but one rooted in the American ideology: the fatal break between idealist declaration and terrorist practice. By the evidence of history, he was not wrong.

Appendix: Jean Toomer's *New York Call* Articles

Ghouls

June 15, 1919

Hither and thither among the dead and dying of the battlefield moved the crouched shadow of the ghoul. His practiced hands went about their business with a precision almost machine-like. In the gray dawn his trained eyes missed no valuable. Now and then he would have to turn a corpse that he might rifle its pockets. Infrequently he would bend lower, dislodge from the mud a severed hand, and pluck from it a ring. Only once did he hesitate; as he was about to jerk a heart-shaped locket from a slender neck, two eyes, luminous in their death stare, seemed to plead with him to spare that remembrance. His hesitation, however, was but momentary, for quickly snatching the locket he hurried on with his business. But suddenly a flash and a sharp report; the ghoul straightened, whirled, and fell amongst the misshapen forms of his helpless prey.

*   *   *

Seated around a hard-grained table sat the war profiteers. Their cheeks were full and their eyes glowed with the light of conquest. Slaves entered obsequiously and deposited upon the broad table a heap of coins. Coins of all shapes and sizes there were, coins stained with the tears of children, coins wrung from the breasts of mothers. The slaves retired. The profiteers rubbed their hands and swept the loot into their coffers. Many slaves entered and piled a more varied assortment upon the ample table—and withdrew. Here and there a bright red coin shone out and seemed to fascinate the profiteers. But they broadly smiled and swept the mass into their coffers.

Slaves, with more gold bearing heavily upon their weary shoulders, struggled to the table and disgorged their weighty burden. The coins rolled out, red and gory with the blood of men. The slaves stared, but their masters drove them from the room and hastened back to divide the spoil. Slaves, with a peculiar light in their eyes, stalked in and placed upon the table a bundle—but they did not retire. The profiteers, mindful only of the treat before them, ripped open the bag and grabbed at its contents. But they recoiled, afraid, for they had touched there the hearts of men.

Reflections on the Race Riots

August 2, 1919

The central fact emerging from the recent series of race riots is not so much that the Negro has developed an essentially new psychology, characterized by a fighting attitude. The Negro has always been conspicuous for his aggressiveness when arrayed against a foreign enemy. What is significant is that the Negro, for the first time in American history, has directed his "fight" against the iniquities of the white man in the United States. It is, of course, obvious that this fighting spirit received a decided stimulus in the form of the world war. It is likewise clear that the manifest disinclination of civil authorities to protect Negro life went far to crystalize a long smouldering resentment. Yet the outstanding feature remains, not that the Negro will fight, but that he will fight against the American white.

As long as the Negro was here passive the true solution of the race problem could wait. The South burned and lynched, and the North aided by its silence. But now, with the Negro openly resolved and prepared to resist attacks upon his person and privileges, the condition assumes a graver aspect. Immediate steps toward co-operative relations are imperative. It now confronts the nation, so voluble in acclamation of the democratic ideal, so reticent in applying what it professes, to either extend to the Negro (and other workers) the essentials of a democratic commonwealth or else exist from day to day never knowing when a clash may occur, in the light of which the Washington riot will diminish and pale. Clearly, then, this is no time for appeal. This is no time for academic discussion and presidential meditation. This is essentially a time for action.

Amongst those who would offer a fitting solution there is a motley group so deep in the pit of prejudice, and with vision so circumscribed by the walls of their confinement, that they would eliminate racial differences by increasing the very acts which immediately caused them. They would have the fist of the white man educate the brain of the black. And where common, everyday American brutishness proved to no avail, lynching-bees and burning-fests would be substituted. Thus would they hold up to the eyes of the world the salutary effects of depravity. As those in this class are their own and only counsellors, none may advise them, nor can they counsel others wisely.

Then there is a second group which limits its suggestions to the worn-out method of "constitutional rights for the Negro," who seem to believe that therein lies the sole solvent of racial antagonisms. Quite naturally, believing as they do in the adequacy of our governmental machinery, and certain as they are of the essential goodness of all Americans, they deplore the Negro's fighting psychology, contending with irrefrangible logic that "two wrongs never make a right."

As to the extension of constitutional rights—it should be apparent that under this very constitution the country has come to this crisis. To fit a worn-out coat on the Negro will not alter the essential character of things. Race riots are prevalent in Chicago, where Negroes enjoy political privilege. In effect, the constitution gives no more. The solution, then, must lie deeper than mere suffrage.

As to deploring the new spirit and attitude of the Negro there is much to be said. Not a few who condemn the Negro's "fight" would be themselves the first to fight under like circumstances. Their quarrel is not with fight, per se (a war with Mexico would meet with their hearty approval), but with the Negro (or any other worker), who displays an active unwillingness to submit to injustices. Such a Negro is difficult to exploit.

But over against those whose rhetoric covers their intention are individuals who, in all sincerity, believe physical resistance or aggression, as a means to an end, a discredited institution. And, on the whole, they are in the right. But this one conditioning factor should be noted. In this instance the choice of means—the prerogative—is not with the Negro. If a man would shoot you, and there be no one to prevent him, you must shoot first. Life permits of nothing less. In substance, just this condition prevailed in Washington. Not only did the civil authorities offer little or no protection, but in all too numerous cases were themselves the assailants. Those, then, who would aid in the present crisis would do well to focus attention and action upon those fundamental and determining causes which have irresistibly drawn the Negro into his present position. To do this brings one adjacent to the thought and action of the labor movement.

In the literature of the Socialist movement in this country there is to be found a rational explanation of the causes of race hatred, and, in the light of these, a definite solution, striking at the very root of the evil, is proposed. It is generally established that the causes of race prejudice may primarily be found in the economic structure that compels one worker to compete against another and that furthermore renders it advantageous for the exploiting classes to inculcate, foster, and aggravate that competition. If this be true, then it follows that the nucleus of race co-operation lies in the substitution of a socialized community for a competitive one. To me, it appears that nothing less than just such an economic readjustment will ever bring concord to the two races; for, as long as there are governing classes and as long as these classes feel it to their gain to keep the masses in constant conflict, just so long will a controlled press and educational system incite and promote race hatred. Where there is advantage to be secured by racial antagonisms, heaven and hell will be invoked to that purpose. Demagogues may storm and saints may plead, but America will remain a grotesque storm-center, torn by passion and hatred, until our democratic pretensions are replaced by a socialized reality.

Americans and Mary Austin

October 10, 1920

Though we are some distance from a realization of the race to be known as the American, yet in general contour and aspirations it is visible to those who see. It is certain that it will be a composite one, including within itself, in complementing harmony, all races. It will be less conscious of its composite character than the English are of theirs, and it will be considerably more aware of the grandeur of its destiny. The splendid fire of this latter will effectively coalesce what straggling tendencies to antagonism and disruption may still be hanging over from the former individual race consciousnesses. The resultant temper will be broad, inclusive, aware of one race only, and that the American. In fine, in our future national type humanity will have again achieved the constructive association of its varied elements.

If this be true, then it follows that, individually and collectively, we are distant from the true American (racially) in just that proportion as we are mindful of former race affiliations. Applying this test to the United States of today, some idea of the assimilative processes yet required to produce our ideal type will be manifest. Street conversations quite generally revolve around "nigger," "cracker," "wop," "kike," "polak," "greaser" and "foreigner" and the like. While in the drawing rooms where esthetic pretensions gloss over a poverty of moral and human values, the same sentiments find expression in a weaker but less offensive vocabulary. It is a bitter dose for a certain class of Gentiles to think of the future American including Jewish blood; and it is equally galling for the Orthodox Jew to contemplate the fusion of the Hebrew and the Christian. It would occasion a rupture of friendship, if not a fight, to suggest to the average white man that the blood of his future grandchildren will commingle [with Negroes. In addition there is the] current nonsense among Negroes of the white race being degenerate. Asiatic eyes in the progeny of the Californian is a frequent and current coast nightmare. And all who are American citizens in name are at one in crying horrors at the foreigner. And yet there is nothing more certain than that these seeming ill dreams, frightful to the narrow and the prejudiced as are nature's elements to the uninformed, will come to pass. And there is tremendous good inherent in their certainty. In them rests the seed of the true American, the evolved spiritual pioneer of humanity.

National ideals, varied, and more or less partial and confused, have a host of followers. It is claimed by all the foremost of our institutions and societies that they are integral in the formation of our national character. Our arts are dynamic in their desire to produce something uniquely American. And then, too, there is a body of workers, known as the Americanists, who are devoting energies to research in aboriginal society, art and culture. From the materials thus released many are making deductions as to the future of our present country and the lines along which it may be expected to progress. Thus, it is clear that much effort is being spent to crystallize a national type. But an effort, even when sincere, need be neither intelligent nor sympathetic: it quite frequently omits both these happy attributes, contenting itself with mere functioning. And so, many energies, directed at our evolution, have been degraded, producing no salutary or compensating effects. An interesting case in point recently appeared in the columns of the Nation. In an article, entitled "New York: Dictator of American Criticism," Mary Austin, an American, and undoubtedly having at heart the interests of the national culture, protests to New York against its obvious ascendancy in the matters of criticism and intellectual initiative.

Any centralized control exasperates the provinces, especially if these provinces be conscious of their identity and zealous of their local rights. So it is not surprising that Miss Austin should voice a protest against the usurpation of democratic prerogatives by a group centered in New York. The validity of this protest, as respects New York, however, seems to me to revolve around the question: Is the ascendancy of this group due to an exclusive control of the means of expression; i.e. the publishing houses and the reviews, or does the dominancy of the group rest solely on its intellectual attainments? If the South and the West may not be heard because of the former, then the protest is a serious one and should commend itself to the sense of economic freedom of thoughtful Americans. If, on the other hand, the combined voices of all "extra-New Yorkers" is not sufficient to be heard above a small Manhattan group, then the protest loses none of its seriousness, but its appeal should be transferred from the economic sense to the shame of every one concerned with the cultural growth of his country.

As I read Miss Austin's article I am led to conclude, in absence of clear proof to the contrary, that New York and the New Yorkers are dictators of American criticism for the same reason that Moscow and the Bolsheviki are dictators of the present course of Russia, namely, that they are doing the job better than any others are now capable of doing it. Thus, it seems to me that Miss Austin's quarrel is not so much with New York as with that "vast extra-Manhattan territory" of which she speaks. Such an address to them would undoubtedly spur them toward an articulate consciousness of their own strength and responsibilities.

Miss Austin is decidedly positive in her indication of the Americans. Whether the expression, the form and the substance of an attained American consciousness will be derived from the cultural resources of the Indian or not is a matter of question, the solution of which cannot concern us here. What is of moment is that a group of workers have turned over a body of knowledge, the essence of which is unknown to America at large. This omission places a handicap on every effort at a true interpretation and understanding of what is comprehensively American. Energy directed toward the removal of this handicap is in the nature of a national service. Miss Austin, in this instance, has rendered just such a service.

My next point is pertinent. It regards her stated attitude toward the Jews. Miss Austin opens this phase of her subject by wondering "what part is played in this schism between literature and the process of nationalization by the preponderance of Jews among our critical writers." I cannot for a moment admit that such a schism does exist between literature and the process of nationalization, as I know them. But, as this subject can only adequately be handled in a more extensive paper, I shall have to leave it an undetermined possibility and pass to her next passage.

"There is nothing un-American in being a Jew," says Miss Austin. Certainly not. But why state the obvious? Once made, such statements are never without their contrary implications. And, when sincerity is the question, one feels it better to have left such things unsaid. But to continue: "It is part of our dearest tradition that no derivation from any race or religion inhibits a contribution to our national whole." Nor is this passage effective. Miss Austin knows that in practice it does not now obtain. She need look no further than her own California and its relation to the Japanese to feel the error of this remark. "We could not without serious loss subtract the Jewish contribution from our science or our economics, or dispense with the services of the younger Jewish publishers. It is only when the Jew attempts the role of interpreter of our American expression that the valadity [*sic*] of the racial bias comes into question."

Frankly, I know of no immediate analogy to the sentiment here expressed other than that of the average Southern white in his attitude toward the Negro. I can imagine him saying: "No, th' nigger ain't un-American, so far as that goes; a good nigger's all right. An' he's damn useful pickin' cotton. But let him keep away from them polls. I ain't going to have no nigger legislating for me." Nor does the difference in the phases of the human effort lessen the force of the analogy. In both cases there are prejudice and racial consciousness, whereas a national consciousness without prejudice is the aim.

Miss Austin then asks: "Can the Jew, with his profound complex of election, his need of sensuous satisfaction qualifying his every expression of personal life, and his short pendulum swing between mystical orthodoxy and a sterile ethical culture—can he become the commentator, the arbiter, of American art and American thinking?" From the position taken at the beginning of this article it is clear that no racial or religious unit thus conscious of past affiliations can truly reflect America, the evolved American. The point in question is, Are the Jews such a unit? Is Miss Austin exact in her conception of them? To support an implied negative answer to her question, Miss Austin cites Waldo Frank's "Our America." Her short review of it does not convince me. As to the "complex of election," admitting a want as regards the Americanists, which want, by the way, I can picture most Catholics or Protestants capable of, how many men are there to name other than the "gentlemen" Mr. Frank chooses? A single volume may not be inclusive. Selection is imposed upon it. And in justice preference must be given those whose known output demands it. I think Mr. Frank's choice admirable, and fail to see in it any strict evidence of a peculiar complex of election. Turning to the pages of his book, I am deeply convinced as to the essential American origin and nurture of its fibres. Evidence of a distinct "need of sensuous satisfaction" and "pendulum swing" in this case is not available.

It thus appears to me that what was nominally a valid protest against the one-sided development of the American intellect degenerates into a force misdirected against the intellect vested in a single race. Desiring the inevitable amalgamation and consequent cultural unity, Miss Austin's article has given new cause for old race consciousness. Aiming at a community of cultured differences, she serves the cause of disunion. With her soul toward the realizable ideal, her eyes still focus on the unfused metals of the melting pot. And what is true of this writer obtains for millions of those who live within the political boundaries of the United States, augmented in these latter, of course, by the crudity of their expression and the essential poverty of their lives. Yet, and nothing is more certain, from just such stuff will a continent of Walt Whitmans evolve, universal in their sympathies and godlike of soul.

Notes

Introduction: The Witness of History

1. Robert A. Bone, "Cane," *New York Times Book Review,* January 19, 1969, pp. 3, 34.
2. Therman B. O'Daniel, "Jean Toomer: A Classified Bibliography," in Therman B. O'Daniel, ed., *Jean Toomer: A Critical Evaluation* (Washington, D.C.: Howard University Press, 1988), 505–28. O'Daniel's work is usefully supplemented by the bibliography in Robert B. Jones, *Jean Toomer and the Prison-House of Thought: A Phenomenology of the Spirit* (Amherst: University of Massachusetts Press, 1993), 155–83. For the continuity of reference to Toomer in surveys of African-American literature, see Sterling A. Brown, *The Negro in American Fiction* (Washington, D.C.: Associates in Negro Folk Education, 1937); J. Saunders Redding, *To Make a Poet Black* (Chapel Hill: University of North Carolina Press, 1939); Hugh M. Gloster, *Negro Voices in American Fiction* (Chapel Hill: University of North Carolina Press, 1948); Robert A. Bone, *The Negro Novel in America* (New Haven: Yale University Press, 1958); Arna Bontemps, "The Negro Renaissance: Jean Toomer and the Harlem Writers of the 1920's," in Herbert Hill, ed., *Anger and Beyond: The Negro Writer in the United States* (New York: Harper and Row, 1966). An interesting account of the reaction to Arna Bontemps's paper on Toomer at a 1964 conference on black writing is given in Kenneth Rexroth, "Panelizing Dissent," *Nation* 199 (September 7, 1964): 97–99. Toomer also receives several mentions in the survey *The Little Magazine: A History and a Bibliography*, by Frederick J. Hoffman, Charles Allen, and Carolyn F. Ulrich (Princeton, N.J.: Princeton University Press, 1946), not as the author of *Cane*, but as a notable contributor to the magazines being surveyed.
3. Waldo Frank, *Our America* (New York: Boni & Liveright, 1919), 197. Cary Nelson, *Repression and Recovery: Modern American Poetry and the Politics of Cultural Memory, 1910–1945* (Madison: University of Wisconsin Press, 1989), 6–7.
4. Robert A. Bone's 1969 article in the *New York Times Book Review* provoked two letters of response which offer some measure of the distance Toomer had traveled from *Cane* by the end of his life. One was from Gorham Munson, applauding the belated recognition of Toomer's writing but devoting most of its length to correcting Bone's mistaken information about Gurdjieff and affirming Toomer's devotion to the "Caucasian Greek who grew up in Armenia." The second letter was from Thomas Hancock, a Quaker acquaintance of Toomer, who objected to Bone's description of *Cane* as Toomer's "affirmation of his blackness" and asserted that he had known "Jean Toomer as a well-regarded, happy Quaker, who never was thought about by others in terms of white or black." Ironically, all three—Bone, Munson, and Hancock—managed to essentialize *Cane*, if only by implication. For Bone, "it was Toomer's genius to discover and essentialize the qualities of 'soul,'" just as

Munson and Hancock remembered him primarily as a Gurdjieffian or a Quaker. See "Letters," *New York Times Book Review*, February 16, 1969, pp. 54–55.

5. Cynthia Earl Kerman and Richard Eldridge, *The Lives of Jean Toomer: A Hunger for Wholeness* (Baton Rouge: Louisiana State University Press, 1987). Even borrowing directly from Darwin T. Turner's assembled autobiography in *The Wayward and the Seeking: A Collection of Writings by Jean Toomer* (Washington, D.C.: Howard University Press, 1980), Kerman and Eldridge get some things wrong, as in their description of the important meeting between Waldo Frank and Jean Toomer in Central Park. They also make the undocumented claim that Toomer wrote "Bona and Paul" in 1917 (he was revising that story as late as 1923), and they have Toomer suggesting the trip to Spartanburg in the summer of 1922, when in fact Waldo Frank proposed it. They claim that Toomer wanted to publish in the *Call* under an assumed name, when in fact this was a ploy initiated by his publisher, Horace Liveright, who wanted to use an essay of Toomer's to generate publicity for *Cane*. Some of these factual errors are major and some are minor, but their sheer number makes *The Lives of Jean Toomer* a very unreliable source for information about Toomer and *Cane*.

6. Waldo Frank to Jean Toomer, October 21, 1920, Jean Toomer Papers, Yale Collection of American Literature, Beinecke Rare Book and Manuscript Library, Yale University (hereafter cited as Jean Toomer Papers); Jean Toomer to Waldo Frank, April 4, 1922, Waldo Frank Papers, Special Collection, Van Pelt Library, University of Pennsylvania (hereafter cited as Waldo Frank Papers); Biographical Publicity Sketch, Box 26, Folder 612, Jean Toomer Papers. Toomer's *New York Call* articles are reprinted at the end of our text as an appendix.

7. Kerman and Eldridge, *The Lives of Jean Toomer: A Hunger For Wholeness* (1987; reprint, Baton Rouge: Louisiana State University Press, 1989), 102. Kerman and Eldridge do not cite a page number for their quotation from *Our America*. For a similar neglect of Frank's social criticism, see Frederik L. Rusch, ed., *A Jean Toomer Reader: Selected Unpublished Writings* (New York: Oxford University Press, 1993), xii–xiii; Mark Helbling, "Jean Toomer and Waldo Frank: A Creative Friendship," in *Jean Toomer: A Critical Evaluation*, 85–97; Rudolph P. Byrd, *Jean Toomer's Years with Gurdjieff: Portrait of an Artist, 1923–1936* (Athens: University of Georgia Press, 1990), 50, 96. Byrd also suggests (p. 50) that the "omission" of African-Americans from *Our America* reflects Frank's narrow thinking. But, of course, in *Our America* Frank freely admitted his lack of "knowledge" about the presence of "the African on the American continent" and in fact suggested that "some one fitted for the task" write the "Chapter" on this subject that he was unable to write. See Waldo Frank, *Our America*, 97.

Misreading Frank, or not reading him at all, is related to the problem of reading *Cane* as the product of a "spiritual" Toomer. For Byrd, *Cane*'s unity lies in "Toomer's most important theme—human development, or man's lack of and search for wholeness" (15). For Rusch, "The restless searching and aching discontent displayed by many of the characters of *Cane* were representative of its author, and so it's not surprising that by 1924 Toomer had abandoned black writing in favor of more didactic and philosophical work" (xi). Even Robert B. Jones, who has a much more complex view of the meanings of *Cane*, believes the book is primarily a spiritual autobiography. See Robert B. Jones, *Jean Toomer and the Prison-House of Thought*, 61.

8. Waldo Frank, *Our America*, 138, 146.

9. See Charles Scruggs, "'My Chosen World': Jean Toomer's Articles in *The New York Call*," *Arizona Quarterly* 52 (Summer 1995): 114, nn. 9, 10.

10. Darwin T. Turner, ed., *The Wayward and the Seeking*, 111. Turner uses "Outline of An Autobiography" as "the basis for Toomer's life from 1909 to 1922" (11). Jean Toomer Papers, Box 22, Folder 561.

11. Jean Toomer Papers, Box 22, Folders 560, 561. Arguably, the most interesting works of Toomer's post-*Cane* writings remain unpublished—little in Toomer's later work which has been published is as vivid and powerful as his 1936 description of working in the shipyards.

12. See our discussion of this question in Chapter 2.

13. In dealing with Toomer's life up to 1924, Kerman and Eldridge relied primarily on "Outline of an Autobiography" and "On Being an American." After sorting through the Jean Toomer Papers at Yale, with the help of Karen V. Peltier's detailed catalogue of this material, we chose three further versions of Toomer autobiography: in addition to "Outline of an Autobiography" and "On Being an American," we have used "Book Ten," which has been edited as a Ph.D. dissertation by Isaac Johnny Johnson III, "*The Autobiography of Jean Toomer:* An Edition" (Ph.D. diss., Purdue University, 1982). This 1935 autobiography exists in typescript and ends circa 1917; our supposition is that the materials in Box 22, Folders 558, 560, and 561 represent a continuation of this autobiography, probably written in 1936 in notebooks and never transferred to a typescript. These materials deal with the years 1917–1920 in a way that is significantly different from Toomer's treatment of the same period in "Outline of an Autobiography." The last autobiography we use is "Incredible Journey," probably written between 1937 and 1941, which contains a brief but important anecdote of his residence in Sparta. There are, of course, other biographical fragments in the Jean Toomer Papers, detailed in Peltier's Yale catalogue (9–11) and outlined in *The Wayward and the Seeking* (9–14), in *The Autobiography of Jean Toomer: An Edition* (1–2), and in *The Lives of Jean Toomer* (393–94).

14. In general, it is necessary to use the unpublished correspondence as a check against the 1931–32 biography and the other fragments that make up Turner's selection. Even reading the Toomer-Frank letters can be difficult, however. The correspondence is divided between two libraries, and after August 1922 Toomer and Frank dated very few of their letters. Kerman and Eldridge sometimes read the letters in the wrong order, and this leads them to say, for instance, that Waldo Frank sent Toomer part of *Holiday* to read early in 1922, although the book was not begun until that fall.

15. Vera M. Kutzinski, "Unseasonal Flowers: Nature and History in Placido and Jean Toomer," *Yale Journal of Criticism* 3 (Spring 1990): 153–79; George B. Hutchinson, "Jean Toomer and the 'New Negroes' of Washington," *American Literature* 63 (December 1991): 683–92; George B. Hutchinson, "Jean Toomer and American Racial Discourse," *Texas Studies in Literature and Language* 35 (Summer 1993): 226–50; Michael North, *The Dialect of Modernism: Race, Language, and Twentieth-Century Literature* (New York: Oxford University Press, 1994), chapter 7; Barbara Foley, "Jean Toomer's Sparta," *American Literature* 67 (December 1995): 747–75; Barbara Foley, "Jean Toomer's Washington and the Politics of Class: From 'Blue-Veins' to Seventh-Street Rebels," *Modern Fiction Studies* 42 (Summer 1996): 289–321. On the "ideology of racial uplift," see Kevin K. Gaines, *Uplifting the Race: Black Leadership, Politics, and Culture in the Twentieth Century* (Chapel Hill: University of North Carolina Press, 1996).

16. See S. P. Fullinwider, "Jean Toomer: Lost Generation, or Negro Renaissance?" *Phylon* 27 (4th quarter, 1966): 396–403; Nellie Y. McKay, *Jean Toomer, Artist: A Study of His Literary Life and Work, 1894–1936* (Madison: University of Wisconsin Press, 1984), 27–28 and passim. Kenneth S. Lynn, *Hemingway* (New York: Simon and Schuster, 1987), 332–33. Lewis Mumford, *My Works and Days: A Personal Chronicle* (New York: Harcourt, Brace, Jovanovich, 1979), 163.

17. Lewis Mumford, *Findings and Keepings: Analects for an Autobiography* (New York: Harcourt Brace Jovanovich, 1975), 103. Van Wyck Brooks, "On Creating a Usable

Past," *The Dial* 64 (April 11, 1918): 337–41, quoted in Claire Sprague, ed., *Van Wyck Brooks: The Early Years—A Selection from His Works, 1908–1921* (New York: Harper and Row, 1968), 223.

Chapter 1: Sparta

1. *Sparta Ishmaelite*, November 11, 1921. Toomer would have been living in Sparta when the *Ishmaelite* reported its census.

2. Allen D. Candler and Clement A. Evans, eds., *Georgia: Comprising Sketches of Counties, Towns, Events, Institutions, and Persons, Arranged in Cyclopedic Form*, vol. 2 (Atlanta: State Historical Association, 1906), 191–92.

3. Thomas Jesse Jones, ed., *Negro Education: A Study of the Private and Higher Schools for Colored People in the United States* (1917; reprint, New York: Arno Press, 1969), 228.

4. Jean Toomer published two books in his lifetime: *Cane* (New York: Boni & Liveright, 1923), the work for which he is primarily known, and *Essentials: Definitions and Aphorisms* (1931), a privately printed collection of aphorisms (edited by Rudolph P. Byrd and reprinted by the University of Georgia Press, 1991). Five other books that print selections from Toomer's mostly unpublished writings have appeared since 1980: Darwin T. Turner, ed., *The Wayward and the Seeking: A Collection of Writings by Jean Toomer* (Washington, D.C.: Howard University Press, 1980); Darwin T. Turner, ed., *Cane: An Authoritative Text, Backgrounds, Criticism* (New York: W.W. Norton, 1988 [hereafter referred to as Turner, ed., *Cane*]); Robert B. Jones and Margery Toomer Latimer, eds., *The Collected Poems of Jean Toomer* (Chapel Hill: University of North Carolina Press, 1988); Frederik L. Rusch, ed., *A Jean Toomer Reader: Selected Unpublished Writings* (New York: Oxford University Press, 1993); and Robert B. Jones, ed., *Jean Toomer: Selected Essays and Literary Criticism* (Knoxville: University of Tennessee Press, 1996).

5. Darwin T. Turner, ed., *The Wayward and the Seeking*, 124. Also see Jean Toomer Papers, Yale Collection of American Literature, Beinecke Rare Book and Manuscript Library, Yale University, Box 19, Folders 507–8 (hereafter referred to as Jean Toomer Papers). In "Notes" for his unpublished "Autobiographical Writings," Toomer says that he arrived in Sparta in September and left "November 25." See Jean Toomer Papers, Box 17, Folders 476–77. Also see Nellie Y. McKay, *Jean Toomer, Artist: A Study of His Literary Life and Works, 1894–1936* (Chapel Hill: University of North Carolina Press, 1984), 32–33, 45; Cynthia Earl Kerman and Richard Eldridge, *The Lives of Jean Toomer: A Hunger for Wholeness* (Baton Rouge: Louisiana State University Press, 1987), 81–85. McKay, Kerman, and Eldridge put his stay in Sparta at two months.

The August 19, 1922, letter to *The Liberator* is typical of one kind of lyric response Toomer gave: "I heard folk-songs come from the lips of Negro peasants. I saw the rich dusk beauty that I heard many false accents about. . . . And a deep part of my nature, a part that I had repressed, sprang suddenly to life and responded to them." He repeated variations on this theme in letters to Waldo Frank, Sherwood Anderson, and John McClure (editor of *The Double-Dealer*). On April 26, 1922, he wrote Waldo Frank: "There [Sparta], for the first time I really saw the Negro, not as a pseudo-urbanized and vulgarized, a semi-Americanized product, but the Negro peasant, strong with the tang of fields and soil. It was there that I first heard the folk-songs rolling up the valley at twilight, heard them as spontaneous and native utterances. They filled me with gold, and tints of an eternal purple. Love? Man they gave birth to a whole new life." Jean Toomer to the editors of *The Liberator*, August 19, 1922, Jean Toomer Papers; Jean Toomer to Waldo Frank, April 26, 1922,

Waldo Frank Papers, Special Collections, Van Pelt Library, University of Pennsylvania (hereafter referred to as Waldo Frank Papers). Toomer's correspondence shows that he had already submitted material to *The Liberator* before he left Sparta. (See note 20, below.) Also see Jean Toomer to Sherwood Anderson, December 18, 1922, Jean Toomer Papers (reprinted in Turner, ed., *Cane*, 148–49). Jean Toomer to John McClure, July 22, 1922, Jean Toomer Papers, reprinted in Frederik L. Rusch, ed., *A Jean Toomer Reader*, 12.

6. Jean Toomer to Waldo Frank, April 26, 1922, Waldo Frank Papers; Jean Toomer to Waldo Frank, August 2, 1922, Jean Toomer Papers.

7. Jean Toomer to Waldo Frank (probably 1923), Jean Toomer Papers; reprinted in Turner, ed., *Cane*, 156. Jean Toomer to Waldo Frank (probably January 1923), Waldo Frank Papers.

8. A description of the system of syndication for rural Southern newspapers appears in Thomas D. Clark, *The Southern Country Editor* (New York: Bobbs-Merrill Company, 1948), chapter 3. Clark makes the point that most of the syndicated rural "hometown" features these papers carried originated from bureaus in Chicago or New York.

9. For the South's reaction to Roosevelt's dinner with Booker T. Washington, see Thomas Clark, *The Southern Country Editor*, 307–13.

10. W. Fitzhugh Brundage, *Lynching in the New South: Georgia and Virginia, 1880–1930* (Urbana: University of Illinois Press, 1993), 278–79. In 1923, however, two black men were lynched in Hancock County. Also, see Pete Daniel, *The Shadow of Slavery: Peonage in the South, 1901–1969* (Urbana: University of Illinois Press, 1972), chapter 6.

11. See Numan V. Bartley, *The Creation of Modern Georgia*, 2d ed. (Athens: University of Georgia Press, 1990), 169: "In 1920 cotton prices dropped precipitously, and, worse, the fields teemed with boll weevils. The terrifying insect arrived in Georgia in 1913 but not until 1919–20 did it become a problem and not until the early 1920s did it become a plague. . . . The destruction from 1921 to 1923 was devastating. Georgia's annual cotton production (in 500-pound bales) during these years was: 1918, 2,122,000; 1920, 1,415,000; 1921, 787,000; 1922, 715,000; 1923, 588,000." Also see Wilbur Cash, *The Mind of the South* (1941; reprint, New York: Random House, 1969), 263–64, 279–80.

12. Wilbur Cash, *The Mind of the South*, 312; C. Vann Woodward, *Origins of the New South, 1877–1913* (1951; reprint, Baton Rouge: Louisiana State University Press, 1971), 212–15; Jacqueline Jones, *The Dispossessed: America's Underclasses from the Civil War to the Present* (New York: HarperCollins, 1992), part 2; Pete Daniel, *The Shadow of Slavery*; Charles L. Flynn, Jr., *White Land, Black Labor: Caste and Class in Late Nineteenth-Century Georgia* (Baton Rouge: Louisiana State University Press, 1983); John Dittmer, *Black Georgia in the Progressive Era, 1900–1920* (Urbana: University of Illinois Press, 1977), 72–89. On the association of lynching and the Southern economic system, see especially Stewart E. Tolnay and E. M. Beck, *A Festival of Violence: An Analysis of Southern Lynchings, 1882–1930* (Urbana: University of Illinois Press, 1992), 255: "Our evidence suggests that lynching was an integral element of an agricultural economy that required a large, cheap, and docile labor force. Compromises following the Civil War led to an organization of agricultural production that was built more around the tenant farmer than upon yeoman farmers working their own land. At least at first, this niche was filled primarily by newly freed African-Americans. Any shocks or threats to the arrangement carried the potential for conflict and violence." On the convict lease system, which ended in Georgia in 1907, see Alex Lichtenstein, *Twice the Work of Free Labor: The Political Economy of Convict Labor in the New South* (London: Verso, 1996).

13. The effort to control the movement of African-American labor was always an important element in Southern legal systems and local custom, both during slavery and afterward. That control joined the economics of white supremacy with its "social" claims, as, for instance, the claim that "vagrant" black men were responsible for most crime in the South, particularly rapes of white women. George M. Fredrickson points out that the black codes established by Southern states immediately following the Civil War "meant that blacks ceased to be slaves of individual masters only to become the quasi-slaves of the white community in general. This system required that legislation, law enforcement, and the judicial system be under exclusive white domination so that they could be used for the explicit purpose of black subjugation. A key feature was the attempt through draconian vagrancy laws to deny blacks access to a free and competitive labor market." George M. Fredrickson, "The South and South Africa: Political Foundations of White Supremacy," in Numan V. Bartley, ed., *The Evolution of Southern Culture* (Athens: University of Georgia Press, 1988), 70. For a discussion of the qualified nature of white control over black labor, see Jacqueline Jones, *The Dispossessed*, chapter 4.

14. John Dittmer, *Black Georgia in the Progressive Era*, 101–4; Forrest Shivers, *The Land Between: A History of Hancock County, Georgia to 1940* (Spartanburg, S.C.: The Reprint Company, 1990), 283–84. Shivers also mentions the rejection by Sparta citizens of a Carnegie Library grant in 1907, on the grounds that it would be too expensive to maintain a public library. See p. 307.

15. Elizabeth Wiley Smith, *The History of Hancock County, Georgia* (Washington, Ga.: Wilkes Publishing, 1974), vol. 1, viii. Also, see Forrest Shivers, *The Land Between*, 237–38.

16. W. J. Cash, *The Mind of the South*, 140. Cash takes a rather different view later in his book when he says that "the most powerful single consideration in the South's adoption of the idea of public education for him [the Negro] had been the will to take control of his instruction away from the Yankees who were swarming in to start schools, and to fit him to stay in the place intended for him" (321). This comes closer to the real Southern fear of the "schoolmarm." James D. Anderson points out that the Northern "schoolmarm" was as much a symbol of the South's rejection of Northern interference as she was an element in the education of Southern blacks. In Anderson's view, the main impulse and achievement for the education of the former slaves came from within their own communities. That achievement, of course, was undercut by the end of Reconstruction: "With both state authority and extra-legal means of control firmly in their hands, the planters, though unable to eradicate earlier gains, kept universal schooling underdeveloped. They stressed low taxation, opposed compulsory school attendance laws, blocked the passage of new laws that would strengthen the constitutional basis of public education, and generally discouraged the expansion of public school opportunities. . . . Indeed, between 1880 and 1900, the number of black children of school age increased 25 percent, but the proportion attending public school fell." James D. Anderson, *The Education of Blacks in the South, 1860–1935* (Chapel Hill: University of North Carolina Press, 1988), 23.

17. C. Vann Woodward, *Origins of the New South*, 373. On the exchanges between Dorsey and the Ku Klux Klan, see Nancy MacLean, *Behind the Mask of Chivalry: The Making of the Second Ku Klux Klan* (New York: Oxford University Press, 1994), 125–28. MacLean's book, which is centered around the post–World War I Klan in Clarke County, Georgia, about forty miles north of Sparta, provides an excellent background to the economic, social, and political settings of race in the Georgia of 1921. The Dorsey controversy was the subject of pieces in *The Crisis* 22 (June 1921):

53–54, the *Nation* 112 (May 25, 1921): 727, and the *Literary Digest* 69 (June 4, 1921): 19. The article in *The Nation* makes specific reference to the Mary Turner lynching, which becomes the Mame Lamkins lynching in "Kabnis," a story that also mentions the *Literary Digest* by name.

18. Forrest Shivers, *The Land Between*, 276–77.

19. Darwin T. Turner, ed., *The Wayward and the Seeking*, 123. The *Ishmaelite* in the early 1920s routinely published white supremacist pieces, ranging from outright declarations to favorable treatments of local Ku Klux Klan organizing and stereotypical depictions of African-Americans. See, for example, "Uncle John's Poem," July 1, 1921; on the Ku Klux Klan, see January 28, February 18, and February 25, 1921. For depictions of African-Americans, see "He Is Now Safe for Twelve Months," January 14, 1921, or, especially, "A Millionaire Negro Woman Still Washes," June 3, 1921. This last story contains all the contradictory elements of economic modernism and old-fashioned racism ("She's worth $8,000,000, probably $10,000,000, but she is up before the break of day each morning to do the work for 'muh whi' folks'"), of the conflict between a disruptive economic system and the urge to preserve a rigidly hierarchical social system.

20. Darwin T. Turner, ed., *The Wayward and the Seeking*, 123. Jean Toomer to Floyd Dell, November 22, 1921, and Claude McKay to Jean Toomer, December 6, 1921, Jean Toomer Papers. McKay's description of "Georgia Night" sounds as if the story might be an early version of "Kabnis." Unlike T. S. Stribling's Hooker's Bend in *Birthright* (1922), Waldo Frank's Nazareth in *Holiday* (1923), or James Baldwin's Plaguetown in *Blues for Mr. Charlie* (1967), Toomer in *Cane* does not split Sempter into black and white sections—total segregation of the population in Sparta would have been almost impossible—but he does distinguish between town and country. Toomer's Sempter suggests a town very much like the Sparta of today (which is now 85 to 90 percent African-American). In *Cane*, Jim Crane's grocery store, "Nat Bowle's place" (the local black whorehouse), and Halsey's workshop as the "village meeting-place" are signs of a black presence in the heart of the city. Charles Scruggs visited Sparta, Georgia, in May 1995, and gathered the materials on which our comparisons here are based. Also see Barbara Foley's informative article, "Jean Toomer's Sparta," *American Literature* 67 (December 1995): 747–75.

21. Scruggs learned the name "Sander's Quarters" by accident when he asked local African-Americans what the dirt road was called. They responded that the road had no name, but that this area where they lived was "Sander's Quarters." None of the people he talked to knew who "Sander" was, and when he asked the white editor of the *Sparta Ishmaelite* where the name might have come from, the editor said that he had never heard of "Sander's Quarters," though he had worked in Sparta as the newspaper's editor for the past eleven years. Dr. Carlton Morse, a graduate of the Sparta Agricultural and Industrial School (1942) and its former principal (1948–1957), told Scruggs in a telephone conversation (July 1996) that a man named Sander ran a juke-joint in the area in the 1940s. Dr. Morse also informed Scruggs that Highway 22 to Milledgeville did not exist in 1921, thus making the black community on the western edge of town even more distinct.

22. Ingraham, who was born in slavery, died in 1935, and his wife, Anna Ingraham, kept the school open until her death in the 1950s. See Forrest Shivers, *The Land Between*, 277. The school's last year was 1959. Contrary to his portrait in *Cane* as Hanby, Ingraham seems to have been well loved and respected by his students. On July 2–5, 1992, a school reunion was held in honor of both husband and wife, and Scruggs talked to several former students of the school, now in their eighties, who had fond though vague memories of its founder. Dr. Morse, however, remem-

bers Ingraham well. According to him, Ingraham made great personal sacrifices to maintain the school, and he also brought in outside teachers like Toomer to enrich the curriculum.

23. Jean Toomer, *Cane* (1923; reprint, New York: Harper and Row, 1969), 17. In this chapter, page numbers of subsequent citations from *Cane* are put in parentheses and appear in the text. We use this edition of *Cane* because it is a facsimile of the original Boni & Liveright edition. We are mindful of the fact, as John Callahan has noted (*In the African-American Grain: The Pursuit of Voice in Twentieth-Century Black Fiction* [Urbana: University of Illinois Press, 1988], 112, n. 11), that this 1969 edition lacks the curve like a "crescent moon" on one of the two blank pages that precedes "Karintha." The reference to "old Pap's store" in "Fern" (18) is probably to the same store (now white-owned) that exists today near the point where the James Hunt Jr. Road divides from Dixie Street.

24. Richard Johnson eventually tried to "pass" in Atlanta but failed because a white Spartan recognized him. He and his family then migrated to California, where they melted into the anonymity of American life. Information and quotation provided by Mark Schultz in a letter to Charles Scruggs, December 12, 1995. The source of his information is James McMullen, a former black businessman in Sparta, and Katie Hunt, African-American born in 1890 who has lived in Sparta all her life. Charles Scruggs had the pleasure of interviewing Katie Hunt with Mark Schultz in May 1995. Elizabeth Wiley Smith, *The History of Hancock County, Georgia*, 54–55, 58–59.

25. Forrest Shivers, *The Land Between*, 210; Elizabeth Wiley Smith, *The History of Hancock County, Georgia*, 101. The factory was probably still standing in 1921; the *Sparta Ishmaelite* referred to it twice (February 23, 1917; September 13, 1918) in the context of an illegal crap game that had taken place there and a theft in which several black men were caught by the police tearing up the factory's floorboards for lumber. On antebellum "cotton factories" using slave labor, see Robert S. Starobin, *Industrial Slavery in the Old South* (New York: Oxford University Press, 1970), 12–14. Also see James Oakes, *The Ruling Race: A History of American Slaveholders* (1982; reprint, New York: Random House, 1983), chapter 6.

26. See Forrest Shivers, *The Land Between*, 239. During a conversation with a barber in Sparta, Toomer discovered that his father "stayed at the best white hotel" when he was in Sparta courting a woman, probably Amanda America Dickson. Toomer claimed not to know who the woman was, and the barber said the two never married. See Autobiographical Writings, Box 18, Folder 487, Jean Toomer Papers. Elizabeth Wiley Smith, *The History of Hancock County, Georgia*, 241; Eugene Victor Walter, *Placeways: A Theory of the Human Environment* (Chapel Hill: University of North Carolina Press, 1988), 202.

27. William Boelhower, *Through a Glass Darkly: Ethnic Semiosis in American Literature* (Venice: Edizioni Helvetia, 1984), 48, 75. Also see David Harvey, *The Condition of Postmodernity: An Enquiry into the Origins of Cultural Change* (Oxford: Blackwell, 1989), 253. Simon Ryan, "Inscribing the Emptiness: Cartography, Exploration and the Construction of Australia," in Chris Tiffin and Alan Lawson, ed., *De-Scribing Empire: Post-Colonialism and Textuality* (London: Routledge, 1994), 124. Pierre Nora, "Between Memory and History: *Les Lieux de Memoire*," in Genevieve Fabre and Robert O'Meally, eds., *History and Memory in African American Culture* (New York: Oxford University Press, 1994), 298. Also see Craig Hansen Werner, *Playing the Changes: From Afro-Modernism to the Jazz Impulse* (Urbana: University of Illinois Press, 1994), chapter 8.

28. Thomas Jefferson, *Notes on the State of Virginia*, ed. William Peden (Chapel Hill: University of North Carolina Press, 1955), 97. See Roy Harvey Pearce, *The Sav-*

ages of America: A Study of the Indian and the Idea of Civilization, rev. ed. (Baltimore: Johns Hopkins University Press, 1965), chapter 1.

29. Kirk Savage, "The Politics of Memory: Black Emancipation and the Civil War Monument," in John R. Gillis, ed., *Commemorations,* (Princeton, N.J.: Princeton University Press, 1994), 131. Jane Gallop, "The Problem of Definition," *Genre* 20 (Summer 1987): 115.

30. James Haskins, *Pinckney Benton Stewart Pinchback* (New York: Macmillan, 1973); Kent Anderson Leslie and Willard B. Gatewood, Jr., "'This Father of Mine . . . a Sort of Mystery': Jean Toomer's Georgia Heritage," *Georgia Historical Quarterly* 77 (Winter 1993): 789–809.

31. *New York Times,* July 15, 1892, cited in Kent Anderson Leslie and Willard B. Gatewood, Jr., "'This Father of Mine,'" 790. Ibid., 789–809. On the David Dickson will, see Jonathan M. Bryant, "Race, Class and Law in Bourbon Georgia: The Case of David Dickson's Will," *Georgia Historical Quarterly* 71 (Summer 1987): 226–42. As Bryant makes clear, the struggle over Dickson's will (his white relatives attempted to have it invalidated) was a contest between the New South's respect for property rights and the Old South's assumption of white priority; in this case, property won out. Also see Adele Logan Alexander, *Ambiguous Lives: Free Women of Color in Rural Georgia, 1789–1879* (Fayetteville: University of Arkansas Press, 1991), 185–90; Kent Anderson Leslie, *Woman of Color, Daughter of Privilege: Amanda America Dickson, 1849–1893* (Athens: University of Georgia Press, 1995), 84–104, 117–33.

32. Jean Toomer Papers, Box 18, Folder 491. Kent Anderson Leslie and Willard B. Gatewood, Jr., "'This Father of Mine,'" 793.

33. Darwin T. Turner, *The Wayward and the Seeking,* 33. Jean Toomer Papers, Box 18, Folder 487 and Box 19, Folder 488. Kent Anderson Leslie and Willard B. Gatewood, Jr., "'This Father of Mine,'" 794. For an illuminating history of miscegenated relationships in Hancock County, see Mark R. Schultz, "Interracial Kinship Ties and the Emergence of a Rural Black Middle Class, Hancock County, Georgia, 1865–1920," in John C. Inscoe, ed., *Georgia in Black and White: Explorations in the Race Relations of a Southern State, 1865–1950* (Athens: University of Georgia Press, 1994), 141–72.

34. Joel Williamson, *New People: Miscegenation and Mulattoes in the United States* (New York: The Free Press, 1980), 56. Williamson's discussion of this pattern is on pp. 42–56. This practice was well understood by African-Americans themselves, of course; see, for example, Alexander Crummell's remarks of 1883, in *Africa and America: Addresses and Discourses* (1891; reprint, Miami: Mnemosyne Publishing, 1969), 62–63. Some excellent grammar schools in the antebellum North were open to black students, notably the Gilmore School in Cincinnati, which "attracted blacks from throughout the nation, including a sizable group of mulatto children of southern planters. Among the latter were P. B. S. Pinchback, James Monroe Trotter, and John Mercer Langston, whose descendents were also well educated." Willard B. Gatewood, Jr., *Aristocrats of Color: The Black Elite, 1880–1920* (Bloomington: Indiana University Press, 1990), 251.

35. Pinchback's fortune, which had been considerable in 1890, was largely gone by 1920. In an autobiographical passage included in *The Wayward and the Seeking,* Toomer says that in 1920, "grandfather sold my house in order to get back what he had loaned me on it. He said he needed the money. I think he did." From the sale "there was about six hundred dollars left over. This he sent to me. I decided to live on it." At that point Toomer quit his job in New York and devoted himself "to music and to literature" (112). The house which Toomer borrowed against and then received a final cash settlement for must have been the one his father purchased for Nina when they were engaged in 1893; thus it was his indirect inheritance from

the Dickson estates in Hancock County. After Pinchback's death Toomer discovered, as he wrote to Frank, that his grandfather's money had "slipped through his hands." There was barely enough left to support his grandmother. Jean Toomer to Waldo Frank, April 4, 1922, Waldo Frank Papers. In a summary of his mother's petition for alimony from Nathan, Toomer recorded "that N.T. told her he owned two plantations at or near Sparta, Georgia." And in the autobiographical passage describing his conversation in the Sparta barbershop, Toomer reflected, "I thought to myself—well, it would seem that [Nathan] Toomer did have some money. You can't take it away from a man unless he has it." Box 18, Folder 491, Jean Toomer Papers. Adele Logan Alexander, *Ambiguous Lives: Free Women of Color in Rural Georgia, 1789–1879*, 70; Mark R. Schultz, "Interracial Kinship Ties," 158.

36. Mark Schultz, "Interracial Kinship Ties," 166.

37. Barbara J. Fields, "Ideology and Race in American History," in J. Morgan Kousser and James M. McPherson, eds., *Region, Race, and Reconstruction: Essays in Honor of C. Vann Woodward* (New York: Oxford University Press, 1982), 151. Stephen Jay Gould, *The Mismeasure of Man* (New York: Norton, 1981), chapters 1 and 2. Joel Williamson, *New People: Miscegenation and Mulattoes in the United States* (New York: The Free Press, 1980). John G. Mencke, *Mulattoes and Race Mixture: American Attitudes and Images, 1865–1918* (Ann Arbor, Mich.: UMI Research Press, 1978). On the parallel development of slavery and racial definition, see Barbara Jeanne Fields's "Slavery, Race and Ideology in the United States of America," *New Left Review* 181 (May–June 1990): 101–8.

38. Deborah Gray White, *Ar'n't I a Woman? Female Slaves in the Plantation South* (New York: Norton, 1985), 34. See White's discussion, pp. 27–46. Joel Williamson, *New People*, 6–59.

39. Deborah Gray White, *Ar'n't I a Woman?* 39.

40. Ibid., 41.

41. Joel Williamson, *New People*, 61–75.

42. Barbara J. Fields, "Ideology and Race," 154–55.

43. John Mencke, *Mulattoes and Race Mixture*, 107–14. In her diary of the 1860s, Mary Chesnut famously described the Southern system, where "our men live all in one house with their wives and their concubines; and the mulattoes one sees in every family partly resemble the white children." The system of open concubinage of black women largely disappeared after the Civil War. See Mary Boykin Chesnut, *A Diary from Dixie*, ed. Ben Ames Williams (Boston: Houghton Mifflin, 1949), 21. For a discussion of resistance to sexual violence by African-American women during Reconstruction, see Laura F. Edwards, "Sexual Violence, Gender, Reconstruction, and the Extension of Patriarchy in Granville County, North Carolina," *North Carolina Historical Review* 68 (July 1991): 237–60. Edwards examines court records and observes that black women's legal resistance to sexual attack became problematic after a redemptionist government assumed power in North Carolina (239, 243 n. 10).

44. John Mencke, *Mulattoes and Race Mixture*, 108. Certainly this apocalyptic theme can be traced from Nott to Madison Grant (*The Passing of a Great Race*, 1916), D. W. Griffith (*The Birth of a Nation*, 1915), and Lothrop Stoddard (*The Rising Tide of Color*, 1920) where extermination and origins become linked—one race's birth is predicated on the other's extinction. Thomas F. Gossett, *Race: The History of an Idea in America* (Dallas: Southern Methodist Press, 1963), 15; John Mencke, *Mulattoes and Race Mixture*, 50, 107–14; Mencke locates 1890–1915 as the years that define the antimiscegenation hysteria in the South (p. 62).

45. Albert Bushnell Hart, *The Southern South* (New York: D. Appleton and Company, 1910), 154–55. A similar description of postbellum miscegenation in the South appears in Ray Stannard Baker, *Following the Color Line: An Account of Negro*

Citizenship in the American Democracy (1908; reprint, Williamstown, Mass.: Corner House Publishers, 1973), chapter 8. A book by a Southern white woman offers a reluctant but significant admission in its discussions of postbellum race relations. After a long chapter in defense of lynching ("Crime Against Womanhood"), the author goes on to say, regarding African-American women: "The South did not do her whole duty in teaching chastity to the savage, though making more patient, persistent and heroic struggles than accredited with. The charge that under slavery miscegenation was the result of compulsion on the part of the superior race finds answer in its continuance since. Because he was white, the crying sin was the white man's, but it is just to remember that the heaviest part of the white racial burden was the African woman, of strong sex instincts and devoid of sexual conscience, at the white man's door, in the white man's dwelling." Myrta Lockett Avary, *Dixie After the War, An Exposition of Social Conditions Existing in the South, During the Twelve Years Succeeding the Fall of Richmond* (New York: Doubleday, Page & Company, 1906), 395.

46. Albert Bushnell Hart, *The Southern South*, 155.

47. The lynching of African-American men who attempted to defend black women from white sexual attack was not unknown, and was no doubt more common than the historical record shows. See Gerda Lerner, ed., *Black Women in White America: A Documentary History* (New York: Pantheon Books, 1972), 162–63, 188–90.

48. Alexander Crummell, *Africa and America*, 66, 68–69; Anna Cooper, *A Voice from the South* (1892; reprint, New York: Negro Universities Press, 1969), 24–25, 32; on Fannie Williams, see Paula Giddings, *When and Where I Enter: The Impact of Black Women on Race and Sex in America* (New York: William Morrow, 1984), 85–87. Cooper, born in North Carolina, was educated at Oberlin and later became a teacher at M Street High School in Washington, where she taught Latin when Toomer attended the school. See Sharon Harley, "Anna J. Cooper: A Voice for Black Women," in Sharon Harley and Rosalyn Terborg-Penn, eds., *The Afro-American Woman: Struggles and Images* (Port Washington, N.Y.: Kennikat Press, 1978), 87–96; and Kevin K. Gaines, *Uplifting the Race: Black Leadership, Politics, and Culture in the Twentieth Century* (Chapel Hill: University of North Carolina Press, 1996), chapter 5. At about the time Myrta Avary published her book, *Dixie After the War*, a member of Washington's mulatto elite, Mary Church Terrell, wrote an essay for the *North American Review* which offered a different perspective on the same history: "The only object lesson in virtue and morality which the negro received for 250 years came through the medium of slavery, and that peculiar institution was not calculated to set his standards of correct living very high. Men do not gather grapes of thorns nor figs of thistles. Throughout their entire period of bondage colored women were debauched by their masters. From the day they were liberated to the present time, prepossessing young colored girls have been considered the rightful prey of white gentlemen in the South, and they have been protected neither by public sentiment nor by the law. In the South, the negro's home is not considered sacred by the superior race. White men are neither punished for invading it, nor lynched for violating colored women and girls." Mary Church Terrell, "Lynching from a Negro's Point of View," in Beverly Washington Jones, *Quest for Equality: The Life and Writings of Mary Eliza Church Terrell, 1863–1954* (Brooklyn, N.Y.: Carlson Publishing, 1990), 177–78. Terrell's topic, of course, had originally been raised by Ida B. Wells.

49. Williamson suggests that, besides opportunity, inclination decreased, as evidently "after slavery white feelings against miscegenation soon came to be fully as virulent as those among Negroes." The evidence for this is in the laws banning miscegenation and interracial marriage and in the public pronouncements of Southern commentators, editors, preachers, judges, and others. Williamson cites, for instance, an "Anti-Miscegenation League" in Mississippi and a similar "vigilance

committee" in Louisiana, formed in 1907. Such groups may well have been part of the anti-black hysteria of the time, but they might equally well indicate the continuity of black-white sexual relations in the postbellum world. In fact, Ray Stannard Baker's examples in *Following the Color Line* (pp. 167–68) illustrated how the South had "begun to organize against the evil." For quotations, see Joel Williamson, *New People*, 90–91; for the argument for the decline in miscegenation, see ibid., 91–100. Examples of Freedman's Bureau records appear in Dorothy Sterling, ed., *We Are Your Sisters: Black Women in the Nineteenth Century* (New York: Norton, 1984), 352–55. Also see Herbert G. Gutman, *The Black Family in Slavery and Freedom, 1750–1925* (New York: Random House, 1976), 385–402; Jacqueline Jones, *Labor of Love, Labor of Sorrow: Black Women, Work and the Family, from Slavery to the Present* (1985; reprint, New York: Random House, 1986), 150.

An excellent summary of miscegenation in the economic, social, and political contexts of the post-Reconstruction South is in Nell Irvin Painter, " 'Social Equality,' Miscegenation, Labor, and Power," in Numan V. Bartley, ed., *The Evolution of Southern Culture* (Athens: University of Georgia Press, 1988), 47–67. A classic description of the sexual exploitation of African-American women in the twentieth-century South is John Dollard, *Caste and Class in a Southern Town* (1937; reprint, New York: Doubleday, 1957), chapter 7; on the "tradition" of such exploitation, see Lillian Smith, *Killers of the Dream* (1949; reprint, New York: Doubleday, 1963), 97–119.

50. Peter W. Bardaglio, *Reconstructing the Household: Families, Sex, and the Law in the Nineteenth-Century South* (Chapel Hill: University of North Carolina Press, 1995), 191, 193–94. John Dittmer, *Black Georgia*, 119. Also see Mary E. Odem, *Delinquent Daughters: Protecting and Policing Adolescent Female Sexuality in the United States, 1885–1920* (Chapel Hill: University of North Carolina Press, 1995), 32–33. Odem quotes a representative from Kentucky who wrote in 1895, "We see at once what a terrible weapon for evil the elevating of the age of consent would be when placed in the hands of a lecherous, sensual negro woman, who for the sake of blackmail or revenge would not hesitate to bring criminal action even though she had been a prostitute since her eleventh year!" Even a study of mulattoes by a member of the Chicago school of sociology adopted the Southern mythology, arguing that black women felt "honored" by having sexual congress with "a man of a superior race." See Edward Byron Reuter, *The Mulatto in the United States* (Boston: Gorham Press, 1918), 163.

51. Jean Toomer Papers, Box 18, Folder 491. This barbershop story was important enough to Toomer that he wrote two versions of it. The version we have quoted differs from the second version in some details and in the style of its writing. The second version ends: "Then a third man said one of those things that are never said in the South, yet sometimes are said: The white boss of this town is called a nigger behind his back, by his enemies. They say he has some Negro blood. What do you make of that? No one wanted to make anything of that. Not a single word was spoken thereafter. Every man in the shop felt that too much had been said as it was." Jean Toomer Papers, Box 18, Folder 487. Nellie Y. McKay says of Nathan Toomer that "people were reluctant to talk about the man because of issues surrounding his racial identity. Nathan Toomer had lived like a white man, Jean Toomer was told, but behind his back his enemies called him 'nigger.' " Nellie Y. McKay, *Jean Toomer, Artist*, 228. The epithet, however, was directed not against Nathan Toomer, but against "the leading white man in this town."

52. See James Haskins, *Pinkney Benton Stewart Pinchback*, 257. Haskins records the drop in the registered black vote in Louisiana, a figure which, of course, measured Pinchback's political influence. The vote fell from 130,334 in 1896 to 5,320 in 1900 and 1,342 in 1904. Willard B. Gatewood, Jr., *Aristocrats of Color*, 39.

53. Darwin T. Turner, ed., *The Wayward and the Seeking*, 85.

54. Willard B. Gatewood, Jr., *Aristocrats of Color*, 64–68; Gatewood says that one reaction to the new Jim Crow system among some members of the black elite was to retreat "into the safe oasis of their own making in an effort to isolate themselves from the conflict and tensions of race" (300). Constance McLaughlin Green, *The Secret City: A History of Race Relations in the Nation's Capital* (Princeton, N.J.: Princeton University Press, 1967), chapter 8, esp. 170–77; Joel Williamson, *The Crucible of Race: Black-White Relations in the American South Since Emancipation* (New York: Oxford University Press, 1984), 364–95. Kevin K. Gaines, *Uplifting the Race*, 89.

55. Willard B. Gatewood, Jr., *Aristocrats of Color*, 29. Also see ibid., 151–75; Kevin K. Gaines, *Uplifting the Race*, especially chapter 3. For an example of the arrogance of elitism, see Mary Church Terrell's remarks on "negroes who are known to have been guilty of assault": they are "ignorant, repulsive in appearance and as near the brute creation as it is possible for a human being to be." Mary Church Terrell, "Lynching from a Negro's Point of View," 169.

56. The story of his friend Mae Wright, which Toomer related in a letter to Waldo Frank, also offers a different view of the "color line" among Washington's mulatto elite: "Mae. Came down for the Thanksgiving holidays. I took her to the Howard-Lincoln football game. Surrounded by friends of mine — near-whites. As prejudiced as 'real' whites. Mae's loveliness didnt get a chance to show. Only her skin. She really seemed insignificant, — and black. And my friends didnt fail to take her (or rather, not take her) in terms of her color and in terms of what she seemed." Jean Toomer to Waldo Frank, undated letter (circa January 1923), Waldo Frank Papers. Barbara J. Fields, "Ideology and Race," 146. Constance McLaughlin Green, *The Secret City*, 174. Pinchback was still well known enough in 1918 to be one of the leaders invited to a "Conference of Colored Editors" convened to solidify black support for the Wilson administration during World War I. See Mark Ellis, "Joel Spingarn's 'Constructive Programme' and the Wartime Antilynching Bill of 1918," *Journal of Policy History* 4 (1992): 158.

57. Willard B. Gatewood, Jr., *Aristocrats of Color*, 334. See Charles Scruggs, *Sweet Home: Invisible Cities in the Afro-American Novel* (Baltimore: Johns Hopkins University Press, 1993), chapter 2; Ann Douglas, *Terrible Honesty: Mongrel Manhattan in the 1920s* (New York: Farrar, Straus and Giroux, 1995).

58. Willard B. Gatewood, Jr., *Aristocrats of Color*, 336. Darwin T. Turner, ed., *The Wayward and the Seeking*, 269, 303.

Chapter 2: The New Metropolitan

1. Darwin T. Turner, ed., *The Wayward and the Seeking: A Collection of Writings by Jean Toomer* (Washington, D.C.: Howard University Press, 1980), 91, 94–106; also see Nellie Y. McKay, *Jean Toomer, Artist: A Study of His Literary Life and Work, 1894–1936* (Chapel Hill: University of North Carolina Press, 1984), 21–27. Cynthia Earl Kerman and Richard Eldridge, *The Life of Jean Toomer: A Hunger for Wholeness* (1987; reprint, Baton Rouge: Louisiana State University Press, 1989), 63–75.

2. Darwin T. Turner, ed., *The Wayward and the Seeking*, 95, 100. Isaac Johnny Johnson III, *The Autobiography of Jean Toomer: An Edition* (Ann Arbor, Mich.: University Microfilms International, 1982), 247. Toomer's memoir is probably somewhat idealized. The Chicago school provided background for his story "Bona and Paul," which suggests a more complicated situation.

3. Ibid., 273.

4. Two important books on the subject of economic control and cultural hier-

archy during this period are Allan Trachtenberg, *The Incorporation of America: Culture and Society in the Gilded Age* (New York: Hill & Wang, 1982), and Lawrence W. Levine, *Highbrow/Lowbrow: The Emergence of Cultural Hierarchy in America* (Cambridge, Mass.: Harvard University Press, 1988). On the general historical background, see Richard Hofstadter, *The Age of Reform: From Bryan to F.D.R.* (New York: Vintage Books, 1955); Robert H. Wiebe, *The Search For Order, 1877–1920* (New York: Hill & Wang, 1967); Robert H. Wiebe, *Self-Rule: A Cultural History of American Democracy* (Chicago: University of Chicago Press, 1995), especially part 2; David W. Noble, *The Progressive Mind, 1890–1917*, rev. ed. (Minneapolis, Minn.: Burgess Publishing, 1981).

5. John Higham, *Strangers in the Land: Patterns of American Nativism, 1860–1925* (1955; reprint, New York: Atheneum, 1966). Page Smith, *The Rise of Industrial America* (New York: McGraw-Hill, 1984), 336, 344.

6. Alan Trachtenberg, "Conceivable Aliens," *Yale Review* 82 (October 1994): 54.

7. For a history of the qualified support and crucial steering given Progressive reform by "large corporations and financial institutions," see James Weinstein, *The Corporate Ideal in the Liberal State: 1900–1918* (Boston: Beacon Press, 1968). As Weinstein convincingly demonstrates, corporate intentions were to forestall more radical changes. On the gap between Progressives and immigrant populations and the political consequences, see Paul McBride, *Culture Clash: Immigrants and Reformers, 1880–1920* (San Francisco: R and E Research Associates, 1975); John F. McClymer, *War and Welfare: Social Engineering in America, 1890–1925* (Westport, Conn.: Greenwood Press, 1980); Rivka Shpak Lissak, *Pluralism & Progressives: Hull House and the New Immigrants, 1890–1919* (Chicago: University of Chicago Press, 1989).

8. Nina Silber, *The Romance of Reunion: Northerners and the South, 1865–1900* (Chapel Hill: University of North Carolina Press, 1993), 124. Gilbert Osofsky traces the course of this development in New York City in *Harlem: The Making of a Ghetto, Negro New York, 1890–1930* (New York: Harper & Row, 1968), chapter 3.

9. C. Vann Woodward, *Origins of the New South, 1877–1913* (1951; reprint, Baton Rouge: Louisiana State University Press, 1971), 323. Also see C. Vann Woodward, *Tom Watson: Agrarian Rebel* (New York: Rinehart, 1938).

10. Philip S. Foner, *American Socialism and Black Americans from the Age of Jackson to World War II* (Westport, Conn.: Greenwood Press, 1977), 105–6, 124–27.

11. Ibid., 201.

12. William A. Link, *The Paradox of Southern Progressivism, 1880–1930* (Chapel Hill: University of North Carolina Press, 1992), 68.

13. Herbert Shapiro, "The Muckrakers and Negroes," *Phylon* 21 (Spring 1970): 76–88. Ray Stannard Baker, *Following the Color Line: An Account of Negro Citizenship in the American Democracy* (1908; reprint, Williamstown, Mass.: Corner House Publishers, 1973). In his study of the new mass culture of popular magazines in the 1890s, a culture that would become important to the "muckrakers," Richard Ohmann writes, "Where were black people on this beachhead of mass culture? The short answer is, outside the arena of public discourse organized by the new cultural producers." Richard Ohmann, *Selling Culture: Magazines, Markets and Class at the Turn of the Century* (New York: Verso, 1996), 255.

14. Herbert Croly, *The Promise of American Life* (New York: Macmillan, 1909), 81. It is likely that Croly's father, David Croly, a Copperhead publicist at a New York newspaper during the Civil War, actually coined the word "miscegenation." The word was first used in a faked Abolitionist pamphlet intended to frighten voters away from Lincoln's Republican Party in the election of 1864. See Sidney Kaplan, "The Miscegenation Issue in the Election of 1864," in Allan D. Austin, ed., *American Studies in Black and White: Selected Essays, 1949–1989* (Amherst: University of Massachusetts Press, 1991), 47–100. Despite the racialist attitudes of the author, Jean

Toomer regarded *The Promise of American Life* as an essential text, even noting in an autobiographical passage the coincidence of its publication and his return to Washington, D.C., after his mother's death. Toomer's esteem for Croly may have originated with Croly's interest in Gurdjieffism in the 1920s. See Isaac Johnny Johnson III, *The Autobiography of Jean Toomer: An Edition,* 79, 305.

15. Herbert Croly, *The Promise of American Life,* 95, 318, 344. Also see Jane Lang Scheiber and Harry N. Scheiber, "The Wilson Administration and the Wartime Mobilization of Black Americans, 1917–18," *Labor History* 10 (Summer 1969): 433–58, for a description of "lily-white progressivism."

16. Elisabeth Lasch-Quinn, *Black Neighbors: Race and the Limits of Reform in the American Settlement House Movement, 1890–1945* (Chapel Hill: University of North Carolina Press, 1993), 3. Lasch-Quinn surveys a number of books written by settlement workers about the "emerging black ghetto" in the North (pp. 11–23). She also demonstrates how Progressive liberals were able to reject a biologically determined racism only to replace it with an environmentally determined one.

17. August Meier, *Negro Thought in America, 1880–1915: Racial Ideologies in the Age of Booker T. Washington* (Ann Arbor: University of Michigan Press, 1963), 10. For a detailed narrative of the violence associated with the restoration of Southern white supremacy after the Civil War, see Allen W. Trelease, *White Terror: The Ku Klux Klan Conspiracy and Southern Reconstruction* (New York: Harper & Row, 1971). An excellent general history is Herbert Shapiro, *White Violence and Black Response: From Reconstruction to Montgomery* (Amherst: University of Massachusetts Press, 1988).

18. August Meier, *Negro Thought in America,* 101, 23–24, 100–2.

19. On Washington, Du Bois, and uplift ideology, see Kevin K. Gaines, *Uplifting the Race: Black Leadership, Politics, and Culture in the Twentieth Century* (Chapel Hill: University of North Carolina Press, 1996), chapters 3 and 6. William Jordan claims that even after the 1890s Du Bois was often forced into an accommodationist role, a position especially evident in his editorship of the *Crisis* and in his ideological stance toward black participation in World War I. See William Jordan, " 'The Damnable Dilemma': African-American Accommodation and Protest During World War I," *Journal of American History* 81 (March 1995): 1563–83. Moreover, like Washington, Du Bois was also capable of "making deals" if it was to his personal advantage; the promise of an officer's rank in the armed forces was tied to his famous "Close-Ranks" editorial in the *Crisis.* See David Levering Lewis, *W.E.B. Du Bois: Biography of a Race, 1868–1919* (New York: Henry Holt, 1993), 555–56. Yet no matter how contradictory Du Bois's actions sometimes were, there was no doubting his fierce stand on the Negro's civil rights. See chapters 17 and 18 in *W.E.B. Du Bois: Biography of a Race, 1868–1919,* and Mark Ellis, "W.E.B. Du Bois and the Formation of Black Opinion in World War I: A Commentary on 'The Damnable Dilemma,' " *Journal of American History* 81 (March 1995), 1584–90. For a discussion of Du Bois and his intellectual relationship to the Progressive Age, see Adolph Reed, Jr., "DuBois's 'Double Consciousness': Race and Gender in Progressive Era American Thought," *Studies in American Political Development* 6 (Spring 1992): 93–139.

20. Abby Arthur Johnson and Ronald Maberry Johnson, *Propaganda and Aesthetics: The Literary Politics of Afro-American Magazines in the Twentieth Century* (Amherst: University of Massachusetts Press, 1979), 8. Abby and Ronald Johnson point out that the original story of Hopkins's dismissal appeared in the *Crisis* in 1912.

21. Louis R. Harlan, *Booker T. Washington: The Wizard of Tuskegee, 1901–1915* (New York: Oxford University Press, 1983), 106. See also Willard B. Gatewood, Jr., *Aristocrats of Color: The Black Elite, 1880–1920* (Bloomington: University of Indiana Press, 1990), chapter 11.

22. Page Smith, *The Rise of Industrial America,* 625. For the context of Pinchback's

Louisiana political career, see Ted Tunnell, *Crucible of Reconstruction: War, Radicalism and Race in Louisiana, 1862–1877* (Baton Rouge: Louisiana State University Press, 1984).

23. Louis R. Harlan and Raymond W. Smock, eds., *The Booker T. Washington Papers, Volume 6, 1901–2* (Urbana: University of Illinois Press, 1977), 85–86. *The Booker T. Washington Papers*, in 14 volumes (1972–84), are hereafter cited as BTW Papers, with volume and page numbers. Whitefield McKinlay, a wealthy descendant of a Charleston free black family, was Washington's most trusted ally in the capital. Heading a real estate and loan business, he was also in contact with Toomer's father, Nathan, to whom he loaned money. See Willard B. Gatewood, Jr., *Aristocrats of Color*, 304, and Kent Anderson Leslie and Willard B. Gatewood, Jr., " 'This Father of Mine . . . a Sort of Mystery': Jean Toomer's Georgia Heritage," *Georgia Historical Quarterly* 77 (Winter 1993): 789–809.

24. BTW Papers, vol. 6, 370–71. For representative letters that follow the Pinchback-Washington relationship from 1901 to 1915, see BTW Papers, vol. 8, 462–63; vol. 9, 458–59, 568–70; vol. 10, 153–54, 392–93; vol. 13, 485. On Pinchback's fortune, see Willard B. Gatewood Jr., *Aristocrats of Color*, 44.

25. Darwin T. Turner, ed., *The Wayward and the Seeking*, 23–24, 22, 110, 111. In an entry from his autobiographical writing "Incredible Journey," Toomer reflected on his grandfather's politics at the time of the 1894 "Coxey's Army" march of the unemployed to Washington, D.C.: "My grandfather was downtown the day the men marched in. Years later he used to tell of it in a half-serious, half-laughing way. I imagine he was all-serious at the time it happened. For he, then, was among the 'haves,' and the 'haves' then as now were sufficiently upset by any demonstration of solidarity and power on the part of the 'have-nots.' " Jean Toomer Papers, Yale Collection of American Literature, Beinecke Rare Book and Manuscript Library, Yale University, Box 18, Folder 491. Hereafter cited as Jean Toomer Papers.

26. Thomas Bender, *New York Intellect: A History of Intellectual Life in New York City, 1750 to the Beginning of Our Own Time* (New York: Knopf, 1987), 224.

27. Page Smith, *Rise of Industrial America*, 364–65.

28. Martin Shefter, "Political Incorporation and Containment: Regime Transformation in New York City," in John Hull Mollenkopf, ed., *Power, Culture, and Place: Essays on New York City* (New York: Russell Sage Foundation, 1988), 136. Thomas Bender, *New York Intellect*, 207.

29. James Burkhart Gilbert, *Writers and Partisans: A History of Literary Radicalism in America* (New York: John Wiley and Sons, 1968), 1. Julian F. Jaffe, *Crusade Against Radicalism: New York During the Red Scare, 1914–1924* (Port Washington, N.Y.: Kennikat Press, 1972).

30. Among the many discussions of Greenwich Village and its literary radicals we have relied especially on Thomas Bender, *New York Intellect*, chapter 6; Martin Green, *New York 1913: The Armory Show and the Paterson Strike Pageant* (New York: Scribner, 1988), 11–27, 49–61; Caroline F. Ware, *Greenwich Village, 1920–1930* (Boston: Houghton Mifflin, 1935); Leslie Fishbein, *Rebels in Bohemia: The Radicals of the Masses, 1911–1917* (Chapel Hill: University of North Carolina Press, 1982); Douglas Clayton, *Floyd Dell: The Life and Times of an American Rebel* (Chicago: Ivan R. Dee, 1994).

31. On class divisions in the Greenwich Village community, see Carolyn F. Ware, *Greenwich Village*, 3–8, 404–21. More generally this division is the subject of Martin Green's book, *New York 1913*.

32. On the origins of the Cooper Union, see Thomas Bender, *New York Intellect*, 113–16. On the Rand School, see ibid., 300; also, Julian F. Jaffe, *Crusade Against Radicalism*, 15–16. On the background of the Rand School's founders, see Page Smith, *The Rise of Industrial America*, 563–67.

33. James Weinstein, *The Decline of Socialism in America, 1912–1925* (New York: Monthly Review Press, 1967), 99.

34. On *Seven Arts* and other small magazines of the period, see Frederick J. Hoffman, Charles Allen, and Carolyn F. Ulrich, *The Little Magazine: A History and a Bibliography* (Princeton, N.J.: Princeton University Press, 1946), chapter 6.

35. John Tebbel, *A History of Book Publishing in the United States*, 2 (New York: R.R. Bowker, 1975), 389. For the background of the Liberal Club, see Douglas Clayton, *Floyd Dell*, 105–7.

36. Walker Gilmer, *Horace Liveright: Publisher of the Twenties* (New York: David Lewis, 1970), 19.

37. Ibid., 8.

38. Ibid., 22, 242 n.9. When royalty payments for Liveright's edition of *The Waste Land* were late, Eliot remarked in a letter to his anti-Semitic lawyer and patron John Quinn, "I am sick of doing business with Jew publishers." Quoted in Tom Dardis, *Firebrand: The Life of Horace Liveright* (New York: Random House, 1995), 98.

39. Waldo Frank, *Our America* (New York: Boni & Liveright, 1919), 176.

40. Darwin T. Turner, ed., *The Wayward and the Seeking*, 108; Jean Toomer Papers, Box 22, Folder 558. Lester Ward was a Progressive critic of laissez faire theories of government and economics in the late nineteenth century. His *Dynamic Sociology*, published in 1883, argued for policies to improve social conditions and especially for programs of universal education. As Page Smith describes, "The only remedy for the capitalistic excesses that in Ward's view caused poverty was for labor to 'retain possession of its products, and only transfer them to the consumer, making the processes of distribution wholly dependent upon and subservient to those of production.'" Page Smith, *Rise of Industrial America*, 156.

41. Donald L. Miller, *Lewis Mumford: A Life* (New York: Weidenfeld and Nicolson, 1989), 107–8. Jean Toomer Papers, Box 22, Folder 558.

42. Darwin T. Turner, ed., *The Wayward and the Seeking*, 108–11.

43. Jean Toomer Papers, Box 22, Folder 560.

44. Biographical Publicity Sketch, Jean Toomer Papers, Box 26, Folder 612. Toomer's three articles are printed as an appendix following our main text. They were reprinted earlier in Charles Scruggs, "My Chosen World: Jean Toomer's Articles in the *New York Call*," *Arizona Quarterly* 51 (Summer 1995): 103–26. Walter Goldwater says the *Call* was the "daily organ of the Socialist Party. During World War I it was under government censorship (some issues appeared with large blank columns), but it continued publication until lack of funds forced suspension." *Radical Periodicals in America, 1890–1950* (New Haven: Yale University Library, 1964), 30. Goldwater probably means the Socialist party of New York, which was largely autonomous from the American Socialist Party. Toomer looked at the *Call* as a possible outlet for his writing up until its closure. In *The Lives of Jean Toomer*, Kerman and Eldridge say Toomer reveals his "growing disassociation from his former life" by a plan "to use an assumed name when he submitted his article 'The South in Literature' to the *Call*" (125). Their source for this statement is a letter from Toomer to Waldo Frank, dated September 9, 1923. However, what the letter actually says is, "Liveright also said he thought my paper, The South in Literature, a humdinger. Under a faked name, he's sending it to Ryan Walker of the Call. Phamplets [*sic*] are to be printed. Well old soldier, it looks as if *Holiday* and *Cane* are *going over*." In other words, it was not Toomer who proposed the use of a false name in the *Call*, but Horace Liveright, who hoped to use Toomer's essay as a promotional piece for *Cane* and so wished to conceal the fact that both essay and book were by the same author. This plan came to nothing, probably because the *Call* ceased publication the day after Toomer wrote his letter. See Waldo Frank Papers, Special Collec-

tions, Van Pelt Library, University of Pennsylvania. Hereafter cited as Waldo Frank Papers.

45. See Lloyd M. Abernethy, "The Washington Race War of 1919," *Maryland Historical Magazine* 58 (December 1963): 309–24, for a thorough account of the riot, its background, and its aftermath. Cyril V. Briggs, "The Capital and Chicago Race Riots," *The Crusader* 2 (September 1919): 437–40, describes an edition of the *Call* (August 1) which printed the famous photographs of black men being stoned to death by the white mob in Chicago. Toomer's article appeared in the next day's edition of the *Call*. Also see Lee E. Williams II, *Post-War Riots in America, 1919 and 1946*, (Lewiston, N.Y.: Edwin Mellen Press, 1991). The Washington, D.C., address of the Pinchbacks and Toomer was 1341 You [U] Street N.W. (Toomer always spelled the "U" as "You" in return addresses for his correspondence.) Williams records that at the height of the fighting on July 21, "shots blazed all through the night at the corners of Seventh and U Street and Fourteenth and U streets" (34).

46. Pinchback may well have contributed to the article on the Washington riots. Some phrasings in the piece are unlike the article's general style, or the style in Toomer's other writings, for example, the sentence, "It now confronts the nation, so voluble in acclamation of the democratic ideal, so reticent in applying what it professes, to either extend to the Negro (and other workers) the essentials of a democratic commonwealth or else exist from day to day never knowing when a clash may occur, in the light of which the Washington riot will diminish and pale." The rhetorical elegance here sounds like the work of the practiced, famous political orator Pinchback. There is also the curious phrasing Toomer uses in his notebook autobiography, where he says his grandfather objected to his leaving Washington "at just this time when I was going well and he with me." It's possible that Toomer's writing, as well as the crisis of the Washington riot, had revived Pinchback's political engagement.

47. Ernest Allen, Jr., "The New Negro: Explorations in Identity and Social Consciousness, 1910–1922," in Adele Heller and Lois Rudnick, eds., *1915, The Cultural Moment: The New Politics, the New Woman, the New Psychology, the New Art and the New Theatre in America* (New Brunswick, N.J.: Rutgers University Press, 1991), 48. The term "New Negro" has a complicated history, which Allen traces from the New York radicals to Alain Locke's cultural proclamations. James A. Miller summarizes the "contested" nature of the phrase "New Negro" during the war and the 1920s: "If we see the 'New Negro' as initially an expression of *political* insurgency, which will later find its cultural counterpart in the careful construction of the "Harlem Renaissance" by Alain Locke and others, it becomes possible not only to recover the radical content of the original usage of the term but also to recognize how sharply contested and coveted the term was among various strata of the black community: black leftists, nationalists, and the black bourgeoisie." James A. Miller, "African-American Writing of the 1930s: A Prologue," in Bill Mullen and Sherry Lee Linkon, eds., *Radical Revisions: Rereading 1930s Culture* (Urbana: University of Illinois Press, 1996), 81. Du Bois himself was sometimes faulted for lacking the political radicalism of the "New Negro" because, as a member of the educated mulatto elite, he was out of touch with the black masses. In other words, the "contested" term could be tied to class and color. See William Ferris's review of *Darkwater* in the *Africa and Orient Review* (June 1920), reprinted in Theodore G. Vincent, ed., *Voices of a Black Nation: Political Journalism in the Harlem Renaissance* (San Francisco: Ramparts Press, 1973), 342–48. For the view that "New Negro" refers to a specific cultural tradition within the Talented Tenth of African-American life, see Wilson J. Moses, "The Lost World of the New Negro, 1895–1919: Black Literary and Intellectual Life Before the 'Renaissance,'" *Black American Literature Forum*, 21 (Spring–Summer 1987): 61–

83. Henry Louis Gates, Jr., traces its use as a "trope" in the process of opposing white racist images of black people. See "The Trope of a New Negro and the Reconstruction of the Image of the Black," *Representations* 24 (Fall 1988): 129–55.

48. For surveys of the national press reaction to the Washington riots, see Arthur I. Waskow, *From Race Riot to Sit-In, 1919 and the 1960s: A Study in the Connections Between Conflict and Violence* (New York: Doubleday, 1966), 33–37; Lee E. Williams II, *Post-War Riots in America*, 55–59.

49. Randolph's article from the *Messenger* is reprinted in August Meier, Elliott Rudwick, and Francis L. Broderick, eds., *Black Protest Thought in the Twentieth Century*, 2d ed. (New York: Bobbs-Merrill, 1971), 85–91.

50. For the continuity of Toomer's thought on this matter, see his essay "Race Problems and Modern Society," published in 1929: "There is no need to present new facts to support the statement that race problems are closely associated with our economic and political systems. . . . It is well known that whenever two or more races (or nationalities) meet in conditions that are mainly determined by acquisitive interests, race problems arise as by products of economic issues." Jean Toomer, "Race Problems and Modern Society," in Baker Brownell, ed., *Problems of Civilization* (New York: D. Van Nostrand Company, 1929), 89. For the socialist view of the causes of racism, see Philip S. Foner, *American Socialism and Black Americans*, especially chapters 5 and 12. On the economic causes of the race riots, see William M. Tuttle Jr., "Labor Conflict and Racial Violence: The Black Worker in Chicago, 1894–1919," in John H. Bracey, Jr., August Meier, and Elliot Rudwick, eds., *Black Workers and Organized Labor* (Belmont, Calif.: Wadsworth Publishing Company, 1971), 72–92, and James R. Barrett, "Unity and Fragmentation: Class, Race, and Ethnicity on Chicago's South Side, 1900–1922," in Dirk Hoerder, ed., *"Struggle a Hard Battle": Essays on Working-Class Immigrants* (DeKalb: Northern Illinois University Press, 1986): 229–53.

51. Phillip S. Foner, *American Socialism and Black Americans*, 290. Jean Toomer Papers, Box 22, Folder 560. There were exceptions to the white indifference about attacks on black people, notably Max Eastman's magazines, *The Masses* and its successor, the *Liberator*. See Philip Foner's discussion, pp. 254–55; also see Leslie Fishbein, *Rebels in Bohemia: The Radicals of the Masses, 1911–1917*, 160–67.

52. The best background discussion of the Harlem radicals is Ernest Allen Jr.'s article, "The New Negro." Other useful discussions are in Theodore Kornweibel, Jr., *No Crystal Stair: Black Life and the "Messenger," 1917–1928* (Westport, Conn.: Greenwood Press, 1975); Philip S. Foner, *American Socialism and Black Americans*, chapters 13 and 14; and Jervis Anderson, *A. Philip Randolph: A Biographical Portrait* (New York: Harcourt Brace Jovanovich, 1973). The association of Randolph and Owen with the Rand School is discussed in Anderson, pp. 115–16. Anderson cites the *Call* editorial in the notes to chapter 8, page 361.

53. Jean Toomer, "Banking Coal," *Crisis* 24 (June 1922): 65. In the text printed in *The Collected Poems of Jean Toomer*, ed. Robert B. Jones and Margery Toomer Latimer (Chapel Hill: University of North Carolina Press, 1988), line 2 has "Fire" instead of the lower case "fire" of the *Crisis*. *Fire!* of course, was the title given the single issue of one of the important small magazines of the Harlem Renaissance. The title was taken from a spiritual refrain by Langston Hughes, but the magazine's foreword seems to allude as well to "Banking Coal." See *Fire!* (1926; reprint, Metuchen, N.J.: The Fire!! Press, 1982). The damping "ashes" of the poem will reappear in the final scene of "Kabnis."

Chapter 3: Cultural Politics, 1920

1. Darwin T. Turner, ed., *The Wayward and the Seeking: A Collection of Writings by Jean Toomer* (Washington, D.C.: Howard University Press, 1980), 111.

2. Jean Toomer, "Race Problems and Modern Society," in Baker Brownell, ed., *Problems of Civilization* (New York: D. Van Nostrand Company, 1929), 71, 72, 102. See also chapter 2, n. 54. For the biographical treatment of Toomer's reaction to the shipyards, see Darwin T. Turner, *In a Minor Chord: Three Afro-American Writers and Their Search for Identity* (Carbondale: Southern Illinois University Press, 1971), 9–10; Nellie Y. McKay, *Jean Toomer, Artist: A Study of His Literary Life and Work, 1894–1936* (Chapel Hill: University of North Carolina Press, 1984), 28; Cynthia Earl Kerman and Richard Eldridge, *The Lives of Jean Toomer: A Hunger for Wholeness* (1987; reprint, Baton Rouge: Louisiana State University Press, 1989), 71; Rudolph P. Byrd, *Jean Toomer's Years With Gurdjieff: Portrait of an Artist, 1923–1936* (Athens: University of Georgia Press, 1990), 3.

3. Jean Toomer Papers, Yale Collection of American Literature, Beinecke Rare Book and Manuscript Library, Yale University, Box 22, Folders 560–61 (hereafter referred to as Jean Toomer Papers).

4. Toomer had no illusions about the white-collar working class at Acker, Merrall, either. He recognized that while their working conditions were much better than those in the shipyards, "these grocery men also, of course, were doomed. Doomed to low salaries and long hours every day of their lives, without hope of change or betterment." Their wages, which "barely keep them from starving," locked them into a system where "the grocery clerk also knows he is doomed unless *he* and others like him in similar positions *can do* and *do do* something about it." Jean Toomer Papers, Box 22, Folder 561. His experiences in the shipyards and at Acker, Merrall confirmed the radical ideas that Toomer's boxing instructor at the American College of Physical Training in Chicago had helped introduce him to in 1917. See Isaac Johnny Johnson III, "The Autobiography of Jean Toomer: An Edition" (Ph.D. diss., Purdue University, 1982), 264–79.

5. Jean Toomer Papers, Box 22, Folder 561.

6. Darwin T. Turner, ed., *The Wayward and The Seeking*, 114. In *The Lives of Jean Toomer*, Kerman and Eldridge say that at the Lola Ridge party, "Toomer met Waldo Frank, one of his literary idols. . . . The following day, meeting by chance in Central Park, they engaged in talk about music, literature, art, and American values" (73). They also suggest Toomer had been reading Frank before this meeting (72), and that it took place in August. Their source for this statement is the passage from "Outline of an Autobiography" published by Turner, which, as we have quoted, is substantially different in the details of the meeting. Toomer's memoir also indicates that the meeting was in the spring, for in the paragraphs immediately following he says that after the meeting he returned to Washington, where he spent "the summer of 1920." Toomer's correspondence with Frank confirms the significance given their meeting in the autobiographical passage; in his letter of March 24, 1922, Toomer, commenting on his sense of isolation in Washington, says "Almost the first, and surely the last real talk was the one I had with you in Central Park." Jean Toomer to Waldo Frank, March 24, 1922, Waldo Frank Papers, Special Collections, Van Pelt Library, University of Pennsylvania (hereafter referred to as Waldo Frank Papers).

7. Darwin T. Turner, ed., *The Wayward and the Seeking*, 114.

8. H. C. Peterson and Gilbert C. Fite, *Opponents of War, 1917–1918* (Madison: University of Wisconsin Press, 1957), 8–9. The declaration of war was not rejected by all prominent socialists, and some, in fact, left the party over the decision to oppose the American entry. See John A. Thompson, *Reformers and War: American*

Progressive Publicists and the First World War (Cambridge: Cambridge University Press, 1987), 179–80.

9. As early as 1915 Woodrow Wilson had been attacking "citizens of the United States . . . born under other flags . . . who have poured the poison of disloyalty into the very arteries of our national life." Harry N. Scheiber, *The Wilson Administration and Civil Liberties, 1917–1921* (Ithaca, N.Y.: Cornell University Press, 1960), 6.

10. Robert K. Murray, *Red Scare: A Study in National Hysteria, 1919–1920* (Minneapolis: University of Minnesota Press, 1955), 85. David M. Kennedy, *Over Here: The First World War and American Society* (New York: Oxford University Press, 1980), 31–32, 67–68. For a detailed history of the Progressives and World War I, see John A. Thompson, *Reformers and War*. On the general pattern of government suppression during the period, see Harry N. Scheiber, *The Wilson Administration and Civil Liberties*; H. C. Peterson and Gilbert C. Fite, *Opponents of War*; William Preston, Jr., *Aliens and Dissenters: Federal Suppression of Radicals, 1903–1933* (Cambridge, Mass.: Harvard University Press, 1963). The specific case of New York state is the subject of Julian E. Jaffe, *Crusade Against Radicalism: New York During the Red Scare, 1914–1924* (Port Washington, N.Y.: Kennikat Press, 1972). African-Americans were among the groups most suspected of disloyalty during the war; as Mark Ellis records, "At least five investigative agencies of the federal government engaged in a detailed secret scrutiny of black American opinion and leadership," a surveillance that "not only continued but escalated during the post-war Red Scare." Mark Ellis, "Federal Surveillance of Black Americans During the First World War," *Immigrants & Minorities* 12 (March 1993): 1, 17–18. See also Mark Ellis, "America's Black Press, 1914–18," *History Today* 41 (September 1991): 21–27.

11. Harry N. Scheiber, *Wilson and Civil Liberties*, 57.

12. Calvin Coolidge, "Whose Country Is This?" *Good Housekeeping* 72 (February 1921): 14. On the background of pseudo-scientific racism, see Stephen Jay Gould, *The Mismeasure of Man* (New York: W. W. Norton, 1981), especially chapters 3, 4, and 5. See also our discussion in Chapter 2, above.

13. John Higham, *Strangers in the Land: Patterns of American Nativism, 1860–1925* (1955; reprint, New York: Atheneum, 1966), 204. Higham's book remains the best history of nativism. Madison Grant's most influential book was *The Passing of the Great Race* (New York: Charles Scribner's Sons, 1916).

14. John Higham, *Strangers in the Land*, 310. David H. Bennett, *The Party of Fear: From Nativist Movements to the New Right in American History* (Chapel Hill: University of North Carolina Press, 1988), 193, 205–6, 208–14.

15. Frederic C. Howe, *The Confessions of a Reformer* (New York: Charles Scribner's Sons, 1925), 278–79. Howe had earlier written a key Progressive text, *The City: The Hope of Democracy* (New York: Charles Scribner's Sons, 1905). He had celebrated the future of the American city as the hope for local authority and culture, but as he painfully discovered, the gravitation of power was away from the local and toward the national. See especially Gerald E. Frug, "The City as a Legal Concept," in Lloyd Rodwin and Robert M. Hollister, eds., *Cities of the Mind: Images and Themes of the City in the Social Sciences* (New York: Plenum Press, 1984), 233–90.

16. The *New York Call* had been denied second class mailing privileges in 1917, and this denial was extended well into 1920 by the government's tactics of delay and legal evasion. See "Burleson and the Call," *New Republic* 21 (January 7, 1920): 157–58. The suppression of the *Seven Arts* was less direct; as Thomas Bender puts it, Randolph Bourne's antiwar essays "caused the magazine's angel to withdraw support, ending its brilliant career after little more than a year." Thomas Bender, *New York Intellect: A History of Intellectual Life in New York City, from 1750 to the Beginnings of Our Own Time* (New York: Alfred A. Knopf, 1987), 241.

17. Mary Austin, "New York: Dictator of American Criticism," *Nation* 111 (July 31, 1920): 129–30. The essay is reprinted in Reuben J. Ellis, ed., *Beyond Borders: The Selected Essays of Mary Austin* (Carbondale: Southern Illinois University Press, 1996), 56–61. On Liveright's publicity for *Our America,* see Walker Gilmer, *Horace Liveright: Publisher of the Twenties* (New York: David Lewis, 1970), 25–26.

18. The major biographies of Mary Austin are Esther Lanigan Stinemen, *Mary Austin: Song of a Maverick* (New Haven: Yale University Press, 1989), and Augusta Fink, *I-Mary: A Biography of Mary Austin* (Tucson: University of Arizona Press, 1983). Austin was well known enough in literary circles of the day to be included in an advertisement for the *Dial* published in the *Nation* of August 28, 1920, along with John Dewey, Robert Frost, Amy Lowell, Waldo Frank, and others listed as important American "collaborators" in Scofield Thayer's magazine.

19. The term "New Humanist" came to be applied to the reactionary professors Irving Babbitt, Paul Elmer More, and, in 1917, their follower Stuart Sherman. Late holdouts for a continuing nineteenth-century tradition, as against modernism, they also affirmed their class's ethnic and racial orders. Richard Ruland suggests that "Santayana is largely responsible for the widespread identification of the Humanists with the earlier Genteel critics. There are only surface resemblances between the two groups." However, the connecting link of class and ethnic prejudice was more than a "surface." It could emerge viciously, as in Sherman's 1918 pamphlet, *American and Allied Ideals,* or more "genteely," as in Ellery Sedgwick's objections to Randolph Bourne. See Richard Ruland, *The Rediscovery of American Literature: Premises of Critical Taste, 1900–1940* (Cambridge, Mass.: Harvard University Press, 1967), 12, 65–67; Thomas Bender, *New York Intellect,* 247–48. Chapter 6 of Bender's book provides an excellent overview of the New York literary scene during the period of the *Seven Arts.*

20. See especially Stuart P. Sherman, *Americans* (New York: Charles Scribner's Sons, 1922), 1–27. In 1917 Sherman published his scurrilous attacks on Mencken as a kind of literary Hun. For Sherman's criticism of Ludwig Lewisohn as being outside the Anglo-American tradition because of his "quick Semitic intelligence," see his "The National Genius," *Atlantic Monthly* 127 (January 1921): 3. For Lewisohn's position, see "Tradition and Freedom," *Nation* 111 (December 8, 1920): 651–52, and *Upstream: An American Chronicle* (New York: Boni & Liveright, 1922). For a defense of Sherman against the charge of anti-Semitism, see Jacob Zeitlin and Homer Woodbridge, *Life and Letters of Stuart P. Sherman* (New York: Farrar & Rinehart, 1929), vol. 2, 486–87.

Before 1900, dialogue concerning the nature and future of American literature would most likely have occurred within the groves of academe among male professors (preferably at Ivy League universities) or in the pages of a respectable magazine like the *Atlantic Monthly,* but after 1910 the intellectual arena expanded considerably. This intellectual and cultural revolution has been the subject of a good many books, perhaps the best known being Henry May, *The End of American Innocence: A Study of the First Years of Our Own Time, 1912–1917* (New York: Knopf, 1959). For an intelligent defense of one member of the genteel tradition, see Lawrence J. Oliver, *Brander Matthews, Theodore Roosevelt, and the Politics of American Literature, 1880–1920* (Knoxville: University of Tennessee Press, 1992).

21. Ludwig Lewisohn, *Upstream,* 237. Lewisohn also was subject to a Mary Austin attempt to "Americanize" him. When, in a letter, Austin offered to explain American culture to him, he responded: "You offer me access to the American mind. To have access to your mind and opinions I shall count—I speak with the simplest sincerity—a privilege. But access to the American mind I have always had and have now." Ludwig Lewisohn to Mary Austin, March 11, 1921, in T. M. Pearce, ed., *Liter-*

ary America, 1903–1934: The Mary Austin Letters (Westport, Conn.: Greenwood Press, 1979), 145.

22. Remarkably, what Austin said about Jews, culture, and "nationalism" has passed almost without comment in contemporary criticism of her work, even by the editor of the *Selected Essays*, who reprints her anti-Semitic piece. Yet her remarks clearly belong with the line of thought running from the attacks on Alfred Dreyfus, to the Nazi film "The Eternal Jew," to Paul de Man's "Les Juifs dans la litterature actuelle," an essay which might be usefully compared to "New York: Dictator of American Criticism." The "sensual" Jew, disrupter of "national" harmony, ersatz artist, polluter of Aryan (or Anglo-Saxon) culture, is a figure behind each of these works. For an excellent discussion of the Dreyfus and de Man cases, see Alan B. Spitzer, *Historical Truth and Lies About the Past: Reflections on Dewey, Dreyfus, de Man, and Reagan* (Chapel Hill: University of North Carolina Press, 1996).

Austin's attack on the New York Jewish writers and Mencken and Hackett apparently did nothing to speed her acceptance by similarly minded conservative critics such as Stuart Sherman. They probably remembered her formerly avant-garde associations and her feminism and resented her demand to include little-known Western writers in their canon or to imagine an American literature somehow based on the poetic "rhythms" of Native Americans. See, for instance, Sherman's dismissive lines in his chapter "Tradition," in *Americans*, 14.

23. Atherton believed American literature and criticism should be based on Madison Grant's racial theories. She felt, too, that the "Alpines," one of Grant's racial categories, were an inevitable part of the American scene since "so far we are too unenlightened to sterilize such groups and exterminate them." Gertrude Atherton, "The Alpine School of Fiction," *Bookman* 55 (March 1922): 28. Before attacking Frank and *Our America*, Austin had "protested" a *Dial* review by Louis Untermeyer of an anthology of translations from Native American poetry, *The Path on the Rainbow*. Austin had written an introduction for the anthology, and her letter claimed a special expertise in the field, as opposed to the reviewer "whose mind has so evidently never visited west of Broadway." Untermeyer had been the poetry editor of the *Seven Arts*. See Louis Untermeyer, "The Indian as Poet," *Dial* 66 (March 8, 1919): 240–41; "Communications," *Dial* 66 (May 31, 1919): 569–70.

24. Austin's quarrel with New York would continue in the pages of *Freeman*. See her "The Culture of the Northwest," *Freeman* 2 (September 22, 1920): 33–35, in which the manly West is pitted against the effeminate East. Van Wyck Brooks would answer her *Freeman* article, in a manner similar to Toomer's, by juxtaposing New York's vital intellectual life with the soul-deadening commercial orientation of the provinces. See Van Wyck Brooks, "A Reviewer's Notebook," *Freeman* 2 (December 1920): 286–87. In *No. 26 Jayne Street* (New York: Houghton Mifflin, 1920), Austin's heroine (Neith Schuyler) has "the clean Anglo-Saxon instinct" as opposed to her politically radical lover (Adam Freer), who has been contaminated by the foreign ideologies associated with New York City (304).

25. John Higham, *Strangers in the Land*, 156. The Japanese and Chinese were denied immigration rights to the United States well before any Europeans, in 1907 and 1882, respectively. See Thomas F. Gossett, *Race: The History of an Idea in America* (Dallas: Southern Methodist University Press, 1963), 291, 308–9. Toomer may have been too frank for the *Call*'s presumably socialist typesetters. The single garbled passage in "Americans and Mary Austin" occurs at just the line where Toomer suggests there will certainly be a mixing of white and black blood in the future American "race." See "The Call Magazine," in the *New York Call* (October 10, 1920): 2.

26. Ironically, the course description appeared in the same October 10, 1920, issue of the *Call* as Toomer's article on Austin. For an example of Austin's Ameri-

canism as the process of eliminating difference, see her anecdotes about African-Americans in her autobiography, *Earth Horizon* (1932; reprint, Albuquerque: University of New Mexico Press, 1991), 346–48. For her racialist thinking on the question of American identity, see her essay "Sex in American Literature," *Bookman* 57 (June 1923): 385–93. In her 1923 article, "Arizona: The Land of Joyous Adventure," she was pleased that "social control [is] in the hands of the superior racial groups," and at how "Anglo" the Arizona "pioneers" looked. She also described the illegal Bisbee Deportations of 1919 as necessary "to throw the drunken cowboy out of the dance." In fact, they were murderously racist, antilabor attacks directed mainly against Mexican-American miners. See the *Nation* 116 (April 4, 1923): 385, 387–88.

27. Philip Gleason, *Speaking of Diversity: Language and Ethnicity in Twentieth-Century America* (Baltimore: Johns Hopkins University Press, 1992), 18. In an afterword published in a revised edition of his play, Zangwill discussed the "inconvenient element in the crucible of God—the negro." That phrase was taken from William Archer, friend of Mary Austin and producer of her play *The Arrow-Maker*. Archer was in favor of creating a separate state within the United States and moving all African-Americans into it. Zangwill, while retaining many of the racial stereotypes attached to black people, did recognize how central their influence was to American culture, a phenomenon he referred to as "spiritual miscegenation." See Israel Zangwill, *The Melting-Pot* (New York: Macmillan, 1926), 204–7.

28. Higham, *Strangers in the Land*, 276. Higham discusses how one prominent "proof" of non-Nordic inferiority became the analysis of intelligence tests given by the army to recruits during the war. "Inspired by reading the books of Madison Grant and Charles W. Gould, the psychologists realized how neatly their own studies might serve to substantiate the conception of a hierarchy of European races in America. Thus Brigham's book, *A Study of American Intelligence*, triumphantly concluded: 'The intellectual superiority of our Nordic group over the Alpine, Mediterranean and negro groups has been demonstrated.' With such authority to sustain them, it is little wonder that not only many eugenicists but also a broad segment of literate opinion in America accepted the tenets of racial nativism as proved truths of science" (275–76). Notable in such work was the linking of African-Americans to "inferior" white ethnics. Of course, by the time of *The Bell Curve*, those inferior white ethnics had been lifted, presumably by a hasty evolution, up to the level of Nordics.

29. After the end of Reconstruction, arguments over amalgamation, racial intermarriage, and "racial integrity" were sometimes quite bitter among people defined as "black," especially when they involved a class distinction between the lighter mulatto elite and darker freedmen or their descendants. The increasing segregation African-Americans were subject to promoted a black nationalism that argued for black racial integrity against either amalgamation or social equality, and which attacked the elite mulatto class of Washington, New York, and Cleveland as "would-be whites." As Willard B. Gatewood, Jr., says, a black person who married a white "was almost certain to prompt an outpouring of criticism from opponents of amalgamation in the black community." Jean Toomer never seemed to waver in support of his own ideal of racial fusion, a position Gatewood regards as not uncommon among "fair-complexioned aristocrats of color": "Tied by blood and culture to both black and white society, they viewed themselves as people uniquely capable of building a bridge between the two." In the early 1900s a mulatto member of the Washington elite, Daniel H. Murray, described the ideal "composite man" (a phrase Toomer picked up)—a product of African and Anglo-Saxon amalgamation—in terms similar to Toomer's generic "Walt Whitmans." He spoke of mulattoes as the "only

true Americans outside the Indians." Willard B. Gatewood, Jr., *Aristocrats of Color: The Black Elite, 1880–1920* (Bloomington: Indiana University Press, 1990), 178, 173, 174. Of course, defenders of "racial purity" saw the intermediate status of mulatto people as a dangerous contamination rather than as a social bridge; thus the Mississippian Alfred H. Stone argued that mulattoes broke down the clear demarcation of the races and were thus the major source of racial friction. See Alfred H. Stone, "The Mulatto Factor in the Race Problem," *Atlantic Monthly* 91 (May 1903): 658–62.

30. Thomas Bender, *New York Intellect*, 241. Oppenheim's remarks show how ethnic and racial tensions had heightened by the 1920s. As he says, "It did not occur to us [in 1916] that we were, as it now appears in the camp of the Humanists, a bunch of 'foreigners.'" James Oppenheim, "The Story of the *Seven Arts*," *American Mercury* 20 (June 1930): 157.

31. James Oppenheim, "*Seven Arts*," 158, 163. James Hoopes, *Van Wyck Brooks: In Search of American Culture* (Amherst: University of Massachusetts Press, 1977), 121–26.

32. James Hoopes, *Van Wyck Brooks*, 110; Van Wyck Brooks, "On Creating a Usable Past," *Dial* 64 (April 11, 1918): 337–41, reprinted in Claire Sprague, ed., *Van Wyck Brooks: The Early Years—A Selection from His Works, 1908–1921* (New York: Harper & Row, 1968), 221.

33. Claire Sprague, ed., *Van Wyck Brooks*, 220, 221, 223. Brooks coined, or at least made current, the phrase "Young America," which Toomer used in his unpublished play, "Natalie Mann" (1922). Van Wyck Brooks, "Young America," *Seven Arts* 1 (December 1916): 144–51, reprinted as a chapter in Van Wyck Brooks, *Letters and Leadership* (New York: B. W. Huebsch, 1918), 49–61. Brooks knew that "Young America" was the name given an earlier literary movement. See Perry Miller, *The Raven and the Whale: The War of Words and Wits in the Era of Poe and Melville* (New York: Harcourt, Brace, 1956). Also see Darwin T. Turner, ed., *The Wayward and the Seeking: A Collection of Writings by Jean Toomer* (Washington, D.C.: Howard University Press, 1980), 303. Toomer no doubt got the phrase from Waldo Frank or from Brooks's original essay in *The Seven Arts*. In an undated letter (circa summer/fall 1922), Toomer told Frank he had "just finished Van Wyck Brooks' Letters and Leadership. He is real, no doubt about it." Waldo Frank Papers.

34. Claire Sprague, ed., *Van Wyck Brooks*, 224, 225.

35. Ibid., 219, 221; James Hoopes, *Van Wyck Brooks*, 119–20. For Brooks's influence on Alain Locke's anthology, *The New Negro*, see Nathan Irving Huggins, *Harlem Renaissance* (New York: Oxford University Press, 1971), 60, 65, 70–71.

36. Claire Sprague, ed., *Van Wyck Brooks*, 55.

37. Van Wyck Brooks, *The World of H. G. Wells* (1915; reprint, New York: Haskell House Publishers, 1969), 167; Van Wyck Brooks, *Letters and Leadership*, 50–51.

38. In 1927 Lewis Mumford wrote an unproduced play on the Brooklyn Bridge, "The Builders of the Bridge," subsequently published in his *Findings and Keepings: Analects for an Autobiography* (New York: Harcourt, Brace and Jovanovich, 1975), 215–312. On "pontification," see Kenneth Burke, *Attitudes Towards History* (1937; reprint, Berkeley: University of California Press, 1984), 224–25; 364–65; idem, *Language as Symbolic Action: Essays on Life, Literature, and Method* (Berkeley: University of California Press, 1966), 187; idem, *A Rhetoric of Motives* (1948; reprint, Berkeley: University of California Press, 1969), 301. In *The Blue Meridian* in Darwin T. Turner, ed., *The Wayward and the Seeking*, 219, "the arch of our consciousness" is Toomer's metaphor for bridging earth and heaven, finite and infinite. Also see Alan Trachtenberg, *Brooklyn Bridge: Fact and Symbol* (New York: Oxford University Press, 1965).

39. Claire Sprague, ed., *Van Wyck Brooks*, 9; Van Wyck Brooks, "The Culture of

Industrialism," *Seven Arts* 1 (April 1917): 655. Brooks used the figure as the title of his essay, "The Splinter of Ice," *Seven Arts* 1 (January 1917): 270–80.

40. Van Wyck Brooks, *The Ordeal of Mark Twain* (New York: E. P. Dutton, 1920); idem, "The Literary Life," in Harold Stearns, ed., *Civilization in the United States: An Inquiry by Thirty Americans* (New York: Harcourt, Brace, 1922), 182; idem, *The Pilgrimage of Henry James* (New York: E.P. Dutton, 1925); idem, *Letters and Leadership*, 40. James Hoopes, *Van Wyck Brooks*, chapter 8.

41. Waldo Frank, *Our America* (New York: Boni & Liveright, 1919), 133; Harold Stearns, *America and the Young Intellectual* (New York: George H. Doran, 1921), 31; Darwin T. Turner, ed., *The Wayward and the Seeking*, 216.

42. Jean Toomer, *Cane* (1923; reprint, New York: Harper & Row, 1969), 132, 133, 21, 191. Darwin T. Turner, ed., *The Wayward and the Seeking*, 182–96; Frederik L. Rusch, *A Jean Toomer Reader: Selected Unpublished Writings* (New York: Oxford University Press, 1993), 121–37.

43. Claire Sprague, ed., *Van Wyck Brooks*, 223.

44. Van Wyck Brooks, *Days of the Phoenix: The Nineteen-Twenties I Remember* (New York: E. P. Dutton, 1957), 34; also see idem, *Fenollosa and His Circle With Other Essays in Biography* (New York: E. P. Dutton, 1962), 309. For Brooks's continued concern with Bourne, see Van Wyck Brooks, *History of a Literary Radical and Other Essays* (New York: B. W. Huebsch, 1920), ix–xxxv; idem, *Emerson and Others* (New York: E. P. Dutton, 1927), 121–45; idem, *The History of a Literary Radical and Other Papers by Randolph Bourne* (New York: S. A. Russell, 1956), 1–20; idem, *Days of the Phoenix*, chapters 1 and 2; idem, *Fenollosa and His Circle*, 259–321. Also see Robert E. Spiller, ed., *The Van Wyck Brooks–Lewis Mumford Letters: The Record of a Literary Friendship, 1921–1963* (New York: E. P. Dutton, 1970), 296. In 1946, Brooks wrote to Mumford that "I felt as I have felt before in reading this *phase* of your work that no one had written with such passion since Randolph Bourne." For Brooks's critical attitude toward Bourne's writing on the war, see Brooks, *Emerson and Others*, 142–43; idem, *History of a Literary Radical*, 17; idem, *Fenollosa and His Circle*, 309–17; idem, *Days of the Phoenix*, 34.

45. Bourne's letter quoted in Leslie J. Vaughan, *Randolph Bourne and the Politics of Cultural Radicalism*, (Lawrence: University Press of Kansas, 1997), 121. Vaughan's book is an excellent and much needed study of Bourne's political culture and cultural politics. James Hoopes, *Van Wyck Brooks*, 132; Thomas Bender, *New York Intellect*, 240–41. Also see Paul Rosenfeld, *Port of New York: Essays on Fourteen American Moderns* (1924; reprint, Urbana: University of Illinois Press, 1966), 49, 211–36. In his essay on Brooks, Rosenfeld notes Brooks's evasion of Bourne's antiwar articles, but in his own essay on Bourne, Rosenfeld finesses Bourne's political insights in these articles by viewing them as satire that should not be mistaken for Bourne's final word on America; moreover, he fails to see their implications for his own optimistic assessment of America's future. Brooks himself may have come to understand something of Bourne's concern for the American polis; see the letter he wrote to Lewis Mumford in 1923 discussing a possible meeting of younger intellectuals about a "symposium on censorship—to work out some sort of serious, philosophical treatment of the subject." Robert E. Spiller, ed., *The Van Wyck Brooks–Lewis Mumford Letters*, 23.

46. The contradiction in Brooks is pointed out by Harold Stearns: Brooks the determinist took a negative view of American culture, whereas Brooks the optimist willed the American renaissance. See Harold Stearns, *America and the Young Intellectual*, 24–33.

47. Olaf Hansen, *Randolph Bourne: The Radical Will, Selected Writings, 1911–1918* (New York: Urizen Books, 1977), 434.

48. See especially Randolph Bourne, "Maurice Barres and the Youth of France,"

Atlantic Monthly 114 (September 1914): 394, 396. Randolph Bourne, "An Hour in Chartres," *Atlantic Monthly* 114 (August 1914): 215, 217.

49. Claire Sprague, ed., *Van Wyck Brooks*, 149. Despite his quarrel with Matthew Arnold, Brooks, as Harold Stearns observed, shared Arnold's fastidiousness when it came to including the common life in his definition of "culture." See Harold Stearns, *America and the Young Intellectual*, 30. For useful distinctions between the outlooks of Bourne and Brooks, see Olaf Hansen, *Randolph Bourne: The Radical Will*, 67–68; also see Casey Nelson Blake, *Beloved Community: The Cultural Criticism of Randolph Bourne, Van Wyck Brooks, Waldo Frank, and Lewis Mumford* (Chapel Hill: University of North Carolina Press, 1990), 76–121.

50. Horace Kallen, "Democracy Versus the Melting-Pot," *Nation* 100 (February 18 and 25, 1915): 190–94, 217–20. Kallen's essay is framed as a reply to a book by Edward Ross, *The Old World in the New*, criticizing the "un-Americanism" of the new immigrants. Ross was a populist and a La Follette supporter, but in the heat of the war debate he wrote to present "the anti-immigrant case from the Anglo-Saxon Progressive standpoint." See Richard Hofstadter, *The Age of Reform: From Bryan to F.D.R.* (New York: Random House, 1955), 179–80.

51. Olaf Hansen, *Randolph Bourne: The Radical Will*, 251, 249.

52. Ibid., 250. Also see David A. Hollinger, *In the American Province: Studies in the History and Historiography of Ideas* (Bloomington: Indiana University Press, 1985), 59.

53. Olaf Hansen, *Randolph Bourne: The Radical Will*, 261.

54. Ibid., 256.

55. Ibid., 260, 264, 123; Edward Abrahams, *The Lyrical Left: Randolph Bourne, Alfred Stieglitz and the Origins of Cultural Radicalism in America* (Charlottesville: University Press of Virginia, 1986).

56. Carl Resek, ed., *War and the Intellectuals: Essays by Randolph S. Bourne, 1915–1919* (New York: Harper & Row, 1964), 131.

57. Olaf Hansen, *Randolph Bourne: The Radical Will*, 523, 525, 527.

58. Ibid., 520, 254; Bourne admired Theodore Dreiser because both of them understood that the electrical energy of the city could fragment the human personality and dissolve communal relationships, and both were concerned as to what might replace that community. See "The Art of Theodore Dreiser," in Olaf Hansen, *Randolph Bourne: The Radical Will*, 462–71.

59. Ibid., 264.

60. Stuart I. Rochester, *American Liberal Disillusionment in the Wake of World War I* (University Park: Pennsylvania State University Press, 1977), 10; Max Lerner, *Ideas for the Ice Age: Studies in a Revolutionary Era* (1941; reprint, Westport, Conn.: Greenwood Press, 1974), 131.

61. Stuart I. Rochester, *American Liberal Disillusionment*, 33.

62. Olaf Hansen, "The State," in *Randolph Bourne: The Radical Will*, 355–95.

63. It's not clear how early Toomer was reading Bourne, or how familiar he was with Bourne's work when he wrote *Cane*. Since he was reading such New York magazines such as the *New Republic* and the *Seven Arts*, it's likely that Toomer saw at least the occasional Bourne essay. Bourne was given lengthy attention in Frank's *Our America*, and in 1924 Toomer would characterize him in an unpublished review as "against all that is vicious in this nation." See Robert B. Jones, ed., *Jean Toomer: Selected Essays and Literary Criticism* (Knoxville: University of Tennessee Press, 1996), 40.

64. "The Will-to-Lynch," *New Republic* 8 (October 14, 1916): 262. For Bourne's authorship of the unsigned article, see Leslie J. Vaughan, *Randolph Bourne*, 213 n. 56. Bourne considered writing on African-Americans in the last months of his life, and in "The State" referred to "a white terrorism . . . carried on by the government

against pacifists, socialists, enemy aliens, and a milder unofficial persecution against all persons or movements that can be imagined as connected with the enemy." Olaf Hansen, *Randolph Bourne: The Radical Will*, 367.

65. Olaf Hansen, *Randolph Bourne: The Radical Will*, 262. For Young America's comments on Bourne, see Waldo Frank, *Our America*, 198–201; Paul Rosenfeld, *Port of New York*, 211–36; Lewis Mumford, "The Image of Randolph Bourne," *New Republic* 64 (September 24, 1930): 151–52. Mumford's essay showed the diminution of Bourne's actual influence by 1930; for Mumford, "Randolph Bourne was precious to us because of what he was, rather than because of what he had actually written."

Chapter 4: Whose America?

1. Toomer virtually ceased to publish any new work at all after the mid-1930s, though short pieces of his devotional writing were printed in connection with his service in the Quakers fellowship. Some attention has been given to *The Blue Meridian*, published in Mumford and Rosenfeld's last *American Caravan* (1936) as *Blue Meridian*, but even that piece traded on the inspiration of 1921–22, the year the poem was originally drafted as "The First American." Jean Toomer, *Blue Meridian*, in Alfred Kreymborg, Lewis Mumford, and Paul Rosenfeld, eds., *The New Caravan*; (New York: Norton, 1936), 633–53. A revised version of the poem, titled *The Blue Meridian*, appeared in Langston Hughes and Arna Bontemps, eds. *The Poetry of the Negro* (Garden City, N.Y.: Doubleday, 1970), 107–33.

2. On the matter of Toomer's identity as an African-American, see especially George B. Hutchinson, "Jean Toomer and the 'New Negroes' of Washington," *American Literature* 63 (December 1991): 683–92. Also see Toomer's letter to Mae Wright, August 4, 1922, Jean Toomer Papers, Yale Collection of American Literature, Beinecke Rare Book and Manuscript Library, Yale University (hereafter cited as Jean Toomer Papers). Toomer obviously felt that he was not part of Anglo-Saxon America. "Paradoxically as it may seem," he told Mae Wright, "we who have Negro blood in our veins, who are culturally and emotionally the most removed from the Puritan tradition, are its most tenacious supporters." But, he argues, if black people learn to "prize" their own "qualities," they can escape "the dominance of the Anglo-Saxon ideal." Also see Jean Toomer to Claude McKay, July 23, 1922, Jean Toomer Papers, where Toomer refers to "this southland of my ancestors." See Jean Toomer to Sherwood Anderson, December 29, 1922, Jean Toomer Papers, also published in Darwin T. Turner, ed., *Cane: An Authoritative Text, Backgrounds, Criticism* (New York: Norton, 1988), 149–50 (hereafter cited as Turner, ed., *Cane*).

3. Michael North makes a brief but useful assessment of Toomer's relation to the "Young America" group in *The Dialect of Modernism: Race, Language, and Twentieth-Century Literature* (New York: Oxford University Press, 1994), chapter 7. The discussion in Kerman and Eldridge is incomplete and frequently inaccurate. Cynthia Earl Kerman and Richard Eldridge, *The Lives of Jean Toomer: A Hunger for Wholeness* (1987; reprint, Baton Rouge: Louisiana State University Press, 1989), 72–73, 86–91, 93–94, 101–16. Jean Toomer Papers, Box 22, Folder 558. Darwin T. Turner, ed., *The Wayward and the Seeking: A Collection of Writings by Jean Toomer* (Washington, D.C.: Howard University Press, 1980), 19. For the mention of how his identification as a black person hindered his Gurdjieffian work, see Frederik L. Rusch, ed., *A Jean Toomer Reader: Selected Unpublished Writings* (New York: Oxford University Press, 1993), 103.

4. For Toomer's readings in the *Seven Arts*, see undated letter to Waldo Frank from 1922, and September 29, 1923, letter to Frank, Jean Toomer Papers. See also Darwin T. Turner, ed., *The Wayward and the Seeking*, 117. It is evident from remarks

scattered through the Jean Toomer Papers that he was regularly reading the little magazines where he hoped to get his own work published.

5. Toomer's biographers mention his visits to New York in 1922. Nellie McKay states that Toomer "had returned to New York" in early 1922, and even wrote part of *Cane* there. Kerman and Eldridge say Toomer met Gorham Munson "on one of Jean's visits to New York," but don't give a date for the meeting. Toomer's autobiography *and* his correspondence, however, suggest that after he returned from his grandfather's funeral in December 1921, his only trip in 1922 beyond the environs of Washington, D.C., was the visit to Spartanburg with Waldo Frank in September. Toomer was living in an apartment with his grandmother, subsisting on a small stipend she gave him, and he could not afford to travel. The Spartanburg trip, in fact, was financed by an "advance" from Frank against a pension Toomer said his grandmother would be receiving. (See Jean Toomer to Waldo Frank, August 21, 1922, Jean Toomer Papers.) Toomer's letters are filled with laments that he can't afford to visit New York and with schemes and proposals to arrange such a visit. His correspondence with Munson predated their meeting in person, and they probably didn't meet until Toomer visited New York in the early summer of 1923. Although Munson's views of Toomer's work were often obtuse, Toomer's response to them indicates how immensely valuable "Young America" was as a source of motivation: "Your letter came this morning. It stimulates. It contains just what I want: criticism that rubs me against myself; opinions, appreciations, interests, whose inherent fuel sets me going; thoughts that I value to the extent that I must test myself against them." Toomer's actual isolation from the intellectual ferment and literary politics of New York no doubt had both advantages and disadvantages, but it certainly emphasized his dependence on Waldo Frank as mentor, editor, and agent. Nellie Y. McKay, *Jean Toomer, Artist: A Study of His Literary Life and Work, 1894–1936* (Chapel Hill: University of North Carolina Press, 1984), 47; Cynthia Earl Kerman and Richard Eldridge, *The Lives of Jean Toomer*, 92; Darwin T. Turner, ed., *The Wayward and the Seeking*, 126; Jean Toomer to Gorham Munson, October 31, 1922, Jean Toomer Papers.

6. Waldo Frank, *Our America* (New York: Boni & Liveright, 1919), 196. Subsequent citations refer to this edition and will appear within the text. Alan Trachtenberg, ed., *The Memoirs of Waldo Frank* (Amherst: University of Massachusetts Press, 1973), 92: "Bourne's essays began with 'The Puritan's Will to Power,' a theme developed by Brooks and taken over later by me in *Our America*." It is almost certain that Toomer had been reading the *Seven Arts* during his early years in New York. The magazine's original issue of November 1916 printed a Robert Frost poem, "The Bonfire," which is probably the model for Toomer's poem "Banking Coal." That same issue opened with a short story by Barry Benefield, "Simply Sugar-Pie," set in rural Louisiana during an outbreak of racial violence. The story's protagonist, a young African-American woman, flees the white mob in her town and buries the body of her mulatto child in a pine wood; much of the story's effect comes from the suppression of narrative action or explanation. In "Karintha" Toomer would make that suppression even more effective. See *Seven Arts* 1 (November 1916): 3–14, 25–28.

7. Frank would restate his antitranscendentalism in the final chapter of *The Rediscovery of America*, where such "escapism" would be specifically identified with the "theosophic cult" of Gurdjieff. Frank describes the "transcendental danger" as a method of "objectively" observing the self until a sense of division is created, and "soul becomes separate from body." The effect "takes all value" to the "observing 'I'": "This transcendental dualism is the greatest curse of man; it has debauched almost all his highest efforts to know himself and to know life. By means of it, soul and its values are cut off from life and life—the observed—becomes a valueless do-

minion." Waldo Frank, *The Re-Discovery of America and Chart for Rough Water* (1929; reprint, New York: Duell, Sloan and Pearce, 1947), 299–300. Of course, Emerson's version of transcendentalism was not always as otherworldly as Frank presented it.

8. "Alienation," originally a religious (and a legal) term, was secularized by Hegel, Marx, and others as a sociological concept in the course of the nineteenth century; the term does not appear in Frank's book, but the concept clearly does. See Nasir Khan, *Development of the Concept and Theory of Alienation in Marx's Writings* (Oslo: Solum Forlag, 1995), 25–28, 34. Alan Ryan's remarks on the language of John Dewey are also relevant to Frank's writing: "This readiness to use the language of traditional Christianity helped Dewey to communicate with a public that would have turned away from a more aggressively secular or skeptical writer. It was a surprising achievement, given that Dewey early on decided that the 'supernatural' elements in traditional Christianity were superstitious, incredible, and outmoded. It was even more surprising that Dewey could so successfully use the language of religious belief in the process of arguing for a view of the world that is commonly thought to be squarely at odds with religion." Alan Ryan, *John Dewey and the High Tide of American Liberalism* (New York: Norton, 1995), 20.

9. Kerman and Eldridge initially describe Waldo Frank as holding "a somewhat mystical vision of the connections among nature, humanity, and the American Dream." In a later discussion they say he was interested in a "cultural 'revolution,'" but they characterize this revolution as "centered on the 'organic, mystic Whole,'" and "a deep sense of brotherhood rooted in a divine Oneness." None of these vague formulations is helpful for understanding the politically specific cultural criticism of *Our America.* Cynthia Earl Kerman and Richard Eldridge, *The Lives of Jean Toomer*, 73, 102–4.

10. On Frederick Jackson Turner, see David W. Noble, *The End of American History: Democracy, Capitalism, and the Metaphor of Two Worlds in Anglo-American Historical Writing, 1880–1980* (Minneapolis: University of Minnesota Press, 1985), 16–26; Richard Nelson, *Aesthetic Frontiers: The Machiavellian Tradition and the Southern Imagination* (Jackson: University Press of Mississippi, 1990), 82–85, 249–50.

11. See also Waldo Frank, "Mid-America Revisited," *American Mercury* 8 (July 1926): 322–23. For Frank, Chicago was a microcosm of America; in this upstart city, "you see America . . . not as a new world but as an old one." That world—"industrialized Chicago"—had to die first before it could be reborn as "green life." Frank's conception of Chicago as containing the possible seeds of renewal would be critiqued in Toomer's "Bona and Paul."

12. Frank's concentration on the cities of New York and Chicago also reflects the urban concentration of Jewish immigration. "The country's Jewish population increased from 250,000 in 1881 to nearly 3.5 million by 1920; or from less than 0.5 percent of the population of the United States to some 3.5 percent. . . . However impressive, data of this kind cannot capture the unevenness of the ties forged with American society by this wave of immigrants. Despite their dramatic demographic and institutional growth, they remained invisible in much of the United States. By contrast, in the leading urban centers, they became a major presence. By 1910, Jews constituted nearly 20 percent of New York City's population and 10 percent of Chicago's." Ira Katznelson, "Between Separation and Disappearance: Jews on the Margins of American Liberalism," in Pierre Birnbaum and Ira Katznelson, eds., *Paths of Emancipation: Jews, States, and Citizenship* (Princeton, N.J.: Princeton University Press, 1995), 187–88.

13. A prominent example of this mixture of theater and street life is Toomer's early play, *Natalie Mann* (1922); Toomer also hoped to have the dramatic version of "Kabnis" performed by the Provincetown Players. Not only had Frank addressed

the subject of the "little theater" in America in the *Seven Arts* (1916), but he had written a long essay in 1918 on the revolutionary repertory theater founded by Jacques Copeau on the rue du Vieux Columbier in Paris. This essay, "The Art of the Vieux Columbier," focused on a favorite theme of his: the city should be the home for a vital theater and should be revitalized in turn by that theater. See Waldo Frank, "Concerning a Little Theater," *Seven Arts* 1 (December 1916): 157–64, an essay which Frank reprinted in *Salvos: An Informal Book About Books and Plays* (New York: Boni & Liveright, 1924), 41–52. For "The Art of the Vieux Columbier," see *Salvos*, 119–67, which also reprints four other essays on the theater. Ira Katznelson observes of Jewish city life that, "by this period [the 1930s], Jews had also begun to establish publishing houses (such as Knopf, Simon and Schuster, Random House, and Viking, which did not yet rival the non-Jewish houses); they dominated the new media of radio and movies; and they had taken on a growing share of the theater, located as it was in New York. In each of these instances, the training ground and model for Jewish activity was the Yiddish theater and Jewish entertainment zones of the big cities, especially New York." Ira Katznelson, "Between Separation and Disappearance," 196.

14. Jean Toomer, *Cane* (1923; reprint, New York: Harper & Row, 1969), 38–39. In his foreword to *The New Negro* Locke poses the question of whether race attitudes are really changing among African-Americans: "But are we after all only reading into the stirrings of a sleeping giant the dreams of an agitator?" That is, does the New Negro represent a mass movement or an intellectual illusion? Locke replies to his own question, that "the answer is in the migrating peasant. It is the 'man farthest down' who is most active in getting up." See Alain Locke, ed., *The New Negro* (1925; reprint, New York: Atheneum, 1969), 7.

15. Frederick J. Hoffman, Charles Allen, and Carolyn F. Ulrich, *The Little Magazine: A History and a Bibliography* (Princeton, N.J.: Princeton University Press, 1946), 92; editorial [by Waldo Frank], *Seven Arts* 1 (November 1916): 52.

16. Gorham Munson, *The Awakening Twenties: A Memoir-History of a Literary Period* (Baton Rouge: Louisiana State University Press, 1985), 54. Of course, a significant part of *Our America*'s success had to do with Horace Liveright's imaginative publicity campaign for the book.

17. Paul J. Carter, *Waldo Frank* (Boston: Twayne, 1967), 22; Howard M. Sachar, *A History of the Jews in America* (New York: Alfred A. Knopf, 1992), 282; John Higham, *Send These to Me: Jews and Other Immigrants in Urban America* (New York: Atheneum, 1975), 126, 133, 144; Willard B. Gatewood, Jr., *Aristocrats of Color: The Black Elite, 1880–1920* (Bloomington: Indiana University Press, 1990), 24–29; 333–35.

18. Howard M. Sachar, *History of the Jews in America*, 300–334; John Higham, *Send These to Me*, chapters 2, 6, 8, and 9. Albert Lee, *Henry Ford and the Jews* (Braircliff Manor, N.Y.: Stein and Day, 1980). Nattan C. Belth, *A Promise to Keep: A Narrative of the American Encounter with Anti-Semitism* (New York: Times Books, 1979), especially chapter 4. Dan A. Oren, *Joining the Club: A History of Jews and Yale* (New Haven: Yale University Press, 1985), 37. An excellent summary of Jews and racial ideology during this period is Robert Singerman, "The Jew as Racial Alien: The Genetic Component of American Anti-Semitism," in David A. Gerber, ed., *Anti-Semitism in American History* (Urbana: University of Illinois Press, 1986), 103–28. The *Saturday Evening Post* articles are reprinted in David A. Shannon, ed., *Progressivism and Post-War Disillusionment, 1898–1928* (New York: McGraw-Hill, 1966), 273–78. For a selection of American anti-Semitic writings, see Michael Selzer, ed., *Kike: A Documentary History of Anti-Semitism in America* (New York: World Publishing, 1972). For discussion of the Leo Frank case, see Leonard Dinnerstein, *The Leo Frank Case* (New York: Columbia University Press, 1968), and Nancy MacLean, "The Leo Frank Case

Reconsidered: Gender and Sexual Politics in the Making of Reactionary Populism,"
Journal of American History 78 (December 1991): 917–48. For the confused racial
definitions between Jews and African-Americans associated with the Frank case,
see Eugene Levy, "Is the Jew a White Man?: Press Reaction to the Leo Frank Case,
1913–1915," *Phylon* 2 (June 1974), 212–22.

19. John Higham, *Send These to Me*, 152.

20. Jean Toomer to Waldo Frank, March 24, 1922, Waldo Frank Papers, Special
Collections, Van Pelt Library, University of Pennsylvania (hereafter cited as Waldo
Frank Papers).

21. Toomer's attention to the "history, traditions and culture" of African-Americans was probably related to his organization of the Washington, D.C., study group
which included Georgia Douglas Johnson and perhaps on occasion Alain Locke.
See Ronald M. Johnson, "Those Who Stayed: Washington Black Writers of the
1920's," in Francis Coleman Rosenberger, ed., *Records of the Columbia Historical Society of Washington, D.C.: The Fiftieth Volume* (Washington, D.C.: Columbia Historical Society, 1980), 493. George Hutchinson suggests that the "literary evenings"
would have begun in 1920. Toomer had already met Locke in 1919. See George B.
Hutchinson, "Toomer and the 'New Negroes,' " 683, 684, 686. Toomer may well
have introduced Locke to the ideas of *Our America*, perhaps as early as August 1920;
a year later he would write Locke from Sparta that he "learned alot" from his experience there, "especially from an economic, sociological standpoint. 99 percent
of the people who write and talk about the Negro hardly know his name. Artisti-
cally, the field is wide open." Jean Toomer to Alain Locke, August 23, 1920, November 8, 1921, Alain Locke Papers, Manuscript Division, The Moorland-Spingarn Research Center, Howard University.

22. For Tom Watson's attacks on Leo Frank, see C. Vann Woodward, *Tom Watson,
Agrarian Rebel* (1938; reprint, Savannah, Ga.: Beehive Press, 1973), 378–89. In her
essay "Sex in American Literature," Mary Austin blames what she sees as a perverse
treatment of love in literature on a Jewish influence: "Sometimes I suspect that this
engagement of the love interest with the secret forces of the dark only appears to be
Semitic because here in the United States we are for the moment confronted with
Semitized examples of it." She then adds, however, that these "forces of the dark"
may emerge anywhere because of widespread miscegenation: "Now this dark-white
strain [from around the northeastern shore of the Mediterranean] has so mixed
with all European peoples that it cannot always be traced by blood or political relationships." Mary Austin, "Sex in American Literature," *The Bookman* 57 (June 1923):
390. For the continuing argument in nineteenth-century Europe about whether or
not Jews were "white," see Sander Gilman, *The Jew's Body* (London: Routledge, 1991),
chapter 7. For the cultural association of Jews and African-Americans in music, see
MacDonald Smith Moore, *Yankee Blues: Musical Culture and American Identity* (Bloomington: Indiana University Press, 1985), especially 66–71 and 130–35.

23. Jean Toomer to Waldo Frank, August 15, 1922, Jean Toomer Papers.

24. Perhaps the fullest published statement of Toomer's views on race appear in
the long essay "Race Problems and Modern Society," published in Baker Brownell,
ed., *Problems of Civilization* (New York: D. Van Nostrand Company, 1929), 67–111.
There, Toomer cites the authority of anthropologists Franz Boas and A. L. Kroeber
and the sociology of Louis Wirth and Melville Herskovits to argue that "the term
'race' in its strict biological sense . . . mean[s] an hereditary subdivision of a species,"
and that it is necessary for "the purely sociological aspects of racial matters to be
distinguished and seen for what they are" (76, 77). If this is done, Toomer suggests
(quoting Herskovits), it appears that "a race is something social rather than biologi-

cal. A race, it turns out, is a group of people that we treat as if they were one. You belong to a certain race, if you feel yourself to be a member, and if others treat you as if you were" (78). If "race," then, is socially constructed, Toomer felt he could deconstruct the racial definition others tried to apply to him.

25. Waldo Frank to Jean Toomer, undated letter (circa July 1922), Jean Toomer Papers.

26. Michael Rogin, "Blackface, White Noise: The Jewish Jazz Singer Finds His Voice," *Critical Inquiry* 18 (Spring 1992): 439. Rogin's analysis, much more detailed and extensive than our brief summary, is part of a series of articles about the conflicted connections of black and white culture in the history of Hollywood film. See especially Michael Rogin, "Making America Home: Racial Masquerade and Ethnic Assimilation in the Transition to Talking Pictures," *Journal of American History* 79 (December 1992): 1050–77. These essays are collected in Rogin's book, *Blackface, White Noise: Jewish Immigrants in the Hollywood Melting Pot* (Berkeley: University of California Press, 1996). Eric Lott analyzes similar connections in the nineteenth-century minstrel shows in *Love and Theft: Blackface Minstrelsy and the American Working Class* (New York: Oxford University Press, 1993).

27. Waldo Frank to Jean Toomer, undated letter (circa July 1922), Jean Toomer Papers. Frank suggested the trip to the South in a letter of July 17, 1922, Jean Toomer Papers.

28. Jean Toomer to Waldo Frank, July 25, 1922, Jean Toomer Papers; Waldo Frank to Jean Toomer, July 26, 1922, Jean Toomer Papers.

29. Jean Toomer to Waldo Frank, July 27, 1922, Jean Toomer Papers. In the discussions of *Holiday* in his correspondence with Toomer after their return from Spartanburg, Frank repeatedly placed his friend as the book's only judge. Thus in one undated letter he said, "I am going to submit Holiday to you, when it's done, as to a judge." In another undated letter he announced the book's completion and his intention of sending it to Toomer for a reading. He added, "O I shall TRRRREMBLE." When he finally sent some of the manuscript to Toomer on January 16, 1923, he said, "I await your verdict—it is really that—with fear and trembling." Jean Toomer Papers. On the relationship between black and white popular culture, note Toomer's remark to Frank in the undated letter about the Negro "in solution": "For the shows that please Seventh Street make their fortunes on Broadway." For remarks by Zora Neale Hurston on Paul Whiteman, see Kathy J. Ogren, *The Jazz Revolution: Twenties America and the Meaning of Jazz* (New York: Oxford University Press, 1989), 133–38.

30. Sherwood Anderson to Jean Toomer, quoted in Darwin T. Turner, "An Intersection of Paths: Correspondence Between Jean Toomer and Sherwood Anderson," in Therman B. O'Daniel, ed., *Jean Toomer: A Critical Evaluation* (Washington, D.C.: Howard University Press, 1988), 99. Jean Toomer to Waldo Frank, undated letter (circa January 1923), Jean Toomer Papers.

31. Waldo Frank to Jean Toomer, undated letter (circa January 1923), Jean Toomer Papers.

32. Jean Toomer to Waldo Frank, undated letter, Jean Toomer Papers.

33. Jean Toomer, *Cane* (New York: Boni & Liveright, 1923), xi. Jean Toomer to Waldo Frank, undated letter (circa 1923), Jean Toomer Papers. See Darwin T. Turner, ed., *The Wayward and the Seeking*, 125–26. Also see Jean Toomer to Minnie Lomax, February 14, 1931, Jean Toomer Papers. It's possible that Frank was writing the foreword for Horace Liveright as well as for Toomer. Liveright had already predicted a "limited market" for *Cane*, and both he and Frank were to urge Toomer to help find ways to publicize *Cane* and *Holiday* to black readers. Frank's characteriza-

tion of Toomer might have been intended partly to attract the African-American middle class. See Waldo Frank to Jean Toomer, undated letter (circa January 1923), Jean Toomer Papers.

34. Jean Toomer, "Waldo Frank's Holiday," *Dial* 75 (October 1923): 383–86, reprinted in Robert B. Jones, ed., *Jean Toomer: Selected Essays and Literary Criticism* (Knoxville: University of Tennessee Press, 1996), 7–10. Waldo Frank to Jean Toomer, September 29, 1923, Jean Toomer Papers.

35. It is worth noting that Toomer wrote a second (unpublished) essay on *Holiday* in which he sees its primary focus as a satire of the spiritual and emotional sterility of the white South. See "Waldo Frank as Ironist," Waldo Frank Papers.

36. Alan Trachtenberg, ed., *Memoirs of Waldo Frank*, 107. Toomer was not always able to maintain hope about his racial ideal. In one later unpublished essay, he noted that America had become "retrogressive" since World War I, that she "may soon wake up to find herself considered a backward nation." He went on to juxtapose Waldo Frank's optimistic prophesy in *Our America* with Andre Siegfried's more realistic *America Comes of Age*; even though he thought Siegfried "false" in arguing that "America is tending toward separatism and contradiction," he called him "a penetrating social observer." See Box 51, Folder 1106, Jean Toomer Papers.

37. Darwin T. Turner, ed., *The Wayward and the Seeking*, 128–31. One brief version of Toomer's post-*Cane* racial position is his essay "The Crock of Problems," written in 1928. See Robert B. Jones, ed., *Jean Toomer: Selected Essays and Literary Criticism*, 55–59. In Beinecke's catalogue of the Jean Toomer Papers, its compiler, Karen V. Peltier, lists two pages of files dealing with unpublished material on race relations (pp. 58–59). For evidence of Toomer's withdrawal from African-American writers and intellectuals of his acquaintance after 1923, see his correspondence with Jessie Fauset, especially Jessie Fauset to Jean Toomer, May 29, 1923, and August 20, 1923: "Why all the mystery and silence? Ever since you've been in New York, I've been thinking and hoping that you'd come to see me." Also see Toomer's replies to Fauset, June 13, 1923, and August 22, 1923, Jean Toomer Papers. Also see Cynthia Earl Kerman and Richard Eldridge, *The Lives of Jean Toomer*, 110–12.

38. Herbert Aptheker, ed., *The Correspondence of W.E.B. Du Bois, Volume I, Selections, 1877–1934* (Amherst: University of Massachusetts Press, 1973), 295–96. Part of the letter appeared in *The Crisis* 29 (January 1925): 118.

39. On the *Opportunity* magazine dinner, see David Levering Lewis, *When Harlem Was in Vogue* (1981; reprint, New York: Random House, 1982), 89–90. George B. Hutchinson, "Toomer and the 'New Negroes'," 691–92. Countee Cullen, ed., *Caroling Dusk: An Anthology of Verse by Negro Poets* (New York: Harper & Brothers, 1927), 93–94. Cullen says in his foreword that the "biographical notices . . . have been written by the poets themselves" (xiv). Jean Toomer to James Weldon Johnson, July 11, 1930, Jean Toomer Papers. Printed in Frederik L. Rusch, ed., *A Jean Toomer Reader: Selected Unpublished Writings*, 105–6. Toomer was not consistent about this policy, however; he later allowed parts of *Cane* to appear in anthologies designated as "Negro." Moreover, as late as 1925 he would inform Carl Van Vechten, the leading white patron of black arts, that he was "working on material that is enough for a novel," perhaps the same novel about black life that he had outlined in 1922 to Margaret Naumburg. See Jean Toomer to Carl Van Vechten, March 9, 1925, Jean Toomer Papers; Jean Toomer to Margaret Naumburg, September 14, 1922, Jean Toomer Papers. Also, see "Notes for a Novel," Box 48, Folder 1002, Jean Toomer Papers.

40. Darwin Turner describes the unfinished manuscript titled "On Being an American (The Brief Statement of a Human Position)" as an attempt by Toomer to

explain "his attitude about race." Darwin T. Turner, ed., *The Wayward and the Seeking*, 11. Frederik Rusch prints part of an "undated typescript titled 'This May Be Said/The Inside Story,'" which he believes to have been written in 1931, and which may be a preliminary outline for "On Being an American." The typescript, which Rusch titles "Fighting the Vice" in his excerpt, offers a much truncated version of how *Cane* was written. It emphasizes Toomer's difficult circumstances in Washington, D.C., and gives a rather more generous treatment of Waldo Frank than appears in "On Being an American." The excerpt also discusses Toomer's differences with Horace Liveright over the matter of racial identity, his attitude toward the "New Negro in literature movement," and his two objections to appearing in anthologies of Negro writing: he didn't wish to see *Cane* dismembered, and he had discovered that his identification as a Negro "tended to hinder my work" as a Gurdjieffian teacher. See Frederik L. Rusch, ed., *A Jean Toomer Reader*, 80, 101–4.

41. Darwin T. Turner, ed., *The Wayward and the Seeking*, 124. While he was still in Sparta, Toomer had already submitted a piece written about Georgia to the *Liberator*.

42. Jean Toomer, "Song of the Son," *The Crisis* 23 (April 1922): 261; Jean Toomer to Waldo Frank, April 26, 1922, Waldo Frank Papers. W.E.B. Du Bois reprinted "Song of the Son" in 1931 as part of a selection titled "Masterpieces of Crisis Poetry, 1910–1931." See *The Crisis* 28 (November 1931): 380–81. Toomer published one later poem in *The Crisis*, "As the Eagle Soars." That title was actually a regular entry appearing each month in *The Crisis* above a half-page column called "As the Crow Flies." Du Bois printed "uplifting" poems or quotations under the "eagle" and his own witty and sarcastic remarks about the month's news under the "crow." Perhaps by accident but probably by intention, the month Toomer's poem appeared there also appeared, two pages further on, a poem by Harry J. Warwick titled "Passing." See *The Crisis* 32 (April 1932): 116, 119.

43. John McClure to Jean Toomer, July 5, 1922; Jean Toomer to John McClure, June 30, 1922; Waldo Frank to Jean Toomer, April 25, 1922, Jean Toomer Papers.

44. Darwin T. Turner, ed., *The Wayward and the Seeking*, 125.

45. Waldo Frank to Jean Toomer, April 25, 1922, Jean Toomer Papers. On the dates of composition for "Theater" and the other stories of *Cane*'s second part, see Jean Toomer to Waldo Frank, letters undated but written after their return from Spartanburg. Toomer didn't send Frank a completed rough draft of *Cane* until December 12, 1922. See Jean Toomer to Waldo Frank, December 12, 1922, Jean Toomer Papers, printed in Turner, ed., *Cane*, 152.

46. Darwin T. Turner, ed., *The Wayward and the Seeking*, 125; Waldo Frank to Jean Toomer, April 25, 1922, Jean Toomer Papers.

47. Darwin T. Turner, ed., *The Wayward and the Seeking*, 126; Jean Toomer to Waldo Frank, undated letter (circa 1923), Jean Toomer Papers. For Toomer's identification with Kabnis, see also Jean Toomer to Lola Ridge, undated letter (circa 1922), Jean Toomer Papers: "Lewis, in point of origin, is as authentic as Kabnis. For I myself am frankly the source of both of them."

Chapter 5: Writing *Cane*

1. Waldo Frank to Jean Toomer, undated letter (circa July 1922), Jean Toomer Papers, Yale Collection of American Literature, Beinecke Rare Book and Manuscript Library, Yale University (hereafter referred to as Jean Toomer Papers). Waldo Frank to Jean Toomer, undated letter (circa July 1922), Jean Toomer Papers: "tell

Williams [editor of *Rhythmus*] I told you to [submit poems] . . . that you were the man I referred to at Lola Ridge's." For the *Seven Arts* reference, see Waldo Frank to Jean Toomer, April 11, 1922, Jean Toomer Papers.

2. Waldo Frank to Jean Toomer, undated letter (circa October–November 1922), Jean Toomer Papers; Jean Toomer to Waldo Frank, undated letter (circa November 1922), Jean Toomer Papers; Waldo Frank to Jean Toomer, undated letter (circa October 1922), Jean Toomer Papers: "It's the mysterious rule of life: and yet not so mysterious either when you think of the *physics* of true creation, of its inevitable and functional displacement of material already there, and of the inevitable resistance-inertia of that material (the powers that be) to being displaced. Good hunting, brother."

3. Waldo Frank to Jean Toomer, October 21, 1920, Jean Toomer Papers.

4. Jean Toomer to Waldo Frank, March 24, 1922, Waldo Frank Papers, Special Collections, Van Pelt Library, University of Pennsylvania (hereafter cited as Waldo Frank Papers). Citing a November 1921 letter from Toomer to Alain Locke, George Hutchinson has said that "Toomer was sharing the material that went into *Cane* with Locke from early on, that he in fact turned to Locke as an advisor and supporter during the crucial period in which his book was taking shape." Toomer may well have shared his *Cane* materials with Locke and other African-American friends in Washington, but there seems to be no evidence that Locke or anyone else besides Waldo Frank and a few editors of little magazines significantly influenced the shaping of those materials into the book. There is no doubt, however, that the background study of African-American history and life that Toomer did was important for *Cane*. Hutchinson says: "Toomer wrote Alain Locke that he had held two meetings at [Georgia Douglas] Johnson's home of a group 'whose central purpose is an historical study of slavery and the Negro, *emphasizing the great economic and cultural forces which have largely determined them.* The aim is twofold, first, to arrive at a sound and just criticism of the actual place and condition of *the mixed-blood group in this country,* and second, *to formulate an ideal* that will be both workable and inclusive' " (emphasis added). The quotation includes Toomer's socialist background, his concern with miscegenation, and his activist hopes. See George B. Hutchinson, "Jean Toomer and the 'New Negroes' of Washington," *American Literature* 63 (December 1991): 686, 690.

5. Waldo Frank to Jean Toomer, April 3, 1922, Jean Toomer Papers.

6. For Frank's opinions on the older and younger New York critics, see Waldo Frank to Jean Toomer, undated letter (circa July 1922), Jean Toomer Papers: "Yes, as you feel, Munson is real. Burke is too, but in a far more limited manner. Josephson is the merely clever man of the triumvirate. . . . Brooks had a glimpse of such, but he lacked the power to create, and he lacked the courage to criticize. His career is a wistful retreat."

7. Jean Toomer to Waldo Frank, April 4, 1922, Waldo Frank Papers. Waldo Frank to Jean Toomer, April 11, 1922, Jean Toomer Papers.

8. Waldo Frank, "A Note on the Novel," in *Salvos: An Informal Book About Books and Plays* (New York: Boni & Liveright, 1924), 223–31. Jean Toomer to Waldo Frank, April 10, 1922, Waldo Frank Papers.

9. Waldo Frank, *Salvos*, 226.

10. Ibid., 226–27. The influence of *unanimisme* in this passage is something Frank took from the French poet, playwright, and novelist Jules Romain. Kerman and Eldridge confuse Jules Romain with Romain Rolland, the author of the novel *Jean-Christophe*, which Toomer admired. Cynthia Earl Kerman and Richard Eldridge, *The Lives of Jean Toomer: A Hunger for Wholeness* (1987; reprint, Baton Rouge: Louisiana State University Press, 1989), 101–2.

was "spherical"—that the stories "fit into an inevitable circle" and that there was "a curve cementing them together and giving the Whole a dynamic propulsion forward." Jean Toomer, "The Critic of Waldo Frank: Criticism: An Art Form," *S4N* 30 (January 1924): no pagination. Although this review was not published until January 1924, Toomer had probably confronted the idea of spherical form in Frank, via Burke, before he read it in Munson. Toomer told Frank on December 12, 1922, that *Cane* was "finished," but he kept revising it for at least another two months. We can only conjecture how useful Munson's remarks about Frank's book were to Toomer while he was working out the final form of *Cane*.

26. Jean Toomer to Waldo Frank, July 19, 1922, Jean Toomer Papers.

27. Waldo Frank to Jean Toomer, July 26, 1922; Waldo Frank to Jean Toomer, undated letter (circa July 1922); Jean Toomer to Waldo Frank, July 25, 1922, Jean Toomer Papers.

28. Jean Toomer to Waldo Frank, August 2, 1922; Waldo Frank to Jean Toomer, undated letter (circa October 1922); Jean Toomer to Moses (?), October 9, 1922, Jean Toomer Papers.

29. Jean Toomer to Waldo Frank, August 2, 1922, and July 27, 1922, Waldo Frank Papers. Toomer introduced Frank to some of his African-American "study group" when he visited Washington, and Frank found them, as he later remembered, "intelligent, sensitive, neurotic." What they thought of Frank hasn't been discovered, though Georgia Johnson wrote to Alain Locke: "Did you know Jean had things in the Double Dealer and the Liberator? Waldo Frank has been here, came around and spent an evening. Must tell you my impression of him." Alan Trachtenberg, ed., *Memoirs of Waldo Frank* (Amherst: University of Massachusetts Press, 1973), 106–7; Georgia Johnson to Alain Locke, September 31 [*sic*], 1922, Alain Locke Papers, Moorland-Springarn Research Center, Howard University.

30. Toomer must have thought of Kabnis as an answer to Stribling's Peter Siner: both characters are mulatto intellectuals who return to the South. Toomer also intended to write a review of *Birthright*. Jean Toomer to Claude McKay, July 23, 1922, Jean Toomer Papers. Toomer had just read *Harlem Shadows* (1922), and his remarks echo the theme of McKay's poem, "The Tropics in New York." Frederik Rusch mistakenly identifies this letter as one written "to Waldo Frank." *A Jean Toomer Reader*, 13.

31. Jean Toomer to Waldo Frank, July 19, 1922, Jean Toomer Papers: "Here also meet three states: West Va., Virginia, and Maryland. The opportunity for a vivid symbolism is wonderful. I have made a partial use of it in my last long piece." Also see Jean Toomer to Waldo Frank, undated letter (circa January 1923), Jean Toomer Papers.

32. Waldo Frank to Jean Toomer, January 16, 1923, Jean Toomer Papers: "I send you here with Part One of Holiday. I have typed no more, as yet. Will you do me the great favor of reading it at once, and reading it carefully, and then returning it to me." Frank's letter is misdated "1922" (not an uncommon mistake in the first weeks of a new year). Kerman and Eldridge assume Frank's "1922" is correct and so misconstrue the sequence of Toomer and Frank's correspondence: there was no January 1922 letter from Frank to Toomer, and *Holiday* was written after the two men's return from Spartanburg in September of that year. See Cynthia Earl Kerman and Richard Eldridge, *The Lives of Jean Toomer*, 86, 89.

33. With John and Dorris, Toomer probably had in mind Peter and Cissie in *Birthright*. Also see Waldo Frank to Jean Toomer, July 26, 1922, Jean Toomer Papers. On the composition of "Theater," see Jean Toomer to Gorham Munson, October 31, 1922, Jean Toomer Papers: "Theater sprang to life a few weeks back when I was helping to manage the Howard. For a week or so my job kept me from writing it.

The minute I was released, I brought it out. The piece was written in a single day." Also see Jean Toomer to Waldo Frank, October 4, 1922, Jean Toomer Papers.

34. Jean Toomer to Waldo Frank, undated letter (circa October 1922), Waldo Frank Papers.

35. Gorham Munson to Jean Toomer, October 29, 1922; Jean Toomer to Gorham Munson, October 31, 1922; Jean Toomer Papers. Gorham Munson, "The Mechanics for a Literary 'Secession,'" *S4N* (November 1922), no pagination.

36. Gorham Munson to Jean Toomer, October 29, 1922; Jean Toomer to Gorham Munson, October 31, 1922; Gorham Munson to Jean Toomer, November 11, 1922; Jean Toomer Papers. Toomer would complain of Munson's reading of "Theater" that "he came to it through Hope and through what impressions he already had of me. There is more subtlety to it than he thought for." Jean Toomer to Waldo Frank, undated letter (circa November 1923), Waldo Frank Papers.

37. Jean Toomer to Gorham Munson, March 19, 1923, Jean Toomer Papers, printed in Frederik L. Rusch, ed., *A Jean Toomer Reader*, 21–22.

38. Jean Toomer to Gorham Munson, December 20, 1922, Jean Toomer Papers. Toomer would make the same point in his "Open Letter to Gorham B. Munson," *S4N* 25 (March 1923): no pagination. Munson's essay appeared in *S4N* in the *same* month and year that Eliot's *Waste Land* appeared in the *Dial*, and the cultural elitism implied by *The Waste Land* stood in marked contrast to Munson's American future, where everything was accepted and everything was possible. Eliot lamented the fall of civilization because the barbarians had already entered the gates; Munson implied that the barbarians might be society's best hope. While Eliot took a European perspective, especially as it involved "tradition," Munson focused on America—not on Brooks's "usable past" but America's multiple futures. Of course Munson's political attitudes would move away from Waldo Frank and end up very close to those of Eliot.

39. The dating of "Blood-Burning Moon," "Theater," "Box Seat," and "Esther" we can more or less approximate, but one important story, "Bona and Paul," presents a special problem. We can approximate the composition of other stories by their date of publication in magazines or, as for "Theater," "Box Seat," and "Blood-Burning Moon," by their mentions in letters. Cynthia Earl Kerman and Richard Eldridge think "Bona and Paul" was written in 1917 or 1918, but give no evidence for such an early date. Internal evidence, however, specifically a reference to Georgia, suggests it was written, or at least significantly revised, after the Sparta trip. Moreover, Toomer uses one of Frank's favorite words, "clot," in the story, which suggests a date coming after his familiarity with Frank's work. The earliest mention of "Bona and Paul" we found was in the August 20, 1922, letter to Lola Ridge, where Toomer merely says at the end of the opening paragraph, "Thanks- Bona and Paul." Toomer may have sent her the story among his other manuscripts and was thanking her for her comments. Frank may not have seen "Bona and Paul" until Toomer sent him the completed manuscript on December 12. Frank thought Toomer needed to "tighten up" the story, and in his letter of reply Toomer agreed to revise it. It is a city story but the only story in *Cane*'s middle section not to be set in Washington; its characters, with the exception of Paul and the doorman, are white—again an anomaly for the middle section and for *Cane* in general. Kerman and Eldridge also say that "by April of 1922 he completed most of the pieces that were eventually to go into *Cane*." But Toomer had not yet written "Esther," "Blood-Burning Moon," "Theater," or "Box Seat"; nor had he written two of the poems that appear in the Washington section, and he had not yet changed "Kabnis" from a play into a story. See *The Lives of Jean Toomer*, 69, 86. Also see Jean Toomer to Lola Ridge, August 20, 1922, Jean Toomer Papers; Waldo Frank to Jean Toomer, undated letter (circa Janu-

ary 1923), Jean Toomer Papers, printed in Turner, ed., *Cane*, 153; Jean Toomer to Waldo Frank, undated letter (circa January 1923), Waldo Frank Papers.

40. Jean Toomer to Waldo Frank, undated letter (circa November 1922), Waldo Frank Papers.

41. Lola Ridge to Jean Toomer, undated letter (circa spring–summer 1922); Jean Toomer to Lola Ridge, undated letter (circa spring–summer 1922), Jean Toomer Papers. Kerman and Eldridge say of Toomer's initial literary party in New York "in August of 1920" that it was "given by Lola Ridge, an editor for the fledgling 'little magazine' *Broom*." However, *Broom* did not begin publication until November 1921, and Ridge was not an original member of the magazine's editorial staff. Cynthia Earl Kerman and Richard Eldridge, *The Lives of Jean Toomer*, 72.

42. Jean Toomer to Waldo Frank, undated letter (circa October–November 1922); see also Toomer's later letter to Frank (undated, circa October–November 1922), where Toomer says he has been reading "The Unwelcome Man in detail (God but the things that book tells me)." Waldo Frank Papers. On reading *Winesburg, Ohio*, and *Triumph of the Egg*, see Jean Toomer to Sherwood Anderson, letter dated December 18, 1922, Jean Toomer Papers, printed in Turner, ed., *Cane*, 148–49. Toomer's letters to Frank in 1922 are punctuated with requests for copies of Frank's fictional works, nominally in pursuit of a critical study that evidently was never written.

43. Waldo Frank, *The Unwelcome Man* (1917; reprint, New York: Boni & Liveright, 1923), xi; Jean Toomer, "The Critic of Waldo Frank: Criticism, an Art Form," *S4N* 30 (January 1924): no pagination; reprinted in Robert B. Jones, ed., *Jean Toomer: Selected Essays and Literary Criticism* (Knoxville: University of Tennessee Press, 1996), 24–31.

44. Waldo Frank, *The Unwelcome Man* (Boston: Little, Brown, 1917), 176, 177. For the connection between Frank's sense of being an outsider at Yale and his Jewishness, see Alan Trachtenberg, ed., *Memoirs of Waldo Frank*, 37, 196.

45. Jean Toomer to Waldo Frank, undated letter (circa November 1922), Waldo Frank Papers.

46. Jean Toomer to Waldo Frank, December 12, 1922, Jean Toomer Papers, printed in Turner, ed., *Cane*, 152. In a letter of January or February 1923, Toomer told Frank, "I'm incorporating the introduction [of "Kabnis"] into the body of the work. In this way, two or three pages are cut off. I'm wondering if this form wouldnt be best for the book. I dont believe I lose anything essential. And the piece gains in concentration. As I go over it, new lines etc form. I think I'll have a better Kabnis." Jean Toomer Papers. The "introduction" would presumably be what became part 1 of "Kabnis," which Toomer was still revising within a month of the final manuscript's submission to Boni & Liveright.

47. Jean Toomer to Waldo Frank, undated letter (circa November or December 1922), Waldo Frank Papers. Waldo Frank to Jean Toomer, undated letters (circa December 1922 and January 1923), Jean Toomer Papers.

48. Waldo Frank to Jean Toomer, undated letter (circa January 1923), Jean Toomer Papers, printed in Turner, ed., *Cane*, 153. Jean Toomer to Waldo Frank, undated letter (circa January 1923), Waldo Frank Papers.

49. Frank would approve the new poems and leave the disposition of "Prayer" up to Toomer: "copper wire poem . . . a very excellent fantasy, though not so deep as the Georgia portrait by any means . . . I think you should decide about Prayer . . . it certainly is far more deserving than the other poems." Waldo Frank to Jean Toomer, undated letter (circa January 1923), Jean Toomer Papers.

50. Jean Toomer to Waldo Frank, undated letter (circa January 1923), Waldo Frank Papers.

51. Toomer's last remark may seem curious to anyone who has read Frank's fic-

tion: "muddy" and obscure frequently seem fair descriptions of his prose style, yet he was obviously an excellent editor of other people's work.

52. Jean Toomer to Waldo Frank, undated letter (circa January 1923), Waldo Frank Papers.

53. Waldo Frank to Jean Toomer, undated letter (circa January 1923), Jean Toomer Papers; Jean Toomer to Waldo Frank, undated letter (circa 1923), Waldo Frank Papers.

54. Jean Toomer to Horace Liveright, February 27, 1923, Jean Toomer Papers, printed in Turner, ed., *Cane*, 153–54; Waldo Frank to Jean Toomer, undated letter (circa summer 1923), Jean Toomer Papers, printed in Turner, ed., *Cane*, 154; Waldo Frank to Jean Toomer, August 1923, Jean Toomer Papers, printed in Turner, ed., *Cane*, 155; for the tensions between Toomer and Frank, see their exchanges about Flaubert in undated letters from the spring and summer of 1923, and especially the letter from Toomer to Frank of September 9, 1923, Jean Toomer Papers; Jean Toomer to Waldo Frank, October 1, 1924, Waldo Frank Papers; Waldo Frank to Jean Toomer, undated letter (circa January 1923), Jean Toomer Papers.

55. Jean Toomer to Gorham Munson, undated letter (circa November 1922); Jean Toomer to Waldo Frank, undated letter (circa October 1922), Jean Toomer Papers. Toomer's remarks to Munson refer to Anderson's story "Many Marriages," published in the *Dial* (1922).

56. For Frank's later view of Sherwood Anderson, see his postscript to "Emerging Greatness" (first published in *Seven Arts*) in *Salvos*, 38–40. In 1917 Anderson had written to Frank, "We are so different. Something very rank and vulgar in me is lacking in you. We both need growth, but in what different directions." Sherwood Anderson to Waldo Frank, January 10, 1917, in Howard Mumford Jones and Walter B. Rideout, eds., *Letters of Sherwood Anderson* (Boston: Little, Brown, 1953), 6. Anderson probably disapproved of Frank's influence on Toomer. He wrote to Paul Rosenfeld that he thought "Kabnis" was "wonderful," but "when I read of some negro woman, that her mind was a meshbag of pink baby toes, I shuddered. I thought X—had indeed laid his warm fog over the negro's mind." Jerome Mellquist and Lucie Wiese, eds., *Paul Rosenfeld: Voyager in the Arts* (New York: Creative Age Press, 1948), 219–20.

57. Jean Toomer to Sherwood Anderson, December 18, 1922, Jean Toomer Papers, printed in Turner, ed., *Cane*, 148–49.

58. See Walter B. Rideout, "The Simplicity of *Winesburg, Ohio*," *Shenandoah* 13 (Spring 1962): 20–31.

59. Waldo Frank, "Foreword," *Cane* (New York: Boni & Liveright, 1923), x, ix. Jean Toomer to Waldo Frank, undated letter (circa 1923), Jean Toomer Papers, printed in Frederik L. Rusch, ed., *A Jean Toomer Reader*, 23. The best proof that Frank understood *Cane* is his own Gothic detective novel, *Chalk Face*, written in 1923 and published by Liveright in 1924.

60. Waldo Frank to Sherwood Anderson, November 27, 1919, quoted in Jerome W. Kloucek, "Waldo Frank: The Ground of His Mind and Art" (Ph.D. diss., Northwestern University, 1958), 408. The quoted phrases are from Jean Toomer to Waldo Frank, undated letter (circa 1923), Jean Toomer Papers.

Chapter 6: The Gothic Detective Story

1. Terry Eagleton, "Theydunnit," *London Review of Books*, April 28, 1994, 12. A similar connection is made by Paul Skenazy, "Behind the Territory Ahead," in David Fine, ed., *Los Angeles in Fiction: A Collection of Essays*, rev. ed. (Albuquerque: Uni-

versity of New Mexico Press, 1995), 114: "Both gothic and detective fiction remind us that the past exerts a compelling moral force upon the present. The two forms share common assumptions: that there is an undisclosed event, a secret from the past; that the secret represents an occurrence or desire antithetical to the principles and position of the house (or family); that to know the secret is to understand the inexplicable and seemingly irrational events that occur in the present."

2. Jean Toomer, *Cane* (1923; reprint, New York: Harper & Row, 1969), 4. Subsequent citations refer to this edition and will appear within the text. Toomer's essay on the South, which he intended to accompany *Cane*'s publication, gives a misleading impression of that region as it appeared in his book. Thinking of Frank's *Our America*—its attack on the Puritan-pioneer, its failure to talk about either the South or the Negro—he argued that previous American writers "have omitted the peasant-adjustment rhythm of the Southern Negro." To make a case for the South as a subject for literature equal to Frost's New England or Anderson's Ohio, Toomer accentuated the positive aspects of the region: a peasantry adjusted to "its physical environment" ("which the general cultural body stands in sore need of") and an aristocracy possessed of culture, "a tradition of leisure." He did not ignore the South's demonic side ("a land of great passions: hate, fear, cruelty . . . the stark theme of the black and white races"), but these themes took a back seat to the "South's rich complexity." Jean Toomer, "The South in Literature," Box 48, Folder 1008, Yale Collection of American Literature, Beinecke Rare Book and Manuscript Library, Yale University (hereafter cited as Jean Toomer Papers). Also printed in Frederik L. Rusch, *A Jean Toomer Reader: Selected Unpublished Writings* (New York: Oxford University Press, 1993), 233–34.

3. Fred See's observation about John Irwin's *The Mystery to a Solution* is a kind of gloss on *Cane*: texts that "set out" to celebrate "the triumph of reason over subjectivity" can also "spell out how fragile our mastery of fear finally is." Fred See, "Mapping Amazement: John Irwin and the Calculus of Speculation," *Modern Fiction Studies* 40 (Summer 1994): 348; also see John T. Irwin, *The Mystery to a Solution: Poe, Borges, and the Analytical Detective Story* (Baltimore: Johns Hopkins University Press, 1994), chapters 19, 20, 21.

4. Eve Sedgwick, *The Coherence of Gothic Conventions* (New York: Arno Press, 1980), 3, 4. Orlando Patterson, *Slavery and Social Death: A Comparative Study* (Cambridge, Mass.: Harvard University Press, 1982), 8.

5. Robert D. Hume, "Gothic Versus Romantic: A Revaluation of the Gothic Novel," *PMLA* 84 (1969): 287, 290. Stephen Graham, *Children of Slaves* (London: Macmillan, 1920), 200, 212. Also see Albert Bushnell Hart, *The Southern South* (New York: Appleton, 1910), 209; and NAACP, *Thirty Years of Lynching in the United States, 1889–1918* (1919; reprint, New York: Negro University Press, 1969), 7: "Georgia leads in this unholy ascendancy with 386 victims." In addition to these contemporary accounts, see W. Fitzhugh Brundage, *Lynching in the New South: Georgia and Virginia, 1880–1930* (Urbana: University of Illinois Press, 1993); Joel Williamson, *The Crucible of Race: Black-White Relationships in the American South* (New York: Oxford University Press, 1984), 183–89; Trudier Harris, *Exorcising Blackness: Historical and Literary Lynching and Burning Rituals* (Bloomington: Indiana University Press, 1984), 7–11; Stewart E. Tolnay and E. M. Beck, *A Festival of Violence: An Analysis of Southern Lynchings, 1882–1930* (Urbana: University of Illinois Press, 1995), 124, 218. Eve Sedgwick, *The Coherence of Gothic Conventions*, 31.

6. Thomas Nelson Page, "The Lynching of Negroes—Its Cause and Its Prevention," *North American Review* 178 (January 1904): 34. Page numbers for subsequent citations of this work are given in parentheses and refer to this journal.

7. Ida B. Wells-Barnett, *On Lynching* (New York: Arno Press, 1969). Wells's de-

bunking of the Southern rape myth, "A Red Record: Tabulated Statistics and Alleged Causes of Lynchings in the United States," was published in 1895. W. Fitzhugh Brundage, *Lynching in the New South,* 263. Brundage notes that "industrialization, rapid expansion of the market economy, and sharecropping—the distinguishing features of the New South—are all central to the story of mob violence in the postbellum South" (14). Brundage also observes that lynching was "the ultimate sanction against willing sexual liaisons between white women and black men, a practice that defied the most fundamental notions of the southern racial hierarchy" (61–62). Curiously, Page reprints lynching statistics compiled by the Chicago *Tribune* in his essay, and even those statistics refute his thesis about the cause of lynching; either he did not read the *Tribune* figures or he did not expect anyone else to read them.

8. See Vera M. Kutzinski, "Unseasonal Flowers: Nature and History in Placido and Jean Toomer," *Yale Journal of Criticism* 3 (Spring 1990): 153–79. Kutzinski has uncovered the "troubling histories of sexual and economic abuse" (169) that Toomer constantly hints at in the backgrounds of his female characters. On the presentation of rape and lynching in some turn-of-the-century writers, see Sandra Gunning, *Race, Rape, and Lynching: The Red Record of American Literature, 1890–1912* (New York: Oxford University Press, 1996).

9. W.E.B. Du Bois, *Darkwater: Voices from Within the Veil* (New York: Harcourt, Brace, and Howe, 1920), chapter 7. A book of essays, poems, and short stories, *Darkwater* clearly influenced *Cane.* Toomer's line in "Kabnis," "Teat moon-children at your breasts," alludes to Du Bois's visionary poem, "Children of the Moon," where the black children of Isis are hidden in caves, deprived of the sun, and protected by black mothers. "The Comet"—Du Bois's science-fiction short story—bears a striking resemblance to "Bona and Paul," and in his essay "The Damnation of Women," Du Bois describes the white outcast Ide Fuller, perhaps a model for Becky. The literary effect of the two books is nearly opposite, however: Du Bois's attack on Southern mores is direct, by way of satire and ridicule, while Toomer's use of a modernist broken narrative creates the air of secrecy and fear surrounding Southern race relations. Barbara Jeanne Fields, "Slavery, Race and Ideology in the United States of America," *New Left Review* 101 (May–June 1990), 107.

10. W.E.B. Du Bois, *Darkwater,* 163. The treatment of this meeting of sex, race, gender, and power in *Cane*'s first section remains paradigmatic for American culture. The 1991 hearings over Clarence Thomas's nomination to the Supreme Court ended by matching a black woman, a black man, and white male authorities in a nationally televised debate that alluded to both sexual attack and a symbolic lynching. See Toni Morrison, ed., *Race-ing Justice, En-gendering Power: Essays on Anita Hill, Clarence Thomas, and the Construction of Social Reality* (New York: Pantheon Books, 1992), especially the essays by Nellie Y. McKay, Nell Irvin Painter, Kimberle Crenshaw, and Paula Giddings. For an account of how black women created a "culture of dissemblance" to protect themselves from rape, see Darlene Clark Hine, *HINE SIGHT: Black Women and the Re-Construction of American History* (Brooklyn: Carlson Publishing, 1994), 37–47.

11. "Hybridization . . . produces new combinations and strange instabilities in a given semiotic system. It therefore generates the possibility of shifting *the very terms of the system itself,* by erasing and interrogating the relationships which constitute it." Peter Stallybrass and Allon White, *The Politics and Poetics of Transgression* (Ithaca, N.Y.: Cornell University Press, 1986), 58. Mary V. Dearborn, *Pocahontas's Daughters: Gender and Ethnicity in American Culture* (New York: Oxford University Press, 1986), 143. According to Hazel V. Carby, the mulatto functions "as a vehicle for the exploration of the relationship between the races and, at the same time, an expression of the relationship between the races." Hazel V. Carby, *Reconstructing Womanhood: The*

Emergence of the Afro-American Woman Novelist (New York: Oxford University Press, 1987), 89. Also see Judith R. Berzon, *Neither Black or White: The Mulatto Character in American Fiction* (New York: New York University Press, 1978), chapters 1, 2, 9. Homi K. Bhabha, *Nation and Narration* (London: Routledge, 1990), 319.

12. William Wasserman notes that "the word 'pyramid' " has an old association with fire "because, according to Johnson's *Dictionary*, 'fire always ascends in the figure of a cone.' " Since Plato thought the soul "to be of a fiery nature," by analogy "the pyramid signifies the human soul." Paradoxically, of course, the pyramid as a monument signifies death, not life, thus making the pyramid an ambiguous figure. Earl R. Wasserman, *Shelley: A Critical Reading* (Baltimore: Johns Hopkins University Press, 1971), 493–95. In his discussion of Melville's *Pierre*, Edgar A. Dryden points to a further ambiguity in the figure of the pyramid that is directly related to Toomer's "Karintha": "the pyramid situated in the cradle of civilization and the birthplace of the gods . . . marks the point beyond which it is impossible to go and . . . at the same time indicates that the moment of origin is not one of plenitude and presence but the sign of a loss." Toomer's association of Karintha's beauty with the horizon ("dusk on the eastern horizon") connects her with the lost world of origins. Edgar A. Dryden, *The Form of American Romance* (Baltimore: Johns Hopkins University Press, 1988), 96. Hegel thought that what made the pyramid both fascinating and mysterious was its "double architecture, one above ground, the other subterranean." Georges Hegel, *Aesthetics*, trans. T. M. Knox (Oxford: Oxford University Press, 1975), 304–5.

13. Maria Leach and Jerome Fried, *Funk & Wagnalls Standard Dictionary of Folklore, Mythology and Legend*, vol. 1 (New York: Funk & Wagnalls, 1949): "Many fairy stories and legends have to do with changelings. Newborn infants are often snatched away and fairy babies left in their places" (365). Darlene Clark Hine discusses a black slave mother who murdered her miscegenated child: "The woman insisted that she would not have killed a child of her own color." Hine observes that infanticide of this kind was not uncommon: "There are numerous instances in which a slave woman simply preferred to end her child's life rather than allow the child to grow up enslaved." Darlene Clark Hine, *HINE SIGHT*, 33.

14. Jean Toomer to Gorham Munson, October 31, 1922, Jean Toomer Papers. The smoke that "curls up" from the sawdust pile is repeated in a seemingly innocuous image in "Evening Song": "Cloine" is "curled" in the narrator's arms, sleeping (35). A Gothic note is also sounded in this pastoral poem by the words "vesperkeeps," for vesper prayers are not only celebratory but petitionary: God protect us from the beasts that begin to prowl "at the close of day." See *The Book of Common Prayer* (Kingsport, Tenn.: Kingsport Press, 1977), 139–40. The sleeping Cloine foreshadows the "orphan-woman" Avey, asleep in the arms of another Toomer narrator. W. E. B. Du Bois, *Darkwater*, 166, 167. In *Darkwater*, Isis is the life force, the "mother," depicted always with the lunar disc between her cow's horns; but as an expression of the demonic side of Isis, the moon is transformed into Erzulie "the red-eyed" seductress. Her other appearance is as Louisa in "Blood-Burning Moon," when she becomes an agent of death, a femme fatale. See Zora Neale Hurston, *Tell My Horse* (1938; reprint, Berkeley: Turtle Island, 1983), 147.

15. Frederick R. Karl, *Modern and Modernism: The Sovereignty of the Artist, 1885–1925* (New York: Atheneum, 1985), 310, 311.

16. Allon White, *The Uses of Obscurity: The Fiction of Early Modernism* (London: Routledge and Kegan Paul, 1981), 36. Autobiographical Writings, Box 18, Folder 491, Jean Toomer Papers. Also see Chapter 1, n. 51, above.

17. Joel Williamson and others have noted that "by 1920 at least 70 percent of the Negro population was in fact mixed." Joel Williamson, *New People: Miscegena-*

tion and Mulattoes in the United States (New York: The Free Press, 1980), 59; also see F. James Davis, *Who Is Black? One Nation's Definition* (University Park: Pennsylvania State University Press, 1991), 12, 20, 21; Richard Leonard Lempel, *The Mulatto in the United States: Changing Status and Attitudes, 1800–1940* (Ann Arbor, Mich.: University Microfilms International, 1979), 26.

18. Jacqueline Jones, *Labor of Sorrow, Labor of Love: Black Women, Work and the Family, from Slavery to the Present* (1985; reprint, New York: Random House, 1986), 37–38; bell hooks, *Ain't I A Woman: Black Women and Feminism* (Boston: South End Press, 1983), 27–39. In attempting to portray the plight of black women under slavery and afterward, hooks deemphasizes the psychological impact that "terrorism" against black women had on black men.

An earlier unpublished and unfinished version of "Reapers" expressed the poem's political anger more directly. In *Cane*'s version the images work by suggestion; in the unpublished version the idea of transferred aggression is made explicit:

> Black workmen with the sound of steel
> > on stone
> Are sharpening scythes, they swing them
> > through the weeds
> Mules pulling a mowing machine *fill needs*
> A rat with belly close to ground
> A matter *medicinal.* (Emphasis added.)

See Jean Toomer Papers, Notebook (1920–21), Box 60, Folder 1410.

19. In "The Uncanny," Freud used E. T. A. Hoffmann's famous short story "The Sandman" to illustrate his thesis about the nature of dread. The young protagonist associates the mythical sandman with his father, and later with the dismemberment of a young woman who is actually a doll. It is the first association that interests Freud —the father is the figure whom the son fears will castrate him—but the image of the woman-doll's "bleeding eyeballs" is possibly echoed by the "dismembered" Becky, separated from both home and community. Sigmund Freud, "The Uncanny," trans. Alix Strachey in *Standard Edition of the Complete Psychological Works*, vol. 4 (London: Hogarth Press, 1953–64), 378–86. Freud's essay was not given an authorized translation until 1925, but his bibliographers note that there were many unofficial translations of the shorter essays in circulation, and it is certainly possible that Toomer read these. The world of Greenwich Village was saturated in "Freudianism" by 1920, and Waldo Frank was one of the young intellectuals who not only studied Freud but actually underwent analysis. See Alexander Grinstein, M.D., *Sigmund Freud's Writings: A Comprehensive Bibliography* (New York: International Universities Press, 1977), viii, 95; Leslie Fishbein, "Freud and the Radicals: The Sexual Revolution Comes to Greenwich Village," *Canadian Review of American Studies* 12 (Fall 1981): 173–89.

20. Joan Dayan, "Amorous Bondage: Poe, Ladies, and Slaves," *American Literature* 66 (June 1994): 242, 247, 250. In the *Phenomenology of the Spirit*, Georg Hegel also understood bondage to be double-edged; the master depends on the slave for his sense of self, and the slave becomes conscious of freedom because the master possesses it.

21. David Punter, *The Literature of Terror: A History of Gothic Fictions from 1765 to the Present Day* (London: Longman, 1980), 402–27; Leslie A. Fiedler, *Love and Death in the American Novel* (1960; reprint, New York: Dell, 1967), 126–61. Wilbur J. Cash, *The Mind of the South* (1941; reprint, New York: Random House, 1969), 163. See also Lewis P. Simpson, *The Dispossessed Garden: Pastoral and History in Southern Literature* (Athens: University of Georgia Press, 1974), chapters 1 and 2; Richard Gray, *Writ-*

ing the South: Ideas of an American Region (Cambridge: Cambridge University Press, 1986), chapters 1 and 2, and p. 135; John Chalker, *The English Georgic: A Study in the Development of a Form* (Baltimore: Johns Hopkins University Press, 1969), 57–64, especially Chalker's discussion of James Grainger's "West Indian Georgic," *The Sugar–Cane* (1764). Georgia's origins recall Ernest Renan's observation that "historical enquiry brings to light deeds of violence [against others] which took place at the origin of all political formations." See Ernest Renan, "What Is a Nation?" in Homi K. Bhabha, ed., *Nation and Narration* (London: Routledge, 1990), 11, 19; see also Homi K. Bhabha, "DissemiNation: Time, Narrative, and the Margins of the Modern Nation," in *Nation and Narration*, 310.

22. Homi K. Bhabha, *The Location of Culture* (London: Routledge, 1994), 11. Gaston Bachelard, *The Poetics of Space*, trans. Maria Jolas (Boston: Beacon Press, 1969), 52–73. Zora Neale Hurston relates a story of how people who are to become Zombies have their houses violated: the Bocor "rides after dark to the house of his victim. There he places his lips to the crack of the door and sucks out the soul of the victim." Zora Neal Hurston, *Tell My Horse*, 192–93. Sigmund Freud, "The Uncanny," 369–70, 377.

23. Allon White offers an analysis of "obscurity" and modernist literary technique which helps illuminate how Toomer's narrative method works: "Modernist obscurity is not due simply to the unfamiliarity of the protocols upon which it is based. It is rather that a key protocol upon which it is based is obscurity." In modernist literature, "not all the areas of hesitation, vagueness and concealment in these authors are areas of difficulty: difficulty applies largely to the language of a text, its style or syntax, but often in these novels the obscurity is of a visual nature, a matter of oblique point of view or concealed vantage within a scene, and this is not a matter of 'difficulty' but rather one of obscured vision." The "oblique point of view or concealed vantage" occur frequently in *Cane*, as in the narrator and Barlo's attempt to see what happened to Becky or the disappearance of Carma into the cane field. But this obscurity is not only visual impairment, it also appears as an uncertain history, one repressed, "rumored," or contradicted. Allon White, *The Uses of Obscurity*, 17.

24. As Shoshana Felman has asked, how does one bear witness to an event that both the witness and the audience refuse to see? Shoshana Felman and Dori Laub, *Testimony: Crises of Witnessing in Literature, Psychoanalysis, and History* (New York: Routledge, 1992), chapter 6.

25. Of course, artists as different as Raymond Chandler and Rainer Werner Fassbinder have preferred melodrama as a genre over the more "respectable" kinds of art because, in Chandler's words, it is "relatively honest" — it doesn't pretend that violence is not a factor in American life. Moreover, the phrase "crudest melodrama" implies that there may yet be another kind of melodrama, and as recent scholarship has shown, even the "crudest" kind (such as "pulp fiction") can become a modernist vehicle (one thinks of Faulkner's *Sanctuary*) put to the service of revealing what Raymond Chandler calls "a hidden truth." Also, the very nature of melodrama — that it depends upon the "desemanticized language of music" for its effects — suggests that its heightened emotional surface conceals ineffable depths. See Joyce Carol Oates, "The Simple Art of Murder," *New York Review of Books* 42 (December 21, 1995): 40; Raymond Chandler, "The Simple Art of Murder," *Atlantic Monthly* 174 (December 1944): 59; Peter Brooks, "The Melodramatic Imagination," in *Imitations of Life: A Reader on Film and Television Melodrama*, ed. Marcia Landy (Detroit: Wayne State University Press, 1991), 60.

26. Martin Buber, *I and Thou*, trans. Ronald Gregor Smith (1958; reprint, New York: Macmillan, 1987), 55.

27. Bane, like Faulkner's Lucas Beauchamp, believes in a past fated to repeat

itself in the present: "How to God . . . can a black man ask a white man to please not lay down with his black wife? And even if he could ask it, how to God can the white man promise he wont?" William Faulkner, *Go Down, Moses* (1941; reprint, New York: Random House, 1973), 59.

28. The narrator at the end of "Becky" speaks as if he were a native of Sempter — "Our congregation had been visiting at Pulverton" (11) — while the narrators of "Carma" and "Fern" seem clearly to be outsiders in the community. The figure of Fern illustrates Darlene Clark Hine's argument that black women attempted to re- sist the social stereotypes that defined them by constructing "a secret, undiscovered *persona*" to protect them from white men and, to a lesser extent, from black men. See Darlene Clark Hine, *HINE SIGHT*, 43.

29. Toomer no doubt understood that "Fern" could be read as a criticism of *Our America.* He didn't include the story in the first manuscripts he sent to Frank in April, although he thought it good enough to send to John McClure and then to the *Dial.* In a letter to Frank on July 19, 1922, Toomer says, "He [Gilbert Seldes] now has Karintha and Fern. Fern you have not seen." Waldo Frank Papers, Special Collections, Van Pelt Library, University of Pennsylvania (hereafter cited as Waldo Frank Papers).

30. Walter Benjamin, *Illuminations*, trans. Harry Zohn (New York: Schocken, 1969), 94.

31. Toomer structures "Esther" around the ages of her life, as Sherwood Ander- son had structured his *Winesburg* narrative of Alice Hindman ("Adventure"), but Toomer's character is less sympathetic and his story more political. His social per- spective emphasizes class divisions and the satiric view of Esther's family.

32. The small retail business of Esther's father was the sort of occupation the African-American elite of a Southern town might pursue. The store's dependence on black customers alludes to the Booker T. Washington ethos of the "group econ- omy," i.e., black consumers supporting black businesses, although Esther's back- ground doesn't seem to fit the "new bourgeoisie" which was, as August Meier says, behind "the philosophy of racial solidarity, self-help, and the group economy, of the rationalization of the economic advantages of the disadvantages in segregation and discrimination." Members of this new middle class were for the most part not light-skinned mulattos, and Barlo seems intended to represent their rise. As white prejudice against black businesses increased after 1900, the class of Esther's father was forced to adapt to Washington's philosophy if they wanted to make money. Toomer's acid critique of that class anticipates the point of view of E. Franklin Frasier in *The Black Bourgeoisie.* See August Meier, *Negro Thought in America, 1880– 1915: Racial Ideologies in the Age of Booker T. Washington* (Ann Arbor: University of Michigan Press, 1963), 149–52, 156–57, 301. Esther's father (Jim Crane) is probably modeled after Sparta resident Richard Johnson; see Chapter 1, n. 24.

33. Some critics read "Portrait in Georgia" as descriptive of a black man and white woman, but the poem creates a more ambiguous surface: "her slim body" could be that of either the white femme fatale or a lynched black woman. Toomer avoids the identification of the lynched figure (black man or black woman), because both are caught in the mysterious web of white-black relations in the South. In- deed, white and black shade into one another, just as Louisa in her mind "jumbles" Tom Burwell and Bob Stone, or just as Bob Stone confuses Louisa with his sister. See George Hutchinson, "Jean Toomer and Racial Discourse," *Texas Studies in Lit- erature and Language* 35 (Summer 1993): 233; Walter Benn Michaels, *Our America: Nativism, Modernism, and Pluralism* (Durham, N.C.: Duke University Press, 1995), 61.

34. A textile factory was built in 1857 on a forty-acre area in Sparta known as Montour Village; Toomer confirms its urban origins by calling Montour "Factory

Town" in *Cane*, an extension of the agribusiness of cotton and slavery or what James Oakes called "factories in the fields." See Chapter 1, n. 25. Whether or not Toomer's description of the cotton factory was intended as a figure for the Marxist view of an economic base and cultural superstructure, the description fits that pattern. Also see Barbara Foley, "Jean Toomer's Sparta," *American Literature* 67 (December 1995): 754. In his article "Myth and Narrative Fiction in *Cane*: 'Blood-Burning Moon,'" *Callaloo* 8 (Fall 1985): 551–62, Alain Solard discusses other mythological figures associated with the moon: Diana, Hecate, Artemis, and Isis.

35. The moon figures in many blues songs, suggesting as it does the unpredictability of human experience and the impermanence of human relationships. From Charlie Patton's "Moon Going Down" to the Neville Brothers' "Yellow Moon," the image has reappeared continually in black music. "If the [blues] music has a single Great Subject," notes Robert Palmer, "it's impermanence." See *Deep Blues* (New York: Viking Press, 1981), 275. The figure also had religious and apocalyptic associations in the slave spirituals: "The Day of Judgment," published in 1867, begins with the line, "And de moon will turn to blood" on Judgment Day. See Ronald Radano, "Denoting Difference: The Writing of the Slave Spirituals," *Critical Inquiry* 22 (Spring 1996): 536. Bernard Bell has noted that the "red nigger moon/Blood-burning moon" is an allusion to the Book of Revelation (6:12), but perhaps Toomer was thinking as well of the Book of Joel (2:30–32): "The sun shall be turned to darkness, and the moon to blood, before the great and terrible day of the Lord comes." The *Dies Irae* in the Book of Joel is associated with the enslavement of the Jews by Tyre, Sidon, and Philistia. See Darwin T. Turner, ed., *Cane: An Authoritative Text, Backgrounds, Criticism* (New York: Norton, 1988), 30n.

36. W.E.B. Du Bois, "Georgia: Invisible Empire State," *Nation* 120 (January 21, 1925): 65. Also see Du Bois's review of *Cane*: "The Younger Literary Movement," *Crisis* 27 (February 1924): 161–63. Although he praised *Cane*, Du Bois complained of the author's modernist obscurity: "I cannot . . . see why Toomer could not have made the tragedy of Carma something I could understand instead of vaguely guess at." He answered this objection himself in his remarks on Georgia two years later.

37. Maggie Kilgour, *The Rise of the Gothic Novel* (London: Routledge, 1995), 32.

Chapter 7: *Cane* in the City

1. Jean Toomer, "York Beach," in Alfred Kreymborg, Lewis Mumford, and Paul Rosenfeld, eds., *The New American Caravan* (New York: Macaulay Company, 1929), 18. Toomer's characterization of New York occurs in the context of a wish for "the perfect place"; New York is not perfect, but by implication it is the best place he has found. Also see Cynthia Earl Kerman and Richard Eldridge, *The Lives of Jean Toomer: A Hunger for Wholeness* (1987; reprint, Baton Rouge: Louisiana State University Press, 1989), 178.

2. Constance McLaughlin Green, *The Secret City: A History of Race Relations in the Nation's Capital* (Princeton, N.J.: Princeton University Press, 1967), 120–21. Willard B. Gatewood, Jr., *Aristocrats of Color: The Black Elite, 1880–1920* (Bloomington: Indiana University Press, 1990), 23–29, 332–35. Kevin K. Gaines, *Uplifting the Race: Black Leadership, Politics, and Culture in the Twentieth Century* (Chapel Hill: University of North Carolina Press, 1996), chapters 3, 6, and 7.

3. Constance McLaughlin Green, *Secret City*, 207. Willard B. Gatewood, Jr., *Aristocrats of Color*, 161–70. For the M Street High School protest, see Green, *Secret City*, 174. Toomer went to M Street High School (later renamed for Paul Laurence Dunbar), "the leading academically elite, all-black public high school in Washington

from its establishment in 1870 until it was integrated in 1955." James M. Goode, *Capital Losses: A Cultural History of Washington's Destroyed Buildings* (Washington, D.C.: Smithsonian Institution Press, 1979), 404.

4. See Kelly Miller, "Howard: The National Negro University," in Alain Locke, ed., *The New Negro* (1925; reprint, New York: Atheneum, 1969), 312–22. For Hughes's criticism of Washington's African-American elite, see "Our Wonderful Society: Washington," *Opportunity* 5 (August 1927): 226–27. In the same issue appeared a defense of Washington society by Brenda Ray Moryck, "I, Too, Have Lived in Washington," 228–31. Also see the discussion in Ronald M. Johnson, "Those Who Stayed: Washington Black Writers of the 1920's," in Francis Coleman Rosenberger, ed., *Records of the Columbia Historical Society of Washington, D.C.: The Fiftieth Volume* (Washington, D.C.: Columbia Historical Society, 1980), 490–98. The process of forming class distinctions around cultural consumption wasn't occurring only among African-American classes, of course. See Lawrence Levine, *Highbrow/Lowbrow: The Emergence of Cultural Hierarchy in America* (Cambridge, Mass.: Harvard University Press, 1988).

5. William H. Jones, *Recreation and Amusement Among Negroes in Washington, D.C.: A Sociological Analysis of the Negro in an Urban Environment* (Washington, D.C.: Howard University Press, 1927) 131, passim.

6. Ibid., 122, 198–99. On the black elite's view of class differentiation as a sign of "evolutionary race progress," see Kevin K. Gaines, *Uplifting the Race*, 20–21.

7. Darwin T. Turner, ed., *The Wayward and the Seeking: A Collection of Writings by Jean Toomer* (Washington, D.C.: Howard University Press, 1982), 155. In the aftermath of the 1919 race riots in Washington, a retired African-American army major, W. H. Loving, offered military intelligence his assessment of "Conditions Among Negroes in Washington," and included a few lines about the city's racial geography: "Washington, unlike other large cities, has two comparatively large 'black belts.' One in the northwest section of the city extending from S Street to V Street going north and from First Street to Fourteenth Street going west. The other is the well known 'blood field' district in the southwest section of the city." Quoted in Lee E. Williams II, *Post-War Riots in America, 1919 and 1946* (Lewiston, N.Y.: Edwin Mellen Press, 1991), 53. A later commentator extends the north–south range of the elite district from M Street to Florida Avenue. See Ronald M. Johnson, "Those Who Stayed," 485. Toomer lived with his grandparents (his grandmother, after Pinchback's death) in an apartment at 1341 U Street, N.W.

8. Darwin T. Turner, ed., *The Wayward and the Seeking*, 155, 141. Washington's Masonic Temple seems to have been a venue for racist speakers, particularly Southern politicians. For a description of a 1913 speech at the temple by Senator James K. Vardaman of Mississippi, see Joel Williamson, *The Crucible of Race: Black-White Relations in the American South Since Emancipation* (New York: Oxford University Press, 1984), 379–80. On segregation of the Lincoln Memorial dedication, see Constance McLaughlin Green, *Secret City*, 199.

9. Darwin T. Turner, *The Wayward and the Seeking*, 250.

10. Ibid., 325.

11. R. C. Bruce to Josephine Bruce, March 16, 1922, quoted in Willard B. Gatewood, Jr., *Aristocrats of Color*, 327; Darwin T. Turner, *The Wayward and the Seeking*, 294–95.

12. William H. Jones, *Recreation and Amusement*, 122.

13. Ibid., 131.

14. Ibid., 133.

15. Ibid., 167–68; 108, 119, 112. The Lincoln Theater was located on U Street, between 12th and 13th, probably within a block or two of Toomer's apartment in 1922.

The Howard was at 620 T Street, no more than 8 or 10 blocks distant. U Street at that time was the commercial center of the African-American district in northwest Washington. See Mark Tucker, *Ellington: The Early Years* (Urbana: University of Illinois Press, 1991), 11, 69, 5.

16. Jean Toomer, *Cane* (1923; reprint, New York: Harper & Row, 1969), 21 (hereafter all citations to *Cane* will come from this edition and will appear in the text). John Milton, *Areopagitica*, in *Prose Works*, ed. Merritt Y. Hughes (New York: Odyssey Press, 1947), 223. For optimistic readings of "Song of the Son" in terms of Toomer's relationship to the South, see Farah Jasmine Griffin, *"Who Set You Flowin'?": The African-American Migration Narrative* (New York: Oxford University Press, 1995), 148; Charles T. Davis, "Jean Toomer and the South: Region and Race as Elements within a Literary Imagination," *Studies in the Literary Imagination* 7 (Fall 1974): 30-31.

17. Matthew 23:13, 27; Acts 23:3. One of the legends, true or not, which grew up about black resistance to white attacks during the Washington riots of 1919 was that at a moment of crisis bootleggers from the "Blood Plain" ghetto in the southwest of the city went to the aid of the small, upper-class black district in the northwest armed with guns and ammunition. See W. H. Loving's memorandum, quoted in Williams, *Post-War Riots*, 53-54.

18. M. H. Abrams, *Natural Supernaturalism: Tradition and Revolution in Romantic Literature* (New York: Norton, 1971), 39.

19. By implication, it might be added, Toomer is repeating Tocqueville's point that a society that sets up a "monument" to law is in danger of misunderstanding its own foundations: "The government of the Union depends almost entirely upon legal fictions; the Union is an ideal nation, which exists, so to speak, only in the mind." Quoted in Robert A. Ferguson, *Law and Letters in American Literature* (Cambridge, Mass.: Harvard University Press, 1984), 10.

20. According to William H. Jones's *Recreation and Amusement Among Negroes in Washington, D.C.*, the drill competition between Armstrong and Dunbar high schools was the "crowning event of the school year," an exercise Jones saw as the proper kind of entertainment for Washington's black elite, instilling "patriotism" and "a high degree of *espirit de corps*" in the participants and a sense of common cause in the class-oriented spectators (81, 83). Dunbar, of course, was Toomer's alma mater (originally M Street High School).

21. See Charles Scruggs, "Textuality and Vision in Jean Toomer's *Cane*," *Les Cahiers de la nouvelle* 10 (Spring 1988): 104-9. The Capitol's setting within the city was also to be symbolic, "the city's most dominating monument." Although Pierre L'Enfant's geometrical plans for the city were never precisely followed, the Capitol's placement within this urban scheme was realized: "a gridiron arrangement of streets cut by diagonal avenues radiating from the capitol and white house." See *Columbia Encyclopedia* (New York: Columbia University Press, 1963), 338, 2291. In other words, the Capitol and the White House were to be at the center of a circle, with the White House a symbol of the practical seat of government and the Capitol a symbol of its theoretical center: a world of law that guided the ship of state. The symbolism of Washington's official architecture was never without controversy. See Vivien Green Fryd, *Art and Empire: The Politics of Ethnicity in the United States Capitol, 1815-1860* (New Haven: Yale University Press, 1992). Fryd notes that "the virtual absence of blacks and slavery in the Capitol decoration before the Civil War is no accident, but instead resulted from conscious efforts to avoid the very issue that threatened national unity. Ironically, attempts to keep references to slavery out of the Capitol are often connected to images of justice and liberty, which embellished the building" (177). One image of liberty that was to adorn the Statue of Freedom on top of the Capitol dome was the liberty cap of the French Revolution; the cap,

however, was replaced by the militant headdress of Minerva when Jefferson Davis insisted that "armed Liberty wear a helmet" since "her conflict [is] over, her cause triumphant" (193). As Fryd says, "Davis used his position as the person in charge of the Capitol extension between 1853 and 1857 to reject any potential anti-slavery implications" (189).

22. James Baldwin, *The Fire Next Time* (New York: Dial Press, 1964), 59: "In the same way that we, for white people, were the descendants of Ham, and were cursed forever, white people were, for us, the descendants of Cain." Also see Charles Scruggs, "The Mark of Cain and the Redemption of Art: A Study in the Theme and Structure of Jean Toomer's *Cane*," *American Literature* 44 (May 1972), 276–91. Soldiers' Home was established in the 1850s "to provide housing and care for disabled or infirm army veterans." A house on the grounds used by Abraham Lincoln as a summer retreat was where he wrote the final version of the Emancipation Proclamation. James M. Goode, *Capital Losses*, 305–6. Kerman and Eldridge have "Avey" set on Meridian Hill rather than at Soldiers' Home. See *The Lives of Jean Toomer*, 74. Toomer calls it "Soldier's Home" in "Avey."

23. Tony Tanner, *Adultery and the Novel: Contract and Transgression* (Baltimore: Johns Hopkins University Press, 1979), 19, 21, 22. Waldo Frank uses the phrase "illumined city" to refer to the two lovers in his translation of Jules Romains's *Lucienne* (New York: Boni & Liveright, 1925), 122. The "ghost ship" of the story's ending also echoes the opening of Melville's "Benito Cereno" and probably Melville's poem, "The Conflict of Convictions," in *Battle-Pieces*, about the construction of the Capitol dome. See Alan Trachtenberg, *Reading American Photographs: Images as History, Mathew Brady to Walker Evans* (New York: Hill and Wang, 1989), 113–14.

24. Lewis Mumford, *The Culture of Cities* (New York: Harcourt Brace Jovanovich, 1938), 40. Mumford's ideas have continued to be important in American urban studies. See, for example, Edgar Relph, *Place and Placelessness* (London: Pion Limited, 1976); Richard Sennett, *The Fall of Public Man* (New York: Knopf, 1977); Yi-Fu Tuan, *Segmented Worlds and Self: Group Life and Individual Consciousness* (Minneapolis: University of Minnesota Press, 1982).

25. James Borchert, *Alley Life in Washington: Family, Community, Religion, and Folklife in the City: 1850–1970* (Urbana: University of Illinois Press, 1980), 42. One of W.E.B. Du Bois's Atlanta University Studies, *The Negro American Family* (1908; reprint, Cambridge, Mass.: MIT Press, 1970), 58–64, discusses black alley life in Southern cities largely in terms of the pathological; but in contrast to William Jones, Du Bois concentrates on the material poverty of the black masses instead of their "social disorganization." As Toomer was writing the middle part of *Cane*, Ernest Howard Culbertson published his popular play of black alley life in Washington, *Goat Alley: A Tragedy of Negro Life* (Cincinnati: Stewart Kidd, 1922). The introduction was written by Ludwig Lewisohn.

26. James Borchert, *Alley Life in Washington*, 113.

27. William Empson, *Some Versions of the Pastoral* (1935; reprint, New York: New Directions, 1968); Raymond Williams, *The Country and the City* (New York: Oxford University Press, 1973), chapter 3. The germ of the distinction between rural and urban lies in Friedrich Von Schiller's distinction between "naive" and "sentimental" poetry. See his *Naive and Sentimental Poetry and On the Sublime: Two Essays*, trans. Julius A. Ellas (New York: Frederick Ungar, 1966), 148–49.

28. Mark Tucker says that "by 1920 the Howard Theater had become a focal point of activity for Washington musicians." The young Duke Ellington played there, along with his future drummer, Sonny Greer, and trombonist Juan Tizol. The Poodle Dog was a cafe and cabaret that opened in 1920 at Seventh Street and Florida Avenue, around the corner from the Howard Theater. Ellington also played

there, and named his first musical composition "Poodle Dog Rag" after the cabaret. Ellington, born in 1899 in the northwest section of Washington, came from a middle-class background rather than the mulatto elite. Mark Tucker, *Ellington*, 65–67, 34. At the Howard Toomer no doubt met the orchestra leader Will Marion Cook (who would also befriend Ellington and help introduce him to the New York music scene); Cook was the subject of Toomer's enthusiastic letter to Waldo Frank in which he concluded that Cook "is the only person within the negroid segment of this country who has touched me to artistic love, even to reverence." Tucker notes that Cook played the Howard on January 22–28, 1923, with Sidney Bechet in his orchestra (p. 75). See Jean Toomer to Waldo Frank, undated letter (circa February 1923), Special Collections, Van Pelt Library, University of Pennsylvania (hereafter cited as Waldo Frank Papers).

29. For an interesting parallel to Toomer's view of chorus girls, see Siegfried Kracauer, "The Mass Ornament," *New German Critique* 5 (Spring 1975): 67–76. Kracauer's essay was originally published in the *Frankfurter Zeitung* in June 1927.

30. Jean Toomer to Gorham Munson, March 23, 1923, October 31, 1922, Jean Toomer Papers, Yale Collection of American Literature, Beinecke Rare Book and Manuscript Library, Yale University (hereafter cited as Jean Toomer Papers).

31. In 1929 Duke Ellington recorded his own composition, "The Dicty Glide"; four years later, in a short article for a British music magazine, he explained that "every one of my song titles is taken from . . . the life of Harlem." He went on to say that "a 'swanky' person is known in America as 'ritzy,' in Harlem as 'dicty,' and this was the basis of my *Dicty Glide*. Of course, a large part of the meaning is conveyed not only by the music and singing, but by the dance itself, for which certain steps fitting to the rhythm should be used. A lofty carriage is needed for this particular dance." Interestingly, Ellington recorded his "Stevedore Stomp" at the same 1929 session. An early Ellington band member, saxophonist Otto Hardwick, described their breakthrough to high-paying venues as booking "a lot of 'dicty' jobs . . . an embassy or private mansion." "Dicty" (or "dictie," in Toomer's usage), then, wasn't merely middle class. It wasn't the vernacular only in Harlem, either, though whether or not it would have been heard in "Sempter, Georgia" (Toomer's other use of the word is by a woman at Barlo's good-time house [p. 47]) seems uncertain. Gatewood cites Marcus Garvey's references to "upper-class blacks" as "'dicties' or 'dickties,' a term that had become popular by 1920." See Peter Gammond, *Duke Ellington* (London: Apollo Press, 1987), 90; Duke Ellington, "My Hunt for Song Titles," in Mark Tucker, ed., *The Duke Ellington Reader* (New York: Oxford University Press, 1993), 87–89; Mark Tucker, *Ellington*, 56. Willard B. Gatewood, Jr., *Aristocrats of Color*, 321.

32. Darwin T. Turner, ed., *The Wayward and the Seeking*, 43.

33. Toomer submitted "Calling Jesus" to the *Double Dealer*, where John McClure wanted to publish it but was afraid of offending his patrons with religious satire. He eventually ran it with the title "Nora." See John McClure to Jean Toomer, July 5, 1922, and August 14, 1922, Jean Toomer Papers. "Nora" was published in *Double Dealer* 4 (September 1922).

34. William H. Jones, *Recreation and Amusement*, 119; Jones also says of the Lincoln Colonnade (a dance hall located "in the basement of the Lincoln Theater"): "Most of the college fraternities give open and closed affairs here, as do also the various clubs and prominent social leaders" (125). In contrast, vaudeville specialized in "freaks." For instance, "a typical listing of vaudeville acts in the early 1900's included such intriguing names as Burke's juggling dogs, the imperial Japs, the Piccolo midgets, the Zat Zams, Muslinger's Pigs, Drako's Sheep and Goats." In the nineteenth century, minstrelsy—vaudeville's most direct ancestor—often featured

"African" dwarves, the most famous of whom was "Japanese Tommy." See Douglas Gilbert, *American Vaudeville: Its Life and Times* (New York: McGraw-Hill, 1940), 246–47; John E. DiMeglio, *Vaudeville, U.S.A.* (Bowling Green, Ohio: Bowling Green University Popular Press, 1973), 30; Robert C. Toll, *Blacking Up: The Minstrel Show in Nineteenth-Century America* (New York: Oxford University Press, 1974), 136–37, 197–98.

35. For the literary use of the Moses joke, see Mark Twain, *Huckleberry Finn* (1884; reprint, New York: Washington Square Press, 1973), 127; James Joyce, *Ulysses: Annotated Students' Edition* (1922; reprint, New York: Penguin Books, 1992), 860. The phrase "black vaudeville" was picked up frequently by early reviewers of *Cane*, and may have been originally supplied either by Toomer himself or by Waldo Frank. See Box 26, Folder 612, Jean Toomer Papers.

36. Jean Toomer to Waldo Frank, undated letter (circa January 1923), Waldo Frank Papers.

37. One theory as to why the leper came to be thought of as "unclean" in Western civilization is that his or her condition was a kind of miscegenation, a "confusion of proper boundaries": "The leper would be taboo in that sense as someone of mixed dead and living flesh." See Gilbert Lewis, "A Lesson from Leviticus: Leprosy," *Man: The Journal of the Royal Anthropological Institute* 22 (December 1987): 607. Also see Judith Halberstam, *Skin Shows: Gothic Horror and the Technology of Monsters* (Durham, N.C.: Duke University Press, 1995): "The Gothic monster . . . as a creature of mixed blood, breaks down the very categories that constitute class, sexual, and racial difference" (78).

38. Michel Foucault notes that the leper was an ambiguous figure in the Middle Ages, an expression of both God's "anger and His grace," because his pariahood made him a type of Christ. See *Madness and Civilization: A History of Insanity in the Age of Reason*, trans. Richard Howard (1965; reprint, New York: Random House, 1973), 6, 7.

39. One of the sketches Waldo Frank thought less successful in the original batch of manuscripts he saw was titled "Dan"; a probable source of the revised "Box Seat" is in Frank's *City Block*. In the story "John the Baptist," Karl Loer reads "wisdom and godliness" into a group of outcasts in the park, one of them a black dwarf. None of these grotesques is a type of Christ; rather, they shift the focus away from themselves and onto Loer when a bearded man, whom Loer has said looks like a "ridiculous Jesus," claims to be "John the Baptist." The scoffing intellectual becomes Christlike through his spontaneous empathy for life's grotesques, and Frank sees Loer as a means by which the city of law might be redefined as the city of *caritas*. See Waldo Frank, *City Block* (Darien, Conn.: self-published, 1922), 139–165.

40. For two treatments of successful call-and-response patterns that critics have found in *Cane*, see Barbara E. Bowen, "Untroubled Voice: Call-and-Response in *Cane*," *Black American Literature Forum* 16 (Spring 1982): 12–18; John Callahan, *In the African-American Grain: The Pursuit of Voice in Twentieth-Century Black Literature* (Urbana: University of Illinois Press, 1988), 62–144.

41. Carl Sandburg, *The Complete Poems of Carl Sandburg* (New York: Harcourt, Brace, 1970), 85. When Jean Toomer wrote *The Blue Meridian*, of course, Chicago again became the city of the idealized new American of the "Beloved Community."

42. William Jones devoted chapter 14 of his book on Negro amusements to "Negroes Who Pass for White" in Washington, D.C., attempting to identify different motives for passing and to summarize the social consequences of the practice. Jones said a primary reason for passing was to have access to white cultural venues ("gaining contact with the most advanced phases of modern social life"), yet he was

critical of the "class of mulattoes" who "desire to escape from the Negro group." William H. Jones, *Recreation and Amusement Among Negroes*, 147–52.

43. Robert Bone points out the allusion to the Apostle Paul in *Down Home: A History of Afro-American Short Fiction from Its Beginnings to the End of the Harlem Renaissance* (New York: G. P. Putnam's Sons, 1975), 227.

44. Constance Green says that in Washington, "passing was so common in the twenties that the National Theatre employed a black doorman to spot and bounce intruders whose racial origins were undetectable by whites." Constance McLaughlin Green, *The Secret City*, 207. When Toomer wrote directly on the matter of passing in his unpublished 1928 essay "The Crock of Problems," he was as critical of the practice as William H. Jones, though for different reasons. Toomer thought the "great psychic strain" of passing damaged the individual, and he also said that he had "never tried to pass." Of course, the theory of the cosmopolitan culture could not always be put into social practice. In "Bona and Paul," Paul shows all the signs of "psychic strain" in the episode at the Crimson Gardens. In 1932, after his marriage to Margery Latimer, Toomer would be subjected to the agony of "his past life come up to betray him." Robert B. Jones, ed., *Jean Toomer: Selected Essays and Literary Criticism* (Knoxville: University of Tennessee Press, 1996), 57–58.

Chapter 8: The Black Man in the Cellar

1. Terry Eagleton, "Theydunnit," *London Review of Books*, April 28, 1994, 12. W. H. Auden, "The Guilty Vicarage," *Harper's* 196 (May 1948): 406–12. Much of the critical writing on *Cane* describes the book in terms of a neat tripartite structure. Both Robert Bone and Todd Lieber, for instance, see parts 1 and 2 as point and counterpoint, with "Kabnis" as the concluding section. Bernard Bell imposes a Hegelian pattern: part 1 is "thesis," part 2 is "antithesis," and part 3 is "synthesis." See Robert Bone, *The Negro Novel in America*, rev. ed. (New Haven: Yale University Press, 1965), 82–89; Todd Lieber, "Design and Movement in *Cane*," *CLA Journal* 13 (September 1969), 35–50; Bernard Bell, "A Key to the Poems of *Cane*," in *Jean Toomer: A Critical Evaluation* (Washington, D.C.: Howard University Press, 1988), 322.

2. Jean Toomer to Waldo Frank, December 12, 1922, Jean Toomer Papers, Yale Collection of American Literature, Beinecke Rare Book and Manuscript Library, Yale University (hereafter referred to as Jean Toomer Papers). The letter is printed in Darwin T. Turner, ed., *Cane: An Authoritative Text, Backgrounds, Criticism* (New York: Norton, 1988), 152 (hereafter referred to as Turner, ed., *Cane*). At the end of *Our America*, Frank reveals the meaning of America that he had promised his French friends in the book's introductory chapter—an America whose origins had been hidden. This process of revelation uncovers a pattern suggested by the epigraph from *The Dark Mother*: "She is Flesh moving through Flesh. She is Spirit." The "Flesh" of American materialism begins with the Revolution ("the triumph of the capitalistic state"), culminates in the Industrial Revolution, and ends with the disillusionment of World War I. The book's ending insists that true revolution has been delayed until now: "in a dying world, creation is revolution." Waldo Frank, *The Dark Mother* (New York: Boni & Liveright, 1920), title page. Idem, *Our America* (New York: Boni & Liveright, 1919), 3–4, 14, 232, 230. Idem, *City Block* (Darien, Conn.: self-published, 1922); idem, *Rahab* (New York: Boni & Liveright, 1922).

3. Jean Toomer, *Cane* (1923; reprint, New York: Harper & Row, 1969), 2, 204, 239 (hereafter all references to *Cane* are from this edition and appear in the text). In critiquing the rectangular plan of America's city streets, Frank would argue in

1925 that "Nature likes curves," implying that modern art should also reject the linear narrative. For Frank, the curve is "God's favorite architectural design," and the circle is an expression of a "mystical prefiguration of eternity" in that it "cannot exhaust itself, because each step forward is an approach to the beginning." Frank would reiterate this idea in his critique of Oswald Spengler's *Decline of the West*, where he argued that within "a series each integer is at once the conclusion of what came before and the outset of an infinity beyond." Waldo Frank, "Straight Streets," in *In the American Jungle (1925–1936)* (New York: Farrar & Rinehart, 1937), 123. Also see Robert Perry, *The Shared Vision of Waldo Frank and Hart Crane* (Lincoln: University of Nebraska Press, 1966), 45–50. Waldo Frank, *Virgin Spain* (Boni & Liveright, 1926), 42; also see Perry, *Shared Vision*, 47–50. Waldo Frank, "Reflections on Spengler," in *In the American Jungle*, 201.

4. Jean Toomer to Waldo Frank, undated letter (circa January 1923), Jean Toomer Papers. Focusing on this "spiritual entity," some critics have tried to read *Cane* as a spiritual autobiography: as a "search for wholeness" or as "a spiritual odyssey." Two books that have recently taken this approach are Rudolph P. Byrd, *Jean Toomer's Years with Gurdjieff: Portrait of an Artist, 1923–1936* (Athens: University of Georgia, 1990), 15–16; and Robert B. Jones, *Jean Toomer and the Prison-House of Thought: A Phenomenology of the Spirit* (Amherst: University of Massachusetts Press, 1993), 49–50.

5. Jean Toomer to Georgia O'Keeffe, January 13, 1924, Jean Toomer Papers.

6. It is possible that the word "awakening" in Toomer's description of the book's circular form alludes to Sherwood Anderson's story in *Winesburg, Ohio* called "An Awakening." In Anderson's story, George Willard also expresses a oneness with the universe on the night he goes to meet Belle Carpenter, feeling "oddly detached" (especially from the working-class neighborhood he walks through) and uttering "brave words, full of meaning . . . 'Death . . . night, the sea, fear, loveliness.' " But this fusion of opposites is suddenly terminated when he discovers that Belle has used him for her own ends, an ironic epiphany similar to Paul's after he utters his own "brave words" and awakens to find Bona gone. Sherwood Anderson, *Winesburg, Ohio* (1919; reprint, New York: Penguin Books, 1982), 185.

7. W. H. Auden, "The Guilty Vicarage," 408. For another consideration of the conflict between pastoral or "nature" and history in *Cane*, see Vera M. Kutzinski, "Unseasonal Flowers: Nature and History in Placido and Jean Toomer," *Yale Journal of Criticism* 3 (Spring 1990): 153–79.

8. Kari J. Winter, *Subjects of Slavery, Agents of Change: Women and Power in Gothic Novels and Slave Narratives, 1790–1865* (Athens: University of Georgia Press, 1992), 99. Orlando Patterson, *Slavery and Social Death: A Comparative Study* (Cambridge, Mass.: Harvard University Press, 1982), 1–14; Karl Marx, "The Eighteenth Brumaire of Louis Bonaparte," in *The Marx-Engels Reader*, ed. Robert C. Tucker (New York: Norton, 1972), 437.

9. In *Ezra Pound: The Image and the Real* (Baton Rouge: Louisiana State University Press, 1969), Herbert N. Schneidau quotes Pound as saying that imagism has "nothing to do with image-making" (48). Rather, the image as an "intellectual and emotional complex in an instant of time" must strike the reader with the luminosity of insight. See especially chapter 2: "Hulme versus Fenollosa." For an account of Toomer's interest in, and indebtedness to, imagism, see Robert B. Jones and Margery Toomer Latimer, eds., *The Collected Poems of Jean Toomer* (Chapel Hill: University of North Carolina Press, 1988), ix–xiii; and Robert B. Jones, *Jean Toomer and the Prison-House of Thought*, 11–12, 21–27.

10. Toomer's letters to both Waldo Frank and Kenneth Burke often deal with philosophical questions as well as aesthetic ones. One question in particular that

fascinated Toomer was the relationship of "experience" to "essence." Toomer wanted to believe in Burke's aphorism that "Wisdom is the circle we take in getting back to the starting point [essence]," but, as he said to Burke in a letter, he found no way of reconciling the "multiplicity" one was fated to learn from experience with the simplicity of "essence" that Burke believed framed the beginning and end of life. See correspondence between Kenneth Burke and Jean Toomer, circa 1923–24, Jean Toomer Papers; also see Mark Helbling, "Jean Toomer and Waldo Frank: Creative Friendship," in Therman B. O'Daniel, ed., *Jean Toomer: A Critical Evaluation* (Washington, D.C.: Howard University Press, 1988), 88–89.

11. Ralph Ellison, *Invisible Man* (1952; reprint, New York: Random House, 1972), 345–46.

12. The "spectatorial artist" is Gorham Munson's coinage for Toomer's persistent presence in *Cane* as an observer. See his "The Significance of Jean Toomer," *Opportunity* 3 (September 1925): 263. Also see Susan Blake, "The Spectatorial Artist and the Structure of *Cane*," in *Jean Toomer: A Critical Evaluation*, 95–211. Blake argues that the movement in *Cane* is from "spectator" to "artist," but she does not consider the significance of the witness in this process. Kenneth Burke, *Grammar of Motives* (1945; reprint, Berkeley: University of California Press, 1969), 219.

13. Kate Ferguson Ellis, *The Contested Castle: Gothic Novels and the Subversion of Domestic Ideology* (Urbana: University of Illinois Press, 1989), 3. Ellis argues that the castle in Gothic fiction is a metaphor for contested domestic space, but that (white) male and female authors use this symbol for different ends. For male authors, the castle became the place in which female influence was replaced by a masculine rule of shame and honor, while the genre allowed women authors to depict real dangers, albeit encoded in a formula that returned their female characters to the safety of the middle-class domicile. But these conventions don't necessarily work for African-Americans who are not given the assurance of maintaining honor or even finding a safe domicile.

14. Norman N. Holland and Leona F. Sherman, "Gothic Possibilities," *New Literary History* 8 (Winter 1977): 282.

15. Michel Foucault, *Discipline and Punish: The Birth of the Prison*, trans. Alan Sheridan (1975; reprint, New York: Random House, 1979), chapter 2.

16. Mame Lamkins was based on Mary Turner, who was lynched on May 17, 1918, in Brooks and Lowndes Counties, Georgia. Walter White described the grisly details of the death and that of her baby in his article "The Work of the Mob," *Crisis* 16 (September 1918): 222. Another contemporary account of the murders appeared in Stephen Graham, *Children of the Slaves* (London: Macmillan, 1920), 205–7. An English traveler, Graham put the lynchers "on a lower level than cannibals."

17. Foucault argues that Western civilization discovered more effective means than "theatrics" to "discipline" and "punish," and his thesis has a particular application to *Cane*. Beginning in the eighteenth century, "surveillance" would replace "spectacle" as the way in which social control would be achieved—a "modality" rather than an event. Here the faceless gaze of the panopticon is the key metaphor for the dystopian ideal of the "carceral society"—that is, a society modeled on the prison. Indeed, control of the "soul" through the "omnipresent surveillence" of the body becomes the ultimate objective whereby physical punishment per se is less important than its "representation" or the "play of signs" around it. See Michel Foucault, *Discipline and Punish*, 95, 214, 217. The idea of punishment becomes more terrifying than its visual display; the idea of the incarcerated prisoner whose sufferings are hidden but imagined becomes a more arresting figure than the mutilated victim of the "spectacle." Or rather, the two together create an atmosphere of fear

and "discipline" that permeates the social body. Foucault suggests how Toomer's conception of the "grotesque" differs from that of Sherwood Anderson—the difference between social pressure and social terror.

18. Quoted by Kari J. Winter, *Subjects of Slavery, Agents of Change*, 18. Walter Benjamin, "On Some Motifs in Baudelaire," in *Illuminations*, trans. Harry Zohn (New York: Schocken Books, 1969), 188. In a sense, Toomer has anticipated Emmanuel Levinas's idea that the human face penetrates "beyond the *logos*" to a racial "memory" that transcends history. For Levinas, the "nakedness of the face that faces" calls into question the social order—its conception of justice, its hierarchical rankings, its verbal discourses. See Robert Bernasconi and David Wood, eds., *The Provocation of Levinas: Rethinking the Other* (London: Routledge, 1988), 63, 150, 169, 171, 76: "The face is fundamental, a notion beyond thought." Also see Emmanuel Levinas, *Collected Philosophical Papers*, trans. Alphonso Lingis (Dordrecht/Boston/Lancaster: Martinus Nijhoff Publishers, 1987), 55, 57–59, 65: "The epiphany of the face is wholly language." See Emmanuel Levinas, *Time and the Other*, trans. Richard A. Cohen (Pittsburgh: Duquesne University Press, 1987), 18–19, 105–14.

19. "The storyteller takes what he tells from experience—his own or that reported by others. And he in turn makes it the experience of those who are listening to his tale." Walter Benjamin, "The Storyteller," in *Illuminations*, 87. Shoshana Felman and Dori Laub, *Testimony: Crises of Witnessing in Literature, Psychoanalysis, and History* (New York: Routledge, 1992), 101, 204.

20. Walter Benjamin, "The Storyteller," in *Illuminations*, 89, 93, 98.

21. On "historical amnesia," see Nina Silber, *The Romance of Reunion: Northerners and the South, 1865–1900* (Chapel Hill: University of North Carolina Press, 1993), 156. Shoshana Felman and Dori Laub, *Testimony*, 270. Felman and Laub say that Camus's *The Plague* had attempted "to testify from the perspective of the honest witness, and whose narrative [hoped] to transmit a clear *picture* of events, a visual, coherent, legible representation of the Holocaust. But *The Fall* suggests that no one can legitimately claim the ownership or the possession of such a picture: we can only contemplate its trace, acknowledge that we are living, in its absence, on its *site*: 'the site of one of the greatest crimes in history'" (195).

22. See Charles Scruggs, "The Mark of Cain and the Redemption of Art: A Study in Theme and Structure of Jean Toomer's *Cane*," *American Literature* 44 (May 1972): 276–91.

23. Genesis: 4:22. Tubal Cain is "the forger of all instruments of bronze and iron." See Lord Byron, *Cain*, ed. Truman Guy Steffan (Austin: University of Texas Press, 1968). Byron's theme of the sins of the parents being visited upon the children would have appealed to Toomer, as would the Cain Byron created: the poet as rebel, the rebel as a defeated Faust. Moreover, Kabnis's own anger against the metaphysical order bears a striking similarity to Cain's verbal attack on a bloodthirsty deity: "*His pleasure!* What was his pleasure in / The fumes of scorching flesh and smoking blood, / To the pain of the bleating mothers which / Still yearn for their dead offspring?" (243). Stephen Dedalus, too, sees himself as Cain, fleeing Ireland in Joyce's *Portrait* to "forge in the smithy of his soul the uncreated conscience of his race," only to return to his native land in *Ulysses* and become overwhelmed by the nightmare of history. For commentary on Bessie Smith's version of the vaudeville song, see Hayden Carruth, "Good Old Wagon," *Antaeus* 71/72 (Fall 1993): 140–145. On literacy as a class marker for the Talented Tenth, see Evelyn Brooks Higginbotham, *Righteous Discontent: The Women's Movement in the Black Baptist Church, 1880–1920* (Cambridge, Mass.: Harvard University Press, 1993), 43–45.

24. Walter Benjamin, "The Storyteller," in *Illuminations*, 84. Lewis seems a combination of an idealized Jean Toomer and a realistic portrait of Walter White, the man

who investigated lynchings for the NAACP. Toomer is alluding here to a famous peonage case in 1921 in Jasper County, Georgia. Investigation of John S. Williams's plantation not only uncovered a brutal peonage system but nine hidden gravesites, the latter discovery making the pages of every major newspaper throughout the South. It was not, however, mentioned in the *Sparta Ishmaelite*. For an account of the incident and the trial, see Pete Daniel, *The Shadow of Slavery: Peonage in the South, 1901–1969* (Urbana: University of Illinois Press, 1972), 110–31. Toomer could not have known in 1921 that the campaign against lynching would eventually end this practice in the rural South, though it also seems apparent that in the 1930s "legal" executions of African-Americans merely replaced illegal lynching.

25. Box 48, Folder 999, Jean Toomer Papers, printed in Frederik L. Rusch, ed., *A Jean Toomer Reader* (New York: Oxford University Press, 1993), 84. For a discussion of a possible mutual influence between Toomer and O'Neill, see Robert Cooperman, "Unacknowledged Familiarity: Jean Toomer and Eugene O'Neill," *Eugene O'Neill Review* 16 (Spring 1992): 39–47.

26. Brom Weber, ed. *The Complete Poems and Selected Letters and Prose of Hart Crane* (New York: Liveright, 1966), 4. Also, see Victor A. Kramer, "The 'Mid-Kingdom' of Crane's 'Black Tambourine' and Jean Toomer's *Cane*," in *Jean Toomer: An Evaluation*, 121–31.

27. Ralph Ellison, *Invisible Man*, 560. Elizabeth Anne Scruggs reminded us of the subversive nature of Aesop's stories.

28. John Irwin noted a connection between the black man, Aesop, and Crane, mirrored later in *The Bridge* when "floating niggers" become the "floating singer." Thus the Invisible Man's emergence from his cellar at the end of *Invisible Man* could be interpreted not as a subversive rereading of Crane's text but as an interpretation of it. See John Irwin, "Hart Crane's *The Bridge* I," *Raritan* (Spring 1989): 82–85. Crane's cellar, of course, still remains problematic. Although his biographer, John Unterecker, insists that he did not want his poem "to be limited to a single 'meaning,'" Crane himself, in explaining the metaphor to Munson, tended to focus on its sociological implications: "I find the negro (in the popular mind) sentimentally or brutally 'placed' in this midkingdom." See John Unterecker, *Voyager: A Life of Hart Crane* (New York: Farrar, Straus and Giroux, 1969), 191. For Frank's influence on Crane, see *Voyager*, 277–81, and passim.

29. The exchange between Kabnis and Carrie K. is thus additional confirmation of the "call and response" pattern that Barbara Bowen and John Callahan perceive in *Cane*. See Barbara E. Bowen, "Untroubled Voice: Call-and-Response in *Cane*," *Black American Literature Forum* 16 (Spring 1982): 12–18; John Callahan, *In the African-American Grain: The Pursuit of Voice in Twentieth-Century Black Fiction* (Urbana: University of Illinois Press, 1988), 63–113.

30. This may partly explain the appeal that Goethe's *Wilhelm Meister* (which he read before 1920) held for Toomer. He claimed in his 1932 biography that Goethe's portrait of "the aristocrat of culture" was the theme that had appealed to him, but a theme equally important to the novel involves the twin movements of "regeneration and recurrence," or "circularity and progress." In the "Hall of the Past," Wilhelm shouts, "This is how everything was, and this is how everything will be. Nothing perishes except him who observes and enjoys." See Darwin T. Turner, ed., *The Wayward and the Seeking*, 112; Thomas P. Saine, "Was *Meister* To Be a Bildungsroman?" and Michael Minden, "The Place of Inheritance in the Bildungsroman," in James Hardin, ed., *Reflection and Action: Essays on the Bildungsroman* (Columbia: University of South Carolina Press, 1991), 134, 235. For the discussion of a similar question of "circularity and progress," see "Hope in the Past: On Walter Benjamin," in Peter Szondi, *On Textual Understanding and Other Essays*, trans. Harvey Mendel-

sohn (Minneapolis: University of Minnesota Press, 1986), 145–59. The ambiguous circularity of *Cane* also illustrates the "space-logic" that Joseph Frank called modernist. Rereading *Cane* in terms of "snapshots" suspended in time means that "past and present are seen spatially, locked in a timeless unity which, while it may accentuate surface differences, eliminates any feeling of historical sequence by the very act of juxtaposition." But if "spatial form" obliterates those distinctions between past and present, then slavery and its attendant horrors may continually reappear; this is not a means of escaping history but of emphasizing its continued presence. See Joseph Frank, "Spatial Form in Modern Literature," *Sewanee Review* 53 (April 1945): 229, 234–35; idem, "Spatial Form in Modern Literature," *Sewanee Review* 53 (June 1945): 653.

31. Northrop Frye, *The Secular Scripture: A Study of the Structure of Romance* (Cambridge, Mass.: Harvard University Press, 1976), 183. See *Cane*, 2, 207. The "spiral" recalls Pascal's terrifying picture of the universe as an infinite series of concentric circles which "encompasses me and engulfs me *like a point.*" See Georges Poulet, *The Metamorphoses of the Circle*, trans. Carley Dawson and Elliott Coleman (Baltimore: Johns Hopkins University Press, 1966), 39.

32. Toomer's characters not only reflect the "interests" of their class and gender but interact in ways that reflect the "multi-colored leaves" of African-American life. As a member of the new black middle class, the "black-skinned" Hanby is a challenge to the mulatto elite, in a strange way mirroring what Barlo has become as a cotton broker after the war; he is a corrupted representation of Booker T. Washington's "progressive" philosophy, the administrator as power broker. And just as Ralph Ellison would depict the "Founder's" college in *Invisible Man* in terms of the dynamo in the rural garden, so Toomer connects Hanby, as principal of a "progressive" institution like the Agricultural School, with both North and South: "to members of his own race, he affects the manners of a wealthy white planter . . . when he is up North, he lets it be known that his ideas are those of the best New England tradition" (185).

33. John W. Cell, *The Highest Stage of White Supremacy: The Origins of Segregation in South Africa and the American South* (Cambridge: Cambridge University Press, 1982), 170; Randolph Bourne, "The State," in Olaf Hansen, ed., *The Radical Will: Selected Writings, 1911–1918* (New York: Urizen Books, 1977), 381. For a consideration of writing about "the role of the state in establishing and maintaining racial dominance," see George M. Fredrickson, "The South and South Africa: Political Foundations of White Supremacy," in Numan V. Bartley, ed., *The Evolution of Southern Culture* (Athens: University of Georgia Press, 1988), 68–86.

34. Waldo Frank, *Our America*, 210, 228, 92, 230.

35. John T. Irwin, "Foreshadowing and Foreshortening: The Prophetic Vision of Origins in Hart Crane's *The Bridge*," *Word & Image* 1 (July–September 1985): 303. Irwin observes that there is a difference between God's "field" of perception and our own: "Where our field of vision at any given moment is only an arc of a circle, His field of vision at every moment is a sphere."

36. Michel Foucault, *Discipline and Punish*, 221. Toomer wrote an unpublished Gothic short story called "The Eye," which is discussed in detail in Robert B. Jones, *Jean Toomer and the Prison-House of Thought*, 84–92. Orlando Patterson, *Slavery and Social Death*, 3. The idea of the "blues detective," which is implicit in the setting and narrative method of *Cane*, would be developed by other African-American writers. Although he might agree with Albert Murray that the blues detective employs the method of "improvisation" to discover "the source or sources of 'evil,'" Toomer would be skeptical of Murray's insistence that such a discovery keeps chaos at bay. Albert Murray, *The Hero and the Blues* (1973; reprint, New York: Random House,

1995), 99–101. Also see Houston A. Baker, Jr., *Blues, Ideology, and Afro-American Literature: A Vernacular Theory* (Chicago: University of Chicago Press, 1984); Stephen F. Soitos, *The Blues Detective: A Study of African-American Detective Fiction* (Amherst: University of Massachusetts Press, 1996).

Epilogue: "An Incredibly Entangled Situation"

1. Jean Toomer Papers, "Incredible Journey," Box 18, Folder 491, Yale Collection of American Literature, Beinecke Rare Book and Manuscript Library, Yale University (hereafter cited as Jean Toomer Papers).

2. Kevin K. Gaines, *Uplifting the Race: Black Leadership, Politics, and Culture in the Twentieth Century* (Chapel Hill: University of North Carolina Press, 1996), xx.

3. Ibid., 3.

4. Jean Toomer Papers, Box 60, Folder 1413.

5. Jean Toomer, *The Blue Meridian*, in Darwin T. Turner, ed., *The Wayward and the Seeking: A Collection of Writings by Jean Toomer* (Washington, D.C.: Howard University Press, 1980), 223, 229 (hereafter all citations to *The Blue Meridian* will come from this edition and will appear in the text).

6. See our discussion in Chapter 3.

7. Waldo Frank, *The Rediscovery of Man: A Memoir and a Methodology of Modern Life* (New York: George Braziller, 1958), 426.

8. Ibid., 425–26; see also Chapter 4, n. 8. In this late book, Frank specifically mentions "Jean Toomer, the Negro poet" as a follower of Gurdjieff, but he had earlier anticipated, and critiqued, Toomer's flight to Gurdjieffian resolutions. In *Our America* Frank made his crucial distinction between the escapist mysticism of Emerson and the materially rooted mysticism of Whitman. By 1929 Frank knew enough of Gurdjieff to place his movement in Emerson's camp, listing it as a kind of adapted (and debased) Buddhism, by which "soul and its values are cut off from life." Waldo Frank, *The Re-Discovery of America and Chart for Rough Water* (1929; reprint, New York: Duell, Sloan and Pearce, 1947), 300.

9. Langston Hughes, *The Big Sea* (1940; reprint, New York: Hill and Wang, 1963), 241–43; Hughes also satirized Toomer the Gurdjieffian as Eugene Lesche in "Rejuvenation Through Joy," in *The Ways of White Folk* (1934; reprint, New York: Random House, 1990), 69–98. Robert C. Twombly, "A Disciple's Odyssey: Jean Toomer's Gurdjieffian Career," *Prospects: An Annual of American Cultural Studies*, 2 (1976): 448–49. Frederik L. Rusch, ed., *A Jean Toomer Reader: Selected Unpublished Writings* (New York: Oxford University Press, 1993), 103. Kerman and Eldridge refer to Luhan's letter of 1934 requesting repayment of "some money that she [Mabel Dodge Luhan] claimed she had loaned him." However, Luhan's biographer says that in 1926 "Mabel cemented her love [for Toomer] with a loan of $14,000" and cites letters requesting the loan's repayment in 1929 and 1932 as well. She also says that Toomer, in his relations with Luhan, "encouraged her interest and to some extent exploited her feelings." Cynthia Earl Kerman and Richard Eldridge, *The Lives of Jean Toomer: A Hunger for Wholeness* (1987; reprint, Baton Rouge: Louisiana State University Press, 1989), 147; Lois Palken Rudnick, *Mabel Dodge Luhan: New Woman, New Worlds* (Albuquerque: University of New Mexico Press, 1984), 228–29.

10. Jean Toomer, "York Beach," in Alfred Kreymborg, Lewis Mumford, and Paul Rosenfeld, eds., *The New American Caravan: A Yearbook of American Literature* (New York: Macaulay Company, 1929), 80, 81. These passages might remind a reader of Bigger Thomas's similar attraction to Hitler, Mussolini, or Stalin in *Native Son*.

11. Robert C. Twombly, "A Disciple's Odyssey: Jean Toomer's Gurdjieffian Career,"

450. Jean Toomer, "York Beach," 15, 29, 62–76. In a brief memoir of 1941, Toomer remarked on his own reservations in first observing Gurdjieff at work: "He seemed to have everything that could be asked of a developed human being, a teacher, a master. Knowledge, integration, many-sidedness, power—in fact he had a bit too much power for my comfort." "Why I Entered the Gurdjieff Work," in Robert B. Jones, ed., *Jean Toomer: Selected Essays and Literary Criticism* (Knoxville: University of Tennessee Press, 1996), 108.

12. *The Blue Meridian* rewrites from a Gurdjieffian perspective not only *Our America* but also Brooks's *America's Coming-of-Age* (1915) and *Letters and Leadership* (1918). Phrases like "cathedral people," "yeast," "open this pod," and "seed," repeat images first given currency by Brooks in his seminal studies of American culture. It is not by accident that the poem was first published (as *Blue Meridian*) in *The New Caravan* (Alfred Kreymborg, Lewis Mumford, and Paul Rosenfeld, eds. [New York: Norton, 1936], 633–53). Toomer's earlier, shorter version of the poem ("Brown River, Smile," *Pagany*, 3 [Winter 1932]: 29–33) was even more specifically indebted to Frank, Brooks, and Bourne. Walt Whitman, of course, is behind the "locomotive" that initiates the revival in the poem, while its intention and form are specifically indebted to Crane's *The Bridge*.

13. Jean Toomer to Georgia O'Keeffe, January 13, 1924, Jean Toomer Papers; Kenneth Burke, *Rhetoric of Motives* (1950; reprint, Berkeley: University of California Press, 1969), 208.

14. Lewis Mumford, *The Story of Utopias* (New York: Boni & Liveright, 1922), title page. Mumford does not provide the source for his epigraph, which is Oscar Wilde's essay, "The Soul of Man Under Socialism"; in context, the quote reads: "A Map of the world that does not include Utopia is not worth even glancing at, for it leaves out the one country at which Humanity is always landing." Wilde asserts that socialism is one stage along that journey. See *The Selected Essays of Oscar Wilde*, ed. Russell Fraser (Boston: Houghton Mifflin, 1969), 348. Also see Peter Weston, "The Noble Primitive as Bourgeois Subject," in Brian Loughrey, ed., *The Pastoral Mode* (London: Macmillan, 1984), 173: "Marx and Engels argued that the utopian conceptions of society have a value because 'they attack every principle of existing society' and 'correspond with the first instinctive yearnings . . . for a general reconstruction of society.'"

15. William Boelhower, *Through a Glass Darkly: Ethnic Semiosis in American Literature* (Venice: Edizioni Helvetia, 1984), 48, 60–61.

16. Kenneth Burke, *A Grammar of Motives* (1945; reprint, Berkeley: University of California Press, 1969), 87; Kenneth Burke, *Language as Symbolic Action: Essays on Life, Literature, and Method* (Berkeley: University of California Press, 1966), 437; Van Wyck Brooks, *America's Coming-of-Age* (New York: B. W. Huebsch, 1915), reprinted in *Van Wyck Brooks: The Early Years*, ed. Claire Sprague (New York: Harper & Row, 1968), 81–118.

17. This account of the Carmel scandal is based on Robert C. Twombly's "A Disciple's Odyssey: Jean Toomer's Gurdjieffian Career," 454–56; Twombly's sources are a letter from Toomer to Yvonne Dupee, a member of the Portage commune, March 26, 1932; a letter from Margery Latimer to her friend Meridel Le Sueur, March 1932; an interview with Katharine Green, another Portage commune member; and various contemporary newspaper accounts. Kerman and Eldridge give a briefer account, different in detail, but offer no sources except contemporary news reports. See Cynthia Earl Kerman and Richard Eldridge, *The Lives of Jean Toomer*, 201–2. Toomer wrote an unpublished novel called "Caromb" which dealt with this experience. For a short summary of the latter, see Frederik L. Rusch, ed., *A Jean Toomer Reader*, 259–63. Margery Latimer was also disturbed enough to write an

essay about the scandal. She submitted it to *Pagany*, saying: "Since reading, on top of everything, the vulgar article in *Time* about us, I feel more than ever before that I must try to do something. Would you care to use the enclosed essay or review in *Pagany*? I have been so misquoted and we have both been so vulgarized that to have this positive appreciation printed, even if the mass of people does not see it, would mean much—much—to me." Quoted in Daniel P. McCarthy, " 'Just Americans': A Note on Jean Toomer's Marriage to Margery Latimer," *CLA Journal* 17 (June 1974): 477. Latimer's essay has evidently not survived.

18. See Jean Toomer Papers, Box 65, Folder 1489.

19. "Just Americans," *Time* 19 (March 28, 1932): 19.

20. Toomer had developed the metaphor of the "stomach" (which *Time* used as a mocking title beneath the picture of Toomer and his wife) in several unpublished essays, where he had recognized that the metaphor was only a hopeful prediction of a possible American future, similar to the "melting pot" analogy of an earlier day. See Jean Toomer Papers, Box 51, Folder 1108; Box 51, 1106. In his essay "The Americans," he said that "any young country or nation can be likened to a stomach, and, like a stomach, its job is to handle—to digest and assimilate—the materials put into it." He added, via Waldo Frank: "there must be death before there can be new life. . . . When we pick and eat an apple that is the end of the apple. The apple dies. But that is just the beginning of us, in so far as we are embodiments of the elements which previously existed in the apple-form." Printed in Frederik L. Rusch, ed., *A Jean Toomer Reader*, 107.

21. Bertram Wyatt-Brown, *Southern Honor: Ethics and Behavior in the Old South* (New York: Oxford University Press, 1982), 436, 442. For the background and forms of the charivari, see Wyatt-Brown's chapter 16. One of the usual causes of a charivari might be the local reaction to an "inappropriate" marriage.

22. Robert C. Twombly, "A Disciple's Odyssey: Jean Toomer's Gurdjieffian Career," 457; Lois Palken Rudnick, *Mabel Dodge Luhan*, 229–30; Cynthia Earl Kerman and Richard Eldridge, *The Lives of Jean Toomer*, 145–48, 219–22. Rudnick says that after receiving a letter from Toomer that attempted to account for the $14,000, "Mabel never corresponded with nor heard from him again."

23. Alain Locke, "From *Native Son* to *Invisible Man*: A Review of the Literature of the Negro for 1952," *Phylon* 14, 1 (1953): 34.

24. Toomer used the "Authors' Clipping Bureau" to obtain newspaper reviews of *Cane*, which are now part of the Jean Toomer Papers, Box 65, Folder 1489. Most white newspapers noted Toomer's indebtedness to Waldo Frank; one (the *Asheville Citizen* of North Carolina) even asserted that "Jean Toomer is none other than Waldo Frank." Most white reviewers spoke disparagingly of the "style affected by modern writers," but Southern newspapers in particular were sarcastic, attacking Toomer's modernist style perhaps to avoid dealing with his treatment of the South. Interestingly, the *New York Post* (January 12, 1924) was willing to overlook *Cane*'s "broken sentences and cacophonies of thought" because of the "thought-provoking stabs of horror, the nakedness of which one forgives, knowing their essential truth." That "essential truth" no doubt appealed to the young Langston Hughes, who before the book was published asked Alain Locke if he knew Toomer. Hughes said, "I have liked some of his work very much in 'The Liberator' and 'The Crisis,' " and he maintained an admiration for Toomer's work for the rest of his life. Langston Hughes to Alain Locke, Alain Locke Papers, Moorland-Spingarn Collection, Howard University (hereafter cited as M-S Center). Also see Countee Cullen to Jean Toomer, September 29, 1923, Jean Toomer Papers; Countee Cullen to Alain Locke, September 30, 1923, M-S Center. Arna Bontemps recalled that at *Cane*'s publication "a few sensitive and perceptive people went quietly mad, as the saying goes, about

this wholly extraordinary book." See Arna Bontemps, introduction, *Cane* (1923; reprint, New York: Harper & Row, 1969), x.

25. Countee Cullen, "The Dark Tower," *Opportunity* 6 (March 1928): 90. Cullen made it clear that the "guest" was the white reader, insisting that "every phase of Negro life should not be the white man's concern. The parlor should be large enough for his entertainment and instruction." Cullen's warning reflected the views of the man who was about to become his father-in-law, W.E.B. Du Bois, and may have been aimed most specifically at the homoerotic contents of the single issue of *Fire!* On class uplift ideology and sexual morality, see Kevin K. Gaines, *Uplifting the Race*, 80–83.

26. Alain Locke, ed., *The New Negro* (1925; reprint, New York: Atheneum, 1969), 8, 11. Further citations of *The New Negro* refer to this edition and will appear in the text. Locke's description of the New Negro should be compared with the one A. Philip Randolph offered in *The Messenger* for August 1920. See "The New Negro —What Is He?" reprinted in Cary D. Wintz, ed., *African American Political Thought, 1890–1930: Washington, DuBois, Garvey, and Randolph* (Armonk, N.Y.: M. E. Sharpe, 1996), 272–74. A useful discussion of the New Negro as "contested term" is James A. Miller's "African-American Writing of the 1930s: A Prologue," in Bill Mullen and Sherry Lee Linkon, eds., *Radical Revisions: Rereading 1930s Culture* (Urbana: University of Illinois Press, 1996), 78–90.

27. Alain Locke's essays in his anthology are framed by class distinctions based primarily on educational and cultural criteria. See his foreword for the "multitude" versus "the thinking few" (4), the "forward elements of the race" (9), the "more advanced and representative classes" (10), the "thinking Negro" (11, 12), "a relatively few enlightened minds" (13). Locke opens his short piece "Negro Youth Speaks" with an invocation of the "talented few" (47) and closes it with the "promise of the cultured few" (53).

28. Howard University professor Montgomery Gregory had helped set that tone when he reviewed the book for *Opportunity* in December 1923; he argued that *Cane* was not a "realist" text like *Main Street*, whose author "confuse[s] superficial and transitory political and economic conditions with the underlying eternal elements." The "eternal elements" in *Cane* were art as "*self-expression*," the "spirituality" of African-Americans, especially women, and the folk spirit of the race: "Mr Toomer's highest inspiration is to be found in the folk-life of his beloved Southland." Montgomery Gregory, "Our Book Shelf," *Opportunity* 1 (December 1923): 374–75, reprinted in Darwin T. Turner, ed., *Cane: an Authoritative Text, Backgrounds, Criticism* (New York: Norton, 1988), 165–68.

29. In January 1923, Jessie Fauset, literary editor of the *Crisis*, had written to Arthur Spingarn, one of the founders of the NAACP: "I am enclosing the poem by Jean Toomer of which I spoke to you last night. I consider the lines which I have marked proof of an art and of a contribution to literature which will be distinctly negroid and without propaganda. It will have in it an element of universality too, in that it shows the individual's reactions to his own tradition." That poem, no doubt, was "Song of the Son." In Fauset's claim for its "universality" *and* "distinctly negroid" characteristics, the cosmopolitan ideal appears, adapted for African-American literature. Jessie Fauset to Joel Spingarn, January 20, 1923, Manuscript Division, Moorland-Spingarn Research Center, Howard University. Also see Charles S. Johnson's remarks, cited by Arna Bontemps, in which Johnson praised *Cane* for being "detached from propaganda, sensitive only to beauty." See Arna Bontemps, introduction, *Cane*, vii.

30. On Locke's selections for his anthology, see Charles Scruggs, *Sweet Home: Invisible Cities in the Afro-American Novel* (Baltimore: Johns Hopkins University Press,

1993), 54–58. On "The Black Christ," see Gerald Early, "Introduction," *My Soul's High Soul: The Collected Writings of Countee Cullen, Voice of the Harlem Renaissance*, ed. Gerald Early (New York: Doubleday, 1991), 60–63.

31. Alain Locke, "Self-Criticism: The Third Dimension in Culture," *Phylon* 11, 4 (1950): 391–94. When Locke brought *Cane* up again in his *Phylon* piece of 1953, he praised it in the terms of the 1920s: "it soared above the plane of propaganda and apologetics to a self-sufficient presentation of Negro life in its own idiom and gave it proud and self-revealing evaluation. More than that, the emotional essences of the Southland were hauntingly evoked." Locke still couldn't appreciate the modernism of *Cane*, complaining of its formal weakness that it was "a succession of vignettes rather than an entire landscape." Alain Locke, "From *Native Son* to *Invisible Man*," 34.

32. Jean Toomer Papers, Box 60, Folder 1411.

33. Waldo Frank, *Our America* (New York: Boni & Liveright, 1919), 223.

34. Eugene Holmes, "Jean Toomer—Apostle of Beauty," *Opportunity* 10 (August 1932): 252–54, 260.

35. David Bradley, "Looking Behind *Cane*," *Southern Review* 21 (July 1985): 683, 684. David Bradley, *The Chaneysville Incident* (1981; reprint, New York: Avon, 1982), unnumbered page. Other contemporary black novels that followed or participated in the tradition of the Gothic detective story include Alice Walker's *The Third Life of Grange Copeland* (1970), Ernest Gaines's *A Gathering of Old Men* (1983), Gloria Naylor's *Linden Hills* (1985), and Octavia Butler's *Kindred* (1979).

36. Alice Walker, "The Divided Life of Jean Toomer," in *In Search of Our Mothers' Gardens* (New York: Harcourt Brace Jovanovich, 1983), 60–65. Gayl Jones, "Blues Ballad: Jean Toomer's "Karintha," in *Liberating Voices: Oral Tradition in African American Literature* (Cambridge, Mass.: Harvard University Press, 1991), 70–78. Charles H. Rowell, "An Interview with Gayl Jones," *Callaloo* 5 (October 1982): 46. Gayl Jones, "Blues Ballad," 73; Charles H. Rowell, "An Interview," 48. Jones has admitted that Toomer was a major "first" influence on her writing—see Claudia Tate, ed., *Black Women Writers at Work* (New York: Continuum, 1983), 94; Charles H. Rowell, "An Interview," 52. Farah Jasmine Griffin, *"Who Set You Flowin'?" The African-American Migration Narrative* (New York: Oxford University Press, 1995), 188, 194. Toni Morrison, *Jazz* (New York: Knopf, 1992), 40, 133–34, 213, 226.

37. Waldo Frank, *Chalk Face* (New York: Boni & Liveright, 1924).

Acknowledgments

We wish to thank the Beinecke Library of Yale University, the Van Pelt Library of the University of Pennsylvania, and the Moorland-Spingarn Research Center at Howard University for permission to quote from the manuscript collections of Jean Toomer, Waldo Frank, and Alain Locke, respectively. We also wish to thank the *Crisis* magazine for allowing us to quote from Toomer's poem "Banking Coal," as well as the Liveright Publishing Company for allowing us to quote from Hart Crane's "Black Tambourine" and from the 1969 edition of *Cane*.

Index

11. Waldo Frank, *City Block* (Darien, Conn.: self-published, 1922), unnumbered pages. Box 60, Folder 1412 (journals, 1923), Jean Toomer Papers. One of the major stylistic changes defining modernism after the turn of the century was in the nature of narrative, the way in which stories were told. Waldo Frank's "standard of reality" was destabilized in such a way as to demand a new kind of literary narrative. Comparing a nonrepresentational Vasily Kandinsky watercolor with T. S. Eliot's "The Love Song of J. Alfred Prufrock," Frederick Karl observes that the key similarity "is fragmentation, narrative based on discontinuity, perception of objects in movement rather than representation." Karl also notes Kandinsky's remark about Picasso's cubism in 1911, that Picasso didn't destroy the material world in his paintings, but rather rearranged it: "Picasso held onto things, but not in the ordinary way of representation; rather, he located elements (objects, figures, forms) on the canvas in ways not 'represented' before. He had found a new way of narrative, through a process of redistribution." Both of these examples are relevant to Frank's theory and practice of literary narrative. Frederick R. Karl, *Modern and Modernism: The Sovereignty of the Artist, 1885–1925* (New York: Atheneum, 1985), 314, 317.

12. Waldo Frank, *Salvos*, 228.

13. On Coleridge's theory of knowledge, see Gerald McNiece, *The Knowledge That Endures: Coleridge, German Philosophy and the Logic of Romantic Thought* (London: Macmillan, 1992), chapter 4; Toomer compared Frank's plan for *Holiday* with Stribling's novel. See Jean Toomer to Waldo Frank, July 25, 1922, Jean Toomer Papers: "Those unspeakable pale-faces who have been championing Birthright, and who have been clamoring for the black folk in our literature, will hate you for it."

14. Waldo Frank, *Salvos*, 229.

15. Waldo Frank to Jean Toomer, January 16, 1923, Jean Toomer Papers.

16. For another view of Frank's sensitivity to criticism, see Lewis Mumford's introduction to Alan Trachtenberg, ed., *Memoirs of Waldo Frank* (Amherst: University of Massachusetts Press, 1973), xix–xx.

17. Waldo Frank to Jean Toomer, April 25, 1922, Waldo Frank Papers, printed in Darwin T. Turner, ed., *Cane: An Authoritative Text, Backgrounds, Criticism* (New York: Norton, 1988), 157–60 (hereafter referred to as Turner, ed., *Cane*).

18. For George Bernard Shaw's early influence on Toomer, see Darwin T. Turner, ed., *The Wayward and the Seeking: A Collection of Writings by Jean Toomer* (Washington, D.C.: Howard University Press, 1980), 107.

19. Waldo Frank, *Virgin Spain: Scenes from the Spiritual Drama of a Great People* (New York: Boni & Liveright, 1926), 160; Waldo Frank, *The Re-Discovery of America: An Introduction to a Philosophy of American Life* (New York: Charles Scribner's Sons, 1929), 171. Frederick Karl makes an interesting comparison between the use of collage or papier collé in the visual arts and the narrative methods of Joseph Conrad, a comparison similar to Frank's figure of the "unorganized mosaic" describing "Kabnis." See Frederick R. Karl, *Modern and Modernism*, 318.

Frank's connection to Alfred Stieglitz and the circle that formed around the gallery "291" was a major source for his modernist aesthetic. See, for example, his notebook entry cited in Daniel Stern Terris, "Waldo Frank and the Rediscovery of America, 1889–1929" (Ph.D. diss., Harvard University, 1992), 96: "Whatever you think of Cubism as a plastic expression, it contains this truth for all modern-Art: that the Art-parts of the desired picture must be given actual, complete dimensions and that these must be ensured by the *spatial omission of all else* from the Art-milieu or canvass. *Their joining or composition* must, moreover, be attained not by the addition of irrelevant, non-Art parts (episodes, incidents, etc.) but by the fluid, mystical pervasion of the Whole."

20. Jean Toomer to Waldo Frank, July 19, 1922, Waldo Frank Papers. Frederik

Rusch prints this letter in a version from the Jean Toomer Papers, but without setting *Cane* in capitals and without writing out the names of the stories: "Such pieces as K.C.A. ["Karintha," "Carma," "Avey"?] and "Kabnis" (revised) coming under the sub-head of Cane Stalks and Chorouses [*sic*]." See Frederik L. Rusch, ed., *A Jean Toomer Reader: Selected Unpublished Writings* (New York: Oxford University Press, 1993), 11.

21. Jean Toomer to John McClure, July 22, 1922, Jean Toomer Papers. The distinction Toomer made between "Cane Stalks" (including "Karintha, Carma, Avey, and Kabnis") and "vignettes" (of which he mentions only "For M.W.") isn't clear. Probably the pieces "Seventh Street," "Rhobert," and "Calling Jesus" from the middle section of *Cane* would be "vignettes"—prose pieces without traditional plot lines. Yet the difference between the narrative of "Karintha" or "Carma" and that of "Calling Jesus" or "Rhobert" is one of degree rather than kind; Toomer's modernism was eliding generic divisions. Curiously, the title "For M. W." (Mae Wright) is attached to a formally correct Italian sonnet Toomer sent to Frank in July; he may have placed it with vignettes rather than poems in the letter to McClure because he associated it with Washington. See Jean Toomer to Waldo Frank, July 27, 1922, Waldo Frank Papers.

22. Jean Toomer to Waldo Frank, July 19, 1922; August 21, 1922, Jean Toomer Papers. On the publishing of *City Block*, also see Waldo Frank to Jean Toomer, undated letter (circa July 1922), Jean Toomer Papers: "My reason [for publishing *City Block* myself] is that L[iveright] convinced me that he would be in danger of prosecution, since Sumner has just discovered that Limited editions arent privileged." John Sumner was head of the New York Society for the Suppression of Vice. On Sumner and "Limited editions," see Walker Gilmer, *Horace Liveright: Publisher of the Twenties* (New York: David Lewis, 1970), 60–80.

23. Jean Toomer to Waldo Frank, July 19, 1922, and July 27, 1922, Jean Toomer Papers. Waldo Frank, "A Note," in *The Bridegroom Cometh* (New York: Doubleday, Doran, and Company, 1939), 7–8. Also see Charles Scruggs, "Worlds Spinning Within Worlds: *Unanimisme* in Waldo Frank's *City Block* and Jean Toomer's *Cane*," in *La Nouvelle de langue Anglaise* (Paris: Publications de la Sorbonne Nouvelle, 1988), 127–35.

24. Waldo Frank to Jean Toomer, undated letter (circa July 1922), Jean Toomer Papers; Kenneth Burke, "The Consequences of Idealism," *Dial* 73 (October 1922): 450–51; Kenneth Burke, "Enlarging the Narrow House," *Dial* 73 (September 1922): 346–48.

25. Jean Toomer to Waldo Frank, October 4, 1922, Jean Toomer Papers; Kenneth Burke, "The Consequences of Idealism," 452. In a sense Burke had answered his own question about the "inevitable centre" a month earlier in his *Dial* review of Evelyn Scott: "Waldo Frank's characters are meant to be like pebbles dropped into a pool: he tries to draw ever-widening circles around them. His plots are conceived in the same non-temporal, non-spatial tone." Burke, "Enlarging the Narrow House," 347. Toomer no doubt knew this reference if he followed Frank's advice that he read Burke before he wrote his piece on Frank. When Gorham Munson published his book on Frank in 1923, he emphasized the uniqueness of the stories of *City Block*: "an American phrase of unanimisme . . . their arrangement and spacing help to create a unit greater than their sum as short stories. Again, Frank is intent upon a spherical form. . . . With a firm grasp of *Beginning*, the reader, upon reviewing the other units, is likely to see them take their positions on a circle, a circle threaded together by the offsets of stories of victory and defeat." Gorham B. Munson, *Waldo Frank: A Study* (New York: Boni & Liveright, 1923), 50, 51, 53, 54. Toomer reviewed Munson's book for *S4N* and focused on Munson's point that the form of *City Block*

"God has created us to be connected to our bodies, and life has a way of connecting us. Tara has begun a conversation that will be helpful to many who feel alienated or even in conflict with their own bodies."
Dr. Henry Cloud, author of *Boundaries* and *Never Go Back*

"Wise, erudite, loving and tender, *Embracing the Body* will bring true health and wholeness to our theology of our physical bodies as a church. Tara Owens is the perfect guide for this holy journey."
Sarah Bessey, author of *Jesus Feminist*

"Tara Owens's *Embracing the Body* is a gift for anyone seeking to understand how the body—with all of its twitches, itches and bentness toward false notions—is not an enemy of spiritual formation but an amazing gift from God and the ground for personal incarnation—experiencing the reality of the apostle Paul's number one teaching point, Christ within. She makes great use of real-life stories and engaging theological reflection."
Gary W. Moon, executive director, Dallas Willard Center, Westmont College

"Tara Owens offers us a wise and tender exploration of the gifts our bodies offer to us as portals into God's grace and wisdom. This book is much needed and should be required reading in every church's adult faith formation program. Tara doesn't just invite us to read, but to ponder, to engage and to practice so that we might claim the truth of the incarnation in new ways."
Christine Valters Paintner, abbeyofthearts.com, author of *The Artist's Rule*

"Tara M. Owens is a rare find among contemporary writers. Part theologian, part mystic, her insight is bold and rich, and her writing is fine tuned. . . . I'm grateful for the ways Tara's words have revealed some of my own wounds and fears and helped me make space for new ways of encountering God, through the body, in the body. I will be meditating on this book for a long time to come. I hope the same for you."
Micha Boyett, author of *Found: A Story of Questions, Grace & Everyday Prayer*

"Tara Owens writes with warmth and wisdom on a subject that many Christians have at best dismissed or at worst discarded—our bodies as carriers and avenues of spiritual growth and connection with God. We claim to be people of the incarnation but often live as if only our souls mattered and our bodies did not. Owens calls us back to our whole selves—body and soul—and in doing so helps us reconnect with incarnational living both through the central historical event that kicked off Christian movement and our ongoing task of being the disciples of Jesus cloaked in flesh and blood."
Brent Bill, coauthor of *Awaken Your Senses* and *Finding God in the Verbs*

"Truth. Beauty. Revelation. Those are just some of the words to describe *Embracing the Body* by Tara Owens. It is a rare and insightful book written by a poet who longs to love Jesus with every fiber of her being and invites others to do the same."
Stasi Eldredge, coauthor of *Captivating*

"This book is beautiful, learned and wise. It will make you think, and it will make you want to say 'amen'—and, more important, it will enable you more fully to live as a body."
Lauren F. Winner, author of *Girl Meets God* and *Still*

EMBRACING
THE BODY

Finding God in
Our Flesh and Bone

TARA M. OWENS

IVP Books

An imprint of InterVarsity Press
Downers Grove, Illinois

InterVarsity Press
P.O. Box 1400, Downers Grove, IL 60515-1426
World Wide Web: www.ivpress.com
Email: email@ivpress.com

InterVarsity Press® is the book-publishing division of InterVarsity Christian Fellowship/USA®, a movement of students and faculty active on campus at hundreds of universities, colleges and schools of nursing in the United States of America, and a member movement of the International Fellowship of Evangelical Students. For information about local and regional activities, write Public Relations Dept., InterVarsity Christian Fellowship/ USA, 6400 Schroeder Rd., P.O. Box 7895, Madison, WI 53707-7895, or visit the IVCF website at www. intervarsity.org.

All Scripture quotations, unless otherwise indicated, are taken from THE HOLY BIBLE, NEW INTERNATIONAL VERSION®, NIV® Copyright © 1973, 1978, 1984, 2011 by Biblica, Inc.™ Used by permission. All rights reserved worldwide.

While all stories in this book are true, some names and identifying information in this book have been changed to protect the privacy of the individuals involved.

The poem on p. 166 is from David Whyte, "The Opening of Eyes," in Songs for Coming Home, 1984. ©Many Rivers Press, Langley, Washington. Reprinted with permission from Many Rivers Press.

Cover design: Cindy Kiple
Interior design: Beth McGill
Images: esthAlto/Michele Constantini/Getty Images

ISBN 978-0-8308-3593-5 (print)
ISBN 978-0-8308-9679-0 (digital)

Printed in the United States of America ∞

Library of Congress Cataloging-in-Publication Data
Owens, Tara M., 1976–
  Embracing the body : finding God in our flesh and bone / Tara M.
Owens.
   pages cm
  Includes bibliographical references.
  ISBN 978-0-8308-3593-5 (pbk. : alk. paper)
  1. Human body—Religious aspects—Christianity. I. Title.
  BT741.3.O94 2015
  233'.5—dc23
                                                    2014044444

P   22   21   20   19   18   17   16   15   14   13   12   11   10   9   8   7   6   5   4   3   2   1
Y   34   33   32   31   30   29   28   27   26   25   24   23   22   21   20   19   18   17   16   15

For she who remembered in her last losings

For he who learned to touch the world

For You

Contents

We awaken in Christ's body
As Christ awakens our bodies,
And my poor hand is Christ, He enters
My foot, and is infinitely me.
I move my hand, and wonderfully
My hand becomes Christ, becomes all of Him
(For God is indivisibly
Whole, seamless in His Godhood).
I move my foot, and at once
He appears like a flash of lightning.
Do my words seem blasphemous?—Then
Open your heart to Him
And let yourself receive the one
Who is opening to you so deeply.
For if we genuinely love Him,
We wake up inside Christ's body
Where all our body, all over,
Every most hidden part of it,
Is realized in joy as Him,
As He makes us, utterly, real,
And everything that is hurt, everything
That seemed to us dark, harsh, shameful,
Maimed, ugly, irreparably
Damaged, is in Him transformed
And recognized as whole, as lovely,
And radiant in His life
We awaken as the Beloved
In every last part of our body.

—St. Symeon the New Theologian

Introduction

An Invitation to More

IF YOU ASKED ME IF I WAS ALWAYS comfortable in my body (and required that I answer honestly), I would have to say, *No . . . No, I'm not.* I'm of the opinion that there isn't anyone alive who is at home in his or her body 100 percent of the time, and I don't believe that I formed this opinion just to justify my own neuroses. If you'd like to test this (and some of you will), I would suggest that you place your hand on the shoulder of the person nearest you for ten seconds. Just reach out and lay your hand on them lightly, and hold it there. You can count to ten if you want. Not only will this make them wildly uncomfortable, you'll probably want to get out of your chair and run as far as you can from them.

And yet, if you actually did what I suggested, all you've done is put your hand on the shoulder of another person. It may have been your spouse, your child, your friend or, if you're amazingly brave, the stranger next to you at the coffee shop where you're reading this book. You initiated physical contact and connected with another human being using your body. You acknowledged your existence, you acknowledged their existence and you acknowledged the connection between the two of you. And, most likely, the vulnerability that brought up in you was unsettling. (More than unsettling if the stranger consequently slugged you.)

Today, I'm a pale-skinned, freckled woman with blue eyes. I don't look in the mirror every morning and think that I'm lovely; in fact, the moments that I feel most lovely are moments when I'm not looking in the mirror at all. Consciously contemplating my physical exterior isn't something I do very often, unless I'm applying makeup or noticing that I probably need a haircut. But, unconsciously, I do it every day, squinting at myself when I'm brushing my teeth, noticing another fold or crease of skin that indicates I've gained a little more weight when I pass by the mirror on the way to the shower, picking at my fingernails and judging the length and symmetry of my fingers as I wait for dinner to be ready at a restaurant. These are not my finest moments. I would like to fool myself into thinking that these are the moments when I am most cognizant of my embodiment, the fact that it is my very essence, my very self that I'm squinting at, criticizing or judging. But, mostly, they're not.

Mostly those moments are when I'm objectifying myself in order to distance myself from the pain of not measuring up to some standard I internalized at an age too young, because of a voice or voices that told me my body was inadequate, and in order to protect myself from being a disappointment at the very core of who I am, I began to think of "me" as something or someone separate from the physical body that walks, talks, breathes and sweats.

As a result, the moments when I feel most lovely, most true, most whole are those moments when I don't have a mirror in front of me, when I'm not confronted with the physical reality of being human. I should like to think that this is a good thing, just as I should like to think that I'm most aware of my embodiment when I'm looking at myself, even if I'm gazing with cruel eyes. Sometimes it *is* a good thing—I'm holding a child in my lap; being held in my husband's arms; taking the Eucharist into my mouth, chewing and swallowing; or covered with oil splatters, cornmeal and spices as I prepare a meal. In those moments, I'm integrated—all the parts of me are working together and I'm present to them all. Nothing is cut out, nothing is despised, nothing is peripheral to my experience.

On the flip side of that, when I'm lost in thought at a coffee shop, unaware of the mug of tea in my hands, or when I'm caught in a good book, so disconnected from the physical object in my hands that my husband needs to literally take it from me in order to get my attention—those are times when I'm fragmented, gone astray and in need of being found by the One who is about bringing every part of us together into a whole. This whole is me, the me as I was originally designed, envisioned in the eyes of God. It's also the whole of a part, a functioning vital part, of the body of Christ. This larger whole needs *me* to be whole in order for the entire body to function, to be complete and healthy. The body of Christ needs me to be integrated with my body so that we may experience redemption together, not just as individuals but as a people, a colony of heaven here on earth.

Welcome to the Mess

Bodies are messy. They secrete, they bruise, they are fragile and unpredictable. Bodies are strong. They climb, run, grow and exert. Bodies are pliable. They shrink and expand, they adapt to parts being lost; bodies heal parts that have been hurt. Bodies do glorious things and bodies do unspeakably horrible things.

I know, for the most part, I would rather tell other people what to do with their bodies than deal with the crazy mess that is my relationship with my own flesh and blood, my embodied soul. I would rather talk about the fractured way the world and the church relate to the material we're made of than really wrestle with the way I fracture and fall apart when forced to deal with the stuff of myself.

I come by that naturally—we all do, because it's a physiological fact that we don't perceive our own bodies the same way other people see them.

Body schema is the term scientists and doctors use to define our physical sense of ourselves. This is different than *body image*, which involves all the narratives we believe about our bodies based on the cultures and stories we're surrounded with. Our body schema is based on both visual input (the way we see parts of ourselves) and neural-motor input (the amount of sense preceptors we have in parts of our body and the way our bodies move in the world). More recently, researchers have discovered that we also take body schema cues from interpersonal input (the way other people move their bodies changes how we perceive ours, especially when we're children).

But what does all of this scientific language mean? Why does it matter when we're talking about our bodies and God, the stuff of ourselves and the Creator of the universe?

It matters because if you mapped out our body schema, the way we experience our bodies doesn't match the way our bodies look to others. It's been done before, in scientific modeling, this mapping of the way we experience the world versus the way we are in the world, and the results are somewhat shocking. The image is one of a person with huge hands and a huge mouth, but a receding forehead and small skull. The neck, back, arms and legs are small, but the genitals and feet are larger than their actual size.[1] On a biological level, we don't see ourselves rightly.

Now, we do see ourselves in a way that helps us navigate the world. If your body paid too much attention to the back of your neck, for example, you would be paralyzed with sensory input every time your hair got ruffled. And it's important to note that body schema and body image are, as I've said, different things. Yet they do overlap, and in an interesting metaphorical way our body schema says something to us about the path to a whole, holistic relationship with God. Because to see ourselves as we are in the world, with right proportions, right values, rightly ordered parts—well, that requires other people.

Unfortunately, as history and our own living, breathing, walking-around experience tells us, other people aren't always helpful. Throughout history, societies have misrepresented other bodies, classifying some as valuable (white bodies) and others as expendable (black bodies, for example). Women's bodies have been labeled as dangerous or inferior, the bodies of slaves as objects rather than people. Mothers sometimes feel like their whole embodied experience is of service to the children they parent, single people as if their bodies represent only unattached sexuality to others.

The church has been alternately helpful and unhelpful when it comes to a right understanding of our bodies. On the one (somewhat oversized) hand, the reality of the incarnation, the in-breaking of God into the material world, shattered and remade our body schema completely. With our broken relationship with God redeemed through Christ, we've been wholly restored to the level of perception we were created to operate with from the beginning—the spiritual life flows through us fully once more. Nowhere but in the community of God do we learn how to live integrated; nowhere but in the community of God do we learn the life of the Spirit lived out in our very flesh.

On the other hand, the church over the years has also succumbed to or reacted against the world's narratives about our bodies—the culture's misperceptions of the value of our flesh and blood—and become so deeply afraid of infection that we began to attack ourselves. Instead of bodies celebrated and life lived fully in flesh and Spirit, the body of Christ often suffers from a kind of autoimmune disease. We are so afraid of infection from the outside world we've mistaken healthy tissue for unhealthy, sickening ourselves as a result. And, as anyone with this kind of malady can tell you, this kind of pain and affliction throws your self-perception into wild disarray.

I bring all of these things out into the open because each of these narratives, each of these examples have real stories, real people attached to them. These are stories woven into the very fabric of our faith, stories that have leaked into the Christian narrative from our surrounding culture. They are the prohibitions and prescriptions that define how to think about our bodies.

These stories are ones that, for the most part, we don't talk about. We live with them, and they define us, but we don't have a language for discussing them, a way of challenging or reshaping them because we can't even approach them. We stuff them and we ignore them and we relegate them to silence. We shuffle away awkwardly when the subject of our physicality comes up, and we eschew the idea that this uncomfortable, sweaty, noisy, unruly body of ours might indeed be the vehicle for union with the God who loves us beyond anything we could imagine. That children and dance and sex and art and body image and beauty and prayer and touch just might be encoded with something more than fear and danger. That in them we might find the fullness of life in Christ that we've been longing for.

And we affirm the Nicene Creed without ever dwelling for a moment on what it might mean. *I believe in the resurrection of the body*.

Eden and More

During service today we baptized an eight-year-old wonder. All smiles and eager anticipation, Eden stepped forward to the sacrament as if it was the most natural thing to do. Washed in the waters, anointed with oil, holding a lit candle—the light of Christ made visible—Eden was everything that we lost in the fall, and everything that has been and is yet to be restored.

Together we recited the words "I believe in the resurrection of the body." Looking into Eden's bright eyes, I know it's time. It's time to take those words seriously.

It's time to reach for the more that God has for us in relationship with him and with the stuff of our very selves. It's time to risk taking God at his Word when he says we are redeemed, not in part but the whole.

It's time discover why he scooped earth to make man and breathed us into being with bone and blood. It's time to listen to his murmurs along our muscles, his whispers in the wind and his song of delight in our sexuality.

It's time to reach for resurrection, here and now.

A Word About Touch Points

At the end of each chapter, you'll find something called a "Touch Point."

TADY - redemption of body
- salvation of the soul and body

These sections are meant to help you wrestle with the content of the chapter in your own life and, more importantly, your own body. Touch Points include exercises, prayers and ways of making the material yours.

If you're anything like me, you'll be tempted to skip over these sections and move on to the next chapter. It may be my own performance anxiety, but I tend to want to finish a book quickly, to move through the material and get that sense of accomplishment that comes from closing the cover on another book of spiritual insight and challenge read. Been there, done that, moving on.

I'm asking you not to do that here.

It'll be hard, I know, to stop at the Touch Points. You don't have to do every single exercise, and there won't be any extra credit if you've checked them all off by the end of the book. (I know, I threw you with the points thing, but no one is actually keeping score.)

The thing is, this is a book about the body—my body, your body—and like any written communication it runs the risk of being another tumble of words *about* something rather than an encounter *with* that something. My hope, my desire is for you to experience your body, God and God in your body for yourself.

So please, don't skip the Touch Points. Read them through, decide which one calls most deeply to you (or, on the other hand, makes you most uncomfortable) and take the risk of trying it. Some of them will be easier than others, but all of them are designed to get you out of your head (where you process words on the page) and into your messy, unruly, complicated and oh-so-glorious body.

You can do them alone or with a friend, you can bring them to your small group or invite your book club to try them with you. I can't be there with you in person, stepping into the awkward, hopeful, crazy experience of incarnation, but believe me I want to be. I wish I could see your face, smile into your eyes, listen to your heart. I can't be there in flesh and bone, but I can be here in these words. What I *can* give you are my hopes, my heart and my prayers.

And I have been praying. Over each word in this book, and over you (yes, you) before you ever cracked its cover. I've been praying God would meet you exactly where you need to be met and would speak through his glorious creation (you, me, the world around us) just what you need to hear. I've been praying for courage, for hope, for freedom for you, and I believe Jesus wants that for you. Not only do I believe he wants it, I believe that he will accomplish it. Because he promises:

> Ask, and it will be given you; search, and you will find; knock, and the door will be opened for you. For everyone who asks receives, and everyone who searches finds, and for everyone who knocks, the door will be opened. (Matthew 7:7-8 NRSV)

So I bless you with the courage to really enter in. I bless you with a heart willing to risk a transformation that will bring about the more that God wants for you—and for us all. Let's answer it together, God's invitation to more: more redemption, more freedom, more life.

In the name of the Father, the Son and the Holy Spirit,

Amen.

So be it.

Touch Point

Walking with God

Take thirty minutes or an hour to go for a walk with God after reading this introduction. Leave the things that might distract you (mobile devices, mental to-do lists) at home. Take a deep breath as you step out the door, and pray these words: *Jesus Christ, I commit this journey to you. I want to walk with you, God. Let me feel, see and know what you would have for me in this time.*

As you walk, notice in particular how it feels to step across thresholds and over obstacles. Do you feel confident stepping into new spaces on the path? Are there times your body hesitates, not sure that this is the right way to go? Don't try to reach a destination as you walk. Simply be present to what this chapter has stirred in you. Is there a fear about your own body, or the material world, that surfaces as you journey with Jesus in this time? Is there something you are resisting or disagreeing with?

Make space for what arises on the journey. Notice whether your thoughts are churning or if your stomach is in knots. Pay attention to the way the path leads you back to the safety of home.

Afterward, take some time to reflect or journal on your experience of walking out this chapter. Did anything arise for you as you entered the material in an embodied way? Was it confusing or difficult to understand what you were doing in taking this walk? Was it natural or unnatural to notice how you felt as you stepped over cracks in the sidewalk or things in your path? Listen to the whispers of Christ as he gently encounters places in you that are afraid or unsure.

Thank God for the experience of journeying together during this exercise.

P+1 what Mary is
P+2 what Mary does
P+3 What Mary offers

Ask Mary for help on this path

Mary as beloved
unique
job / work / contribution

Mary as friend

1

Where Do Our
Fears Come From?

*Fear is such a powerful emotion for humans that
when we allow it to take us over, it drives
compassion right out of our hearts.*

St. Thomas Aquinas

If a fear cannot be articulated, it can't be conquered.

Stephen King

I'VE ONLY HAD MY KNEES GIVE OUT IN FEAR once my life. Earlier that day, I had been stuffed full of pizza and various sugary substances at the eighth birthday party of one of my friends. The festivities continued with a rare and special treat: we were all going to watch our very first movie in a *real* movie theater.

Now, eight-year-old girls are generally obsessed with a short list of things, often including but not limited to their friends, ponies (real or imagined), their favorite color and their stuffed animals. With the addition of an obsession with reading and a proclivity to being the "good

girl," I was a fairly typical eight-year-old girl. So, when the fluffy creatures that looked remarkably like my collection of stuffed bunnies and
bears began metamorphosing into slimy, scaly, unruly and unrighteous
things that not only stayed up past bedtime but, as far as I could see,
killed people—well, I was terrified.

But this was my first movie on the big screen. The enormous images
had me pinned to my seat, the sound sickeningly reinforcing how real
this experience was. At one point, I vaguely recall the blonde bob beside
me leaning in close, her brow wrinkled in concern. "Are you going to
throw up?" she whispered fiercely. Wide-eyed, I was only able to shake
my head once. *No.* I didn't think so, anyway.

The blonde bob retreated. I sucked in the sickly sweet smell of stale
popcorn and soda-slicked floors through my nose, trying not to do the
very thing I said I wouldn't.

When the movie ended and the credits rolled, everyone got up. Except
for me. Oh, I attempted to get up, to follow the parents in single file out
of the seats. But when I tried to stand, I found my knees had turned to
water, my fear pooling behind my kneecaps, secretly eroding my ability
to hold myself upright, to hold myself together even. So I fell, collapsing
into a small, trembling muddle on the sticky floor. I burst into tears.

I don't recall the details of getting back to my home. I'm also not sure
if I ever knew why my mother and father let me go to that particular
movie in the first place. As I look back, I get the sense that my parents
were grateful for a night out. I know that I returned home to a babysitter
who had already tucked my sister firmly into her bottom bunk and sta-
tioned herself in front of the television.

A bit too solidly, it would turn out.

Upon my return, the babysitter—we'll call her Jenny—told me to
change into my pajamas and get into bed. This was not a suggestion, it
was a command. So, I obeyed. Well, I tried to, anyway. I changed. I
brushed my teeth. I climbed up the short brown ladder to the top bunk.
I crawled under my covers. But when I attempted to close my eyes, the

backs of my lids sneered at me with the gleefully evil grin of the movie's main villain, Spike. In the darkness of our room, it felt like there were gremlins in every corner, ready to grab me, grab my sister, ambush my parents when they returned home. I tried counting sheep with my eyes open, desperately wanting to be obedient. It didn't work. I began to cry.

So I climbed back down the short brown ladder, careful not to wake my sister but afraid to leave her with the menacing darkness. I tiptoed down the stairs to Jenny, and stood at her elbow.

"I'm scared," I told her. "I can't sleep. Spike . . ."

"Go to back to bed," she said. "You're being silly." She had looked away from her television program only once.

"I'm scared," I said. "Spike . . ."

"Go. To. Bed." Jenny commanded.

It was a rare occasion that I had to be told anything twice. It was even rarer that I would disobey.

I crept to the top of the stairs and paused at the landing. I could see my sister asleep, but the top bunk was shrouded in darkness, teeming with an unknown number of creatures bent on torturing me. My tears started up again, and I collapsed, only slightly more purposefully than I had at the movie theater, on the landing. There I sobbed until terror and fatigue combined to drag me unwillingly into sleep.

I'm not certain what my parents thought when they discovered me, crumpled, at the top of the stairs. I doubt they did anything other than smile indulgently at their strong-willed daughter asleep on the carpet, scooping her up and depositing her still-sleeping form onto her bed. They couldn't have known the furrows plowed deep into my imagination by the night's events, perfect conduits for the next fifteen years of fear. Fear of the dark. Fear of falling asleep. Fear, fear, fear.

The Roots of Fear

Most of us have a similar story to some extent or another. Whether it was an overzealous swimming coach who precipitated a lifelong fear of

drowning or a near miss with a neighborhood Rottweiler that left us
dripping with dread every time a poodle walked by, our fears have their
foundations somewhere in our stories. Indeed, they must. Research has
shown that there are only two fears that babies are born with—fear of
falling and fear of loud noises. Every other fear ingrained in our psyches,
consciously or unconsciously, has been enculturated by our family systems,
teachings and experiences. If you think you were born with that fear of
spiders, think again. You *learned* it.

The same can be said of the fears and mores found in the church body
as a whole. As people of faith, we were not birthed into life in Christ with
a requisite compliment of terror. The things that we've learned to fear—
both rightly and wrongly (and there are both)—come from the immediate context of the world in which we live, as well as from a long history
of theological tenets, cultural influence and unexamined assumptions of
our faith tradition as a whole. In the same way you inherited your fear of
flying from your mother's fear of flying, the church has inherited a
number of fears about the body from our church fathers and mothers.

But why focus here, on the fear? The church also started with a deep
belief in the goodness of our knees and fingerprints, our sense of smell
and our desire for touch. Aren't there many, many good things that we've
learned about our bodies from the life of faith?

Ironically, we focus on fear because it's a lot easier to handle. (In fact,
that's part of the problem.) We'll start with fear because fear sets up
fences, boundaries that keep us safe, or at least far away from that which
we've come to associate with being afraid.

Fear was the genesis of my ritual of reaching around a doorway and
turning on the light *before* I entered the room. Fear is the genesis of the
abuse victim's tendency to shut people out when they get to know him
too intimately. Fear motivates strange behaviors and stranger thought
processes. Fear is what patrols the borders of our lives in order to minimize risk, keep everyone safe, prevent whatever happened from ever
happening again. Fear is rigid, restraining and, generally, easy to identify.

Keep off the Tracks

Indeed, fear tells us well-wrought, beautiful and convincing stories. Fear is what feeds headlines in every medium, and fear is what keeps us buying products that we don't need and we'll never use. It's fear of missing out that has us trying to keep up with the Joneses and fear of losing out that keeps us in jobs and in places that we deeply loathe. When we're on the lookout for it, fear is everywhere, but fear is also good at dressing itself up to look really lovely. Alluring, even.

When I was young, probably the same age as my *Gremlins* experience, we lived in a small town in the southern part of the province of Ontario. Across the street from our house was a large, vacant lot. The perfect playground for children with wild imaginations, it was home to a small stream and a series of rocky outcroppings that hid invisible castles, lands of adventure and the occasional broken beer bottle. About a mile away was the local strip mall, the place where we took our allowance money and bought strips of bubblegum and packets of Nerds. Anything sugary, really. The quickest way between point A (our playground) and point B (the mall) was the stretch of nearby train tracks—a mother's worst nightmare.

Although we were reasonable kids who knew how to stay out of the way of large moving objects, the movie *Stand by Me* had just come out. Spurred by the gory images of her children finding dead bodies by the tracks, Mom set out to prohibit us from ever setting foot near this super-highway to sugar. Perhaps it was because she knew that a simple "don't do it" would inspire my sister and me to do just that, or perhaps it was her own poetic imagination, but my mother came up with the most fear-inducing thing she could think of to keep her children safe: invisible trains.

The story started practically enough, with an explanation of the workings of railway signals. She told us that each train on the tracks had a series of invisible train cars before and after the visible train—this was what triggered the flashing light and striped barrier and gave it enough time to be lowered before the real train came rumbling past in all its steam and power. We even sat beside the train tracks (in the car of course) watching the signals precede the train down the line. "Do you see it?" she said, asking the impossible of us. See the invisible train. Of course, invisible trains were there to keep us safe—but they were just as dangerous as the visible ones if you were on the tracks. This meant that if you saw a signal light flashing down the tracks a way, you'd better get off them pronto. The invisible train was bearing down on you faster than you knew, especially since *you couldn't see it.*

What a way to terrify small children into staying away from trains. I don't know why I bought into this fiction of fear, but buy into it I did. Fully, completely. It was ingenious, really, a fence around a fence. Something that not only kept us far enough away from trains that we wouldn't get hurt but had us jumping one step farther than that, just to be safe.

Unbeknownst to her, my mother was dipping back into centuries of Jewish tradition in her attempt to prevent us from becoming child-sized grill decorations. Jews use the word *Torah* to denote the first five books of Scripture—the Law, if you will. In the Torah (which is, by the way, a verb in Hebrew), God gives his people a set of rules for living. Genesis, Exodus, Leviticus, Numbers and Deuteronomy are all shot through with things that get called commandments, rules and laws. Mostly, they are God's utterances over his people, a set of guidelines that lead to a life well lived, a community well formed. Some of them seem silly and needlessly restricting to modern readers, but they cut deeply into the reality of our hearts, reflecting back to us our tendencies to scramble and strive instead of living in the gifts and provision of God.

Jews use the word *Talmud* to denote the centuries of rabbinic writing and teaching on the stories and statements that comprise Torah. While not being considered the direct word of God, the Talmud expounds on the mysterious ways that God sometimes puts things in the Torah. The Talmud explains, points out and seeks to make clear that which God has said.

It's out of the Talmud that most of the restrictions on sabbath activity come. The Torah records that no *melakah* shall be done on the sabbath and that it should be both remembered and honored. The word *melakah* here is often translated as "work," but in Hebrew it connotes the idea of creating, just as God created the world in six days and rested on the seventh.

This makes sense for our souls. Sabbath, or *shabbat*, can be literally translated as "to stop." We are told to cease striving, working, creating for one day to receive the rest and holiness of God for ourselves. This idea of weekly rest was not common in the contexts in which the nation of Israel found itself, and God was setting up something different, something important for the souls of not only the Jews but all people. The sabbath holds the people of God together.

From the prohibition on work or creation spring the teachings of the Talmud. In place of an individual interpretation of what work might be (how close to the train can we get before we need to jump from the tracks?), the Talmud prescribes thirty-nine different activities that are forbidden on the sabbath, from kindling a fire to tearing down a building. Around the original fence that protects the soul from forgetting God on the sabbath, the Talmud creates another fence, so that we're a safe enough distance away that there is no possibility of falling into sin.

The religious leaders in Jesus' time took things even further than this. For the most observant (read: holiest and farthest away from getting smushed by an oncoming train), the prohibition on plowing, for example, included a prohibition on pushing your chair back from the table abruptly. Why your chair? Because in the action of pushing it back, the leg of the chair may rend the dirt floor, creating a furrow. Oops, you just plowed something.

For the Pharisees and Sadducees (two rabbinic groups in Israel at the time), the fact that Jesus' disciples ate heads of grain while walking through a field on the Sabbath (breaking rule number three, reaping) was the equivalent of throwing the Torah back in God's face. *We don't need any flashing lights or barricades! We'll play chicken with the train on our own, thank you!*

It's enough to send them in to apoplectic fits of rage.

It's enough to get Jesus crucified.

It's enough to keep us as far away from the tracks as possible.

Fears Founded

Before we get too far in criticizing either the Talmudic scholars or my mother, let's recognize that the things they feared happening had dire, dire consequences. For Mom, the consequences of children too close to the train meant a lifetime of grief and regret, dreams destroyed, futures cut short. It meant the one thing that horrifies you as you hold a baby in your arms—that you might somehow not be able to protect her. For the rabbis, charged with protecting the spiritual lives of the people of God, the consequences of allowing the people to dishonor the sabbath were even more worthy of fear. God's not stingy with words when he calls his people to the carpet for breaking one of the few true imperatives of the Ten Commandments: honor the sabbath and keep it holy.

Indeed, God sent his prophets to warn the people of God when they broke the sabbath that he would let loose his wrath against them. Jeremiah, Ezekiel, Hosea and Amos all cried out to the people of God that they were playing heedlessly on the tracks with the train bearing down quickly. When they didn't listen, the nation was shattered and sent into exile. Of course you would set fences around fences around fences if you'd seen your people destroyed, the nation meant to be the light of the world scattered to the four winds.

Which is why our fear of our bodies is not to be taken lightly either. The church has, historically, set up fences around how we are to treat and interact with bodies—our own and each other's—for good reason. The statistics on sexual abuse alone are horrifying enough to send us running for the rule books. In the United States and Canada, one in four women have been sexually abused in some way, and one in six men. Think about that the next time that you walk into your church sanctuary or the grocery store.

As one who has experienced sexual abuse, I understand the fear as both victim and someone who longs to protect the ones that I love. As I've wrestled through the effects of rape in my own story, I've lived for a long time in fear's grip. He was my first boyfriend, and the obedient girl from the movie theater had grown up into a teen eager to please, to perform in order to be loved and accepted. That worked fine, too well in fact, right up to the moment when I wasn't given a choice to perform—it was expected of me, no matter whether I was saying no or not.

Unconsciously, I kept myself as far away as possible from the circumstances in which my abuse took place, that hazy middle ground between being awake and being asleep. Although I didn't know that I was doing it, for nearly a decade I ran myself hard into the night, working, watching television, talking to friends right up until the moment I could barely keep my eyes open. Then I would fall into bed and be asleep before my head ever hit the pillow. I used to joke that I could fall asleep anywhere, even on a concrete slab, not realizing I kept myself in a chronic state of sleep deprivation as a form of self-protection. I had put up a fence in order to keep myself off the "tracks" that bore the train named abuse into my life.

I could have kept up that pattern for the rest of my life, if love hadn't interfered. Love, in the form of my husband, began asking gentle questions about how fear was dictating the course of my days—and my nights. Love began to ask if I could live differently, if trust in my own body might be possible, even necessary, for my healing. Love invited me out beyond the fences that fear had erected, into a field of freedom.

I won't tell you that the process was easy. Abuse brings with it strong messages about ourselves, body and soul. Choosing trust in the face of fear is one of the bravest and riskiest things that we can do. My choice to trust brought with it evenings of tears and long discussions as those who loved me let me wrestle through the nightmares and fight lies that felt incontrovertibly true.

But these days, as I fall slowly, slowly to sleep wrapped in my husband's arms, I don't find myself listening for the clack-clack of wheels on steel, alert to impending doom. Instead, I listen lazily to the whisper I hear from both him and God: *I love you, I love you so much. You are safe here. Love, love, love.*

Worlds of Anxiety

As a people both called out of and called into the world, there's a lot to cause anxiety when it comes to our bodies. The messages and ideas around us rush manic-depressively from one extreme to another. Cooking shows nearly deify the stomach, creating a culture of gastronomical pleasure to be pursued at almost any cost (including but not limited to your bottom line, your waist line and your social standing). Social media encourages us to measure up against unattainable standards of beauty, trickling down to our children who compete in informal beauty contests where only the skinniest and prettiest survive. Even apart from the statistics on physical and sexual abuse, the ways that we're encouraged to manipulate and misappropriate the gift of our physicality in order win friends and influence people are in themselves a form of abuse.

So, not only is there a lot to be nervous about, there are many popular conceptions of our bodies (and exactly how they are to look, smell, feel and operate) that are worth rejecting outright, even agitating against. There is a great deal of legitimacy to the idea that separation from the world's conception of the body is a step toward a healthy and holistic embrace of what our bodies have been intended by God to be. The reality is, there is a train. And standing on the tracks as it comes barreling toward you is neither wise nor safe.

And yet.

And yet I still find myself checking over my shoulder obsessively when I change lanes while driving. At inopportune moments, crossing the street makes my palms sweat and forces me to do deep breathing exercises for at least fifteen minutes afterward. Although the invisible trains were completely fictitious, I live as if they (and invisible cars) are real. And because I live as if they're real, they have a life and a power that steals from me. This way of being isn't an inheritance of freedom and life. These responses aren't what God most deeply wants for me as I navigate the world.

Fences for Fences

To the fears of abuse and adultery, over time the church has added fears of corruption, of immodesty, of impurity. Whole cultures have sprung up around "purity," cultures dedicated to ensuring that the risk of becoming "impure" is completely eliminated. There are rules around rules, not only for Christian leaders but for anyone who wants to consider themselves serious about their faith.

All of these rules are couched, quite rightly, in the language of safety. It's not wise to speak to someone of the opposite gender with the door closed. It's not wise to kiss someone you wouldn't want to marry. It's not wise to touch someone who is not your spouse. It's not wise to bare your shoulders when someone could interpret this to mean you have loose morals. In all the rules, we get further and further from the possibility of danger. Our fears are seemingly allayed. We're being safe. We're being wise. We're being good.

Unfortunately, when we turn around, we're also so entangled in the rules of what it means to be "safe," "wise" and "good" that we've cut ourselves off from the life of God in our bodies. We can't hear God's whispers through our physical senses because coming near the messages of our fingers, our eyes, our lips is much too risky. We've fenced the tracks so highly that we can't even step out the front door.

Precious Pictures

Trapped in our houses, hedged in by our fears, something really nefarious starts to happen. We begin to believe that this house is all we really need. Aware of the dangers "out there," we start to make up stories about why it's better to be confined inside these four walls rather than out there in the world. Instead of taking considered and sometimes spectacular risks with God, we content ourselves with smallness, reasoning that our purity, our lack of corruption, our modesty are somehow things of our own making rather than conditions gifted to us because of the incredible work of Christ on the cross. We become self-satisfied with the ways that we have made the world safe, rather than seeing we've stepped into a cell of our own creating.

This contentment with the smallness and safety of our relationship with our body also allows us a dangerous measure of self-deception. I, for one, know that I can be the world's greatest saint in my own head. Without stepping out my front door, I can convince myself that I have great empathy for the poor, that I have conquered my tendency to fall into envy, that I respond easily and charitably even to those I would consider my enemies. Without ever encountering another person, I can believe wonderfully contrived things about how patient I am, how pious I am in prayer, how graciously I accept disappointment or even suffering.

I may be the only one who paints these pretty pictures of myself, but I suspect that I'm not. These glowing self-portraits are possible because we tend to keep ourselves at a remove from embodied experience, pre-ferring instead the sanctuary of the mind.

Our bodies, you see, don't lie.

Oh, they may betray, they may act in unpredictable and embarrassing ways, they may even fail us, but they never lie. When you spend time with your wildly successful sister and your stomach turns into a mass of knots, your envy is exposed (even if you choose to ignore it). When your pulse races and you struggle to reach a hand out to the young man on the street whose body odor reaches you before his palm does, your discomfort with those who are less fortunate than you belies your belief in how responsive you are to the needs of the poor. When your jaw clenches as you listen to the person in line in front of you at the grocery store tell the clerk all about her day, your tendency to impatience broad-casts itself in the grinding of your teeth. Just as it isn't possible to abuse the body without abusing the soul, soul sickness (however it has come to us) gets expressed in the body as well.

This is one of the great tragedies of our fear-filled, rule-bound worlds—in avoiding any hint of risk we not only miss the opportunities to experience the fullness of life, we deceive ourselves into believing that the lives we're living are whole, holy and good.

Don't get me wrong. These small worlds are, on the surface, safer than the alternative. Without invisible trains, my mother ran the risk of losing me under the dark weight of engine and steel. Without the rules around the sabbath, the Pharisees risked watching the people of God turn their backs on the Holy One of Israel. Without the prohibitions we put on experiencing our bodies, we run the risk of misuse, exploitation or assault. Of course protecting ourselves from these things feels like wisdom.

Sadly, caution and wisdom are two different things. Scripture says over and over that the fear of God is the beginning of wisdom, not the fear of the world. In Proverbs, Solomon, who so audaciously asked and received wisdom from God, writes,

> Trust in the LORD with all your heart
>   and *lean not on your own understanding*;
> in all your ways submit to him,
>   and he will make your paths straight. (Proverbs 3:5-6,
>   emphasis added)

This life with God is meant to be a relationship, not a set of rules. While our fears drive us into control and circumscribe our lives with prohibitions, the One who died for us invites us into love and a freedom that comes from trusting him not only with our salvation but with our whole embodied lives as well. Instead of leaving us in the small stories we create for ourselves, God invites us out into spacious places, lavishing us with his delight and fiercely insisting that our delusional self-images be replaced by truth in the inmost places. In this context it's not surprising that the most frequent command in Scripture is "Fear not!"[1]—an imperative that's impossible to obey without the grace and strength of God living in and through us.

Touch Point

How Did I Get Here?

Recognizing the places where fear has taken over our relationship with our bodies isn't a simple task. Fear is slippery and can look a lot like reasonable precaution (except for the fact that it's divorced from a relationship with God). While coming at our fears straight on sometimes surprises them enough that they show their hand, most of the time our fears are cunning enough to hide in other disguises. Take a step into these exercises without trying to force your fears out into the open. Be open to surprises and the gentle revelations of Christ.

Read through the story found in John 5:2-9. Ask Jesus to guide your imagination and speak through the story to your heart.

Begin by imagining in the scene at the Sheep Gate. What are the surroundings like? What about the pool? How big is it? What is the water like? This is the place that people go when they want to be healed. They believe that an angel stirs the waters, and the first ones into the pool will have their physical ailments removed.

Imagine the types of people who have come to find healing. What are they wearing? What are they like? Why have they come? Notice that all of their illnesses are physical. What might it mean that all of these people are seeking restoration in their flesh and blood? What hopes do they have about their own bodies?

Now, invite the scene to come to life. The invalid who as been unable to walk for thirty-eight years is here. How did he get here? Did people bring him to the pool, this supposed place of healing, and then leave him without any way of getting into the waters? How does this relate to how you feel about your body, your way of relating to the world? How does this mirror how those around you (your family story, the story of the church) have brought you to a place that seems so close but so far away from actual healing?

Notice Jesus enter the scene. What are you feeling as you imagine him coming toward you? What hopes or fears are stirred as Jesus approaches?

Jesus speaks to the man beside you. What does he say? He asks the man, "Do you want to get well?" What rises in you when you hear that question? What is your first response?

Pay attention to what happens when Jesus heals the man. Jesus says nothing about his faith or where his friends are. The man picks up his mat and walks. Is there something that you want to say to Jesus at this moment? Something you want to ask him? Are you ill? Are you suffering from something—perhaps in your relationship to your own body—that you want to talk to him about? Is there something you would like Jesus to say to you?

Spend some time conversing with Jesus. Let him speak to the questions and fears in your own heart.

2

How We Lost Our Bodies

I believe what I believe. It makes me what I am.
I did not make it, no it is making me.
It's the very truth of God, not
the invention of any man.

RICH MULLINS

I am very easy of belief when the Creed pleases me.

CHARLOTTE BRONTË

A FEW YEARS AGO, MY HUSBAND AND I became briefly obsessed with our genealogies. Since neither of us had done much digging into our family trees, each discovery brought with it a sense of revelation and understanding. Night after night we sat on the couch piecing together the stories of family members long dead, discerning from old documents and pictures who had married whom or divorced whom or died young.

As we traced the limbs of my husband's tree, for example, we discovered that his sense of stability and desire for simplicity comes from a family who has lived in the same small town in Massachusetts since they came to it on the *Mary Gould*, one of the flotilla of ships that followed in the *Mayflower*'s wake. Whether or not he knew it, Bryan's heartwood draws on four hundred unbroken years of living locally before his father moved out of the area to serve in the Vietnam War.

As we climbed onto the branches of my tree, we discovered that I come by my competing desire for both family loyalty and independent adventure quite honestly. Back in the 1640s, seven of eight brothers seized adventure by sailing off from the Old World to the New. Left behind was Valentyne, who stayed to care for his aging, widowed mother. It's from his line I spring, and I feel the same tension he must have felt: I want to go, but I also want to stay and support those I love. It thrums through my veins every day.

That the apple doesn't fall far from the tree is a cliché, it's true, but it's also a profound statement on how our heritage shapes us both consciously and unconsciously.

It helps to understand where you're from. Not just for a sense of permission to be who you are—or who you aren't—but also because it gives you a picture of what has formed you, what factors have shaped your family and therefore you, what silent assumptions have trickled down through the centuries, finding their way into your own worldview. This isn't always possible to do—especially in the cases of closed adoptions or times when families become so ashamed of their past they swallow it in silence—but in these cases even an understanding of general cultural heritage helps us understand how we're formed.

The same is true of the family of God. Just as we have brothers and sisters in the faith who inform, strengthen and sometimes challenge our daily journey with God, we have forebears whose prayers, study, assumptions and thoughts about life in the kingdom make an impact on us today. Who exactly those forebears are depends in part on the branch of Christianity that we find ourselves on. For the Western church, the main branches split off into Protestant and Roman Catholic, with further varied divisions on both sides of that fork. For the East, Orthodoxy hewed off into branches as diverse as the cultures in which they found themselves: Greek, Russian, Polish, American and more. If we climb back down to the main trunk, the place of original split and the heritage from which it all springs, we find that we're all related, all reaching back to the same source of sustenance and life, our roots in the same soil.

Family history doesn't always deposit us in a good or helpful place, of course. In the same way that we can trace our influences, the heritage that gives us red hair or blue eyes, we can trace our dysfunctions, the tendency to rage or self-protection that comes from decades of deprivation. In the same way that our heritage gives us a bent toward stability, it can also bequeath to us a resistance to change, an inability to see innovation as anything other than a threat to the way things have been.

Tracing family systems in our own lives leads to self-knowledge, which can then empower us to seek better, healthier ways of interacting with the world. It can also fill us with profound gratitude for what we've been given and help us stand on the shoulders of those who have come before us.

It's a little more difficult to trace back what we've been formed by when it comes to the church. Only a percentage of those in the body of Christ are fit, at core, to become historians or theologians. God didn't form everyone with a deep desire to understand the prevailing reasons for the Great Schism of 1054. Nor did he make everyone with a delight in auto mechanics or a desire to research the origins of the sewer system in France.

We each have been formed by God, not just in our mother's womb but in the womb of the church, the traditions passed on to us whether we're Southern Baptist or Pentecostal, Eastern Orthodox or Roman Catholic. As we have developed and grown in faith, the church has nurtured us, formed us in Christ and given us tools for moving forward in our spiritual lives. Some of those tools have been useful, some make everything around us seem like a nail. Some of those tools have caused us to approach the world in a way that has even been hurtful to us and others, and some have been the way God brought great redemption and healing into our communities and ourselves. We intuitively know that we've been nurtured differently by different streams of Christianity.

We see our differences—just as my husband sees my tendency toward drinking tea and I see my husband's proclivity toward daring new things—but more rarely do we ask where they might have come from. My blindness, our blindness, to our origins finds its source in the desire to believe that, somehow, we're the only ones. That our struggles are unique, specific only to us. That desire to be special runs through all of us, on one level or another, because we are seeking our belovedness, our uniqueness in God. It's not a bad thing to want to know that God sees us, but it gets twisted quickly into a sense that no one could understand us, or that we're all alone—both faces of false pride.

My blindness, our blindness, comes from thinking that we are without community or roots and that we can somehow understand ourselves outside of the environment in which we are raised, the places of nurture that have brought us up. When we begin to crawl out of the bias (whether Western, modern or some combination thereof) that we have never been influenced by our context or, in the case of our relationship to our bodies, the history of the church, we begin to learn that our tendencies are not just our own and that the tools we have been given might not be the best ones for moving forward into a healthy, whole, redemptive future.

This process, though, is a process of attention few of us have training in undertaking. It's like being conscious of the air around you on a regular basis or having a constant awareness of the temperature of your skin. As we learn our heritage, we need to be attentive to the ways that heritage has formed us, for ill and for good. That heritage will continue to crop up in the way we do things, and it requires acts of concerted attention to discern where the heritage is informing us well and where God might be calling us to go a different route. This holds as true for our own histories as it does for the story of the church as a whole.

Any telling of history is a simplification. Just as when you tell your own story, you leave things out (what you had for breakfast three weeks ago, that embarrassing but minor incident when you showed up for your chemistry final an hour late), a history of the church will necessarily leave details out, a history of the church's relationship with the body more so. In order to give a history of almost anything, we also tend to create a clean narrative, a relatively clear path to the story we're trying to tell. That means that competing viewpoints, or even events that don't fit into our timelines well, sometimes get left out. At times this is intentional and nefarious, at others it's simply the bias of the context in which the history is written (history is always written, as the saying goes, by the victors, after all).

The thing is, the church's ambivalence toward the body is something woven deeply into our heritage. The body and its goodness (or evil) isn't just something that we've been talking about in recent history. From nearly the first century onward, the church has struggled with heresies and more subtle influences that sprung up about the body, and whether it was, indeed, something capable of being redeemed.

The Creeds and the Gnostics

The first concise definitions of the Christian faith that we have are the Apostles' Creed[1] (which is a derivative of the Old Roman Creed[2]) and the Nicene Creed,[3] confirmed by the First Council of Nicaea which met just after Christianity became the official religion of the Roman Empire. Nicaea was revolutionary because it was the first time the church had attempted to gather all of known Christendom together to discuss and decide on important matters of faith, and the decisions made by those 318 men stand as the foundation of the church to this day. Apart from the totality of Scripture, these creeds are the record of the early church, imprints of the first tottering footsteps of infant Christianity. They give us the necessities of the living faith—lungs, nerves, breath, blood flow—as birthed by those who followed the wandering rabbi from Nazareth.

There isn't anything extra here. What we see in the creeds, what we read in these early affirmations of our church ancestors, is an insistence on the particularity of Jesus (he lived at a particular point in history, he was fully God and fully human), the unity of the Trinity and—something that seems to have gotten tucked away in the folds of history—an unflinching belief in the physical resurrection of our bodies when the kingdom of God comes in fullness.

Much doctrine and theology springs out of the creeds, doctrine and theology that point to very important aspects of the faith, about which tomes and tomes have been written. As the diversity of the body of Christ has increased, our ways of describing and parsing out the true mysteries and the truth of the faith has increased as well, and—no matter how dry you find academia—this diversity is stunningly beautiful. The church continues to exercise all of the faculties given to it by God, to dive deeply and intelligently into the understanding and defense of what it means to believe in the One who sacrificed his very self for our redemption.

But at the beginning, the infant church didn't need the theological clothing that would come to dress it as it grew to adulthood in the centuries to come. Instead, it needed nurture, structure and protection, something the creeds provided. We can tell from the creeds, and the Nicene Creed in particular, one of the most important things that the church needed to be protected from: a belief that Jesus wasn't really human, after all.

Early Christians defended the faith against a particularly insidious infection called Gnosticism. A heresy that sprung up in the second and third centuries after Christ, Gnosticism purports that matter—the stuff our universe is made of—is inherently flawed and, to more ascetic factions, evil. Gnostics also believe in special knowledge, a revelation given to the elite of a particular group, knowledge not available to the majority of us. It's a temptation all of us feel—we want to be the ones "in the know," the ones who have something others don't—but that kind of hierarchy puts a barrier up between the people and Jesus, a barrier that Jesus never erected himself.

Today, *Gnosticism* is used to refer to any time we privilege the spiritual over the material. Although this seems natural to us in some ways—if God is Spirit, and Scripture clearly says he is, why wouldn't the spiritual be better, more holy, more pure than the physical?—that's not the dichotomy God set up. As I wrote in chapter one, the incarnation was a radical rearrangement of the story. God became flesh, and flesh became God.

Doesn't it feel a bit radical to read that? I get the "God became flesh" part. That's in the Bible. But that flesh became God? That one's harder. If we narrow it down, it's a little easier to swallow (and less of a logical fallacy for us). Jesus' flesh became God. But it's more than that as well. Because the flesh that Christ had was real human flesh, human flesh made capable of complete union with God. In the early church, a church not far removed from the Jesus who walked and talked and laughed and sweat and wept with his disciples, this wasn't as hard to swallow. But the further that we got from an embodied experience of knowing Christ, the more apt people were to wiggle away from the radical truth of the redemption of our bodies. It just wasn't comfortable.

Doctors of the Church

The early church fathers, those whose faith grew out of and was formed by that young church protected by the creeds, contended with this discomfort as well. John Chrysostom, Gregory of Nyssa, Tertullian and Augustine in the fourth and fifth centuries all wrestled with what it means to have a body like Christ's, possessing the same capacity for redemption, and still feel the pull toward what is degenerate and dark in that very body. The heresy of Gnosticism, as well as a number of other heresies that contended that Jesus wasn't fully human, continued to swirl around the church, seeking entrances unprotected by the faithful.

The church councils, from Constantinople to Ephesus to Chalcedon, dealt regularly with various theologies that rejected the body.[4] For the most part, these gatherings of the faithful defended against any belief system that attempted to separate Christ's work of redemption from the full restoration of our bodies. And yet, like an infection weakening the systems meant to defend against it, these repeated assaults on the theology of the body made it difficult to completely flush out that inherent mistrust of the physical world. Two hundred years of fighting off attempt after attempt to strip Christianity of its radical belief in the goodness of the body took its toll.

In particular, the prolific theologian St. Augustine labored over the way embodied habits draw us away from God. To say the bishop of Hippo had a checkered history is a bit of an understatement, especially as he is the one most often credited with praying, "Lord, give me chastity, but not yet." As he sought a life of intimacy with God, he found himself drawn back to sexual fantasies rooted in his loose living in Carthage years before.

Augustine did daily battle with lust, something that comes out clearly in his autobiography, *The Confessions*, and in his theological writings that focus on the necessity of denying every bit of our sexual desires, even in marriage. He bemoaned that procreation couldn't occur without a "certain amount of bestial movement"[5] or a "violent acting of lust," believing that sexual expression before the fall was without the shame that he saw as incapable of being separated from sexual desire.

This belief in the shamefulness of sexuality stands shoulder to shoulder with his continual defense of the incarnation and the fact that Jesus lived a fully human life. To paint Augustine as radically against our bodies is to lose his teachings on the work of God in human history and his belief that the body is an essential part of the human person. At the same time, Augustine's views on the inevitability of sin when it comes to our sexuality affect the church's view of the goodness of our bodies to this day.

Gregory of Nyssa, a church father of the East, also struggled, not with the incarnation or human sexuality necessarily but with the idea that humans even had a fleshly body before we were expelled from Eden. In his writings, he explored in depth the idea that our creaturely bodies—

bodies that copulate, procreate and defecate—are the things God clothed us in after eating the forbidden fruit, the "garments of skin" that God provides for Adam and Even in Genesis 3:21. As a result, anything that could be considered an "animal impulse" works against our redemption because it is a result of our sin, a consequence of it. That Jesus inhabited these "garments of skin" was not in dispute for Gregory; instead, Gregory theologized that Jesus took on a body so that the body's inherent post-fall shame was redeemed by the indwelling Christ.[6] Our bodies, therefore, are God's "second best" plan for creation, something that had to be given to us because of sin.

Holding the Tensions

Augustine and Gregory of Nyssa aren't the only relatives in the church family tree who tried to solve the puzzle created by the full humanity of Jesus set against what is yet unredeemed in our humanity—the painful reality that our bodies don't always act in ways that are healthy, good or holy. They are, however, emblematic of the legacy the modern church received. Just as my inherited tendency to want to stay home and look after my responsibilities—the legacy from my forefather Valentyne—sometimes has me missing out on the adventures that God intends for me, the heritage of believing our bodies to be painfully incapable of *certain types* of redemption cripples us to the possibilities God has for the whole of us, bodies included.

There's an adage that says we become what we fight. It is, perhaps, why Jesus calls the peacemakers blessed as the children of God. Those who make peace are free to live out their true identity as beloved of the Almighty instead of being defined by that which they are trying to eliminate or destroy. As much as the church needed to protect against cultural philosophies attempting to strip Christ's physical reality from the faith, fighting that belief over and over again left a mark. A mark that mars our ability to embrace the body as good, a mark that has us patrolling the way our bodies act, ready for any sign that they may betray us, proving the heretics right after all. Over time the scars from those battles have obscured the glory of the body beneath, and we have come to see only the surface wounds. Calling that ugly, twisted, not what God intended misses the very point of the battle in the first place. We've been left with the shreds of the story; what we piece together says that the body is somehow deficient.

But the body is so powerful, and at its best so very good, that it forms and shapes our views of ourselves, others and God. Our bodies are an integral part of our selves and tell us what we most deeply believe—even when our minds and hearts are telling us otherwise. You may think you believe the bridge across that ravine is perfectly sturdy and safe, but your increased heart rate and sweaty palms tell you that your body (and therefore you) believe otherwise. Our bodies don't lie, and what they tell us about how we perceive reality is the key to stepping into actual transformation in Christ. This in itself is a sadly overlooked gift from God, for who at their healthiest wouldn't want to know what's really going on in themselves, in others, in their relationship with God and the world from a source that would never deceive them? We can teach ourselves wrong things by the way we live out our embodied existence—that God will leave us if we aren't interesting or that every impulse is to be fed immediately, for example. Paul's lament in Romans 7—"I do not understand what I do. For what I want to do I do not do, but what I hate I do" (Romans 7:15)—is ours too. There are habits of flesh that lead us away from the very redemption that Christ's embodied life, death and resurrection brought to us.

Of course, the church marched forward through history. As it grew through the ages, the early wrangling over whether or not the stuff of this world was evil seemed to fall away, solved it seemed by the defense of the councils. Other, more pressing threats arose, and the Dark Ages engulfed Christianity in conflict with other conquering societies. As humanity advanced, so did the wielding of power (in domination, in slavery, in financial exploitation), and believers were not immune to its pull, despite the refusal of the Messiah from Nazareth to exercise the power of heaven in the face of his own impending execution. The church split, over and over, bloodied and bruised by the ways it embraced and used the culture of commodification and power around it.

The creeds continued to wend through the ages and stages of the church, circling the sacraments round with the beauty of what it means to be an embodied soul (or an ensouled body). But just as early childhood trauma unconsciously informs how we respond as adults, so did the early heresies persist in influencing modern Christianity's push-and-pull relationship with celebrating the beauty of sexuality, the holy grace of art and artists, the mystery of God's messages in our sense of smell, taste and touch. Instead of explicit attacks on the nature of God, the war against our bodies became more subtle, threaded through with truth but woven into cloth used to cover our bodies, enrobe them in mantles not of dignity, but shame.

Touch Point

Discovering Your History

Knowing where we come from involves both an understanding of our origins as well as an examination of the assumptions that we've inherited without thought or interrogation. Dysfunction, whether it relates to our bodies or to our family systems, doesn't necessarily mean outright abuse (although it can). Dysfunction can sometimes be functional practices that were appropriate for one phase of life translated inappropriately across other phases.

Take some time to practice the prayer of examen. This ancient prayer form is often credited to St. Ignatius of Loyola, who lived in the fifteenth century. This prayer is most often used as a practice for reflecting quietly on the past twenty-four hours. Engaging in examen strengthens our abilities to notice God's presence, to be attentive to the leading and guiding of the Holy Spirit. Examen normally has four phases (presence, thankfulness, review, response) and can be used regularly to notice God's action throughout your life, whether in the daily details or in life's transitions (marriage, birthdays, new years, etc.).

In this case, I suggest using the prayer of examen to notice your own history with your body and the ways you've either encountered or rejected your physicality as an important part of your whole life.

Begin in a quiet place where you're not likely to be interrupted (if possible). There isn't a timeline to examen, but I would encourage you to set aside enough time so you won't be rushed. I also encourage you to journal this prayer and to engage yourself physically in it. This may simply mean putting pen to paper, or it may mean getting up and walking, laying on the floor or moving your body in a way that connects you more deeply to the messages you've received about what it means to be human.

As you enter in, turn your attention toward the presence of God with you. Take a few deep breaths, and settle in to a calm space with Jesus. If you feel yourself anxious or distracted, remind yourself there is no right or wrong way to practice examen. Ask the Holy Spirit for his light, for the grace to pray and the eyes to see.

Spend time in gratitude for the things about your body you enjoy. What's your favorite body part? Give thanks for it. Notice the ways you've been given positive messages about your body from your family and from the church. Focus your attention on each part of your body in turn. Even if it's difficult for you, give thanks as authentically as you can.

Now, review as thoroughly as you can the messages you've received throughout time about your body. It may be helpful to break your life down into decades—what were the messages about your body when you were ten years old? How about when you were a teenager? You might want to look at the messages as they came from different systems in your life: narratives about your body from your family, your church, your culture, your generation. Listen for what the Spirit of God is whispering to you here. Pay attention not to the shoulds and shouldn'ts but to your own experience of your body in the midst of the messages. Where has God been with you in your body? It's important to remember that this isn't about judging or rationalizing but about paying attention to the way you've experienced your body and messages around it during your lifetime.

Now, gently turn your attention to what God might have to say about these messages. Is there a particular message that God wants to highlight as helpful or unhelpful? Is there a place where you were given a message about your body that resulted in harm to you or to others? Is there a way you may have treated your own body God that wants to touch and redeem? What messages is God asking you to embrace? What messages is he asking you to leave behind?

Finally, spend some time responding to God about what you've seen in this time together with the Spirit. You might want to journal about a particular embodied experience and how God met you through it. You may find yourself confessing and asking God for his truth about the goodness of your body in the midst of your own fears and confusion. Don't try to tie everything up in a neat bow. Instead, speak to God about what's on your heart—what you need, what you want and what you might want to walk away from. Beginning today, how do you want to live differently?

End with a simple prayer. You can use the following or something that speaks to where you are in your story with God:

> *Loving and ever-present God, help me to meet you daily in my embodied experience of your glory-filled creation. I want to live into the truth of your redemption of my body, to welcome, serve and love myself and others so that your kingdom may come and your will may be done. I ask you to continue guiding me and helping me grow in being your presence in my spheres of life. In Christ's name, amen.*

Broken Body, Broken Church

We carry a terrible wound: alienation from our embodied life.
Your flesh shall become a great poem.

WALT WHITMAN

Why then, man, are you so worthless in your own eyes and yet so
precious to God? Why render yourself such dishonor when you are
honored by him? Why do you ask how you were created
and do not seek to know why you were made?

ST. PETER CHRYSOLOGUS

IN ISAIAH 61, THE PROPHET INVITES THE PEOPLE of Israel to see God
differently. Historically, the nation is in exile under the Babylonians, the
city of Jerusalem in ruins. Foretold judgment has come, and the people
of God are struggling to find hope. Isaiah speaks poetically into this
place of shame and resignation. He says that God has come to set the
captives free, to release the prisoners, to bind up the brokenhearted.
Isaiah asks a people in exile to believe that God is up to something good.

The Hebrew word for brokenhearted there is *leb shabar*. *Leb* is colloquially translated "heart"—not the physical organ but the concept of personhood that we mean when we say "she took that to heart" or "he is a goodhearted man." It also means "will" or "yourself" in the truest, most encompassing sense of who you are as a unique human being. To use the word *leb* in the Hebrew mind was to invoke that which is your core, that irreducible part that makes you, you. *Shabar* translates as "broken," but the image here is not something that is simply cracked or prevented from functioning. In Hebrew, *shabar* translates more fully as "broken into pieces" like a piece of pottery shattered on the ground.

When Isaiah says that God has come to bind up the brokenhearted, then, the prophet isn't saying that God is about to comfort our sadness or put a bandage on our betrayals. Instead, he is about the work of putting us—every part of us—back together into an integrated whole.

Most of us intuitively know what this "broken into pieces" feels like. We live it every day in our relationships, our vocations, our families and our spiritual journeys. We live our lives putting on different roles (mother, brother, student, friend, employer) and masks (the good girl, the poet, the outdoorsman, the academic), none of which encompass all of who we are, most of which leave us feeling like half a person or, worse, in direct conflict with our true selves, if we could even articulate who that is.

For some of us, the moment of shattering is vivid and easily recollected. Abuse, betrayal, rejection and shaming at the hands of another broke our very selves into pieces. For others, the shattering felt gradual, a series of hairline fractures that laced slowly across our souls, the fissures running deep, rending us apart while the pieces were still pressed achingly close together.

When I journeyed into Christianity in my mid-twenties, I was a woman wracked with fear and self-hatred. A journalist who believed in the power of words to shape and move the world around her, I nonetheless regularly used those words to strip myself bare of dignity. The words I used in my own head to describe myself would have made the harshest taskmaster cringe—I regularly berated myself for being stupid, ugly, socially inept or just plain boring (although I was, and am, none of those things). Driven by performance and a need to be simultaneously approved of by and apart from others, I pushed myself hard. I longed for love and acceptance but categorically refused to give it to myself. I was splintered, at war.

I first walked into Georgetown Community Church in downtown Washington, D.C., looking not for Jesus but instead for a brief détente, just a short hour of peace in which the world might not make any more sense but at least the various parts of myself wouldn't be in pitched battle. It hadn't yet crossed my mind that peace might be a Presence, instead of a temporary lack of combat.

The Christianity I was offered at GCC (now Three Strands Community Church) was at once rare and redemptive. In prayers, music and sermon, I heard about a God who was about the work of loving us into wholeness. Over meals shared after service, people talked openly about their struggles and how Jesus was offering himself into them. Restlessly, I returned each Sunday, unsure of what I was seeking and even less confident of how to open myself to receive whatever that might be.

What was stunning to me then, and is even now, was the complete lack of judgment I received from this ragged community of Christians. To them, my story was holy. The way I saw the world was fascinating, and they actively watched for the fingerprints of God in even my most devastating memories. When I revealed my struggle with depression, they sat with me in it. When I talked about my years as a pagan and then Wiccan, they didn't cringe in fear or categorize that time as evil. Instead, they looked with me for what I might have been searching for, what I didn't find. With them, I discerned that I'd been longing for that wordless something; their care and curiosity freed me from what is often a stifling amount of shame heaped on the spiritual journeys of those who are seeking for God. They also gave me the gift of the well-received question. In this community of love, I saw a wholeness—not complete by any measure—that I was longing for; in them, the life I was seeking took form and shape.

It was the constancy of this community that eventually won me, a sense that I was beloved, not condemned. That here, with Jesus and these other messy but blessed folk, might be a place where I could live in faith instead of fear. It was a kind of communion that brought the grace of God right into the deepest places of my soul, where I myself was *leb shabar*, and salvation took hold of me. I remember the physical sensation in my heart when I turned to God for the first time to tell him that I wanted this life of wholeness that I saw in others, that he seemed to want for me. Although it was an emotional moment, the feeling was physiological, the way a lock tumbles and turns when met with a key, the various pieces rolling to fit together once again, a door opened. Something in my soul was repaired, and I felt it in my body.

Eugene Peterson writes,

> You would think that believing that Jesus is God among us would be the hardest thing. But it is not. It turns out that the hardest thing is to believe that God's work—this dazzling creation, this astonishing salvation, this cascade of blessings—is all being worked out in and under the conditions of our humanity: at picnics and around dinner tables, in conversations and while walking along roads, in puzzled questions and homely stories, with blind beggars and suppurating lepers, at weddings and funerals. Everything that Jesus does and says takes place within the limits and conditions of our humanity. No fireworks. No special effects. Yes, there are miracles. But because they are so much a part of the fabric of everyday life, very few notice. The miracle is obscured by the familiarity of the setting, the ordinariness of the people involved.[1]

Salvation is the work of Christ to bring the whole of ourselves (and also our world) back into alignment with the way God intended. This is a healing. This is a rescue. Salvation, then, is not only on the cross but also a reparation, a restoration to health that is progressively taking place. The binding up that Isaiah speaks of is this very process, where we are saved, are being saved and will be saved by a healing God. It isn't simply a moment of exchange but a lifetime of being brought back to the way we were meant to be, something Paul underlines when he urges the church at Philippi to work out their salvation with fear and trembling (Philippians 2:12).

Tracing the Cracks

In my journeying since that point, I have come to see how difficult it is for a community like GCC to form, what battle and sacrifice it takes to live and offer that kind of grace to one another. Each year, in December, I send a thank-you note to my friends Greg and Molly, who invited me into that journey, who are now pastors of that church, who continue to shepherd it in grace and love.

I have also come to see something that saddens me, a deep fracture that runs through not only my own splintered soul but the heart of the church as well. Admittedly, I stand at a vantage point that only allows me a clear view of the Western church. I suspect that there are those in the East and perhaps the Global South who are allowing the goodness and love of God to heal this rift of self differently, more fully. But as I have thumbed the wound in my own soul, I have traced its lines through the heart of every church I've set foot in, even, yes, from GCC all the way through the place I call my spiritual home now. I've tracked backward, slowly tracing this fissure as one would trace a fault line to its source, watching it run through the history of our faith, all the way back to our first father and mother, Adam and Eve.

There are many deaths precipitated by that first fruit grasped: alienation from God, each other, creation. But the one we still seem to guard as if it is natural and right, as if we must live with this as the "wages of sin" (Romans 6:23) for all eternity *despite* the work of Christ on the cross, is alienation from our bodies.

Now, hear me rightly. I'm not saying that alienation from our bodies is somehow worse or more pervasive than our alienation from God. Nor am I saying that alienation from ourselves was not a consequence of that soul-shattering fall. But I am suggesting that our alienation from our bodies, our refusal to receive God's redemption in our bodies, is a symptom of that state of *leb shabar*. Alienation from our bodies is a form of alienation from God, one that we moderns seem to accept as simply normal, just the way it is.

If you doubt me, tell me this: when was the last sermon you heard on the goodness of our physical selves? Who among your community talks regularly about hearing God in his body? When people you know speak about their bodies (if they ever do), do they talk in a context of condemnation or grace? Who do you know who *hasn't* complained about their latest diet or wanting to lose weight or needing to get stronger? What leader of yours embraces her sexuality as a call to connectedness rather than something to police and restrict?

If you can answer even one of those questions with a name or example that is positive and affirming, you are a rarity in the community of believers in the modern church. Call yourself blessed. Then go out and share this blessing with others, because we are all in desperate need of witnesses to the healing life in Christ that includes our bodies, not just our souls.

We're in need of that witness because the subtle and explicit message we've received over the centuries—woven in through the history of the church—since Jesus walked the dusty paths of Judea is that our bodies are fallen, twisted things, not to be trusted. Subtle, because if someone dear to you told you that your hands, your feet, your thighs were a hideous source of sin, you would likely laugh. Subtle, because we learn instead from glances and silences, from shaming looks and fearful responses that the flesh we walk around with is somehow dirty, corrupt and, worse, dangerous. Subtle, because we are consistently bounded by rules of what we should *not* be doing with our bodies, from parading them around naked to full-frontal hugging of the opposite gender to sexual intercourse before (and in some permutations after) marriage.

The explicit ways that we've been told our bodies are, if not evil themselves, then a very sure source of evil covered by a sheen of sanctification. We get called, we are told, to a standard different than that of "the world" when we choose how to dress and how to present ourselves physically to others. The ways that "secular" society dresses, eats and copulates are presented as clearly unbiblical and leading to sin. I remember attending a large nondenominational church a few years after I had become a Christian. I got involved in a women's small group that gathered once a week in the cramped living room of a single girl whose non-Christian roommates scattered rapidly as soon as we arrived. One of the women had recently been bringing a friend to church in a sincere attempt to offer her life and redemption but struggled with the attention she had been receiving because of it. "She just dresses so ... so ... *slutty!*" she wailed to us one evening. "I don't know how to tell her to dress different and still have her come back to church with me."

No condemnation of our bodies is more harrowing than the silence that entombs our discussion of the body as beautiful and good. Our participation in worship, in community, in Communion is all predicated on our bodies—we can't show up to church or to the soup kitchen without them. But instead of addressing them as part of the whole, a part to be saved and redeemed, we focus on our "spiritual lives" as somehow distinct from our hungering, thirsting, bleeding, sweating bodies. We have sermon after sermon on how to love God with "heart, soul, mind and strength" or "be transformed by the renewing of your mind" without a single consideration of the clause that precedes: "offer your bodies as a living sacrifice, holy and pleasing to God" (Romans 12:1-2). In our silence, we damn our bodies as peripheral to life with God at best and an impediment to redemption at worst. In our silence, we refuse to live in the corporeal reality of humanity, we pretend as if we can be human without being incarnate, and we choose, day after day, to live somewhere other than the present reality of the body, the only place where heaven actively meets earth.

The Right Fight

I took up boxing just after college. Living on my own on an intern's budget in Washington, D.C., meant that I ended up in some pretty seedy neighborhoods, mostly on foot. While I knew that my skills at bobbing and weaving wouldn't hold up if a weapon was involved, it felt good to know I could probably knock an assailant down, if not completely out.

I'm not an aggressive person by nature, but I am competitive, and amateur boxing was just what I needed in the high-pressure world of political journalism to take my mind off the day's stories and use my hands for something other than typing copy. It's impossible to focus on anything else when someone is throwing punches at your head. That, plus my coaches were savvy enough to notice I wasn't just there for the workout. I wanted to improve. I wanted to win.

Stepping into a boxing ring with someone is part chess game, part ballroom dance. In the course of a round (which is, by the way, the longest two minutes known to man), you get a feel for your opponent. You start to see she's going to take a half-step forward before throwing an uppercut, that she turns right when she's a little tired. She learns you tend to follow a left with a double right, if you can, and that you don't like being in the middle of the ring. At the lower levels, there's a greater possibility of getting hurt, because you don't know to keep your guard up and your opponent is more likely to throw wild punches.

I learned a lot more about myself in the ring too. I learned that while I'm not large, I'm quick, and I have a surprisingly wicked right cross. I learned that getting tagged (a boxing term for your opponent hitting you squarely) angers me, and I find it hard to shake that anger off. Some lessons, though, were a slower sort of education.

"Again," she said flatly, pivoting on her left foot.

I squared up and hit the pads she held at shoulder height. Once, twice, we were up to ten before she backed up suddenly.

Eva was my third boxing coach, but the first woman I'd trained under. She looked a bit like the main character from *Million Dollar Baby*, without the victim mentality. When we weren't training, she was usually teasing her business partner, Brice, or enlisting me to clean the studio. Eva knew I was a Christian, even though it puzzled her. She'd never trained a seminary student before, but she didn't think the God-stuff made me any less serious about competing. She'd seen me box.

A pad came out and smacked my shoulder. I blocked it at the last minute, but I'd been somewhere else in my mind.

"Cross," Eva said, backing up a half step.

I advanced and struck out, but she dropped the pads before I got there.

"No." She looked me in the eyes. "No, stay still."

I narrowed my gaze, not sure what she was doing. The pads came up again.

"Cross," she snapped, and I connected with a crisp *whack*.

"Again." She shuffled back.

Whack.

"Again." Another half step.

Whack.

"Again!" She leaned back on her heels.

Whack.

She dropped the pads and grinned, giving me a look no one would be brave enough to call impish. "You don't know the length of your arms, you know."

I wiped the sweat from my eyes.

"You need to learn that you can reach farther than you think."

It wasn't the only spiritual lesson she'd teach me.

I had a fight poster with my face on it, knuckles that no longer bruised easily and an understanding that the best way to win a brawl is just to get out of the way, but it took a few more years for Eva to see and undo what my other coaches had been training into me—closet

Gnostics though they didn't know it.

She caught it during pad drills one evening. I'd had a long day at the office and a long night studying the night before. I was tired but expecting more of myself than was strictly reasonable.

"One, two, duck, cross, hook, hook, uppercut." Eva called the combination and moved back across the canvas, causing me to follow her. She'd cornrowed her hair sometime that week, and she looked meaner than usual.

One-two-duck-cross . . . I growled at myself. I'd lost the sense of where I was supposed to go next.

She repeated the combination to me and pivoted. I followed. One-two-duck. I hooked when I should have crossed. Angry, I stepped forward at the same time she said, "Again!"

One-two-duck-cross-hook-uppercut. My punches were full of power but sloppy. I wasn't thinking, I was lashing out.

"Stop!"

Eva's eyes turned to slits as she looked at me bouncing from toe to toe on in front of her. My guard was up, my breathing shallow.

"Take a break," she said. "Quit it."

"Quit what?" I was mad; I wanted to do it again, do it right.

"Quit being angry at yourself. So you did it wrong, shake it off, do it again."

She paced the edges of the gym as my stormy energy ebbed.

"I've seen you like this, sparring. You get tagged, you get mad. I egged you on, I've seen others egg you on, but I get it now. You're not mad at your opponent. You're mad at yourself."

I felt like I was a balloon untied, my air releasing in a flabby whoosh.

"Angry is a waste of energy." Eva tapped me gently with the pads on each shoulder, a reminder of the strength of my arms. "Angry makes you sloppy, takes the power out. When you're mad you're not present anymore. You gotta stay present. You gotta stay with your body. Keep your hands up. Don't turn on yourself. You already got one opponent in the ring. You don't need another. Stay present. Keep your hands up."

Watch the Signs

In his pioneering teachings titled *The Theology of the Body*, Pope John Paul II wrote that "the body, in fact, and only the body is capable of making visible what is invisible: the spiritual and the divine. It has been created to transfer into the visible reality of the world the mystery hidden from eternity in God, and thus to be a sign of it."[2] It is only in our bodies that we experience God at all; without them, we cease to exist. When we focus only on our "spiritual lives"—the interior realm of thought and feeling— we lack a foundational understanding and attentiveness to that which is at the center of our very lives, the only vehicle through which God reaches us and we reach others: our incarnate, bound-in-time, utterly beloved bodies.

When we try to split ourselves in two, to separate our bodies from our souls, we do violence and make difficult the healing of our bodies. This is something that modern medicine is only recently beginning to realize, as more and more hospitals encourage practices of prayer, meditations and silence as ways of facilitating physical healing. Hospitals have historically been places where worship or faith have no place, especially in the lives of the doctors bringing the healing work, and the split between body and soul is rigid, painful. So often, doctors and nurses burn out because they are not allowed to experience themselves as fully human—body and soul—even as they try to bring holistic healing to those they tend.

So, too, do we feel this fissure in the church. From the opposite side, the church insists through silence that we focus on the soul instead of the body, as if the two could be fully separated. In the church, we insist that the body is somehow separate, not something to be brought into the life of the community. In so doing we watch clergy and those in ministry run ragged with fatigue, living unhealthy lifestyles that lead to the slew of moral and ethical failures that grab headlines today. Whether it's the body without soul (hospital) or soul without body (the modern church), we're living in part, not in full, and at the depths of us, we know it.

Sadly, we have lived with this schizophrenia of self for a long time.

Bound by our bodies but told to ignore or castigate them, the lives of the faithful—mine included—have been marked by a set of false dichotomies that categorize actions into "sacred" or "secular," "spiritual" or "physical," as if the two are not ineluctably intertwined. We live our bodily lives—eating, sleeping, touching, weeping—with a whispering sense that we are experiencing the sacred in these mundane moments, in the taste of soup on our tongue or the tender touch of a friend in comfort. We intuitively feel that the aches in our joints are communicating something larger of God's presence to us, but we are told (explicitly and implicitly) to ignore these murmurs in favor of something more spiritual, more holy.

In the midst of this brokenness, the exile from our bodies in which we find ourselves, Isaiah stands in bold proclamation:

> The spirit of the Lord God is upon me,
>> because the Lord has anointed me;
> he has sent me to bring good news to the oppressed,
>> to bind up the brokenhearted,
> to proclaim liberty to the captives,
>> and release to the prisoners;
> to proclaim the year of the Lord's favor,
>> and the day of vengeance of our God;
>> to comfort all who mourn;
> to provide for those who mourn in Zion—
>> to give them a garland instead of ashes,
> the oil of gladness instead of mourning,
>> the mantle of praise instead of a faint spirit.
> They will be called oaks of righteousness,
>> the planting of the Lord, to display his glory.
> They shall build up the ancient ruins,
>> they shall raise up the former devastations;
> they shall repair the ruined cities,
>> the devastations of many generations. (Isaiah 61:1-4 NRSV)

God is about the work of redemption, he proclaims. He is about binding up our broken pieces—every piece reclaimed from our hearts and souls and minds all the way through our maligned and misappropriated bodies. God is about the work of liberation from the yokes of oppression, and it is in our very bodies that we are to be free, whole, restored. These bodies of ours have been treated as ruined, lost, devastated and unable to be redeemed. And yet the Lord of all creation is coming for them, indeed, has given to each of us the work of rebuilding these ancient ruins, reclaiming the very fortress of our selves, our blood and bones and skin and muscle, from the devastations of the fall and of our mishandled attempts at holiness. God is about this work, and we are called to see it and to receive it.

Touch Point

Every Shattered Thing

Go to the dollar store or a thrift store and pick up a piece of pottery. This could be a ceramic plate or an ornamental figurine. Just ensure it's something you don't want to keep in one piece. In a controlled environment (and preferably out of doors), shatter the piece of pottery on the ground.

Spend a few prayerful moments looking at the pieces. Where did they fall? How did that shattering feel in your soul? Was there resonance, or a feeling of resistance or pushing away?

Now, carefully gather the pieces that have shattered. You may notice that pieces are missing or that some edges have chipped irreparably so they can't be fit back together again. Do these pieces feel too fractured, impossible to redeem?

Spend some time in silence, centering yourself before God. You might want to pray the Lord's Prayer or spend a few moments simply talking to God. Ask God what he'd like to do with these pieces. He might ask you to try to glue the pieces back together, or perhaps his invitation is to create something new out of these splintered pieces—a collage or a piece of art or a remembrance piece. Notice how your body feels as you are invited to make something new out of what has been shattered. Is there a place inside you that feels blocked? If so, I encourage you to put your feet firmly on the ground and breathe deeply, asking God's Spirit to reveal what the blockage or resistance is inside of you.

If you need further guidance, try inscribing a word on each of the pieces, something that represents the way that you've viewed your body until this point. Perhaps they are words like *useless, fat, evil, sinful* or maybe simply *unthought of* or *peripheral.* You may even be the rare person who can use words like *whole, integrated* or *hopeful.* Gather the pieces in a bowl or basket and come back to it over time to see how God is putting the pieces back together, binding up the brokenhearted. Commit these pieces and this process to him in prayer.

4

Dust to Dust

Incarnation, Body and Flesh

The Christian religion is not about the soul; it is about man, body and all, and about the world of things with which he was created, and in which he is redeemed. Don't knock materiality.
God invented it.

ROBERT FARRAR CAPON, *BED AND BOARD*

AS I WRITE, IT'S THE SEASON OF ADVENT. The lectionary, the communal book of Scripture and prayer that guides most liturgical churches, hasn't yet reached the more familiar Christmastime readings in the books of Luke or John. Instead, we have started in Matthew.

> This is the genealogy of Jesus the Messiah the son of David, the son of Abraham:
>
> > Abraham was the father of Isaac,
> > Isaac the father of Jacob,
> > Jacob the father of Judah and his brothers,
> > Judah the father of Perez and Zerah, whose mother was Tamar,
> > Perez the father of Hezron,

Hezron the father of Ram,
Ram the father of Amminadab,
Amminadab the father of Nahshon,
Nahshon the father of Salmon,
Salmon the father of Boaz, whose mother was Rahab,
Boaz the father of Obed, whose mother was Ruth,
Obed the father of Jesse,
and Jesse the father of King David. (Matthew 1:1-6)

Oh, practical Matthew. Dedicated Jew. Fervent, even earnest, in his desire to see his people, the tribe of Israel, understand the salvation offered in Christ. Unlike the impetuous and somewhat terse Mark, Matthew wants to do everything he can to make the connections clear to the Jews. Every part of his Gospel account pulses with the lifeblood of the Old Testament. *We are the people of God*, it calls out. *And this is our God made flesh.*

So what does Matthew start with? What's his first big foray into the story that fulfills, completes, brings to fruition all of the stories that came before? What's his opening salvo in the bid to convince the people of Israel that their God has become Immanuel, God *with* us? The first words that he writes to them outline the birthright and pedigree of the man named Jesus.

I sometimes wonder how Matthew and the esoteric John got along with each other. Their Gospels are so interwoven during Advent, their words shifted back and forth between them, as if they had the same ethos, as if the two were even remotely similar. John, with his "And the Word became flesh and dwelt among us." John, who was mystical and hopeful, who called himself "the one whom Jesus loves" and wrote in poetic metaphor. And Matthew, who insists on the grounding of history, on the grit that settled between Abraham's toes as he trudged up the mountaintop to lay his son Isaac on the altar that he had built with his own hands. Did they even understand each other?

We're used to thinking John starts off his story strangely, yet it's Matthew who begins his good news with this mind-bending clause: *This is the genealogy of Jesus the Messiah.* The word *genealogy* here means "the origin of." Do you hear it? Essentially, Matthew starts with, "This is where Jesus, the Son of God, comes from."

As if that isn't a bold enough statement, Matthew continues on, not with the stars and sky, the deep mystery of the Spirit hovering over the waters in Genesis 1, but with a family tree. Where John moves in mystery, painting with grand gestures that the Greek mind would more readily embrace, Matthew insists on flesh and blood. Jesus, this God-man, came from Abraham. He came from Perez. He came from David. He has the same blood flowing through his veins as you do, Matthew insists. He is Messiah, and he is one of us.

We've grown numb to how audacious this claim truly is, numb to the implications of a God who is also human, a Creator who walked around in the flesh of his creation, who became one of them. We're not shocked or brought up short when the lists of names are read. Instead, we skim, thinking we have the whole story, thinking that we know what's going on, that we need to get on to the good stuff, the part when the angel appears to Mary or the Holy Family flees to Egypt.

But it's here, in the beginning, at this threshold place, that we need to linger. This is the beginning of things in the New Testament, and it is no mistake that the canon begins with this book rather than John's or Mark's or Luke's. It's here in Matthew's account that the crux of Christianity finds its first hard angle, the crossbeam against which the world will nail the Messiah. Because if God becomes human, he's taking on something that we thought was full only of decay and betrayal. If God becomes human, it means that the very stuff of our lives can be infused with the holy, the true, the good. If God becomes human, then there's something essential and true to be found in the human experience—there's something essential and true to be discovered in our very flesh and blood, bone and sinew.

While Christ's genealogy is the place where the New Testament starts, something came before Matthew's beginning, of course—something wondrous and mysterious and grand, something that has been told and retold through the ages as a way of remembering, of recounting the story of our origins. In Genesis 1, the great narrative of creation unfolds. From the Spirit hovering over the deep to the separation of night from day to the population of the world with tree and tortoise, the great and diverse landscape of our world pours forth.

And then God forms humankind. He makes them in his image—male and female—and he sets them in his creation as those who tend and guard. A great and glorious moment, yes, and one in which our purpose is clearly set forth. But it takes until the retelling of this great tale in Genesis 2 for us to recognize what we're really made of. In the second telling of creation, God lets us in on exactly where the stuff of ourselves finds its origin.

The word in the Hebrew is *apar*, which generally gets translated as "dust" in English. God didn't have to create this way. The human race could have sprung entirely from God's imagination—he didn't need to bend down, scoop up some dirt and form it. So something else must be going on, something more than a little poetic license or a bit of theater.

In breathing into the dust of the earth to form humanity, he linked us inexorably with the stuff of this world. If we had sprung whole from his head (as was the tendency in Greek or Roman mythology when a new god needed to be created), we would be free to dissociate ourselves from the world around us. We could use it, manipulate it, abuse it without being born of it. But with that first breath of God into the dust of the earth, we have been tied tight, held, co-mingled with the sand and the stars.

Here is what we resist, what we've been trying to flee for centuries. The stuff around us, the dirt and debris, the mud and the muck—we're made of it. We're not just earth-bound, although we try our best in many ways to overcome that (think of the Wright brothers and our constant fascination with anything that flies), we're earth-made. No matter what we do, no matter how we try, we'll always come back to the crumbling and quotidian, the basic, unglamorous and ashy. The physical and feeble.

Matthew's audacity becomes clear when we remember Genesis, our origins, and hold against it the litany of names. Finite, created people. Members of the family of God. Humans. Through which God became one of us.

I'm belaboring a point here, I know, but I'm doing so because it's something that would bring forth life if we would do the hard work of slowing down to see, to really experience, the great scandal of Christianity in its fullness. We've been so inundated by crèche scenes and angelic-faced Christ-children made of porcelain that we've lost the sweat and blood and tears and flesh of that radical entry into our world. We've put it safely aside as something to be celebrated once a year with candles and carols, to be sealed behind hymns and wreaths. In so doing, we've lost a large part of what God brought into our lives that holy night—the redemption of our bodies and a pathway to knowing God intimately within them, just as he came to know us.

It's radical to say that we've lost something of the work of God, and it takes a great deal of audacity to do so. But this message—that God didn't just wear flesh but *was* flesh—has been hotly contested since the very beginning of the church, almost as soon as Christ ascended into heaven.

It was Thomas, perhaps, that was the first to insist on honestly questioning this God-made-flesh mystery, and for that we owe him a great deal of praise. Sadly, he rarely gets labeled for his courage; Thomas is known most often as the Doubter, but I prefer his other name: Didymus, the Twin. We don't know if Thomas is actually a twin; no brother or sister ever appears on the scriptural scene. That said, biblical scholars often conjecture Thomas's twin isn't mentioned because he's so deeply embedded in the Gospels themselves that the reference would have been understood. It is said that Thomas, the one to insist on flesh and blood, was the twin of the one who starts the canon off with flesh and blood. Close in the womb, they may indeed be reversing the tragic rivalry of Jacob and Esau—Thomas and Matthew, the brothers who received the blessing of seeing Christ as firstborn from the dead.

Even so, *I won't believe unless I touch him* is Thomas's audacious cry. *I won't believe unless I can put my hands in his wounds.* Not just on him, mind you, not just a light brush of body to body to confirm his solidity. No, Thomas needs to enter Christ's body, as Christ enters ours, to confirm what his heart desperately wants to be true. And Jesus, much to everyone's surprise, doesn't count Thomas's request as doubt. Doubt, in fact, is mentioned nowhere in the passage. Instead, Jesus meets Thomas in the flesh and invites him to enter his very body: Here, put your hands in me. Just as I asked you to eat my flesh and drink my blood, to take me within yourself, I will take you in, and you will be transformed.

Perhaps this is why after the resurrection Thomas is the first to cry out, "My Lord and my God!" The first to identify this Messiah as Yahweh himself, the first to fall prostrate before Christ as Isaiah fell down before God in the heavenlies, as Moses hid his face before God on Sinai.

From Beginning to End

My jaw spasmed, clenching tight. Pain rippled through me.

Maundy Thursday. My favorite day of the year.

I had taken the driver's seat on the way to service. We were late. I drove aggressively, careless enough of the cares of others on the road that my jet-lagged husband mentioned it. *I hate being late.*

And so I speed walked my way to the chapel, trying to control the pace, refusing to reach out for my husband's hand, he who I had been without for nearly two weeks, who I professed to missing more than anything in the world. I needed to be on time. I need to be in the right.

But we weren't late. Not really. I had read the time wrong, and we were half an hour early instead, there in time for rehearsals. It was then the first pain shot through my jaw. I rubbed at it absently and went to help fill the tubs for the foot washing with hot, hot water. Hot as we could stand. It would cool as the service progressed.

And then, sitting in the pews, early and woefully unrepentant for my control, my need to be perfect, my desire to save myself by being at the right places at the right times, it was then she came and asked us:

When the time comes, will you help strip the altar?

She used our names. Bryan and Tara. Us in particular. I hesitate even to add our names to the request, to make the sentence a reference to me, in the flesh. Tara, the daughter of Sally, the granddaughter of Francis, the great granddaughter of Reginald.

Bryan and Tara, will you help betray Jesus?

Yes, we nodded. Of course we will help.

When she left, I turned wild-eyed to look at my husband, the muscle in my cheek clenching hard, harder.

Maundy Thursday is my favorite service, my favorite day, because of all that happens in it. After a flurry of activity in Jerusalem, temple-clearing and hosannas and watching a widow give her all, Jesus settles in with his beloveds to something he himself says that he has "eagerly de-sired" (Luke 22:15). We don't get that anywhere else—the idea that the Son of God is looking forward to something. And it's us, in this moment. It's washing our feet, gently, tenderly. It's taking the bread and breaking it, offering the cup and blessing it. Take, eat, he says.

And I do. I receive.

My husband, who I had rejected only hours before in my need to prove my own righteousness, kneels down before me. The water is still hot, hotter than it's ever been before, and I wince in surprise and sorrow. It has to be hot to wash my cold soul clean, to wake me physically to what is to come. He kneads my toes, my arch, my heel, and I remember Christ's words about the serpent and the bruising. It's been a long season of bruising, and suddenly the hands on my feet are Christ's hands, rubbing the ache away. I look into Christ's eyes as he kneels before me. *Oh, how often I betray you*, I think. *You are Christ made flesh.*

Bare-footed, I return to my seat and in the silence, I watch our community knit together in humility. Newlyweds, whose first service together as a couple last year was this service, who married two months ago in this very church, approach the water. She washes him, and as he in turn serves her, I imagine his tears mingling with the water. He washes her clean, and they stand together, embracing.

A new father washes his infant daughter's feet, dangling her above the basin as she is so often held above and away from the cares of this world. I know he would always hold her, if he could. Protecting, guarding, loving. Across from him, his wife kneels to wash the feet of a man without a home, someone on whom the cares of the world weigh heavy and dark. Her mother's heart tenderly embraces him.

Another mother's eyes brim with tears as she watches her husband wash her son's feet, strong hands serving a son grown strong in God. And then the son turns, and the tears spill as he washes his own son's feet, her grandson, who is scooped close in his arms, carried as she once carried him, all of his questions held tight in the embrace of a father.

After this, I watch the arms of the priests and deacons—brown and white, male and female, bearing on themselves disease and desperation, forgiveness and fear, hope and hosanna—rise in worship. I sing with my whole heart, *May I never lose the wonder, the wonder of the cross. May I see it as the first time, standing as a sinner lost.* I remember hearing these words first sung in a cathedral in England, as I stood by my best friend, ourselves both once lost but now found. I remember the moment that he found me, and the tears spill again.

And again my jaw spasms.

The pain dogs me up to the altar. The hands of the priest wrap warmly around mine, and his eyes smile as he hands me the broken bread. The body of Christ, he says. His joy repeats Jesus' words to his disciples, *I have eagerly anticipated this moment, I have eagerly anticipated* serving you.

I bow my head. I can feel the weight of my coming betrayal. My jaw throbs. I open my mouth only wide enough to slip the bread in through the pain. The wine stings as it slides down my throat. My feet chill on the stone floor.

He knows I will betray him, and yet he loves, and loves me to the end. The music swells as the Communion line thins.

Holy God, you are love.
Holy God, you are love.
Holy God, you are love.

It is normally a triumphant song, but the throb and beat is the throb and beat of the soldiers coming to take him away. I can feel it beating in my own blood, knowing that I am the one that will strip him bare. I want to say no, to give back the shiny silver of service that I so eagerly received before this all began. But it has already begun, and he has promised to love me till the end.

In the end, it's the pain that propels me forward. I just want to get this over with.

The priest snuffs the candles with the palms of his hands, and I imagine the dark marks on his palms as he hands me the candle sticks. I walk away quickly with the silver heavy enough to bruise my bare heels once again, my steps on the stone resounding as I retreat.

Next, the stoles, already red with blood. I am handed both and I think, *I have stripped him. I have taken his glory for my own.* I lay them down over the offering baskets, hidden away, as if I could offer it back to him.

Finally, the white over the altar, all innocence and silk. Crumpled, I receive it, and as I walk away I hear the crash that years before I have only watched—the altar tipped over, defiled. It vibrates through me, this sound, and I almost don't want to return to see what was once a table of celebration knocked over with my help.

Still, I return and watch from a place away, to the side. I want to cry out as the cross is covered in black. As I hear the hammer of stake on wood, my soul screams. But my jaw clenches tight again, the stabs of pain keeping me silent. I cannot open my mouth.

And then, it is over. The priest who so warmly embraced me runs, stripped, from the church, fleeing Gethsemane. We who have served and celebrated sidle away silently.

The muscles in my cheek spasm again as I reach for my husband's hand. It's different, I tell him. It's different when it's me stripping the altar, when I take the actions myself, betraying him. On other nights like this, I have felt lost, unsure of where they have taken this man who is everything to me. Unable to return home, we have wandered the city without purpose. Tonight, I feel my complicity. I am not lost. Instead, I want to trail after those who are, haunting them with a warning not to forget, not to fall asleep, not to leave him as I have. As I did. I am living the story—all the pain and the promise—in my own hands and feet.

My jaw spasms, and I stay silent.

This morning, I wake up, and the day is shrouded in fog. I ache all over, my body reflecting what my soul knows to be true. My knees feel pulled out of joint, my neck bearing a yoke of pain. I stay inside, not wanting to be with the crowd. I know my spasming jaw will keep me silent when they yell out, *Crucify him!*

But he has already been betrayed.

Instead, I take more ibuprofen than I should, to numb the pain. And I wait. I wait because he has promised more, he has promised to love me to the end. I wait because this body of betrayal has the possibility of being a body of glory and wonder.

And it is not over yet.

Not yet.

I could easily have dismissed these few days of my journey as ones where my body was fighting off a strange illness that it eventually overcame. Nothing to be concerned about, and definitely nothing that meant more than some minor aches and pains inconveniently timed. But to do so would be to willfully ignore the fact that God is and does communicate through our bodies—through the aches and pains as much as the joys and pleasures.

The smaller sensations of my Maundy story were signposts along the way—physical things that God used to get my attention, to engage my whole person in the story I was living, the story he was knitting deeper into my soul. The unexpected heat of the water on my bare feet jolted me into corporeal presence. I was utterly in the moment, experiencing each touch of my husband's hands—and living the juxtaposition between that moment and the moments leading up to the service when I had rejected and denied him. In the wash of water over skin, I was stepping closer to the incarnation, living in my body the sensations of Maundy Thursday rather than just agreeing in my mind or feeling in my heart the reality of Jesus' story.

It's dangerous to ignore our bodies, to neglect the mumbling of muscle or the beating of blood. I was listening—sort of. I was aware of the way my cold feet and my bruised heels echoed and amplified the betrayal of Christ, feeling my complicity with those who wanted to manipulate Jesus to be the messiah of their dreams rather than God's. My body kept me alive not only to that story—which is gift enough in itself, to be taken deeper into the life of Christ in flesh and bone—but to my own tendency to manipulate and manage who I want Jesus to be for me. And yet, my own pride kept me from asking the question that needed to be asked: What was God saying to me, inviting me to notice in the pain in my jaw?

Mostly I hid from any recognition of this painful messenger. Sure, the ache was hard to ignore, but I was open enough to the implications of the other things going on with my body—why did I need to pay any attention to this inconvenient, if insistent, tenderness?

Self-righteousness is more decadent than the worst sexual sin, says Dan Allender, a noted Christian therapist and author. Self-righteousness is the ugly assumption that I can save myself, that I can somehow arrive at a spotless state of purity that forces both God and others to acknowledge how good I am. And it isn't just the territory of the Pharisees or morality squad. I'm self-righteous when I feel proud about my regular times of prayer, I'm self-righteous when I walk around feeling like I've got it all together. I'm even indulging in self-righteousness when I talk down to myself, telling myself that I'm stupid or lazy or undisciplined—all shaming words designed to keep me trapped in the belief that my actions somehow dictate how valuable I am to God and others.

The tightness in my jaw was screaming out against the ways that I was indulging in this sin, the set of my teeth and thrust of my chin (both physical indicators a person is stubbornly holding on to something) only making the problem more painful and, one would think, more obvious. But I didn't want to look at myself that closely, didn't want to feel how helpless I was in that moment against the power of my desire to be in control—not only of my schedule but of my entire eternal destiny. I didn't want to feel the enormity of what it means to be rescued by this wild God of ours, especially in the face of the story of Maundy Thursday, a story that was already wrecking me.

Yet God wasn't going to let me off the hook. Not because he was being cruel, but because he was after something deeper in this living out of his Passion. God was, as he always is, speaking through the very stuff he created to remind me of what is true and loving and wise. My spasming muscles were telling me that I was carrying something that I was not made to carry—the weight of my salvation—and that pain was the result. My stubbornness and desire for control, my very self-righteousness insisted that I could be something more than just dust, that I wasn't *actually* sustained by the very breath of God. Ironic, really, when I started the Lenten season with my feeble and glorious brothers and sisters, wearing the sign of the cross—remember that you are dust, and to dust you shall return.

The Faith of the Doubter

We forgive the other disciples, Thomas's friends, of course, for not seeing or knowing, for not even asking Jesus for deeper, more physical proof that he has risen. Sometimes we call that lack of asking "faith." Sometimes it is faith. Other times, though, this lack of seeking for what we most need—incarnated presence—is really a lack of belief in the story of God that we're all living in.

Indeed, we condemn Thomas sometimes for his questions. We see those questions as an exercise in missing the point, a lack of faith, an arcane and outdated insistence on something that doesn't really matter—his body, Christ's body, bodies in general. But Thomas, the one who volunteered to follow Jesus into Jerusalem even *after* Christ had promised that the outcome would be death, was feeling around the edge of something that he knew from Genesis but had yet to see be radically played out. Thomas knew that our bodies are the very focus of the story of God.

Wait a minute, you're thinking. Aren't our souls the point of God's plan? Didn't he come to seek and save not our bodies but our souls?

That answer is both yes and no.

We live, you see, in a particular context when it comes to our understanding of what it means to be human, just as Thomas did during the time of Jesus' ministry. We live with an understanding that our bodies are primarily tools, primarily a sort of container for the stuff within them—our mind, our emotions, our awareness. This philosophy is why we struggle so deeply with issues surrounding both the beginning and the end of life. We assume that to be human is something *more* than having a human body.

Last weekend I was traveling back from a retreat center in the mountains. I had just spent almost two hours with a group of weary and hopeful pilgrims. Pastors, missionaries, those who care for the souls of others, who were seeking rest, renewal and a new rhythm of life. Theirs had burned them out, brought them low, and they needed to find a way to live not just *for* God but *with* God. During those two hours, I scratched the surface of what it means to experience our bodies as places of God's redemption, to believe not that our bodies are evil but that they are more wonderful than we could possibly imagine.

On the winding drive down the mountain pass, I turned on the radio to catch the tail end of a radio program about an unusual couple. The two people, a man and a woman, had fallen deeply in love. So deeply, they believed, they no longer wanted to be two people in two separate "restricted" containers. They wanted to live in one body.

So they began the process of attempting to erase the boundaries between them. They had facial surgeries so that they began to look alike. They cut their hair the same way and dressed identically. They grafted pieces of their bodies onto each other—a mole here, a piece of skin there. The husband even chose to have breasts surgically constructed for him.

We consider this an anomaly, a strange story of people so in love with each other that they've probably gone clinically crazy. But it's not so strange if we consider that, for the most part, we view our bodies as containers, as matter into which our consciousness has somehow been poured. During the interview, the husband said more than once that his body was a hindrance to his relationship with his wife—something that was in the way of their union rather than an integral part of it. Substitute God for his wife, and the story sounds a lot like the narrative we're living in our lives with God. Their crazy escape-from-our-bodies-so-we-can-be-together tale is not so far from our own if we believe our bodies are the problem instead of part of the solution.

At root, Christianity insists on particularity. In the very understanding that Jesus was a real historical person who lived and breathed on planet Earth during a span of human history, Christianity insists that the details matter. It wasn't just any human that walked the paths of Judea with a gathering of disciples—it was Jesus, the one about whom the Gospels are written.

This seems in some ways obvious to us—of course the Gospels are written about Jesus. But we've taken to creating Jesus as anything we want him to be, from long-haired and white-skinned to a black woman. Because we don't have photographic or even physically descriptive evidence of what Jesus looked like when he walked around with Peter, Mark and John, we're given to picturing him as whatever we feel like, whatever feels most comfortable in our culture. As a spiritual director, one who walks with others as they walk with God, I don't think this is entirely off base—God does appear to us as we most need him to be, and he created our imaginations for a redemptive reason. However, we've let our lack of photographic proof remove the burden of singularity from the life of Jesus the Christ.

To say that Jesus was born to a woman named Mary, that he came from a certain lineage of people, that before his death he had a conversation with a government official named Pilate—all of these details point to the fact that God was indeed made flesh, and made flesh in particular, historic form. Jesus wasn't generally the Messiah, he was the specific Savior.

Why does that even matter? It matters because God could have come to humanity as a universal truth transmitted through the atmosphere or entered our story in a series of orchestrated events that would have shown everyone his purposes and plans in the abstract. We get so familiar with the arc of Christianity we forget that God entering our story the way that he did isn't the only way he could have accomplished things. We forget he chose the path of intimacy, a path that insists that each person— you, me—isn't simply a cog in a machine or a part to be played in a script that we're all following. God's action in Christ insists that each person matters, and matters deeply, and that mattering has as much to do with our bodies as it does with our souls.

That last part is a stretch for most of us. Why would our bodies matter? Why would my flabby arms or bony knees or acne-prone skin matter to the Creator of the universe? Our bodies matter because without them we aren't human. Without our bodies, we might be angels or demons, but we wouldn't be people. Without our bodies, we simply wouldn't exist. Just like Thomas insisted on touching Jesus, Christianity insists on the importance of our particular bodies, insists on our individuality and the redemption of each of us in particular.

Christ didn't just take on flesh; he became human. It's hard to wrap our minds around—Jesus was both fully human and fully God (a paradox that continues to so confound us that we often prefer heresy to wrestling with the mystery of it all). It's hard to believe that the fullness of God ever had hiccups or sweat on hot days.

Touch Point

Touching Thomas

Read through Thomas's story in John 20:19-29. Start by imagining what it would have been like to be in that locked room with the disciples when Jesus appeared to them. What would your reaction have been? What would it be like in that space full of people to suddenly have Jesus appear? Would someone have noticed right away, or would it take some time, like someone arriving at a crowded party? What would the mood in the room have been like? What would the sounds and smells be?

Now imagine Thomas, who wasn't with the disciples at the time. What would it have been like to have missed out on this miraculous event? What might Thomas be thinking about himself or what other people might believe of him given that Jesus didn't choose to appear when he was in the room as well? Consider the tone of Thomas's voice in verse 25. Is he defensive? Defeated? What does Thomas's expression look like?

Finally, imagine the experience of Jesus again appearing to Thomas and the disciples a second time. What would it be like to be in a locked room and have Jesus appear once more? Consider why the room was locked at all. Was there fear there? Now imagine what it would be like for Thomas to actually put his finger into the wounds in Jesus' hands. Although we aren't told whether or not Thomas actually touches Jesus in the Gospels, let your imagination paint the scene. If Thomas did reach out, what would that look like? What would the physical sensations be? Don't shy away from how forcefully intimate and uncomfortable this encounter might have been. What would it be like for Thomas to put his hands in the wound in Jesus' side? Would Thomas have wanted to pull away quickly? Or would he be so overwhelmed he might refuse to touch Jesus at all? Then shift your attention again. Look toward Christ. What would Jesus' physical posture during the encounter be like?

After you've spent time meditating on the passage, ask God which character you are in this particular Gospel account. Are you a disciple, slightly afraid but there at the beginning? Are you a servant in the room, forgotten and not mentioned in this story? Are you someone to whom the events were told later? Are you Thomas, doubting and wanting physical proof? Although it might feel strange to consider, might you even be Jesus in this particular story, inviting those who struggle with the healing and life, the kingdom of God that you usher in, to touch and see that all of this is true?

What is God asking you to believe about his body and your body? What might be holding you back from trusting Jesus in this way?

Gather some dust or dirt from the area around your home. You can gather it in a small container or simply in your hands. This is the dust that you currently inhabit, the very stuff that forms your day-to-day life. Pay attention to it carefully. Is it soft and sandy? Wet and loamy? How does the ground around where you live reflect the grounding of your own soul? Do you feel like this is a fertile place for you, your family? Does the ground around you reflect that? Or have you felt impermanent, unable to penetrate to the deeper layers of life beyond the rocky soil around you?

How long have you lived in this area? Have you ever spent time with the stuff on which you stand, the land that supports you each day? What might it be like to notice your origins a little more closely?

Ask God to speak through this dust of the earth directly to your heart. What might he be inviting you to in the place that he's planted you right now? What are the ways that he's using your physical surroundings to form and create new life, new character, a new story within you?

fertile season
growth
beauty
lush

5

Angel or Animal

Beyond False Dichotomies

What a piece of work is a man!
How noble in reason! How infinite in faculties!
In form and moving, how express and admirable!
In action how like an angel!
In apprehension how like a god!
The beauty of the world!
The paragon of animals!
And yet, to me, what is this quintessence of dust?

WILLIAM SHAKESPEARE, *HAMLET*

WHEN MY HUSBAND, BRYAN, AND I FIRST MET, you would have been hard-pressed to find two people with such different relationships to their bodies. I'm a kinesthetic learner, someone who needs to touch the world in order to understand, a poet of the particular. The stories I loved were earthy and real, full of appetites and impulses. Bryan, on the other hand, had grown up in a context where his body didn't fit, where the world of ideas was privileged over manual labor. It was in our differences, and in watching Bryan journey toward an embrace of his body, that I began to see how revolutionary God-made-flesh can be.

The Body Ignored

Bryan can't quite articulate when the discomfort with his body began. Was it when his father left, when he was four, something about that stage of development that caught him in between worlds, never quite sure he belonged in either? Or was it the constant attention paid to him because of his red hair—*rub a red head's head for good luck!*—not only from children but from adults who thought they were being cute? Maybe it was when he began growing into his height, the long limbs and gangly growth spurts putting him above his peers, something they needed to tear down in order to feel like they were equally worth the attention he received for being tall.

Whatever the reason, he learned early on to treat his body as something to be ignored at best, minimally accommodated at worst. It wasn't easy as a young man, because he was continually treated as older than his biological age, because of both his height and the ways he took responsibility for himself. The natural process of maturing into adulthood brought with it a surge of new challenges: hormones, facial hair, vocal changes. Everything was to be minimized because he was outside of the norm. He dealt with most things alone, convinced that the changes he went through were particular to him, because he was so particular.

The therapist settled down into his chair, pulling slightly impatiently at his layered shirt. The man in front of him shifted, and he looked from the closed window to Bryan's pinched and somewhat resigned face.

The therapist asked what seemed to him an obvious question. "Are you hot or cold? I can adjust the temperature."

Bryan shrugged in reply.

"No, really." He adjusted his folder of notes, aware of his client's reticence. "It's no problem. Are you hot or cold?"

Bryan looked at him blankly. "Whatever is."

His brow furrowed, and his own awareness of the heat of the day shifted to concern. "Bryan, are you hot or cold?"

He sighed, forced to answer the question.

"I don't know."

"Really?"

Bryan took a deep, sad breath. "It doesn't matter."

By the end of the hour, Bryan was reminded that his physical needs did matter, and he was achingly, increasingly aware of how disconnected he was from what his needs really were.

There are six types of hernias: femoral, umbilical, ventral, inguinal, epigastric and hiatal. They bring with them a sense that something has ruptured, and patients describe feeling that parts of themselves protrude in ways that feel unnatural, frightening, impossible to ignore.

Bryan's hernia was inguinal, not painful but awkward, and close to intimate parts of his body. Doctors recognized it immediately and scheduled surgery, something he initially resisted because it would require rehabilitation, periods of time when he wasn't able to attend to the needs of his very demanding first wife, his children. He needed to be functioning. He didn't have time for his body to be repaired. It would only be a few days. Only a few days of being in pain, being out of commission. Only a few days of healing. But that was too much.

At the same time, something was out of place, and his body was asking him to pay attention. Surgery was the first step in putting things back into right relationship. Bryan's body was a microcosm of his world in ways he wasn't fully aware.

He made minimal concessions for the operation, took as little time off work as possible. He arranged his circumstances as best as he could and told very few people why he would be unavailable. Inguinal hernias occur in the groin area, and pointing out his pain involved owning the reality of both his body and his sexuality in the presence of others—something that made him feel awkward and aware, that forced him to notice his own places of detachment.

The surgeon sent him home with a prescription for powerful pain-killers and instructions not only to rest but to remain supine for at least twenty-four hours.

Aware of the way drugs would make him fuzzy-headed in the face of potential conflict, Bryan didn't take any of the medication. He lay on the couch for a few hours, grimacing through the pain, aware in a new way of the blood pumping through his veins, the way something as small as a scalpel rendered powerless a man of his size, of any size really. His body told him of the way things could be forced back together after an incision, but healing still took time. The surgeon repaired the hernia, but things were not yet correctly placed.

Soon enough, the tension at home erupted around him, the pieces initially held together by his convalescence tearing apart once more. In pain, he got up from the couch to smooth the conflicts over, to sacrifice himself for what he saw as the good of the whole. He looks back and wonders if God was speaking through the surgery and pain about the healing that he was going to bring in the years to come—the ways the Father was putting systems back into place, stitching in new support in weak and weary tissues. The unhealthiness at home made healing hard, both symbolically and literally. The reality of Bryan's body avoidance made it difficult to see these messages at the time, but he looks back to see both struggle and salvation at work in his flesh.

After the divorce, he threw himself into work on the house as a kind of physical grieving—the rending of one flesh demanding a response in body

as well as soul. The cement patio split and cracked as he applied the weight
of what felt like his failure. The sloped backyard gave way to shovel and
pickax, and the aches of muscles overused reminded him that life was still
beating within him, life that he hadn't been able to deny or escape.

Repentance doesn't always mean confessing your sin to God (or others).
Sometimes repentance means engaging in the opposite of what you've
been doing to hide or avoid or, in Bryan's case, pretend you don't exist. But
how do you enter a world that you've been avoiding for so long? How do
you let go of the control you've needed to manage, to repress, to minimize
the experience of your body? How do you stop being such an angel?

You start with the little things.

At first, Bryan's repentance—freely chosen—took the shape of willfully encountering the world with his body. It took conscious effort, intentional action, but each day he would purpose to experience the world
physically as well as mentally, emotionally and spiritually. For a period of
time, when his eyes fell on something (or someone) long enough to really
see it, he would ask himself the question, *I wonder what that feels like?* and
if it was appropriate, he would reach out and touch whatever it was in
front of him—door frames, the sweaters of colleagues, a flower petal, the
screen of his computer.

It might not seem like much, but these touches took effort and intention,
a deliberate choice for redemption for Bryan. He began stepping out of his
isolation kinetically, refusing what had been his dominant filter for physical
interaction for so long: it would be better if you didn't have a body at all.

There are so many ways that Jesus chooses to meet us in our world, in
our isolations, and draw us into him. For Bryan, each choice led him

inexorably closer to an invitation that God had set out before him. It was time to start learning how to make bread.

When you've learned to minimize your body, making messes of any sort is a big no-no. In addition to the self-imposed invisibility, Bryan's family had the fastidiousness of those who have fought their way out of social and financial need. Every item in the household was to be cared for carefully, cleaned immediately after use, put away in its proper place as soon as possible. Flour, Play-Doh, dishes—none were left to linger for any period of time. And *deliberately* getting messy? Choosing to be covered in anything that shouldn't necessarily be there? Not even an option.

Making bread is a study in contrasts. There's no wonder that bread shows up over and over in Scripture as metaphor. Bread is God's provision, bread is comfort, bread is offering and bread is redemption.

Bread, or the making of it anyway, is also a big mess.

For the uninitiated, bread making is intimidating. Activation, kneading, resting, rising. It all sounds very complicated. New bakers are often surprised that a simple bread can be made with four ingredients, a cracker with three. And new bakers are often fooled into believing that the simplicity of the recipe means that making a loaf appear out of the oven is a basic task. Combine ingredients, knead, put in oven—voilà, bread.

Never one for seeking the easy road to redemption (if one actually exists), Bryan decided early in this journey that in order to truly learn how to make a good loaf of bread—one that sits lightly in your hand with a soft, slightly sweet interior and a crust that crackles but isn't tough—he needed to learn how to make it completely by touch.

Eschewing the bread maker, the thermometers, even the measuring cups, this path of restoration to the goodness of his body needed something more than getting messy with flour—it needed touch. Instead of learning a recipe, Bryan chose to learn bread by knowing it in his hands, feeling it on his skin, coming as close to bread as you can before you consume it. He learned to tell the temperature of water by feel—warm enough to activate the yeast, cool enough that the heat wouldn't kill it. He chose to face the messiness and learn not just about bread but about his body and its connection to the world.

He started, though, as everyone must, with a recipe. We like to think that certain things can be intuited, simply discovered through exploration, as if we have within us the answers to life's most basic necessities, like where to find water, how to take care of ourselves when hurt, how to make bread. Perhaps that's where the popularity of post-apocalyptic entertainment originates, this vain hope we all seem to have that, should the world end, at least *I* have the basic skills I need to survive.

We're truly oblivious to how false that assumption is.

The grace of bread is that almost anything tastes good hot out of the oven and immediately slathered with butter. No matter how dense, how coarse, how dry, hot bread covers over a multitude of sins.

But when the heat fades, when the bread must provide its own energy to draw us to eating—that's when you know what you've made sustains not just itself but others as well.

Redemption came slow on this road for Bryan.

One of the first reminders of his isolation on this journey was that he had to use a recipe of sorts—something basic to guide him. As he stepped gently into God invitation of restoration, he had no one in his life to show him how bread is made, no one to knead the dough in front of him to teach him the gestures, no one to guide him into the shaping, or explain what living yeast looks like when activated or what to do when your dough overrises. He had to let his body become his teacher—to experience through feel what worked and what didn't. In some ways, the lack of an instructor helped him to embrace this journey in a way he might not have otherwise. He simply had to live it.

Then there was the flour. He wasn't even sure what type of flour to use, which kind was best. But worse, the flour went *everywhere,* covering the counter, his hands, his clothing. For a boy who kept life under control by controlling the messes in his life, actually spreading flour around needed to be a conscious choice of trust, a belief that out of messes something important could be born, something that he hadn't seen or realized up to this point in his story.

Bryan read books, researched through articles and watched video after video explaining the process of bread making. Yet, as anyone who has learned to ride a bicycle knows, head knowledge is not the same as body knowledge.

While redemption has its own costs, a loaf of bread costs about 80 cents worth of the ingredients required to make. Depending on the type and quality of the bread that you want to produce, you can spend days on the process. Bryan started with simple loaves that took two to three hours to make. Some Saturdays he would begin when he woke, and when the first loaf came out of the oven, he tasted it, let it cool, tasted it again, threw it out, and started the entire process over again. He could get two to three loaves out in a day this way—none of them anywhere near the quality that he hoped for at the beginning of this journey, but slowly, slowly improving.

But this is where things go a bit deeper. Bryan thought that he was learning to make bread, to enter into a process of getting closer to God and his own body, by baking. God, on the other hand, was kneading grace into Bryan's soul, slowly working an awareness of himself in the flesh into skin and muscle, gesture and feel.

This truth came to sharp relief on New Year's Eve. Bryan was alone, not for the first time, for the turning of the year. His soul was longing for ritual, a way to mark this year of destruction as finished, and an offering to God on the cusp of the next year as a kind of desperate prayer for something new. What better way than Communion? A remembrance of Christ's sacrifice, a commitment to take in what God gave, and a shaping of the year to come with bread and wine. Bread. His heart leapt.

He started kneading and forming shortly after 9 p.m., hoping for the loaf to come hot out of the oven just before midnight, a fresh sacrifice to God. As he worked, he mumbled prayers of release and forgiveness, hope and pain. Nothing overly scripted, but as he leaned into the dough, he felt something inside him shift and realign, just like the proteins shifting and forming beneath his hands, gluten mirroring the repaired elasticity of his own soul.

It would be poetic to say that this loaf came out of the oven light, golden, flavorful and strong. That the offering at midnight became a new start, and everything was shaped by that moment of redemptive baking.

But that's not what happened.

Instead what came out of the oven was misshapen and dense—one of the worst loaves he had made so far. Betrayed by his inexperience, the bread was heavier than he wanted it to be, imperfect and, he felt, a cruel reminder of his inadequacy. Still, there wasn't time to bake another loaf. The new year was approaching quickly, and the offering needed to be given.

Except that he wept to offer such pitiful fare to God. His heart had been to offer his best, to give back to God the graces he had been receiving in this journey of reconnection. Aching at his failure, he sat on the floor with his loaf and a glass of wine, forced to offer to Christ the imperfection of both himself and what he had made.

Body and blood.

Angel and Animal

We love our dichotomies. Yes-no, black-white, right-wrong. This simple classification system has been around since the Egyptian empire, and allows us to judge and respond quickly to threats without much thought. It also traps us into either-or thinking without leaving much room for God's more expansive both/and responses.

It's easier to think of our bodies as either completely good or completely bad than it is to walk in the daily tension of discerning which bodily experiences lead us toward God and which lead us away. It's easier to listen to the narratives modern society weaves around the body and react against those, choosing the other side of the dichotomy as the "right" option. What do I mean by the narratives modern society weaves around the body? Think for a moment about the last advertisement you experienced (willingly or unwillingly). If it didn't explicitly use sex or sexuality to sell a product, it probably used physical comedy or a play on a particular appetite to catch your attention. Advertising works by prompting us to feel a certain lack or fear, and then posing a product as a solution to that problem. More often than not, the people portrayed don't display any form of impulse control, let alone a desire to practice any kind of personal deprivation. There's no waiting in sales—if there were, you wouldn't need to *Buy Now*.

Advertising, of course, isn't the entirety of our cultural self-awareness, but how we try to persuade one another to think or act certain ways is usually a good indication of our underlying assumptions. While it's more nuanced than this in most of its expressions, the primary assumption of modern society when it comes to our bodies is that they are simply animal (the root of the word *animal* is, interestingly, "having breath"): instinctive, demanding and capable of being trained but not fully controlled. For the most part, the message that we receive is some variation of "if it feels good, do it," which is a capitulation to the notion that our bodies are the ones that dictate our desires to us. These desires are either stymied or fulfilled, but either way, we're not in control of them. From this perspective we are incapable of transcending them because we *are* our desires, be they for food, sex, alcohol or any other form of pleasure.

Have you ever been at the mercy of something? Completely helpless to respond to anything other than what the conditions were creating for you? I know I have. I was in a hospital gown, attached to IVs and monitors. The events of the day had been dramatic, and I was under doctor's orders to remain immobile in my bed. I wasn't sedated, wasn't incapable of movement, but the nature of what had occurred meant that healing would only happen if I stayed completely still. I was at the mercy of my body, waiting for it to do what doctors believed it would do on its own: clot, heal, protect me from further danger.

But I needed to pee. Desperately. I'd been pumped full of fluids for the past forty-eight hours, and those fluids were ready to be expelled. I held everything in for as long as I could, but eventually I had to call a nurse in and ask how exactly I could go about answering the demands of my body without disrupting the delicate healing process it was tackling at the same time.

The answer, as you might have guessed, was a bed pan. Several nurses lifted me carefully and slipped it underneath me. They kindly turned their backs as I lay atop the plastic container, a generous gesture meant to preserve my dignity. They knew what they were doing and had positioned it appropriately. But neither they nor I knew exactly how much fluid had been stored up in anticipation of this moment of release. Soon enough, the sheets were soaked.

If you asked me to name one of the most despairing moments of my life, that would probably be it. Wet with my own urine, pinned there by dictates of a body that neither the doctors nor I could consciously control, I felt both disheartened and humiliated. Sure, some of that was a reaction to being revealed as weak, but more of it was an unvarnished response to the fact that I was helpless in the face of my body's actions. There was nothing to be done.

And that, consciously or unconsciously, is where most people who believe in the animal narrative of our bodies live. While they may not be confronted with their powerlessness in the face of their impulses to the extent that I was, the daily imperative to meet impulse as if it was a mandate, stripped of the ability to say anything but "not yet" to their desires, brings with it a barely discernible daily disgrace. Without the agency to say no, we lose the agency to truly say yes at all, and we are enslaved. Cumulatively, these small shames bring on hopelessness or anxiety—we feel trapped in our bodies and want to do almost anything to escape them, if even for a moment.

I look back at that episode now with deep empathy for myself. The humiliation was anything but inconsequential, but it also revealed how deeply I believed that my body was simply animal. There wasn't anything I could have done differently at the time, it's true, but the despair I felt showed me how absent I felt of God in my body, absent of redemption or hope in a place where I had been brought low. Absent of God, absent of the Spirit's movement and messages through our bodies, absent of Jesus in us, what else can we do but believe our bodies to be beasts to control or obey?

Unfortunately, the binary response to the animal narrative that we're creatures only without any higher sense of the spiritual gives us an equally destructive opposite: that we're *only* spiritual. This has been called the angel narrative,[1] and while the church isn't the only proponent of it (Buddhist philosophy hinges on the idea that we are spiritual beings moving through a temporal world over and over again, for example[2]), it's the place where its destructive power is most felt (Christianity rests on the incarnation, after all).

It's facile to say that all of Christianity responds to the animal narrative in our culture by pursuing the idea that we're purely spiritual (we're deeply nuanced and multifaceted, after all), but the reality is that if you walk into almost any church on a Sunday morning you'll see the angel narrative threaded through the service. Instead of embracing the tension of our bodies, the call is to transcend them, to move beyond the physical into a realm of pure spirit. Instead of listening to God's voice in and through our physicality, we're told to ignore it completely. Did you walk into church after a long night battling a toddler who thought 2 a.m. was a great playtime? Suck it up. Single and in desperate need of a real hug from someone to remind you that you're not alone? Don't you dare express that.

Many who grew up with this Christian narrative of spiritual-is-higher-than-physical end up with distorted views of themselves and the world around them. Bryan's story with his body and bread is a prime example. Because holiness was linked with repression of desire, he, like many brought up with the angel narrative, sought rules and control as the highest form of spiritual maturity. The less you needed, the more you sacrificed your desires for the desires of others, the more pure and sanctified you proved yourself to be. Instead of dealing with the ambiguity and the tension and the mess, those brought up with the idea that our bodies aren't holy or good simply ignore the issue, sidestepping it or cloaking it in a shaming silence. Which, if we're honest with ourselves, only works if our repressions are increasingly harsh, increasingly sublimating, increasingly powerful. Unfortunately, this isn't a vigilance we're meant to maintain, and as mental health professionals tell us, what is sublimated always comes out—even if sideways and in unintended ways.

Sarx and *Soma*

Before we go much further, we need to get an important distinction in place. This is a defining of terms, yes, but it's also an assumption on which this book is based, an assumption underpinning all of orthodox Christianity. And it has to do with *particularity*.

As a writer, I think a lot about the words that I'm using to convey what I'm trying to communicate. Some authors talk about writing as a kind of telepathy, an act of transferring to your mind the image that's in my mind at the moment. If I'm thinking of a table, and I want you to think of a table too, I use words like *round*, *squat*, *varnished*, *low*, *ornate* and *teak* to get that image into your mind. While the pictures that we both have in our heads of that table aren't going to match exactly, I've given you enough in those descriptive words that we're thinking about roughly the same table.

The same is true of the writers of the Old and New Testaments. The words they used were chosen to convey, in as finite detail as was necessary, the concepts to us, concepts that form the foundations of our lives in Christ. Their word choice, though, mattered much more to them than describing a table to you does to me. They knew they were articulating what it means to be a follower of Christ, to believe in and follow the Messiah. Their words weren't sloppy, and when things were left vague or less clear than we would like, that wasn't an error either. The Spirit may be messy by our standards, but he isn't sloppy.

I set this up because thousands upon thousands of words have been written analyzing and attempting to explain the differences in the New Testament between the words "body" and "flesh." Scholars more brilliant than me have debated, and continue to debate, the meanings of these words. Professors of systematic theology have picked apart the verses to find meanings that are complete variants of one another. There are those who study ancient Greek with such exacting rigor that they can detect dialectical differences between the various ancient manuscripts that we have copies of.

I am not that scholar or professor or language expert. As Dallas Willard said whenever he lectured, one of my assumptions is that I've got some of this wrong. I assume that because very smart people over the ages have gotten parts of things wrong in what they have believed and taught, and it would be a very strange and anomalous thing for me to somehow buck that trend.

The words for body and flesh used in the New Testament are *soma* and *sarx*, respectively. They aren't interchangeable, necessarily, because they mean slightly different things. Translated directly, *soma* means "body" and refers to the whole of a physical being, whether human, animal or plant. When the authors use it to describe something, they are most often talking about the physical, corporeal nature of the person or thing about which they are writing. Jesus uses it when he commands the disciples to take and eat. This is my *soma*, he says. Paul, too, uses *soma*, although not quite as often as Jesus.

The word *sarx*, by contrast, directly translates as "meat" or "meat without skin" in Greek literature of the time. There wasn't any value placed on that word, just like the words "steak" or "meat" don't automatically connote anything positive or negative to us. More often than not, however, translators have replaced the word *sarx* with the word "flesh," eliminating the distinction. (I don't know about you, but I find it a bit disconcerting to refer to myself as meat or talk about the habits of my meat, so I'm a little bit grateful for the substitution.) Yet the distinction is important because the writers of the New Testament make a distinction. Standing with the writers of the New Testament in insisting that the distinction is important is to value the words that they were using and to translate them as clearly and as meaningfully as we can.

Interestingly—and here's where things get tricky—there's very little evidence of the word *sarx* being used outside of the New Testament to mean anything other than "meat" or "flesh." This is predominantly why scholars have made the decision to keep continuity with the meanings of the age and stick with the prevailing definition, sticking with the more palatable "flesh" over the more disconcerting "meat," of course. But Paul was doing something different with the word—as evidenced by the context of his usage many times in his letters to churches and communities. Our crafty Paul, for whom the meaning of words was deeply important (remember, he, like Matthew, was a good Jew and the specific was also the sacred for him), was doing his best to carve out a distinction in a culture that didn't have words for the difference.

There's an interesting phenomenon that happens when a language doesn't have a word for something. Imagine, for example, that English didn't have a word for *blue*. Now, of course we have a word for the shade we called *blue*; I've just used it, and you've got a color in your mind that ranges from off-green to almost-black. But stay with me here. Anthropologists have discovered that if a culture doesn't have a word for something—*blue*—the people of that linguistic group physically lose the ability to distinguish that thing (color, concept, feeling) from other things that actually have a name. In cultures that don't have a word for *blue*, everything is simply a shade of green. There is no such thing as blue, and those cultures physically cannot see a difference between something that is green and something that is blue. Over time, though, as a group begins to distinguish between one thing and another, between, say, off-green and something that is darker than off-green, their eyes begin to make a distinction. They actually begin to see differently.

The writers of the New Testament, from Matthew through Paul to John and back again, were working in a language and a culture that had no way of seeing that the physical world was not inherently morally corrupt. In Greek thought and philosophy, the material world was, in essence, evil. Greek philosophers taught that there was, out in the heavenly realms, a perfect form of everything on earth. These perfect forms aren't actually physical—they are signifiers of everything around us. So, somewhere there is a perfect table, an ideal, of which every other table (including the one I'm writing at right now) is simply a poor copy.

If you follow that thought, everything material has mistakes in it, is imperfect. Everything that is made of stuff falls short and pulls us away from knowing and experiencing the ideal that we are ascribing to. For the Greeks, then, everything physical is, in some way, evil. So, even while the word *sarx* (think "steak," just for a minute) gives us an idea of the flesh, to a Greek mind there's an immaterial, insubstantial idea of flesh that is more perfect, more desirable, than the physical stuff of this world. It's as if we're to desire the perfect, immaterial world of video games in place of the physical reality of day-to-day life.[3]

How do you explain the most revolutionary, most world-changing event—the incarnation of Christ, the perfect made material—to a group of people in whose language the concept of the ideal becoming physical is like saying a circle became a square? Or worse, the most perverse, ugly thing imaginable being revered as holy?

How could a Jew who thinks, eats, breathes in Hebrew begin to explain something as holy and beautiful as the incarnation to a people who don't see the body as good, who don't really have a way of even *saying* the body is good? Paul, clever Paul, pushes the words around a bit. He puts concepts together that haven't been placed side by side before. To say it a different way, Paul says "three-sided square" to get at concept of triangle, putting words in contexts that Greeks would have rarely seen before. He works hard to give them a glimpse into a reality they can't possibly imagine—the goodness of God in human form. And we've been having trouble with the concept ever since.

Paul, you see, had to translate. Although he most definitely knew Greek, and most likely Aramaic, Hebrew was the language of his devotion to God, the language of his heart, how he'd studied. Paul most definitely had the first five books of the Bible, the Torah, memorized in Hebrew, and probably much more. Hebrew was the language of his heart, and it was *this* heart Christ encountered on the road to Damascus.

So when Paul wrote in Greek, he was at one remove. And I know from my own experience of being in a culture whose language I don't speak natively, sometimes I'm searching for a word that doesn't exist in this second language, trying to express a concept that my listeners simply have no framework for. I'm trying to make the words fit, and sometimes I come up with hybrid concepts that don't quite express the idea but start getting at it in a way that helps my hearers begin to know what I'm saying and make the leaps on their own.

This is, most likely, what Paul (and the other writers of the New Testament) had to wrestle with in expressing the difference between our bodies (*soma*) and our flesh (*sarx*). Our *bodies*—whole, animate and encompassing so much more that just the material that makes up our skin, bones and blood. Our *flesh*—the stuff of our bodies, stuff that is neither good nor evil but is capable of bearing habits that move us away from or toward God. This distinction would have been difficult for Greek hearers. Paul, in his Holy Spirit–given audacity, was trying to help them see differently.

The challenge with this separation of *sarx* and *soma* is that over the years the church has committed the same kind of error that Greek hearers would have been wrestling with. As teaching has shifted over time, instead of hearing *body* and *flesh* neutrally, *flesh* has come to be defined as evil or corrupt and *body* as neutral or marginally good.

The slide is understandable. As the church grew (and it grew quickly), issues of immorality and sin needed to be addressed. In the cultures of the time, a lot of that sin was sexual immorality. As we've seen, even early theologians like Augustine of Hippo struggled with lust. Because it grew outside the bounds of Judaism, something that the disciples had to wrestle through themselves, Christianity welcomed in people who didn't have a history of purity codes and religious law governing their lives. The church had an influx of believers who didn't hold the same understandings of holiness, of morality, of conduct that the early disciples held.

As I've experienced, and you probably have as well, there are habits of flesh that are difficult to resist. No matter how much we know it to be unhealthy, we crave things that give immediate satisfaction to our appetites (cupcakes, soda, casual sex). Our bodies, it seems, betray us. In that, it's easier to blame our bodies than our selves. It's easier to call the stuff of our bodies evil than to own the hard work of training—not just our minds but indeed our very flesh—to want something different. Even then, the training feels imperfect, and we watch ourselves hawkishly, assuming that we're going to choose poorly, that our bodies will betray us.

We want the perfect picture, don't we?

We want the loaf to come out well, the redemption to be easy and effortlessly attained. We squirm (or at least I do) when the process isn't without its bumps, false starts and repeated do-overs. *What are we doing wrong?* we ask with alarming regularly.

If we get betrayed by our bodies or the world around us in any way—from earthquake to earache—we assume that we have once again been let down by the feeble, false stuff of this world.

Animal. Angel.

There's no space in between.

Or is there?

In Genesis, God creates humankind from the dust of the earth. He creates us *after* he creates the angels and the animals, and he creates us distinct from them both. Into our earth-formed bodies he breathes his own breath, touching us with divine life, and that divine life sparks and flares in every single one of us to this day. There *is* space between angel and animal because we were created in that very space. And it's that space we're meant to inhabit.

Bryan has moved on from making bread, although he occasionally returns to the playground on which he learned to see his body and his messes as imperfect and holy, all at the same time. After that New Year's Eve, the loaves he made became increasingly consistent, increasingly light, crisp and tender. He learned to make bread by touch so instinctively that he can throw a loaf of bread in the oven as easily at sea level as he can at the rarified altitude of Colorado Springs.

He still slips occasionally into angel mode, but for the most part he lives in the messy middle where redemption takes place—listening to his body and the bodies around him, living in the unruly reality of God-breathed mud. And the journey isn't over. In the kitchen, he's leaned into other places of sacramental grace, creating meals and offering himself to God and others plate by plate.

Touch Point

Standing on the Edge

Together, we have entered into a journey that is both simple and complex, hopeful and frightening. In this place, we're saying yes to the risk of encountering God in our bodies and the world in ways that we may never have done before. There will be tensions and unresolved places, there will be life and hope. There will be resurrection.

In this place of tension between angel and animal, you are invited into a meditation involving your body. First, find a place where you can physically stand on an edge. This might be the edge of your porch, the edge of a stair or even just the edge of your carpet. Standing with your toes on (but not over!) this edge, I invite you to close your eyes. Take a few deep breaths in this place, noticing the air flowing into and out of your lungs.

Breathe all the way down to your toes, in through your nose and out through your mouth.

With your eyes closed, pay attention to any place in your body that is feeling tension. Starting at the top of your head and scanning slowly all the way down to your toes, notice the places of emotion or tension that might be behind your eyes, in your neck, in the pit of your stomach or the backs of your legs.

As you stand on the edge of this journey of facing your fears, simply make note of the parts of your body that are reluctant to step forward and the parts of your body that seem to want to move. Listen carefully to anything they may be telling you about your willingness or unwillingness to encounter old stories, messages or fears from your past.

Say a quiet prayer for God's guidance, wisdom and healing as we step into this journey together. Take as long as you want to talk to God about how you're feeling.

Then after another deep breath, take a step over the edge at which you are standing. Let this step be an embodied act of entering into the journey that God has for you. Notice how you're feeling. Relieved? Startled? Joyful? Frightened? Hopeful? Let this step over the edge be the first step in your embrace of God's work in and through your body.

6

Beauty or Beast

Living with an Unglorified Body

In my deepest wound I saw your glory, and it dazzled me.

ST. AUGUSTINE OF HIPPO

ALL THIS TALK OF HOW GOOD OUR BODIES ARE CAN ring hollow in the face of pain and suffering. My friend Eric, for example, has been suffering for the past five years with digestive issues that leave him exhausted, sick, unable to get out of bed. This beautiful body of his needs to be managed carefully if he wants to be able to sit on his porch and read a book. Hannah lives with the chronic pain of rheumatoid arthritis at an age when she should be chasing around after her eighteen-month-old son. Joints flame with pain so fierce that it feels like she's housing a wildfire within her. She can't button up a shirt, let alone feed herself or her boy.

It would be easy enough to brush away these examples, to focus on the gifts of the body, if they weren't all around us. Think for a moment about your family—is there anyone in pain, anyone ill, anyone in the hospital or hospice care? Or how about your friends—does anyone come to mind who has a chronic illness or a life-threatening allergy? Is there anyone who goes through a day needing to manage her pain levels? Deeper still, have you lost someone you love and felt the tearing loss death is to the living?

Unless you live in a cave or in a peculiarly pain-free community, you've probably thought of a handful of people you know who are personally wrestling with their bodies. Which is why all this talk of the goodness of our bodies call stall in the place of pain. What use is it to say the body is good when so much of what it does, what it goes through, seems so inherently evil?

The Beastly Body

I want to think that it started in my early twenties; a time when I tried— at parties, at work, in the awkward moments standing beside people in a crowded bookstore—to be someone else. I want to think that I wanted to be *anyone* else, but that's not true. I just wanted out of my skin, this membrane that kept me trapped inside my own limitations. I didn't want to be thin or popular or even professionally successful. I was just out of college, just out on my own, and I knew that this bottom-of-the-pecking-order lifestyle was only temporary, a kind of dues that we all pay in one way or another.

In a new town, and without the usual moorings of family or social circles that knew me well, I had the opportunity to remake myself, to choose to be a seductive socialite one moment and a caring do-gooder the next. I remember one embarrassing evening that I pretended, for the sake of a guy I thought attractive, to be a rabid fan of Sebadoh, a band I'd neither heard of nor enjoyed after I listened to their entire discography in the next twenty-four hours in an attempt to look at least marginally knowledgeable. Unfortunately, that relationship lasted nearly two and a half years. I never told him.

But the remaking wasn't working. Every role I tried on, every new persona I became only reinforced how much I didn't know who I really was—and how much I didn't want to find out. And I didn't want to find out because I was pretty sure that what would be revealed wouldn't be worth anyone's time or attention.

It started with my back. I'm not entirely sure why—maybe because it was the least conspicuous, the least likely to draw scrutiny? Whether it was that or just a convenient entry point doesn't really matter. My fingers began exploring, looking for imperfections, places where the skin puckered or bunched, concealing clots of white blood cells huddled together. Everywhere I found one, I picked at my skin. At first, gently, but soon it was enough to draw blood.

Anyone who has passed through adolescence knows the temptation of squeezing a zit. As disgusting as it sounds on paper, there's a certain thrill to the popping of a pimple, a thrill that teenagers need to be trained to ignore—unless morphing into a scarred, pock-marked social outcast sounds deeply appealing.

Unfortunately, that thrill, the psychological satisfaction of finding an imperfection and squeezing it out of you, doesn't stop with adolescents. Whether it's dermatillomania (the technical term for the obsessive skin-picking cycle), cutting, anorexia, bulimia or any other host of self-injuring habits, many of us have ways of trying to squeeze our perceived imperfections out of us.

Soon enough, my back became a latticework of scars. More often than not, by the end of the day my shirts would be stained with tiny pricks of blood from my compulsion. I began wearing turtlenecks more often, until they became a wardrobe staple well beyond wintertime.

Ironically, the long-sleeved shirts uncovered a whole new territory for my picking—my arms. In the early years, I avoided my face, for the most part. Despite struggling with bad skin and going through three to four rounds of treatment with the acne drug Acutane, I'd absorbed the dermatologists' commands to keep my hands off my face fairly well. Instead, I took to my arms with unintentional delight, my fingers itching to eradicate every rough patch, every raised pore, every enlarged follicle.

If you've never picked your skin, I suspect that you're about ready to put this book down in disgust. Frankly, I'm with you. Despite unconsciously finding satisfaction in my compulsion, consciously I consider it revolting and destructive. That I can't tell you exactly when it started is also distressing.

What I can tell you is that the satisfaction comes not from the actual action but from the rush that results from getting something unworthy, something impure, something imperfect *out of my body.* If I could consciously impress upon myself the reality that picking creates even more imperfection than it eliminates, I would.

Instead, somehow, picking made the membrane between myself and the outside world permeable. When I picked, the sense of constriction within myself eased, the feeling of being limited by this organ that kept the inside in and the outside out blurred for a moment, an instant.

And that's the thing, really. The blurring wasn't real. It wasn't a magical shift in my reality, allowing, for a moment, that I could physically fix the things about me that were imperfect, that weren't enough. Even though serotonin surged within me when I chose this form of self-destruction, I wasn't actually creating anything new or removing anything old. I was only tearing myself apart, refusing to reflect on the beauty of my own skin.

I find myself picking, even to this day. It happens when I'm stressed or tired, when I feel the least secure about myself. Because it's become a neurological pathway in my brain, it's easy to return to my old haunts, ignoring the paths of life that God has laid out for me before time even began. Sometimes, I'll be alone, trying to sit quietly in meditation or prayer, and my hands will start shifting, moving, seemingly on their own.

And there, there is the gift of it all. I know it's radically uncomfortable to suggest that there might be gift in mutilation. That, somehow, this obsessive practice birthed from insecurity and doubt might have a blessing from God woven into it. But I believe that it does.

You see, the picking happens when I'm least attentive to the whole of myself. I may be searching for imperfections in my body, but by the time I'm picking my soul is already out of alignment. I'm lost, instead, in a false world where I must be perfect and beautiful, strong and good in order to be loved. I've taken the lies of performance and perfection so deep within myself they seem to be the only true thing left. I'm telling myself I have to do it right, I have to achieve, I have to be so much better than I am right now, and yet my body's telling me that I can't, that I wasn't meant for perfection. My body is telling me I need something different, something more, something outside of myself in order to make all of that happen.

Which is, ultimately, true.

What I'm scratching into my skin in those unconscious, almost hypnotized moments—when my actions are seeking the endorphin release of picking—is the sign of the cross. When I'm not consciously choosing it (and sometimes when I am), these pin-pricks of blood bring me to Golgotha, the darkest moment in history, and I am living that darkness out. God's radical grace is present in that very same moment; he's right there, ready to rescue me, and the blood, the cross is a reminder that without help, without his help, I'm doomed, I just can't do it.

The horror of it comes not when I pick but when I refuse to notice that I'm picking, when I continue along these paths of self-injury that are somehow supposed to produce self-righteousness, a success of self-improvement. When I don't see that the very flesh and blood God gave me is crying out for his redemption, I'm turning away from the only One who can make the life that he died for possible, and possible in these very hands that are betraying him once again. It's when I refuse his presence, his cohabitation with me that I am truly betraying God, not with a kiss, it's true, but still with my own two hands.

The grace of it all is, God still lets me do it. While I'm injuring myself, he looks on me with compassion and kindness. He doesn't condemn me or turn from me, even when I'm denying him in my actions. Even when I've participated in my rituals of denial enough times that it's just habit, so easy to ignore, to tune out, that I don't even see I'm doing it until I literally have blood on my hands.

This, too, is the world of those who self-injure by cutting, or those who punish themselves with anorexia or bulimia. While the paths to these types of self-harm are many and varied (nail biting is dermatillomania's close cousin), neither the embodied action nor the kindness of God are any different.

Whether we're starving out our perceived imperfection, vomiting it up or cutting it into our skin so that we can feel the pain of it, these forms of self-injury are, in their deepest places, a reach toward something holy, something pure, something good. This doesn't mean that self-harm is redemptive—it isn't, and it's not God's desire for us at all. But just as God loved as while we were yet sinners, so does his love reach into the most desperate places of our lives, the places where we turn against our own bodies, looking to transcend our own limitations. We're going about that transcendence all wrong, but he knows the desire to transcend is at root a desire for him.

And that's the disorder of it all, isn't it? We're humiliated by the practices, aware that they're not the right things to do, not the appropriate ways to God, but biochemistry or abuse or shame or some horrific combination of all three have us trapped on a path we can't seem to leave. We know it doesn't lead where we want to go, but we're still traveling it, just in case it might.

It's here where we live with the reality that are bodies are unglorified, not yet perfected.

The Body Blamed

One of the places most prone to seeking perfection in modern society—perfection that we're simply not meant to attain—is in our body's weight and shape. Up to 60 percent of girls in elementary school (ages 6-12) are concerned about becoming "too fat." Nearly twenty million women and ten million men in the United States suffer from some form of eating disorder. Anorexia nervosa and bulimia have the highest mortality rate of any form of mental illness.

So much of this struggle stems from how we seek to control and perfect our unruly and often unresponsive bodies. Cultures over time have held up a variety of standards of beauty and desirability, most of which have resulted in attempts by both men and women to fit into cultural norms that have nothing to do with the healthy functioning of their God-given flesh. The message of perfection (whatever standard that is measured by) is repeated over and over again in the media, through peers and, sadly, in the home. We swallow the image of desirability because it's the water we swim in, and we can't help gulping it down, no matter how hard we try to keep our mouths shut.

Try asking a friend or colleague what they'd like to change about their body—I can almost guarantee you that the list will be at least three items long. Weight, hair color, the size of their nose—it doesn't matter if they're male or female. Now try asking them what they like about their body. I suspect they'll struggle to give you even one thing they feel good about.

Our distorted body image changes how we interact with the world and, I believe deeply, how we interact with God. Psychological studies have shown that those suffering from anorexia nervosa routinely overestimate the size of their body (by a shocking extra 20%) and that the estimate isn't conscious—they actually interact with the world as if they are physically larger than they are. In the same way, the manner in which we see and treat our bodies (as unglorified as they are) affects how we interact with the world around us and affects how we live the love of God in the flesh to those who need it desperately.

It's hard to believe we follow a loving God when our image of our very bodies is colored by a lens of "not enough," "too fat," "too tall" or "too short." In the same way I pick at my skin, most people pick at their body image, getting a strange sense of control and even thrill from putting themselves down physically. It's a way to hold on to self-righteousness (I'll be better/good/lovable when I'm 5/10/25 pounds lighter), a way to hold on to the false belief that our value is somehow self-determined and that our bodies just need to be shaped differently to match up to whatever standard of beauty is currently deemed valuable.

The grace of it all is the same grace that God offers me when I'm in my most self-destructive, wounded places—the very weakness we feel in our image of ourselves is the place God will meet us most deeply. The way toward a healthy body image isn't by ignoring our desires to be thin or muscular or shapely, but by stepping in closer to them. Every time we think "fat" when passing by a mirror is an opportunity to notice and attend to our own sense of loneliness and inadequacy, a place that God's love and presence can meet us—if we'll open the door.

One of my favorite stories about how our bodies can speak to us of the redemption God offers is in an interview Amy Frykholm writes about in her book *See Me Naked: Stories of Sexual Exile in American Christianity*. Frykholm tells the story of Ashley, a young girl struggling to heal from anorexia brought on by a lifetime of trying to be holy by repressing every desire—especially hunger. At one point in the book, Ashley is trying to learn who to listen to and how to listen on her journey toward wholeness. She sits at the kitchen table, stilling herself, trying to get in touch with the sensation that she's denied for so long, a physical sensation called hunger. As she begins to identify that she does, in fact, feel hungry, she decides that orange juice sounds good, and drinks a glass slowly, tasting and attending to the experience the whole while. Frykholm writes:

> Gradually, desire by desire, Ashley built herself back up. "My body was talking to me, but I had to practice to hear it."... To name and to satisfy one's desires was not, contrary to what she had long believed, to be at the mercy of selfishness and sin. On the contrary, naming and satisfying took her step-by-step onto a path of life and goodness.[1]

In the same way, naming the ways that we struggle with our own image of our bodies, young and old, healthy and unhealthy, can lead us into a deeper experience of God's grace and goodness. The ways that we find to temporarily silence our longings for belonging or love by binging or purging may bring momentary physiological relief, but the damages they wreak have long-term effects. We can numb ourselves and keep picking at our image as a way to produce perfection, or we can step toward the pain of feeling lonely, tired, despairing or inadequate. This step will feel like the grave, but on the other side of the valley of the shadow of death is the One who will protect, guide, redeem and bless us.[2]

Sense and Suffering

Self-harm is only one way in which this tension of good but unglorified, beauty and beast plays itself out. If you've lost a loved one, especially to the ravages of cancer or the cruelty of a stroke in old age, you know the way our bodies seem to betray us. Whether it's Eric with his extremely restricted diet, Maria with breast cancer or Hannah with an auto-immune disease, these are paths we did not choose, and our bodies lead us into the valley of the shadow of death in ways that are totally out of our control.

I can't tell you why some suffer for so long and in such deeply difficult ways. Tome after tome has been written on why pain exists in God's world at all. C. S. Lewis called pain God's "megaphone to rouse a deaf world,"[3] but try telling that to the mother who has lost her child to an in-utero genetic malformation or the husband whose young wife just died of brain cancer. It would be cruel to suggest in those places that God is simply trying to wake us up.

It would be easy, and perhaps even kind, to choose in these places to retreat to the Platonic divide that says our bodies are bad and our souls good. It is tempting, indeed, to blame death, disease, disorder, pain on the way this evil world turns. Easy, tempting, but achingly off the mark.

Yes, death and disease are part of the fall. When God warns Adam and Eve not to eat the fruit of the tree of the knowledge of good and evil, he tells them that if they do, they will surely die. Since neither of the two drop dead after that first bite, we know that the death God was speaking of was much larger, more far-reaching than the death of the body. What comes after that fateful choice is separation from one another, from the world around them and from God. Indeed, they are separated from their own bodies by shame, a kind of self-alienation that has us hiding from all the functions of our bodies that we don't inherently feel are worthy or good. This hiding ironically leaves us vulnerable to the very things that we are trying to avoid—a sense that we are somehow unholy, that we are shameful.

Just as my self-injury is a cry for the cross, so too is each person's journey through the valley of the shadow, the place of pain. Our bodies are the very place where all of the theological talk about suffering becomes personal, physical and inescapably real. The glory of our bodies is that they are better than we could ever imagine; the mystery of them is that they house such suffering and disorder as well.

This tension between glory and the world that is, the pain that we don't choose, that we don't want, holds us squarely before this mysterious and great God of ours.

Living Weakness

This year, God asked me to give up contact lenses for Lent. I remember the moment clearly. I was laden with too many bags, heading to my office for the day to meet with those whom I journey alongside in spiritual direction. Loading the car with books, my computer and paperwork, I caught my reflection in the rear window.

And I winced.

I was wearing my glasses. I'd gotten something in under my contact the day before, and I needed to give my eyes a rest. Normally, I wear my contacts constantly; my vision is bad enough without them that I can't

drive or read anything that is more than four inches from my face. At
the time, I tended to feel claustrophobic in my glasses, because the edges
of my sight outside of their lenses blurred and softened, restricting my
peripheral vision completely and restricting me to what's directly in
front on me.

When God tapped me on the shoulder, I was looking at my glasses
(and myself) with contempt. *Ugly. Helpless. Weak.* Those were the words
running through my head. *Glasses make my deficiencies, my need for help, so
obvious. I don't feel beautiful in them at all,* I thought.

Exactly, said God.

In that moment, the Lenten discipline I'd been fishing around for—
maybe gluten? or how about giving up television?—became blindingly
clear. I needed to give up contacts, because I'd become dependent on
hiding this weakness that is simply a part of who I am. I'd become hooked
on appearing perfect, appearing capable, appearing without need of help,
and contact lenses had allowed me to do that.

Now, I know that almost no one who looked at my glasses during the
season before Easter thought, *Oh, wow. She must be repenting of her addiction to appearing strong, embracing the reality of her unglorified body.* It
wasn't that obvious for others. But, boy, was it obvious to me.

This is the other side of the practices of physical self-harm, the side
that is so much more acceptable, so quickly encouraged by the world
around us. Think you don't have it together? That you're not attractive
enough, strong enough, interesting enough? Just fake it. Project what you
think other people want, especially when it comes to your body. If you
can't mold it to the current norm, you can cut your way there with surgery.
And if you can't cut your way there, cover it up with these revolutionary
products that are designed give you brighter skin, firmer abs, shinier hair
(or hair at all)—whatever it is that you think you're in need of.

What I believed I was in need of was beauty, strength, some elusive
combination of allure and power that would help me feel accepted, desirable, enough.

Of course, this way of thinking wasn't something I operated in consciously. The affliction of the self-aware is that we think we know ourselves. Instead, the ways of grasping and striving, of making life happen or hiding from life as acts of self-protection go underground, masked behind seemingly small choices like constantly wearing contact lenses or always being the one in charge.

The interesting thing about the ways we hide, the way I hide, both from the beauty that we fear we don't have or the beastliness that we fear we do, is that they are, more often than not, physical actions, ones that involve the very bodies we feel conflicted about. Hiding under baggy clothes for fear we fall short of some physical standard; cutting to express the darkness we feel inside. These choices express our need in louder ways than if we were to own the lack we are feeling and speak it aloud.

This is why so many people experience the losses and physical difficulties of aging as a shaming. Instead of owning the vulnerability, pressing into the way aching knees and loosening muscles bring to bear the weight of weakness, we camouflage aging with dyes and devices. Out of our sight and mitigated by technology, the sometimes gentle and always difficult gifts of loss are ignored in favor of the fantasy of cost-free immortality. Getting stripped of our delusions about death and dying feels truly beastly. Especially in an age when we can corral the elderly in facilities designed to make both them and, more heinously, *us* more comfortable in their degeneration, confronting the weakness of the body rips from us our safe distance and forces an encounter with mortality.

Does that sound like a bit much to stuff into forty days of wearing glasses? Perhaps. But the wilderness time that Lent represents is a stripping away of all that we've clung to instead of God, the ways that we've arranged to make our slavery comfortable, the ways we've made a home there. God took the Israelites out of slavery in Egypt and into a place devoid of all the things they'd used to make their prison bearable—

food, furnishings—but full of his voice, his leading, his presence. We may not have the comfort that convinces us we're okay enslaved to Pharaoh, but what we have instead is relationship with the One who will lead us to the land that he is giving us.

Forty days without contacts meant forty days of dependency for me, forty days living into the truth that I can't do it on my own, that I'm physically limited, in need of help, and that it's perfectly all right to be that way. The wilderness was, for me, a place where I could hear God in the very weakness that I despised, where I left the slavery to appearance and control behind to be with him in all that I wasn't. Leaving Egypt (which literally translates as "the narrow place") meant leaving behind the ridiculous standards of fashion and figure, the changing vogues around style, weight and general appearance to meet God in this freedom of his delight over me, his definition of what it means to be attractive.

Staying with the Story

None of this makes a cancer diagnosis any easier to bear, nor aging any less brutal a journey of surrender. It doesn't make genetic diseases anything but grueling or sudden illness any less surprising or painful. The world that we live in, the very flesh that makes us human, is subject to decay and death, brought in by the fall and conquered only by the work of Christ. Our bodies are, as yet, unglorified, and living with the pain of that has us scrambling for any relief we can get—even in the form of blaming God.

It is no surprise that we fear the flesh when it so often betrays. It is no surprise that we self-harm or mask our pain instead of standing in the awkward place between the weakness that is and the strength that is yet to come. It is no surprise that we hide away rather than step into the risky place of fear and failure.

Yet, it is in this wilderness of the body, this place of utter frailty and dependence that we find ourselves freed by God. We may not be healed of our illnesses (although sometimes he does that), but we will be healed of the reliance on perfection and performance. We may not find ourselves with answers as to why some people suffer and others do not, but we will find ourselves in relationship to the One who has suffered it all so that we can be redeemed. We may not be transformed into the world's ideal of physical beauty, but we will find ourselves reflected in the eyes of the One who finds us so alluring that he left the heavenly realms to be with us, the One whose very breath sustains this figure of dust and dreams.

Touch Point

Blessing Your Body

Spend a few moments centering yourself before God in your body. Get yourself in a comfortable position, feet flat on the floor, and when you're ready, close your eyes.

We're going to take a journey into body awareness, a journey into the deepest beliefs about yourself and your body.

Begin by taking a few deep breaths, all the way down to your toes. Feel the love of Christ present in you, he who is our hope of glory (Colossians 1:27).

Slowly bring your attention to those parts of your body that you enjoy the most. Whether that's your waist, your eyes, the slope of your cheek, your arms or any other part of your body, imagine your breath moving to that part of your body, breathing God's life into it.

Now move your hand to that body part, covering it gently with your palm. Experience the covering and blessing of Christ's hand touching you, even as your own hand rests there. Say, silently or aloud, *I bless my body* or *My body is blessed.* If you're able, name the specific part of your body, saying, for example, *I bless my eyes* or *My eyes are blessed.*

When you're ready, release your hand, and sit silently for a few more minutes, noticing what it felt like to have your body specifically blessed in this way. If there's another part of your body that has drawn your attention, repeat this exercise there.

Now, as you've returned to this centered place, resting in the love of the One who gave everything for you, notice the parts of your body that you particularly dislike or that you're particularly dissatisfied or uncomfortable with. Spend some time with that discomfort, making space for it, breathing in slowly and deeply.

Resting here, ask God what it is about that part of your body that he particularly likes or enjoys. Why did he craft you in this way? Why does he love this aspect of your flesh and bone? Listen carefully for any words, images, impressions or Scriptures that come from the Holy Spirit. Continue breathing slowly and deeply.

Finally, once again take your hand to rest on your body, this time on the part or parts that you like the least about yourself. As you place your hand on that part of yourself, do so gently and slowly, as you would gently touch a sleeping child or put your hand on someone you didn't want to startle. Don't rush past this part of the exercise; breathe and move slowly.

Notice with compassion any feelings you have about touching this part of your body. Do you want to move away? Are there aspects of this part of your body that aren't pleasurable to touch? Stay there, in that sensation, noticing what, if anything, changes as you leave your hand gently there.

Yet again, you are invited to bless this part of your body with God's love and regard. This may be difficult to you or may feel silly or embarrassing. Let those feelings come, but also acknowledge within your heart that blessing is a powerful act—one that we're given to do throughout Scripture—and that the blessing of God changes and hallows things around and in us. This blessing is holy and important, no matter what your emotions or conditioning says to you.

With you hand resting gently, say silently or aloud, *I bless my body* or *My body is blessed.* Then name again the part of your body specifically that you are blessing. If you feel any resistance in yourself to this blessing repeat it, slowly, gently, several times over.

If there's another part of your body that is asking for attention now, move your hand there, and attentively repeat the blessing process again.

When you're ready, return your attention to your breath, breathing in through your nose and out through your mouth. Breathe deeply, once, twice, three times. Silently or aloud, repeat the Lord's Prayer or another simple prayer of your choosing to end this time in gratitude and peace.

7

Touch or Temptation

Issues Around Sexuality

*Alienating as it sometimes feels, this non-home
is my home, and on a good day I count a sense
of disequilibrium among my greatest gifts.*

JULIA KASDORF, *THE BODY AND THE BOOK*

THE MOST OBVIOUS PLACE WHERE FEAR POINTS the finger when it comes to our bodies is our sexuality. We've already touched on the horrendous amount of abuse that we experience in our society and, sadly, in and through the church. As a result, fear says that we mustn't touch one another, mustn't acknowledge sexuality except in safe, prescribed places (namely, within marriage). While there are some clear and healthy guidelines around the genital expression of sexuality (namely, the various forms of intercourse) the Bible teaches, we fail to recognize that our sexuality encompasses much more than just genital sex. As a result of our fears, sexual feelings, the grounding power of sexuality itself, are more often than not deemed too dangerous to be acknowledged. The assumption here is that acknowledging our sexual feelings brings them out into the open where they can damage and maim.

As a result, most Christians have unspoken rules about touch in general. We fear the power of sexuality, so we put a fence around it to protect ourselves and our children. We stand beside the tracks and talk them into imagining invisible trains. Touch, one step out from sexuality, is sensual. It's difficult to use the word *sensual* without it being imbued immediately with a sense of the titillating.

The sensual is about our senses, the interactions of our bodies with the outside world. Jesus touched people quite a lot—and in ways that the religious culture around him didn't permit. He touched prostitutes and allowed them to touch him. Worse, he touched lepers—the ritually unclean and possibly biologically contagious. In Christ's time, those suffering with leprosy were required to live outside the town limits and cry out "Unclean! Unclean!" wherever they went, so that travelers could avoid even the potential of accidentally touching them. Most lepers went to their deaths without another single human touch after "diagnosis."

Sadly, our fears around touch and what it might lead to have us labeling one another, consciously or unconsciously, as lepers. A hand left too long on a shoulder or a full-frontal hug seems to carry with it the contagion of misinterpretation, and so we skip it entirely. Even the brush of fingers as the offering plate passes has us recoiling as if we're in danger of catching something fatal.

Much like the Talmudic laws, these unwritten rules of interaction multiply upon themselves, tangling us in coils of our own spinning. Because we are not comfortable with our own bodies and those around us, we struggle, often consciously and with some shame, to make room for those whose bodies are significantly different than ours: those who have handicaps of one form or another, and those for whom body awareness is simply not yet a part of their consciousness—children.

I happen to have the blessing of being part of a church body that welcomes children into the daily life of the congregation. While we still have children's church and a nursery, the wiggling, squirming, touching bodies of our children are invited up each Sunday to be blessed by the whole body. Their small hands are invited to touch the waters of baptism in blessing as it is consecrated, and their weak arms are asked to hold bread and wine before us all as our pastor proclaims, "These are the gifts of God for the people of God. . . . Feed on him in your hearts by faith, with thanksgiving."

In our body, children aren't just the future church—they are the church of today. It is in their innocence and wonder that we see the kingdom of God at work. As G. K. Chesterton writes in the fourth chapter of *Orthodoxy*,

> A child kicks his legs rhythmically through excess, not absence, of life. Because children have abounding vitality, because they are in spirit fierce and free, therefore they want things repeated and un-changed. They always say, "Do it again"; and the grown-up person does it again until he is nearly dead. For grown-up people are not strong enough to exult in monotony. But perhaps God is strong enough to exult in monotony. It is possible that God says every morning, "Do it again" to the sun; and every evening, "Do it again" to the moon. It may not be automatic necessity that makes all daisies alike; it may be that God makes every daisy separately, but has never got tired of making them. It may be that He has the eternal appetite of infancy; for we have sinned and grown old, and our Father is younger than we.

So we honor and cherish our children's little bodies, their unconscious and glorious manifestation of God's care. We make room for the dis-ruption of impulse and guilelessness. We choose to see their boundless, inconvenient energy as an excess of life, a sense of the abundance of God, not an interruption to the life we have planned out.

This is nonetheless rare. In the life of faith we're not far off from the disciples' reluctance toward Jesus gathering the little children to him, touching them, holding them. At home, we teach our children to explore and interact with the world physically. At church, we segregate them from anything that might disrupt the orderly—and rather disembodied—worship of God.

This fear of being disrupted, of perhaps being touched, bleeds into the things that we allow into not only our public but our private relationship with God. It's something that much of the church in the Global South has to teach the Northern and Western churches—the involvement of our bodies in worship. We are afraid to move, to dance, to weep. We raise our hands only in prescribed and acceptable ways. We invite only sterilized forms of art into our communities and our own communion with God. Nothing that might make a mess or cause us to rethink our body boundaries. We pray in words, and only occasionally on our knees. The standing and sitting that happen in liturgical communities can be done also, in rote form, without a foundation in a rich understanding of the importance of physical movement toward God.

Power and Privilege

I always touch people with permission. I don't go in for a hug without asking first, and I'm not already moving forward in such a way that whoever I'm hugging almost has no chance to refuse. I touch with permission—only, always—because I've been touched without permission, without wanting to be touched, and the violation that is goes so much deeper than the surface of my skin.

Think of any group of people—your friends, your church, your workplace. Statistically, of the people that you're imagining, at least one in four have experienced some kind of assault. At least one in four live with at least one experience (and sometimes more, sometimes horrifically repeated) that haunts them, whether it lives in their consciousness or not. I always ask permission before I touch someone.

Touch, you see, like anything else, can be used or misused. It's no use saying that we're touch-deprived (we are) and that we should all just touch each other more (we probably should), because that gives us no compass to guide us toward touch that heals and away from touch that owns, touch that uses, touch that destroys.

We don't necessarily come by our understanding of touch that heals naturally, not in our disordered and desperate world. Watch any parent of a small child around animals, and you'll hear repeated cries of "Gentle! Gentle!" as a little one yanks an ear or pokes her fingers into an eye socket. At the same time we are learning impulse control as infants, we are also learning the power of our bodies. It's why one of the most enjoyable games for a one-year-old is to knock over the stack of interlocking cups you just meticulously reordered. They are beginning to understand their ability to re-form their world with their bodies.

It takes much longer to understand that we have the power to re-form other people's worlds with our bodies as well; some of us never learn. "Sticks and stones may break my bones, but words will never hurt me" is a ridiculous children's rhyme on so many levels—both broken bones and words can wound us in ways that go far beyond syllables and stitches. Rhymes like these encourage children (and adults) to make hurts of the body purely physical and hurts of the soul purely metaphysical, when our physical wounds shape our souls and the pains of the soul are borne deep within bone and muscle. Our bodies and souls are so much more complex and important than that.

Jesus' encounter with the woman with the issue of blood is fascinating when it comes to an understanding of touch and our effect on other people. We find her story in Matthew, Mark and Luke, told from slightly different perspectives. In each case, there is something about this woman's touch that is unique, something that Jesus feels.

The day, no doubt, was hot. Sweaty, sticky, sandy and loud, Christ's followers would have formed a phalanx around him as supplicants and onlookers alike pushed in for a sight of this prophet, this rabbi who was yet another wandering messiah in a context of many such claimants. The itch of rough wool on skin, the stink of men pressed together after at least a day of walking on hot roads, the residue of oil meant to freshen beard and hair would have all combined in a crowd pressing and leaning in to this God who had become man-handled.

So what was different about this touch? What about this reach of hand for rough wool, this movement of flesh to reach out and find substance caused Jesus to turn around in search of who made contact? Luke records Peter's incredulity: "Master, the people are crowding and pressing against you" (Luke 8:45). In other words, how could you possibly ask "Who touched me?" when we all were touching you?

We don't get the detailed description of what it was about this woman's touch that made such a difference, but we do get Jesus' explanation of what happened when he was touched. Power went out of me, he says. That's how he knew something was different. There was a movement of power, of life, from one to another because of touch—and faith.

You've had an experience like that, haven't you? One where the touch you received was more than something casual; it drained life out of you or fed something into you. In that hug from a friend at church who is deeply in need of comfort, or the way the solicitor at your front door grabs your hand just a little too tightly as he shakes it, the way you can feel that he wants to draw something out of you, that he's interested in using you.

Casual touch doesn't feel that way. It's bumping into someone in a line at the store or being pressed against your neighbor on an overcrowded subway. There isn't any exchange of power because neither of you are seeking it. Instead, you're trying your hardest to stay within your self-contained bubbles of personal space.

What a difference it is when someone touches you with intent, whether it's the touch of a lover, the anguished handclasp of a suffering friend or the insistent pressure of a child who wants your attention. In each case the touch is a conduit of request or invitation, something that turns your will, attention, spirit and body toward the other person.

The power that Jesus and his disciples speak of here is *dynamis* in the Greek, which is the root for the English terms "dynamic," "dynamism" and "dynamite." The sense is a movement of the miraculous, the explosive. Power is a particular combination of heat, light and energy.

No wonder we worry so much about touch.

We have at our disposal, contained in these frail and fraught bodies of ours, the power to heal or to destroy, to open a way where there was no way or to bury in such a manner as to make the excavation of the soul a lifelong endeavor.

Doing It Wrong

Funny how we remake our own experiences over again.

If I had to guess, I would say this was the sixth or seventh time I'd taught the class on sexuality and spiritual direction in a seminar setting. The words were familiar in my mouth, the rhythm of the teaching a pattern I could follow easily. I wasn't rigid in my scheduling—I was willing to be surprised by my students and by God. But that day, I also wasn't fully present to them, and as a result, someone suffered.

The exercise I lead students in is designed specifically for spiritual directors in training. These folk have intentionally placed themselves in a program designed to shake their foundations, to help them know and realize what is true and real and pure about their faith and their desire to walk with others in the holy territory of the soul. Because of this, I knew I was operating outside of the regular bounds when I asked them to follow me. I knew that I was stretching them into unfamiliar and potentially dark territory.

Written out, the exercise I led them in is deceptively simple. After a period of silence to quiet their souls, the students are to take the hands of a fellow student with whom they'd been paired. Using only their hands and touching only the hands of their partner, they were to explain their day to one another, describing when they got up, what they had for breakfast, where they went and who they encountered. I asked them to stretch, as well, beyond the bare details of their schedules. As far as was possible, they were also to share how they *felt* about the day's events, not just what happened. And all of this to be undertaken with their eyes closed.

I've seen some pretty intense reactions to this exercise over the years. I've had students tacitly refuse it—their hands remaining in their laps. And I've had students who could only nominally participate, their trembling fingers barely brushing their partner's own fingers, pinky resting against pinky and no more.

What saddened me as I reflected on the exercise later was that, at least at first, I didn't notice anything different was happening in this class. I led the exercise as I do, slowly, tenderly, allowing for the giggles and the deep breaths and the sense of awkwardness and heat that flushes over everyone when we begin. Happily, every student seemed to be entering in, speaking in touch, gently explaining their day to one another. For once, the room seemed to be willing to take this risk, to notice what touch could do and how deeply it connects us.

It wasn't until afterward that she spoke up. I hadn't seen the anger in her at all until she began to use her words, and when she did, she was livid. She felt betrayed, she said, by my leadership (or lack thereof). She felt like she'd had no option, and that she was forced into an experience that felt violating to her heart and even to her marriage vows. Partway through her denunciation, she broke down in tears and needed to leave the room. I didn't need to argue with her. I felt every criticism in my gut. I felt like I'd failed her.

In point of fact, I had failed her.

I carried this regret around for nearly a week before she came to me again, while I was leading a retreat in which she was also participating. I was sitting in a patch of sunlight, eyes closed. Nothing reminds me to rest like a stray sunbeam (growing up in a house with cats, I had a daily picture of what stopping for sabbath time looks like), and when I'm in need of a deep breath, I'll find a ray of light in which to rest. It was there that she searched me out, and I didn't see her coming. When she sat down beside me, I flushed with guilt and shame, preparing myself to apologize to her once again for stewarding her story so badly.

She cut my apologies off abruptly.

"I've spent the past ten years of my marriage working through the sexual abuse that I suffered as a child," she began, charging in as if the story was overtaking her. "I've gone to counseling, both with my husband and on my own. It's been hard—a fight really—but God has done some amazing healing. The touch I receive from my husband no longer reminds me of my abuser's hands; we both feel the work of God in the way we love each other freely and physically."

I drew in a breath, ready to affirm the fact that I should have realized that in any room with more than two people in it, chances are that someone has been sexually abused. I wanted to bury myself in recrimination, grovel in apology for hurting her.

She wouldn't let me.

"I'm not going to say that the exercise that you led was easy—and I think that you should show more care in the future telling people more explicitly that they can choose whether to participate or not." She paused, thinking. "But if you hadn't led it the way that you did, I wouldn't have been forced to confront the fact that I've missed out on a huge amount of healing that God wants me to step into."

I blinked at her.

"In limiting my story of touch to my husband alone, I've limited my interactions with others. I don't let people hug or touch me. Even a good friend's hand on my shoulder feels oppressive sometimes. Instead of letting God into those places, I've run away from them. I haven't seen them as invitations, I've seen them as intrusions."

She took my hand in hers. I could feel how unpracticed she was at this kind of touch, as well as how much courage it took to reach out of her self-imposed safety bubble to encounter me physically.

"I wanted to say thank you. Thank you for asking us to do that exercise. Thank you for not backing down when I got angry and tearful. Thank you for listening to the Spirit when it seemed like you did the wrong thing.

If you had validated my indignant withdrawal, I wouldn't have been forced to talk through it with my husband and with God. I would have gone on as I was—living, enjoying, but not to the full. Not the way God wants me to. I'm excited about the healing he has for me. I'm frightened too. I know my therapist and spiritual director will journey alongside me in it. But something new has opened up, and I believe that God has more redemption for me than I otherwise imagined."

She withdrew her hand, and I wiped at tears.

Yes, she had been triggered. Yes, we had pushed the envelope. But the envelope needed to be pushed beyond what was "safe" in order to find what was truly good.

Sometimes doing it wrong is the only way to get it right.

Doing It Right

The woman who reached out for Jesus in that crowd was doing it wrong. Not only was she a woman reaching for a man (a radical reversal of roles at the time), she was a woman who, biblically speaking, was to be without touch, without contact, without company of any kind. Because of her bleeding, she was considered as unclean as the lepers society so quickly rejected.

Everything about her desperate touch was against social norms, and Jesus called it an act of faith.

What kind of God do we have who would pack the kind of explosive power touch has into the human body? What kind of God would risk our using for destruction that which he pours into us for our redemption?

There aren't many of us who haven't felt the fire touch can light along our veins. Some of us have had that fire touch a dry and ready wick, and the resulting burn was so violent and quick that it seemed like nothing could stop it—and lives exploded. Some of us have felt that fire smolder within us for so long that we felt consumed. What would make God risk this kind of power in us?

I don't know for certain, but I suspect that the answer can be found in Christ's response to the woman with the issue of blood and his words to the disciples the night before he was crucified. When Jesus responds to her that her faith has healed her, the word he uses is *sozo*. Used throughout the New Testament, *sozo* means to heal or make whole, but it's often translated in contexts to mean God's work of salvation. And when Jesus is in the upper room with his disciples, after he has washed their feet and described to them what is to come, he tells them, "Whoever believes in me will do the works I have been doing, and they will do even greater things than these" (John 14:12).

Put those two things together for just a moment in your mind. Jesus healed a woman who had been bleeding for twelve years, a woman who had spent her entire fortune looking for cures, and he healed her through the power of touch. And Jesus, knowing he was about to die, tells the disciples a radical, crazy thing—if you believe in me, you'll do what I've been doing, and greater things too.

So maybe, just maybe, God imbued this flawed, fractious body of ours with this kind of wacky power not because he likes playing with explosives but because he truly believes that we can do what he did, because he made us to be agents of healing in this broken world.

The powers of touch, of the sensual, of our sexuality are heavy, holy things. Those powers have been used to desecrate one another, to harm, to use and abuse. Such is the ache and the paradox of our free will—we have the ability to choose away from God, to choose away from others, to choose away from the good, the right, the true.

But we also have the power to choose to use our bodies for healing, and in doing so our touch becomes the conduit of God's love, grace and power. The gift of this power running through us—sometimes named sexuality, sometimes named sensuality—is that it can and will bring life to others if stewarded well and wisely. It can and will bring about the healing of emotional scars, the healing of long-held lies about our bodies and self-worth, and even the healing of our very flesh through the sacred union of touch. We were made to touch one another, and that touch matters, deeply.

Desperate to Connect

As a spiritual director, I've been given the gift of walking with hundreds of individuals as they journey toward God and toward their truest selves. Listening to someone as they share their story with me is a holy experience. In my spiritual direction office, I've sat with people who came from deeply conservative Christian denominations, with people who came from fundamentally liberal Christian denominations, with people who came from other faith traditions and with people who had no faith tradition or understanding of God at all. Tragically, the common denominator in each of those stories was each person's profound sense of disconnection—usually expressed as a dissatisfaction or discontent.

The more I saw this discontent, the more I began to understand that something much larger was going on. In his book *Sex God*, Rob Bell writes that "our sexuality is our awareness of how profoundly we're severed and cut off and disconnected."[1] Sadly, most of us, myself included, aren't only disconnected from our world and our God—we're disconnected from *ourselves*. We're disconnected from our desires and drives, we're disconnected from the earthy reality of our physical bodies. We live our lives trying to control or sometimes completely suppress the things that our bodies ask for so insistently—intimacy and connection.

Whatever our underlying theological differences, as Christians we've been taught certain things about our sexuality along the way. On the whole, we've been taught that sexuality means sex, however we define the physical boundaries of that act. We've been taught that any expression of our sexuality (because, after all, it's all about sex) is meant to be confined to the marriage bed. If we came from more restrained Christian circles, as I did, we've also been taught that any personal experience of our sexuality—whether it's a slight flush of the skin when our partner touches our hand or, more scandalously, that heat we feel when we begin to pray with that friend we care so deeply about—is wrong. Very, very wrong. And that internal not-quite-right voice in our heads says stridently, we need to stop it *right now.*

Amélie, the main character in the 2001 movie by the same name, is an odd young woman. Shy and observant, she sets about to bring life and happiness to those around her after she witnesses the joy of an old man reunited with childhood memories. Despite Amélie's quirky and isolated upbringing, she is deeply connected to the world around her. One of her secret pleasures is to thrust her hands into the bags of legumes in the market, to feel the different textures slide over her skin, connecting her to her body and to beans.

Why does she do this? Should we really be enjoying the fact that she does?

The answer to the second question is yes, and the fact that we need to ask the first shows how deeply severed we are from our bodily need to connect with the world around us—the *many* bodies with whom we interact on a daily, hourly basis. Amélie was a girl stunted in her social interaction by the social phobias of her father. Instead of the touch-and-tumble world of toddlers, she got the sterility of her solitary room. Instead of the giggly wonder of preteen girls beginning to experience the changes of puberty, she sat at supper staring down her aging parents in awkward silence. Like Amélie, we have been living in a world almost completely devoid of touch. For most of us, physical interaction is limited to the "side hugs" officially sanctioned by most Christian literature and an occasional handshake. Even our marital relationships are focused, or at least encouraged to be focused, almost entirely on intercourse. We're rarely encouraged to get out and feel the way rain physically speaks of God or to discover the way our bodies respond to being held kindly by a friend. We're stuck staring at our aging parents, while our bodies are screaming to feel connection.

Unlike Amélie, however, we don't go sticking our hands in bags of black-eyed peas in order to remember that we're really *here* and so is the rest of the world. Instead, we suppress—and repress—every desire we have to be touched, every noticing we have of our physical body and the urges that we experience in it. Some of us end up in accountability groups, trying desperately to pretend that we don't have *any* desires or, if we do, that we need to confess them and repent of feeling any physical desire, any embodied longing. We're practical Gnostics.[2] While we confess with our mouths that we believe Christ became human, we live as if the stuff of this world can't be redeemed or, worse, is actively working against holiness.

Which is where sexuality comes in.

While it seems the most unlikely and scandalous place to start in the recovery of our connection to our bodies, sex and sexuality is one of the best places to start. We can be practically disconnected, or generally disordered, about the way we eat, how much we drink or how much sleep we get a night. We're pretty good at ignoring God's command to rest on the sabbath, and for all intents and purposes we've completely ignored the fact that gluttony is one of the besetting sins not only of the Western culture but of the Western church. Sex, however, we find difficult to ignore.

I once heard a pastor friend joke that the way to pack the pews on a Sunday morning was to preach a sermon series about sex. Ironically, he was in the middle of preaching just such a series and, lo and behold, church attendance was up. While sales of the Christian classics (Teresa of Ávila's *Inner Castle* or Thomas à Kempis's *The Imitation of Christ*) remain almost flat-lined, books on purity or self-control or how to have great Christian sex are more than hot off the presses. We're driven to decode where the "lines" are in our dating relationships (not in itself a bad thing unless it's taken to legalistic extremes) and what the latest wisdom is on how to control our drive to ogle the opposite sex.

All of this talk about sex and purity and self-control titillates us quite thoroughly, and even occasionally convicts us about what God's best designs for our desires are in a way that provides lasting change. But it essentially misses our point of deprivation, this odd disconnect that we still experience between the life we live in our bodies and the life we live in the Spirit. It misses the point because in all of this talk we keep skirting around a fact that we all know but are too busy covering up to admit: *we are sexual beings.* Our sexuality is an essential part of being human, a part that has been sadly unintegrated by the church and scandalously over-exposed by society.

Before we get hung up on the fact that Jesus never got married and never had sex, however, let me restate that what we're talking about when we talk about sexuality is so much more than genital intercourse. While sex is one way that we express our sexuality, it is not the only way—and we've been tied up in knots about this ever since, oh, the time of St. Augustine in the mid-400s (as we talked about in chapter two). To say that sexuality is only about genital sex (or our thoughts about genital sex) is to strip the millions of single people in the world of their sexuality. A single person has just as many desires and longings and embodied feelings as a married person does—he or she is just as human. Just as Jesus was fully human. Which means that he was also a sexual being.

For some of us, that's a scandalous and difficult thought—that Jesus had longings and felt desires just as we did, just as we do. Even more scandalous is that Jesus went about his life being a human being *fully alive* to his sexuality. He didn't shuck it off as irrelevant. He didn't live without the touch of others to keep himself more pure and holy. He was fully God and fully human, and he welcomed touches that the world around him thought thoroughly improper. (Think about the women who wiped his feet with her hair and anointed him with oil.) He connected with those around him because he loved us so much and knew how profoundly we were (and still are) cut off from ourselves, from one another and from our God.

There's another truth about our sexuality that is important for us to grasp, twinned to the first that our sexuality is our awareness of how profoundly we are cut off—by sin, by the world—from one another. In my spiritual direction practice, I've seen this truth acted out in both healthy and unhealthy ways, but it is nonetheless at work most of the time. Sexuality is also all of the ways we go about trying to *reconnect*, with ourselves, with others and with our world. Apart from being an important broadening of the way we see what is sexual and what isn't, this definition opens us up the possibility that our sexuality is pointing to something much larger and more central to who we are—our spirituality, our longing for God.

The Need for Touch

And that's the thing. For the most part, we *just don't see it*. If you've come from almost any Protestant spiritual tradition, the connection between our sexuality and God is less than clear. If you've come from a conservative tradition, especially a conservative evangelical tradition, not only is the connection difficult to see, it's almost antithetical to what you might perceive as a biblical understanding of spirituality. Unfortunately, whether it's tradition or a simple neglect of the subject, the impulses of our bodies (be they toward food, drink or physical intimacy) rarely make their way into the pulpit on a Sunday morning. Or, better said, they're there, in the body of the pastor or the priest, but he or she does their practical best to make sure they don't interfere. This despite the fact that Jesus says, "Eat. This is my body, broken for you. Drink. This is my blood poured out for the forgiveness of sins." Even as he instituted the Last Supper, what Anglicans and other liturgically structured churches call the Eucharist, he addressed our deepest needs—food, drink and intimacy. Take my body into your body. (Perhaps this is why we can be so confused and conflicted about whether or not Christ is truly present in the elements. The discussion itself requires us to talk about the stuff of our bodies—blood and flesh, wine and bread—and we have trouble putting the spiritual and the corporeal together with our disordered view of our physical selves.)

We still need to be shocked back into the realization that we are bodies that need, and need to touch.

Compared to common life a century ago, we in the West are a shockingly touch-deprived society. The study of "personal space" didn't develop until the twentieth century and was based originally on observations of the interactions of zoo animals. It wasn't until Edward T. Hall, an anthropologist and crosscultural researcher, wrote about "proxemics" or "personal spaces" in 1966 that we even had words to describe what it meant to be uncomfortable in close proximity to someone else. By this time, technology and transportation improvements afforded the luxury of a bubble of space all to ourselves in which we could live, controlling the ways in which we touched or were touched by others. Today, we can go through days, weeks and even months without touching another human being. We correspond electronically, which detaches us from the physicality of communication. More often than not, we drive rather than walk to the places we need to visit, and with bench seats faded from the auto design landscape, you won't even slide into your driving companion on a sharp curve anymore.

More often than not, we protect ourselves not just from any kind of person-to-person touch, but any other kind of unbidden touch as well. We are less and less likely to simply deal with the inconveniences of the weather; instead we isolate ourselves from it almost completely. Most office buildings no longer have windows that can open—we can watch the wind blow, but we can't feel it ruffle our hair. Even our clothing industry reflects this trend toward physical isolation. The more affluent and isolated we become, the less our clothing is designed to stand up to any weather conditions other than those brought about by the vagaries of air conditioning and central heating. You can't walk through a blustery parking lot, let alone a muddy field, in most of today's fashions. We are disconnected from earth, wind, rain, and, more and more, from our own bodies.

Sadly, the church as a whole has not been of great help, especially recently. The fact is, most Christians have grown up with, or, if they converted as I did in adulthood, grown into, a set of behavioral standards that make touching and being touched—healthy expressions of intimacy and sexuality—even less possible. Instead of seeing the crying need of people to have their physical existence in the world acknowledged, instead of following the incredible loving-kindness of Jesus as he touched those who were deemed completely untouchable, we, on the whole, see touching of any kind as suspect and potentially immoral. Functionally, we act as if it would be a lot more convenient if we just skipped the whole body thing altogether.

Which is ironic, really, given that our whole theology revolves around the fact that Jesus lived and breathed and sweated and walked around and touched people. Most other faith traditions can get away with an aversion to or attempt to escape from the reality of our physical incarnation. Not Christians. The Nicene Creed—whether or not we recite it regularly—states that we believe in Christ's physical birth, death and resurrection. None of that happens without a body.

Stepping out from under cultural and historically accepted ways of acting is, however, extremely difficult. Especially if we don't have any understanding of why behaving or thinking any differently will help us to live a better life, understand God, be more connected to one another. And so on.

Frankly, there is good reason to be scared. Touch (our sensuality) and connection (our sexuality) are two desires that, left unbridled, lead to the kinds of ravenous behaviors that destroy marriages and disgrace churches. The reasons that Christians have developed such a reputation for prudish mores and strict standards are both manifold and valid. Illicit affairs, addictions to pornography, inappropriate touching of small children—all have disastrous effects on families, churches, perpetrators and victims. Disordered sexuality quite often leads to addiction, which can feed into other destructive behaviors and systems.

Avoiding the Mess

One of the places where we've allowed our sexuality and sensuality, our understandings of our bodies and how we connect with each other, to be defined not by original design or God's story of redemption but by those things that keep us safe and secure is the emphasis on purity. This is the theology behind much of the courting literature found on the bookshelves of Christian stores. It's safer to avoid this intimacy thing altogether until we know it's what God deems good. This in-the-middle-of-things muckiness is just not worth fumbling through. Keep the lines clear. Don't connect. Don't touch. Don't desire.

While choosing sharp boundaries around our physical and emotional interactions is a valid way of living, I believe that it's also resulted in the kind of disconnection that had my friend from the spiritual direction class stuck in her process of healing. Instead of having safe experiences of touch within the context of friendships and families, her only redemptive experiences were with her husband, and those were primarily centered around sexual intercourse. She had lived nearly twenty years without having the assumptions about sexuality and sensuality that were created by abuse challenged. In my mind, that is a failure of Christian community, a failure of the body of Christ to offer healing to someone who deeply wanted it.

So how do we approach the topic of our sexuality? How do we live without the lines, as scary as that sounds?

Redemption, Not Control

Wrestling is a messy, intimate act. Whether you've wrestled at the level of Olympic sport or merely gotten down and dirty on the living room floor with your kid brother, you've taken part in something that forced you into knowing another person quite thoroughly. In the tangle of legs, arms and effort, you touched and were touched. Depending on your level of exertion, you were either covered with sweat (your own and your opponent's) or giggles. In the awkward dance of dominance, fingers were jammed, egos were bruised and someone ended up on the bottom. Whether your goal was to pin your opponent to the ground or to allow your five-year-old niece the pride of "besting" her aunt, you also discovered the inevitable truth: triumph didn't mean control.

We really do love control, though, and we ache when it isn't achieved. In the ring or on the living room floor, some of the shine comes off our victories when our opponent gets up and moves on. Even medals don't guarantee that we've mastered something—records are broken, our bodies age, and time flows inexorably forward. That which we thought was pinned underneath our superior maneuvers squirms away, and we are left empty-handed.

Jacob knows something of this wrestling and the desperate desire to own something after victory gets up, dusts itself off and walks away into the night. Genesis 32 presents a brief but intimate picture of the patriarch's struggle with control. Jacob, after besting his crooked father-in-law, is traveling with his family and all his household goods to be reunited with the brother that he so famously cheated out of the family inheritance. It's easy to imagine the apprehension in Jacob's soul; rightly, his brother could meet him with armed men and revenge in mind. We could guess that Jacob's feet get heavier and heavier as he approaches his brother's homeland. No wonder he sent his wives, children and livestock across the river first. Alone as night falls, he decides to linger a little bit longer, rather than cross in the darkness. A bit cowardly, yes, but which one of us doesn't want now and then to delay what seems so very inevitable?

There, without help or witness, Jacob is met by what different translations of Scripture alternately call a man, an angel or God himself. Shrouded in mystery, it's unclear how this encounter gets started. There's no indication of a preceding shouting match or if this divine visitor simply jumps Jacob (or, perhaps, given his predilection for grabbing what isn't his, Jacob jumps him). What we do know is that they wrestle all night. Which, if we think about it, is a long, exhausting time of struggling for victory.

How many times did Jacob find himself near defeat, only to somehow turn the tide of the fight? Did the match break apart occasionally, as the opponents regrouped to find their bearings, reassessing what they knew of each other in this dark night? Was Jacob the only one truly exerting himself, or did he get covered in God's sweat as well as his own?

We don't know. We don't even know, as morning approaches, the name of this stranger. God came so close that Jacob couldn't see exactly who or what had gotten a hold of him. At yet, in the wrestling, Jacob knew and was known by this mystery. The reason we don't get a detailed picture of what happened that night, I would suggest, is because our own wrestling with God is as individual, intimate and holy as Jacob's night with the divine. It would be like participating at a peep show to have the details revealed to us. Not only would it not help our understanding of God, we would end up trying to push ourselves into Jacob's mold instead of learning how to wrestle in our own ways. This mysterious night was a holy time of testing, of being known, of contending, discovering, revealing.

Not only was he known, not only was he tested, Jacob, it seems from the text, was winning. Whether this is the kind of prevailing that happens when a small child sits on his father's chest and announces his victory or a bloody, sweaty, painful realization that Isaac's son simply wasn't going to give up, well, again, we don't know. We do know that when it became clear that Jacob wasn't going to let go, the divine power gets unleashed. Just a little.

With only a "touch," Jacob's hip is dislocated, gracing him with a permanent reminder of the fact that he wasn't and isn't the one in control. We often gloss over the fact that it didn't take this visitor a great deal of effort the pull a full-grown man's leg from the socket.[3] As if that's an easy thing to do. All this time, Jacob has been wrestling with someone vastly more powerful than himself, and yet that someone, in his grace, withheld his power and met Jacob on even ground. He could, I would guess, have killed Jacob easily, and yet he left him with both a limp and enough strength to continue on. As morning began to break over the horizon and the wrestling continued, Jacob, victorious yet so aware how fleeting and sometimes deceiving victory can be, demanded a blessing.

Strong's Concordance says that the Hebrew word used to describe Jacob's request, *barak*, carries within it the notion of breaking or breaking down. Jacob was asking for a fundamental thing, a blessing that spoke to his core and, perhaps, to his brokenness. Mystery obliges, but not with a reparation of damaged sinew and joint. Instead, he removes Jacob's old name—which means "takes by the heel, overreacher, supplanter"—and gives him the name by which he and his descendants would from thenceforth be known: Israel. "God rules," "God preserves," "God protects," "God strives" are some of the translations. More colloquially Israel translates "one who wrestles with God and with people; one who is able."

So often, we are known by our wounds. Not only do we allow them to define us, we allow them to control, guide and mock us. Knowing that we chose unwisely—whether it be sliding into an addiction, giving ourselves over to a besetting temptation or choosing to look the other way when injury is done to another—we very often let ourselves be trapped into believing that choice, whatever it was, defines who we are to our very core. Instead of letting guilt prick us into confession and reconciliation, we make friends with guilt's poisonous bedmate, shame, and wear our sins with something akin to false pride.

Jacob knew this way of being quite well. Having cheated his brother out of his inheritance, something his mother seemed set in having him do even as she named him, Jacob chose to live exiled from his family instead of seeking to lay down his sin and be reconciled. Over time, his betrayal became so much a part of his identity that it seemed to come as little surprise to him when others betrayed him—after all, hadn't he done the same thing (Genesis 26–32)? And don't we, consumed even unconsciously by how we've acted or what we've done, do the same as well, especially when it comes to our sexuality?

And yet, on the eve of confronting that which he believed to define him (his brother and his own betrayal), Jacob ends up wrestling with God. And instead of being confronted with his sin and self-definitions, Jacob is confronted instead with his own brokenness and lack of control. He begins, perhaps for the first time, to see himself as he really is: wounded, alone, dependent. As he demands a blessing, we can almost hear the desperation in his voice: *Don't leave me like this. Give me something that I can hold on to.*

What God does is surprising, backward and redemptive. Knowing Jacob not only from a night of wrestling but from the foundations of all time, God sees him completely. Instead of meeting what might seem to be an obvious need—physical healing—God hears what Jacob is crying out for. Even the words Jacob uses harken to what he most deeply needs: Jacob asks God for a blessing when he took that very blessing from his own brother. *Barak* is exactly the same word that Isaac uses to bless Jacob-as-Esau. What Jacob took from Esau by trickery and deceit, Jacob, surrendered at last, asks of God. But God doesn't give it to him.

God gives Jacob a new name. He redeems all that had defined Jacob by, in essence, reframing it. The blessing that he bestows on Jacob is that Jacob is seen, utterly known, completely broken, and mercifully, in the face of all that Jacob believes to be true about himself, God sees and speaks a different truth over him. "Taker" becomes "given by God." "Overreacher" becomes "preserved (one might say hemmed in) by God." "Supplanter" becomes "God protects." "Inadequate" becomes "one who is able."

Jacob goes forward from his wrestling changed and blessed, not because he has triumphed but because he has been known, wounded and renamed. What came out of his encounter was not control but redemption, a deep transformation of that which was once wayward and warped by the voice and touch of God. Jacob named the place of his transformation Peniel, which means "facing God."

Facing God is the very place of our transformation as well.

Sadly, when we wrestle with our sexuality, we are much less interested in being known and transformed in the presence of One so close we cannot name than we are interested in controlling and dominating. If we grew up in a Christian context that emphasized avoidance as a path to sexual purity, more often than not we have found ourselves deep in the throes of this wrestling match with our desires and drives. Sometimes directly framed for us as a battle, this fight has taken all that we have to "win." Married or single, constant vigilance, accountability and redirection are the hallmarks of our relationship with our sexuality. Frustratingly, each time we emerge from these battles victorious, our erstwhile opponent slips out from under our pinning moves—sometimes the same day, or the next month, or after a year or two.

Others of us have lived in contexts where wrestling with our sexuality wasn't even a category. On one end of the spectrum, we were taught to ignore our desires completely, to blush and giggle when those topics came up and then quickly move the discussion in a different direction. Sex happened behind closed doors and was not to be discussed, never mind encountered and struggled with, talked or prayed about. We are meant to be angels. On the other end of the spectrum, we were taught to give our sexuality free rein. Whether this came through our parents or peers, the message was to indulge whatever felt good—or, ironically, even what felt bad but seemed to be a good idea at the time. We're meant to be animals.

In both of those cases, we got jumped in the night by something we couldn't see or name. Whether we even recognize it as our sexuality, the things that we ignored or indulged came back (or will come back) to demand our attention, to demand to be known and engaged. For some of us, that looks like unexpected physical longings or desires that have either snuck up gradually or knocked us over with their intensity. For others, it's a nagging sense that something is missing, that each time we indulge our appetite, there's a part of us that remains unsatisfied, unfulfilled and wanting more.

In the complex muddle of ways that we've handled our sexuality and
its demands on our attention, it is often difficult to see why any other
method of dealing with our desires would be better than the one we've
been using. If you've been living well in a context of avoidance and accountability, succeeding in resisting temptation and living within limits,
engaging with the story of sexuality sounds sort of dangerous. For those
living in the land of indulgence, whether that means a life of sexual mo-
nogamy or diversity, really encountering your sexuality is frightening
because it means a possible loss of control. And if you've lived life with
the belief that these things shouldn't be talked about, looking at what it
means to be a sexual being could be so foreign to you that it feels like
drowning in an ocean of impulses and jargon and mores without any
hope of rescue.

But hold on—there is rescue. In fact, rescue is the point.

God didn't get down and dirty with Jacob on that fateful evening just
because he was bored and had nothing else to do. He spent time knowing
and being known because his goal was redemption. He didn't give Israel
a permanent reminder of his identity because he wanted to ensure he'd
be remembered as a cruel and arbitrary deity. He left a mark because
that's what an encounter with the divine does to us—strips us of our old
ways of being and gives us a new, syncopated movement, something that
sounds a lot like grace notes. He renamed not because he was ashamed
of who Jacob was but because he was calling him to more—to a relationship, a reliance and a reimagining of what the future could look like.
God didn't wrestle with Jacob to control him. That would have been easy
to do. He wrestled instead to redeem.

Our sexuality—the ways we connect with each other and with our
embodied selves—is something that needs that redemption. In the
places that we've forbidden ourselves from feeling, longing, desiring; in
the places that we've ignored, refused or hidden from our bodies and
drives; in the places that we've indulged, experimented and misdirected,
we need to invite the presence of God. We may be afraid, just as Jacob

was terrified of what his brother Esau might do to him. And we will inevitably feel quite alone in this place where forces that we've considered both dark and secretly attractive come out to play. We may, in fact, worry that what we're wrestling with isn't anything that we've ever encountered before—so close to the core of who we are that we don't even know how to name it.

The journey, though, is about letting go of control and instead inviting redemption to have his way. It's about being known, deeply, in places that you never thought to be known. It's about the struggle, the explosion of the idea that life with God is something that's easy to manipulate. And it's about allowing our sexuality, one of the primary driving forces of our embodied lives, to be renamed as "God rules," "God preserves," "God protects" and "God strives."

Touch Point

I Wanna Hold Your Hand

For this exercise, you'll need to find someone safe and mature who is willing to participate in an exercise of redemptive touch. This may be tough for you, and it may feel like quite a risk, but the resulting revelations, and the connections that you feel with others, will be worth it.

If it's more comfortable for you, you're welcome to choose your spouse or a good friend, but it would be helpful if it is someone with whom you don't actually live on a day-to-day basis (the mundane and holy reality of living in each other's spaces tends to break down our false cultural and ethical standards around touch). Don't ambush the person—let them know that you're on a journey to reclaim the goodness of your body and of touch and that you're wanting more than anything to listen to God in this exercise.

With your partner, find a quiet space to be before God together. Spend some time praying for God's presence and guidance, naming and releasing any fears that you may have. Covering the time with the sacrifice and work of Christ will be important here, as well.

Read aloud either Psalm 23 or John 17:6-19.

Now, hold each other's hand. You may do this with both hands or simply hold hands side by side. Remain holding each other's hands for at least two to three minutes (you may need a timer for this; you'll probably want to let go sooner). Breathe through the time, being aware of how the other person's hand feels in yours.

Notice in yourself any sense of connection or disconnection as you sit in this space. Do you want to pull away? Do you feel like resting in this touch? Dialogue silently with God about the push and pull you feel in your body. What messages are being triggered by this touch? Are they positive or negative?

When it comes time, release hands without squeezing or grasping tightly—simply let go openly. Notice how your hand feels now that you are no longer connected to another person. Is there relief? Loss? Emptiness? Presence?

Spend some time dialoguing with your partner about what you heard from God in that time. Were your experiences similar or different? Let the conversation flow as you are able—the more you are willing and present to the experience, the more you will discover the underlying messages and the power of touch and connection in your own story. This dialogue, too, is prayer.

When you're ready, conclude the time with a prayer of gratitude to God for his movement in and through your bodies and conversation. Touch each other's hands in the center of each palm, blessing those hands with the power to bring the healing touch of Christ into the world.

Desire or Destruction

Exploring Our Impulses

Give me a man in love; he knows what I mean. Give me one who yearns;
give me one who is hungry; give me one far away in this desert,
who is thirsty and sighs for the springs of the Eternal Country.
Give me that sort of man; he knows what I mean. But if I
speak to a cold man, he just doesn't know what
I'm talking about.

St. Augustine of Hippo

SO, MAYBE NOW YOU'RE READY TO GET DOWN on the mat with the confusing mess that our sexuality seems to be. You're ready for it to be redeemed, renamed, reframed—whatever needs to happen in this vulnerable place of intimacy and brokenness. You're ready, you're willing, but you're really not sure what to do with this thing that seems both insatiable and unpredictable: desire. And I have to say, you're not alone in that confusion.

My husband and I love to cook together. We are particularly enchanted with creating meals that feed people in ways that they weren't expecting—the extravagance of homemade angel food cake with crème anglaise at a budget meeting, the rich exuberance of potato chips made from scratch and scented with truffle salt at a backyard barbecue. There's something transcendent about meeting a desire people didn't know they had, something of the taste of the kingdom of heaven in awakening an appetite that was otherwise laying dormant.

The reaction of most of my friends to this awakening, though, is both baffling and sadly typical. When the physical sensations hit and the pleasure centers of their brains light up, we hear exclamations of joy and contentment—and people head back for seconds. But, almost without fail, the mumbles of "Mmm . . . marvelous" turn to comments about how fattening this type of food must be or how they wish they had someone like my husband as a live-in chef.

While I'm certain they don't know that they are doing it, my friends are attempting to stuff these newly birthed desires away. With the reality of the laundry stacking up and the kids that need to be run to soccer practice looming before them, very few of them want to live with this newly found appreciation of the quality of fresh hollandaise sauce. Looking forward, however briefly, into their own lives, they see no way this appetite for a new flavor can be met. Whatever it is just isn't in their skill set or time constraints or budget. So, instead of sitting in the tension that desire births in us, in them, they shut it down with deprecation and dismissal, a combination that controls desire by killing it.

When it comes to our bodily desires, we're used to either appeasing them or denying them—not living in them. We do this most often because we've lost the distinction between *desire* and *impulse*.

I'm following an impulse when I head to the grocery store when I'm sad or the bookstore when I'm feeling lonely (my two go-to places). Impulse is something we often feel powerless in the face of, something that drives us from within. The root of the word is to impel, and that's what we feel in our bodies—a drive that compels us to act.

People who are ruled by their impulses are difficult people to be in relationship with. Caught in the present moment by whatever is driving them, they rarely make plans and often act in a way that gets themselves (and others) into trouble. Impulsive people seem incapable of thinking through their actions, and often talk about their experience of life as something of a whirlwind. A body ruled by impulse is a body in imbalance. There is no harmony of mind, soul and flesh; instead, the constant drive of impulse often exhausts, frustrates and eventually sickens our internal systems.

Impulse, for the most part, drives us toward things and people without thought, care or presence. We live not whole but in fragmented parts, pushed forward helplessly and sometimes irrationally. It is because of these impulses, and the way that they seem to war against wholeness and holiness in God, that we find ourselves so often disgusted with what it is that we seem to want, what it is that our bodies gravitate toward without our conscious thought.

Because, our bodies indeed gravitate. Impulse control is difficult precisely because the habits of flesh, those unconscious impulses, lead us toward death instead of life, sin instead of holiness. Impulse doesn't care about its means, just its ends.

It's this Paul is talking about in Romans 6 when he exhorts the church, "Therefore do not let sin reign in your mortal body so that you obey its evil desires" (Romans 6:12). "Desire" here is an unfortunate translation, as the Greek reads *epithumia*, which is perhaps better rendered as covetousness or lust. Although we tend to shy away from the word *lust*, defining it narrowly as inappropriate sexual desire, lust is better understood as a desire that seeks to posses or fully consume its object. Which is to say lust will use people as objects to get what it wants, without regard to their vulnerability or humanity. Lust treats people as tools, emotions as disposable, and elevates the desires of the self over the desires or needs of anyone else. By definition, lust and love can't ever coexist.

Couple lust with impulse and you have a deadly and chaotic combination, one that leads to disintegration and destruction.

But Paul continues on after his well-worded warning about letting sin reign in our bodies: "Do not offer any part of yourself to sin as an instrument of wickedness, but rather offer yourselves to God as those who have been brought from death to life; and offer every part of yourself to him as an instrument of righteousness. For sin shall no longer be your master, because you are not under the law, but under grace" (Romans 6:13-14).

There's an interesting twist there at the end: sin, in our bodies, in our desires, can be an instrument of wickedness, but we can also offer everything, including our bodies and our desires, as instruments of righteousness. As followers of Christ we're not ruled anymore by impulses we can't control, desires that lead to destruction. We don't have to categorize everything we want as automatically bad, because, beyond the first faltering steps of our walk with God, our desires tend more and more to coincide with his.

Spiritual director and professor of Christian spirituality Janet Ruffing puts it this way,

> I am convinced that many Christians never entertain their desires long enough to know what they really want. If we habitually suppress our wants, we may never discover the true core of our longing that could lead us more deeply into God. It takes courage to allow our desires to become conscious. When they do, we become responsible for either participating in their fulfillment—moving toward that which we desire—or participating in their frustration— failing to act on our desire. Many of us have been conditioned to expect our desires to be frustrated anyway. . . . Beyond the beginnings, however, our wills tend to coincide with God's.[1]

Isn't that both horrifying and hopeful? Horrifying because healing involves taking the risk of being awake to our desires, alive to them in ways we've been trained by our culture and sometimes, sadly, the church, to ignore, repress, even kill. Hopeful because as you and I both know, those desires just won't stay dead. They rear their heads in strange and con-fusing ways, coming out when we least expect them or in forms that we would hardly identify as our desires.

Desire and Rest

I have several friends at the moment with children under two—my younger sister included. One of the fascinating and, often for parents, frustrating things about these pint-sized people is that they make their desire for rest abundantly clear. Most of these parents guard naptime with a fervor that nonparents find bewildering (although a similar fervor of nonparents for say, a particular television show, is equally bewildering to those with children). The midday rest period for little ones is so sac-rosanct that I sometimes meet friends on my porch for a quick chat while the car is running and the little one sleeps inside. Another friend of mine has given up going to church for a season because the start of service coincides precisely with the beginning of a ten o'clock snooze.

This dedication to honoring the need to sleep is based on hard learning. If parents are lucky, the tinies will fall asleep wherever they are, depleted, but if they're not, the ensuing storm is difficult to weather. Exhausted toddlers are unable to control their emotions and reactions, resulting in dramatic meltdowns in inopportune places.

However well managed our adult emotions are, the consequences of sleep deprivation as well as a general lack of rest affect us in the same way they affect toddlers. We've just learned to ignore our fatigue.

That studied ignorance finds its roots in a mistrust of our what our bodies ask us for most often—food, sleep, sex. Because we've been encul-turated to believe that our physical desires are at best neutral or at worst destructive, listening to the subtle messages of a system ready for a little more sleep or in need of a day of rest is nearly impossible.

Our fears in trusting our desires are so strong that we often have to reach a full-on meltdown of our own in order to pay attention to the physiological need for sleep. It's why people regularly get sick the first day of a vacation or after a wedding—the body's *desire* for rest morphs into a *need* for rest that, unheeded, results in vulnerability to pathogens and diseases. The minute the adrenaline surges produced by stressful events (the classic fight-or-flight hormone) leave our system, illnesses are right there, and a depleted body is unable to fight them off.

That is as true for us on a mental and emotional level as it is physically. When we've trained ourselves to mistrust the desires of our bodies, we've cut ourselves off from some deeply important sources of information about how we're doing—our emotions are primarily physiological, after all—and we're unable to access the reality of what's going on inside our souls. The belief that giving in to our desires leads to destruction is so well patterned in us that a day of rest brings with it a host of voices declaring that we're lazy, indolent, unable to take anything seriously. While these aren't physical pathogens, they are mental and emotional ones, tearing at our self-worth, our image of God and our ability to care for others. Instead of pressing deeper into physical rest and letting the Spirit do the work of restoring our souls, we often dive instead into more work, tiring ourselves further, or succumb to the messages of guilt and shame that we receive, taking on an identity as lazy, worthless or unproductive, rather than leaning into the grace and the gift of God.

I wouldn't be telling you this if I hadn't experienced it myself, more than once. Today, in fact, I spent the morning struggling with the amount of free time that I had, telling myself that I needed to get to work, berating myself for not doing the laundry faster or getting to my emails in a more timely way. Instead of embracing the leisurely day head, instead of listening to my body's desire for a slower pace and an unhurried approach, I let myself get sucked into the vortex of what I "should" be doing. Even when faced with a clear message—the ache of a lower back that collects stress when I'm not caring for myself—I faced my desire for rest with a suspicion borne of years of earning approval through productivity. I let the messages win—until an encounter with Scripture brought me up short and returned me to the center of myself, body, soul and mind.

In the words of the psalmist I heard my own fractious complaint that I was surrounded by enemies, unable to find relief. And the Father stepped in to remind me that it was he who was my shield and salvation—not my ability to impress others by meeting deadlines and answering demands. "But You, O LORD, *are* a shield for me, My glory and the One who lifts up my head. . . . I lay down and slept; I awoke, for the LORD sustained me" (Psalm 3:3, 5 NKJV).

There's a reason God created us with the need to sleep at least one-third of our lives away. The simple fact of our need for at least six hours (and ideally eight to ten) of enforced helplessness reminds us that we aren't the Creator of the universe and that one higher and more powerful than ourselves is at work, holding it all together. We can't do anything while asleep—even our unconscious minds are not exactly under our control. Instead, we are at the mercy of systems that are supposed to work automatically (respiration, circulation, digestion), systems we think little about before we slip into slumber. The world carries on around us, and God continues his great God-ing in the world entirely without our input. It's a humbling and reassuring truth that we get to live into physically each day. If only we trusted that desire for sleep just a little more fully.

Discerning Desires

St. Ignatius of Loyola lived in Europe in the mid-fifteenth century. A man of passion and promise, he was wounded in battle as a young knight of the Spanish court. During his recuperation—he lay immobile for long periods of time as the cannonball wound to his leg healed—he read widely, from historical fiction to the lives of the saints. During this time, how he responded to what he read gave him direction and focus, later shaping his desire to follow God and, more than that, to provide guidance and discernment for others as they chose to pursue God in all aspects of their lives.

What Ignatius discovered as he read was that there were certain books that caused a deep unrest in his spirit. It wasn't that they incited lust (although that may have been part of it), but that they drew him away from a sense of interior peace. There were other topics that made him feel discontented, disconnected and ill at ease. These, too, drew him away from that interior peace, from a sense of God. In contrast, there were subjects and materials that drew him into God's presence, and away from the shoals of restlessness.

Ignatius began to notice that it wasn't so much his appetites that were causing discontentment—or, as we would say, his desires. Instead, his desires and drives were simply pointing to or away from things that incited them. When he read stories of battles and women of court, Ignatius ended up restless and focused on what he wasn't getting or was missing out on. When he read about the lives of the saints, he found himself wondering how to get closer to God.

From these observations, Ignatius developed his concepts of *consolation* and *desolation*. It wasn't the stories themselves that changed Ignatius, but how he personally responded to them. He could have been reading about botany and culinary techniques for cooking fish. The times when his desires were turned toward God, whether he was seeking to be closer to him or even just wanting to talk to him, Ignatius called consolation. On the other hand, when Ignatius felt himself driven to places of distraction, self-focus or discontent, those moments he called desolation—he was oriented away from God.

Ignatian scholar and spiritual director Margaret Silf puts it this way:

Another way of looking at the effects of our inner movements is through the example of the tide ebbing and flowing onto a beach. If we imagine that the beach represents our true center and home in God, and the destination of our journeying, we can see that the sea is either moving toward the beach (flow tide) or away from it (ebb tide). In the same way, our hearts, our truest centers, are directed either toward or away from God. This represents the general orientation of our lives. Now look at the effect of the winds, which we might compare to the action of what Ignatius calls "the spirits." Imagine the effect on a swimmer who is moving, in general terms, with the tidal flow, when the wind is blowing against the direction of the tide: If the wind is blowing out to sea, then it will impede the process of the person swimming with the flow tide by working in the opposite direction; If the wind is blowing in from offshore, it will accelerate the swimmer's progress. The opposite effects can be seen in the way these same winds work on a swimmer who is moving out to sea on an ebb tide.[2]

What, though, do these tides have to do with our bodies and, more pressingly, with our unruly desires? For, as many of us have experienced, all the logic and good intentions we've amassed often seem like the smallest anthill in the face of our physical desires and drives when we're in the arms of our girlfriend or sitting in front of the computer trembling to click on that next link. And you know which link I mean.

Desire is the seemingly unmanageable element when it comes to our bodies and our sensuality (not to mention our sexuality). It's easy enough to be overwhelmed by desire at any given moment, and it is a powerfully addictive force.

But the fact is, it's a force. Something that impels or compels us—like hunger or thirst, which are instinctual desires often called appetites— isn't in itself inherently evil or inherently good. The motor in the car can be said to be powerful, broken or revved, but it can't rightly be said to be either good or bad. Just like our wills, our desires are forces that move us, but they are not the ultimate arbiters of how we act or how close we are to God.

Even though the modern church is somewhat afraid of desire and what it means to awaken desire (sexual, sensual or otherwise), awakened desire, true longing, is what motivates us in any given direction and, paired with our wills, causes us to act. As Simone Weil says, "The danger is not lest the soul should doubt whether there is any bread, but lest, by a lie, it should persuade itself that it is not hungry."[3]

We can and often do pretend that we don't have desires, but suppressing those desires, lying to ourselves, only results in those passions appearing elsewhere. Whether it's road rage, yelling at your spouse or compulsive hand washing, what we suppress in terms of our desires cries out for our attention in other ways. This is true whether we're talking about a desire for recognition or a desire for intimacy. Desires that aren't acknowledged control us far more regularly than acknowledged desires do.

This is where fear often rears its ugly head.

We'd much prefer the safety of repressed desires to the risk of living alive to longings and understanding that not all longings are meant to be fulfilled. Indeed, in our microwave, consumer-oriented society, it's difficult to wait for anything, let alone to long for something that might not be fulfilled. What's the point of *that*?

"Two things contribute to our sanctification: pains and pleasures," says Blaise Pascal. In our journeys, "the difficulties [we] meet with are not without pleasure, and cannot be overcome without pleasure."[4] Living alive to desire means allowing the possibility of pleasure (as well as pain), and understanding that pleasure is neither reprehensible nor our main goal. It isn't wrong to feel desire, whether for your spouse or for a life of deep meaning.

At the same time, there *are* some desires that society would call wrong (sexual desire for animals being one example) and classical writers and the saints would call disordered. What St. Ignatius illustrated through his understanding of consolation and desolation, and what he later provided for the church writ large in his *Spiritual Exercises*,[5] is a method of self-awareness, a way to know whether our desires are ordered or disordered, attached to things that take us away from God or free from the competing pulls of the world. Consolation and desolation are tools that can help us understand the direction that these interior forces orient us toward, whether the desire for food or the desire for touch.

When Bryan and I were dating, together we had to consciously decide that our physical desires for each other were something that could be rightly or wrongly ordered, either pointing us toward each other or pointing us away as we sought to build our relationship. That meant not running away from the feelings, the physical sensations that we roused in each other when we kissed, touched or even just held hands. It meant welcoming them into the dialogue and refusing to be ashamed of them when they arose. It meant consciously asking questions like: Is this building unity and respect and moving us toward God? Are we oriented in the right direction? And, importantly, are we treating each other in this moment like a person or like a method of getting our physical desires fulfilled?

Checking Out

Every now and again, Bryan will call me while I'm in the middle of a writing project or responding to a particularly urgent email. Most of the time, I pick up the phone but continue what I'm doing. In less than thirty seconds, he's well aware that I'm not fully present to him, despite the fact that I haven't said anything to him about what's distracting me—or whether or not *he* is. Most people would call that multitasking, the hallmark of the modern age. But neuroscientists, as well as my disgruntled husband, tell us that our brains simply aren't able to multitask. We can't pay attention to two things at one time, no matter how hard we try. Mostly this results in scary commercials insisting that we stop texting or talking on our cell phones when we drive. But there's something else that our single-tasking brains are telling us.

In order to survive, whether in traffic or in romantic relationships, we need to be fully present to whatever we're doing. When we're not attentive to what's in front of us—the email or the oncoming truck—we lose our ability to interact with the world as it is and begin to act on a hybrid of instinct and habit. Most of us, though, live split, and I'm no exception. When we divide our attention between multiple activities at once, we fail to be fully engaged and present to any one of them. We are, in essence, checking out of our lives.

Now, there are many reasons why we do this, as psychologists and marketing managers can tell us. And we've been doing this—narrowing our worlds down—for most of human history. Sometimes it's just that we're so overloaded with stimuli that we don't know *how* to make the decision to be present to one thing over another. We're so interconnected that we're not actually making any connections worth the word *connection* at all. Sometimes we're so driven by the expectations of others and ourselves that we spread our attention and energy over many more things than we can cover. As Bilbo Baggins said, we "feel thin, like butter spread over too much bread."

While those reasons are nefarious enough, sometimes we disengage because we're simply afraid to be seen and known. We purposefully hide from others, and from ourselves, because being present risks being seen for who we really are, rather than the persona that we present on a regular basis. We only half-listen to a conversation with a friend because we're nervous that her pain is going to make us wrestle publicly with our own woundings. We play the "dutiful spouse" because we suspect that if we were to really express what's going on with us we'd be exposed as inadequate or, worse, weak. And we check out from our desires because we're afraid of what they may lead us toward, afraid of what might come if we open the door to that Pandora's box.

God asks us to risk that, though. He doesn't implore us to give him our deadened hearts, our repressed desires. He asks us to present our bodies to him as *living* sacrifices—fully alive, fully present (Romans 12:1). David Benner, a spiritual director with a doctorate in clinical psychology, puts it this way: "Until we can be at home in our bodies, we can never truly be at home anywhere. Until we can return to being grounded in our self as a biological organism, we will be forever vulnerable to looking for substitute anchors for our being."[6]

We have those anchors everywhere—whether it's the "good girl" persona or a political party affiliation, a belief that our impulses are impossible to control, or an inability to connect with our desires as mechanisms for pointing us to God. We hold on to multiple ego identities other than Christ when we are unable to ground ourselves in our bodies, the core reality of our selves, and it is those identities, those selves, that Jesus calls us to die to in order to find true life and wholeness.

It's time for us to put away our fears of our desires, or at least to step out in trusting God, and come home to ourselves.

Touch Point

Neither Compass nor Map

One of the great questions of spiritual direction is *What do I want?* This question is central to our lives of faith not because wanting world peace is somehow holier than wanting some financial security in your life, but because the true answer to that question for each of us is revealed progressively, layer by layer. We've put up so many levels of defense against our true desires that, more often than not, we cannot consciously answer the question of what we really want the first time around.

We've been given great tools in the spiritual life: Scripture as map and pattern of what life in the kingdom of God can be, the life of Christ and the companionship of the Holy Spirit as a compass directing toward the fulfillment of all that we have been created in God to be. Yet, as anyone who has been lost in unfamiliar territory can tell you, a compass and a map can't help you unless you know where you are.

This is where our embodied desires are so helpful—if we take the time to listen to them rather than respond to well-worn and often unhelpful patterns of impulse. And listening does take both time and attention. Like noticing carefully your surroundings, listening to our desires can tell us a great deal about where we are in our journey with God, which in turn helps us know what direction to turn as we follow the map, with the compass as our guide.

Your challenge over the next twenty-four to forty-eight hours is this: make note of all of your desires. This will require a prolonged and prayerful act of attention (twenty-four hours may be difficult; if you're easily distracted, forty-eight hours might give you a better scope of field). Every time you want something strongly, take note of it. That doesn't mean you immediately fulfill that desire, but that you pay attention to its presence and direction.

Don't try to whip yourself up into some state of unreasonable piety in this exercise: if you want an extra slice of cake, write it down. If you notice yourself wanting to admire your neighbor's [insert part of anatomy here], note that too. This is neither a list of acts of holiness nor of sin—it's simply an observation of where your desires have been touched in the course of a day or two. Write things down even if they seem small to you: *I wanted to lay on the floor rather than fold the laundry* or *I wanted to go for a walk in the park even though there wasn't time* or (an interesting and unusual desire I've been feeling recently) *I wanted to do a headstand, even though I'm not good at it*, for example.

After you've compiled your list, find some time to quiet yourself before God in prayer with it. Ask the Spirit of God to reveal himself to you through your desires, and to reveal to you the deeper messages of your own embodied longings.

As you center yourself in the presence of Christ, scan the list before you. Spend some time noticing anything in particular in the list in front of you. Does anything stand out, as if highlighted? Is there a desire God seems to want to speak to you about? Attend to his voice there. If there's nothing specific that stands out, take some time to review where your desires were pointing you, what their messages are. Was another slice of cake a true desire of your heart? If not, what was it masking or pointing toward—loneliness, anger, some other emotion that you are wanting to stuff or silence? Was the desire to admire your neighbor's body one that found its root in fulfilling your own pleasures or sense of loneliness or, on the other hand, was it more about admiring and taking in the beauty of another person without having to consume or use that beauty?

Reflect prayerfully on each of your desires and what they spoke about where you were in each part of your day. Listen openly to the creative ways the Spirit might be speaking to you about desire and what it shows you about where you are.

Conclude this time of reflection by thanking God for your desires and asking him to accompany you more deeply in them in the days and months ahead. Consider sharing your list and findings with a spiritual friend or small group, others who are along the journey with you.

Tension Taming

Embracing Our Fears, Finding Redemption

*For me it is the virgin birth, the Incarnation, the resurrection which
are the true laws of the flesh and the physical. Death, decay,
destruction are the suspension of these laws. I am always
astonished at the emphasis the Church puts on the body.
It is not the soul she says will rise but
the body, glorified.*

FLANNERY O'CONNOR, LETTER, SEPTEMBER 6, 1955

THE LAST REMAINING PARENT OF MY PARENTS, my maternal grandmother, passed away recently. Moyra was the pivot point of our family. The
mother of five children, each of whom she birthed in a different country,
she was a woman of grace and law, faith and fear, consistency and contradiction. As the family matriarch, she connected us all, drawing us together
in a way that transmitted not only her love but our love to one another.

Granny's funeral had to it a rhythm that reflected the stuttering syn-
copation of our new life without her. The morning began with a short
family service at the funeral home, a time for us each to say our personal

goodbyes. A woman of humble means and heart, Moyra had insisted on nothing more than a pine box for a coffin. As each family member, some individually and others in tight knots of collected grief, approached the open casket they seemed to wilt, visibly shrinking at the sight of her body.

I remember running my hand lightly over the unfinished wood as I stepped up to what remained of my grandmother. My fingers registered *coffin*, but my heart registered *ark*. I was struck by the strange similarity of the vessel that carried Noah through destruction to new life and this strange, rectangular container that carried my grandmother's body. I stepped a half step closer, ready to say a final goodbye, and gently touched the hands that had been folded genteelly over her chest, as if she was simply in repose.

If you've ever touched a corpse, and in our modern society many of us have not, you know it's not a physical sensation that translates as natural in any way. A body that's no longer producing any neurological activity—there's simply no fire in the nerves—feels wrong. There's no other way to say it.

I knew my grandmother's body would feel this way when I reached out. I was not expecting her skin to still be the same crepe-paper soft I felt the last time I'd held her trembling hands in mine. I wasn't looking hopefully for breath or movement, I wasn't asking for her to return to us. Instead, my body was seeking confirmation of what my mind and heart already knew—she was gone.

Touching the remains of one that you love is one of the most intimate and honoring rituals of grief. As I lay my hands over my grandmother's hands, my body honored hers while at the same time registering the presence of death. Her flesh no longer had any spark, no messages to be sent from skin to skin, no connection to be made anymore. I withdrew almost a little too abruptly, chilled.

The rest of the day passed quickly and slowly. The pastor said a few words, the casket was closed, tears were shed. We reluctantly returned to my aunt's house to wait out the day—Granny's remains were to be cremated and laid to rest beside those of her husband, who preceded her in death by nearly fifteen years. Awkwardly, the family chatted and waited, ate and reflected. There were no plans, and the hours passed slowly. The fires of cremation licked at us even as it consumed her, and we tried not to think about what was happening as we ate lunch on the patio or napped on the couch.

When my aunt and uncle returned from retrieving her ashes, the burial box radiated warmth. Before we began the rag-tag and solemn procession to the cemetery, I held the velour-covered urn box between my splayed palms. The heat from the fire that had reduced my vibrant grandmother to ash felt somehow more comforting than the cool unresponsiveness of her body earlier in the day. However awkward it was to be feeling the lingering heat of the crematorium, here was energy, something that transferred itself to me like the pulse of a neuron.

Although it may seem unpleasant, I'm so glad that I didn't pass up that last chance to be in physical contact with the remains of my grandmother, and I'm equally glad the day's schedule didn't allow any time for the ashes of her remains to cool to dormancy. I could have allowed the fear of the physical to stop me, I could have stepped away from that which jarred me into being fully present in my body to what remained of hers—the body from which I came.

Instead, I felt the fear and stepped forward, embraced the tension and discomfort, and received a gift I didn't know was being offered. That last warmth will linger with me not out of morbid fascination with the mechanics of cremation but because that heat was transferred to me by the atoms and electrons that comprised my grandmother. The energy that matter held was not hers—it was the transfer of kinetic energy—but for a moment what was left of her was animated by fire.

I've heard it said the only body completely without tension is a dead body, and having encountered more than one corpse, I'd have to agree. The tragedy of our relationship with our bodies, however, is that we're constantly trying to eliminate the tensions we feel around them, instead of stepping onto the fertile ground of our fears. Yes, we may falter or fail, we may fall into sin or choose the wrong path, but in so doing we will be embracing the tension of truly living, awake and aware of all that swirls within and without us. It's in this state, connected rather than cut off, that we can feel the power of a fire much greater than that which consumes the flesh—the fire of God.

Feet on the Ground

In childhood, my friend Jennifer was a free spirit, a wisp. Whip-smart and prone to adventure, she flummoxed her parents regularly with her make-believe worlds and tendency to burst suddenly into song. She loved deeply—everything and everyone—and her pixie-bright eyes sparkled with delight every time she was invited onto a stage to perform (whether that stage was a field of stubbly grass or a tabletop didn't matter). A younger sibling, she was both the baby and a daughter determined to have her share of the attention. She wanted to *live* life, to taste, to feel, to touch and hear it, as much as possible. Unsurprisingly, Jen's middle name is Joy.

As an adult, Jen hasn't lost any of that precociousness, although she'll pretend like she has. She's still whip-smart and prone to adventure, still most at home on a stage, still a lover of life. If you watch, her pixie-bright eyes will sparkle when she's invited to share herself with you (although you'll have to watch carefully, because she's learned to hood those eyes quickly enough that you'll miss that beautiful flash of light).

Jen suffers the way that a lot of us do though. She suffers from a kind of self-hatred whose roots originate not in her own story, although they've reached out and dug deep there, or even in her parents' story, although the taproot coils through that soil, but in the story that we all share, the story of the church stumbling its way back to God, the story of humanity picking the wrong tree, picking our own way over God's way.

"Can I go outside?"

The bob of brown hair appeared beside her mother's elbow at the sink.

She looked down.

"Can I go outside, *puhleeze?*" the voice repeated, obediently.

"Yes, but keep your shoes on. I don't want you to get hurt."

The slight shoulders fell and she sucked her bottom lip into her mouth, chewing on it with her upper teeth.

"Ohhhhhhkay," she drawled, quietly calculating the consequences of disobedience.

And then she disappeared into the world outside her door.

It seems like a simple interaction, doesn't it? Something minor, a child asking for adventure while her mother does the dishes. Nothing that appears inappropriate or wounding, nothing that would catch a sensible parent off-guard.

And yet in it there is something of the fall, something of not really understanding, something of not being seen, heard or understood. There's something of fear laced through the edict to keep your shoes on, and that fear is something that laces through not only Jen's heart but the heart of her mother, and the hearts of all mothers before her. There's something that says, *Protect yourself from the world, fear it, because it is dangerous and will hurt you.*

This is what Jen would do though. After tumbling out her front door into the wild of what was to come, she would approach the field she was about to play in with awe and delight. And instead of obeying, of being the good girl who does what she's told, she would take off her shoes, carefully tucking her little socks safely within them.

And she would play and play and play and play. Her toes curled into the earth, her heels striking real ground. With her shoes off, she knew where she was—right where she was meant to be. With her shoes off, she was home. With her shoes off, she stood on solid ground, encountering the reality around her with her whole self, the fullness of her desire and who she was. As David Whyte says, "A good definition of innocence is an ability to be found by the world. Innocence is not a state that is meant to be replaced by experience. Innocence is a kind of faculty, a way of paying attention, whereby the revelations of the world are allowed to be heard in their own voice, and you are allowed to be transformed by them."[1]

Of course, that same earth that welcomed her so readily would also give her away. Even as her small fingers wiped off everything she could from her soles and her toes, dirt found its way into crease and crevasse. No matter how clean she thought her feet were, she would have to hide her sand-filled socks when she took them off at night.

Take Off Your Shoes

In Exodus 3, Moses leads his flock around the back of Mount Horeb, the mountain of God. Later in the story, Horeb will be renamed as Sinai, the place where God gives the Ten Commandments to his people, telling them who they are as a people of God. For now, though, we aren't told by what or whom Moses is being impelled. It isn't normal for him to head all the way across the wilderness and wildness with his flock—it would be safer at home.

But off he goes, and what follows is an encounter with an angel of God and a burning bush that is not consumed. Both are incredible windows into what it means to pay attention, to be present to the world around us. That Moses spent enough time looking at a bush on fire to notice it was not consumed is as much a miracle as the bush not being burnt up. As a man with a flock of sheep on the top of a mountain, his attention would had to have been somewhat divided (there are cliffs, after all, at the top). But he looked, and what he saw made him stop long enough to ask what was really going on here.

It's at that point that God calls Moses' name, not once but twice. And Moses says one of the most dangerous and beautiful things in response in all of Scripture, something that Isaiah later says in the presence of the Lord and Christ says in Gethsemane: "Here I am."

This isn't just a statement of fact, as if God didn't know where Moses was and might be wondering if he'd called the wrong name. There are a few things going on here (as is the case with all of Scripture).

First, Moses has heard the God of the universe call his name. If you've never had this experience (and most of us haven't), imagine with me the idea of being called by name by the person who loves you most and knows you best in the world. The person who knows all of your faults and struggles, the whole of your story from beginning until this moment, who knows your joys and your dreams and the wild hopes that you only dare whisper in the dark to someone who knows you utterly. Imagine that person, who is the safest person in whose mouth your name could rest, saying your name in a way that carries with it all of the love, grace and profound acceptance you could ever hope to enjoy. Imagine them saying your name in a way that causes you to know, without doubt or confusion, that you are deeply loved for who you are right in this moment, that you couldn't be more perfect or more cared for, that you are loved for everything that you are and everything that you are not. Imagine hearing your name *that* way.

Then imagine hearing it a *second* time, a time that builds on the first time. In that second hearing imagine the first time you heard your name being amplified. Because you have already heard, already know with every fiber of your being that you are loved beyond every measure you could come up with, that every way of gathering love into one place has been expressed in the way your name was said the first time. When you hear your name a second time, what you hear in the calling of your name is a calling forth of everything that you know that you are but want to become, a calling forth of your purpose, of what you have been uniquely crafted to be and do, an answer to every *why* you've ever asked when it comes to your purpose and presence on this planet. Imagine hearing yourself named in such a way that you resonate so deeply your soul thrums with it—a sense of a note being chimed that is the very note that your soul is meant to sound when struck with the things of this life, with your very purpose. This naming is powerful—it's the naming of Genesis, and it's God calling Moses back to the Garden.

That is just a taste of what it might be like to hear your name called by God, not once but twice. And that taste points to Moses' response to that calling—a calling of both what is and what is to be. He was named by God (yet again), a naming that was so much more than repetition for emphasis.

"Here I am" is what comes tumbling forth from Moses' lips. *Here. I. Am.*

In that context, it makes perfect sense that Moses would in essence say, *Yes! Yes! That is me, what you have called me is true! Yes! That is who I am, and who I am is fully present here to you right now.*

"A thing resounds when it rings true, ringing all the bells inside of you," sings Andrew Peterson in his song "More." I could imagine that is what Moses felt as he heard God call his name—that resounding within him that rang every bell, until he felt himself to be something he'd never experienced: a cathedral of truth.

To respond with the words "Here I am" was to respond the only way possible: a falling forward with the agreement that was ricocheting within him. It was a tumbling forth to service and worship and a willingness to be used completely by the One who had just named him and known him completely. I suspect if he could have launched himself into the fire of God at that moment, he would have.

And so, God responds with a gentle hand, "Do not come any closer."

Without this understanding of what has come before, the command to stay away feels a little like a rebuff. It's like your lover asking you to stand on the other side of the room, or asking your child not to tackle hug you when they come home from school. *Don't get close to me, it's dangerous,* is what we sometimes read into the text. Or, worse, *you're not worthy, stay over there.* That is intimacy cut off, intimacy aborted. And yet that is the opposite of what God is saying to his child. The text reads us as we read it. How we read the text tells us where we are.

Instead, what God is saying is, *Don't throw yourself so fully into me that you are annihilated, Moses. Don't come closer, because you are where you are meant to be. Don't come any closer, because to throw the fullness of who you are into who I am is only the very beginning of what you are meant to be and do in this world.*

And so, God pulls Moses, and therefore us, back into the physical reality around him by asking him to do something that has become familiar idiom to most Christians, familiar to the point that we don't see how strange, how radical, how deeply physical the act is.

Take off your shoes.

Wait, what? Take off my shoes?

Imagine the one who loves you most returning from a long trip. Appearing before you not only with love and knowledge of who you are and who you are meant to be but also with gifts to show you how much they've been thinking of you, how much they've missed you and known you and want you to be all that they know you deeply to be. You are about to launch yourself into their arms, to fall into them and your desire to be with them. That person is smiling and laughing and delighted and says this one phrase: take off your shoes.

Wouldn't you be pulled up short? Wouldn't you be suddenly jerked into the reality of your physical body and an awareness of your surroundings? Wouldn't your focus be split in a way that made you rethink what was happening around you at that moment?

Precisely.

Because as much as Moses would have wanted to be fully consumed by God, he was also standing in the world, a world that needed more of God, his work and his rescue. And at the same time, Moses was standing at the entrance to the very place humanity has been searching for since the fall—he was standing at the entrance to Eden, to the place we are meant to inhabit, which is not so much a place as a state of relationship, walking and talking with the One who made us.

Poet David Whyte writes it this way:

That day I saw beneath dark clouds
the passing light over the water
and I heard the voice of the world speak out,
I knew then, as I had before
life is no passing memory of what has been
nor the remaining pages in a great book
waiting to be read.
It is the opening of eyes long closed.
It is the vision of far off things
seen for the silence they hold.
It is the heart after years
of secret conversing
speaking out loud in the clear air.
It is Moses in the desert
fallen to his knees before the lit bush.
It is the man throwing away his shoes
as if to enter heaven
and finding himself astonished,
opened at last,
fallen in love with solid ground.[2]

Taking off his shoes is a physical act, one that probably involved more than just kicking off some flip-flops. He would have had to bend down, to bow in a way, and to remember the reality of the places that his shoes had carried him. He would have had to fumble with straps and, at least momentarily, take his eyes off of the fire out of which God was speaking.

This is the gift and the duality of God's work in our physical bodies. It is because of them that we experience the great gift of encounter with God—without them, we wouldn't be human. And it is because of them that we remember that we are not yet with God completely, that there is a world around us that both stains us and needs us, a world into which we are invited as those who redeem and bless.

GHI

God also invites Moses to take off his shoes because the ground he is standing on is *kadesh*, or holy. The same word appears in Genesis when God rests on the seventh day and calls it holy. To call the place where Moses stands holy implies not only that Moses is in the presence of God but also that he is exactly where he is meant to be. He is, in essence, in the Garden.

To take off your shoes, therefore, is an act of radical trust, a belief that you are where you are meant to be, that you are safe, that you are welcome. Indeed, it means that you believe you are done traveling, a pilgrim and outcast no longer. You are home.

Keeping Them On

We've all been walking around, whether we know it or not, with our shoes on. For some of us, it's because we truly believe we're not home, and this world is a waiting place, a byway until death brings us more fully into the kingdom of God or Christ returns. For others, our shoes are simply a symbol of how we mistrust God and his heart for us, a way that we keep ourselves safe by putting a barrier between us and reality. If wars occur, if children are kidnapped, if jobs are lost and if diseases ravage those we love most deeply—what good does it do to take off our shoes and call this place safe? We could do it, but in our heart of hearts, it wouldn't be true. This place of death and pain isn't home, isn't safe, and we'd rather be ready to depart it as quickly as possible *thankyouverymuch*.

Still others of us keep our shoes on because we like our privilege, even if it's mostly secretly. We like that we can change the style of our footwear, and we have the choice to be separate, elevated, able to keep our feet clean and clear of this world. We even like that we can strategically choose when to go barefoot—while running, for example—and feel in those times like we're both somehow more enlightened and set apart. We are in solidarity with the poor, we think; we are feeling what our brothers and sisters feel.

In some ways we are. In some ways we are feeling the same earth, knowing the same connection to our humanity, to the essential reality of our common heritage and participation in life on this planet. But in other ways, we're simply choosing this place of humility as a temporary respite from our life of pride. Which makes it no respite at all.

The fact is, we have to wait for God to tell us to take off our shoes. We neither get to determine where holy ground is, nor do we necessarily simply hallow it by our physically being on that ground. Although I do believe hallowing takes place—merely because by our presence as sons and daughters of God we bring redemption to creation on a physical and spiritual level—it's not we alone who bring holiness into those spaces. As co-heirs with Christ, we bring the manifest reality of the kingdom of God in and through who we are because of the work of the Spirit, not because of our works. As a result, we don't get control over when it's time to take off our shoes.

To live barefoot is a physical act with a profound integrative and re-demptive effect—an effect that takes place only because God is there. To live barefoot, to be called at any given moment (or at every given moment) to strip ourselves of things that separate us from safety, stability and home is to live in that state of self-emptying that denotes a true union with God. To live barefoot means that you're living as you're meant to live, in the places that you're meant to live, in the ways that you're meant to live, with Christ present as your forerunner and guide. To live barefoot is to live aware of God before you, beside you and within you. I believe it's the way that we're meant to live.

Although the injunction to keep your shoes on, especially for a small child, makes practical sense, sometimes children know something more deeply than we adults, who have language and logic and implicit control, could ever hope to. That Jennifer preferred to play barefoot, to feel the world underneath her feet, wasn't just a whim or stubbornness. She em-bodied something that she didn't have words to articulate—that she, like Moses, was safe, that she was known, that she was exactly where she was meant to be.

We often get lost when we don't listen to our body's own impulses and desires—the innocence of the body itself. We find ourselves without mooring when we aren't able to listen to, for example, a craving for a particular type of food or the need to get our feet on earth. Children are more apt (before the inculcation of consumerism) to listen to their body's desires and heed them, to be present. Children, too, are more likely to think themselves immortal, unaware, somehow, of the days of death that lie ahead of them, the consequences of actions, the way the world will reach out to wound a body unaware of its limits.

Living Sacrifices

Moving into this space of embracing our bodies, of living as if they matter, of choosing to feel the anxiety of listening to our emotions, needs and desires as they come to us in physical form requires risk. It's a kind of sacrifice to step into this place, an act of trust that God may, indeed, be interested not in controlling us, but in redeeming us—all of us.

> I appeal to you therefore, brothers and sisters, by the mercies of God, to present your bodies as a living sacrifice, holy and acceptable to God, which is your spiritual worship. Do not be conformed to this world, but be transformed by the renewing of your minds, so that you may discern what is the will of God—what is good and acceptable and perfect. (Romans 12:1-2 NRSV)

Paul's impassioned plea to the church in Rome is familiar to us. You've probably heard more than one sermon on verse 2—do not be conformed to this world, renew your minds. We know how to do this; there are bookshelves full of how-tos on study, renewal, the battlefield of the mind. But there is something in Paul's words that precedes the renewing of our minds, something that we rarely talk or think about, something we tend to avoid because of the tension it creates within us. We are to be transformed first by presenting our bodies to God. The word there is *soma*—a very clear indication that this isn't just a pretty metaphor. Paul means our bodies, the actual stuff of our lives.

Paul also says that presenting our bodies as living sacrifices is our act of spiritual worship—that what we do with our bodies, how and whether we present them to God, really present them, is something that is spiritual as well as physical. In fact, the King James Version translates that phrase "reasonable service." (It says something, doesn't it, that more modern translations move as far away from the embodied act of sacrifice as possible by calling it "*spiritual* worship.") The word there is *logikos*, a Greek cognate that you could almost translate without any knowledge of the language whatsoever. *Logikos*. Logical. Reasonable. Something that we should understand as completely rational and straightforward. How have we come so far from that place?

More often than not, the answer is shame. It stretches as far back as the Garden, and shame separates us from one another, and from God. Shame keeps us from reaching out to touch Jesus' garment and be healed. Shame disintegrates us—not only emotionally but on a physical level. Our brains are actually disordered by shame, the synapses unable to make the connections necessary.[3]

But there's something more in this verse, something deeply important to that shame, something God is saying to us about our bodies. The words Paul uses for how we are to present our bodies are *zōsan thysian*, or living sacrifice. This is a whole new way of understanding not only our relationship to God but God's relationship to and activity in our bodies.

For the first time, God is saying that the sacrifice we are to give him is to be a *living* sacrifice. In the Old Testament, the sacrificial system was described in detail, from the meaning of different sacrifices to the time of year to what the priests should be wearing as the sacrifice was undertaken. But one thing was consistent about these sacrifices—whatever animal was brought needed to be killed, brought to the altar dead, or about to be. Blood was needed. In fact, in the Old Testament, sacrifices weren't something that had relationship *with* God—they were given *to* God.

So *zōsan thysian* is a new thing. A *living* sacrifice. This sacrifice is capable of making a decision to be sacrificed. In fact, because it continues to live (whatever "it" is), the decision to remain in the position of sacrifice and surrender must be a continual one.

You've felt that, haven't you? That our relationship with God is a continual decision, a living choice not made just once but over and over again? It's hard, isn't it? The need to continually give our lives over to God, to surrender our desires for control, for perfection, for achievement, for judgment, for (here's the big one) independence over and over again. This kind of giving over, of sacrifice, is so difficult, in point of fact, we *can't* do it by ourselves. We are only able to be living sacrifices in our bodies because of the work and embodiment of Christ.

But let's get back to *living*, shall we, because it's the part we most often miss, the part where we're not giving over our lives to be destroyed, cut open, consumed. We act like we're doing this, giving ourselves over to destruction. We so often squirm away as if God's going to slit us stem to stern, forgetting that his plans for us are radically different than any other sacrifice we've ever seen before. We can be forgiven our doubts and concerns, because *we haven't ever seen it before*, but God doesn't want us to die. However much this giving over feels like dying, ending your life isn't his aim. As Oswald Chambers writes, "It is of no value to God to give Him your life for death."[4]

Paul tells us to offer God our bodies as living sacrifices not because our bodies are worthless, or because we are to die to them, but because in Christ we are meant to have life abundant running in and through us. The word for "living" in this verse is a derivation of the word *zoe*—eternal or divine life, as opposed to the other Greek words for life: *bios* (physical life in general or sometimes the works of our hands) or *psuche* (life of the soul). There is a holiness, a divine aspect to the sacrifice that we offer to God in our bodies. This act of giving our bodies over to God is imbued with God himself, and he supports us, enabling us to give over the bodies we feel unruly, the life we want to control, the whole of ourselves over to him—not for destruction but for redemption and wholeness. For the coming of the kingdom of God.

Because we're so far from the days of the sacrificial system, our understanding of what it means to offer anything to God sacrificially tends to involve images of knives and burning, altars and priests. Although those are components of sacrifice in the Old Testament, the spirit behind sacrifices to God has been lost in translation.

I experienced this most graphically during my Old Testament Theology and History class in seminary. Filled with pastors and would-be pastors, my class nonetheless squirmed when told we would be required to read through *all* of the Old Testament during the course. Including, the professor underlined, Leviticus. I understand why most Christians avoid this book full of instructions on how to properly slaughter the animals to be sacrificed to God, but I was surprised at how few had ever read through it.

The professor, obviously, was not surprised, having spent his career focused on these books of the Bible, and the questions my classmates had about what they saw as the vengeful, capricious God in its pages came as no shock to him. I'll never forget the explanation he gave of what the sacrificial system was and did during that period of history with God.

To the people of the ancient Near East, be they Jew or Gentile, Greek or Roman, he explained, the spiritual world was very real. Their experience of the world around them included the power of the physical world, as well as another layer of reality in which the power of God (or gods, if they were Greek) existed like a current. The most helpful analogy for this power and its availability for modern thinkers, he explained, is electricity.

In First World countries, electricity is readily available. Wires conducting it run overhead and underground. We flip a switch when we walk into a room, and lights turn on. At the same time, we understand electricity to be dangerous to our physical bodies. Useful to light rooms and cook food, yes, but we know not to stick our fingers in electric outlets or, worse, grab live power lines. We'd be killed. Our bodies simply can't handle that type of current. Power of that magnitude fries our systems.

In the same way, the Jewish culture and those around them understood the spiritual realm to be real, powerful and available—if you had the right instruments to conduct it. To simply walk up to God (if one even could) would be to expose yourself to live electric current or to walk around holding a lightning rod in a violent thunderstorm. A pretty good way to get killed. This wasn't thought of as God's cruelty or vindictiveness any more than we would think of the wires around a major transformer being cruel or vindictive.

This makes sense of some of the more troubling passages of Scripture, like 2 Samuel 6, for example, where the priest Uzzah is killed when he touches the ark of the covenant—something he did because the oxen had stumbled and the ark was in danger of falling. A simple and reasonable enough gesture, we think. Why did he have to die for that? Those closer to the realities of the sacrificial system would have understood more clearly that well-meaning Uzzah just tried to touch live current.[5]

In bringing us back to Leviticus, the professor explained that the sacrificial system acted as a sort of current converter, the way a transformer or a fuse box allows the strength of the electricity in the power towers to be converted into a current useable for our home appliances. The sacrifices made it temporarily safe for the people to approach God, in holiness and purity, and receive spiritual life, support and power.

Another way to look at it is to describe the sacrifices as a type of "adapter" between the spiritual world and the physical world. If you've ever traveled internationally, you know that different countries work on different systems of voltage for their electricity. The United States operates on 120 volts, Japan 100, Afghanistan 240, the United Kingdom 220. This difference in voltage means you can't just plug your devices (whether a laptop or an electric razor) into any outlet you see. Devices made for one level of current won't operate properly, or will overload and ruin the machine, on a different level.

Most travelers solve this with a current converter, an adapter meant to change one type of current to another, either concentrating or reducing the flow of energy so the device is able to function and get power from what would otherwise destroy it. In the Old Testament, the sacrificial system was the adapter that kept our devices (our very bodies) safe.

Without going too far into Christology, this too is why the sacrifice of Jesus makes so much sense, both to an ancient Near Eastern understanding of the spiritual realm and to us. The sacrifice of Christ wasn't just a one-time deal, something to plug into God so we could have temporary access to him. In Christ's death and resurrection, he became what we are so that we could become what he is—universal adapters. He made the power of God accessible to us by changing humanity forever in Christ. Jesus was the first among many who make it possible to have access to God without repeated sacrifice being necessary. Jesus is our universal converter, and he also gives us the power to be that conduit of God's power and life to the world.

In writing about rituals of cooking and eating, of mindfulness around food, Jewish author Jay Michaelson writes, "The Talmudic sages teach that the dinner table is like the altar in the Temple, and the meal we eat like the offerings that brought us close to God. (The Hebrew word for such offerings, *korbanot*, comes from the same root as *l'karev*, to be brought close. Rather than 'sacrifices,' a better translation might be 'joiners' or even 'unifiers.')"[6] This makes sense with the idea of the spiritual world as something that we're meant to be joined to, God's power at work in and through us.

When Paul says we are to give our bodies as living sacrifices to God, he's talking about this kind of joining ourselves with the work of Jesus. We are to be the ones who bring the living power of God to the world by being joined to him in the sacrifice of Christ. We are meant to make the incredible, inexpressible power of the Almighty One, the power that would otherwise destroy, manifest to the ones that he loves by giving over our very bodies to God.

Which is why embracing our bodies and living in their tensions matters so very much. When we are continually giving over our bodies to God, not just in our heads but in our prayers and our actions, we are able to be conduits of the power of heaven on earth. Where we walk becomes hallowed ground, those we touch have the possibility of being touched by the very life of God.

It is the power of Christ that allows us to make this sacrifice—and sacrifice it is, when we so desperately want to be in the ones in charge—and the power of Christ that charges this sacrifice with his power and love. So much of that sacrifice is made possible by our choices to live aware of the fears and uncertainties we experience when it comes to our bodies. The more we live in the fertile space of desire, attention and risk, the better able we are to give all of ourselves to God rather than just the "pretty," "acceptable" or "pure" parts.

Touch Point

Walking It Out

Go for a short walk without shoes on. If it's cold outside, you can walk around your home, but be sure to do it without anything between your feet and the floor.

Be attentive to what's different without shoes and socks on. As you shed the barrier between you and the world around you, how do you feel? Vulnerable? Grounded? Connected? Aware?

If you're able to get outside, how do you find yourself walking? Are you tentative, walking on tiptoe, or able to stride out, your heels hitting the ground squarely? Try to walk in a way that uses your whole foot, rolling from heel to ball with every step.

You're likely to step on something uncomfortable along the way. How does this make you feel? Does it seem wrong? Upsetting? Does it make you doubt the wisdom of walking around barefoot? Notice what happens when your journey isn't as pain-free or smooth as you might want it to be. Where do you go internally? What questions rise up in you?

Is there anything that you feel is holding you back as you walk around the world with bare feet? Are there things that make you feel more or less connected to God and the world around you?

Consider making barefoot walking a regular part of your prayer practice. The idea isn't to suddenly lose the tension or vulnerability you feel walking in the world in such an intimate way, but rather to acknowledge the work of Christ in and through that very vulnerability. Is there a part of your life that needs to be offered to God with that kind of trust, or something that you desire to see be made holy? You might prayer walk around that place or space barefoot, as a way of saying to God and yourself that this is holy ground, hallowed by the steps of one who bears Christ into the world.

10

At Home in Your Skin

Exploring God's Messages in Your Body

Your body needs to be held and to hold, to be touched and to touch. None of these needs is to be despised, denied, or repressed. But you have to keep searching for your body's deeper need, the need for genuine love. Every time you are able to go beyond the body's superficial desires for love, you are bringing your body home and moving toward integration and unity.

HENRI NOUWEN, *THE INNER VOICE OF LOVE*

THIS WEEKEND I HAD A THERAPEUTIC MASSAGE. I'd never met the therapist before, and she asked me very little about my life outside of what it was that brought me in for treatment. Deadlines and illness had twisted my body tight, and I needed some help unwinding the knots I'd tied into myself.

Deep tissue work is unlike massage for relaxation in that it digs into the substructures of the muscles to break up adhesions—bands of rigid, painful tissue that are often the source of a sore back, neck or shoulder. The movement is slow, precise and focused on small but important change in the connections of your body.

"Do you sit at your desk straight on?"

The question from the masseuse interrupted my slow breathing. I'd forgotten that I'd told her I did a lot of sitting for work.

"Yes, mostly," I mumbled toward the floor. "Why?"

"Do you turn at all? Perhaps toward the right?"

This surprised me. As I sit with people in spiritual direction, my chair is positioned such that in order to face my directee I have to turn gently toward them on the couch. A couch positioned to my right.

I shared this with her and I felt rather than saw her nod.

"The small muscles along your spine are tighter on the right than the left. It tells me that you're not sitting balanced. You might want to think about changing that."

It's amazing what our bodies tell other people without us having to say a word. Psychologists say that more than half of regular communication is nonverbal, and much of what we read from others is based on things like body posture, tone and proximity. The massage therapist was trained to notice the subtle shifts in my muscle structure and movement, shifts that told her more about my life than I could have imagined.

Why, then, would we imagine that our bodies would communicate anything less to us? If others can read our emotional states by the way that we smell (pheromones), what would it be like if we actually tuned in to the things going on in our own bodies, the ways that our very flesh and bone are speaking to us—and the ways that God is speaking, inviting and redeeming through those messages too?

Finding Breath

Mark has been under a lot of stress recently. As if being the father of four delightful and active children isn't enough, he and his family have experienced a lot of alienation and betrayal. Top that off with his desire to start his own business in order to get out of a difficult situation, and it wasn't surprising that Mark's stomach was constantly in knots.

It's amazing how our bodies respond to our psychological states, isn't it? Headaches, stomach aches, ulcers. It's even possible to have a heart issue because of the stress that we experience in our daily lives—there's even a name for it: broken heart syndrome. Our bodies are incredible conductors of messages, both emotional and physical.

It works the other way around, too, as I'm sure you're aware. When we're feeling pain or some kind of bodily unrest, our emotions, our mental state, even our spiritual lives can be deeply affected. Psychosomatic illnesses—unexplained nausea, pain or fatigue—are no less real body states simply because we've created them with our minds. As David Benner writes,

> Emotions present us with a crucial connection between mind and body. They are the brain's representations of body states. Just as objects in the external world cause patterns of activation of sensory receptive cells that we experience as sensory perceptions, so too do activation patterns in the internal world result in body states that we experience as emotions.[1]

It shouldn't come as a surprise, then, that God uses this superconductor of information to speak to us about ourselves, about him and even about others.

Mark has been aware for some time that he carries his stress in his gut, the emotion and tension forming knots deep in his abdomen where no one's fingers can reach to untangle them. Our bodies tell us a lot about what's going on with us mentally and emotionally, whether it's stress headaches or stomach aches, easy tears when we're overtired or an urge to eat when we're feeling empty inside.

What *was* a surprise to Mark was the idea of seeing this ache in his gut as an invitation from God, a gentle (or not-so-gentle) tapping of the Spirit through his physical senses that signaled something was going on that needed his attention and prayer. It wasn't until Mark keyed in on the concept of breath and breathing that he began to understand that more was happening than just his reaction to stress.

In the ancient Hebrew texts, the name of God was too sacred to be written out in its entirety. The holiness of God was something to be preserved, so scholars and rabbis acknowledged the human inability to encompass or understand the fullness of God by writing God's name only sparingly. When God's name appears in the biblical text or in our own writings about God, it's time to sit up and take notice. Something important is going on. Pay attention.

This makes the story of the burning bush in Exodus—a story that we began to explore in chapter eight—all the more interesting and important. In the Old Testament, when Moses asks the voice in the burning bush for a name, something he can say to the Israelite slaves when they ask Moses who sent him, God replies directly. Tell them I am Yhwh, he says.

The words are *ehyeh asher ehyeh*, which most directly translates as "I will be what I will be." Most English translations render God's first-given name in this instance as I AM. We have a phrase (I am) in the English, but in the original language, God's name isn't a noun (like Sally or Violet or Tara) but a verb (like *run* or *dream* or *redeem*). This has far-reaching implications for what it means to be made in the image of God-as-verb, but he doesn't stop there. God isn't content with revealing himself in verb form (as if that isn't stretching enough). He follows up that mind-bending announcement with a second, one that feels to me a little more intimate. Tell them I am Yhwh, *yod he waw he*. In English, as in most other languages, we pronounce that name "Yahweh."

Before you read on, take a few moments and get your lips and tongue and throat around that name. Yahweh. Say it a couple of times. Say it on the in breath and on the out breath. Say it a few times loudly, louder than your normal speaking voice. Now say it quietly, in a whisper. Finally, separate the syllables a little bit, slowing yourself down to really absorb what's happening when you say God's name. Start with your in-breath—*Yah*. Next the out-breath—*Weh*. Do that a few times. *Yah-Weh. Yah-Weh.*

Are you beginning to hear it?

The name of God, said slowly and deliberately, sounds a lot like our breath. In, out. In, out. God made us to breathe him in, to pray his name with every sustaining intake and outflow of air. When we breathe, we testify to God's care and support. That's been the plan, I suspect, from the very beginning. When God forms our frame out of the dust of the earth in Genesis 2, he puts his own breath into us—the Hebrew word is *ruach*, also translated as "spirit," as in the Holy Spirit—and the very first sound we make as living beings, as the air rushes into our lungs to nourish us, body and soul, is *Yah-Weh*.

How, though, does this connect to Mark and his anxious stomach? Physiologically, most of us only use about 15 to 40 percent of our lung capacity at any given moment. We breathe shallow, quick breaths instead of the nourishing, slow, deep inhalations and blood-cleansing exhalations that keep our bodies operating on optimal levels. We're meant to take between four and six breaths a minute. Most of us are up somewhere in the vicinity of sixteen to twenty. We don't slow down and take the breath of God, perhaps even God himself, into the deepest places of ourselves. We'd prefer God to only go so deep, just to the top 40 percent of our lives. Nothing deeper.

As Mark and I spoke about this concept of breathing in God's name, his countenance lit up. *That's it*, he said. *That's what's wrong.*

Mark went on to explain that he finds himself most stressed when he is not connecting on a regular basis with God. Although in this season of his journey God isn't far removed, Mark nonetheless tends to take the responsibility for how things are going in his life squarely on his own shoulders, as if God were not fully capable, fully in charge.

Together we wondered if Mark's stomachaches weren't just a symptom of stress (although they were that) but were also an invitation from God to breathe more of him in when the pain appeared. Instead of hustling more, trying to make more of life happen the way he wanted it to, maybe Mark's tight tummy was a request to slow down and receive God's nourishment and care.

Feeling God

These are the multilayered messages of God in our bodies. The relaxing feeling of being held as the hammock beneath us sways gently in the breeze is both an indicator of God's delight in our ability to rest in him and a message of how he's holding and nurturing us even through the stringed support beneath us.

When people feel stuck in their journey with God, unable to attend to what's going on or struggling to hear the heart of the Father for them, I often lead them gently back to their bodies, their lived experiences. In slow, purposeful prayer, we let the worries and wonderings melt away. Into that place of stillness, I invite them to listen to what their bodies might be saying at this precise moment. Is there tension somewhere? At the back of the spine, wrapped around the throat or hidden behind the eyes? Are your hands unconsciously twisting together, crying out for attention? Or is there a sense of fullness in your chest, a sense of bursting in your heart?

Instead of jumping into an analysis of what these bodily sensations mean, together we first turn to Christ—the One who knows us better than we know ourselves—to reveal what might be going on in these interior spaces. In cooperation with one another, we ask him to show us what these tensions or fullness or feelings are speaking. Are they telling us about the way that we feel voiceless before the boss that degrades us, or are they a prompting from him to speak when we fear we will not be heard?

Sometimes this presence to what's going on in our bodies takes a little more time. Most of us have spent so long trying to silence or manipulate our bodies that the messages they have to give us are muted or mixed. Often, there are layers of shame to be peeled away before listening to the messages of our bodies is even possible. It's nearly impossible, for example, to listen to the quiet whispers of a stomach that is empty and craving both comfort and God when every demand for food has been met with a message that you weigh too much and you mustn't put more on your plate. It's hard to receive the comfort of God through food when bare hunger is laced with condemnation, let alone desiring a texture or taste that brings feelings of nurture or memories of being cared for by the people around you.

In the same way, it's easy to miss the messages of the body when we're used to simply meeting their demands without thought or prayer.

Recently I drove up to the mountains to lead a retreat for pastors and missionaries on the goodness, the redemptive nature, of our bodies. I'd just gotten back into the country from a trip overseas, and I was still readjusting to both the time zone and my work schedule. As I stopped by a drive-through coffee shop, my body screamed out for sugar.

It would have been easy enough to say this impulse was a result of bad habits while traveling (probably) or to remind myself that sugar isn't the best thing for my health right at this moment (it wasn't). Both of those things are patently true. However, there was a deeper message that my body was graciously trying to get through to me, one that I would rather not hear but that needed to be communicated to me: I was tired.

I know this seems overly simple, but my body was telling me that I was pushing too hard. When I shared this with my audience at the retreat they reacted with humor and disbelief. Of course I was tired, they affirmed. Yet when I suggested that they listen to the fatigue in their own bodies when they find themselves craving sugar or looking for another coffee at 3 p.m., they squirmed. It wouldn't be practical just to listen to my body, one woman protested. I wouldn't get anything *done*!

More Than Productive

Unfortunately, the imperative to *get things done* is one of the very things that cuts us off from our bodies in the first place. Without the ability to unplug from the need to produce, we live at the behest of others and at a pace that makes it impossible to pay attention to the more subtle movements of God in our lives. When we protest that listening to our bodies will prevent us from getting to our to-do list, we're actually proving that listening to our bodies is exactly what we need to do.

To this end David Benner explains,

> Our alienation from our bodies as adults is so thorough that rather
> than thinking of our self as *being* our body we have come to believe
> that we *have* a body. Often we do not like the body we happen to
> have, and so we do things—surgical and otherwise—to change it
> and make it into something closer to our ideal body self. But, rather
> than improving our relationships to our bodies, this just increases
> the distance between us and our actual somatic self. Alienation
> from our bodies lies at the core of our alienation from our deepest
> self and from the world.[2]

My friend at the retreat who complained so quickly about listening
to her body had found a substitute anchor for her being—productivity.
Instead of being integrated with her deepest self, she had attached her
purpose, her very worth, to getting things done. It was her anchor, and
letting go of it threatened who she believed herself to be.

Coming Home

But what does living without being alienated from your body look like?
What does it mean to be at home in your own skin?

Because God is infinitely creative and infinitely wise, being at home
in your body will look different for different people. For one person, it
may mean taking up a competitive sport that you've always wanted to
participate in as a way of stepping into trust of a body you never believed
would support you. For another, it may mean a loving acceptance of
knees that just don't move the way that they used to, coupled with making
space for the grief for all the activities that are no longer possible. "Our
emotions and senses offer us crucial ways of remaining in contact with
our bodies," says Benner.[3]

Being at home in your own skin doesn't mean that you think yourself
ravishingly attractive at all times or even believe that you're at the right

weight no matter your size. It doesn't mean never wanting to stuff emotions with food or knowing exactly what's going on any time you feel an unusual ache or tension. Moving away from body alienation doesn't have to mean complete acceptance of yourself—although that's a good thing, something worth pursuing—but instead means that you're willing to develop a sensitivity to and awareness of the messages of your own body.

Just as outside factors influence how our bodies feel—the smell of homemade chicken broth bubbling with sweet thyme, salty chicken and buttery, rich noodles causing our stomach to growl and our salivary glands to kick into high gear, for example—so do internal factors create body realities as well. The most obvious of these connections is the fact that we produce tears when we're sad. But emotions manifest in our bodies in a variety of ways, some of them as unique as we are. Indeed, our bodies tell us how we're feeling often more accurately and with less guile than our minds. The clench in your jaw muscles tells you you're feeling stress more accurately than the overworked mind that wants to be the best mom possible for your kids. The frisson of chill across your forearms is a pretty clear message that you're afraid, even when you seem to have no reason to fear.

Your emotions provide a critical path to maintaining connection with and grounding in your body—they are internal states which manifest themselves in physical realities. You can't feel something emotionally without feeling it in your body, just as you can't perceive something with your mind that you haven't perceived through at least one of your senses. Maintaining awareness of what we're feeling emotionally and experiencing sensually keeps us connected to our bodies, anchored in the unique physical creation that God made us to be.

My MI

Although I wouldn't by any means say that I am someone who ignores my body, I do have a tendency to push it beyond reason. It takes me much too long, I'm embarrassed to say, to notice that I'm tired or hungry or thirsty. I live in high desert, and most people around me are so dehydrated that they mistake thirst for hunger, eating when they should drink. I am no exception.

The morning it happened was like any other morning, really. I woke up, got dressed, made the bed. My husband had already gone to work, and I puttered around at home before getting in the car to head to my office downtown.

It was a Thursday, like any other Thursday, really, but it was the end of April and the warmth of spring after a long winter thrilled me on a soul level. There's something about birdsong and the thawing of the earth that births gratitude, and I was almost giddy with it as I headed into my day.

Something of this fullness needed to be shared, so I picked up the phone to call my husband. I remember the gesture because of what came later, and it felt like cruelty for the two to have happened on the same day.

I didn't get through—he was busy in a meeting or away getting coffee. So I left a message instead. "Hi, love, it's me. I'm driving to work, and I just wanted to tell you how much I love our life. I know that we don't live lavishly, and we make a lot of sacrifices, living without things, but I just am so proud of you, and the way we choose to live together. I'm so grateful that we get to journey with people the way we do, to help them find healing, to bring the love of God into their lives. I know it's hard sometimes, but I love our life, I really do. And I love you very much. Thank you for everything you do to make the way we live and love others possible."

I didn't think anything of the message until much later. Instead, I headed into the office to start my day of companioning others. I had a few appointments, ate lunch, nothing strange or unusual.

The pain started just after 4:30, as I was praying for someone. Sharp, stabbing, I tried to ignore it even though it made breathing difficult. Almost as soon as it began, it moved to my chest, and unbidden tears sprung to my eyes. Years later, I still struggle to describe the tearing pain, bereft of words big enough to hold the sensations.

This is the point at which I had a choice to soldier on—or try to—or to acknowledge my body wasn't just trying to get my attention gently, it was screaming bloody murder. I ended the appointment as gracefully as I could (difficult when the explanation you have to give is "chest pains") and placed another call to my husband. This time he picked up, and as soon as he did I began to weep with the pain.

I'm grateful that he reacted even before he knew what was going on. Maybe it was in the tone of my voice or the weeping, but whatever it was, it told him something was desperately, horribly wrong. He was halfway to his car before he even understood that I was weeping from physical hurt. He told me he would be right there.

I'm not sure why I didn't just call 911. It would have made sense, an acknowledgment that something terrible was happening in my body. I could have owned the pain. But I squirmed away from my own knowing, the core of myself, even in this place of deep need. Instead, I reached outward, making my body into a public square, a place open to debate.

I lay on the couch in my office, trying to breathe through the pain, as if this invasion were simply a set of contractions giving birth to a life that I didn't realize I'd been carrying. I had a brief but heartfelt (in more ways than one) conversation with God about my life and possible death.

Surrender in those moments has everything to do with acceptance. If you haven't gone through a moment when you looked death in the face, you might say surrender has to do with submission. But even in its darkest, most rapacious moments, death is not a conquering force whose power overwhelms. I suppose that's why Dylan Thomas counsels us so adamantly to rage against the dying of the light—one does not rage against that which will always have the last crushing word.

I remember very clearly having a conversation with Jesus as I lay on the green couch my clients usually occupy, my elbows going numb. I hesitate to write about it, both because it was a private moment between me and my God and because those moments lay bare the deepest parts of ourselves. It would add some dramatic irony, no doubt, to say that I did rage against death, that I fought it with passion and vigor, pleading with God to save me. But that just isn't true. The conversation was quiet. Simple. Brief. It went something like this: *Jesus, if you are going to take me now, okay. I'm okay with that. But I would really like to live. I would like to stay here. But it really is up to you.*

The irony of that conversation is that it happened concurrent to a conversation with myself that went something like this: *You're fine. Stop being a baby. Stop crying. You're making a big deal out of nothing. You're causing all sorts of trouble. Just handle this, and stop whining. You're fine. You're fine. You're* fine.

Strange how the deepest parts of me knew enough to have a conversation with God about death while my mind was intent on ripping my soul to shreds. Strange how my raging against the dying of the light wasn't so much a surrender to death as an acceptance of God.

Strange how even the loudest cries of our bodies can be so quickly engulfed in shame and self-condemnation, even when embodiment is something we value deeply.

When Bryan arrived, I was still doubting myself, wondering if I was being too sensitive, too self-focused. He wisely took the decision from my hands and drove me to the nearest emergency room, where I was whisked immediately into triage, connected to IVs and a portable EKG. Doctors and nurses asked me rapid-fire questions, which I tried to answer through the pain. My blood pressure was 220/190, but I fit no one's profile of a woman in cardiac distress. The physician on rotation assured me I'd be home by midnight but later returned to my gurney to sheepishly inform me that he'd been wrong, that something serious had happened though they weren't sure what.

I know now that I was having a heart attack. At thirty-three, healthy, fit and without any congenital history, an artery to my cardiac muscle was being blocked, leading to what doctors clinically refer to as tissue death. Starved, my heart was dying.

In God's economy, death will lead to resurrection. Three years on, I'm more aware of my body, more cognizant of little shifts in my heartbeat or blood pressure, more alert to each change in my physical state than I ever was before the heart attack. My senses, my awareness were resurrected that frightening afternoon and in the days and tests that followed. Until the final resurrection I'll always carry around a small part of my heart that simply won't revive, dead muscle that won't live until Jesus calls it forth like Lazarus from the grave.

You don't have to walk through that kind of dramatic event to experience a resurrection in your relationship with your body. In fact, I hope you've already begun to feel stirrings of new life in places that have felt dead, buried under guilt or shame, trapped behind a gravestone of fear. We may need to unwrap some grave clothes in order to give you a full experience of this resurrected life, but Jesus is calling for that life to come forth.

Slowing Things Down

What does this listening, this attentiveness, actually come down to practically? Beyond being aware that I'm overtired or stressed, what would God's messages in my body really feel like? How can I tell if it's God speaking through my aching muscles or just the fact that I'm getting older and can't do what I used to on a daily basis?

It starts with a willingness not to dismiss automatically any sensation or action as "just" physical. As God's redeemed creation, we are living in several dimensions at once, not the least of these being the kingdom of God here and now. Believing that what you feel in your body matters is a first step in being able to listen attentively to what it's saying, and what God might be whispering through it.

Touch Point

Full-Body Prayer

One way to begin is to sit quietly in a place that you'll be uninterrupted for at least ten minutes. Start by acknowledging God's presence and provision in prayer, and thank him for the gift of your body. Close your eyes and breathe deeply, noticing your breath going in and coming out. Don't try to stop all your thoughts (although it will be fairly obvious the first time you try this that it's difficult to quiet them down); just let them pass by you without interacting with them or mulling them over.

Once you feel like you're in a quiet, centered place, begin paying attention to your feet. Flex your toes and roll your ankles. Notice any tension, pain, pleasure, any sensations in particular that come to the forefront. Don't worry if there's nothing dramatic or obvious—just keep your awareness there. After a while begin noticing your legs, then knees and then hips. What sensations are housed there? Is there anything pooled or collected in any place in your joints or muscles? Do you feel any shame or a specific awareness of these parts of your body?

Continue moving upward through your pelvic area. Keep breathing deeply, imaging the flow of air—the breath of God—moving into the places that you've turned your awareness to. Is there anything here that feels different or worth noting? Tightness? Openness? Move your attention up to your waist, then stomach and then low back, staying for a while in each of these places and noticing any sense of connection or disconnection, any numbness or life speaking in these parts of you.

Then bring your awareness to your chest and shoulders. Roll them gently if you need to—most of us hold a great deal of tension here. What do you feel as you pay attention to this part of your body? What's the predominant emotion or sensation? Before moving up to your neck, face, scalp, take some time to notice your arms, wrists and hands. Bend your elbows and rotate your wrists. Curl your hands into fists and then flex them out into open palms. Wiggle your fingers and feel the joints move. Are there any clear sensations lodged in your upper body? What feelings are being carried in the palms of your hands?

Finally, rotate your neck slowly and move your facial muscles any way that feels natural to you. Our faces both hold and express a great deal of our emotions—many of them we haven't taken the time and attention to be aware of. Is your jaw tight or clenched? Do you feel able to move it and feel openness? What about your throat? Is it relaxed and elongated, or clogged with unspoken thoughts? Notice the muscles of your cheeks and eyebrows, the feelings around your eyes. Do you feel sensations or emotions there or in the top of your head? What does this slow noticing of your body's main command center bring to your attention?

Before you come back to your surroundings, spend a few moments appreciating the grace of your body. It may not work the way that you most deeply hope, and it may not be molded the way you would like, but it is who you are. You are this flesh and blood and muscle and bone that you've been contemplating for these minutes, and the essence of who you are is embedded in every cell. Express gratitude to God, as you can, for the gift that is your embodied soul, unique in every way.

When you're ready to return to your surroundings, spend some time thinking about the sensations and emotions you noticed in various places within you. That sadness that you felt in your pelvic area, the sort of empty oddness that resided there—can you put a name to it? Does it have a color or a word associated with it? Don't try to force things, but notice if it has anything to say to you. If you feel stuck, turn to God and ask him if he has anything to reveal about this place in your body and what he might be communicating through it to you. This flesh of ours is an incredible gift, and the sensations we feel in and through it carry wisdom and grace to us. The simple fact that we are being physically renewed—we have a physiologically new body every seven years as each cell dies and is replaced with new life—speaks of God's care, kindness and attention to our bodies.

One of the things I find when I begin to pay attention to my body in this way is the places that have the most energy, ache, emotion or intention behind them tend to dissipate after I've listened to them. I've often found the tension in my shoulders begin to melt away when I slow down enough to listen to the message that I've been carrying burdens too heavy for me to bear. This attention doesn't make the struggles or cares I am holding disappear, nor does it necessarily bring resolution, but it does remind me of the reality of God's presence and protection, his desire to lift those burdens alongside of me.

I liken the effects of this type of body awareness to the way children tend to interrupt conversations in order to share something. They keep pulling and pulling on a pant leg or skirt, insistent even in the face of discouragement, until they are the object of your focus. Sometimes the message they want to convey has been forgotten in the wait, and perplexed, they simply wander away. Other times, they have a simple observation, a mud-and-grass-splattered treasure or a need for tenderness to communicate, and once those gifts have tumbled forth, they are content to melt away into the world once more.

If we've numbed or deadened ourselves to the messages of our bodies, we tend to live with these emissaries of God clinging desperately to every part of us they can hold, screaming and wailing for the attention they actually deserve. It's time to bring these wayward parts home. It's time to listen to the wisdom of our bodies.

11

Sensing His Kingdom

Encountering God's Physical Creation

Only miracle is plain; it is in the ordinary that
groans with the weight of glory.

Robert Farrar Capon, *The Supper of the Lamb:*
A Culinary Reflection

For the past four years I've been attempting square-foot gardening, growing vegetables and herbs in two small, raised garden beds in our backyard. We're in a short-season zone for growing, so attention to the plants and their needs is particularly important. One week of neglect and we may not get peas this year. Each morning before the sun gets too high I go out to my garden to water.

It's a small thing, really, this embodied experience of the cycles of sowing and reaping, planting and pulling up. But it's also a glimpse of the wonder of God in creation, a daily way of physically encountering God's kingdom.

Sensing God's goodness is something that we intuitively understand, even if we don't allow ourselves to experience it all that often. We get the fact that the natural world is God's "second book," a testament to his wonder, his beauty, his grace to us all. Stepping outside on a crisp night to look up at the stars, taking deep gulps of air that chills us from the inside out, we instinctively respond with awe. It's why the natural world draws us so regularly, and places like Iguazú Falls and the Grand Canyon become vacation destinations for us. We know that when we tumble into awe, when we experience the wonder of the physical world around us, we are being restored, body and soul.

One of the great gifts of God is the wonder and diversity of the world that is all around us. From the book in your hands to the sky above you, the physical world invites amazement. In Romans 10 Paul says that we are without excuse precisely because of the glory that shines forth from everything that God has made. It's a stunning thing to be surrounded by all of these windows into the divine, these glimpses of glory.

Spend a moment, just a moment, looking around you right now. Whether you're in a coffee shop, on a subway in a city center, sitting at home on your couch, sitting on the edge of forested trail or nursing a fussy infant with a book in your hand, lift your eyes from page or screen and notice. Take a deep breath. Close your eyes briefly and open them. What do you see? What's around you that invites wonder?

At the moment of this writing, I'm sitting in a tea house in Santa Fe, New Mexico. The particulars of the world around me right now will never exist again. The temperature of the air, the faint scent of sage on the wind, the way the steaming cup of jasmine tea beside me catches and refracts the light. No matter how mundane, this pause for reflection reminds me, as Gerard Manley Hopkins writes, that "the world is charged with the grandeur of God. / It will flame out, like shining from shook foil."[1]

But observing is only the beginning. I can sit here and admire this place, existing at a slight remove from it, or I can enter in, letting the sensations move and change me, speak something of God and his kingdom present here—but only if I let them.

I reach out to touch the green ceramic pot recently filled. I can hold my hand over the small lid for a few seconds before the heat begins to communicate pain. As I take my hand away I feel the energy now in my palm, and I flex my fingers, aware once again that I am fragile and that not every beautiful thing can be safely held, caressed, possessed.

It's your turn now. What around you has caught your attention? What in the sweep of your vision has asked you to slow down, look deeper, come closer? It may be the pattern in your wallpaper, the way the wind is bending the trees, the stubble-strewn face of the barista feverishly filling orders or the margins of this very page. Dare to step a little closer, to reach out and touch or somehow physically encounter what the world is offering to you. (I wouldn't actually recommend accosting the barista, mind you.) There's an invitation in creation here for you; reach out to receive it physically.

Just like my green teapot, the message may not be purely positive—a reminder the world is still to be fully redeemed and our role is to be both open and discerning. Or, leaning into the sensation of bark beneath your hands or the awareness of the weight and downy reality of the child in your arms, you may find yourself receiving the comfort and beauty of the present moment, reminded by God of the steady grace of things that grow, the tender embrace of the One who humbled himself to the point of being small enough to hold.

It's so easy to hide behind a window or a computer screen, watching the world instead of experiencing it, sensing it. It's tempting to keep ourselves safe from what is, quite frankly, the work of experiencing the world. But here's the rub: the less we engage with the physical world around us, the less we are present to reality. And reality is the only place we find God, who is the ultimate Real. Sure, keeping a step back feels safer, more comfortable. I won't burn my fingers, you won't risk splinters. And when we're tired, tuning out, stepping away, finding escape seems the only route that will provide what we so desperately need: refreshment.

Sadly, escape provides everything except renewal. Temporary relief, yes, but lack of presence is the drug addiction of our time. We have so many ways to numb, check out, disappear, from hours spent on social media to the literal days we spend in front of the television, from consuming beauty captured in pictures to time spent completely unaware of what's around us in bumper-to-bumper traffic, the radio spewing out the day's complement of bad news.

It's hard to remain present to the world around you when the baby screamed all night long or the worries of caring for a parent slowly descending into dementia fill your thoughts. Being present forces us into those pains, not away from them, and away from them is where we would so much rather be.

Even our unconscious choices to refuse embodied presence to ourselves and the world around us are products of repeated hits of unreality, our response to the invitations to hide behind the fig leaves of busyness and boredom.

Knitting Redemption

I met Helen at a day retreat in the Colorado mountains. A quiet woman of great faith, Helen and her husband, Dale, are deeply grateful people. They speak of God in hushed, warm tones that denote intimacy and familiarity. They've walked enough pain between the two of them to know that each day is gift, and as Helen and I spoke, she began to share, shyly, about a recent shift in her priorities.

Over a well-prepared meal, Helen told me how she'd become aware that her children and their children didn't have much in the way of family heirlooms to tie them to their history. As she herself looked out onto the autumn of her life, she saw her own lack of connection to those who came before in her family line—a legacy that she didn't want to leave to her children. Newly retired, she knew that she wanted to do something, make something, that would be a tangible thread between past, present and future.

"I've started knitting for them," she said, almost embarrassed. I know it's not much, she continued, and they probably won't care, but it matters to me that they have something.

Helen was on the cusp of a deeper trust in the physical world and the work of her hands. It's a trust that many artists have developed and must continue to cultivate in order to do the work that they do. Those who create, whether it's a knitted sweater or a sonnet or a canvas of paint and light, must first trust their materials, believe that the medium in which they express themselves will carry the weight of their intention.

I'm speaking here not of skill or talent—those are things to be nurtured by the artist herself—but of paint and pixels and paper and dance floor. Creation is an act that says, implicitly, that the physical world can bear the weight of glory, glory expressed through us and in us and with us, glory made manifest through beauty.

Whether or not Helen's knitting resulted in something glorious, whether or not it is ever seen by anyone other than her family is not the point. Helen was choosing to believe that the kingdom of God, and her love, can be woven into the warp of this world, that simple threads can be redeemed to physically bear messages of goodness and kindness.

Janet and I have only met once, at a retreat in the Colorado Rockies. I enjoyed her sweet, calm manner, the way she quietly observed those around her. Unlike Helen, Janet had been knitting for some time, and after meeting with God in the mountains she returned home with a renewed desire to let her stitch work speak something of him to the world.

Many months later, I received a package in the mail unexpectedly. Janet's careful yet whimsical printing spilled out of the parcel, followed by a skein of soft blue thread that resolved itself into a shawl.

Months before, Janet had been captured by something I shared from a spiritual formation exercise in seminary. Asked to create or bring something for our peers that iconized our experience in some way, I brought long lengths of felt. Imperfect, ragged things *meant* to resemble scarves, these pieces of fabric had cartoonish hands at each end—they were hugs made of fleece.

That small story—a hug materialized—bloomed into inspiration. Knitting projects became prayers. Those prayers breathed life and connection into yarn. And the beautiful blue creation in my hands spoke, she wrote carefully, kindly, of the love of God for me during a very dark period of my story. Instead of creating more expectation, the weight of it on my shoulders would press something more precious into my body and soul. Each stitch held within it Janet's hopes and prayers for me, each bobble a textural insistence on redemption.

That shawl, unlike almost anything I've ever received, clothed me in support made manifest. Although not flesh and blood, when I wrap it around myself I physically know myself beloved. Here it was, incontrovertible proof that time had been spent, care had been taken, and by someone who was a virtual stranger to me, someone who trusted the material world enough to let it speak for her, and for God.

Windows of Fire

Sometimes we create icons in our lives and stories—ways of remembering God in the physical world, ways of creating little windows into heaven—and sometimes God gives those icons to us.

It was a Tuesday, and I'd been aware of the forest fire burning not far from our city. It was on the news, and all of us had been advised to at least prepare for evacuation, choosing the things from our home that mattered the most to us, packing up important papers, food for the dog, the right amount of clothing. Bryan and I were lackadaisical about the whole thing, believing that we'd have enough time—hours definitely—to gather our needed items if we were to evacuate. Fires move slowly.

I was supposed to be elsewhere that afternoon, hours away at an appointment with a mentor, but I'd woken that morning with an inkling that I needed to stay home. It wasn't fear or a haunting sense that something was going to happen. It was a simple, clear, "Don't go." Often I ignore these types of impressions, thinking that I'm making it up or that I'm overdramatizing things. But this morning, this twice-blessed day, I listened and I stayed. Unsure what God was saying, I nonetheless canceled my appointment.

We'd been smelling smoke for days, wisps of it on the wind, just a sense that someone must be burning something nearby. It wasn't overwhelming, but it was there and the horizon often host to plumes of smoke, beacons of where the activity was strongest.

Around 5 p.m. the sky turned orange-black. Much too early for a late June afternoon. I'm not one to watch the news regularly, so nothing was on in our house. I'd been getting some work done, writing, editing, and it was only the rapidly descending darkness that told me something was wrong.

I padded barefoot to the end of our driveway and looked up. We live surrounded by two ridges. Behind us is Ute Valley Park, a warren of rocks and scrub oak, populated by deer, rattlers and the coyotes we occasionally hear howling over their kill on summer nights. The highest ridge of the park juts up to the east of us, shadowing our back yard, delaying sunrise each morning. To our west, roughly, begin the foothills of Pikes Peak, a series of rises and valleys that become more and more sparsely populated the higher in elevation you go.

Two days before, Bryan and I had a discussion about when urgent concern about the fire should set in. We were sitting on our front porch, and a neighbor had been packing up his car, leaving for the other side of town, despite the fact that no evacuation had been called and none was pending. It felt like the town was in hysterics, when the fire had only been burning for a few days and was hundreds upon hundreds of miles away.

Bryan rocked the porch swing gently beneath me. He pointed up to the hills to our west, hills belted by houses. "When you can see fire there," he said, "then you can be scared."

His words came back to me as I stood feeling the warm cement beneath my toes that Tuesday evening. Smoke obscured the band of houses that cinched the range of hills before me. As I watched, fingers of fire gouged their way down toward us, grasping at fuel.

There's little of our hurried evacuation I remember as clearly as that moment. The surge of adrenaline and bile, the excitement and frenzied activity that followed. We packed everything quickly, haphazardly, accidentally leaving behind things like pajamas and a few treasured pictures on our walls. We took both cars, filling them with our most valuable possessions. When we drove out of our neighborhood, flames were licking the roadside, burning the dry grass at the curb as emergency vehicles wailed past us toward the blaze.

All of that leaving, all of that scrambling and intense action, the flames by the side of the road, even the reverse 911 call we received only after we'd left our home what felt like for the last time—all of that was just an underline of what I felt at the bottom of the driveway, the cry of my heart as I tried to make sense of what was happening on my horizon.

> I lift up my eyes to the hills—
>> from where will my help come?
> My help comes from the LORD
>> who made heaven and earth. (Psalm 121:1-2 NRSV)

I will never read or hear that psalm again without being taken back to that precise moment at the bottom of my driveway, flames racing their way toward our home. In the Old Testament, the hills are the places of worship to other gods—gods who cannot save or defend their worshipers. Looking to the hills, therefore, is to the psalmist a futile act, because no help would originate there. As in any mountainous area, lifting my eyes to the hills is a regular occurrence, but I can no longer scan the horizon without being aware of the destruction that can wait just beyond its crest. While the devastation of the wildfire was not God's desire for our community, the raw, dark silhouettes of burned pines that make the backdrop of our neighborhood nonetheless speak eloquently of the dangers of looking anywhere other than to the Father for help and support.

The Eastern Orthodox say that icons are windows into heaven. Henri Nouwen calls them holy places. It is easy enough to believe them pretty things, safe inanimate items to be hung on walls and admired. They may be windows, but what they reveal and what they let into our lives has the power to transform everything that we've believed about God, everything that we've ever wondered or wanted about the holy in our world. Icons aren't the lion exhibit at our local zoo, carefully constructed tableaus that give us safe access to what we pretend is the savage wildness of real savannah. These tableaus domesticate and deprive, making of these great cats bored captives who only vaguely remember their primal purpose. This fabricated safety fools us into believing we have actually engaged desert and danger when we get to *ooh* and *aah* in undisturbed peace.

On a hike last weekend, my husband and some friends climbed a remote rock formation to explore some elevated caves. The drive out into the wilderness, at least two hours from anywhere civilized, had filled us with frisson and delight. That the trail was filled with hikers and campers despite the distance from home gave us a semblance of security, so exploring seemed like a good idea. When pint-sized Owen asked permission to crawl into the low cave it was given without thought. But when his hand nearly found purchase in a pile of fresh scat, the adults abruptly remembered that the wilderness is not easily controlled. Before their eyes, the caves transformed from playground into lair, and the softly bedded-down ledges resolved into the signs of danger they truly were. Gathering the younger boys quickly, the adults moved purposefully away. Suspicion was enough to cause appropriate flight from what was later confirmed as an active mountain lion den.

Icons, wherever they are found, aren't plexiglass-enclosed observation bubbles where we watch heaven's invasion of earth at a remove. They are instead the caves into which we unthinkingly blunder, reminders not necessarily of the danger of our God but of his immense power and presence. Reminders he is watching. Indications he is near. Proof he has the capacity and opportunity to devour us. But that he does not. We like to think ourselves safe observers of the world, sometimes even zookeepers, but icons remind us we are not so distant from the beauty, danger and glory. It is all around us, God is all around us, in every moment.

Coming to Our Senses

With a fresh awareness of God's presence all around us, we are released to experience him through all of our senses. Touch, taste, sight, smell, hearing—however we feel or encounter the world around us physically, we have the opportunity to experience within that encounter the work and wonder of God.

Opening up to the messages of God through our senses isn't a new practice for the church, just one that seems to be repeatedly buried and then excavated over time. With history's recent focus on the mind as the most important (and, in some theologies, only) tool for experiencing God, we lost focus on the reality that our bodies receive him through so much more than theory. The savor of God can be tasted in a good meal, smelled in the scent of wet, forested soil on a fall day, felt in the embrace of a friend, seen in the dancing light of a roaring fire. But what does it take to really come home to our senses as an avenue of encountering God through creation? How do we become attentive and present to the gifts of the given moment through our bodies?

Although the answer is, in its most general form, mindfulness, the monastic ideals of solitude and silence are infrequently available to us in day-to-day life. Detoxing from the daily overload of information to our senses is an important spiritual discipline, one that I believe grounds us deeply in ourselves and in God. However, hours of silence are not always a reality in a life filled with regular responsibilities like laundry and the making of meals.

We can, nonetheless, make icons out of those daily duties, experiencing in them the contours of the kingdom of God here and now. Whether or not you're aware of them, you have a number of daily rituals that can be transformed by attentively engaging your senses in something you already do. Take a moment to think about the tasks that you do daily or weekly. It could be brushing your teeth, doing the laundry, walking to the bus stop or class, preparing a meal. You may consider them chores or they may simply weave themselves into the fabric of your life, but they

are rituals in the classic sense of the term—a series of actions or behaviors regularly and invariably followed.

Choose one of those rituals—the one that feels the lightest or the one
that naturally gives you the most enjoyment—and begin paying closer
attention to your senses as you undertake it each day or week. If it's
bathing or showering, take the time to notice what the water feels like
falling on your skin. Do you experience the flow of water differently on
your back than on your scalp? What does your shampoo smell like? Be
present to the way the soap feels on your hands and the drip of water over
your closed eyelids. Don't rush through bathing as a necessity—feel it as
a baptism, a gift, a concert of the senses.

This choice to be present to your senses, fully present, needn't be one
that you exercise every moment of every day. Starting with the rituals
that you regularly undertake gives you a circumscribed way to enter into
what your senses are telling you all the time. Keeping yourself limited to
those activities that you do regularly and, in fact, only one of those rituals,
allows you to grow in your ability to attend to the messages around you.
Like learning to listen in a noisy environment, deliberate and limited
times of attention to your senses teach you to distinguish between one
voice and another. Whether it's noticing the way touch plays a part in
your preparation of a meal for your children or encountering the world
around you in a meditative walk to the bus stop, starting with those daily
deliberate actions opens you to the wonder of your senses in more accessible, manageable ways.

Another window into the experience of being present to the goodness
of God through your senses is to choose a particular sense that you'll pay
attention to for a day or week or even a month. Whether it's touch, smell,
sight, sound or taste, choose one avenue of experience you'd like to focus
on. Then, throughout the day or week pause at regular intervals to review
what you've experienced through that particular sense. Much like the
discipline of fixed-hour prayer, this noticing is a form of liturgical
worship, a way of attending to the gift of your senses and the gifts of God

through them. Even if what you've experienced hasn't necessarily been pleasurable, make note of it. You can journal those noticings or share them with God in prayer or simply let your act of attention itself be a type of prayer—a prayer that honors the work of God in creation by the pure act of awareness.

I'm coming to believe that my dog might be solar powered. After a good half hour in the backyard in the morning, during which he barks at anyone who walks the path behind our house, running up and down with a kind of exuberance that only four-legged creatures and children can embody, Hullabaloo returns inside to find the largest available patch of sunlight and promptly falls asleep. Throughout the rest of the day, he follows the sun around the house, seemingly absorbing its energy through his skin.

If you've ever sat in the sunlight, though, you might have other ideas about what our dog is doing. Hullabaloo knows what comforts and what brings rest. The energy of the sun, the warmth of that light, gives him a physical sensation, an awareness of his own body and the way it interacts with the world around him. Solar energy changes him physically, moves his body to react by tightening his pores and prompting his nervous system to trigger panting when his internal temperature reaches uncomfortable limits.

In the same way, awareness of our senses—whether it's just one or all of them[2]—helps us to delight in the glory of the world around us (the infinite variety of smells and sounds, the refreshing complexity of tastes) and to consciously respond to our place in that world, our place in relationship to God. Attention to your sense of smell, for example, can give you greater insight not only to what's going on around you (bread is baking two doors down, there's a rainstorm on its way) but also to what's going on within you (the smell of the crusty loaf kicks up a memory of the day that you saw your grandmother for the last time, the scent of rain brings with it anxiety around how your relationship with your spouse is going because you fought the last time it thundered). If you've trained your awareness deeply enough, you may be able to follow the messages of your senses into the holy places that God is leading you. As you slowly choose to breathe in the wet tang of precipitation, Christ invites you to release your relationships to him, an act of repatterning your sensual connections that will allow you to move through the world more freely and lightly, tethered less tightly to trauma or fear.

Touch Point

Taste and See

There are many ordinary ways we engage our senses to navigate our world, whether in the meals we eat or the way that we observe God's beauty in sunrise and sunset. Each of these mundane moments—the chill of cold water as you swallow, the way laundry smells just out of the dryer—can be filled with holiness and power if we are attentive to them.

As an act of exploratory prayer, choose one of your senses that you will be most attentive to this week. Before you begin, make a list of the things that you regularly do that engage this sense so that you'll be more present to those actions when they occur.

Each time you use your sense of taste, for example, notice closely what you're experiencing. What are the flavors your tongue registers? What are the textures in your mouth? What does savoring those sensations tell you about God, his kingdom, his heart?

Whatever sense you've chosen, listen attentively to your body as you use it in everyday life. Try not to judge or categorize what you're experiencing—live in it first for a while before you make meaning out of it. Once you've grown in your attentiveness to this sense, begin to give thanks for the sensations you're experiencing. Slow down internally as you wash the dishes and notice the way the water feels on your hands, the bubbles of soap bursting against your skin. What kind of gratitude does this raise in you? What does the sinkful of sensations tell you about God's affection for you right in that moment? What would you like to say to Christ about this? What does Jesus have to say to you?

The insights don't have to be radical, but the more attention you pay to them, the more profound these simple sensations will become. The mystery of the gospel is that it is a reversal of the world's insistence on the big, loud and popular. Instead, the revelation of God is found in the small, the quiet and often the deeply personal interactions of the Holy Spirit with our everyday circumstances and senses.

You might want to keep a journal of these observations over the course of the week and make a sensory "meal" of them once you're finished with this experiment of prayer. Return to your experiences and savor them deeply—they are places where you met and felt the work of God in your body. The particularity of these things to you and your story can't be written in a book, but they are inscribed on your heart by the One who loves you more than life itself.

Flesh of My Flesh

Union, Sexuality and God's Design

*The sensuous is sacred. When we begin to awaken to the beauty
which is Sensuous God, we discover the holiness of
our bodies and our earth.*

JOHN O'DONOHUE, *BEAUTY: THE INVISIBLE EMBRACE*

BEFORE WE BEGIN WRESTLING WITH THE COMPLEX, beautiful, juicy
and difficult topic of sexuality, I'm going to acknowledge that if I were
the one reading this book I would have flipped to this chapter first. Not
that I don't think all that comes before it is important (and, welcome, if
you're starting here—we've covered a lot of ground before this point, but
I'm glad you're here), but because how to live well with our sexuality is a
question most of us live with daily. To that end, there is precious little
out there leading us toward a positive ethic of sexuality, one that focuses
not on the *don't* but on the *do*.

Hovering Over the Chaos

Our sexuality feels chaotic, doesn't it? I often think that we've developed such a robust purity culture in the church precisely because we're fundamentally aware of the power embedded in our bodies, power we can't help but encounter when we identify and express our sexual selves.

There's something so risky, so fraught in acknowledging the power of our sexuality. If we name that power, if we own it, we also have to admit, to ourselves and to others, that we can't really control it, that everything about our sexuality resists control. When we feel that wildness—the drive for connection in our bodies resulting in physiological arousal—our predominant reaction, as we've talked about at length, is to clamp down in fear. When we're flush with attraction, when we're struggling to think about anything other than the way that person's body makes us feel, we're more likely than not to tighten the screws on ourselves rather than realize we're not fully in the driver's seat of our lives after all.

The most fundamentally true thing about our sexuality is that it is good. Stop for a minute and read that sentence again. Your sexuality is fundamentally, at root, beyond all else, *good*.

Do you really believe that? What would change if you did?

Oh, but it feels so dangerous to step toward that idea that our sexuality is a beautiful, good, fundamental part of who we are, something that we're meant to bear, meant to live in, doesn't it? So quickly we want to run back to the reality of our fallenness, to point at the ways sexuality leads us astray, the things that go wrong when we give desire free rein.

Here's the thing: the problem isn't that we've given sexuality free rein, but that we haven't encountered it enough. As C. S. Lewis writes in *The Weight of Glory*, "It would seem that Our Lord finds our desires not too strong, but too weak. We are half-hearted creatures, fooling about with drink and sex and ambition when infinite joy is offered us, like an ignorant child who wants to go on making mud pies in a slum because he cannot imagine what is meant by the offer of a holiday at the sea. We are far too easily pleased."[1] We fool around with sex and sexual expression, stepping in only so far, letting our desires be only so keenly felt. We insist on holding on to control, deeply afraid of the shame and disruption we may feel if we move toward what we *really* want.

But what is it that we really want, after all?

I know what you've been told—I've been told it too. Over and over I've heard from the world that I'm just a bundle of appetites, willing, if given the freedom to do so, to sacrifice everything, including my marriage, for more pleasure. Over and over I've heard from the church that I'm a mess of contradictory desires, many of which lead me away from holiness, away from God—so I'd better watch out. (These messages aren't too far apart from one another, sadly.)

Yet, if I'm a temple of the Holy Spirit (1 Corinthians 6:19), if you're a temple of the Holy Spirit, then God is inhabiting our very selves right now. The very same Spirit that hovered over chaos at the beginning of all time is within us both, inhabiting, holding and hovering over what feels like a very chaotic realm within us: our sexuality. He is the one who is meant to form and direct that power, and he both wants to and will do so if we give him the opportunity.

Just as in the creation account in Genesis, God has formed our sexuality into something he calls both good and blessed. God created us in the image of himself—in the image of the interwoven Trinity—and made us distinct from one another in such a way that our desires draw us together in union. Our sexuality, our desire not just for pleasure (we don't really need another person for that) but for connectedness and intimacy is a reflection of the very heart of God—for us and toward us. As Lisa Graham McMinn writes in her book *Sexuality and Holy Longing*:

> Sexuality is intended by God to be neither incidental to nor detrimental to our spirituality, but rather a fully integrated and basic dimension of that spirituality. . . . Human sexuality . . . is most fundamentally the divine invitation to find our destinies not in loneliness but in deep connection. . . . We experience our sexuality as the basic *eros* of our humanness that urges, invites, and lures us

out of our loneliness into intimate communication and communion with God and the world.[2]

In the same way that God has given us free will, he's not particularly interested in locking down our desires under some kind of robotic restraint. Sexuality feels so deep and out of control precisely because it is meant to be.

Does that mean we throw caution to the wind, let our sexual desire rule our lives and get on with the fun? Not at all (although the fun part has something to do with it). Just as there is no Jew or Gentile, no slave or free in Christ, a holistic, healthy and holy expression of our sexuality involves giving it over to be inhabited, directed, formed by God. It means dying to what feels like the way to do things—either fiercely repressing (which we do more often) or blindly obeying (which we don't actually do as much) our sexual desires. It means surrendering our tight-fisted control, our desire to manipulate, our very ownership of ourselves to the One who is still able to create divinely ordered beauty out of teeming chaos. It means giving over our models of sexuality to God's wilder purposes (remembering, of course, that God's order often looks a lot messier than what "order" means to us).

Making Love

When my husband and I first started dating, we talked a lot about our sexuality and how we hoped to honor each other in relationship. This wasn't simply a discussion of how to stick to the "rules" or do as much as we wanted physically without sinning. Although sin mattered to us, what mattered more was honoring Christ in each other and starting our relationship with the kind of care and love for the other that would result in union between us, rather than a relationship of two people trying to get what they wanted. We were dissatisfied with the various models of dating and courtship around us, especially in the church, because for the most part they were based on what *not* to do, instead of setting up a healthy picture of what sexuality in a relationship that wasn't yet marriage might look like.

Very early on, Bryan wrote me a long letter that would have shocked me if we hadn't had a basis for talking about the fullness of our lives together. We'd talked through our stories and understood together that God is about redemption, not control. We'd encountered how strong our feelings and arousals were around each other and knew this attraction wasn't just something we were trying out. We were growing in love for one another, and we wanted to put each other first. Still, the first line of his letter took me aback a little. It started with the line, "How long should we take when making love the first time?"

He continued,

It may seem on the surface to be a premature question, but I don't think it is. I've never really used the term "making love" except as a euphemism for sex. I don't think I have understood its fullness. Let me tell you what I see.

Making love is creating unity. Creating oneness. I believe we have begun.

A man that seeks a sexual experience or simple pleasure is not creating unity. He is meeting a need for release or relief or pleasure. It is not oneness.

A man and a woman who mutually seek pleasure are perhaps creating oneness in shared experience, but even that shared experience is just a shadow of what "making love" is supposed to be. They aren't seeking unity.

A husband and wife have been unified—have been made one already—but need to reestablish unity between them. They need to repair what has been broken by the harshness of life, sin, and the world. They need to re-unite their minds, hearts, wills and bodies. They look into each other's spirits, tune their hearts to each other, and step in. They remember the unity they once established and re-create it. They create oneness again. And they create it by touching each other's spirits and bodies. They find deep security, pleasure, and they know each other again.

They make love in every way....

For us, I am thinking a year or so. I believe that even now, you and I are beginning to make love for the first time. Not a re-union, but a first union. I'm not asking you into bed with me, but into a journey that may culminate in that final union after marriage. We do not know how or if we will finish making love, but we should acknowledge that we are beginning.

We should begin this first union with as much care as we would any re-creation of it in the future. All thoughts of what it "could be" need to become grounded in how to make love now.

We have talked about how to "stay pure." We have talked about lines that we need to have with each other to ensure holiness. I am asking you to a new place with me—a place I have not been. Instead of lines, I am inviting you to explore with me how we can spend this year "making love" for the first time....

To begin making love, we need to learn each other, trust each other, pace with each other. We need to learn what unites, what calms, what arouses, and what heals. Emotionally, spiritually, socially, mentally, physically. It is dauntingly complex. It will take quite some time.

Making love is creating oneness. Sexual arousal is powerful in creating that oneness. We must be careful. To intentionally create arousal now would be premature and invasive—almost violent to the beautiful innocence we find ourselves in at the moment. We do not know each other yet. Our sexual attraction might be too strong—might destroy the fragile oneness that we are growing. It will be a powerful ally as this journey continues, but for now, we must be careful or we will divide rather than unite.

The other areas of making love must come together first. Minds, spirits, wills, passions, and even our social selves. All these things must be in place before we can complete the first creation of love between us. After the social union of marriage, we may reach climax. The last union of our bodies can happen, and with sexual union is complete. It is then that we have created oneness and really made love for the first time....

If we know this is what we are making, I believe we will honor God
and each other sexually. We will not take short cuts to create oneness too
early. If we know what we are creating, then we will measure our ac-
tions and words with each other to honor our journey.

So . . . how is that for an invitation? Will you join me?

State of Union

Our sexuality is in all of its manifestations an image of union, of
oneness. We see that most clearly in sexual intercourse, the place where
we offer ourselves in nakedness and vulnerability to one another,
seeking to enter and know one another in a deeply intimate way. There's
a reason that Scripture repeatedly uses the term "know" in place of "had
sex," and it isn't because the Bible is particularly modest (Song of Songs,
anyone?). We impose our own puritanical impulses on the text when
we make those assumptions, placing barriers between us and what the
Word is speaking.

The first time the word "know" is used in the sense of knowing another
person, it's in the context of Adam knowing Eve. Up until this point, the
verb has only been used to describe God's knowing. When Adam knows
Eve, life comes forth. This knowing involves Adam's whole self, Eve's
whole self, and reflects the image of God placed within them both. This
is the first reparative act outside of the Garden of Eden, a movement
toward one another in body and soul, an enactment of the unity that was
lost and a hope for more intimacy restored.

Our sexuality isn't simply an expression of our animal selves, God's
way of underlining the fact that we're not in Eden anymore. The power
of knowing, the grace of intimacy reminds us of the intimacy in which
we're intended to live, intimacy with each other and with God. The first
thing our sexuality and sexual expression do in the story of creation is
produce *life*, something only God has done up to this point. Hear that
again. Up until this point, only God has brought forth life. Now, through

knowing, through intimacy, new life has come forth from humanity. This is radical, beautiful, revolutionary. It's worth pausing over, because it's the first creative act that we see from humanity. And it involves our bodies. Sexual expression, held as it is in the knowing of lip and thigh, openness and entering, is a gift that creates life in all its forms.

It is the radical grace of God, his wild, self-giving love, that he imbues us with the ability to create life through union. Outside of the Garden, apart from our relationship with God, we are deeply aware of our own loneliness, the fact that we're cut off from something we deeply desire. Our bodies yearn for connectedness and intimacy—things that can't be fulfilled merely by genital stimulation (although we try). We are created to know and be known, to express and give love in ways appropriate to the union, the life that we're seeking to create.

When Jesus offers his revolutionary challenge to discipleship in Luke 14, he uses the analogy of a man building the foundation of a house he ends up not being able to complete. Consider the cost, Jesus says, think about the life that you're choosing when you decide to follow me. The foundation you're laying down when you become my disciple is one of self-giving love, and that encompasses all that you are, all that you will ever do.

Jesus reminds us to count the cost, not to tell us to be prepared (although many a sermon has been preached on being ready), but to illustrate to us we could never even hope to be. If we were to sit down and honestly ask ourselves if we have everything we need to follow this passionate, unruly God of ours, we would have to say no. We love our lives too dearly, we seek ourselves over others more often than we like, we choose expediency instead of love time and again. The invitation of God isn't to get it together so we can follow him, but to leave all of our preparations behind so that we can.

This is his invitation in our sexuality as well. We like our rules, our guides, our ways of knowing what will be healthy and healing and what will be hurtful and dividing. We like our purity culture with its holiness codes (or society's emphasis on personal freedom with its disregard for sacrifice, for loving one another), and we like to be able to judge whether other people are doing it right or wrong. He invites us to lay down the life of knowing and judging and to walk with him in every decision, every movement, every action, to the place where he restores us into the image that he first created us in, the unique reflection of God's glory that we were meant to bear. He invites us into the dialogue that brings us more into line with who we are meant to be, closer and closer to that life of living naked, unashamed, fully capable of the union we so desperately desire.

Our sexuality points us toward union, and when we surrender our desire to control, our desire to force union to happen, when we begin living in the awareness of the other in such a way that we want to know them so much more than we want to be known, we embody the union that God desires so deeply with us. In the Orthodox tradition, this union is called *theosis*, an intimacy close enough that two become one. In Protestant traditions we tend to flinch away from this, reacting with fear and suspicion to the implication that we could somehow become gods ourselves. We can't become God, just as you can't become your spouse— there's an integral difference between who you are and who they are. But life together, a life of learning one another, knowing and being known, makes the sacrament of marriage a reality—two become one.

The progressive reality of this union is exactly the image that Christ uses in talking about his intimacy with the church. It's an intimacy that we're invited to with each other in the holy covenant of marriage, seeking union with one another in the mysterious intimacy of making love—in body, in heart, in soul, in mind. And this union doesn't come without repeated movement toward one another, a practicing of the self-giving love and vulnerability that builds oneness. The sacrament of marriage doesn't happen once at the wedding ceremony. It may begin there, but it is built into a full reality over years of choosing for one another in all areas of our lives, but most clearly sexually.

It's tempting to simply set up another set of rules for what this looks like in a marriage, what steps to take to make this progressive union possible. And while there are some practical things that help in the journey of union, much like there are some practical things that help in our relationship with God, the unique character and life experiences of each couple must be the guide for this journey if it is to remain personal, incarnate and unique. Just as no one else bears your particular similarity to God, no one else bears your partner's particular similarity to God. To see your partner as a type or set of expectations that you ought to fulfill strips lovemaking and sexuality of their power and turns them into expediency and performance.

When Bryan invited me into a journey of making love, that journey didn't end on our wedding night—it only began. Even with our awareness of what we were building, our first steps into union were both delightful and fumbling. With the witness of friends and family, we had said no to all the other people to whom we could commit our bodies and, more concretely, our nakedness. We turned our backs on every other option when we said yes to each other, choosing to embody for one another what love is—a covenanted, safe space of nakedness, the place where we enact love in the "connected momentum of life-giving communion."[3]

This doesn't mean that every night is filled with ecstatic lovemaking, each encounter building on the other. Intimacy in marriage isn't about greater and greater heights of pleasure—just like intimacy with God isn't about greater and greater ecstatic experiences of him. Intimacy in marriage is much like intimacy with Jesus and, in fact, is meant to lead us deeper into it.

Intimacy in marriage, healthy expression of sexuality, means continuing to risk my desire for my husband when the flush of the first explorations have worn off. It means being known even more fully—when I'm snotty and sick with the flu, when I'm self-focused and angry for no reason, when I'm expressing self-hatred by pointing my disappointment at him, and even when I'm rightly hurt by something that he has done and said. And that is deeply risky, even riskier than it was for Bryan to ask me to start making love before we were first married.

My sexuality in marriage, our sexuality in marriage, is about all the ways that I feel lonely and separated and cut off, just as it is about all the ways that I feel and desire togetherness, connection, presence and oneness. Living out my desire for union with my husband involves being willing to say that sex last night was disappointing or to hear him tell me that the ways we relate sexually feel unfulfilling to him. It involves seeking not *my* pleasure or *his* pleasure—neither of those things were what we were seeking when we began this journey years ago. Engaging my sexuality fully in marriage involves my dedication to and pursuit of *our* pleasure, something that means I need to die to my own agendas and begin living in this new reality that is my husband and me *together*.

To say that sexual expression, whether it's touches or intercourse or the way we make meals together, is simply an upward path to union after wedding vows is to leap into madness. As we've talked about earlier, bodies age and ache, children are born and need attention, things that once aroused no longer do. Being connected to our sexuality means being connected to our desires and being willing to offer them even when they have been disappointed before. Being connected to our bodies means noticing when things are being aroused in us, even if they aren't being immediately aroused by our spouse, and stepping toward rather than away from those desires.

In some ways, it seems that this should get easier in marriage, because the person knows us well. And yet, the reality of our own fallenness and self-seeking is such that when we get into any kind of close relationship we end up hurting one another. Sometimes this is unintentional; other times, sadly, it's intended, and instead of reaching out in vulnerability and nakedness to seek restoration, instead of stepping toward healthy conflict, most of us simply retreat behind walls of silence or blaming, walls that get built higher and higher until risking real intimacy with your spouse seems like the stupidest possible thing to do.

And yet our bodies, if we listen to them, keep urging us toward each other. As with our appreciation of the world around us, most of us deal with these desires—urges and arousals that are hard to ignore—by deadening them with busyness, productivity or distraction. It's why we're so addicted to our technology or our schedules, our need to have a clean home or our desire to be seen as a successful achiever. To step away from those numbing agents means to feel, really feel, how deeply we long for connection and how profoundly lonely we feel.

Sex is worship—if it's about more than just yourself. Sex is a creative act, whether or not physical life is borne of it, and we need to let that creation be as fumbling and wonky and awkward as it sometimes is. Demanding sexual perfection of yourself or your spouse is akin to demanding Christ transform you perfectly right now—it's not going to happen because that demand comes from a position of entitlement and self-absorption.

The grace of it all is that it's exactly in our embodied longings and lonelinesses that we can find the love of Christ meeting us and empowering us to offer our nakedness and vulnerability once again. Intimacy is only possible if we take off our masks and show up to our partner, real body to real body. Just as intimacy with God is only possible when we're not hiding, intimacy in our sexual relationships isn't really possible when we're performing or pretending. We may get pleasure, our spouse may get pleasure, but the pleasure produced wasn't *ours*, and ultimately it will leave us feeling even more lonely and cut off.

I would be sad if someone told me that they had a completely satisfying sex life, that they were constantly satiated. In the same way I would feel sad if someone told me that they felt no desire for their spouse; a sense of satiation means that there are no desires to draw us deeper and little to no risks being taken. (I'd also, frankly, think that the person was either lying or completely delusional.) The tension of our sexuality—the unending well of desire we feel for connection—is that it is always urging and inviting us into *more*.

In that way, I can say that I'm glad that my sex life with my husband isn't perfect, that we're still working on making love well, because we're continually in the process of expressing desires, experiencing disappointments, grieving the places we wound and are wounded, naming things honestly, confessing what we want deeply, blessing one another, and doing it all with humility. To really know and be known by another requires that I encounter all of my story, including the ways my sexuality has been shaped generally by my culture and more specifically by the sexual stories of my mother and father. Naming those narratives means naming the violences that I have experienced myself and the violences I have perpetuated against others. Naming, stepping into real nakedness, means letting go of the ways I cover myself, the ways I hide or deny the story that I'm living out. That's a tall order for any marriage, and it's one that we're stepping into in broken, blessed, beautiful and bruising ways.

We *can* step into this because we believe in the power of the resurrection; we believe that Christ's resurrection can be experienced in and through our bodies—if we're willing to die. Some days, I'm okay with that. Other days, I run the other way. But my body is an engine of hope—it asks, seeks and knocks even when my ego least wants it to, and I can choose to embrace that hope and believe that together my husband and I are moving toward unity, toward ecstasy, toward a taste of what the full *theosis* of heaven can be like here on earth.

Sexual, Intimate

This type of encountering, naming and redeeming isn't restricted to married couples. Although the physical nakedness of the marriage bed is both symbol and reality of what it means to vulnerably offer our bodies to one another in covenant safety, that offering, that union, isn't the exclusive territory of marrieds.

We don't suddenly become sexual beings when we commit ourselves to someone—our sexuality has been a present and vital reality for all of our lives. We each have sexual stories to live into, to acknowledge as both broken and beautiful, and to bless and see resurrected. Married, single, widowed, divorced, we are meant to delight in one another, and that delight includes an awareness of our desires.[4]

To live into the full reality of our sexuality, we need to name and embrace the story of our bodies—skin, breasts, penises, lips, hips. As those living singly, we do that not by repressing our desires but by naming and delighting in them, even when they cause us to ache in loneliness or struggle with self-centered hunger. The most whole and holy single people I know are the ones most in touch with their bodies and their desires, the ones who step toward delight rather than away from it. They ask for touch when they need it and refuse to live or believe in fantasy worlds where there is no suffering or death but only pleasure and self-satisfaction. They do the hard work of encountering God in questions like that of the appropriateness of masturbation, and refuse simple right-wrong, either-or prescriptions for holiness.

In the same way, those I know with the most gratifying marriages allow for the delight in people other than their spouse. This doesn't mean sexual intercourse; it means that each spouse is free to delight and touch and encounter others in a way that increases rather than decreases their appetite for being known by their partner. "You can't misuse people you delight in," says Dan Allender, and sensuality is a framework for delight.[5] In these marriages, the couples talk openly about sexuality in a way that isn't crude or exploitative, and they encourage playfulness and humor. They are, more often than not, involved in projects and places that are larger than themselves, that bring God's redemption into this world. In this way, they practice dying to their own pleasure in order to taste hope, to experience redemption.

When the warp and woof of our understanding of sexuality is honor, humility and hope, we experience the urges and longings of our body without shame and refuse to box our longings into restrictive categories. Whether we're single or married, the expression of our sexuality brings with it the recognition that we need and are meant for connection with one another, and that desires can be met without dishonoring or transgressing the boundaries of other people. When union, *theosis*, and the creation and experience of pleasure that is neither mine nor yours but *ours* is our aim, we no longer find ourselves playing by rules of "right" and "wrong" but instead find ourselves living in intimacy with the Father and therefore with one another. It's risky, true, to step away from the old narratives of separation and repression, but the risk of redemption is worth the cost of death.[6]

Touch Point

Owning Your Story

Whether you are married or single, part of moving toward union and intimacy is owning your own sexual story. This isn't easy for most of us to do because we've been taught and taught ourselves that our desires are to be repressed or, worse, shamed. So we go into hiding or we blame others, refusing to look at or bless our sexual history. This refusal ties us to cycles of misuse and abuse, of violence and lust that move us away from God, not toward him.

Spend some time writing out your own sexual history and exploring God's story woven through it. Begin with prayer, asking for the Lord's guidance and presence:

> *Abba, my body is yours, redeemed and more beautiful than I have yet been able to own. Help me to encounter you in my sexual story. Protect me from shame or hiding, and allow me to see and bless my desires. Show me where I need to grieve or feel anger, and let me name truly and accurately all that has happened to me and through me. Lead me into redemption that I may know your glory, for the sake of your Son Jesus Christ, in whose name I pray. Amen.*

Draw a timeline across one or several sheets of paper, dividing it in sections of five to ten years, from birth to present. If you need to, you might make longer sections for certain periods of your life. Write down the events of your life as they relate to your sexuality—both genital sexual expression and your awareness of sexuality in your family and social circles.

As you recall events in your life, notice what's going on inside you. You might want to draw symbols indicating fears or anxieties, or other visual indicators that represent joy or contentment.

Write down where each encounter leads you in prayer. For example, try to understand the event, noting all the consequences in your life—good or not good. With each event or encounter, talk to God about the joy and the pains. Ask God to speak to difficult places in your story; ask him to show you his place and perspective.

In the places where you feel shame, try to attend not to your own narratives but to what the Holy Spirit is saying to you about these events.

Ask yourself what you were looking for in your sexual encounters, no matter how small. Was it love? Belonging? Protection? Escape from pain? Try to notice what your underlying desires were, not just the surface actions.

Notice as you explore your story the gifts and blessings that you have received from God in your sexuality.

Are there places where you need to confess what you were longing and looking for, not as a place of shaming but as an articulation of what you were driving toward, even if it was in a harmful direction?

Are there places that you need to grieve, to truly feel sorrow or anger at the choices you made or the choices made against you? Can you encounter that grief and pain knowing that God is grieving with and for you? What would stopping to grieve those places look like right now?

Are there places you need to bless (or work toward blessing) your arousal—the pleasure you felt in your body—no matter the circumstances of that arousal? Are there places where you need to bless (which is not the same as condoning) those who have done violence against you or the places that you have done violence?

Even if there are places of sin (missing the mark) in your sexual story, what would it mean to bless those places as capable of being redeemed by God? Will you bless what sin has brought you to now know?

You might also want to write down the sexual stories of your mother and father—how did the way each of them spoke about and lived out their sexuality model what sexual expression was to you? How did your mother's relationship to her body affect you? How did the way your parents physically interacted send messages about what sexual intimacy in marriage should look like? What about your father's sexual story? How did he speak about sex and sexuality, if at all? What did his actions tell you about how he related to his body and yours?

Ask God to show you how he is redeeming these narratives and what knowledge he'd like you to start living out as a result of this reflection. Where is he most at work right now in your story? Is there an aspect of your body's story that he's inviting you to listen to? Is there a way in which you've learned about sexuality that he's inviting you to die to so that your sexuality can be more fully redeemed?

Thank God for the time together in reflection and prayer, and give him permission to continue working and bringing redemption in your shared story of union and healing through your sexuality.

Finally, you might want to seek out a safe and confidential person with whom to share your story. Often we hide our stories from others, and the very act of hiding increases our shame and isolation. This doesn't mean you broadcast your story from the rooftops; instead, seek out a spiritual director, mentor or therapist who can walk you deeper into redemption. Be wise in whether or not this person is your spouse—seek honesty without inflicting violence to the one who has shared their deepest vulnerability and nakedness with you. If God does call you to speak your story candidly with your spouse, do so gently and slowly, in a position of humility and hope, without asking them to fix you but instead inviting them into a process of healing, struggle, redemption and resurrection with you.

This Is My Body

Connection and Communion with the Body of Christ

Christ has no body now but yours. No hands, no feet on
earth but yours. Yours are the eyes through which he looks
compassionately on this world. Yours are the feet with
which he walks to do good. Yours are the hands
through which he blesses all the world.
Yours are the hands, yours are the feet,
yours are the eyes, you are his body.
Christ has no body now
on earth but yours.

TERESA OF ÁVILA

I WAS A LITTLE BIT NERVOUS ABOUT THIS CLASS, I'll have to admit. There were more men in the room than I'm used to seeing in a spiritual direction seminar—a good thing and a grace that more men are seeing the gift of spiritual direction in their lives and communities. The class was also more multicultural than I'd yet experienced; again, a good thing, but as I come from a white, North American cultural experience I knew that I'd be sailing into waters that were unknown to me.

The room was close, which gave my students the ability to see one another and feel my nervous energy as well. As I spoke and led, I prayed silently for the Spirit of Pentecost to be in this space that we shared together—a Spirit that would allow people to hear the teaching in their own language, crossing the boundary between my cultural assumptions and theirs, without a need for my clumsy attempts at translation.

After leading the class in an exploration of what it means to be aware of our sexuality in spiritual direction and guiding the exercise I described in chapter six, I invited the class to reflect on their experiences. I'm guessing they could tell I was holding my breath.

What happened next surprised me. In fact, I think it surprised everyone in the room, including the person telling the story. After a few reflections on the intimacy of touch in an increasingly digital and distanced society, an older gentleman in the corner of the room spoke up. Despite the informality of this seminary group, he wore dress slacks and a white collared shirt, buttoned to the neck. Although he wasn't yet greying at the temples, lines etched his face deep enough to underline the difference in years lived between him and most of his classmates.

"First," he started, "I have to tell you that I'm from Korea, and in my culture and class, touch outside of friendship and intimate relationship is rare. So I knew that this exercise was going to be difficult for me. I entered in, though, because I could feel God here with us. I asked him to speak to me through the exercise."

He paused. "I've been living in Canada for more than ten years. I've done everything that I can to try to be involved in this country and connect with the people that have welcomed me here. I've been part of small groups, I have tried to connect in community."

One of his hands reached out, involuntarily it seemed, to smooth the surface of the table in front of him. He brushed at imaginary crumbs, clearing a space for himself to continue. "No matter what I've done, though, I've always felt disconnected. I've always felt like an outsider, not welcomed in or a part of Canadian culture. That's been very difficult for me, and I've often prayed to God, asking him to show me how to connect.

"When I began the exercise with my partner, it felt awkward. I didn't know how to explain my day using only my hands. Like other classmates have said, I wasn't sure that I was communicating myself in a way that could be understood."

His hand stilled.

"But as I continued the exercise, I began to understand what my partner was saying. And suddenly, I felt connected in a way that didn't need words. I felt accepted and listened to."

The room had fallen hushed. A single tear tracked its way down my student's face, an indication of the vulnerability and trust that he was offering to us all.

"I feel a part of Canadian society for the first time in ten years," he said quietly. "I feel like I belong, and it was all because I was able to connect my need to belong with my body, to say, *I am here, please notice me*, not with my words but with my hands. And my partner met me there, saying, *You are here, I notice you*, with her hands."

He fell silent for a moment.

"This is such a gift from God. I don't know how to explain how much this means to me."

Here is where I pause to wonder: Could we take this as more than an isolated experience of a second-culture citizen longing to belong? Could we see this not as God generously meeting the need of a man struggling to connect but as Christ bursting forth from within our veins, singing through our blood a song of unity, of hope, of redemption? The unity of all people, brought together by the body?

Sharing the Gift

I've held the cup a handful of times. When mine was the chalice for dipping, I've settled the heavy bowl tight against my palm, securing it so that I can kneel easily to serve the smallest, can stretch out my hands to offer it a little bit closer to those whose reluctance to approach Christ is palpable. I'm a little less sure when I'm holding the chalice meant for drinking, and I wrap my fingers around bowl and base like one who's had a little too much spirit. More than once I've felt myself overtip the cup of salvation, and chagrined, I've watched friends and strangers lick the excess from lip and chin.

Whatever your tradition, whatever Communion, Eucharist, the Lord's Supper is for you, the act of partaking in the body and blood is a communal act of embodied worship. Whether you come to the altar to receive one by one or receive the cup and bread from ushers who pass the gift down the aisles as those who bring manna to the people, this taking of Christ into yourself radically breaks you from other communities, other ways of being in the world. The early church was accused of cannibalism because of this wild act of obedient worship—*eat my flesh, drink my blood*—and paid for it, sometimes with their lives.

We are still paying with our lives, no matter how comfortably we think we are living, no matter how far from martyrdom we believe we are. The truth of Paul's words to the Galatians echoes into our lives as well—"it is no longer I who live, but Christ lives in me; and the *life* which I now live in the flesh I live by faith in the Son of God" (Galatians 2:20 NKJV)—and we are forced into a recognition of the life of Christ in our bodies, at work in the world and in our lives whether or not we can even see to acknowledge it.

Died and Raised

Nearly two years ago I had the gift of being witness to the installation of a friend of mine as the abbot of an ecumenical monastic order of Grey Robe Benedictines. The vows to this order, which allows marriage and whose monastery is without walls, are nonetheless lifelong. The commitment is to obedience, stability, simplicity and conversation—the path of a monk in the world. The service itself was simple; song, prayer, a few words from Scripture. Simple except for the physical acts those professing vows took. Before they came forward to recite their covenant, each man and woman lay prostrate for a time before the altar. As they did so, their brothers and sisters from the order covered them gently with white cloths—symbolic of grave clothes—that hid them from any eyes but Christ's. In the physical reality of entombment, the work of the Spirit took place. We held silence, I held my breath, as transformation took place. One of the prostrate forms trembled, shaking with sobs. After a time, the abbot of the order called each man or woman by name, a new monastic name chosen by each as representative of the way they felt called to live, and the veils were lifted as they were helped to their feet, raised to new life.

These physical actions were symbolic, yes, but they were also profoundly real, an acknowledgment that they were giving their whole selves, heart and sinew, to this way of living, far beyond mere words. The memory of that interment in linen will linger with them long after the words of their professions have receded from their memories. And we who witnessed their commitments hold the memory of them being raised to their new monastic lives more vividly than the vows that were spoken.

This is true of any ceremony of which you've been a witness, isn't it? Think of the weddings and funerals you've attended, the times you've been at a christening or a baptism. Do you remember the words that were spoken over the child or the deceased? Do you recall what she said when she slipped the ring on her beloved's finger? Or do you remember the way the water ran down his temples in streams when he was raised from the river by the hands of his friends, the way the light fell across the old man's face as he ran his hand along the side of his wife's casket one last time?

Perhaps this speaks to how our memories are visual, how we remember what we see more often than what we say. But I would also suggest there is something integral about witnessing that involves our bodies and that we remember with our bodies more fully than with our minds alone. We grasp concepts and make meaning intellectually—you're reading this and understanding it because of the incredible power of intellect—but we integrate experiences into ourselves by using every one of our faculties—we have full-bodied experiences.

This is what we're asked to do when we participate in the ritual of witnessing. It's why most weddings are more than just a signature at a government office; they involve flowers and food, music and movement. You can't call in your presence—you have to be there physically, or you haven't been a witness at all. There aren't many places left in our culture where we value this way of knowing, but rituals of beginning and ending are one of those places.

Church, the gathering together of believers, is another. Whether or not we're thinking about it, the fact of gathering together at a specific place for a specific period of time is an insistence on this truth. We witness the work of God in one another, not just in the singing of songs or the words of the pastor, but in the weekly way we bring our bodies together. We may not touch physically, but we coagulate, binding the wounds the world has inflicted on us during the week, drawn together by the redemption call of Christ, the One for whom we all long.

Which brings me back to my friend and his installation. After we processed from sanctuary to chapel, after we watched them buried and raised anew, after we sang in hope of Christ to come and Christ among us, we went forward to receive the body and the blood. It was gift to be there, gift to have taken part in the service itself, and here was the deeper gift—the work of Christ, the life of Christ, given to me so that my own life might be strengthened and preserved. It was a gift, but one I have received so often that, on that particular day, I was less than attentive to the unique reality of the moment.

It's interesting, isn't it, that words which can on the one hand be so easily forgotten, so easily pushed aside by our own distractions and preoccupations, can also snap us swiftly to attention, shock us back into the hour at hand.

I held my hands before me, cupped, the left over the right in an acknowledgment that I am so quick to take rather than receive, a holding of my weaker member over the stronger. This choice of left over right is a habit now, when once I chose it intentionally, symbolically, my own physical submission to God. I waited, rather than grasped, for the bread, and the brother before me placed the wafer in my palm, pressing it slightly into my flesh. I looked up into his eyes, expecting words I knew, words I knew how to respond to.

"Receive what you are, the body of Christ."

Instead of something I was used to hearing, he said this strange and beautiful phrase. My whole body thrilled with awareness.

Receive what you are, the body of Christ.

This was the Word made flesh, small enough to be pressing into my palm, large enough to be resonating through this monk's mouth. This was the Word who died for me and who has come to live, co-substantial, within me. The Word I held in my hand and who arced through my neurons, within and without. In that minute stretched into millennia, I felt the truth of God's sacrifice once more. How he so longed to be with me, to be with us, that he became one of us and lives within us, within me even now.

I trembled as I put the wafer to my tongue, aware anew of the holy calling of being the body, of the way this act of receiving is also an act of remembering who I really am.

The monk with the cup smiled widely at me, as wide as my eyes had become. I reached tentatively to touch the chalice he held, unable to trust wholly enough to let him steady it to my lips all on his own. I want to say I was participating in community, touching my fingertips to his own around the pewter bowl, insisting on his particularity and my own. That would be poetic, but it wasn't my motivation, rattled as I was by the wafer and the words. I sought to steady myself.

"Receive what you are, the blood of Christ."

If it was possible, his smile widened, and the kiss of the cup to my lips was the kiss of Christ, the kiss of Magdalene as she washed her Lord's feet, the kiss of Judas in the garden, over all of which spilled the forgiving, healing, cleansing blood of Jesus.

Receive what you are, the blood of Christ.

That We May Be

There's a blessing we receive at my church at the end of the service. It seems a small moment, when we open our hands toward the front, eager for the words from Numbers 6:24-26,

> The LORD bless you
> > and keep you;
> the LORD make his face shine on you
> > and be gracious to you;
> the LORD turn his face toward you
> > and give you peace.

We respond, sometimes bored, sometimes hopeful, sometimes tired, sometimes simply wanting the service to be over so we can take the children home: "We receive this blessing that we may be a blessing." Our hands move toward our hearts and then open again, spilling outward, a gesture that might appear rote and perhaps meaningless, a child's repetitive mimicking without real understanding. It might appear that way, if you don't see what's really going on.

It would be easy enough to think that nothing had happened in that moment. It is, truly, easy enough to dismiss that we are the body of Christ and that Christ deeply coexists with each of us, no matter our experiences to the contrary. It is easy enough to believe that the blessing we receive from Scripture is a mere washing with words, the end of the time of worship and a release to the rest of the day.

But here's the thing. Whether we raised our hands or not during the songs, whether we moved to the music, sat or stood, shuffled or strode toward the offered Communion table, whether we played absently with a notebook during the sermon or wept on our knees during the prayers, we have been woven together in physical presence during this time. This unity, this bringing together, depended not primarily on the willingness of our souls to be present to God but on the very presence of our physical bodies. Whether or not we *felt* present, we were—and this in and of itself is a means of grace.

There's a line in some of the more traditional sets of wedding vows: *With my body, I thee worship.* You'd probably be hard-pressed to find it in a ceremony these days; it's long removed from the modern Book of Common Prayer, but it says something important not only about marriage but about the life of the church(To bring our bodies to one another, to be physically present, no matter our emotional or spiritual state, is to insist on the power of the incarnation to heal us and make us whole.)

This isn't something that we're conscious of most of the time. We hurry through our days, pulled by competing desires, needing to fulfill obligations and accomplish things, missing the sacrament that is actually available in us in every single moment—the real presence of Christ. We like to quote Matthew 18:20 ("For where two or three gather in my name, there am I with them"), but we don't seem to believe it. And yet, the Scripture doesn't say, "Where two or three gather in my name, there am I with them if they pay attention." The letters to the churches in Colossae and Rome both insist it is Christ *in* us that brings transformative power and hope, without the caveat that we must be attentive, aware, present to this reality for it to be made manifest (Colossians 1:27; Romans 8:10).

Now, awareness, presence, a sense of what is actually happening when we physically gather together makes a difference, to be sure. Just as my attentiveness to what is happening in the gift of Communion changes the way I receive it, changed how I received it from my brother monks, attentiveness to the sacredness of the gathering of believers changes the way I receive the gift of community. But that is simply an opening of my eyes, a letting go of distraction in order to see what is already there.

This is what I want you to know, deep in your bones, as you engage with your community of believers, whether in a small group, a cathedral, an underground church or on a rag-tag mission trip: *it's already there*. The gift of the incarnation, the presence of Christ among you, is active, moving, blessing, bringing forth life based on your very hands, thighs, lips, hair. Christ doesn't require your awareness to be present in you, and he doesn't require your attention to be active among you. This may sound horrible or incredible, depending on your perspective, but the glory of Christ cannot be held back, dimmed or otherwise diminished by our petty inability to notice one another or keep our mind off the day's list of chores.

Your hand is the hand of Christ, your mouth the mouth of Christ, your feet the feet of Christ. And so, too, are the hands and mouths and feet of those who fellowship in Jesus with you, whether they're part of the local group with whom you worship or the ones who gather on an earthen floor thousands of miles away from you.

Kissing, Blessing

Bristled. Burnished and brown. Baby-soft. With each cheek, I pressed my lips in deeper. With each person I became a little bolder.

I looked into eyes shining with hope, heads bowed with heaviness. I wrapped my arms around those who were weary. I stood in tip-toed excitement to receive each one.

Earlier that morning, I was conscripted, deputized as a makeshift monk. In this community of artists and wanderers that I had called home for the week, I was asked to be a stand-in for the holy. I listened carefully as our chaplain explained what I was to do. In a blessing of these who bring beauty into the world, each would approach with a request. In the manner of the pilgrims to the Greek Mount Athos, also known as the Holy Mountain, on approaching a monk, the traveler would call out, "Bless me." In return, I would acknowledge what already is—that they are chosen and called by God—by responding, "The Lord blesses you."

"Then," my chaplain said, "we will kiss them."

I struggle to find words for the joy that sang through me on hearing those words. The surge of delight I felt was disproportionate, sudden and thrilling. While I recognize that most people, when faced with the prospect of kissing the cheeks of more than fifty near-strangers, would not be filled with excitement, I've been thinking, teaching, wrestling with and writing about the wonder of embodiment for more than six years. In today's context, we're rarely given the opportunity to touch others in blessing, let alone get close enough to kiss them. But the act of embodying love, of reaching out of our imperfect, sweaty, awkward humanity to touch the trembling, holy, grace-infused stuff of another is a place of sacrament. As I touch you with my lips, I give form to love. As I lean close to bless, we insist together on the holiness of creation—even as we feel and know its limitations and vulnerabilities.

I've blessed people with oil before, marking them gently with the sign of the cross. I've rested hands on bowed heads, pressed my palm over a heart. I've supported cupped hands as they asked for God to fill them with his love. Until this particular day, I'd never kissed others in blessing, only in greeting, and then only with the anxious fumble of one who grew up in a culture devoid of these ritual greetings. Do I kiss once? Twice? Three times? I never know.

But now I am the moment's monk. As each artist, each pilgrim comes with their brave petition—*Bless me*—and I unconsciously move toward them, grasping their shoulders, holding them in the surety of grace—*The Lord blesses you*—I am the one kissed by love. Assured of our common humanity, the tenderness of skin and lips and hope and blessing, I have embodied Christ, watched him spill out of others and into me. I have fallen in love again and again with each face, and the kissing has become a needful thing, something that is right and good and true. It is a reversal of Judas's betrayal, an embodiment of "not my will but thine be done," and a release into all that they are and all that I am and all that God is in and between and through us.

This is how we begin to create community with our bodies. Not with kissing (although there is great wisdom to be gained in reflecting on

Paul's suggestion to greet one another with a holy kiss—Romans 16:16; 1 Corinthians 16:20; 2 Corinthians 13:12; 1 Thessalonians 5:26; 1 Peter 5:14), but with an attentive awareness of the tenderness of our very selves, the softness of flesh, the hope of movements toward redemption, the aching flaws of bodies that age and ail.

What would it mean to attend to one another's bodies as if they were our own to receive and bless? Not objects to control but members of ourselves, whose gifts and grief are as real as our own. To make safe spaces for the grace of touch—a kiss, a clasp, a hand on a shoulder or arms that encircle—is to create a culture of body that embraces mystery and material together. These spaces, held open at once by our God and our bodies, speak safety—*I see you, I feel you, you can relax now, you are safe*—and incarnate the presence of God, whose love can move through us to bring healing and wholeness.

This is the kneeling of the body of Christ, together as a community. In kneeling, in blessing, we put ourselves in the most vulnerable position possible. We expose ourselves to hurt, we risk betrayal. We open the softest parts of our flesh to others and the world, and we do it with radical trust, not that we will be saved from hurt but that God will move through our vulnerability to bring the power of Christ into the world. This is the kneeling of Christ in Gethsemane, a kneeling not for himself but for the redemption of all, an opening of a way of return to the One who loves us all the way to death.

This is the risk we must take with our bodies, our selves. We must offer a hand to the one we fear to touch, a shoulder to the one whose load seems impossible to bear. These aren't metaphors; we have to get up and move, to let sweat and smell make us uncomfortable, let words become meals shared and savored, let the promised prayers become bedside vigils beside the cots of the dying.

This isn't a list of things to do, another heavy requirement of a life of holiness. It isn't anything further from you than the next deep breath, the way the air fills your lungs and oxygen rushes through your arteries to sustain life. We are meant to live this incarnate life together, and however dysfunctionally we do so, the togetherness lets the blood of Christ flow freely, doing what our own blood does so well: it brings sustaining energy, washes us of what is wasteful; it gives us rhythm and movement, maintains warmth and holds us open to what is needed; it defends against what will infect, closing wounds so that the life within can heal and make new.

These are things to recognize in our life with Christ and with one another, not manufacture. The wonder of kneeling, of blessing, is that it is something that we receive instead of produce, it is not what we earn but what we make known.

The Body Kneels

This is what I fumble toward as I talk about the church, the community of believers, this flawed, messy, holy reality that we call the body of Christ. I fumble toward blessing, *berakah*, whose root isn't happiness or gift or some ephemeral sense of beauty but the word for "knee," a part of the body.

So blessing, too, is rooted in our very joints and sinew, a kneeling down to receive from the One who knows how difficult it is for us to bear weight too long in this frail flesh. When my congregation of holy miscreants reaches out in word and body to receive, the blessing finds its way into not just our hearts but our hands as we move into a sense of ourselves as the enfleshed ambassadors of the kingdom of God. When I take Communion from a monk, I am not just receiving a symbol but enacting and receiving a truth that I experience with my taste buds, my stomach, with the blood that carries the nutrients of the elements to my waiting cells.

Most modern Protestant churches have done away with kneelers, those padded pieces of plush and plywood. There is mostly sitting during the service, with some standing during the songs; for the most part, the time together is sedentary (formed, one might conjecture, by the mostly sedentary nature of our modern lives). I'm not agitating for a return to an hour spent kneeling and standing (although I'm a fan of what many like to call liturgical calisthenics), but it's important to be aware of the messages that we're living in our bodies, even as we come together in worship. It's why I love and learn from the worship of my brothers and sisters in the Global South—they move their bodies so freely when they gather together in God's presence, whether they are mourning or rejoicing. There is a lesson that we learn from our collective physical movement (or lack thereof), and it's a lesson caught, not taught.

Indeed, if you want to discern how the church you're in views the body, watch how the community treats those with mental or physical disabilities, children, artists and the poor (both within and without). Oh, there might be good rhetoric about the gospel being given to the little ones and service projects to encourage members toward generosity, but how often are the artists allowed to speak from the margins? How often do the children spill over into the regular worship of the body, instead of finding themselves corralled into programs specific to their age?

I'm not speaking against children's church or age-specific learning—I think both are deeply valuable, deeply needed, as we raise up a generation to love God and love people. At the same time, how we collectively treat those whose bodies are other than our own, different in some way, capable of expressing something that might not fit into our common ways of being, evidences what we believe about the value of the body itself. Do we believe that God's kingdom can be experienced by those we consider broken, or do we want only people who appear physically whole? Are we closer than we think to a culture that refuses the leper access to the courts of the Lord, or can we believe the body of Christ that we are, that we receive, will do the work of healing and bringing wholeness regardless of what our culture says is "normal"?

Here we are brought low again, here we are invited to receive the calling to be the humble, holy ones.

Receive what you are, the body of Christ.

We receive this blessing, that we may be a blessing.

We kneel, we receive, in our bodies, with our bodies, and we open ourselves to the bodies of those around us, filled with the breath of God, formed as they were before time began by the One who chose and called them by name. We begin to make room for the things that don't seem to fit into the world's perfect picture—the blind, the lame, the paralyzed (John 5)—and in making room, we feel the heartbeat of God begin to thrum through us all, a pulse that invites us to create safety, dignity, trust in community. In our bodies, through our bodies, with our bodies together we are the body of Christ.

Touch Point

 ### *Giving Blessing*

Here is this last place we linger together before we part ways. Recall what blessings you've received as you've considered, wrestled with, journaled about and lived in the embrace of your body and the bodies around you. In what ways has your experience of your own embodiment changed? In what ways have you heard God in your body?

Over the next few days, I invite you to look for opportunities to bless the bodies of those around you. This may be through a simple touch on the shoulder of someone who is hurting, or lightening someone's load by carrying their groceries to their car for them. It may be a laying on of hands (something Scripture tells us has real and lasting power) or anointing someone with oil.

You might think about having a small bowl or vessel of oil beside your bed or in your bathroom and receiving the anointing of your body before you start your day—an act of receiving blessing so that you may be a blessing to others, a sacramental reminder that you have the power to touch in holy, healing ways.

Remember to always touch with permission, but seek out opportunities to hold the hands of others, to look into their eyes, to embrace them with God's love through you. Insist on presence by turning toward those speaking to you, meeting their eyes, giving them your whole face.

Notice those you are reluctant to bless, for whatever reason. Are there places that seem unsafe and make you recoil? Or is it an ego place, a place of fear of rejection or hurt, that causes you to step back from blessing someone? What of those whose bodies are different from yours? What are the ways that blessing those bodies is difficult or easy?

Pay attention also to those places where people gather together, bringing their bodies into proximity with one another. At the gym, the grocery store, the bank or at school—what does coming together physically mean? Is there a way that these bodies together are a blessing, a way that God is present, or is this a place of gathering where God (though always present) is unwelcome or unacknowledged? How does this feel different than gathering in a space or place where God is drawing our bodies together?

Attend to how you, too, receive blessing by being a blessing to others. What shifts in you as you reach out? What is called out in you, what do you learn about yourself, about God, about others? What are the ways that blessing others physically brings deeper freedom and wholeness to your own body? What are the new places of love and grace that open up within you in this process?

This is an exercise that can easily go on for the rest of your life—your body is a blessing to others whether or not you are attentive to the fact that it is—but this period of intentional awareness of blessing others with your body is important. After you've finished, you're invited to write or create a kind of Ebenezer to say, "Thus far the Lord has brought me." Whether that's an actual stone or pile of stones with the words and blessings you've received, a journal list of those blessings, a bracelet you wear regularly, or a picture you hang on your wall, make a concrete, physical marker of this work of God in your life: the blessing and embrace of your body and the bodies of those around you. This has been and will continue to be your spiritual act of worship, offering your body as a living sacrifice to God, a place where your body, your very self, becomes the conduit of God's redemptive power and love in the world.

Appendix

Group Discussion Guide

1. The author says on page 13 that the body of Christ as a whole needs you to have a holistic, healthy relationship with your own body in order for it to function as it was designed. Do you agree with this? Why or why not?

2. In chapter one, the author tells a story of being warned against invisible trains as a way of keeping her out of danger. In what ways have you seen rules placed around interactions with the body in Christian culture to keep us out of danger? Do you believe they are helpful or unhelpful?

3. On page 55, the author writes, "No condemnation of our bodies is more harrowing than the silence that entombs our discussion of the body as beautiful and good." Do you agree with this statement? Why or why not?

4. In chapter three, the author asserts that "our bodies are the very focus of the story of God" (p. 75) and that we cannot be human without a body. What is meant by these assertions?

5. In using the terms *sarx* and *soma*, flesh and body, in the New Testament, Paul is using terms without implying that either one is good or bad. How have the words "flesh" and "body" come to have moral implications?

6. How do the terms *sarx* and *soma* connect (or not) with the "angel" and "animal" narrative in the church?

7. While our bodies are the image of the invisible God, the only thing that can bear Christ into the world, we regularly experience pain,

betrayal, illness and death in our bodies. What does the author suggest we do with this seeming contradiction?

8. On page 117, the author implies that we can discern how comfortable we are with our bodies by how we make space for those whose bodies are different from our own. Do you find this to be a helpful tool in discerning your own comfort level with your body?

9. "God imbued this flawed, fractious body of ours with this kind of wacky power not because he likes playing with explosives but because he truly believes that we can do what he did, because he made us to be agents of healing in this broken world," writes the author on page 126. How have you seen the power of Christ move in people's lives?

10. Do you believe that the healing touch that the woman with the issue of blood received from Jesus in John 5 is within our power to give to others today? Why or why not?

11. In chapter seven, the author suggests that the energy and risk it takes to be present to our desires is so fraught that most people would rather check out than be present to their body's yearnings. Do you agree? If so, how have you seen that play out in the lives of those around you?

12. Looking at chapter eight, "Tension Taming," would you say that the tension of our embodied lives is positive (healthy) or negative (unhealthy)?

13. On page 183, the author writes, "Most of us have spent so long trying to silence or manipulate our bodies that the messages they have to give us are muted or mixed." Explain what the author means by silencing or manipulating our bodies and the messages they are sending.

14. In an exercise in chapter ten, the author encourages readers to pay serious, prolonged attention to their current surroundings, including reaching out to touch them and experience God in them. What would you say is the intent of this exercise? Why was it included in this chapter?

15. Chapter eleven asserts that our sexuality can be redeemed and that our sexual desires can point us toward God. Do you find this idea compelling? Why or why not?

16. "Receive what you are, the body of Christ" is a phrase that jolts the author into sudden awareness of what's happening in the Eucharist and in herself (p. 231). How are our bodies part of the body of Christ?

Author's Note

TO PROTECT THE PRIVACY OF THOSE with whom I journey in spiritual direction, as well as to honor the stories of those with whom I live in community, some names of people and institutions have been changed, and some minor characters are composites.

Acknowledgments

WHEN I BEGAN TO TAKE SERIOUSLY the writing of poems, I decided to take part in a poetry workshop lead by the redoubtable Scott Cairns. This was a courageous and foolish decision, and I've been grateful for it ever since. During the week of looking at and loving words together, Scott underlined over and over the necessity of being aware of the conversation into which the poet enters when she picks up the pen. Poetry—great poetry, terrible poetry, mediocre poetry—has been written since the advent of writing itself. To even hope to produce something not just of quality but of meaning to the reader requires respecting the poets who have come before enough to listen to them and, one can only hope, to respond to them with intelligence and craft.

I went home from that workshop and immediately quit writing poems. (This made Scott very sad, I will admit, when I told him a year later. Scaring an amateur poet out of writing was not his intent.) I quit not because I was discouraged but because I was naive, and I had been humbled enough to be made aware of that fact.

To undertake the writing of a book, a book about God and our bodies no less, is a similarly humbling endeavor. I am aware that these words are part of a much larger dialogue that the people of God have been having throughout the ages, and the only thing that makes me confident enough to enter into that vast and beautiful conversation is the work and love of my Lord and Savior Jesus Christ. It is he who stands at the center of it all, he to whom all the honor and glory and praise and thanksgiving goes. It is his incarnation that pushes me forward to speak and his Spirit that, I pray, infuses these words with transformative meaning.

There are so many in the great cloud of witnesses to whom I'm indebted, so many whose cadences and diction echo in my own writing. Julian of Norwich, my foremother in spiritual writing, the first woman to write in English; Evelyn Underhill, my cranky patron saint; Simone Weil, because of whom my acts of attention are keener and more purposeful. St. Francis, St. Antony, St. Benedict, Teresa of Ávila, St. Ignatius, Bernard of Clairvaux, St. John of the Cross, Catherine of Siena—I could go on and on. And this leaves out the many moderns whose writings influence my thoughts and journey toward God—C. S. Lewis, George MacDonald, Eugene Peterson, Richard Foster, Frederick Buechner, David Benner, Brennan Manning, Dallas Willard, David Whyte, Christian Wiman.

And then there are those saints with whom I gather regularly in the beautiful, broken and blessed mess that is the International Anglican Church, my spiritual family. I'm grateful to Ken and Sallie Ross for their care and commitment to both me and the church, to the leadership team, to the IAC artist's group and to every member of the body. Each of you is a part of these words, making them possible.

The community of Story Sessions, founded by Elora Ramirez, is another cloud of witnesses who gathered around, reminded me of the holiness of this calling and prayed these words into being. I'm especially grateful to Tanya Marlow for the reading of first drafts and the reminder that these words matter when my own will and words failed me.

It was my friend Anne Overstreet, whom I met first in Scott Cairns's class at the Glen Workshop, who drew me back to the creative community that meets in Santa Fe each year. Anne's belief in my words, her quiet insistence that I am, indeed, a poet, and her continual support of my writing process—no matter how ragged—has made her one of the chief champions of creativity in my life. She and her husband, Jeff, will have my gratitude—and friendship—forever.

There are so many who picked me up as I stumbled along this path: Rachelle, Heather, Laura, Elisabeth, Erin and Susan from my book club who knew exactly when to ask how the book was going and when not to, and Elisa, from the same phalanx of amazing women, who encouraged me as I cried over a cup of tea in Pike's Perk.

Jennifer, David, Leta, Margie and Todd from my peer group, whose prayers, promptings and *anam cara* friendship have reminded me who and Whose I am.

Laura Brown, whose late night conversations and songs sung into my voicemail reminded me of the way a love of words and the Word ties hearts tight together no matter the distance between them.

John Blase, whose poetry calls me back to the warp and woof of this world and whose evaluation of my ideas were the scrim through which I began to see the back end of God in this process.

Steve and Gwen Smith and the folks of Potter's Inn, who provided a place for this writer to retreat and find herself when I needed it most.

Lauren Winner, without whose blunt insistence I craft these thoughts into a book nothing would have happened, is another friend to whom I'm indebted.

Mark and Lorrie Hostetler, who have helped me to see as God sees (and taught me how to avoid ginger snaps at 60 miles per hour).

Alan Ullman, who came into my life like the *ruach* of God, taught me what *tov* means, mirrored back to me who I'm called to be and became the spiritual father I never thought I'd have.

Lorraine Wheeler, into whose constant friendship, understanding, love, support, permission, grace and open arms I've fallen again and again, is the best friend a woman could ever have along this winding road. I'm under no illusions my stumbling is over, so each of you have been warned.

Speaking of stumbling, it was Preston Yancey whose belief in my writing and incredulity at my lack of faith in myself finally helped me out of the woods and into the words once more. His daily emails, wise guidance and skillful encouragement (coupled with some real talk butt-kicking) made him the kind of companion on this journey that only God could have ordained. This book couldn't have been written without him.

Even as there are those who walk with me, I am deeply shaped by those who have given me the honor and privilege of walking alongside them. Each person who has shared their God-story with me in spiritual direction is an incredible gift to my heart, and I've been transformed in witnessing your courage, vulnerability, authenticity and desire for God, no matter the cost.

I owe a debt of gratitude to Cindy Bunch and the skillful team at IVP. Your patience with me was the patience of Christ, and your belief in the importance of these words have made all of this possible.

I'm so blessed to have a family that has supported my writing from my first published poem (in grade four) until today. Mom, Dad, thank you for believing in me and my dreams. Bryony, you inspire me each day, I love you (and Joey, Violet and Willa) deeply. Ron and Joanne, Janna and Avery, I couldn't ask for better in-laws. Andrea, Ryan, Luke, Evelyn and Raechel—it's your courage and grace that made me into a mother and grandmother. We may not have been made family by blood, but God's kindness has knit us together in love.

And, above all, Bryan. This journey began in conversations had deep into the night, when distance separated us and marriage was a dim dream. I didn't know what it was to truly love another person until you came into my life. You offer yourself to me daily, sacrificially, as a partner, as a friend, as a man of God. You make it possible for me to be more of myself, more of God's beloved every day. You delighted in this project from the beginning, believed in my voice in the conversation, and lived the flesh-and-blood sacrifice that made it possible. I'm forever grateful.

Notes

Introduction

[1]The research was done in the 1930s on male patients by Dr. Wilder Penfield, and the resulting model is called the corticol homunculus. More recent research in Germany has mapped the female body as well.

Chapter 1: Where Do Our Fears Come From?

[1]N. T. Wright, *Following Jesus* (Grand Rapids: Eerdmans, 1994), p. 66.

Chapter 2: How We Lost Our Bodies

[1]I believe in God the Father, Almighty, Maker of heaven and earth.

And in Jesus Christ, his only begotten Son, our Lord; who was conceived by the Holy Ghost, born of the Virgin Mary, suffered under Pontius Pilate, was crucified, dead and buried; he descended into hell; the third day he rose again from the dead; he ascended into heaven, and sits at the right hand of God the Father Almighty; from thence he shall come to judge the quick and the dead.

I believe in the Holy Ghost; the holy catholic church; the communion of saints; the forgiveness of sins; the resurrection of the body; and the life everlasting. Amen.

[2]A statement of belief that was used before baptism in the early church in and around the second century.

[3]We believe in one God, the Father Almighty, Maker of heaven and earth, and of all things visible and invisible.

And in one Lord Jesus Christ, the only-begotten Son of God, begotten of the Father before all worlds (æons), Light of Light, very God of very God, begotten, not made, being of one substance with the Father; by whom all things were made; who for us men, and for our salvation, came down from heaven, and was incarnate by the Holy Ghost of the Virgin Mary, and was made man; he was crucified for us under Pontius Pilate, and suffered, and was buried, and the third day he rose again, according to the Scriptures, and ascended into heaven, and sitteth on the right hand of the Father; from thence he shall come again, with glory, to judge the quick and the dead; whose kingdom shall have no end.

And in the Holy Ghost, the Lord and Giver of life, who proceedeth from the Father, who with the Father and the Son together is worshiped and glorified, who spake by the prophets. In one holy catholic and apostolic Church; we acknowledge one baptism for the remission of sins; we look for the resurrection of the dead, and the life of the world to come. Amen. (Philip Schaff, *The History of Creeds*, vol. 1 of *Creeds of Christendom, with a History and Critical Notes* (New York: Harper & Brothers, 1877).

[4]Docetism (a belief that Jesus only appeared to have a body but didn't actually), Marcionism (a belief that the God of the Old Testament and New Testament were different Gods, and that the Old Testament needed to be rejected to be truly Christian), Montanism (a fanatical movement that radically embraced martyrdom, rejected the authority of the church and insisted that the end of the age was imminent) and Manichaeism (a radical sect of Gnosticism) are four other movements that affected the early church.

[5]Augustine, *De Gratia Christi* and *De Peccato Orginali Contra Pelagium,* cap.43, xxxviii, ed. and trans. Marcus Dodd, vol. 2, The Works of St. Augustine (Edinburgh: T & T Clark, 1895); Augustine, *City of God,* xiv, 26, ed. and trans. Demetrius B. Sema and Gerald C. Walsh, The Fathers of the Church (New York: Image Books, 1950).

[6]Jean Danielou, *From Glory to Glory: Texts from Gregory of Nyssa's Mystical Writings,* trans. and ed. Herbert Musurillo (Crestwood, NY: St. Vladimir's Seminary Press, 1998), pp. 11-13.

Chapter 3: Broken Body, Broken Church

[1]Eugene Peterson, "Why Spirituality Needs Jesus," in *The Christian Century*, March 22, 2003, pp. 30-37.

[2]Pope John Paul II, *The Theology of the Body: Human Love in the Divine Plan* 19.4 (Boston: Pauline Books, 1997).

Chapter 5: Angel or Animal

[1]Rob Bell, *Sex God: Exploring the Endless Connections Between Sexuality and Spirituality* (Grand Rapids: Zondervan, 2007), pp. 49-67.

[2]This is necessarily a deeply reduced explanation of the Buddhist worldview, which is varied and nuanced, but it gets at the core tenants.

[3]This is an oversimplification of Greek thought, to be sure. The Greek mindset is more nuanced than this, but the analogy does serve to illustrate the ways in which Greek, and particularly Platonic, thought conceived of the physical over the ideal.

Chapter 6: Beauty or Beast

[1]Amy Frykholm, *See Me Naked: Stories of Sexual Exile in American Christianity* (Boston: Beacon Press, 2012), p. 118.

[2]It is important to note here that eating disorders are classified mental illnesses, and most require the intervention of mental health professionals in order for healing to occur. If you suspect you or someone you know is suffering from anorexia or bulimia, please contact the National Eating Disorder Association to find help in your area: www.nationaleatingdisorders.org/find-help-support.

[3]C. S. Lewis, *The Problem of Pain* (London: Geoffrey Bles, 1940), p. 81.

Chapter 7: Touch or Temptation

[1]Rob Bell, *Sex God: Exploring the Endless Connections Between Sexuality and Spirituality* (Grand Rapids: Zondervan, 2007), p. 40.

[2]Gnosticism, as we spoke about in chapter two, is a complicated and varied set of beliefs that suggest there is "secret knowledge" given to only a few through specific, hidden means. This stands directly in opposition to biblical revelation. Some of the tenets of Gnosticism are that knowledge is the highest good and that Christ only appeared to have a body. This belief sprung from the idea that all matter is inherently base and evil, and that the spirit, mind and intuitions are, in fact, where all that is pure and good resides. Since Christ was without sin and uncontaminated by evil, Gnostics conclude that Jesus must have only *appeared* to have a body. Many Christians today treat their bodies as if they are evil, base things, only meant to be endured until the resurrection, without redeemable qualities or faculties. This is, very simply put, practical Gnosticism.

[3]The word in the passage (Genesis 32:25), *naga,* is sometimes translated as "to strike," as well as "to touch." It's most often used (92 times versus less than 20 times in all other instances) to mean touch or handle, a much (startlingly so) gentler word.

Chapter 8: Desire or Destruction

[1]Janet Ruffing, *Spiritual Direction: Beyond the Beginnings* (New York: Paulist Press, 2000), pp. 12-13.

[2]Margaret Silf, *Inner Compass: An Invitation to Ignatian Spirituality* (Chicago: Loyola Press, 1999), p. 42.

[3]Simone Weil, *Waiting for God* (New York: Putnam, 1951), p. 210.

[4]Blaise Pascal, *Thoughts on Philosophy and Religion* (Glasgow: W. Collins, 1838), p. 255.

[5] *The Spiritual Exercises* were written by St. Ignatius in the 1520s and are comprised of prayers, meditations, Scripture readings and exercises designed to take the reader through a series of four "weeks." The *Exercises* are meant to be undertaken over a period of approximately thirty days, and not only deepen one's relationship with Christ but provide useful tools for self-reflection, discernment of one's interior movements and hearing the voice of God.

[6] David Benner, *Soulful Spirituality: Becoming Fully Alive and Deeply Human* (Grand Rapids: Brazos, 2011), pp. 78-79.

Chapter 9: Tension Taming

[1] David Whyte, "A Great Invitation: The Path of Risk & Revelation" (Langley, WA: Many Rivers Company & David Whyte, 2013), audio recording.

[2] David Whyte, "The Opening of Eyes," in *Songs for Coming Home*, 1984. ©Many Rivers Press, Langley, Washington. Reprinted with permission from Many Rivers Press. See www.davidwhyte.com.

[3] If you'd like to read a great book on the neuroscience of spiritual formation, a look into how our bodies and brains aren't just a house for our souls, I highly recommend Curt Thompson's book, *Anatomy of the Soul: Surprising Connections Between Neuroscience and Spiritual Practices That Can Transform Your Life and Relationships* (Carol Stream, IL: SaltRiver, 2010).

[4] Oswald Chambers, *My Utmost for His Highest: Selections for the Year* (Grand Rapids: Marshall Pickering, 1986).

[5] It's important to note that this isn't the only thing going on in this passage. God's wrath isn't just mindless power unleashed in the world. However, a contextual look at how the Jewish people would have understood this story is important for us to grasp the unchanging nature of God.

[6] Jay Michaelson, *God in Your Body: Kabbalah, Mindfulness and Embodied Spiritual Practice* (Woodstock, VT: Jewish Lights, 2006), p. 2.

Chapter 10: At Home in Your Skin

[1] David Benner, *Soulful Spirituality: Becoming Fully Alive and Deeply Human* (Grand Rapids: Brazos, 2011), p. 82.

[2] Ibid., pp. 78-79.

[3] Ibid., p. 83.

Chapter 11: Sensing His Kingdom

[1] Gerard Manley Hopkins, "God's Grandeur," in *Gerard Manley Hopkins: Poems*

and Prose (New York: Penguin Classics, 1985).

[2]There's some interesting debate in the medical community about how many senses humans actually have.

Chapter 12: Flesh of My Flesh

[1]C. S. Lewis, *The Weight of Glory* (New York: HarperCollins, 2009), p. 26.

[2]Lisa Graham McMinn, *Sexuality and Holy Longing: Embracing Intimacy in a Broken World* (San Francisco: Jossey-Bass, 2004), p. 6.

[3]Dan Allender, "The Design of Desire," talk given at the Design of Desire conference, Windsor, Colorado, November 16, 2013.

[4]Ibid.

[5]Ibid.

[6]Ibid.

About the Author

Tara M. Owens is a certified spiritual director and the founder of Anam Cara Ministries (anamcara.com), where she practices the art of holy listening with pilgrims from all over the world. She holds a master's of theological studies in spiritual formation from Tyndale Seminary, teaches in the Benedictine Spiritual Formation program at Benet Pines Monastery, and is a sought-after speaker, supervisor, consultant and retreat leader. Formerly a professional journalist, Tara believes in the power of connecting our story to God's story, and she is the senior editor of *Conversations Journal*, a spiritual formation journal founded by David Benner, Larry Crabb and Gary Moon. Canadian by birth and British by blood, she has made her home in the mountains of Colorado, where she lives with her husband, daughter and rescue dog. If you'd like to continue the conversation with Tara or book her as a speaker or retreat leader, she can be reached at tara@anamcara.com or on Twitter (@t_owens).

*f*ormatio

TRADITION. EXPERIENCE.
TRANSFORMATION.

Formatio books from InterVarsity Press follow the rich tradition of the church in the journey of spiritual formation. These books are not merely about being informed, but about being transformed by Christ and conformed to his image. Formatio stands in InterVarsity Press's evangelical publishing tradition by integrating God's Word with spiritual practice and by prompting readers to move from inward change to outward witness. InterVarsity Press uses the chambered nautilus for Formatio, a symbol of spiritual formation because of its continual spiral journey outward as it moves from its center. We believe that each of us is made with a deep desire to be in God's presence. Formatio books help us to fulfill our deepest desires and to become our true selves in light of God's grace.